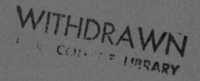

DATE DUE

MAR 4 '75			
GAYLORD			PRINTED IN U.S.A.

A HISTORY
OF THE WORLD

A HISTORY OF THE WORLD

Volume II - 1500 to the present

CHESTER G. STARR
University of Illinois

CHARLES E. NOWELL
University of Illinois

BRYCE LYON
University of California

RAYMOND P. STEARNS
University of Illinois

THEODORE S. HAMEROW
University of Wisconsin

Rand McNally & Company
Chicago - 1960

RAND McNALLY HISTORY SERIES

Fred Harvey Harrington - Consulting Editor

(*Rand McNally*)

Copyright © 1960 by Rand McNally & Company

All rights reserved

Book design by Georgette Roux

Printed in the United States of America
by Rand McNally & Company

Library of Congress Catalogue
Card Number 60-5001

PREFACE

⌁ A HISTORY OF THE WORLD *is a textbook for the study of all the world's people—although the major portion of the work is devoted to the development of Western civilization. Every important period has been covered, and every geographical area represented. The authors are, for the most part, specialists in the topics they treat. In writing this book, they have considered the latest research and interpretations and, whenever possible, have presented their own views.*

The authors of these two volumes were all, at the time of writing, members of the Department of History at the University of Illinois. The close association had many advantages, for it gave opportunity for conference and discussion of problems that arose regarding organization and co-ordination. Each author has read and criticized the work of the others, always bearing in mind the need for clarity and readability as well as accuracy. The styles of presentation are understandably different, but each contributor has endeavored to write with vigor. The authors have been listed on the title page of each volume in the order in which their contributions appear in the work.

In Volume II the division of authorship is as follows. Professor Nowell writes on "The Great Discoveries" (Chapter 16), "The Orient in Decline" (Chapter 22), and "The Europeanization of the Earth" (Chapter 25). Professor Stearns contributes the greater part of the sections entitled "The Transformation and Expansion of Europe" (Chapters 17 and 18) and "Absolutism and Revolution" (Chapters 19–21), and Chapter 23, "The Factory System and the Rise of Industrial Society." Chapter 24, "The Liberal Era, 1815–1871," Chapter 26, "Nationalism and Democracy, 1871–1914," and the four chapters of the final section, "The Contemporary World," are the work of Professor Hamerow, now of the University of Wisconsin.

The history of the world is too enormous a subject to be covered fully in these two volumes, or in any other two volumes. Careful selection of material has been necessary; much has been omitted; much that was first written has been deleted. The authors hope that what they have chosen to include will throw light on the absorbing history of human development and will lead the readers on to investigate further aspects.

C. G. S.
C. E. N.
B. L.
R. P. S.
T. S. H.

CONTENTS

PREFACE   vii

PART FOUR

The Transformation and Expansion of Europe

Chapter 16 - THE GREAT DISCOVERIES   5

Medieval Geography and Travel, 6 / The Sea Route to the
Indies, 11 / The Western Hemisphere, 22 / The Spaniards
in America, 30 / Other European Discoveries, 42

Chapter 17 - CONFLICTS AND DIVISIONS IN
                   WESTERN CHRISTENDOM   49

The Role of the Roman Catholic Church on the Eve of the
Reformation, 50 / Martin Luther and the Rise of Lutheran-
ism, 56 / John Calvin and Calvinism, 67 / The Rise of the
Church of England, 72 / The Catholic Reformation, 77 /
Some Results of the Reformation, 81

Chapter 18 - BEGINNINGS OF THE MODERN
                   STATES SYSTEM   93

The Dynastic State, 93 / The French Dynasty — from Valois
to Bourbon, 97 / England — the Tudor Dynasty, 104 / The
Habsburg Dynasties of Germany and Spain, 112 / Conflict
Among the Growing States, 123 / The States System, 128

PART FIVE

Absolutism and Revolution

Chapter 19 - THE TRIUMPH OF ABSOLUTISM   143

The Northlands and the Emergence of Russia, 143 / Central and Southeast Europe — Hohenzollern and Habsburg, 158 / Western Europe — the Age of Louis XIV, 166 / Curbs to Dynastic Absolutism, 177

Chapter 20 - THE WORLD OF THE ENLIGHTENMENT   193

The Rise of Early Modern Science, 193 / John Locke, Sage of the Enlightenment, 202 / The Optimism of the Enlightenment, 206 / Religion and the Church, 210 / The *Philosophes* and Reform, 214 / Enlightened Despotism, 220 / The Arts and Literature of the Enlightenment, 233

Chapter 21 - THE FALL OF THE OLD REGIME   238

The American Revolution, 239 / The Emergence of the United States of America, 246 / The French Revolution, 1789–1799, 250 / Napoleon and the French Imperium, 266 / Napoleon and the Coalitions, 272 / The Settlement at Vienna and Its Aftermath, 277 / The Revolutions in Latin America, 281 / Summary, 289

Chapter 22 - THE ORIENT IN DECLINE   293

India under the Great Moguls, 294 / China to the Manchu Decline, 306 / The Ottoman Turkish Empire, 318

PART SIX

The Golden Age of the West

Chapter 23 - THE FACTORY SYSTEM AND THE RISE OF INDUSTRIAL SOCIETY   339

The Backgrounds of the Industrial Revolution, 342 / The Agricultural Revolution, 346 / The Factory System, 350 / The Industrial Revolution, 355 / The Revolution in Transportation, 360 / Effects of the Industrial Revolution, 366

Chapter 24 - THE LIBERAL ERA, 1815–1871   378

The Conflict of Ideologies, 378 / Western Europe, 385 / Central and Southern Europe, 392 / Eastern Europe, 400 / The New World, 407

Chapter 25 - THE EUROPEANIZATION OF THE EARTH   419

The Extension of the European Empires, 422 / The Partition of Africa, 438 / The Far East, 445 / Oceania, 454 / Results of Global Europeanization, 457

Chapter 26 - NATIONALISM AND DEMOCRACY, 1871–1914   461

The Indian Summer of the European Age, 461 / Western Europe, 467 / Central and Southern Europe, 472 / Eastern Europe, 477 / The New World, 484 / The Coming of the War, 490

PART SEVEN

The Contemporary World

Chapter 27 - THE PASSING OF THE EUROPEAN AGE, 1914–1945   505

The First World War, 505 / The Rise of Communism, 513 / Fascism on the March, 519 / Democracy on the Defensive, 525 / The Pipe Dream of Peace, 532 / The Second World War, 535

Chapter 28 - THE WANING OF COLONIALISM   548

Europe and the World, 548 / The Far East, 553 / India, 559 / Southeast Asia, 563 / The Middle East, 565 / Africa, 571

Chapter 29 - NEW PATTERNS OF CULTURE   581

The Scientific Image of Nature, 581 / The Scientific Image of Society, 587 / Philosophic Thought, 594 / Religion, 598 / The Arts and Letters, 603 / Changing Ideals of Learning, 610

Chapter 30 - THE POST-WAR SCENE   619

The New International Order, 619 / The Recovery of the West, 628 / The Orient in Revolt, 635 / The Cold War, 644 / The Meaning of the Twentieth Century, 650

LIST OF PHOTOGRAPHS   659

INDEX   663

List of Maps

Maps in Black and White

CARTOGRAPHY BY WILLIS R. HEATH

	page
Activity of the Portuguese in the East	20
Indian America	23
Religious Divisions about 1550	65
Catholic Reformation	79
Established Churches and Religious Minorities about 1600	82
Dynastic Inheritances of Charles V	95
Division of the Netherlands, 1579	121
Growth of Russia to 1725	148
Growth of Brandenburg-Prussia, 1415–1815	159
Expansion of France during Reign of Louis XIV, 1643–1715	173
The English Revolution, 1640–1690	185
The World after 1763	226
Partitions of Poland	231
British North America on the Eve of the American Revolution	243
Mogul India at Its Greatest Extent under Aurungzeb, 1707	299
Manchu Empire at Its Greatest Extent under Ch'ien Lung, 1795	313
Ottoman Empire, 1529–1789	322
English Waterways, 1837	362
English Rail Routes, 1846	364

Population Changes, England and Wales 367

Unification of Germany — Bismarck's Empire 394

Unification of Italy 397

Westward Expansion, 1800–1850 408

Resource Comparison — North-South, 1860 410

Nineteenth-Century Australia and New Zealand 428

East Indies — Spread of Dutch Rule in Nineteenth Century 436

Ethnic Groups of Austria-Hungary (Dual Monarchy) 476

Expansion of Russia in Europe 479

Balkan Peninsula to 1914 482

Dominion of Canada 488

Territorial Divisions of the Austro-Hungarian Empire after the First World War 512

Russian Civil War — Furthest Advance of the Counter-Revolutionary Armies 515

Europe, 1941 — Spread of Axis Power 538

The Pacific Theater of War, 1941–1945 540

Japanese Expansion in China, 1871–1935 558

The Middle East between the World Wars 566

Africa after the First World War 573

Central and Eastern Europe in 1947 622

Germany after World War II 623

India and Pakistan, 1950 638

Israel 641

Maps in Color

following page

The Age of Discovery 14

Europe about 1560 94

The Holy Roman Empire after the Peace of Westphalia, 1648 110

LIST OF MAPS

Europe in 1721   174

European Civilization in the 18th Century   206

Europe in 1810   270

Revolutions in the Atlantic World, 1776–1826   286

Europe in 1815   398

Latin America after Independence   414

The Partition of Africa   446

Europe after the First World War   510

European Civilization in the 19th Century   590

A HISTORY
OF THE WORLD

PART FOUR

The Transformation
and Expansion of Europe

Introduction

§ NEAR THE END *of the fifteenth century Europe stood on the threshold of a mighty transformation. It exhibited a many-sided leadership, whose dynamic qualities soon outshone those of the rest of the world. As we have seen in Volume I, the revival of trade, the growth of urban communities, and the rise of commercial and manufacturing guilds altered the economic, social, and political structure of feudalism. Building upon the knowledge of their predecessors, Europeans pushed ahead in the search for new trade routes and trading centers. Their explorations led them to find new all-water routes to Asia and to discover the New World. Soon Portugal and Spain, and later France, England, and Holland, had established trading posts and colonies in the Far East and in the New World, through which they could extend European civilization and reap the rich profits of expanding trade. No longer was Europe isolated, ingrown, and provincial; suddenly it had become worldwide, cosmopolitan, aggressive, and the pioneer in new world relationships.*

While these events took place, Europe was transformed within. The feudal ideal of one church and one state was shattered by the Reformation and by the rise of dynastic states. The western church fell into dissensions, divisions arose, and these hardened into conflict until the unity of western Christendom was permanently destroyed. Instead, there arose a variety of Protestant churches which, existing alongside the Roman Catholic church, created a religious and ecclesiastical scene similar to that of the Modern Age. Simultaneously, ambitious kings and princes, assisted by the new bourgeoisie, built upon the late feudal monarchies to set up new dynastic states, with increased centralization of power and a personal absolutism which at once doomed feudal institutions and buried the old ideal of one state in Christendom. Feudal Europe fell into a series of dynastic states, with here and there a suspicion of local sentiments presaging the nationalism of the Modern Age. A states system replaced the imperial ideal, and the machinery and processes of international relations were begun.

But if the old unity in church and state was lost, the dynamic qualities of the new European society excelled that of the earlier age and placed Europe in the forefront as the prime mover in world affairs.

3

THE GREAT DISCOVERIES

THE GREATEST geographical discoveries in human history took place between 1400 and 1650. During those two centuries and a half sea and land explorers from western Europe discovered the New World and investigated many hitherto unknown parts of the Old. At the close of the era much had still to be learned: the great African hinterland remained as mysterious as ever, central Asia contained many dark spots, and no human eye had yet beheld Antarctica. Even so, Europe had by then gained an approximate idea of the size of the planet and the shape of its principal oceans and land masses. There would be further exploration, extending into the twentieth century, but this would consist largely of filling in the details of a pattern already known.

When European man commenced his great search for geographical knowledge, he knew accurately only the western half of his own continent, for Russia remained almost as much of a mystery as China. His knowledge of Africa stopped at the northern edge of the Sahara Desert, and eastward his information scarcely extended beyond Persia. To the west, European acquaintanceship with the Atlantic reached to Iceland and in some individual cases to Greenland. Although Scandinavians had touched North America around the year 1000, the existence of this western land had been forgotten by all but a handful of learned persons in Iceland and Scandinavia.

A few Europeans had crossed Asia to China and the Pacific in the late Middle Ages, and the most famous of these travelers, Marco Polo, had even learned something of Japan. Polo and others had left written accounts of their adventures, yet the reliable information they furnished had somehow failed to penetrate the European mind. Maps survive which show that Europeans could not be even roughly accurate when they attempted to draw maps of Asia from data furnished by the travelers. A glance at any of them will show that the baffled maker had no idea of the shape and extent of Asia. With Africa the situation was even worse, because no one—at least no one known in Europe—had ever crossed the vast Dark Continent.

This explains why the Europeans, when they undertook the systematic exploration of the earth, started with little information that could aid them. Instead, they held many false beliefs which they had to discard in order to comprehend the true nature of their discoveries. In some cases demonstration failed to upset established belief for many years. In the meantime a curious blend of fact and fiction passed for geography. In this chapter we shall follow the principal explorers and empire builders as they enacted one of the great adventure stories of human history. Only if mankind is some day able to reach and explore other planets can he relive those thrilling years when a world existed ready for exploration.

1 : Medieval Geography and Travel

BELIEF IN a spherical earth dates back at least to the Greeks of the fifth century B.C. With the coming of the Middle Ages, however, ideas that were considered to embody true Christian doctrine prevailed, and the ancient, flat-earth idea of the primitive Homeric Greeks came back into fashion. Yet believers in a round earth were never wholly lacking, and even during the centuries called the Dark Ages such persons lived and expressed their views. The church, contrary to today's popular belief, never took a doctrinal stand on the question of the flatness or roundness of the earth, though some priests thought it sacrilegious to believe in antipodes, the word invented to describe human beings dwelling on the other side, whose feet are opposite to ours. These priests argued that people separated by impassable physical barriers from the rest of mankind could not be descendants of Adam and Eve, and that belief in their existence meant denial of the authority of the Bible.

Until Copernicus and Galileo worked and wrote in the sixteenth and seventeenth centuries geographers and other scientists agreed that the earth was the center of the universe, with all heavenly bodies from the moon to the fixed stars revolving about it. Medieval scholars never fully agreed on the question of whether land or water occupies most of the earth's surface. General opinion long favored water, but in the centuries just before the great discoveries, experts veered to the belief that land covers the larger area. This opinion, though mistaken, had an important bearing on expedition plans. It enabled the believers in a spherical earth to maintain that a western voyage from Europe to Asia would be neither long nor particularly hazardous.

THE NORSE VOYAGES

Even during the so-called Dark Ages the peoples of northern Europe pushed into previously unknown seas and discovered new lands. Irish monks and seamen before the year 800 visited the Hebrides, northern Scotland, the Faroes, and Iceland. During the next two centuries the Scandinavians discovered the White Sea, colonized Iceland, and pushed westward to Greenland. Naming the latter land for the one patch of green grass they found growing, they planted several settlements along the western coast, directly facing North America. From these locations they could scarcely fail to encounter the continent, and their first contact with it, an accidental one, occurred about 986.

The discoverer was a Norse ship commander who attempted to reach Greenland from Iceland in bad weather. Losing course in a fog, he missed Greenland and encountered a land, "flat, covered with trees, on which no hill was to be seen." From the description it appears to have been Newfoundland. Turning northward, he and his seamen continued for days to behold other stretches of coast, which the commander refused to explore, because the lands seemed worthless. He insisted on turning back to look for Greenland, which he eventually reached.

About fifteen years later Leif Ericson, an adventurous young Greenland captain, sailed with one ship to explore the reported land. Leif proceeded southward far past the coasts his predecessor had seen, and touched at several points whose descriptions suggest New England. He and his crew went ashore and wintered in a country they named Vinland, or Wineland, because of the wild grapes growing there. The Norsemen, from rugged Iceland and barren Greenland, knew nothing of grapes, but a German crew member, possibly a Rhinelander, could identify the berries as being similar to those used for making wine in his country. Vinland was probably a part of Massachusetts, not far from Cape Cod. The climate reported by the Norsemen bears this out, and the story of the wild grapes is confirmed by their existence there to this day. Norse accounts of Leif's experience make no mention of human inhabitants of Vinland, although it is almost certain that Indians occupied the Massachusetts coast at the time.

Leif visited the grape country no more himself, but during the next fourteen or fifteen years others from Greenland went to the newly-discovered coasts. They seem not to have confined their efforts to Vinland, and at least one expedition may have entered the St. Lawrence River. These later explorers met Indians, who at first seemed friendly but soon quarreled and fought with the Norsemen. The fighting proved costly to the badly-outnumbered white men, whose eleventh-century weapons gave them no decisive superiority over the savages. The danger from Indians probably accounts for the Norse loss of interest in Vinland. At least one of the voyagers, an individualist called Thorhall the Hunter, proclaimed his dislike of the country because the wine-producing grapes promised him had not been forthcoming. According to report, he declaimed:

> *When I came, these brave men told me*
> *Here the best of drink I'd get.*

Now with water pail behold me
Wine and I are strangers yet.

Stooping at the spring I've tested
All the wine this land affords.
Of its vaunted charms divested
Poor indeed are its rewards.[1]

With their Greenland home so far from Europe and with only its sparse populations from which to draw, the Norsemen had neither resources nor manpower to spare for conquest or colonization.

The Greenland colonies endured for centuries, and their inhabitants never quite forgot Vinland. Later they may have visited North America more often than is commonly supposed. No thought of a New World or Western Hemisphere ever occurred to Leif and the other Norsemen. Vinland to them was but another land in the distant west, probably an island like Iceland or Greenland. Being unlearned and only recently converted Christians, they had no thoughts on the question of whether the savages were antipodes or descendants of Adam and Eve. When the new region, after first looking valuable, proved a dangerous one, they did not apparently regard further contact with it as worth the effort.

EUROPEAN INTEREST IN THE EAST

The crusades to the Holy Land (1096–1291) reawakened European interest in the Middle East but did not extend Western knowledge far into Asia. The crusaders opened new stations in Syria and Palestine for commerce with the Orient and learned to bypass Constantinople and the Byzantine Empire. Yet they handled only the western part of the trade themselves, while Asiatics bore the Chinese and other Far Eastern products by relays to the Mediterranean ports.

In the twelfth century, with the crusades turning into a losing battle, Europeans built the legend of Prester John, an imaginary Christian ruler of great riches, might, and virtue who supposedly dwelt eastward of the Moslems. The legend was based on reports of the Asiatic Nestorian Christians, on the garbled account of a twelfth-century Asiatic conqueror, and on the equally garbled but basically authentic report of a Christian ruler in Abyssinia. European Christians believed in Prester John because they desperately needed him. In their eyes he loomed as an ally in the rear of Islam, eager to aid them in downing the followers of Mohammed and in

---

[1] Arthur Middleton Reeves, *The Finding of Wineland the Good* (London: Henry Froude, 1895), p. 45.

regaining the holy places. For had he not said, in a supposed letter to western Christians, that when he went forth to war thirteen large crosses made of gold and jewels were carried before him and each was followed by ten thousand knights and one hundred thousand footsoldiers?

When Genghis Khan began his colossal sweep through the Kwaresmian Empire in 1220, leveling cities and destroying their populations, Europe heard magnificently inaccurate reports of him. With an upsurge of hope, the West decided that Prester John was coming to crush the Moslems at last. Genghis, however, retired to Mongolia without pushing westward, and after his death the Mongols made their great invasion of Russia and central Europe. Reports of their behavior proved that they could not be Christians, yet hope persisted that these heathen, who at least were not Moslems, might somehow bring benefits to the Roman Catholic religion. Therefore, when the Mongols abandoned Germany, Hungary, and Poland to consolidate their power in Russia Pope Innocent IV (1243-1254) sent a religious mission that he fondly hoped might persuade them to accept Roman Christianity. The mission, headed by the elderly Franciscan John of Pian del Carpine, managed to make the dreadful journey from Italy to the Great Khan's court in Mongolia. Here the papal envoys were snubbed by the Mongol ruler, who threatened to make war on the Pope unless he accepted his own overlordship.

The Mongol khan did not make good his threat against the Papacy, but his vast empire in Asia and Russia endured for several generations. Other Europeans, both priests and traders, crossed the Mongol dominions. Ultimately, some of them penetrated to China. The first to enter China were evidently the two Polo brothers from Venice. They went as merchants, first to Constantinople and then to Russia, where they found their way home blocked when the Byzantine Greeks recaptured Constantinople in 1261 and destroyed the Latin Empire which Venice had dominated. Marooned in the Russian land and deciding to try their fortunes in the east, the Polos traveled by stages to China, where they found Kublai Khan reigning as emperor. The khan welcomed the Venetian gentlemen, gave them good trading opportunities, and at length sent them home with the request to hurry back bringing a hundred missionaries from the Pope to teach his people Christianity.

Making their way across Asia, by a more southerly route, the Polos reached the Mediterranean and Venice. Owing to a church quarrel, there was no Pope enthroned at the time of their return, so the hundred religious teachers proved out of the question. They finally obtained two Franciscan friars, and with these and the seventeen-year-old Marco Polo, the son of the older brother, they started again for China in 1271. The friars grew alarmed at the prospect of meeting "Tartars" and deserted before going far, but the two elder Polos and Marco persevered and reached Kublai's court in four years. Here they received a gracious reception, despite the conspicuous absence of the desired missionaries.

The Polos this time remained fifteen years in the Great Khan's empire, where the maturing young Marco became an official in Mongol service. He traveled over much of the east on official business, and before departing for home saw more of the empire than Kublai himself had seen. Marco Polo was a keen observer with an eye for detail, and very little escaped his notice. Though he never visited Japan, he learned what he could of this interesting island empire, which he called Cipangu, and heard a somewhat garbled story of the unsuccessful Mongol attempt to conquer it. As for China, which he called Cathay, Marco never learned its language, though he did master that of the Mongol conquerors. Kublai became a hero to the young Venetian, who later gave this description of him:

> He is of middle stature, that is, neither tall nor short. His limbs are well formed and in his whole figure there is just proportion. His complexion is fair, and occasionally suffused with red, like the bright tint of the rose, which adds much grace to his countenance. His eyes are black and handsome, his nose is well shaped and prominent.[2]

The wonders of nature and the great works of man interested Marco Polo. The Venetian described the "black stones" (coal) used for fuel in the empire, the enormous wealth and shipping of a Chinese harbor, and the extended system of charitable relief by which the khan assisted those of his subjects who were in want. Polo obviously considered Kublai's government a benevolent one, although this opinion would not have been shared by the poorer Chinese classes.

When the aging father and uncle felt it time for the family to return to Venice, they had trouble persuading the septuagenarian Kublai to part with them. Opportunity came, however, when the old ruler wished to send a young female relative to be married to another relative, the khan of Persia. Conditions in central Asia being then too disturbed to make a land journey safe, Kublai decided that the princess should go by sea, with the Venetians, who understood seafaring, as her escort. Sailing from a Chinese port, the Polos took their princess by way of Indo-China, Malaya, Sumatra, Ceylon, and India to the Persian Gulf. Though the khan she had come to marry had meanwhile died, they bestowed her on his son and successor, who is reported to have been less handsome than the father. The travelers were at home in Venice by 1295, rejoining friends and relatives who had long given them up for dead. They returned with comfortable fortunes, though by no means with the fabulous wealth some historians have reported.

---

[2] *The Travels of Marco Polo,* rev. from Marsden's translation and ed. with introduction by Manuel Komroff (New York: Horace Liveright, 1926), pp. 124–25.

Soon after his return Marco commanded a Venetian galley in a battle with the rival Italian republic of Genoa. The Genoese won the fight and took Polo, with many others, to their city as captives. While awaiting ransom Marco had as his cellmate a literary man from Pisa, who, on learning what an interesting life the other had led, suggested that they collaborate on a book. With the traveler dictating and his companion writing, they produced in a few months' time what is known as the *Book of Ser Marco Polo*. In it Marco tells the story of all three Polos and describes every Oriental land seen or learned of at first hand by any of them. The book has remained a masterpiece of travel literature for over six centuries, and there is scarcely a language into which it has not been translated. Yet at first this honest and essentially accurate account proved too much for the credulity of most Europeans. Because Polo truly reported the vastness and wealth of the Mongol Empire, he acquired a reputation as a liar and was contemptuously called "Marco Millions." Once ransomed and home in Venice, he became known as a windy bore to be avoided. Years later, as he lay dying, friends urged him to retract the tall stories for the sake of his soul's salvation. Even in the face of death he refused, saying, "I have not told half of what I saw." Only later did his book receive the respectful study it deserved.

The Polos were not the last Europeans to visit the Far East in Mongol times. In the fourteenth century several Chinese cities contained small communities of Italian merchants. Roman Catholic missionary effort finally had some success, and the Pope appointed an archbishop for Peking and bishops for two lesser cities. But with the end of Mongol rule in 1368 every sign of European visitation and influence vanished. China, now known to the West as Cathay, became again an Oriental land of mystery.

2 : The Sea Route to the Indies

COMMERCE BETWEEN China and the West began in ancient times. The oldest known route, called the Silk Road or Silk Route, started from the Chinese province of Kansu, near the western end of the Great Wall. It wound by way of mountains and deserts through the Lob Nor, Khotan, Yarkand, Kashgar, and across Ferghana to Samarkand. From here the silk was taken by a variety of routes to points of destination in the Middle East.

As centuries passed, some alternative roads were developed between China and Turkestan, but Kansu and Samarkand remained the chief terminals of the silk trade. This was a luxury traffic, profitable only because the product was light in weight, small in bulk, and high in price. The Chinese themselves did none of the carrying and appeared strangely unenterprising, as though they cared little whether the trade died or continued. Central Asian middlemen felt differently, and it was they, with their woolly, two-humped Bactrian camels, who for centuries bore silk from Kansu over the desolate road to Western Turkestan and Persia. In return for the silk, later supplemented by Chinese tea and jade, western Asia sent eastward such assorted merchandise as gold, blood horses, metal products, raisins, musicians, and girls.

Political and military disturbances sometimes closed or partially blocked the ancient road. The conquests of Genghis Khan did not disturb the route for long, as the Mongols made it their policy to protect and further commerce. Those of Tamerlane, on the other hand, had a blighting effect, and after his death the road through Persia seems never to have regained its old importance.

The sea routes between East and West developed later. Most of those involving the spice trade had their starting point east of the Malacca Strait, from which goods proceeded by water to cities on the west coast of India. From there they passed across the Indian Ocean and into the Persian Gulf to Bassorah (modern Basra), whence they continued in boats up the Tigris River to Baghdad. They next sailed up the river in smaller craft to a point opposite Antioch. They went on to Antioch in dromedary caravans, though they might be diverted to more southerly cities such as Beirut or Acre. A variant of this route also brought goods up the Tigris, but then took them over the mountains of Asia Minor and Armenia to Trebizond on the Black Sea. Here Venetian galleys picked up those parts of the cargos destined for Europe and carried them via Constantinople to Venice for distribution in the western lands.

The bulk of Oriental trade passed through Egypt in the years just before the great discoveries. Arab shippers brought their eastern cargos to Aden and up the Red Sea to a point from which they could be easily transported to the Nile and Cairo. From Cairo the goods passed to Alexandria, where Italian merchants waited to buy the highly-desired cloves, cinnamon, nutmeg, camphor, dyewood, sugar, perfumes, jewels, gum, oil, cotton, and silk. European traders often went eastward to Damascus, which had important local manufactures for sale. The city produced saddlery and harness, the finest steel weapons in the world, fabrics of silk and velvet, and fragrant perfumes. Because Damascus lay so close to the Mediterranean seaports, a visit to it involved neither hardship nor great personal risk.

What had Europe to give in exchange for these Oriental luxury products? Its exports to Asia in the main consisted of cruder goods, such as wool, tin, amber, copper, honey, and salt. The value of what Europeans sent eastward seldom, if ever, equaled the value of what they bought from Asia. Thus an unfavorable balance constantly existed, to be made up in gold. The Western peoples had but a limited gold supply, and by the opening of the fifteenth century this constant drain to Asia was creating a gold famine which threatened the whole European economy with collapse.

EARLY ATLANTIC EXPLORATION

With the capture of the Galilean city of Acre by the sultan of Egypt in 1291, the European Christians lost the last stronghold gained by them in the Crusades. Not only was this a disaster for the faith but it threatened to bring commercial loss, for no mainland port of the eastern Mediterranean remained in Christian hands. The Egyptians were now in a position to profiteer as middlemen in the valuable Oriental trade, unhampered by any competition with their Red Sea route.

For some years Christians thought of reopening the Crusades with Egypt as the objective, but before long their attention turned to the possibility of developing new routes as compensation for the lost eastern ones. In 1291, the very year of Acre's fall, the Genoese brothers Ugolino and Vadino Vivaldi attempted, with two galleys, to open a western road to the "Indies." Though they appear to have been the precursors of all Western explorers, we know only that they sailed through the Strait of Gibraltar and were never heard of again. Just what they meant by "Indies," and precisely what sailing course they expected to follow, we can never expect to learn.

In the early decades of the fourteenth century voyagers from Genoa rediscovered the Canaries, an island group populated by savages and known vaguely since ancient times. They likewise visited the Madeiras, and the possibility exists that they reached the distant Azores about 1351. Indications are that the maritime Catalans of eastern Spain had by then coasted along Africa as far south as the modern Sierra Leone.

Europeans at that time could push no farther into the unknown waters of the Atlantic. For more distant discoveries they needed ships adapted to oceanic conditions, because the shallow-draft, oar-propelled Mediterranean galleys required more rowers and provisions than could be taken on long voyages. Moreover, if Europeans were to venture far from land for extended periods, as they had never had to do along their Mediterranean and Atlantic coasts, they must have better methods of navigation and improved map-making techniques in order to trace newly-discovered coastlines.

Nautical improvements materialized in answer to the need. By the fifteenth century the galley ship, built for short voyages in the mild Mediterranean, was being replaced for Atlantic use by the round sailing vessel. The compass, borrowed in crude form by the Europeans from the Arabs, who had likely borrowed it earlier from the Chinese, had been adapted to shipboard use. The astrolabe, for determining latitude by the position of heavenly bodies, had also become fairly standard equipment at sea. Computation of longitude remained difficult and was largely a matter of dead reckoning, but dead reckoning by an experienced pilot could be remarkably accurate. As for cartography, the portolanic or compass chart had been developed during the fourteenth century. Such a chart provided a remarkably accurate survey of coastal contours together with close estimates of distances and directions between points. As fast as new coasts were discovered, their main features could be incorporated into these charts. Because of these advances, Europe stood ready soon after 1400 to undertake voyages that would have been impossible a hundred years earlier.

THE PRINCES OF PORTUGAL

King John I (1385–1433) ruled Portugal in the early fifteenth century. His predecessors had consolidated the realm by defeating and expelling the Moslems, who had once been lords of the whole Iberian peninsula. The danger from them seemed not altogether to have vanished, as they still faced Portugal from Morocco, just across the Strait of Gibraltar. The Moroccan city of Ceuta especially tempted the king, for it possessed a good port and had commercial relations with the rich Moslem world to the east. Partly for strategic reasons and partly for adventure, John led a Portuguese army across the strait in 1415 to capture Ceuta. With this accomplished and the city garrisoned against counter-attacks, the king's interest in Africa somewhat waned. With his two ablest sons, Pedro and Henry, the case was far different, as their interest had been stimulated by the Ceuta expedition. The fact that they were younger sons, not in line for the throne, was a positive advantage, as it gave them leisure to satisfy their curiosity and to sponsor a program of geographical discovery.

What explains this activity on their part, beyond the fact that Portugal's position in the southwest corner of Europe was ideal for African exploration by sea? Pedro's motive appears to have been discovery for its own sake and the advancement of knowledge; Henry's was the increase of Portuguese wealth and the discomfiture of the Moslems. European belief in Prester John still existed, but as travelers in Asia had failed to find him, it had become common to identify his kingdom with the Christian land of Abyssinia. As Prince Henry did not know the exact location of this land, he hoped to find it south of Morocco within reach of the west African coast. A search for gold was the most important part of Henry's program. Because of the high prices of Oriental products now reaching the Mediterranean by way of the Red Sea and Egypt, Europe was being drained of its gold supply and suffered a severe shortage. Most of the gold Europe could obtain came northward by caravan across the Sahara. Henry knew this but did not know the precise location of the mines, which were situated near the Niger River, not far from Tombouctu. The prince hoped that his

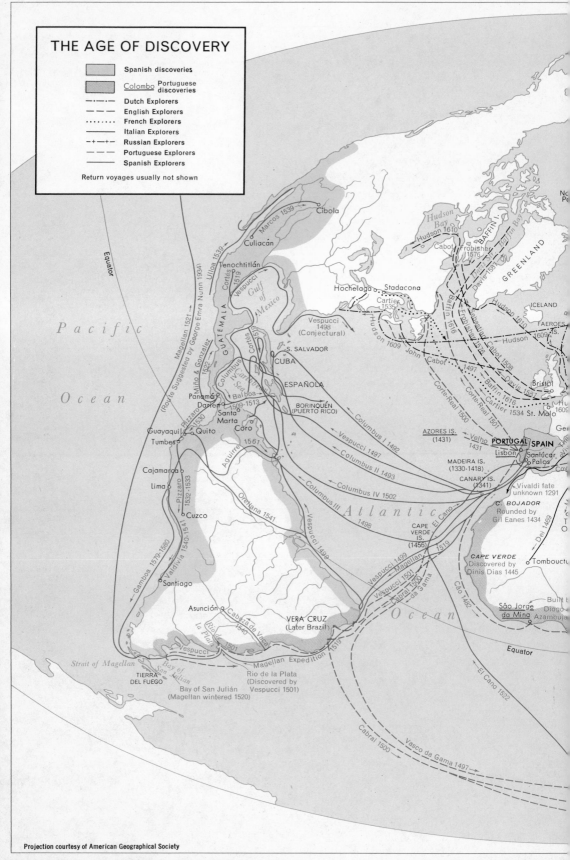

THE AGE OF DISCOVERY

Spanish discoveries

<u>Colombo</u> Portuguese discoveries

—·—·— Dutch Explorers

— — — English Explorers

········· French Explorers

————— Italian Explorers

—+—+— Russian Explorers

– – – Portuguese Explorers

————— Spanish Explorers

Return voyages usually not shown

Equator

Pacific

Ocean

Cibola

Marcos 1539

Culiacán

Ulloa 1539

Tenochtitlán
Cortés 1519

(Route Suggested by George Emra Nunn 1934)

Magellan 1521

Miño & Gonzalez 1522

Cortés

GUATEMALA

Vespucci 1519

Gulf of Mexico

Hochelaga
Cartier 1535

Stadacona

Vespucci 1498 (Conjectural)

S. SALVADOR

CUBA

ESPAÑOLA

Columbus IV 1502 Caribbean Sea

Panamá
Darien
Santa Marta
Coro

Balboa
1509-1513

BORINQUÉN (PUERTO RICO)

Guayaquil
Tumbes
Quito

Pizarro 1526
Pizarro 1530

Aguirre 1561

Columbus I 1492

Vespucci 1497

Cajamarca
Lima

Pizarro 1532-1533

Cuzco

Orellana 1541

Columbus II 1493

Columbus III 1498

Columbus IV 1502

Vespucci 1499

Gamboa 1579-1580

Valdivia 1540-1541

Santiago

Asunción
Cabeza de Vaca 1540

Rio de la Plata
la Plata

VERA CRUZ (Later Brazil)

Vespucci 1499

Vespucci 1501

Strait of Magellan
TIERRA DEL FUEGO

Bay of San Julián

Vespucci 1501

Bay of San Julián
(Magellan wintered 1520)

Rio de la Plata (Discovered by Vespucci 1501)

Magellan Expedition

Magellan 1519

Cabral 1500

Vasco da Gama 1497

Hudson Bay
Hudson 1610

BAFFIN I.

Cabot
Frobisher 1576

GREENLAND

Davis 1587

Baffin 1616

ICELAND

FAEROES IS.

Hudson 1610

Hudson 1609

Cabot 1497

Baffin 1616

Davis 1585

Corte-Real 1500

Corte-Real 1501

Cartier 1534 St. Malo

Bristol

Hudson 1609

AZORES IS. (1431)

Velho 1431

PORTUGAL SPAIN

Lisbon
Santúcar
Palos

MADEIRA IS. (1330-1418)

CANARY IS. (1341)

Vivaldi fate unknown 1291

CAPE VERDE IS. (1456)

El Cano

C. BOJADOR
Rounded by Gil Eanes 1434

Dias 1469

Atlantic

Magellan 1519

Cão 1482

CAPE VERDE
Discovered by Dinis Dias 1445

Tomboctu

Vespucci 1499

Vespucci 1501

Cabral 1500

da Gama

Ocean

São Jorge da Mina

Built by Diogo Azambuja

Equator

El Cano 1522

El Cano 1522

Projection courtesy of American Geographical Society

From R. R. Palmer, *Atlas of World History* (Chicago, 1957), pp. 62-63.

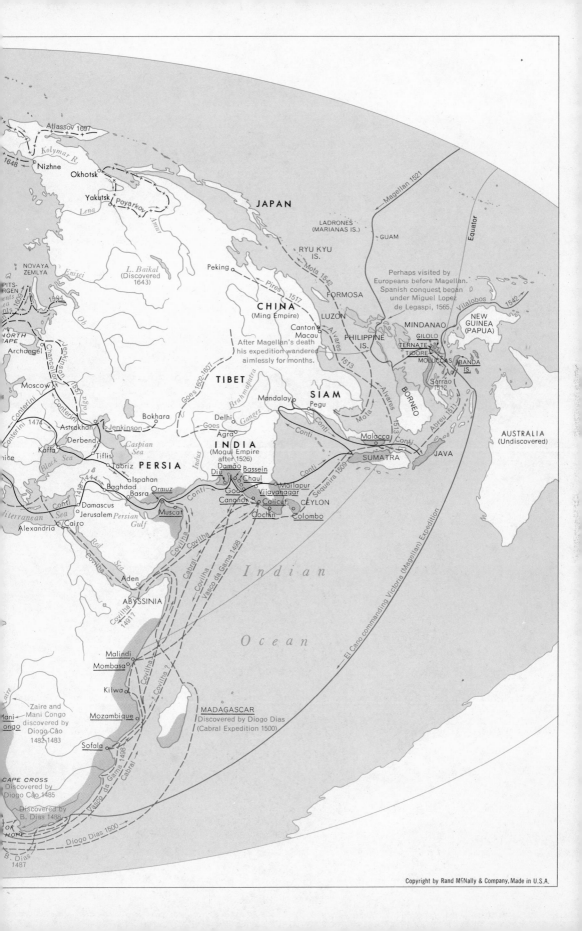

Atlassov 1697

Kolymar R.

1648

Nizhne

Okhotsk

Yakutsk Poyarkov

Lena Amur

JAPAN

LADRONES
(MARIANAS IS.)

GUAM

Magellan 1521

Equator

NOVAYA
ZEMLYA

Enisei

L. Baikal
(Discovered
1643)

RYU KYU
IS.

Mota 1542

Peking

FORMOSA

Perhaps visited by
Europeans before Magellan.
Spanish conquest began
under Miguel Lopez
de Legaspi, 1565.

Villalobos
1542

PITS-
BERGEN

1591

Ob

CHINA
(Ming Empire)

Pires 1517

Canton
Macau

LUZON

PHILIPPINE
IS.

MINDANAO

GILOLO

NEW
GUINEA
(PAPUA)

NORTH
CAPE

Archangel

Chancellor

Jenkinson

After Magellan's death
his expedition wandered
aimlessly for months.

Alvares 1513

TERNATE
TIDORE

MOLUCCAS

Sarrao
1512

BANDA
IS.

Abreu 1511

Goes 1602-1607

TIBET

Brahmaputra

Mandalay

SIAM

Pegu

Conti

Malacca

Conti

BORNEO

Moscow

Bokhara

Delhi

Ganges

Mota

Alvares 1513

AUSTRALIA
(Undiscovered)

Contarini 1476

Astrakhan

Jenkinson

Derbend

Caspian
Sea

Goes

Agra

Conti

SUMATRA

JAVA

Kaffa

Tiflis

Volga

Contarini

Contarini

Black Sea

Tabriz

PERSIA

INDIA
(Mogul Empire
after 1526)

Damão
Diu

Bassein

Chaul

Goa

Meliapur

Vijayanagar

Sequeira 1509

Conti

CEYLON

Conti

Ispahan

Baghdad

Basra

Ormuz

Cananor

Calicut

Damascus

Jerusalem

Persian
Gulf

Muscat

Conti

Cochin

Colombo

Mediterranean Sea

Alexandria

Cairo

Red
Sea

Covilha

Covilha

Conti

Indian

Aden

Covilha

Cabral

Covilha

Vasco da Gama 1498

Ocean

ABYSSINIA

Covilha
1491?

El Cano commanding Victoria (Magellan) Expedition

Malindi

Mombasa

Covilha ?

Kilwa

Zaire and
Mani Congo
discovered by
Diogo Cão
1482-1483

Mozambique

MADAGASCAR
Discovered by Diogo Dias
(Cabral Expedition 1500)

Mani
ongo

Sofala

CAPE CROSS
Discovered by
Diogo Cão 1485

Vasco da Gama 1498

Cabral 1500

Discovered by
B. Dias 1488

OF
HOPE

Diogo Dias 1500

B. Dias
1487

explorers would find rivers leading inland from the Atlantic to the gold region.

Because Pedro became regent of Portugal soon after their father's death and governed the country in behalf of a young nephew, Henry took principal charge of the discovery program. For this reason, his fame has eclipsed that of his brother, who nevertheless retained an interest in Henry's activities and gave them every encouragement in his power.

Prince Henry established headquarters at the Sacred Promontory (Sagres) at the southwestern tip of Portugal. There for most of his remaining years he acted as planner, organizer, and financier of maritime expeditions. His explorers followed two main lines of endeavor: discovery of islands in the Atlantic and progress southward along the African coast. In the ocean one of his voyagers in 1418 rediscovered the Madeiras, visited nearly a century earlier by Genoese seamen and since forgotten. About 1431 a Portuguese captain sighted the easternmost Azores, which may also have been found earlier, but which likewise had dropped out of memory. Both island groups were uninhabited, and so the Portuguese were able to colonize them without opposition and with profit. Henry also attempted to acquire the populated Canaries, but as Castile had already commenced the conquest of the Canarian savages, the prince ultimately withdrew his claims.

Beginning in 1434 the Portuguese mariners managed to push southward along the African coast beyond Morocco. They advanced by slow steps, hugging the shore as closely as possible, each captain sailing only a little beyond where his predecessor had gone. They found few traces of gold, and instead of the Christians they sought, they encountered at first the dark-white Moslems of the western Sahara. A few captives taken from among these tribesmen furnished the Portuguese with their first cargos of slaves, but when brought to Europe they proved to be of slight commercial value. Even for these, Henry devoutly gave thanks to God.

In the later stages of the prince's career his voyagers discovered the Senegal and Gambia rivers, which enter the Atlantic through the Negro country. As one of Henry's early historians writes:

> Going farther . . . they came to a very notable river, which we at present call Çanaga [Senegal], because the principal trade that commenced at that time was with a leading Negro of the country called by this name of Çanaga. However, the true name of the river there at its mouth is Oodesh, according to the speech of the Negroes who live there, and as one goes farther into the interior one hears still other names from the people who live by its waters.[3]

The Negroes were more satisfactory slaves than the northern tribesmen,

---

[3] João de Barros, *Da Asia* (Lisbon: Na Regia Officina Typografica), Vol. I, p. 109.

and the Portuguese pressed some distance up the rivers in search of Prester John and gold. There was no sign of the Prester, though sufficient wealth could now be gained in trade to make the voyages show a profit. Exploration did not progress far beyond the Gambia in Henry's time. A final discovery, in 1456, was that of the uninhabited Cape Verde Islands, where the pigeons were so trusting that they allowed the seamen to catch them with their hands.

When Henry died in 1460 his explorers had probably not traversed any part of the African coast not earlier seen by Europeans. Yet between his well-organized discoveries and the previous haphazard ones there was a great difference. The voyages he sponsored were planned, organized, and accompanied by careful mapping. Their results would never be lost or forgotten, and the next generation would proceed from the sound basis he had laid.

THE WORK OF KING JOHN II

When Henry died, having survived Pedro by eleven years, Portugal did not immediately produce another great patron of geographical discovery. Exploration nevertheless went on through the work of private shippers and capitalists. Portuguese captains pressed beyond Sierra Leone and followed Africa eastward to reach the Ivory Coast, the Gold Coast, and the Slave Coast. Revenue could be gained from all of these places, and the Portuguese also discovered an African pepper which they could sell in Europe as a substitute for the expensive East Indian brand. The African coast, known by the general name of Guinea (Ghana), now yielded such profits that Castilians and Frenchmen began sailing there to encroach on the Portuguese monopoly.

The throne of Portugal passed to Prince Henry's great-nephew, John II, in 1481. This sovereign, probably the ablest man ever to govern Portugal, made his fourteen-year reign memorable in many ways, but most of all for its achievements in geographical discovery. Like Henry, he was a man of inflexible purpose, totally dedicated to carrying out his plans. The plans had expanded by his time, for the king no longer meant to confine Portuguese energies to exploration of western Africa, when a greater world lay within reach. He knew the true location of Prester John's Abyssinia and meant his captains to reach it. As this would require the circumnavigation of Africa in any case, he intended them to press beyond to Hindustan. Europeans then mistakenly believed Hindustan to be the home of the most valuable spices.

John first ordered the construction of a fortified castle on the Gold Coast to anchor the region to Portugal, and next sent out an explorer who in 1482 proceeded beyond and to the south. While many miles out to sea, this captain encountered quantities of mud and floating vegetation, and he realized that the mouth of a mighty river lay nearby. Turning shoreward to investigate, he discovered the Congo, named for the Mani Congo, an interesting African potentate who lived and ruled some miles upstream. Making friends with this sovereign, the Portuguese filled him with stories of their own power and greatness and also with a desire to turn Christian with all his people. The desire for Christianity and civilization was later realized to some extent, though not so fully as had been planned in the first rush of enthusiasm.

THE CAPE OF GOOD HOPE

King John planned two expeditions for the year 1487. On one of them two Arab-speaking Portuguese were to go via Egypt to investigate the Indian Ocean and the land of Prester John. On the other expedition a small fleet should attempt to round Africa and enter the Indian Ocean. One of the two travelers died on the journey, but the other, Pedro de Covilhã, carried out the greater part of the mission alone. After visiting India and returning as far as Egypt, he sent the king a letter describing Hindustan. He next went southward to Abyssinia, but conditions in the realm of Prester John (the Abyssinian Negus) were troubled and the Portuguese traveler, taken for a spy, was not allowed to depart. He accordingly spent the remainder of his days in this remote land, and, despite memories of his languishing wife in Portugal, married again. If a Portuguese priest had not entered the country years later and found him there, we should never have learned Covilhã's story.

King John's fleet, commanded by the renowned navigator Bartholomeu Dias, accomplished the greater part of its assignment. After following Africa beyond all points previously reached, the ships were blown by a storm out to sea and past the southernmost point of Africa. The winds then subsided, and Dias, who had kept his squadron together, turned eastward to continue his tracking of the coast. Several days' sailing failed to reveal land, and the Portuguese then realized that they had passed Africa and were in open water to the south. Turning northward, they struck land considerably east of the great promontory of Good Hope. As the continent now bent northward, the seamen followed it until they knew themselves to be heading into the Indian Ocean. Dias would have persevered to Hindustan, but his weary seamen now resorted to a sit-down strike in their determination to return home. The commander reluctantly yielded. As an old Portuguese writer put it, "one might almost say that he saw the land of India, but, like Moses with the Promised Land, he could not enter it."

During the return voyage Dias sighted and passed the Cape of Good Hope on a forgotten date in the year 1488. An unreliable tradition says that he first called it Cabo Tormentoso ("Stormy Cape") because of its tempests, but that King John changed the name to Boa Esperança ("Good Hope") "because it promised that discovery of India so hoped for and so many years desired."

VASCO DA GAMA AND INDIA

Although John II lived until 1495, he did not send an expedition to reach India. Home troubles kept him occupied, and meanwhile he had started the construction of new ships which experience indicated would be better adapted to the wind and weather of the south Atlantic. Then, in 1493, Christopher Columbus returned to Europe, having discovered the West Indian islands of Cuba and Hispaniola for Ferdinand and Isabella of Spain. This meant that two nations were now engaged in the business of discovery and, as competition threatened to be keen, the Spanish sovereigns appealed to Pope Alexander VI, himself a Spaniard, for a ruling in their favor. Alexander responded with a series of papal bulls, in which he gave Ferdinand and Isabella jurisdiction over most of the Atlantic, unrestricted rights over new lands that might be found in the west, and the privilege of dispossessing the Portuguese of the gains thus far made by them in Africa.

John II naturally objected to such an outrageous award and resorted to threats of war against Spain. The Spanish monarchs then decided to grant better terms, and in 1494 signed the Treaty of Tordesillas with John's envoys. The most important clause of the treaty read:

> It being the pleasure of their Highnesses, they, their said representatives, acting in their name and by virtue of their powers herein described, covenanted and agreed that a boundary or straight line be determined and drawn north and south, from pole to pole, on the said ocean sea, from the Arctic to the Antarctic pole. This boundary or line shall be drawn straight as aforesaid, at a distance of three hundred and seventy leagues west of the Cape Verde Islands.[4]

Discovery and conquest rights east of this line belonged to Portugal; westward, the same privileges were conceded to Spain. This Demarcation Treaty, as it is called, made no mention of the extension of the line to the other side of the globe. The omission merely postponed a dispute that inevitably arose when Spain and Portugal, each proceeding by its own route, later met in the East Indies.

At the time of the treaty nothing in America had been explored other than a few islands of the West Indies. Yet, unknown to both parties, the Tordesillas line was so drawn as to bisect the shoulder of Brazil and place

[4] Francis Gardner Davenport (ed.), *European Treaties Bearing on the History of the United States and Its Dependencies, to 1648* (Washington, D.C.: Carnegie Institution, 1918), p. 95.

the eastern segment of that country in the Portuguese sphere. This was the historical origin of Portugal's later ownership of Brazil.

Manuel I (1495-1521) of Portugal, surnamed the Fortunate, carried out John's plan of a voyage to Hindustan. Selecting as his captain the rough but able Vasco da Gama, he dispatched him from Lisbon with a fleet of four ships in 1497. Da Gama, instead of hugging the African coast in the manner of Dias and earlier predecessors, thrust boldly out into the Atlantic and sailed in mid-ocean until reaching almost the latitude of the Cape of Good Hope. Next, turning eastward and rounding the promontory, he passed up the east African coast, where he made stops at the Moslem cities of Mozambique and Mombasa. Following a series of narrow escapes from the unfriendly Arab inhabitants, he secured the services of a Hindu pilot, who conducted the ships to Calicut on the Malabar coast.

During their considerable stay at Hindu Calicut the Portuguese thought themselves in a Christian city, as they mistook the Brahman temples and depictions of the gods for churches and saints' images. Although bothered by the fact that the "saints" often had elephants' tusks and a half-dozen arms, they remained under this misapprehension and failed to understand why the ruler of Calicut did not esteem them more highly. This Hindu sovereign was, in truth, under the thumb of Moslem merchants who for centuries had dominated Indian foreign trade. Knowing more about Europeans, whose competition they dreaded, than did the Hindus, they at once began to turn the ruler's mind against the intruders. Amid such strained relations the ordinarily tactless Vasco da Gama had to steer a cautious diplomatic course in dealing with the Hindu ruler. By a display of unaccustomed skill, he managed to avoid confiscation of his ships and goods and to push off finally with a small cargo of spice in his holds. The return voyage, though long, proved uneventful, and in July, 1499, the commander and the two ships that had survived the journey were again in Lisbon. As a voyage, this great journey to India and back far outclassed that of Columbus to the West Indies a few years earlier.

PORTUGAL'S EMPIRE IN THE EAST

King Manuel was delighted with Vasco da Gama's achievement despite the smallness of the cargo. During the next few years he sent annual expeditions to India for the purpose of buying and bringing home spice for sale in Europe. The first to follow da Gama was Pedro Álvares Cabral, who departed for India with a large fleet in 1500. For reasons not precisely understood, Cabral veered farther west in the South Atlantic than his predecessor had gone, and encountered the Brazilian coast at about 17° S. He and his pilots realized that under the Treaty of Tordesillas this land belonged to Portugal, and they formally proclaimed the sovereignty of their king. While portions of northern Brazil had a little earlier been coasted

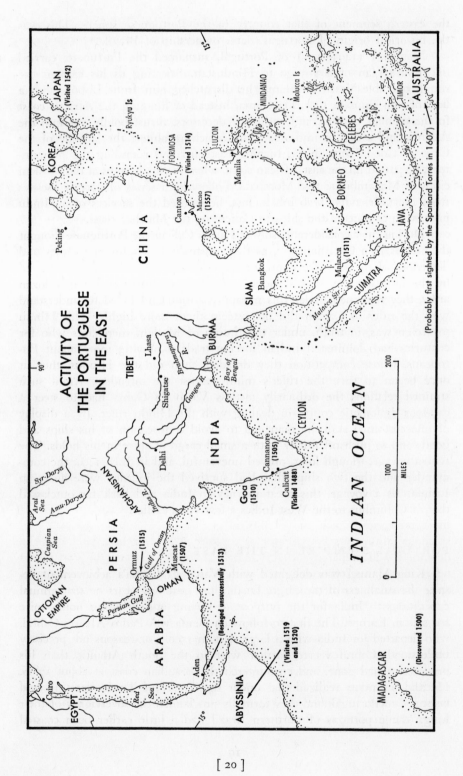

ACTIVITY OF
THE PORTUGUESE
IN THE EAST

JAPAN (Visited 1542)

KOREA

Peking

CHINA

Ryukyu Is

FORMOSA (Visited 1514)

Canton

Macao (1557)

LUZON

Manila

MINDANAO

Moluca Is

CELEBES

BORNEO

JAVA

AUSTRALIA

(Probably first sighted by the Spaniard Torres in 1607)

TIMOR

TIBET

Lhasa

Shigatse

Brahmaputra R.

Ganges R.

BURMA

SIAM

Bangkok

Bay of Bengal

Malacca (1511)

Malacca Str.

Malacca Str.

SUMATRA

90°

Delhi

INDIA

Cannanore (1505)

Calicut (Visited 1488)

Goa (1510)

CEYLON

INDIAN OCEAN

Syr-Darya

Aral Sea

Amu-Darya

AFGHANISTAN

Indus R.

PERSIA

Caspian Sea

Ormuz (1515)

Gulf of Oman

Muscat (1507)

OTTOMAN EMPIRE

Persian Gulf

OMAN

(Besieged unsuccessfully 1513)

Cairo

EGYPT

Red Sea

ARABIA

Aden

ABYSSINIA

(Visited 1519 and 1520)

MADAGASCAR

(Discovered 1500)

15°

15°

0 1000 2000
MILES

by several pilots in Spanish service, this landfall by Cabral is considered the official discovery. Proceeding next to India, the Portuguese expedition touched the island of Madagascar on the way.

Within a few years pilots of Portugal learned both the geography and the sailing conditions of the South Atlantic and the Indian Ocean. They learned, for instance, that they must leave Portugal early in the spring and round the Cape with all possible speed in order to catch the monsoon winds that would blow them quickly from Africa to India. They soon realized their mistake in believing Hindustan to be Christian, and learned that the most valuable spices came not from there but from the remote East Indies, by way of Malacca on the Malay peninsula. They also presently understood that the Arab middlemen poured spice into the Middle East and Europe through the Red Sea and the Persian Gulf, and that most of the cargos went by the latter route. These facts, plus the implacable hostility of the Arabs, who had the backing of the Mameluke sultans of Egypt, soon taught the Portuguese that they could not confine their activity in the East to peaceful commerce. To gain the monopoly of the spice trade, as they now sought to do, they must move ashore and seize a number of land footholds as bases for their power.

In 1505 Portugal began the acquisition and fortification of seaports, both in east Africa and in Hindustan. Several of these, including African Mozambique and Indian Goa, are still Portuguese possessions. The new imperial policy also required the capture of Malacca, guarding the eastern entrance to the Indian Ocean, as well as Ormuz and Aden, commanding the approaches to the Persian Gulf and the Red Sea.

Afonso de Albuquerque, who governed for King Manuel in the East from 1509 to 1515, was the greatest of the Portuguese empire builders. Although elderly and in ill health when he shouldered the task, Albuquerque displayed an iron will and ruthless determination in subduing the enemies of Portugal. Besides keeping the Arabs terrorized, he captured the cities of Goa, Ormuz, and Malacca, thus giving his country bases in the center and at each end of the Indian Ocean. Albuquerque's one conspicuous failure was his attempt to conquer Aden, for here he found the defenders well prepared and suffered a repulse. As a result, the Portuguese never closed this important trade route, through which the Egyptians and their Venetian partners continued to draw some profitable spices. Had Albuquerque lived another year, he would probably have renewed the assault on Aden and might have taken it in a second attempt.

The Portuguese entered the East Indian archipelago beyond Malacca. Here they established trade relations with Java, the Bandas, and the Moluccas, the latter the home of clove, the most valuable of spices. They opened commerce with Siam, and as early as 1514 one of their traders visited Canton in China. In 1542 a group of Portuguese reached Japan, where the missionary effort began that ended so sadly under Hideyoshi.

By this contact with Japan, the Portuguese had reached the extreme eastern limit of civilization. Their great poet, Camões, was largely right when he later sang: "And if there had been more world they would have found it." But east of Japan there could be no more world for them, unless they crossed the Pacific into the Spanish zone. This they never attempted. By reaching the Asiatic shores of the Pacific they had covered the maximum area allotted them at Tordesillas.

3 : The Western Hemisphere

UNKNOWN TO the peoples of the Old World, America had been inhabited for thousands of years. No one knows the full story of human migration to the New World, but the evidence suggests that the Indians and their predecessors came from eastern Asia. The time of their coming is uncertain. Conjectures range as high as one hundred thousand and as low as four thousand years ago, but these are extreme surmises and the truth must lie somewhere between. The migration is thought to have proceeded from Siberia to Alaska by way of Bering Strait and the Aleutian Islands. Because of the immense amount of water absorbed by the last glacier, a land bridge once existed where the strait now lies; if the immigrants crossed before the melting of the glacier ice caused the bridge to disappear, they did not need to traverse water. If they came later, they may have walked on the ice of the frozen strait during the winters. The theory most favored is that two human waves came from Asia, both before the appearance of civilization anywhere on earth. The first consisted of people quite unlike the later Indians and perhaps related to the modern white races. A branch of this group may have been diverted to Japan where it became the Ainu. The second wave consisted of Mongoloids—offshoots of the early stock that later settled in China, Korea, and Japan.

The primitive whites and Mongoloids met and mingled in the New World, where the Mongoloids predominated because of their greater numbers. The resulting dark-skinned mixture became the American Indian. This fusion must have taken place long ago, as the Indians preserved no memory of it in their legends. Thousands of years of residence in America must have been required to produce the great differences in language, culture, customs, and even physical appearance that developed among them. Despite variation in skin texture and pigmentation, all Indians are brown, as the word "redskin" originally referred merely to the paint with which they daubed their faces and bodies.

The Indians, or Proto-Indians, first spread from Alaska through North America, some pushing down the Rockies and the Pacific coast and others moving eastward to the Mississippi and the Atlantic shores of the United

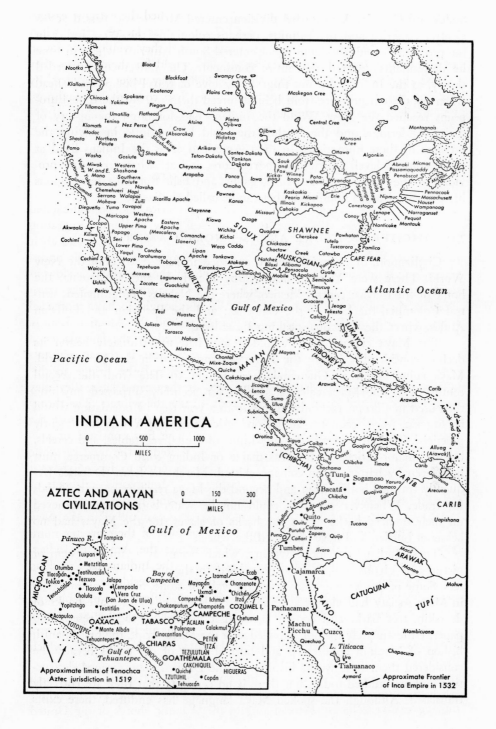

INDIAN AMERICA

0   500   1000
MILES

AZTEC AND MAYAN CIVILIZATIONS

0   150   300
MILES

Approximate limits of Tenochca
Aztec jurisdiction in 1519

Approximate Frontier
of Inca Empire in 1532

Pacific Ocean

Gulf of Mexico

Atlantic Ocean

Gulf of Mexico

Gulf of Tehuantepec

States and Canada. A vanguard division entered Mexico and passed across Central America and the Isthmus, perhaps colonizing the West Indies in the process. The advance contingent entered South America, where in time its descendants covered the entire continent. The movement proceeded slowly, as the Indians did not migrate for love of travel but pushed ahead when population pressure from behind forced them on. By the time Europeans reached the New World the Indians had forgotten the history of their wanderings, and the legends they told helped little in solving the problem of these migrations. In most American areas the Indians lived at a low cultural level, practiced no agriculture, and ate whatever nature provided in the way of edible plants, game, and fish. But in a few regions life proceeded under conditions that can be called civilized.

THE HIGHER CULTURE AREAS—NORTH AMERICA

Civilization, or near-civilization, emerged in four districts of the New World. These were Yucatan and nearby Honduras and Guatemala, the home of the Mayas; central Mexico, where the Nahuas predominated; central Colombia, the land of the Chibchas; and the Peruvian and Bolivian Andes, where the Quechua-speaking Incas lived.

The Maya culture was the oldest and had unfortunately begun its decline considerably before the Europeans appeared in the New World. Maya ruins found in Guatemala are thought to date from the second century A.D. The Maya calendar, which for accuracy surpassed anything then used in Europe, reckoned events from a year that by our dating would be 613 B.C. Maya economy rested on agriculture, which was intelligently practiced. The farmers raised many kinds of fruits, vegetables, and cereals, but the major article of diet was maize or Indian corn. Commerce must have been by barter, as no coinage existed. Merchants from the cities frequently traveled both within and beyond the Maya territory carrying goods for trade. Whenever products could not be water-borne they journeyed on their owners' backs or on the backs of slaves, for the Mayas had no beasts of burden and never invented the wheel.

These Indians developed writing, which began as a simple system of pictures or glyphs and in time progressed to the use of phonetic characters. Some of the writing was carved on walls or stone, but the priests, who in Maya society had almost a monopoly on learning, could make books of deerskin, tree bark, and certain leaves that yielded a product resembling paper. Unfortunately for our knowledge of the Maya script, the first Spanish bishop of Yucatan confiscated and burned most of the books because he considered them false works inspired by the Devil. A few escaped destruction and are studied today, but there is no certainty that they are correctly translated. Although the spoken Maya language has endured, there exists no reliable key to the written script, which has been forgotten by the present-day Yucatan Indians.

The Mayas were artistically gifted and found their favorite forms of expression in painting, sculpture, and architecture. The painting has mostly perished, but some of the sculptured figures and many of the buildings survive. To the modern eye, they contain little of their pristine beauty, as time has removed the brilliant coloring that once covered them. The Maya religion honored many gods and goddesses, whose worship was presided over by well-organized groups of priests and nuns. Belief existed in an afterlife in which souls received reward or punishment according to their deserts. In earlier stages this religion had not involved human sacrifice, but invaders from Mexico introduced the custom about the twelfth century, and it was never eradicated. Usually the priests cut out the victim's heart, but the god of rain, supposedly dwelling in a sacred well, was sometimes propitiated by having attractive maidens hurled into his watery abode to join and comfort him. The Mayas resembled the classical Greeks in making the city-state their political unit. Whether there was a league or alliance between the numerous cities is uncertain, but as the people were by nature warlike and yet usually lived without fighting among themselves, it seems likely that some loose union existed.

Maya history witnessed two distinct periods of cultural flowering, the first in the south, involving Honduras and Guatemala, and the second in Yucatan. The old southern culture, which was the more brilliant of the two, lasted about four hundred years and came to an end around A.D. 870. No one knows why it expired so abruptly, but a likely explanation is that the overfarmed soil became exhausted. A wholesale exodus then took place to Yucatan, where the Mayas built a new group of cities. This second civilization, or renaissance, also flourished for centuries, though a little less radiantly than its predecessor. It too finally decayed, and when the Spaniards arrived in the sixteenth century Maya culture had become a sad relic of its former self and some of the fine cities stood abandoned and empty.

The plateau of Anáhuac in central Mexico, the home of the Nahuas, developed another interesting culture. This has been popularly named for the Aztecs, who were not its principal builders and who came upon the scene rather late. We cannot here describe the peoples who dominated Anáhuac before Aztec times, but one earlier branch, the Toltecs, certainly contributed more to the culture than did the better-known and better-publicized Aztecs.

When the Spaniards invaded Mexico in 1519 the present Mexico City was called Tenochtitlán. It had been built less than two centuries earlier by the Tenochca Aztecs, originally a single tribe. The earliest traditions of the Tenochcas, which possibly contain kernels of fact, describe them as having wandered for generations in search of a home. They entered

Anáhuac probably from the northwest, led by priests of their foremost god. Reaching the vicinity of Lake Texcoco, they attempted to settle, but the hostility of a neighboring chief forced them to move to an island in the lake, where in 1325 they founded Tenochtitlán. Although a small people at first, they grew and in the fifteenth century made an alliance with two nearby cities for mutual defense and profitable conquest. Under this arrangement Tenochtitlán flourished and soon reduced its two allies to satellite status. Its warriors commenced a series of conquering campaigns which extended Tenochca influence from the Gulf of Mexico to the Pacific and from Guatemala to Tampico. The Aztecs failed to found an empire in the true sense and imposed no system of administration on the cities they subdued. From their vassals—Cholula, Cempoala, Orizaba, and many others—they exacted tribute. Otherwise they left the conquered to govern themselves.

The Aztecs thus fastened themselves on a culture, or civilization, that was very old. Central Mexico had long been a region of extensive agriculture and flourishing cities. Industry and the arts had been nourished, and the people in general appear to have lived busy and happy lives. Like the Mayas, the Nahuas were extensive builders and their cities were adorned with impressive palaces, temples, and pyramids. Much attention was paid to clothing and personal adornment, gaily-colored garments being supplemented with brilliantly-dyed bird feathers, jewels, and ornaments of gold and silver. The priests possessed considerable scholarship and used a form of writing which was cruder than Maya script. The most blighting feature of Tenochca-Aztec domination was the hideous system of human sacrifice it involved. The Tenochcas felt obliged to wage perpetual war against their neighbors to obtain captives to serve as religious offerings and slaves. According to the Aztec religious theory, the great gods had made their people strong and given them domination, yet themselves needed to be strengthened at frequent intervals with the most precious fluid that existed— the blood of human males. With each military success the gods grew more insatiable, and a vicious cycle developed that could not be broken. The peoples who supplied the victims naturally detested their conquerors and awaited a favorable opportunity for getting rid of them.

THE HIGHER CULTURE AREAS—SOUTH AMERICA

The Chibchas in the highlands of present-day Colombia were in the process of evolving a higher culture, though at the time of the European invasion they had not equaled those of Yucatan and Mexico to the north or Peru to the south. Five centers of political power existed in Colombia, although the chief of Bacatá, or Bogotá, was the outstanding ruler. If the Spaniards had delayed their coming a few generations, this sovereign, or Zipa, would probably have overcome the others and founded an empire.

The Chibchas lived principally by agriculture, which they supplemented with hunting. Their chief products were maize and potatoes. They had no beasts of burden, as the central Andean llama did not exist so far north. An interesting feature of the Chibcha economy was a crude coinage, the only one in America, consisting of gold plates hammered thin and used as a medium of exchange. Slavery, though practiced, did not occupy a fundamental place in the society. Slaves ordinarily lived comfortable lives and were even employed for military service against savages beyond the borders. The pleasure-loving Chibchas enjoyed feasts and games. Athletic contests were also popular with them, particularly foot races, whose winners received honors and prizes. No religious occasion was too solemn to culminate in a carousal and the consumption of large quantities of *chicha,* the national beer. Chibcha temples, being merely straw huts, were poor things compared with the mighty structures reared in Mexico and Peru. But temples had no great part in the worship of this people, who preferred such outdoor sites as lakes and groves. Apparently, a Chibcha ruler once planned to build a stone and marble edifice to the gods and collected materials for the purpose. Something prevented the execution of the plan, for the temple went unbuilt and the stones intended for it can be seen to this day. Human sacrifice was practiced in pre-Spanish Colombia but had passed its zenith before the Spanish conquest of the Chibchas. It had grown permissible to use animal victims, and talking parrots were especially welcome substitutes.

The Chibchas believed that souls lived after death and traveled to another land in a boat of spider web. For that reason the spider was an object of veneration, not to be killed. Embalming was practiced in the case of illustrious dead, though the Chibchas customarily burned corpses. The most interesting Chibcha religious ceremony was practiced by the Guatabitas, who became subjects of the Zipa of Bacatá not long before the Spanish conquest. In their days of independence the Guatabitas made their ruler-elect the center of a ritual taking place in a lake bearing their tribal name. People thronged to its shores and started innumerable sacrificial fires, into which they cast incense that rose in clouds. Attendants stripped the new ruler, covered him with some adhesive substance and powdered him thickly with gold dust. Next, accompanied by four important vassals, the chieftain entered a balsa raft, which was gaudily adorned and contained burning incense. The raft sailed to the middle of the deep lake and the ruler plunged in. The next few seconds revealed whether he was able to scrape the gold from his body and rise to re-enter the raft, or whether he sank, leaving his people to choose another sovereign. In either case the raft returned to shore and the day terminated in a feast. This custom furnished the basis of the El Dorado, the gilded-man legend, which fascinated the Spaniards, and which they sought to verify in many parts of South America. It will be clear from this description that the Chibcha culture had many crudities.

It nevertheless had possibilities and a capacity for advancement. Left to itself, it might in a few generations have grown more refined.

THE INCAS

Far older and more important was the culture of the Incas, whose center was in the Andean highlands of Peru. The Incas did not alone create the civilization bearing their name, for like the Tenochca-Aztecs they entered the scene rather late. Their immediate predecessors as culture leaders were the Tiahuanaco builders, so called because of the impressive ruins they have left at Tiahuanaco south of Lake Titicaca in Bolivia. Tiahuanaco apparently gave cultural unity to an area nearly as large as the later Inca state. It declined about A.D. 900, and if there was an empire it broke up.

The following two centuries witnessed a decayed culture in Peru, in which little important political activity occurred. Then the Incas, previously an obscure Quechua-speaking tribe living on the high plateau near Lake Titicaca, migrated to the richer valley of Cuzco. From a primitive economy, based mainly on llama herding, they passed to simple and then to complicated agriculture. As large portions of their new home were deprived of rain for long periods, they devised a system of irrigation canals. Much of the arable land lay on hillsides, which they terraced by a series of long parallel walls, each inclining slightly inward to support the weight. They used guano for fertilizer to grow their principal crop, maize, and to raise such lesser ones as potatoes, beans, manioc, and a kind of buckwheat. From maize came their favorite beverage, the same *chicha* beer that was consumed by the Chibchas. The llama continued to be a mainstay of the Incas in their new environment. Besides this beast there was its smaller kinsman the alpaca, which has a thicker coat but is less useful as draft animal. For wool, the Incas preferred the wild vicuña, a mountain creature related to the llama and alpaca, which they hunted for its coat but never domesticated. Even the tame creatures provided but limited service as beasts of burden; a grown llama can be loaded up to perhaps 100 pounds but cannot carry human beings or be yoked to the plow.

The word Inca has three meanings. Most broadly, it applies to the large empire ultimately created by the conquering emperors and warriors from Cuzco. It also designates the original race of conquerors, who were lords of this empire but who comprised but a small percentage of its total population. Finally, it refers to the *Sopa Inca,* the supreme ruler of the state and the most powerful sovereign in America. According to tradition, the first Sopa Inca was Manco Capac, a culture hero of whom most reports are legendary. He is said to have married his sister, a custom prevalent among the later Sopas, and to have led the way to Cuzco. If such a person existed, he lived around A.D. 1100, though he surely bore small resemblance to the mighty being whom the subsequent Incas imagined as the founder of their greatness. Under a line of reputed descendants of Manco the Inca people built an empire, conquering slowly at first and then with greater speed. National pride demanded that each ruler add something to the realm, and each strove to give satisfaction. The superiority of the Incas over their neighbors was not so much a matter of greater bravery or better weapons as of leadership, discipline, and a tradition of victory in which they took pride.

The Inca state by the middle of the fifteenth century had come to be of truly imperial dimensions. It extended from Cajamarca in northern Peru to Tucumán in northwest Argentina, and by then had probably attained the maximum size for effective government from Cuzco. A wonderfully-ordered, smooth-working despotism, it was held together not only by the godlike prestige of the Sopa Inca but also by efficient armies, a system of excellent roads and fortifications, a capable bureaucracy, and a policy that strove to inspire loyalty rather than abject fear among the conquered tribes and kingdoms. Communications between the center and the outlying parts of this far-flung empire were frequent and rapid. The messages borne by post runners who relayed the Sopa's orders could not be written, for the Andean peoples failed to develop writing. But a knotted thong called a *quipu* could be made to convey statistical information, and in the case of a more complicated message the initial runner memorized the text in order to deliver it accurately to the next courier, who in turn passed the same words on to another. The roads used by these messengers and the high suspension bridges spanning the chasms and gorges of the Andes could also be used by Inca soldiers on their way to quell insurrections or make fresh conquests.

The Incas considered religious conformity highly important. Sun worship being a central feature of their cult, they built sun temples wherever they conquered. Coricancha, the solar temple in Cuzco, was the most impressive building in the city and probably the finest ever erected by the Incas. Though acknowledging many gods, the Incas showed signs of progressing toward monotheism. Viracocha, their creator deity, so far outstripped the rest in importance that this omnipotent spirit came to be virtually an amalgamation of all others. The monotheistic tendency existed mostly in the upper social castes which had a more spiritual faith than the humble folk who characteristically clung to crude interpretations of the gods and their activities. Sacrifice played a part in Inca worship, though the Peruvians generally disapproved of human offerings and forbade them among the peoples they conquered. Yet at times the gods or the souls of the illustrious dead might demand appeasement and on such occasions the Sopa could set aside the usual taboos and designate selected persons for sacrifice.

A Sopa Inca, whom public opinion and the priestly theologians held to be a god, lived in a manner becoming a god. Though understood to be physically mortal and to possess human failings, such limitations did not alter his divine status. During his sojourn on earth he lived in a handsome palace, constructed by his orders at the outset of his reign. After his departure the palace remained sacred to his memory and various of his descendants dwelt there at public expense to make suitable offerings to his spirit, while succeeding rulers built residences of their own. The new Sopa, following the supposed example of Manco Capac, was bound by convention to marry his sister, the *Coya,* and only the sons she bore had the legal right to inherit the throne. Yet the rulers had many concubines who produced numerous male children, and doubtless these lesser princes sometimes succeeded to the power. Once in possession of the throne, it proved possible to juggle one's genealogy a little in order to bring fact and theory together.

Until nearly the end the Sopa Incas continued the policy of conquest, and by the reign of Huayna Capac (1482–1527) the empire extended from northern Ecuador to the Rapel River in Chile, including a territory as great as the Atlantic states of the United States. Population estimates vary considerably: one authority gives it as 16,000,000, but others cut this figure to less than half. The later territorial growth had something unhealthy about it, for the empire was now too large for efficient government by the means at the Sopa's disposal. Overexpansion had weakened the structure and made inevitable the split which came, as ill luck would have it, at the time of the Spanish invasion when it could do the maximum damage. The whole culture, moreover, displayed signs of decay. It had already grown static, and its unchangeable nature indicates that senescence was not far away. The Incas showed no signs of developing a script or alphabet, and their primitive *quipu* could be no adequate substitute for the writing they needed in order to progress. The stage of grand-scale imperialism they had reached is one that history seems to show comes when a culture has exhausted its other potentialities. We must conclude, then, that the Inca culture was not a young one full of latent vigor but an old one that had spent most of its force.

4 : The Spaniards in America

IN THE AUTUMN of 1492 Christopher Columbus (1451–1506) of Genoa, commanding three small ships in the service of Ferdinand and Isabella of Spain, discovered the Bahamas, Cuba, and Hispaniola. Inspired by Marco Polo and other authorities, and underestimating the circumference of the earth, he had persuaded the Spanish sovereigns to back him by arguing

Nuno Gonçalves was a fifteenth-century Portuguese painter. In the religious scene shown above, several of the characters are members of the Portuguese royal family. Prince Henry the Navigator is in the right center of the group, wearing a religious habit and a round black hat. This is believed to be the only authentic portrait of the great prince who was the world's first systematic promoter of voyages of geographical discovery.

Tikal is a ruined Mayan city in the Petén department of Guatemala. It is believed to have been founded in the second century of the Christian era, although the pyramid temple shown here was built about A.D. 700. The temple proper is the square edifice resting on top of the steep pyramid. City and temple belong to the earlier period of Mayan culture.

The ruins of Chichén Itzá, located about a hundred miles from Mérida, the capital of modern Yucatan, are in a fairly good state of preservation. The Temple of the Warriors is one of the chief architectural features of the city. Chichén Itzá, along with Mayapán and Uxmal, was one of the power centers of the Mayans during their final, or Yucatan, period.

The "Victoria" was the only vessel of Magellan's fleet to make the entire voyage around the earth. Commanded by Sebastián de Elcano and with a surviving crew of eighteen men, this small ship returned to its original point of departure, Sanlúcar in Spain, in 1522, having spent approximately three years in the voyage of circumnavigation.

that a westward voyage from Europe to Polo's Cipangu (Japan) and the Great Khan's Cathay (China) would be neither long nor particularly difficult. Although the primitive people he found in the islands seemed a far cry from the peoples Polo had described, Columbus had the courage of his convictions and returned to Spain confident that in Cuba he had reached China and that in Hispaniola he had found Japan. The Ming Dynasty and the Ashikaga Shogunate for years remained unconcerned by all this, but the New World felt the impact of Columbus' discovery at once. On reaching Europe with news of his findings, Columbus encountered the opposition of John II of Portugal. The result was the Treaty of Tordesillas (see page 18) which gave the Portuguese a monopoly of the East and insured their future possession of Brazil. By this treaty Spain obtained a free hand in the exploration and exploitation of the remainder of the Western Hemisphere.

Columbus made three later voyages, in which he discovered more West Indian islands, the coast of Venezuela, the eastern shores of Central America, and the Panama Isthmus. Though he several times changed his mind regarding the exact Asiatic pattern of his discoveries, he clung to the main idea that he had made contact with eastern Asia. He died in this belief, although by the time of his death several Spanish pilots and geographers had progressed beyond him in their thinking to the point of gaining some inkling of the truth.

Foremost among these was Amerigo Vespucci of Florence (1454–1512), a businessman who in middle life turned pilot and cartographer. Amerigo made several voyages to the New World in the service first of Spain and then of Portugal. His most famous expedition, under the Portuguese flag in 1501–02, carried him down the South American coast to a point south of Río de la Plata. Everything he saw there—the flora, the fauna, and the inhabitants—convinced him that this could be no part of Asia as described by ancient authorities and medieval travelers. Shortly thereafter he used the expression *Mundus Novus* (New World) in a letter to a friend in Florence, a letter that soon found its way into print and became highly publicized through Europe. With no wish to steal the laurels rightly belonging to Columbus, Amerigo found himself generally regarded as the discoverer of the New World. As early as 1507 the geographer Martin Waldseemüller, writing in the town of St.-Dié in Lorraine, proposed that the new continent, meaning South America, be named for its illustrious discoverer. Waldseemüller first discussed the three continents previously known, Europe, Asia, and Africa, and then continued:

But now these regions have been extensively revealed and another fourth part has been found by Amerigo Vespucci (as will presently be seen), and I do not see any reason why we should not call it

31

Amerigen or America, meaning the land of Amerigo, after its discoverer Amerigo, that sagacious man, as both Europe and Asia have obtained their names from women.[5]

Waldseemüller's proposal soon gained acceptance with most geographers, who began by applying the name America to the southern continent and within a generation attached it to the northern one as well. The Spaniards and Portuguese resisted the name for many years, possibly because they were in a better position than others to know the origins of the great discovery. To them the New World remained merely "the Indies."

THE CIRCUMNAVIGATION OF THE GLOBE

Once the Spaniards grasped the fact that America was not the Asia they sought, they regarded it as an obstacle to be somehow surmounted in order to reach the land, or islands, of spice. Their principal hope for a time was that a strait might be found leading through the apparently useless *Mundus Novus*. This, they thought, should bring them easily to the treasures of the East, for their calculations entirely excluded the enormous width of the Pacific Ocean. The important Spanish voyages of discovery for over a decade after the death of Columbus were therefore principally devoted to the search for this strait. South America's coast was again traced as far as the Río de la Plata, while other expeditions explored the contours of the Gulf of Mexico. Voyagers for England, particularly John and Sebastian Cabot, had meanwhile taken a hand by traversing parts of the coast of North America. All such efforts led to disappointment, and the Spaniards at length concluded that if the strait existed it must lie in the extreme south. At this point the Portuguese Magellan appeared in Spain with a plan for conducting an expedition to the Spice Islands.

Ferdinand Magellan (1480–1521) had spent some years in the Portuguese East. He believed that his own countrymen, by reaching the eastern end of the Indian Ocean, had covered all the longitude allotted them by the Treaty of Tordesillas and that what lay beyond was in the half of the globe belonging to Spain. Therefore the clove-growing Moluccas and the nutmeg-yielding Bandas were legitimate Spanish possessions if only Spain could reach them by a western approach. Magellan thought that, once around South America, the distance to the Moluccas should be short, as he too had no conception of the width of the Pacific. He might never have offered his plan to Spain had he not been snubbed and slighted by his king,

---

[5] Author's translation from Latin text in John Fiske, *The Discovery of America* (Boston and New York: Houghton, Mifflin and Company, 1898), Vol. II, p. 136.

Manuel I of Portugal, who refused him what he considered a merited promotion and raise in pay. As this deprived Magellan of any opportunity to be of further service to his own country, he considered himself a free agent and transferred to the other major maritime power, Spain, whose benefactor he meant to be. He quickly convinced the officials and the new young monarch, Charles, that the Moluccas were rightly theirs and would be found not far west of the Panama Isthmus, which Spain had recently occupied. He asked for a fleet to find the South American strait, whose location he thought he knew, and to make the supposedly short run from there to the Spice Islands. He had no intention of circling the globe, and if he had found the Moluccas where he expected he would simply have laden his holds with cloves and returned to Spain by retracing his outward course.

Magellan obtained a fleet from the Spanish government with speed and ease, and in 1519 left the port of Sanlúcar with five ships. The first course lay southward through the Atlantic to the Brazilian coast and down it to the Río de la Plata. Although this estuary had been explored twice before, Magellan made another reconnaissance in the hope that the desired strait might still be found there. Disappointed, as others had been, to encounter only fresh-water rivers flowing from the interior, he continued southward to winter in San Julián Bay on the Patagonian coast. Here, with the aid of the numerous Portuguese accompanying him, he suppressed a dangerous mutiny led by Spanish officers whom enemies of Magellan in Spain had taught to hate their commander. The principal trophies of the sojourn were two Patagonian giants, whom the mariners captured by a stratagem but who died when the expedition re-entered the tropics.

Magellan sailed southward in the spring and discovered the strait that still bears his name. Sailing through it, he emerged into the Pacific with a fleet reduced to three ships, one having been wrecked and another having deserted. The expedition sailed northward, until the commander thought he had reached the latitude of the Moluccas, and then turned to the west. As days stretched into weeks and weeks into months Magellan realized his great mistake and miscalculation. Until now, all his expectations had been borne out, but he had not counted on this immense expanse of ocean. Food spoiled, water spoiled, and men daily fell ill or died of scurvy and privation. "The sea biscuit we ate was not bread," later wrote one of the voyagers, "but a powder mixed with worms which had devoured all its substance, and it had an unbearable odor from being soaked with rats' urine." More vigorous crews nearer home would have mutinied, but now the simplest sailor realized that the only hope lay in pressing on. Bad weather would have caused the expedition to vanish forever from the knowledge of men, but on this first crossing the ocean merited the name Pacific. Just when further endurance seemed impossible, the voyagers sighted the Mariana Islands. The Micronesian natives clambered aboard the ships stealing everything they could lay hands on, and thus caused Magellan to give the name Ladrones (Thieves) to the entire island group. After a brush with the inhabitants the voyagers obtained food and, strengthened by the nourishment, resumed the westward voyage and next reached the southern Philippines. A Malay interpreter with the expedition could make himself understood by the inhabitants, proving that the ships had reached the vicinity of the Spice Islands.

Magellan now made the mistake of taking sides in a native war to aid a chieftain he had personally converted to Christianity. The battle, on the island of Mactan, ended in defeat for the Spaniards and death for the commander in April, 1521. The Christian chief then repented of his conversion, turned against the white men, and drove them with heavy loss from his island. The survivors elected new leaders and for several months sailed among the East Indies, finally reaching the Moluccas. Here they loaded the holds with cloves and considered the question of their return to Spain. There being no longer manpower enough for the three ships, they destroyed the least seaworthy and distributed crews, spice, and provisions between the other two. It was determined that one of these should sail eastward and attempt to reach the Spanish settlements on the Panama Isthmus. The commander set out, but unfavorable winds forced him back to the East Indies, where he and his crew fell prisoners to the Portuguese.

The remaining ship, *Victoria,* commanded by the Basque Sebastián de Elcano, made the home journey by way of the Indian Ocean, the Cape of Good Hope, and the Atlantic. The element of risk was as great as ever, for there was no friendly port for Elcano to visit, as he was now crossing the zone reserved for Portugal by the Treaty of Tordesillas. Again food and water ran low, and the men suffered severely. Yet perseverance triumphed, and the *Victoria* with Elcano and seventeen others reached Sanlúcar on a day which the voyagers reckoned as September 6, 1522, three years less two weeks after Magellan had departed with five ships and about two hundred fifty men. So weak and few were the returning mariners that they needed the assistance of a towboat to enter the harbor. They could not at first understand why those in Spain called their arrival date the 7th of September, but a learned gentleman straightway explained that by following the sun's course steadily since departure they had inevitably lost a day in their reckoning.

Elcano's completion of Magellan's voyage furnished proof to any remaining sceptics of the sphericity of the earth and, by introducing the width of the Pacific into calculations, gave Europeans some idea of its circumference. Concerning the immediate and practical aims of the expedition, it showed that the Moluccas, while accessible from Spain, could only be reached after a perilous, heartbreaking voyage. Following a second expedition to the islands, which cost Elcano his life, the Spanish government understandably despaired and sold its Moluccan claim to the king of Portugal for cash. Yet as these Moluccas, by a literal interpretation of the Treaty of Tordesillas, belonged to Portugal, the Spaniards sold islands they did not own for a good round sum. The same rules of ownership rightly applied to the Philippines, but Spain continued to claim them on the strength of Magellan's visit. Over forty years after the death of the explorer on Mactan an expedition from Mexico began the Spanish occupation of the islands that lasted until 1898.

THE SPANISH EMPIRE—
THE ISTHMUS AND NORTH AMERICA

For seventeen years following the first voyage of Columbus the Spaniards confined their New World conquests to the West Indies and refrained from colonizing the mainland. They began the island occupation with Hispaniola, which they quickly overran and on which Bartholomew Columbus, the brother of the discoverer, founded the city of Santo Domingo (today Ciudad Trujillo) in 1496. In the opening years of the sixteenth century they occupied Cuba, Jamaica, and Puerto Rico, exterminating or enslaving the unwarlike Arawak Indians who made up the bulk of the population. In parts of Puerto Rico they had more trouble with the fierce Caribs, or Caribales, whose name, slightly modified to Canibales, furnished a new word to Europeans because of the man-eating habits of these unpleasant people.

In 1509, in the expectation of opening gold mines, a Spanish expedition founded a settlement on the Caribbean side of the mainland Isthmus of Darien, or Panama. Gold proved scarce and the colony suffered for want of competent leaders. At this point Vasco Núñez de Balboa, an able, unscrupulous young Spaniard, took control. By a combination of clever frontier politics and strong-arm tactics, Balboa ousted his legal superiors and became for several years ruler of the Isthmus, his position being always precarious because of the unfavorable view of his procedure taken by the Spanish crown. Knowing that he might at any time be superseded as governor, he felt anxious to perform some outstanding deed that would place him in King Ferdinand's good graces. He learned of the adjacent Pacific Ocean from Indians, one of whom told him that on its shores ruled a powerful king who had abundant gold. The native undoubtedly referred to the Sopa Inca of Peru, whose fame had spread as far north as the Isthmus. Balboa, expecting to find these riches nearer at hand, led an expedition across the Isthmus in 1513 and on September 25 caught sight of the Pacific from a hilltop. Quickly understanding that this was not the region of riches he sought, Balboa planned to use the Pacific as a highway to the Incas. He might have been the discoverer and conqueror of their interesting empire, had he not by royal order been superseded as governor of the Isthmus in 1514 by Pedrarias de Avilés.

Pedrarias, a jealous ancient of seventy-four, had other ideas. He regarded Balboa as a rival and took an early opportunity of trying and judicially murdering him on trumped-up charges of treason. He next transferred headquarters to the Pacific side, where in 1519 he founded Panama, named for a local chief called Tubanamá. Turning his exploring energies in another direction, he sent expeditions which discovered Costa Rica and Nicaragua. Pedrarias, who had committed various tyrannical acts, felt uneasy concerning his own standing with the Spanish government. To be farther from the royal reach, he moved to Nicaragua and spent his last years superintending the colonization of that country. He died there in 1530, aged about ninety.

The conquest of the Mexican Aztecs came as the result of another line of Spanish endeavor, starting from Cuba. Governor Diego Velázquez of the island sent two preliminary expeditions to explore the Yucatan and Gulf coasts, each of which returned with reports of riches and civilization inland. Velázquez determined to possess this apparently valuable area and prepared a fleet and several hundred armed men to undertake the conquest. Unable to leave Cuba himself, he selected as his commander Hernán Cortés, an island settler thirty-four years of age, whom he believed able but without personal ambition and entirely devoted to himself.

Seldom has one man misjudged another as completely as Velázquez misjudged Cortés, who possessed ambition second to none and despised the governor, whom he regarded as the tool who could provide the men and material he needed. Cortés had all the qualities required by a *conquistador* (conqueror): diplomacy, ability to command, ruthlessness, intrepidity, and education enough to give him a fair understanding of the importance of his undertaking. He began by making another investigation of the Yucatan and Gulf coasts, finally landing in 1519 and founding the settlement of Vera Cruz. Here he scuttled the ships, not, as frequently stated, because he meant to cut off all hope of retreat, but because he realized his manpower shortage and wished to add the crews to his small army. Leaving a small garrison at Vera Cruz, he began the inland march to Tenochtitlán to meet Moctezuma II, who was now ruler of the Tenochca Aztecs and the most powerful sovereign in Mexico. Fortunately for Cortés and his enterprise, Moctezuma was the sort of man who is easily conquered. The first reports concerning the Spaniards awakened his fears and brought out all the weaknesses of his superstitious, vacillating nature. He first thought the strangers to be gods and heard with alarm of their sixteen horses, certain that only deities could tame and dominate such fearsome beasts. He lent his name and prestige to a conspiracy to entrap and destroy the Spaniards at Cholula, and when this failed with heavy loss to the Mexicans his remaining courage evaporated. Denying all complicity, he allowed Cortés' small army to march unopposed over the causeway separating Tenochtitlán from the mainland. The Spaniards entered marveling at the beauty of the landscape, the splendor of the birds, trees, and flowers, and the height and magnificence of the temples, palaces, and pyramids.

THE CONQUEST OF MEXICO

Cortés, at the first opportunity, arrested Moctezuma, confined him in the Spanish quarters, and began using him as a puppet for governing the country and collecting the treasure he sought. He next hastened to the coast with the bulk of his force to defeat and win over to his side an army Velázquez had sent from Cuba to capture and punish him. Returning to the city with this substantial reinforcement, Cortés found that the Aztecs had repudiated the authority of captive Moctezuma and were preparing to close in and destroy the white men. When the attack came the Spaniards resisted for days and then evacuated Tenochtitlán, a maneuver that proved so costly as to be known thereafter as *La Noche Triste* (The Sad Night). The survivors then retreated eastward to the friendly city and people of Tlascala, old enemies of the Tenochcas, with whom Cortés had made an alliance during his first march on the capital. The Tlascalans proved men of their word and kept to the alliance they had made. They assisted with preparations for a new attack on Tenochtitlán, and soon fresh contingents of Spaniards arrived from the West Indies, eager to take part in a conquest that promised to be both glorious and lucrative.

When Cortés, with many Indian allies, moved again on Tenochtitlán in 1521 he took boats that could be launched on the lake and used for blockade. He destroyed the aqueduct that furnished the Aztecs with their main supply of drinking water. His Spaniards, assisted by the Tlascalans and other Indians, fought their way forward on the causeways. The Tenochcas, under a brave new ruler, resisted heroically, but famine and plague were at work among them, and when the defense collapsed it collapsed suddenly. Cortés found himself full master of the city, whose ruler attempted to escape in a boat. Captured and brought back to face his conqueror, the young Aztec leader vainly asked for a merciful death. But Cortés had no intention of killing his prisoner before learning the truth of a story, already afloat, to the effect that the defeated chieftain had caused a great treasure to be carried away and hidden. It is almost certain that the story had no foundation, although the "Lost Aztec Treasure" has been discussed for centuries and occasionally still awakens interest among the credulous.

Cortés' next tasks were to recreate Tenochtitlán as a Spanish city and to conquer the surrounding area. The conquistador worked at these objectives as long as he remained in Mexico. The city, renamed Mexico, became superficially Spanish, and missionaries baptized hordes of uncomprehending natives into the Christian faith. Conquest of the outlying parts was mainly accomplished by the lieutenants and subordinates of Cortés. Guatemala, the home of a Maya-type culture, early succumbed to one of the conquerors of Mexico. Yucatan, where the degenerate civilization of the Mayas in a measure continued, resisted for two generations the conquering efforts of a family whose founder had been with Cortés.

In the generation following the fall of Tenochtitlán Spanish adventurers roamed over northern Mexico and parts of the United States in the hope of finding another civilization as rich as that of the Aztecs. They lived in a credulous age, in which every kind of tall story not only found believers but stimulated men to action. Six years before the invasion of Mexico Juan Ponce de León had discovered Florida in a vain search for a Fountain of Youth. Following the Aztec conquest new stories, or variants of very old ones, cropped up to tempt would-be explorers. Belief in a rich island of Amazon women, belief in a northern strait connecting the Atlantic and the Pacific, and reports of such mythical wonderlands as the Seven Cities of Cibola and Golden Quivira all mingled in the Spanish mind to produce intrepid feats of exploration. Hernando de Soto traversed the southeastern United States and discovered the Mississippi, though what he really sought was a greater "Florida," possessing golden kingdoms for plunder. Francisco Vázquez Coronado, who crossed Arizona, New Mexico, Texas, Oklahoma, and Kansas, cared little for what he saw, for he traveled with his mind's eye focused on Cibola and Quivira. Juan Rodríguez Cabrillo, who sailed up the coasts of Lower California, California, and Oregon, had his hopes set on the non-existent strait across North America. Before 1550 it had become evident that these mirages would never materialize, and the Spaniards thereafter turned their attention to the exploitation and colonization of the territories they already possessed.

THE SPANISH EMPIRE—SOUTH AMERICA

The conquistadores used their Panama colony as a base for expeditions into South America, and the first region to draw them was naturally Peru. Balboa had heard of the Inca Empire, but his successor, Pedrarias, lacked interest and turned his own attention elsewhere. Yet within a decade a group of Spaniards on the Isthmus decided to pursue the quest that Balboa's death had caused to be temporarily abandoned. At their head was the elderly soldier, Francisco Pizarro, who had been twenty years in the New World without gaining either wealth or fame. The almost penniless adventurers, by borrowing and lavish promises, scraped together money and recruits to make two preliminary expeditions from Panama. The second of these reached northern Peru and abundantly verified reports of Inca treasure. Encouraged, Pizarro now went to Spain and secured from the king a patent granting him the right to govern Peru as soon as he should conquer it at his own expense. Late in 1531 he left Panama to invade the Inca realm with a force of about two hundred men. His lieutenants were principally his three brothers.

The Spaniards found the Incas in the aftermath of a civil war. The conquering Sopa, Huayna Capac, had recently died leaving the state divided between two sons. They could not co-exist in peace, and Atahualpa, ruler of Quito, resented the fact that his brother possessed Cuzco and the title Sopa. Atahualpa made his preparations secretly and struck with speed, defeating and dethroning the Inca and attempting to seize the entire empire. But at the time of the Spanish invasion he had not fully consolidated his power. Unrest persisted, and he resorted to a policy of terrorism to prevent a counter-rebellion.

Pizarro and Atahualpa met at Cajamarca, where, under pretense of a friendly parley, the Spanish leader arranged for an interview. Behaving much as Cortés had done with Moctezuma, Pizarro broke the truce, slaughtered the followers of Atahualpa, and took the ruler prisoner. For months the Spaniards used the Inca as a pawn in governing the country and in collecting a huge treasure. When they considered his usefulness at an end, they put him to death on charges of rebellion and fratricide, worship of false gods, and polygamy. Advancing to Cuzco where he enthroned another puppet Sopa, the Spanish leader began organizing Peru as a Spanish possession and sent an advance expedition to investigate Chile. News of the magnificent Inca spoil had now spread through Spanish America and other soldiers and colonists came flocking into Peru by the thousand. To serve as the capital of the new colony, Pizarro founded Lima, "The City of the Kings," near the coast, because he considered this a better location for the purpose than Cuzco.

Hard fighting was necessary, however, before the Spaniards could call themselves masters of Peru. Pizarro's latest Inca puppet did not prove to be the supine creature that had been expected. Plotting behind his masters' backs, he raised a formidable rebellion in 1536 that required a long time to suppress. When finally defeated, he retired to the remote hinterland where he and his successors maintained a truncated Inca state for several generations, although it finally submitted and made peace with the conquerors. Pizarro ruled Peru until his assassination by Spanish enemies in 1541. He lived long enough to send Pedro de Valdivia with an expedition to undertake the conquest of Chile, previously reconnoitered by the advance party. Valdivia devoted his remaining years to the task, conquering the northern two-thirds of the country, but being finally captured and slain by the ferocious Araucanian Indians of the south.

Meanwhile, with Peru as a focus, other conquests and explorations had gone on. A Spanish expedition had occupied Quito and the northern Inca provinces. There followed an interesting piece of exploration which ended with the traversal of the Amazon River's main course by Francisco de Orellana, a cousin of the Pizarros. Having crossed the Andes from Quito in search of cinnamon forests rumored to lie to the east, Orellana found a return too difficult. Instead he built a large boat in which he embarked his entire company. Following the course of a tributary, they finally entered the main stream, and sailed and fought their way down it to the Atlantic. Because they at one time battled a group of warrior women, the river basin became known as the "Land of the Amazons," and later generations bestowed the Amazonian name on the river itself.

The conquest of the Colombian Chibchas proved easy. A Spanish expedition ascended the Magdalena River from the Caribbean, experiencing great hardships on the way. Once in the Bogotá vicinity, the Spaniards easily disposed of Chibcha resistance, for this normally warlike people knuckled under rather ignominiously. By 1538 their slight resistance had ended, and the Indian capital Bacatá had been refounded as the Spanish city of Santa Fé de Bogotá. Eastward of Colombia King Charles of Spain for some years farmed out the Venezuelan coast to a German banking firm, the Welsers of Augsburg. The Germans, knowing their tenure of Venezuela would be short, endeavored to extract from it every scrap of wealth in the form of gold and slaves in the briefest possible time. From their coastal base, Coro, they conducted exploring expeditions that for intrepidity and harshness to the natives equaled or surpassed any Spanish efforts. Their leaders Alfinger, Speyer, and Federmann, though they did not molest South America long, caused Spanish contemporaries to speak of their cruelties with a sort of grudging admiration. Like the conquistadores, they had great interest in El Dorado, the gilded man. One of their expeditions in search of this personage ascended the Andes and appeared on the plain of Bogotá, only to find that the Spaniards had arrived there first and had no welcome for German intruders. The Welsers held Venezuela from 1529 to 1546, when the crown of Spain evicted them and turned their holdings into a Spanish colony.

Colonization proceeded slowly and unspectacularly in the Río de la Plata. The name, meaning River of Silver, bears witness to the fact that it was first considered a gateway to wealth, but the truth was that no large quantity of silver existed closer than Bolivia. The future in the Río de la Plata lay in cattle raising and grain growing. The first Spanish generation nevertheless proved unwilling to accept such a humdrum existence and preferred to expend its energy in quest of the Bolivian silver range to the northwest. This explains why, after the preliminary foundation of a Buenos Aires settlement in 1536, the tide of colonization at once leaped far up the Paraná River to Asunción in Paraguay, which possessed advantages as a base for expeditions westward to Bolivia. But once the conquistadores of Peru had fastened their grip on the Bolivian mines, attempts to beat a path across the Chaco and Andes to the silver land had to cease. The Plata area then accepted economic realities. Livestock were introduced, agricultural colonists replaced the earlier adventurers, and Buenos Aires, abandoned soon after its beginning, was refounded in 1580 to become the metropolis of the great river system.

The Portuguese did little with their Brazilian possession during the early sixteenth century. With its small manpower and limited resources overcommitted to the empire in the east, the Portuguese government largely turned Brazil over to private enterprise. Sundry concessionaires established agricultural settlements at Recife, Baía, São Vicente, and other points. For the time being the Portuguese attempted few interior explorations, especially after they learned that the Peruvian and Bolivian mines could not be reached by a short journey across the hinterland. Threats to Brazil by foreign powers finally caused Portugal to strengthen its hold, and in the seventeenth century realization came that many forms of wealth lay in the apparent wastelands of the interior. The coastal Brazilian settlers then engaged in a long series of forays and explorations which furnished many interesting adventures.

SPAIN'S WORK IN AMERICA

The thrilling age of discovery and conquest soon passed, and the Spaniards next faced the problem of what to do with their vast new dominions. Organization naturally came first, and Spain abandoned the governmental makeshifts that had been briefly used, to form two large viceroyalties. These were New Spain, including Mexico and the other territories north of the Isthmus; and Peru, embracing all Spanish possessions in South America. Much later, in the eighteenth century, two new viceroyalties, New Granada and Río de la Plata, were formed when the overly-large Peruvian jurisdiction required paring in the interest of efficiency.

The viceroyalties had various subdivisions and had large staffs manning their numerous offices, each bureaucrat appointed by the Spanish king's Council of the Indies. To the end of the colonial régime European-born Spaniards held an almost total monopoly of these posts, as the policy of Spain was to permit few high-salaried positions to be held by colonials. Control and guidance of the Indians was attempted through the *encomienda* system, which Spain had used earlier for dealing with conquered Moslems and Canary Islanders. Spanish magnates, usually landholders, took charge of Indian groups for the supposed purpose of Christianizing, civilizing, and generally improving them. But as the law allowed the Spanish proprietor to profit from the labor of his Indians, he often turned them into slaves and neglected his responsibilities. Such abuses developed in the system that reforming voices clamored against it, and the government attempted to curb the worst evils. The well-meant efforts failed in the main, as the Spanish New World landholders demanded labor and regarded all other issues as secondary. Encomiendas were finally abolished by law, but in practice many continued because no equally-convenient substitute could be found.

What the swords of the conquistadores superficially accomplished, the patient work of missionaries, parish priests, and royal officials in time achieved more satisfactorily. Christianity took a firm hold on the Indians, and European civilization to some degree affected their daily lives. The staunchest apologist for Spain will not deny that along with progress in America went corruption, extortion, and abuse of the natives. But, on the whole, Spaniards may point with pride to the accomplishment of a civilizing mission. Something like civilization had previously existed in isolated parts of America, yet in all of these the dominant classes were either decadent or semidecadent, as among the Mayas and Incas, or utterly bloodthirsty, as among the Aztecs. Against the cruelty of a Cortés or a Pizarro may be balanced the devoted life of an Antonio de Montesinos or a Bartolomé de las Casas, the great Dominican friars who saw the evils of the encomienda system and who spent their lives working for its abolition. Neither faltered in his course, although in their sixteenth century success was unattainable.

Perhaps the most important result of the Spanish occupation of large parts of America was the appearance of a new branch of the human race, the *mestizo,* a cross between the European and the Indian. When this group made its appearance in the generation following the conquest it was small, and because of its newness, despised. Inevitably, it grew until by its numbers it required and obtained a place in the social system. During more than four hundred years the mestizo class has steadily grown in size and importance. It is the largest blood group in most Spanish American countries, and in several it has become the dominant political class.

5 : Other European Discoveries

THIS CHAPTER has dealt mainly with the Portuguese and Spanish discoveries, because the Iberian peoples for several generations had almost a monopoly of exploration. During the busiest period they moved so rapidly that they made the basic contributions before others were ready to take part. A boy eighteen years old at the time of Prince Henry's death, when only a limited stretch of the African coast had been discovered, could, if he lived to be eighty, learn of the return of Magellan's *Victoria* from the voyage around the globe. He could meanwhile have appreciated the discoveries of Columbus, da Gama, and Vespucci and could have been thrilled by accounts of Albuquerque's empire building in the east, Balboa's march to the Pacific, and Cortés' conquest of the Tenochcas. These were all Iberian achievements, and they came with such startling rapidity as to give Europeans less trained and equipped for overseas adventure small opportunity to offer competition. In time the neighbors of Spain and Portugal in Europe refused to be left out and endeavored to emulate the two leaders.

France, England, and the Netherlands ultimately became the leading rivals of the Iberians. At the time of the discovery of America France was hampered by European entanglements, England needed time to achieve internal stability, and the Dutch had not emerged as an independent people. Only as these handicaps were overcome could these three turn their attention overseas.

FRENCH EXPLORATION

The maritime heart of France was its northern provinces, particularly Normandy and Brittany. These had long been fishing and shipping centers, as well as the home of freebooting marauders. Naturally, then, when the great Iberian discoveries became known, the north of France felt the earliest impulse to share and emulate the exploits.

The flag of France was first borne across the Atlantic by Giovanni da Verrazano, a Florentine engaged by a group of French investors including King Francis I to discover for them a strait leading through North America to the land of Cathay. Departing from Normandy in 1523, Verrazano with a single ship scouted the American coast from South Carolina to Nova Scotia, and in the process discovered New York harbor, which he called Baía S. Margarita. While coasting the narrow Hatteras sandspit off North Carolina, he believed himself near the Pacific because he mistook Pimlico Sound, which he could see but not enter, for the ocean recently crossed and named by Magellan. Verrazano was back in Normandy in 1524 with his news. Evidently the backers did not take the Pacific Ocean possibility very seriously, as the next French move was to send a voyager to investigate farther north. The navigator this time was Jacques Cartier of St.-Malo in Brittany. On his first voyage, in 1534, Cartier explored the Gulf of St. Lawrence, and on his second, a year later, he entered the St. Lawrence estuary, thinking that this might be the strait leading to Cathay. The estuary turned into a river, and at the site of the future city of Quebec the explorer left his ships and ascended by small boat to "the Canada," which was the Huron Indian name for Montreal. Cartier wintered in the river and the following spring, having acquired the tobacco habit and learned an Indian cure for scurvy, he returned with his three ships to St.-Malo. A few years later, with the aid of a partner, he attempted to found a settlement along the St. Lawrence, but the colonists quickly grew discouraged and abandoned the enterprise.

For the remainder of the sixteenth century the French gave little attention to the New World beyond planting small colonies in Brazil and Florida, which the Portuguese and Spaniards immediately destroyed. At the turn of the century they again became interested in America and resumed work in the north. Headed by the indomitable pioneer Samuel de Champlain, they began the penetration of the hinterland. Champlain founded Quebec in 1608, explored the lake later named for him, and pushed westward to Lake Huron. His own discoveries and others for which he was largely responsible opened the way for later Frenchmen, who explored the interior of the continent, descended the Mississippi River, and in time reached the Rockies and the Spanish settlements in New Mexico. Their work came considerably later, however, and belongs to another period of history.

ENGLISH EXPLORATION

England, for many reasons unable in 1492 to engage in large-scale explorations, displayed a spurt of vigor soon after. An association of Bristol merchants, whose interest had been aroused by Marco Polo's report of Cathay, engaged the services of a Genoese captain, John Cabot, to discover this land for them by a westward voyage. Cabot does not appear to have been a mere imitator of Columbus, and had probably turned the project over in his mind independently for years. In 1497 he sailed from Bristol with a single ship and a crew of eighteen men. He was back in three months, having visited North American coasts that have been plausibly identified with Cape Breton Island and Newfoundland. Though he had found neither wealth nor human inhabitants, the English business world rejoiced and King Henry VII took notice to the extent of rewarding Cabot with £10. The following year the explorer sailed again to America with several ships, but nothing is known of the outcome of the expedition or the further career of Cabot. He may have lost his life on the voyage; we know only that his son, Sebastian, who evidently inherited John Cabot's plans and discovery ideas, next occupied the center of the stage. The family theory was that Asia and Cathay would be most easily reached by northern voyaging. As the North American coast now seemed unlikely to offer a strait, Sebastian in 1508 made an attempt to sail around it and very likely passed the entrance to Hudson's Bay. Cabot probably considered this promising as a waterway to Asia but had to turn back because of ice-infested sea. England had now apparently lost whatever limited interest it had possessed in discovery and could give Sebastian no further employment. He therefore transferred to Spanish service, in which he rose to positions of power and responsibility.

During the reign of Queen Mary (1553–1558) the aged Sebastian returned to England, still bent on the discovery of Cathay by a northern route. Though his own sailing days had passed, he succeeded in sending an expedition, commanded by Hugh Willoughby and Richard Chancellor, to reach east Asia by what was called the Northeast Passage. Willoughby died en route and Chancellor fell far short of the goal, although the latter did discover the White Sea and Archangel, through which the English opened trade with Ivan the Terrible's Russia.

In Elizabeth's time (1558–1603) England grew formidable on the sea, as the queen's daring captains, headed by Francis Drake, preyed on Spanish commerce, raided Spain's colonies in America, and ultimately defeated and largely destroyed the impressive Armada sent by Philip II against their country. Geographical discoveries by the English were few, however, principally because the waters in which they explored lacked possibilities. Martin Frobisher made several northern voyages to America in search of treasure, but his only discovery was the barren waste called Baffin Island. Frobisher's successors, John Davis, Henry Hudson, and William Baffin, explored the icy waters between Greenland and North America and further investigated Hudson's Bay, but they were groping in a blind alley. By this time English colonization of the North American coast had begun, and the energies of the nation could find their outlet here. Although there would be much important exploration later to the credit of England, it did not come in the era properly known as the Age of Discovery.

DUTCH EXPLORATION

The Dutch Netherlands escaped by a revolution from the control of the Spanish crown in the late sixteenth century. Although their background had not been maritime, the Hollanders took to the sea partly as a consequence of their war of independence. Being commercially minded, with a growing prosperity which they felt anxious to increase, they jealously eyed the colonial empires of Spain and Portugal, coveting them less as territorial possessions than as trade outlets.

Like most European peoples, the Dutch at first felt greater interest in the Far East than in the New World. In an attempt to find the Northeast Passage, which the English had sought forty years earlier, Willem Barents sailed into the Arctic in 1594, and his expedition was followed by two others. Nothing but the Barents Sea and desolate Nova Zemlya rewarded these efforts, and the Dutch next turned to the Cape of Good Hope route, which for a hundred years had been all but monopolized by the Portuguese. With some difficulty an expedition of Netherlanders succeeded in making its way around the cape and across the Indian Ocean to the East Indies. Once they had learned the route, the Dutch poured men and ships into the East Indies, and within a few years had virtually ousted the Portuguese from the islands. Capitalists in the leading cities of the Netherlands formed the heavily-capitalized Dutch East India Company for trade with the Orient, and their government granted them a monopoly of the only two known routes leading to the east—the Cape of Good Hope and the Strait of Magellan.

This official favoritism, which made all Dutch commerce to the East Indies the privilege of a comparative handful, naturally aroused resentment among other Hollanders. Some thought that there must be a way of evading the government's decree and of opening Oriental trade to a greater number. The logical step seemed to be to find, if possible, another route to the islands that would involve neither the cape nor the strait. With this end in view, a group of merchants in the small city of Hoorn organized a company and sent out an expedition to discover any route into the Pacific that might lie south of Tierra del Fuego, the island forming the southern shore of Magellan's strait. In 1616 Willem Schouten, commanding this expedition, passed below Tierra del Fuego to discover and round Cape Horn. Schouten then triumphantly crossed the Pacific, but his exultation ended when authorities of the East India Company refused to believe the story of the cape and, taking him for an interloper, confiscated his two ships. By finding a route into the Pacific that under some conditions was better than the strait, the Hoorn adventurers had made an important discovery, but they derived no personal profit from it.

The Dutch, now installed in Java and neighboring islands, several times made accidental contact with northern Australia, which had earlier been sighted by a Spanish captain en route from Peru to the Philippines. The Hollanders still knew little of the South Pacific and shared a belief then prevalent to the effect that a vast continent, both populous and rich, lay somewhere in the south. In 1641 the governor of the Dutch East Indies sent one of his captains, Abel Janszoon Tasman, to make a survey of these waters and to look for the continent. In carrying out his mission, Tasman circumnavigated Australia and knew he was doing so, though he scarcely sighted it and did not take it for the much greater, imaginary continent he sought. His major discoveries consisted of Tasmania to the south and New Zealand to the east of Australia. While returning to Java, Tasman made the accidental discovery of the Fiji group. But as nothing he found seemed financially promising, the Dutch did not follow up his voyages and left Australasia to be occupied later by the English.

CONCLUSION

The Tasman voyage furnished the closing episode of the great Age of Discovery. From the time of Prince Henry of Portugal to that of Tasman exploration progressed through a series of related achievements whose continuity is easily apparent. Discovery after Tasman lost this continuity and usually sought the solution of lesser problems. Although the world was far from fully known by the middle of the seventeenth century, it was then possible to construct a global map that for all its crudities and inaccuracies would have been instantly recognizable to a half-trained modern eye. In 1400 European man dwelt in a small corner of the Eurasian continent and knew little of the earth outside this corner. By 1650 he conducted activities on a global scale. Exploration would continue, but the future could unfurl nothing as important as the recent past had revealed.

Further Reading

An excellent work on medieval geography is George H. T. Kimble, *Geography in the Middle Ages* (London: Methuen, 1938). This deals with geographical theory, notions of the earth, and travel up to the time of the beginning of the Renaissance. A brief coverage of the principal material in this chapter is provided by Charles E. Nowell, *The Great Discoveries and the First Colonial Empires* (Ithaca: Cornell Univ. Press, 1954). Marco Polo, *The Travels of Marco Polo,* trans. by Aldo Ricci (New York: Viking, 1931), is an English translation of the most accurate French version of Polo's original text. Henry H. Hart, *Venetian Adventurer* (Stanford: Stanford Univ. Press, 1942), provides a biography of the discoverer that is scholarly and readable, if at times somewhat fanciful. William Hovgaard, *The Voyages of the Norsemen to America* (New York: American-Scandinavian Foundation, 1914), is unique because it brings the point of view of a veteran seaman to bear on the problem of the Norse discoveries. Einar Haugen, *Voyages to Vinland: the First American Saga* (New York: Knopf, 1942), offers a new translation into present-day American English of the Norse sagas dealing with the Vinland discoveries. Good works relating to the Portuguese discoveries are Kingsley G. Jayne, *Vasco da Gama and His Successors, 1460–1580* (London: Methuen, 1910), and Edgar Prestage, *The Portuguese Pioneers* (London: A. & C. Black, 1933). Henry H. Hart, *Sea Road to the Indies* (New York: Macmillan, 1950), is virtually a biography of Vasco da Gama, although the book deals with other Portuguese exploits as well.

The problem of the original Indian population of the New World is explored by D'Arcy McNickle, *They Came Here First* (Philadelphia: Lippincott, 1949). George M. Valliant, *The Aztecs of Mexico; Origin, Rise, and Fall of the Aztec Nation* (Garden City: Doubleday, 1941), is probably the best work in any language on the Aztec culture. Philip Ainsworth Means in *Ancient Civilizations of the Andes* (New York: Scribner, 1931) and *Fall of the Inca Empire and the Spanish Rule in Peru, 1530–1780* (New York: Scribner, 1932) describes the native civilizations of Peru until the Spanish conquest, the conquest itself, and the Spanish régime.

The best up-to-date biography of Columbus in English is undoubtedly Samuel E. Morison, *Admiral of the Ocean Sea; A Life of Christopher Columbus* (Boston: Little, Brown, 1942). The work, which is principally concerned with the nautical side of Columbus' career, is printed in a two-volume edition with footnotes, as well as a one-volume edition without notes. Good accounts in English of Amerigo Vespucci are more difficult to find, but German Arciniegas, *Amerigo and the New World,* trans. by Harriet de Onís (New York: Knopf, 1955), is probably the best. The great explorer Ferdinand Magellan is well handled by Charles McKew Parr, *So Noble a Captain: the Life and Times of Ferdinand Magellan* (New York: Crowell, 1953), in a way that brings out many hitherto neglected aspects of the first voyage around the globe. An old but ever interesting work on the first French explorations and their original impact on America is Francis Parkman, *The Pioneers of France in the New World,* various editions. This is the opening volume of a series covering the exploits of the French in North America; succeeding volumes are outside the scope of the present chapter. William Bennett Munro, *Crusaders of New France* (New Haven: Yale Univ. Press, 1921), covers the same material more briefly and also describes the later building of the French empire in North America.

Chapter 17

CONFLICTS
AND DIVISIONS IN
WESTERN CHRISTENDOM

VENTUALLY, exploration and world empire wrought changes in European life and produced a new outlook, but the effects of the great discoveries and conquests were not felt widely at the beginning. In the sixteenth century most of Europe was rocked by religious dissensions which touched the lives of individuals as no upheaval had done since the barbarian invasions. The broad lines of the pattern of western Christianity as we see it today were set during the Protestant Reformation and the Catholic Counter-Reformation. The major religious developments that came later were the growth of interdenominational tolerance and the idea of the separation of church and state. Both of these developments were implicit in the early religious conflicts, although they were not immediately apparent.

Doctrinal arguments and reform movements were not new in Christendom. The story of the Albigensians and the Waldensians, of Wycliffe and Huss, and of the great mystics of the thirteenth and fourteenth centuries were told in the first volume of this work. Some of these will be briefly reviewed in what follows as a means of gathering together the various strands of dissatisfaction which underlay the Protestant Revolt. The main elements that entered into the religious revolt of the sixteenth century were present when Martin Luther posted his ninety-five theses in 1517. Apparently, Luther himself had no intention of starting a revolution when he protested against the sale of indulgences. But it was soon evident that some of his basic doctrines diverged from the official views of the church, and these opinions became the center of conflict while the issue of indulgences sank into second or third place.

1 : The Role of the Roman Catholic Church
on the Eve of the Reformation

IF WE SEEK to understand the magnitude of the changes wrought by the Reformation, we must appreciate the powerful and exclusive position of the church in western Christendom immediately prior to it. Today in many places, as in the United States, several Christian denominations exist side by side, apparently with equal, though different, approaches to Christian living. In some countries, either because of custom or because of legal establishment, or both, a single church exists to which all the people must lend support, at least financial support, although other denominations may be permitted to exist on a voluntary, self-supporting basis. Both of these conditions arose during and after the Reformation. Prior to that time there was but one church among all the peoples of western Europe, accepted almost universally and acclaimed as the only true church of Christ. This was the Church of Rome, the Roman Catholic church.

The Church of Rome had successfully weathered many storms of controversy in its climb to ecclesiastical supremacy in western Europe. Over the years it had also perfected a theoretical justification for its dominant position as well as for its system of sacraments. Headed by the Pope, as "Christ's vicar on earth," the Roman Catholic church stood as the only divinely-appointed mediator between the individual person and the Saviour, holding the keys to salvation which became available to all mankind by means of the sacramental system, a system which the church had perfected in obedience to divine law. Of the seven sacraments, three were most important to the layman: baptism, penance, and the Holy Eucharist. The first wiped out the stain of original sin; the second granted forgiveness to a genuinely contrite sinner; and the third, by celebrating the Last Supper, as Jesus had enjoined his followers to do, miraculously fed the soul of the communicant with the very body of Christ, ever renewing Christ's saving grace. By the sacrament of confirmation a young person of the age of discretion was received into the church; by marriage, a Christian entered into holy wedlock; by extreme unction, a dying person was given the last rites of the church in this world as final preparation of his soul for the next; and by ordination, the church created new priests who alone could administer the sacraments, except baptism, which might be performed by a layman, and confirmation and ordination, which could only be administered by a bishop or his superiors. All of these miraculous things the priesthood could perform by virtue of powers believed to have been passed on by Jesus to his disciples, especially to Peter, the founder of the church at Rome. To Peter, Jesus said, according to Matthew 16:18–19, "Thou art Peter [a Greek name, meaning "rock"] and upon this rock I will build my church and the gates of Hades shall not prevail against it. I will give unto thee the keys of the kingdom of heaven; and whatsoever thou shalt loose on earth shall be loosened in heaven." This was the theory of Apostolic Succession, upon which the Church of Rome grounded its exclusive and universal ecclesiastical dominion.

An individual was born into the church. He did not voluntarily "join" it—although for cause he might be excommunicated, that is, damned and rendered an outcast from Christian society. However, the individual man possessed the power to choose between Good and Evil, and the church, as the only dispensary of heavenly grace, was the sole means whereby man might be so fortified in his choice as to avoid Evil. Man's personal efforts were valuable, to be sure. But of themselves they were powerless to save him without the mediating grace of the church, a grace which proceeded from Christ through the church to man, never to man directly from Christ.

Inevitably, such an institution, believing firmly in its own divine origin, in its exclusive ministry of grace, and in its universality, held itself, its mission, and its hierarchy in high esteem. Moreover, it won the high esteem of others. As it had managed to quiet most of its adversaries from within (the "heretics"), it achieved wide, if not really universal, sway over western Europe, aligning itself with emperors, kings, and princes, and claiming a spiritual sovereignty over them. Its hierarchy, especially in the upper reaches, intermingled with, and sometimes became dependent upon, the aristocracy. Indeed, the church usually accepted the secular order and the state as long as it was accepted by them, and its own existence became interwoven with that of the secular order. In many instances the state and the church became coterminous geographically and institutionally. In the high Middle Ages the Roman Catholic church extended over all of western Europe as an official and public institution. It was maintained by taxes and dues, was everywhere supported by the state, and a Christian child was born into it just as he was born subject to a temporal ruler.

Still, any institution as large as the Roman Catholic church had become is prone to some errors, scandals, abuses, and criticisms arising both from within and without. To these we now turn, because out of them grew the larger doctrinal differences which split western Christendom asunder.

SEEDS OF DISSENT IN THE WESTERN CHURCH

At base the Reformation was a series of religious disputes, but they were so intertwined with political, economic, and social partisanship that the religious threads sometimes became obscured by the larger fabric into which they were woven. Probably this was inevitable, when we consider the far-flung functions and institutions of the church. But developments outside the church as well as those within it affected the course of events.

Back of the religious unrest of the sixteenth century lay a variety of events of the late Middle Ages and the Renaissance. The Papacy itself had been severely shaken when temporal rulers challenged the claims of universal domination set forth by such Popes as Boniface VIII (1294–1303). The prestige of the Papacy was greatly weakened by the "Babylonian Captivity" of the Popes at Avignon in France (1305–77) and by the shocking spectacle of two Popes, puppets respectively of French and Italian temporal interests, simultaneously claiming to be the rightful successors to the Apostle Peter in 1378. This unrewarding situation ushered in the "Great Schism," which lasted from 1378 until 1417. It was followed by the Conciliar Movement (1409–1442), whereby a series of church councils managed to heal the breach within the church and restore the Papacy to Rome, though in a shattered, impoverished condition. And in the meantime emperors, kings, and princes had meddled with some success in ecclesiastical politics, and the powers of the Popes had been challenged by councils of churchmen often influenced by lay authorities. Moreover, an Oxford professor named John Wycliffe (1320?–1384) had attacked the church on many doctrinal and ecclesiastical grounds, translated the Bible into English, insisted upon the supreme authority of the Scriptures as the source of all belief, and founded a widely popular movement in England known as Lollardy, which anticipated many of the teachings of the Protestant reformers and demonstrated powerful individualistic tendencies.

Wycliffe's teachings had in some measure been anticipated in France by Pierre Dubois (1250–1312), who held that the temporal powers of the Popes should be transferred to the king. Similar teachings were advocated in Bohemia by John Huss (1369?–1415) who, condemned by the Council of Constance and burned at the stake, exerted a powerful influence long after his death. Shortly after Huss's martyrdom, a new group of Christian mystics arose in the Rhineland and spread into the Low Countries, and thence into the German states of the Holy Roman Empire. Before the end of the fourteenth century the group had produced a leader in Gerard Groote of Deventer (1340–1389), who founded a sort of lay monastic group known as the Brothers of the Common Life. The Brothers were laymen. They took no irrevocable vows, but they lived together, shared their goods, and supported themselves by their own labors. They studied, copied, and wrote tracts on religion and morals, and they founded schools in the Low Countries and in the empire. By their emphasis upon moral living, together with constant study of the Scriptures, the Brothers taught that the ordinary lay Christian, without church or clerical intercession, could effect an immediate, direct, personal, and mystical union with Christ and through his mercy attain eternal salvation. One of their works, the *Imitation of Christ* by Thomas à Kempis (Thomas von Kempen, 1380–1471), became a religious classic, imparting spiritual inspiration and comfort to countless Christians to the present day, although the religious communities founded by the

Brothers of the Common Life fell into decay after about 1550. Still, these mystics, though they generally accepted the church as a means of salvation and never openly broke with it, promoted essentially a sectarian view. They required no particular ritual or ceremonies, no sacraments, no public worship, no priests, and no church. They offered to all a gripping personal religion in which the church played no essential role; and by their splendid examples they affected the lives of thousands who sought to emulate them. Though they did not rebel against the church they cultivated a soil in which militant reformation and even rebellion took root.

CRITICISMS OF THE CHURCH

Alongside these divisive tendencies there also developed many severe criticisms of the church both from inside and outside it. In the course of the Renaissance a whole catalogue of grievances had arisen against the church. The burden of many of the works of humanist writers was to propose reforms in Christian society and to point out existing evils in the church. Many priests were abysmally ignorant, unable to understand the Latin in which they tried to celebrate the Mass. The clergy, both high and low, often lived scandalous lives. Some of the Popes and bishops lived in princely magnificence, avoiding the inconvenience of celibacy by keeping "celestial wives," as their concubines and mistresses were called. Pope Alexander VI (1492–1503), of the infamous Borgia family, had at least eight illegitimate children, only seven of whom were born before his elevation to the Papacy. Both monks and secular priests frequently ignored their vows of chastity, the latter sometimes supplementing their inadequate parish incomes by keeping taverns, gaming houses, and other unpriestly establishments. Such scandalous behavior outraged pious folk, who felt that the clergy above all others should lead exemplary and virtuous lives.

Rising costs in the sixteenth century probably made the upper clergy appear more rapacious than they intended to be. After the Great Schism the restored Popes found the Roman chapels, churches, and other clerical establishments in a disgracefully run-down state, unbecoming and inadequate for the court of the Vicar of Christ. As we have seen, many of the Renaissance Popes ranked high among the patrons of architecture and the decorative arts, and the extravagant examples set by wealthy Italian Renaissance merchants and bankers led them to set new, expensive models for their new buildings. In consequence, the Popes, like the lay monarchs, were chronically short of funds; and they resorted to many extraordinary and religiously distasteful means of raising money. They sold offices in the church to the highest bidders (who usually sought to recover their money by charging high fees for their services). They sold dispensations, that is, exemptions from laws of the church or from vows previously made (some of the most common were exemptions from laws of consanguinity in mar-

53

riage). They also trafficked in *indulgences* or remissions of all or part of the temporal punishment due to sin which had been forgiven by means of the sacrament of penance. The punishments remitted related only to those of this world or in purgatory; they had nothing to do with punishments in hell. The church exercised this power as keeper of the keys to the treasury of grace wherein are deposited the superabundant merits of Christ and the saints. Properly applied, indulgences were no evil, and originally they had been granted only in return for charitable deeds. But when indulgences came to be sold, overenthusiastic agents often failed to explain their limitations to eager, guilt-smitten buyers. In consequence, the traffic became a profitable source of papal revenue, and unwary purchasers were allowed to believe that they had obtained passports to sin without impairing their eligibility for heaven. By 1500 the sale of indulgences had became a major scandal in the church.

Almost as serious was the traffic in sacred relics which, with the sale of indulgences, Erasmus attacked in his famous *Praise of Folly* (1511). Superstitious souls believed that to touch—or even to see—objects used by Christ, the Virgin Mary, or the saints gave miraculous healing or protection from harm. Such beliefs opened the way for fraud, as ignorant persons easily could be persuaded that any old chunk of wood was a piece of the "true cross." Hucksters of sacred relics took full advantage of such credulities, and some churches and cathedrals accumulated large collections of these objects—with graduated fees to see them or to touch them. According to Erasmus, enough wood of the "true cross" had been collected in European churches to build a ship; and the locks of saintly hair, nail pairings, and many heads of John the Baptist could have been accepted only by the untraveled and extremely credulous person.

To these criticisms of scandals and abuses in the church must be added the opposition arising from political and economic sources. Political opposition to the church, which was often combined with economic considerations, stemmed from the growth of national consciousness and from the growing absolutism of national monarchs. From the late Middle Ages the peoples of Europe exhibited a growing spirit of independence bordering upon nationalism. How much this was fostered by the monarchs and how much the monarchs were fostered by it is impossible to determine; but both peoples and monarchs increasingly showed resentment against the Pope as a foreigner who meddled intolerably in the affairs of their kingdoms and whose revenues impoverished their states for the enrichment of Rome.

During the Babylonian Captivity the Papacy witnessed the beginnings of national opposition in specific ways. The English, hostile to the Francophile Popes, passed statutes (1351 and later) to stop the influx of alien clergy, to forbid appeals to courts outside England (that is, to papal courts), and to refuse payment of further royal tribute to the Popes. In 1438, after the return of the Papacy to Rome, the king of France set forth the law known as the Pragmatic Sanction of Bourges. This law declared that a church council is superior to a Pope, forbade payment of papal revenues in France, and made the appointment of French churchmen subject to royal approval—in fact, the law essentially established the autonomy of the French national (Gallican) church in isolation from Rome. To a lesser extent, the queen of Castile, by the concordat of 1482 with the Pope, restricted the power of Rome over the Castilians. Even in the German states—where the empire provided no such solid political unity as in England, France, or Spain—emperors, princes, and towns grumbled against papal revenues, occasionally forbade the sale of papal indulgences, and often sought to control ecclesiastical appointments.

Added to their growing unwillingness to share their power and wealth with the Roman church was the desire of lay rulers to acquire ecclesiastical properties. Thanks to legacies of pious Christians over the centuries, the church had become much the largest landowner in Europe, and its splendid gold and silver plate, together with its richly jeweled furnitures and furnishings were tempting items of movable wealth. To ascetic reformers such wealth in the hands of the church appeared unseemly. As church lands were exempt from taxation—in Germany and France the church owned from one-sixth to one-third of all lands—the tax burden fell correspondingly more heavily upon private owners. Kings and princes hard pressed for funds, manorial lords struggling against the impending collapse of the manorial economy, and private taxpayers all resented, or coveted, the wealthy, tax-exempt position of the church.

All this became more galling in view of the variety of fees, taxes, and other payments exacted by the church. The *tithes,* nominally one-tenth of every Christian's income but actually often less, were paid for the support of the parish church. The church also levied a tax called *Peter's pence* upon every household. Then the moneys collected from the sale of church offices, as well as the *annates,* or percentages levied upon the first year's income of every priest and bishop, were simply passed on to the people through larger collections. Add to these the payments made for dispensations, indulgences, sacred relics, ecclesiastical court fees, and the like, and the church could be made to appear a greedy monster. Yet the main grievance was not so much against the number or the amount of church levies as against the fact that so much of the money of western Europe was going to Italy where, instead of being devoted to religious purposes, it was being squandered by worldly Popes in luxurious living.

In summary, then, political needs and dynastic jealousies on the part of national monarchs, fortified by scandals and abuses within the church itself, and strengthened further by economic grievances common to monarchs and their subjects alike, created widespread criticism of the church.

At the same time questions about faith and doctrine were revived and asserted on a wide front. All of these converged in the challenge of the Protestant Revolt first sounded by Martin Luther in 1517.

2 : Martin Luther and the Rise of Lutheranism

THE MOTIVATING FACTORS in the Protestant Revolt have become associated with social, economic, and political events, but in the minds of the principal leaders it was simply and solely a religious reform movement. To none of these was the religious impulse more completely in the ascendancy than to Martin Luther.

Martin Luther was born on November 10, 1483, at Eisleben, in Thuringia, of peasant stock, although his father had turned to mining and refining copper and the family became moderately prosperous. Within a year after Luther's birth the family moved to Mansfeld, a nearby copper-mining center, and here young Luther spent his youth and received his early schooling. Later he attended grammar schools at Magdeburg and Eisenach before entering the University of Erfurt, from which he graduated bachelor of arts in 1502 and master of arts in 1505. In July of the latter year Luther, knocked down by a bolt of lightning in a thunderstorm, became terrified and cried out in fright, "St. Anne help me! I will become a monk." Soon afterwards he entered the Augustinian cloister at Erfurt and kept his vow.

Luther's decision displeased his father, who had counted on his son to become a lawyer. But it was in keeping with Luther's own interests and disposition. Reared in a German village atmosphere highly charged with both superstition and religion, he was a highly intelligent young man unusually sensitive to and cognizant of religious problems. Further, like many young people, he felt insecure in his own personal religious condition, burdened by a growing sense of unworthiness and sinfulness from which he could find no peace. In the monastery he hoped to find release from his inner religious crisis.

In this he failed. His brother monks testified that Luther spent more time in devotions and study than any of them, and he was repeatedly honored. He was appointed to a lectureship in the new University of Wittenberg (1508) and sent on a trip to Rome (1510–11); but still his inner religious conflict was unresolved. Soon after his return from Rome his religious mentor, John von Staupitz, vicar of the Augustinian Order, persuaded him to complete his studies for a doctor's degree in preparation for a professorship offered at Wittenberg. He received the degree of doctor of theology from Wittenberg in 1512, and the next year began his duties as professor of Bible. Here, in the course of his studies and lectures on the New Testament, Brother Martin found the answers for which his soul had so long cried out.

Luther found his soul's peace only after years of inner tortures, earnest study, and reflection.

> "My situation," he wrote, "was that, although an impeccable monk, I stood before God as a sinner troubled in conscience and I had no confidence that my merit would assuage him . . . .
>
> Night and day I pondered until I saw the connection between the justice of God and the statement that 'the just shall live by faith.' Then I grasped that the justice of God is that righteousness by which through grace and sheer mercy God justifies us through faith. Thereupon I felt myself to be reborn and to have gone through open doors into paradise . . . . This passage of Paul became to me a gate to heaven."[1]

In St. Paul's Epistle to the Romans Luther had found a new view of salvation which placed God, Christ, man, and the role of the priest in a new relationship. Eternal salvation is achieved by faith alone; man is an unworthy sinner whose very faith is a gift from God and whose salvation depends, not upon his own merit or good works, which at best are puny beside the infinite greatness and goodness of God, but upon the grace of God. Faith is a gift which comes to man by the intercession of Christ through prayer and by a knowledge of the Word as set forth in the Scriptures and as heard in the sermons of preachers. It must be firm and complete faith, "to believe things incredible, to hope for things delayed, and to love God even when He seems angry." Man becomes worthy in the sight of God only by a full surrender to the divine will. The so-called good works of the church—fasts, pilgrimages, and sacraments—are of no vital importance, and the intercession of priests and saints accomplish little for man's salvation. This doctrine of justification by faith was the compelling force of Luther's life and the keystone of his revolt.

THE NINETY-FIVE THESES

Luther had hardly mastered the full force of his discovery when a scandal arose on the borders of Saxony which impelled him to action. To raise money toward the completion of St. Peter's in Rome, Pope Leo X proclaimed an indulgence. The next year Archbishop Albert, a young Hohenzollern prince who already held two sees, won the archbishopric of Mainz. It cost him nearly 30,000 ducats for permission and for confirmation in the new post. Most of this money he borrowed from the famous Fugger bankers and, in order to repay the loan, he arranged to proclaim the indulgence of 1513 throughout all his ecclesiastical domains. Half of the proceeds was to be turned over to Pope Leo; the other half went to Al-

---

[1] Trans. by Roland H. Bainton in *Here I Stand: A Life of Martin Luther* (New York: Abingdon-Cokesbury Press, 1950), p. 65.

bert to discharge his debt. Thus an indulgence originally proclaimed for the pious purpose of building a church to St. Peter was employed in part for the crass purchase of a province for a prince already guilty of pluralism.

Naturally, the promoters wanted to raise as much money as possible, and among their agents was a Dominican friar, John Tetzel of Leipzig, who, while he demonstrated unusual qualities of salesmanship, also aroused wide criticism by his sensational methods and careless unconcern about what the lay purchasers might believe regarding the spiritual nature and ecclesiastical efficacy of the indulgences sold. One of his favorite devices was to play upon his hearers' sympathies for departed relatives and friends whom they might release from the tortures of purgatory by buying an indulgence. His plea was summed up in his jingle:

> As soon as the coin in the coffer rings,
> The soul from purgatory springs.

Frederick III (the Wise), the elector of Saxony from 1463 to 1525, who had a fine collection of sacred relics and indulgences of his own in the parish of Wittenberg, forbade the sale of the papal indulgence of 1513 in his lands. Still, the vendors came close by, and the Wittenberg students as well as the parishioners of the village church in which Luther was priest were tempted by them. As a challenge to the proceedings—and in the hope of reformation—Luther posted his ninety-five Latin theses as topics for debate and sent a copy to Archbishop Albert on October 31, 1517. Writing in indignation, Luther—who was following the usual method of the time in seeking discussion of a subject—was bold and his theses were unqualified. He objected to the purpose of the expenditure ("We Germans cannot attend St. Peter's"); he denied the powers of the Pope over purgatory ("Christ did *not* say to Peter, 'Whatsoever I have bound in heaven you may loose on earth'"); and he argued that indulgences corrupted the purchasers by diverting charity and inducing a false complacency.

Luther made no effort to spread his theses among the people. He merely invited scholarly discussion and, he hoped, official redefinition. But friends translated the theses into German and distributed them in printed form. Soon they became the talk of Germany, and Brother Martin emerged unwittingly into the public eye. Still, he had no stomach for controversy, and if the Pope at once had issued a bull clearly to redefine the doctrine of indulgences and to correct the abuses—as was done ultimately—very likely Luther would have let the matter drop and he would have slipped back into obscurity. But a variety of factors intervened to prevent such an easy outcome. The Pope was at first disposed to dismiss the case simply as the dangerous prattle of an obscure monk, and he appointed a new general of the Augustinians to "quench" Brother Martin. But the order itself was widely persuaded by Luther's arguments, and became the more loath to suppress him because their rivals, the Dominicans, pressed him so severely.

Thus almost a year passed, during which Luther was emboldened to make further remarks questioning the scriptural bases of the sacraments, the divine ordination (as opposed to the mere historical development) of the primacy of Rome in the church, and the power of the papal ban to consign a man to hell unless God had already so consigned him.

These pronouncements roused the Pope, who gave Luther sixty days to appear in Rome for trial. Luther then appealed to the Elector Frederick, who managed to have the trial transferred to Germany. The hearing was to be private, before Cardinal Cajetan serving as papal legate to the imperial Diet of Augsburg (Sept.–Oct., 1518). The cardinal had other assignments also. In the course of the meeting of the Diet he not only failed to rally the Germans to undertake a new crusade against the Turks and to submit to a new tax for the enterprise, but also he learned a good deal about the German temper. This led him to tread warily in the hearing of Luther, although his instructions were to secure Brother Martin's recantation, without discussion, and so to reconcile him with the church. But Luther refused to recant without discussion, and protested against being condemned unheard and unrefuted by scriptural authority. When the cardinal asserted that the Pope is above Scripture, Luther denied it flatly. Whereupon Cajetan appealed to Frederick of Saxony either to send Luther bound to Rome or to banish him from his territories. The request greatly embarrassed Frederick who, though devoutly Catholic, was also founder of the University of Wittenberg upon whose faculty he leaned heavily for advice in such matters. Luther was of that faculty, which as a whole had not condemned him. Rather than believe his own doctor of Holy Scripture was in error, Frederick temporized and begged the emperor either to drop the case or to grant a hearing before unimpeachable German judges. Before anything could be decided Emperor Maximilian died (Jan. 12, 1519). Imperial action was postponed until a new emperor could be elected and assume control. The election took place on June 28, 1519, but the new emperor, the youthful Charles V, already king of Spain, was too occupied in his Spanish possessions to concern himself with Germany until the spring of 1521.

Meanwhile, amidst the plaudits of his admirers, Martin Luther gradually matured the logic of his position, and the gulf between him and Catholic orthodoxy steadily widened. Late in 1518 he called for a hearing before a general church council, thereby cleverly conjuring up the old conciliar hopes and fears about papal absolutism in the church. During the following summer he entered the lists at Leipzig amid a stronghold of bitterly critical Dominicans in a three-cornered debate among Dr. John Eck, Andrew Carlstadt—one of Luther's Wittenberg colleagues—and Luther himself. Dr. Eck was one of the ablest German Catholic polemicists, and after he had sparred for a week with Carlstadt over the depravity of man Luther entered to discuss the position of the Roman Papacy, especially whether it was of human or divine origin. Luther did not deny the supremacy of the Pope. He merely argued that the Pope ruled by human, not divine, right, and that a Christian who refused to submit to papal authority might still be saved. But Eck skillfully forced Luther to admit that these opinions were similar to those formerly condemned in John Wycliffe and John Huss. Luther had been led into a clearly heretical position, forced to argue out the logical consequences of his belief in justification by faith, and to approach more closely the idea of the superiority of individual believers over any church organization. Here was the core of religious individualism to which Lutheranism led. If Christ is head of the church, why have a Pope? Insofar as every believer had faith and had been justified by God's grace through this faith, he was a priest—although Luther was never willing to accept the full implications of the priesthood of all believers, which to some came to mean that no priests or hierarchy of churchmen is necessary at all. Still, Dr. Eck had forced Luther to conclusions which surprised even Brother Martin. "We are all Hussites without knowing it," he mused. But the Papacy knew it, and by the bull *Exsurge Domine* (June 15, 1520) Luther was given sixty days to submit or be condemned as a heretic. Conviction left him no choice. Before the whole assembled body of the University of Wittenberg, Luther consigned to the flames the bull which had placed him outside the church, a revolutionary outcast.

LUTHER'S PRIMARY WORKS

But Martin Luther did not stand alone. The university and town of Wittenberg stood with him, and he had won sympathizers and adherents in many parts of Germany and even beyond. To plead his case even more widely, he now turned to the printed word, using the recently invented printing press for propagandizing as it had never been used before. This continued throughout his life, but the decade of the 1520's witnessed the height of Luther's efforts. Three great tracts of 1521 set forth his principal religious ideas. The first, entitled *Address to the Christian Nobility of the German Nation Respecting the Reformation of the Christian Estate,* was an appeal to the German princes to defy the church and to institute by state authority much needed reforms in Christian society—an appeal which, as we have seen, could hardly fail to find eager listeners ready to act. The second, called *On the Babylonian Captivity of the Church,* attacked the sacramental system of the church and reduced the sacraments to two—baptism and the Lord's Supper—as the only two specifically instituted by Jesus. The abolition of ordination for priests severely attacked the clergy as a special caste and placed them on a footing equal to other believers. It also reduced the Holy Eucharist to a celebration of communion (the Lord's Supper) in which all believers—not just the priest alone—were allowed to perform the miracle in both kinds, that is, by partaking of both the bread *and* the wine.

The third essay, *On the Freedom of the Christian Man,* treated the seeming paradox found in the statements,

A Christian man is the most free lord of all, and subject to none;
A Christian man is the most dutiful servant of all, and subject to every one.

In short, Luther dealt not with outward political or social freedom, but with inner spiritual freedom, which derives from a well-founded faith in God. This is the freedom of soul which comes from a complete surrender to God, whereby a man performs good works in consequence of his justification in God, although good works have nothing to do with the justification: "Good works do not make a man good, but a good man does good works." Such a man, made worthy by true faith, will do everything to please God and will serve his neighbor as Christ gave himself to mankind. By these tracts Luther burned his bridges behind him and stood revealed in the eyes of the church as a heretic. The church had already excommunicated him; now the temporal authorities were to take a stand. In the spring of 1521 Luther was summoned before an imperial Diet at Worms presided over by the young Emperor Charles V.

When Luther first stood before the emperor (April, 1521), Charles was unimpressed and exclaimed, "That fellow will never make a heretic of me." But before Luther's hearing had finished, his stubborn refusal to repudiate his beliefs impressed (and infuriated) Charles:

"Unless," said Luther, "I am convicted by Scripture and plain reason—I do not accept the authority of popes and councils for they have contradicted each other—my conscience is captive to the Word of God. I cannot and I will not recant anything, for to go against conscience is neither right nor safe. Here I stand, I cannot do otherwise. God help me. Amen."[2]

After this outburst the emperor persuaded the Diet to draw up the Edict of Worms, which condemned Luther as a heretic and placed him under the ban of the empire. But two of the electors, Ludwig of the Palatinate and Frederick of Saxony, refused to sign the edict, and the latter whisked Luther away to a safe hiding place in his remote castle known as the Wartburg. The edict was repudiated by Luther's sympathizers because it had been passed by a rump, and not even the emperor could execute the ban while Luther could not be found. Meanwhile, public opinion hardened on both sides. The empire had been split into factions—factions that represented more than religious differences. For in them were found also the political and economic stresses of the German states.

---

[2] The words "Here I stand, I cannot do otherwise" may have been added by Wittenberg admirers. See Roland H. Bainton, *Here I Stand,* p. 185, and R. H. Fife, *The Revolt of Martin Luther* (New York: Columbia Univ. Press, 1957), p. 666.

Luther became increasingly restless during his retirement in Wartburg Castle (1521–22). He completed a German translation of the New Testament, but reports of confusion and even of violence at Wittenberg troubled him. His friend Carlstadt assumed leadership during Luther's absence and introduced innovations which led to disturbances. Monks and nuns forsook their cloisters, laid aside their vestments and their vows, even married; the old fasts were forgotten, sacred relics, images, and indulgences were rejected as rubbish; Mass was conducted in German, and the Lord's Supper was given in both kinds to all communicants. But differences of opinion arose, blows fell, and in Luther's absence no one could control the situation. Learning of these things, Luther risked his personal safety and returned to Wittenberg in March, 1522, hoping to restore order and to build a new church in conformity with God's Word.

The remainder of Luther's life was devoted to this work. Private and public support made it possible to construct a Lutheran church which, by the time of Luther's death (Feb. 18, 1546), had been adopted by the northern German states and by the Scandinavian countries. But it was a difficult task, beset as it was by rival leaders and radical sects, the unremitting opposition of the Catholic church, and the red herrings of economic and social reform movements and of political intrigue.

LUTHER AND THE RADICALS

Until his break with the church became irrevocable, Luther had had support and encouragement from a number of moderate Catholic reformers, including such prominent persons as the great northern humanist Erasmus. But while Erasmus promoted reform of Christendom, he could not endorse further division of it, nor could he accept Luther's views regarding the depravity of man. Still, some humanists cast in their lot with Luther, notably Philip Melanchthon (1497–1560). Melanchthon was professor of Greek at Wittenberg, a learned, gentle soul, able often to temper Luther's vehemence. Ulrich von Hutten (1488–1523) was another humanist supporter of Luther, but Luther found him an embarrassment in the end. Hutten sprang from the German knightly class which was being harried from all sides. Gunpowder and mercenary troops had robbed them of their useful employment, and they were usually heavily in debt to city merchants. The levies of the Papacy made Rome the symbol of their troubles, and they tended to embrace Luther's views for reasons often far removed from religious reform. In 1522 Hutten joined with Franz von Sickingen to rise up in rebellion against the princes and clergy, clothing their rebellion with appeals to German nationalism and setting themselves forth as champions of the poor and of Lutheran reform. But Luther would have none of it, and when the rebellion failed Sickingen was killed, Hutten fled from Germany,

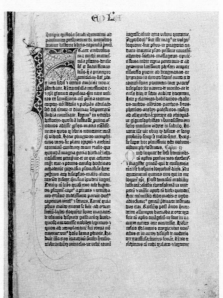

WYCLIFFE BIBLE

LUTHER'S BIBLE

GUTENBERG BIBLE

ERASMUS' NEW TESTAMENT

Humanists' efforts to establish pure texts of ancient documents and the biblicism of the Protestant Reformation combined to give rise to many new translations and editions of the Christian Bible. Shown here are pages from four of these: a manuscript page from the early English Bible (c. 1380) by John Wycliffe, the father of English Lollardy; a page from an early (perhaps the first) printed Latin Bible, called the "Gutenberg Bible" from its printer, John Gutenberg (c. 1450); the beginning of the Book of Job from Luther's German Bible (1544–1545); and a page from Erasmus' New Testament, which was printed in parallel columns of Greek and Latin texts (1516).

MARTIN LUTHER

ULRICH VON HUTTEN

JOHN CALVIN

PHILIP MELANCHTHON

Here are likenesses of four of the early Protestant leaders of the Reformation. There were many contemporary portraits of Luther; this one is by Lucas Cranach the Elder, who moved from his native Franconia to Vienna and became a masterly painter and portraitist of the Danube school shortly after 1500. Later he was court painter at Wittenberg, where many of the early Lutheran leaders posed for him. Ulrich von Hutten, the "mad knight," was drawn by an unknown hand about 1517. Comparatively few pictures of Calvin exist, but they agree in depicting his thin, ascetic face, bearing traces of the ill health from which he suffered most of his life. Philip Melanchthon, Luther's friend and adviser, was also painted by Lucas Cranach.

CARDINAL WOLSEY   ARCHBISHOP CRANMER

EDWARD VI   ILLUSTRATION FROM FOXE'S "BOOK OF MARTYRS"

Prominent in the early stages of the Reformation in England was Thomas, Cardinal Wolsey, Henry VIII's ambitious ecclesiastic who failed in his large objectives. This engraving is based on a portrait by Hans Holbein (see also Plates XI and XII). Archbishop Thomas Cranmer, the "father" of the Church of England's service book, posed for this panel by Gerlach Flicke in 1546. John Foxe's Book of Martyrs *was an enormously influential Protestant propaganda volume depicting in picture and story the allegedly evil deeds of Catholics. Here a Catholic priest preaches in defiance of law and public opinion. A drawing by Holbein was the basis of this portrait of Edward VI, the Tudor boy king.*

COUNCIL OF TRENT

ST. PIUS V (POPE)

POPE PAUL III

ST. IGNATIUS LOYOLA

Here are illustrated some of the personages and events which were high-lights of the Catholic, or Counter-, Reformation. Pope Paul III, who pre-pared the way for the Council of Trent, was among those painted by Titian (see Plate IX). St. Pius V was the "reforming Pope" of the latter years of the sixteenth century. St. Ignatius Loyola, soldier founder of the militant Society of Jesus, is shown in an engraving by Lucas Vorstermann. The Council of Trent met at intervals between 1545 and 1563 and reaffirmed Catholic doctrine while reforming many abuses in the church. This copper engraving was published at Venice in 1565.

and Luther, having repudiated the scheme, avoided being destroyed with the ill-fated knights.

In Wittenberg, too, Luther was embarrassed by his self-proclaimed disciples. Even before his return from the Wartburg some "prophets" arrived from nearby Zwickau who claimed to have had conversations with the Lord. By virtue of these conversations, they claimed a new authority direct from the Holy Spirit which rendered the Scriptures obsolete. They proclaimed themselves to be of the only true Kingdom of God, rejected infant baptism, and proposed a holy war to slaughter the ungodly. Here was naked religious individualism at its height, and Luther turned against it indignantly, labelling the "prophets" charlatans and firebrands. Surely the King of Peace never intended to establish his church by violence and bloodshed! Still, the enthusiasts were hardly silenced before Thomas Müntzer, another of the Zwickau "saints," proclaimed a religious war against the clergy and the nobility. Banished from Saxony for a time, he returned to stir up a violent peasant uprising in 1525. The Peasants' Revolt, like scores of similar rebellions in the late Middle Ages, originated in economic and political unrest. But the peasants had also been strongly attracted by Luther, whose priesthood of believers could be interpreted to mean political and social equality. Indeed, Luther sympathized with the peasants' mean condition, although he warned them against the use of violence to better their lot. Revolt by private subjects against their magistrates was contrary to God's Law, and it would result only in murder and destruction. Luther's judgment as to the outcome was right. At the Battle of Frankhausen (1525) the princes defeated the principal peasant group, butchered five thousand of them, took six hundred prisoners, and ran down Müntzer who was tortured and beheaded. It took little more to quiet the remaining peasants in arms.

The effect on the Lutheran movement was tremendous. Catholic princes and common people blamed Luther for revolt; the former ever after associated church reformation with revolutionary uprisings, and the latter were widely alienated from Luther because, as it seemed to them, he had acted traitorously. Luther himself became increasingly afraid of chaos, fearful of all reform movements other than his own, intolerant of other reformers lest they turn out to be Thomas Müntzers in disguise.

Meanwhile, as it was evident that the Edict of Worms could not everywhere be enforced, each succeeding imperial Diet was forced to consider the Lutheran question. Catholic and Protestant princes took sides, political alignments began to emerge, and, as no agreement could be made, compromise became essential. In 1524 a temporary formula was adopted to the effect that "Each prince in his own territory shall enforce the Edict of Worms in so far as he might be able." This, in effect, made religion a territorial matter to be decided by the temporal powers. It was only a respite, but it lasted until 1529. In the interim the emperor was too embroiled in wars with France to give active attention to internal imperial problems, and most of northern Germany became Lutheran. Further, the German princes in favor of reform joined together in the League of Torgau (1526) in order better to combat Catholic forces in the empire. In April, 1529, at the Second Diet of Speyer (the first was in 1526), the Edict of Worms was reasserted only for Catholic territories. Lutheranism was to be tolerated where it could not be suppressed without tumult; but liberty for Catholics must be granted in Lutheran lands, whereas none would be granted to Lutherans in Catholic lands. Against this arrangement the Lutherans drew up a written protest, and from this document they and other reforming groups as well received the name "Protestants."

This action, together with the fact that the emperor made peace with France in August, 1529 (the Peace of Cambrai), caused Protestant leaders to fear the consequences of the next Diet, to be held in Augsburg in 1530. Accordingly, Philip of Hesse, who had joined with Frederick of Saxony as a leader of the Lutherans, called a meeting of Protestant leaders at the castle at Marburg in October, 1529 (the Colloquy of Marburg). The object was to formulate a common policy for the approaching Diet where, it seemed certain, Protestants would have to defend their views once more. By this time the number of reformers had increased: Martin Bucer (1491-1551), a Dominican who had been converted into a reformer by Luther's teachings, had won many adherents at Strassburg and vicinity; Ulrich Zwingli (1484-1531), a Swiss humanist scholar and former Catholic priest, had taken over Zurich and spread Protestant doctrines into neighboring Swiss cantons; and there were others.

But Martin Luther had no desire for a political confederation lest it lead to bloodshed; moreover, the various reformers could not agree on a common statement of faith. The chief difference arose over the nature of the Lord's Supper. Although Luther denied *transubstantiation,* the Catholic "miracle of the Eucharist," whereby the bread and the wine after having been blessed for the sacrament miraculously became the actual flesh and blood of Christ, he upheld a halfway interpretation known as *consubstantiation,* which maintained the "living presence" of Christ in the bread and wine. Zwingli, on the other hand, refused both transubstantiation and consubstantiation, and held that the bread and wine are merely symbols of the flesh and blood of Christ. Thus the effort to establish a confession common to all Protestant groups failed, and the Marburg Colloquy brought forth no alliance among the Protestants.

Already Protestantism was beginning to show that divisive quality which has characterized it to this day. Bucer and Melanchthon managed to find a workable agreement among north German Protestants in 1536 (the Wittenberg Concord), but the Zwinglians were permanently separated from the Lutherans. Three separate confessions of faith were presented to the Diet of Augsburg in 1530, one by Bucer, one by Zwingli, and one by Luther. The last, really the work of Melanchthon, although with the counsel and approval of Luther, set forth in a systematic, firm, yet moderate fashion the central ideas of Lutheranism. But it failed to win Catholic acceptance, and the Diet voted that the Protestants must recant. As Emperor Charles V threatened them with coercion, the Protestant Lutheran princes drew together in a loose alliance at Schmalkalden (1530). But the emperor found his hands tied and, except for local conflicts, an uneasy truce between Catholics and Protestants within the empire continued until after Luther's death in 1546.

THE LUTHERAN CHURCH

During all these years the Lutheran form of worship was spreading and taking shape. Although Luther was indifferent to many forms and ceremonies, the core of the Lutheran liturgy was participation by the congregation in a service of prayer, praise, and Scriptural instruction. It was conducted in German in order to be intelligible to all, and the sermon served as a medium for Scriptural instruction. Luther's own translation of the Bible (both testaments were completed by 1534), his catechism, and his multitudinous tracts and sermons explored nearly every aspect of theology. Moreover, the Lutheran Bible set a new standard for German language and literature which became the universal High German or literary tongue. Luther also loved music and he wrote many hymns, including the still popular "A Mighty Fortress is Our God." Music became an integral—and

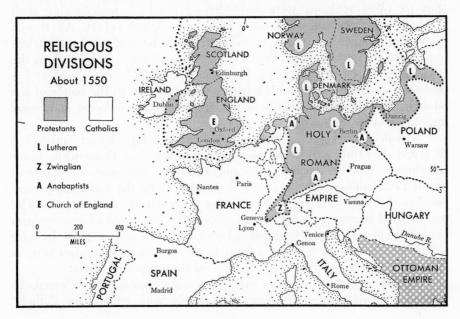

RELIGIOUS
DIVISIONS
About 1550

Protestants Catholics

L Lutheran

Z Zwinglian

A Anabaptists

E Church of England

0   200   400
MILES

popular—feature of Lutheran worship. In all these ways Luther demonstrated an outstanding ability to identify himself and his thoughts with the common man. His own family life (he married a former nun, Catherine von Bora, in 1525) was an inspiration to him and to all who knew him, giving an air of sweet domesticity which further recommended him to German peasants and burghers.

Yet Lutheranism was still insecure at Luther's death. Indeed, in that same year (1546) a religious war broke out between the emperor and the Schmalkaldic League of Lutheran princes. The princes were decisively defeated at the Battle of Mühlberg (1547), and for the moment it appeared that all might be lost. But Charles V overplayed his hand. In a decree known as the *Interim* (1548)—so called because it was to be valid only until a general council was held—the emperor sought to reimpose Catholicism upon the empire. But the Lutheran princes, reinforced by a secret alliance with France, renewed the conflict. Charles was taken by surprise and forced to flee. Such a show of princely strength and Lutheran power forced a settlement.

The result was the Peace of Augsburg in 1555. Charles V refused to deal with the Lutherans, leaving his brother, Ferdinand, to negotiate the settlement. Ferdinand accepted a compromise which spelled the permanent establishment of Lutheranism in the empire. In essence, it was a return to the principle set forth in 1524, known as *cuius regio eius religio,* "the ruler shall determine the religion." Accordingly, each German prince and free city should determine the faith, whether Lutheran or Catholic, and those people whose religion was different from that of the ruler were free to emigrate. But all other religions were forbidden—a provision underscoring both Lutheran and Catholic intolerance of other religious beliefs. All church properties seized after 1552 were to be mutually restored; and an "ecclesiastical reservation" provided that if a Catholic spiritual prince, such as the archbishop of Cologne, became Protestant, he should be deposed and a successor appointed so that his territory might remain in the hands of the church. But this reservation was inserted by imperial decree and never agreed upon by the negotiators.

The Peace of Augsburg was supposed to be a temporary settlement, but it lasted sixty-three years, and the empire remained at peace while bitter religious wars broke out in neighboring states. Yet the emperor's failure to crush Lutheranism and the power demonstrated by the Lutheran princes weakened further the political authority exercised by the emperor. The empire had become an even more loosely federated group of principalities and free cities governed by princes, bishops, and burghers. Thus, in spite of Luther's hopes for peaceful reform in the church, Lutheranism was, in final analysis, imposed by force exercised by the temporal powers.

Outside the German states much the same pattern was followed. In the Scandinavian states the monarchs, largely with an eye for Catholic church properties, adopted Lutheranism by fiat from above, with little apparent concern by their subjects—Sweden in 1527, Denmark in 1530. Slovenia adopted Lutheranism in 1547, and many Poles, Hungarians, and Bohemians became Lutherans. In Poland, however, Catholicism ultimately regained its losses, and in Hungary and Bohemia Lutheranism soon lost out to other Protestant groups.

3 : John Calvin and Calvinism

As WE HAVE SEEN, Martin Luther did not begin by challenging the doctrines of the church, but by attacking a specific abuse, which was later eliminated. He had, however, reached additional conclusions about the Christian faith and the sacraments, which came to the surface as the struggle advanced. These ideas were embraced in the new church that he founded. Subsequent leaders of the Protestant Reformation generally started from a different base. Although they believed that they possessed the essential truths about Christianity and hoped to convert everyone to their views, they did not anticipate that the Roman Catholic church as such would accept those views. John Calvin and his followers resembled Luther in that they worked through governments and tried to build a new Christian commonwealth with the aid of the power of the state. But Calvin was also prepared to accept schism from the outset, that is, to accept the simultaneous existence in western Christendom of more than one Christian church. If Catholics, Lutherans, Anabaptists, and others could not be persuaded to accept his views, Calvin, convinced of his own righteousness, was prepared to forge ahead, allowing the others to suffer the ultimate penalties of their own wrongheadedness.

John Calvin (1509-1564) was born in Noyon, in Picardy, in France, the son of a minor clerk with some legal training. He was educated in the local schools and, being a precocious boy, was granted benefices by the Noyon Cathedral (whose Chapter Calvin's father served as attorney) which enabled him to attend college. In 1523 he matriculated at the University of Paris, first at the Collège de la Marche and then at the Collège de Montaigu, where he graduated with a master's degree when he was only eighteen years old. As his father insisted that he study law, he moved to the University of Orléans and took the degree of doctor of law. But his bent was toward humanistic studies, and when his father died (1531) he felt free to follow his own desires and returned to Paris. There, in 1532, he published his first work, a humanist *Commentary on Lucius Annaeus Seneca's Two Books on Clemency*. So far the young Calvin had exhibited no vital concern with religion beyond that of a well-educated Catholic of his time.

Yet he had been exposed to Lutheran teachings, and Paris buzzed with religious controversy. Indeed, Calvin was a close friend of one of Luther's admirers, and when the latter was forced to flee late in 1533 Calvin also thought it prudent to leave Paris. For a time he was at Saintonge, and he wandered about for several months besides. Somewhere in his wanderings in 1534 he was smitten with a "sudden conversion," sometimes compared with that of Saul of Tarsus (St. Paul), and he became a Protestant. He returned to Noyon, resigned his ecclesiastical benefices, and, because the king of France, Francis I, was then actively trying to root out Protestant reformers, he fled to Basel in Switzerland. There, in 1535, he completed the first edition of his greatest work, *The Institutes of the Christian Religion,* published in 1536. This book, which Calvin repeatedly revised and enlarged until his final version (1559) was nearly five times as large as the original, was one of the most vital works of the Protestant movement. It served as a textbook of theology for Reformed (Calvinist) churches everywhere for more than three hundred years. The work was originally published in Latin, but Calvin himself published a French translation in 1541, and translations were made by others in Italian (1557), Dutch (1560), English (1561), German (1572), and Spanish (1597). Dedicated to King Francis I in the solemn hope that he might be converted, Calvin set forth at once a confession of faith and a book of religious instruction. Vigorous and articulate, Calvin wrote in a simple style which at times rose to great heights of eloquence, immediately marking him as the ablest expositor of the Protestant cause.

THE ESSENCE OF CALVINISM

The final edition of Calvin's great work, though rearranged and expanded when compared to the earlier editions, was not fundamentally altered in its basic thought. It was not original except in style and presentation, for Calvin borrowed heavily from Augustine, Luther, and others. Like the earlier reformers, he recognized the Bible as the only final authority and brought all his humanistic training to bear upon its exposition. Yet his emphasis was different from Luther's, and he created, in consequence, a different conception of the relationships between God, Christ, and man, and of the nature and organization of the true church.

Like Luther, Calvin believed in the justification of sinful man through the mediation of Christ. But whereas for Luther salvation was through faith alone, for Calvin the gulf between the majesty of God and the sinful weakness of man forced a modification of this view. "The chief end of human life," said Calvin, "is to know God"; and knowledge of God requires knowledge of and discipline over ourselves. God is creator of the universe, and all that is in it, including man (his noblest accomplishment), testifies to that fact; and God is redeemer of man, as the Scriptures testify. Man can know God only by means of heartfelt piety and reverent awe;

emotion must be conjoined with reason. Yet when God is known he remains mysterious, aloof, outside mortal comprehension; man may know God's attributes but he cannot penetrate the mystery of divine essence. Man is helpless before the divine judgment, having forfeited all justifiable claim through the original sin of Adam, whereby all men became perpetual sinners. Thus God may justifiably condemn all men. That he does not is due to his mercy. This mercy is extended to those whom, in God's inscrutable will, he has eternally chosen to receive it. These are the elect of God, and all others are consigned to suffer the wages of their sin. This doctrine, called *predestination,* Calvin emphasized more than Luther, and he defined it thus:

> Predestination we call the eternal decree of God by which He has determined with Himself what He would have to become of every man. For . . . eternal life is foreordained for some and eternal damnation for others. Every man, therefore, being formed for one or the other of these ends, we say that he is predestined to life or to death.

Mortal man cannot presume to question or to understand this "dread decree"; that it is God's will is its justification. No one can know for certain whether he is of the elect. But if he earnestly seeks to know Christ through a study of the Bible; if he knows himself in that he develops self-discipline and leads a moral life in conformity to Christ's commandments; if he has faith, that inestimable gift of God, and a conscience clear of hypocrisy in all these matters—then he may expect Christ's mediation and God's election.

But though he be of the elect, he is no saint, free of mortal sin (unlike the claims of the "saintly" followers of the Zwickau prophets, some of the Anabaptists, and other sects); and he has no call for pride or a puffed up spirit, for he is still a sinful man given to a life of penance, suffering, and stern self-discipline. His principal joys are in his grateful praise to God for his mercy and in contemplation of the eternal life to come. Even one who cannot conscientiously lay claim to these things, and may have cause to suspect he may not be of the elect, must nonetheless accept without murmur the justice and wisdom of God's "dread decree." Thus Calvinism demanded faith not only in God but also in the justice and mercy of his omniscient predestination of all men, together with unremitting introspection and self-discipline and a humble acceptance of God's will.

There is a moral grandeur in Calvin's utter surrender to God and readiness to sacrifice all to his will. If later critics found predestination terrifying and the God of Calvin a cruel and capricious tyrant, Calvin himself led men to wonder and worship before God's majesty, power, and grace. His was a call to a faith that transcends reason, that would have us believe in God's justice even when we cannot understand his reprobation. Generations of Calvinists in Switzerland, France, the Netherlands, Scotland,

England, America, and elsewhere found inspiration in these beliefs. The English-speaking world commonly calls them Presbyterians.

THE GENEVAN MODEL OF A CHRISTIAN COMMONWEALTH

Soon after publication of the first edition of *The Institutes* Calvin went on a visit to Italy. On his return in the late summer of 1536 he stopped overnight in Geneva, Switzerland, expecting to go on toward Strassburg the next day. But his presence became known, and William Farel, the breezy, hot-gospeling reformer in Geneva, persuaded him to remain and assist in the church reformation of that badly torn community. "God thrust me into the game," wrote Calvin of this unexpected development. But it was in Geneva that he spent most of the remainder of his life, and the conditions peculiar to that community helped to mold the character of Calvinism.

Beautifully situated along the southwest end of Lake Leman in full view of Mont Blanc, Geneva was on one of the most heavily trafficked Alpine passes through which flowed commerce between France, the Germanies, and Italy. Its citizens, numbering about 16,000, were mostly artisans and tradespeople who were divided religiously and politically and, with the many transients who passed through the town, were a pleasure-loving lot. In the early 1500's the Genevans were struggling to free themselves from the ecclesiastical control of the Catholic bishop of Vienne and the feudal overlordship of the duke of Savoy. Councils elected by the wealthy citizens took over the direction of affairs. In 1526 they formed a league with the neighboring city-states of Bern and Freiberg, renounced the Pope, expelled the bishop, and broke up religious houses. In 1532 William Farel was sent from Bern to assist in church reform and by May, 1536, Farel had persuaded the Genevans formally to renounce the Catholic faith. But pro-Catholic opinion was still strong, and it was at this point that Calvin arrived and was persuaded by Farel to remain and assist in building a new reformed church.

Calvin faced a turbulent, free-wheeling populace who, in spite of internal differences and external pressures, were patriotically determined to establish Geneva as an autonomous city-state. The real power of the city rested in an oligarchy of wealthy citizens who controlled the city councils and were jealous of their position. Through these councils Calvin and Farel worked for church reform, but when, in 1537, they submitted articles of faith to which all Genevans were to swear public allegiance a crisis arose. Many citizens were unwilling to be bound by Calvin's ideas of church discipline, the reformers' supporters were voted out of office, and the new council requested both Calvin and Farel to leave the city within three days (1538). The next three years Calvin spent in Strassburg, where he was persuaded by Martin Bucer to become pastor of the French refugee church. Here, in association with Bucer and other reformers, he compiled a book of French psalms, set to music for his congregation, wrote several works on theology and practical divinity, and generally refined and clarified his pattern of church reformation. Meanwhile the Genevans reversed their position and begged Calvin to return, which with some initial reluctance he did in 1541. Immediately he drew up proposed *Ecclesiastical Ordinances of the Church of Geneva* for submission to the Genevan council. The council adopted them on November 20, 1541. The *Ordinances* served as a constitution for the Genevan church, which became a model of Calvinist church organization everywhere—and, in various perversions, an inspiration for a number of radical Protestant groups. In effect, they held that the true Universal Church of Christ is *invisible,* its only head is Jesus Christ, and its members are God's elect, known only to God. The *visible* church, such as that organized at Geneva, is likely to contain hypocritical reprobates, but this is unavoidable in this world and matters not so long as it is a true church. A true church is one that maintains true preaching and reverent acceptance of the gospel, administers the sacraments according to Scriptural admonition, and supports a discipline to correct wayward members and cast out scandalous and obdurate offenders. Taken altogether, such churches as set up in particular villages, towns, and states form the visible Universal Church. Each has its own disciplinary organization, or consistory, as designated by Christ and the Apostles. This, said Calvin, properly consists of four kinds of officers: pastors and teachers to preach and teach the Word, elders to oversee the discipline of the church, and deacons to care for the poor and the sick. Elders and deacons should be elected by each church; pastors and teachers depended upon a two-fold call, an inward "call" by the spirit of Christ and an outward "call" by the congregation. Such a church organization—that of the Presbyterian or "Reformed Churches"—was republican in form and autonomous in operation. Calvin viewed it as separate from the state, yet the state was expected to defend it and to execute its decrees in matters affecting religion and the welfare of the church. But the Genevan magistrates were never willing to accept this autonomy, and the elders were, in fact, politically chosen by the councils. Thus the church and the state in Geneva became interlocked and, while the final authority nominally rested in the councils, such became Calvin's ascendancy that, in fact, the clergy dominated. In this sense Geneva became a theocracy, a new Protestant "city of God" and model of a Christian commonwealth.

The efforts to overcome opposition in Geneva and to curb the excesses of a pleasure-bent citizenry led the Genevan church to adopt stern measures to repress blasphemy, drunkenness, dissolute songs and dances, and sexual promiscuities. Moreover, as we have seen, Calvin's theology demanded strict self-discipline, and his legalistic mind translated this into a depressing array of do's and don'ts—a feature which many of his admirers in other lands developed into a harsh, gloomy Puritanism. Still, the Genevan original, basking in the first flush of Reformation enthusiasm and inspired by one of the greatest reformers, submitted willingly enough, especially as the Genevan vanity was touched by the adulation it came to receive from other parts of the world. Religious refugees flocked to Geneva in considerable numbers and, as Calvin's fame spread, pious Protestants came from far and wide to sit at his feet. Moreover, Calvin placed heavy emphasis upon schools, in order to have a literate laity capable of reading and discussing God's Word intelligently and "to prepare youth for the ministry and civil government." Accordingly, Geneva developed a remarkable system of schools for both boys and girls, and capped it with an Academy (1559) which supplied trained ministers and teachers to the Reformed churches of Europe long after Calvin's death in 1564. Thus Geneva became a fountain of the Calvinist reform movement from which poured literature, inspiration, and trained missionaries into neighboring states.

4 : The Rise of the Church of England

THE COURSE of the Reformation in Germany, France, and Switzerland was, *in the minds of the reformers,* primarily religious, with political and economic factors playing a secondary, even incidental, role. In England, however, political factors were uppermost—a curious situation in view of the long, pre-Reformation English addiction to Lollardy which, through the works of John Wycliffe, had in some measure communicated itself to John Huss and thence to Martin Luther. Moreover, it seems likely that Lollardy prepared the English mind for church reformation and made the English people supinely receptive to ecclesiastical alterations imposed from above by acts of state. Still, if we except a small group of Lutheran sympathizers at Cambridge University (who were easily brought to recant their views in 1527), there was no loud English demand for church reformation on the part of the clergy or the laity. The king, Henry VIII (1509-1547), wrote a book against Luther which pleased the Pope so that Leo X gave him the title "Defender of the Faith" (1521). Doctrinal opposition to the Catholic church was relatively slight in England, although there was considerable grumbling against Rome's monetary demands and papal influence upon the affairs of the kingdom.

WOLSEY AND THE ROYAL MARRIAGE QUESTION

The immediate background of the Reformation in England stemmed from the ambitions and activities of the royal favorite, Thomas Wolsey, who became a cardinal of the church, chancellor of the kingdom, and papal legate to England (1515-30). In these multiple capacities Wolsey united great political and ecclesiastical authority, and he hoped to employ them for his own election to the Papacy. To this end he fished in dangerous diplomatic waters. In the struggles between the emperor and the king of France, Wolsey first supported France, then, when Charles V won out, he sought to reverse his policy and lost favor with both sides. Meanwhile his high-handed, dictatorial methods of raising money in England aroused bitter opposition at court, in Parliament, and among the English clergy. Ultimately, he lost the king's favor, was arrested for high treason (1529), and died in disgrace in 1530.

Cardinal Wolsey's downfall was hastened by his failure to obtain an annulment of Henry VIII's marriage to Catherine of Aragon, daughter of Ferdinand and Isabella of Spain and aunt of Emperor Charles V. Although Henry VIII had been married for eighteen years, his marriage had been to his elder brother's widow, and a papal dispensation had been necessary to legalize the union. Although a matter of dynastic politics (both of Catherine's marriages had been seals to a diplomatic union between England and Spain), the papal dispensation had been granted in the firm belief that Catherine's first marriage had not been physically consummated and that the Spanish princess was a virginal bride upon her marriage to Henry. Why the king chose to question this after so many years, to seek heavenly forgiveness for having lived in sin with his brother's wife, and to demand papal annulment of his marriage are matters of dispute. However, it is clear that the question of peaceful succession to the throne was prominent in Henry VIII's thoughts. Of six children born to Catherine only one, Lady Mary, survived. After 1525 it became known that the queen could bear no more children, and succession in the female line was not yet secure in England. The king, heavily aware of possible challenges to Tudor succession, needed a male heir. Could the failure to have one have been a divine judgment upon the king for having married his brother's widow? To Henry, who was an amateur theologian, this may have become a serious consideration. Moreover, such a conclusion may have become an easy rationalization after Henry fell in love with Anne Boleyn, a young lady in waiting at the court, and Anne, encouraged by ambitious relatives, would permit no clandestine affair, but must become queen. So Henry appealed to Rome (1527), and Cardinal Wolsey sought to intercede on his sovereign's behalf.

Wolsey attempted to have the case tried in England with himself, as papal legate, empowered to give a decision. The Pope, dominated by Charles V, did not consent, and the case dragged on without settlement until after Wolsey's disgrace and death. But the king was determined, and when Parliament convened in 1529 he found it loud in its denunciation of Wolsey and clerical abuses. Henry was no reformer of the continental variety, but here was a fine opportunity to claim a mandate from the people and to use Parliament to subjugate the church. In 1531 Henry won legal recognition as "Protector and Head of the English Church and Clergy." The next year he graciously allowed a planted petition (against the Ordinaries of the

Realm), whereby the clergy could no longer make church laws (canons) or pay annates to Rome without royal approval. Meanwhile, too, at the suggestion of Thomas Cranmer, the annulment question was referred to the universities of England and Europe. When a number of universities gave approval, Cranmer, now archbishop of Canterbury, declared that the king's marriage to Catherine was null and void; and Henry married Anne Boleyn (January, 1533). In the following September the new queen gave birth to a daughter, the future Queen Elizabeth I. Already the Pope had excommunicated Henry (July, 1533), but Parliament confirmed the annulment, recognized the new marriage, and secured the succession of Anne's children to the throne. In 1534 Parliament also passed the Act of Supremacy which appointed Henry VIII and his successors as "Protector and only Supreme Head of the Church and Clergy of England." Thus the break from Rome was complete. The English church and state became united under the same head, a matter of vast consequence not only in the nationalization of the English church but also in the concentration of powers in the hands of the king.

CRANMER AND THE ENGLISH CHURCH

Still, the king had not discarded Catholic doctrine, Catholic ceremonies, or Catholic church organization. In effect, he had merely put himself in place of the Pope at the head of the English church. To be sure, in 1534 he dispatched a new royal favorite, Thomas Cromwell, as head of a commission to visit monasteries and other religious houses and to report on their condition. On the basis of the commission's report, Henry dissolved all religious houses—the smaller ones in 1536, the rest in 1539—and confiscated their properties for the crown. But most of the efforts to reform the church in England along continental Protestant lines were resisted by the king. In 1539 he procured parliamentary passage of the Six Articles, which reaffirmed the Roman doctrine of the sacraments, including transubstantiation, celibacy of the clergy, and the Mass. Still, Thomas Cranmer, the new archbishop of Canterbury, gave the English church a Protestant bent greater than the king may have realized. Cranmer was a scholar and a theologian, who viewed the English church as part of a vast movement toward the purification of Christendom. He was in constant touch with Melanchthon, Bucer, and other continental reformers, and once asked Melanchthon (without success) to write the English prayer book. His own ten articles of doctrine for the new English church (1536) betrayed Protestant leanings, and he unsuccessfully opposed the Six Articles in 1539. Later Cranmer supervised the production of the English Book of Common Prayer (1548) and promulgated the Forty-Two Articles of Religion of 1552. Afterwards reduced to thirty-nine, these articles remain the basis of the faith of the Church of England to this day.

Henry VIII, disappointed that Anne Boleyn's child was a daughter, soon tired of the queen. His desire for a male heir, together with his mounting appetites, led him to divorce and execute Anne in 1536. His next conquest, Lady Jane Seymour, gave birth to a son, Edward, in 1537, but the queen died soon afterwards. Henry then entered into a diplomatic match with Anne, Duchess of Cleves, but he disliked the "Flanders Mare," as he inelegantly called her, and annulled the marriage in a few months (1540). In the same year he married Catherine Howard, but she was beheaded in 1542 after having confessed to prenuptial unchastity. Then in 1543 Henry married an English widow, Catherine Parr, who outlived him. At his death in 1547 Henry left three heirs whose legitimacy was recognized: Edward, son of Jane Seymour; Mary, daughter of Catherine of Aragon; and Elizabeth, daughter of Anne Boleyn. Ruling in turn, these three completed the Tudor Dynasty in England, and during their reigns the Church of England assumed permanent form.

The structure developed slowly, with a major setback in Mary's reign. Its development was as much in response to political as to religious forces. Edward VI was only nine when he succeeded Henry VIII (1547). He was a sickly boy who died in 1553. His uncle, Edward Seymour, Duke of Somerset, served as regent until he was displaced (1549) by the earl of Warwick (later duke of Northumberland). Both of the regents were Protestants, Somerset out of conviction, Warwick out of desire further to despoil church properties. In consequence, the religious innovations of the continental reformers gained headway in the English church, especially as pushed forward by Cranmer, the archbishop of Canterbury. The Six Articles were repealed, communion in both kinds was instituted, priests were allowed to marry, an English Bible was promulgated, and by the Acts of Uniformity (1549 and 1552) attendance of all Englishmen at the religious services was compelled, with penalties for being present at any other form of service. Furthermore, Books of Common Prayer were set forth, the first in 1549, the second in 1552; and Cranmer's Forty-Two Articles of Faith were adopted in the latter year. The Book of Common Prayer was in English, and it displaced the older service books. Moreover, it was a masterly work in moderation. Its silence on many theological points and ambiguity on others made it acceptable to most moderate Catholics and Protestants alike, permitting wide latitude in vestments, ceremonies, and specific creeds while it retained the episcopal organization of the church with the king as its earthly head. In this, as in the later Tudor settlements, political allegiance and outward conformity were of greater consequence than fine points of Christian dogma.

ROMAN INTERLUDE

When Edward died in 1553 a vain attempt was made to place his cousin, the Protestant Lady Jane Grey, on the throne, but after a few days the effort failed and Mary became queen. Mary was a pious Catholic, embittered by the shabby treatment accorded her mother, Catherine of Aragon, and determined to take the English church back into the Church of Rome. But she faced a reluctant people and opposing Parliaments, and she was forced to move slowly. The Acts of Repeal (1553 and 1554) were intended to undo the English Reformation, but there was no complete English surrender to Rome. The Act of Supremacy of 1534 was repealed, and English bishops once more became obedient to Rome; but confiscated church properties could not be recovered for the Roman church, and papal bulls were given force only if they did not conflict with English laws and the prerogatives of the crown.

Mary's partial restoration of Catholicism might have lasted but for two mistakes which made the queen unpopular, stirred the fires of English nationalism, and prepared the way for a greater emphasis upon Protestant reform in England. The first was her marriage in 1554 to Philip—soon to become Philip II, King of Spain—by which she hoped to secure Catholic succession to the English throne and enlist Catholic Spain's aid in bringing the English realm securely into the Roman orbit. But Philip was unpopular in England, the queen had no heir to succeed her, and the English resented being identified with Catholic powers against continental Protestants. They felt their national independence of action challenged, and identified it with the national church.

The queen's second error lay in her persecution of English heretics. About three hundred Protestants suffered death during her reign, including Archbishop Cranmer and many humble folk who were burned at the stake. These persecutions brought Protestantism more sympathy in England than it had previously enjoyed, and John Foxe's illustrated *Book of Martyrs* (1563) dramatized and chronicled those who suffered for their faith. Moreover, about eight hundred Englishmen, including many prominent churchmen of Edward's time, sought refuge abroad. These men—the "Marian Exiles"—removed to the Protestant centers at Geneva or in the German Rhineland, where they imbibed Protestant doctrine directly from Calvin, Bucer, and others. After Mary's death many of them returned to England determined to construct a reformed English church on the basis of the law of God without regard for political considerations or royal supremacy. Thus they introduced radical Protestantism and prepared the way for the Puritan challenge to the Church of England. Queen Elizabeth, who succeeded Mary in 1558, faced not only a struggle between royal and papal supremacy but also a defense of the Church of England against attacks from Catholics and from Protestant non-conformists heavily indoctrinated with sectarian views of the church.

THE ELIZABETHAN SETTLEMENT

Accordingly, Elizabeth steered a cautious middle course. Political considerations again were uppermost, the queen seeking a church settlement which would at once preserve her royal power and be as inclusive as possible in the interests of national unity. In 1559 a new Act of Supremacy swept away Mary's ecclesiastical legislation and revived the essential points of the antipapal statutes of Henry VIII. The supreme power over the national church was once more vested in the crown, although the title was changed from "Head" to "the only supreme governor" in order to give less offense. At the same time a new Act of Uniformity (1559) required every person to attend church, and penalties for non-attendance were more severe than in Edward's reign. No other forms of church service were allowed. The Edwardian Book of Common Prayer was re-established with slight modifications, and in 1562 the Thirty-Nine Articles of Faith were set forth, modified from Cranmer's Forty-Two to allow even greater liberty for various opinions. The queen firmly rejected, as a threat to royal supremacy, any form of church government but episcopacy. This policy was a source of much dissatisfaction to those who sought the Calvinist, or Presbyterian, form. Indeed this, together with cries for further reformation in ceremonies to cast aside popish vestments and to celebrate the Lord's Supper in a more Protestant manner, were the principal early demands of the more radical reformers. These men sought, as they said, further to purify the English church of popish residues in discipline and ceremonies. From these demands they received the name "Puritan" in 1564, though from the outset they were by no means agreed among themselves as to what they would supply in place of the Elizabethan English church. They were noisy critics, but their divisions rendered them powerless against the broad and inclusive church settlement of Queen Elizabeth I. Similarly, Catholic opposition was ineffective. Indeed, the queen's "soft" policies had early led the Catholics to believe that she might be reconciled with Rome. Several times the Pope appealed to her, and it was not until 1570 that she was finally excommunicated from the Roman church. Thus a political settlement was effected, and the Church of England was broadly and solidly based. Radical Protestants condemned it as too popish, while Catholics protested it was too Protestant. Above all, it was national, perhaps the best example of a political settlement of the religious and ecclesiastical problems created by the Reformation.

5 : The Catholic Reformation

MANY CATHOLICS deplored the abuses that had crept into the church, and they advocated reforms as loudly as the Protestant leaders. Indeed, the beginnings of Catholic reform antedate the Protestant Revolt. Many humanist writers and clerics had advocated it, and in Spain Cardinal Francisco Jiménez (1437–1517) abolished a variety of abuses, set up schools, and greatly strengthened the church against heretics and infidels during the latter years of the fifteenth century. Indeed, it was the church's great misfortune that in the early sixteenth century it had a series of Popes unwilling or unable to take the lead in reform. Most Catholics agreed that the best means to effect reform was by a general council; but while the early Protestant Revolt was gathering force, a variety of factors arose to prevent such an assembly. The Medici Popes, still conscious of the conciliar movement, postponed a council lest it limit their powers and thwart their worldly ambitions; some churchmen warned that political enemies of the Papacy, possibly the emperor or the king of France, might manipulate a council for their own ends; and wide differences of opinion among members of the hierarchy rendered the outcome of uncertain value for the reformation of the church.

By the 1530's, however, the demand for reformation could no longer be postponed, and with the elevation of Paul III in 1534 there was a Pope willing and able to undertake it. Before the end of the sixteenth century the church had five Popes who were zealous for reform: Paul III (1534–1549), Paul IV (1555–1559), St. Pius V (1566–1572), Gregory XIII (1572–1585), and Sixtus V (1585–1590). These Popes appointed to high church offices men known for their virtue and learning rather than for their wealth, family position, or political influence. They dealt severely with clerics who persistently abused their offices. They reorganized papal finances. And they revived and extended the ecclesiastical Court of the Inquisition (1542) to ferret out and try persons suspected of heresies. Pope Paul III also began preparations for a church council which, after much dispute over the place of meeting and other details, assembled for its first session at Trent in December, 1545.

THE COUNCIL OF TRENT

The Council of Trent met, with many interruptions and postponements, until December, 1563. Lutherans refused to attend; Calvinists were not invited; the king of France refused to allow his subjects to participate; and only a few Englishmen, in defiance of their monarch, were present. Spaniards and Italians were most numerous, and Italians dominated the council. Of 225 prelates who signed the council's official acts, 189 were Italians. Moreover, the Italians mostly represented the Curia, thus permitting Roman forces to protect the Papacy against those who might seek to assert the council's supremacy over the Popes. The delicate and rapidly changing state of international affairs occasioned many delays in the council's work, and its meetings were sometimes disorderly. Before its conclusion, however, Protestantism had reached the height of its power—for the moment, at least—and a reaction more favorable to Catholicism had set in. Besides the work of the reforming Popes referred to above, this turn in the tide was also traceable to the work of the Council of Trent.

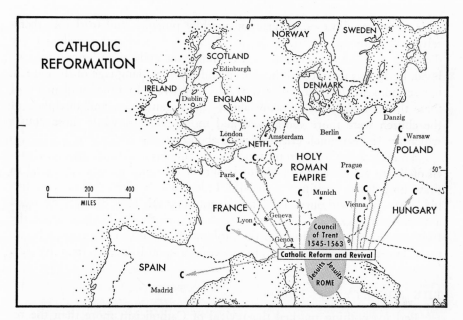

This work fell into four categories: redefinition of Roman Catholic doctrine with defense against Protestant objections; denunciations of specific heretical opinions and practices; reforms designed further to eradicate abuses and set up a more rigid discipline over the Catholic clergy; and protection to Catholics against dangerous Protestant teachings. Taken together, these four can be summarized as dogmatic and reformatory in nature.

In matters of dogma the council reaffirmed Catholic doctrines in flat contradiction to Protestant critics. The Catholic belief in Apostolic Succession, purgatory, clerical celibacy, the invocation of saints, the veneration of images and sacred relics, indulgences—all were reaffirmed, although precautions were set forth to eradicate the abuses that had become associated with some of these doctrines. Protestant teachings about grace, the sacraments, and justification by faith were condemned, and the ecclesiastical authority of the Papacy in matters of faith and church discipline was reasserted even to the point of placing the Pope's power above that of a church council. Interpretations of the Holy Scriptures, the council said, belong exclusively to the church, and they properly rest not only upon the Bible itself but also upon historical tradition as set forth by the Church Fathers and defined by church councils.

The Council of Trent also took measures to eliminate abuses and to strengthen discipline. Although indulgences were approved in theory, their sale was no longer permitted. The sale of church offices and plurality of offices were forbidden; bishops and other prelates were ordered to live in

79

their respective dioceses, to abandon worldly pursuits, and to devote themselves solely to their spiritual labors. Seminaries were authorized in every diocese in order to train priests and eliminate the evils of an ignorant priesthood. Latin was retained as the official and liturgical language of the church, but sermons in the vernacular were also approved. In time—and many of these things took years to bring about—the organization and discipline of the church were more centralized and more effective, while those abuses which aroused so much criticism were abolished.

To protect Catholics from unorthodox and heretical teachings the Council of Trent set up a censorship of books. A commission was appointed to draw up a list of writings, called the Index, which all Catholics were forbidden to read without special permission (1559). This list was enlarged a few years later, and in 1571 Pius V created the Congregation of the Index, a separate office to keep the prohibited lists up to date. Thus began a systematic censorship imposed by the church upon its members to this day.

THE SOCIETY OF JESUS

Perhaps nothing marked the revival of Catholicism more than the renewed strength of the religious orders and the rise of new ones. Both the Dominicans and the Franciscans enjoyed a revival of activity and zealous devotion; and among several new orders, founded among both men and women, none so forwarded the Catholic Reformation as the Society of Jesus. This society was founded in 1534 by a Spaniard, Ignatius of Loyola (1491–1556), and approved by the Pope in 1540. Originally a soldier in the service of Emperor Charles V, Loyola was badly wounded in the leg in 1521. While he convalesced he read a life of Christ and other religious books which led him to renounce his military career and devote himself to the church. For some years he lived as an ascetic, making a pilgrimage barefoot to Jerusalem (1523–24). Upon his return he undertook to complete his scanty education. He studied in grammar school, in Spanish universities, and finally at the University of Paris (1528 and later). Here, in 1534, with a group of pious and dedicated friends he founded the Society (or Company) of Jesus, intended to convert the Moslems and to counteract Protestantism. The members embarked at once on a pilgrimage to the Holy Land, but finding their passage blocked by war with the Turks they enlisted in the crusade for Catholic reform. In 1540 Pope Paul III issued a bull approving their constitution.

The Society of Jesus was by far the most militant order of the church. Founded by a soldier, its organization demonstrated many of the features of a military body, including a special vow of allegiance to the Pope, in addition to the usual vows of poverty, chastity, and obedience. At the head of the order was a general who asserted an iron discipline and gave the society more the appearance of a military company than a monastic body.

Loyola himself served as general until his death. Aware of his own initial educational shortcomings, Loyola made sure that each member was well educated and carefully trained during a long novitiate. Jesuits then set forth as soldiers of the church, serving as priests, as a sort of secret police of the Inquisition to hunt down heretics, as teachers and scholars, and as missionaries to all parts of the world. Their skill, their zeal, and their success soon made them the most hated and feared opponents of Protestantism, and even aroused the envy and jealousy of other Catholic orders. They were foremost in regaining ground lost to Protestants in Poland, Hungary, and southern Germany; they founded colleges and seminaries in Europe and America, and won almost complete control of education in Spain and large parts of France. Their missionary activities extended to the farthest corners of the world to convert to Catholic Christianity the Indians of the Far East and of the New World—Indonesians, Japanese, Filipinos, and Chinese as well. That the Church of Rome recovered so much of its strength in spite of the appeals of Protestantism was due in considerable part to the manifold and aggressive activities of the Society of Jesus.

6 : Some Results of the Reformation

THE REFORMATION set in motion forces which greatly altered the European scene in the sixteenth century, and which have continued to affect the course of events in a variety of ways even in the twentieth century. As is true of most major historical events, what mankind has *believed* to be the nature of the Reformation—that is, the various interpretations placed upon it—have been of greater consequence than many of the events of the Reformation itself. Protestant apologists have seen in the Reformation the restoration of the true church of Christ, the establishment of freedom for the Christian man against the tyranny of the Roman church, a purification of the liturgy and ceremonies of the church, an enrichment of worship through the greater participation of individual Christians, a restoration of the Word of God as the principal guide to church organization and Christian moral behavior, a modification of the rigors of absolute monarchy, and the spread of education for the masses. Catholic observers, on the contrary, have seen rents in the seamless fabric of western Christianity which weakened the church and opened the door for irresponsible sectarianism, bigotry, superstition, witchcraft, fanaticism, immorality, atheism, and poor taste; a destruction of moral and ecclesiastical authority which gave rise not only to heresies and the denial of the true church but also to social and political disorders and rebellions, the aggrandizement of temporal at the expense of spiritual power, and a presumption on the part of individuals both in

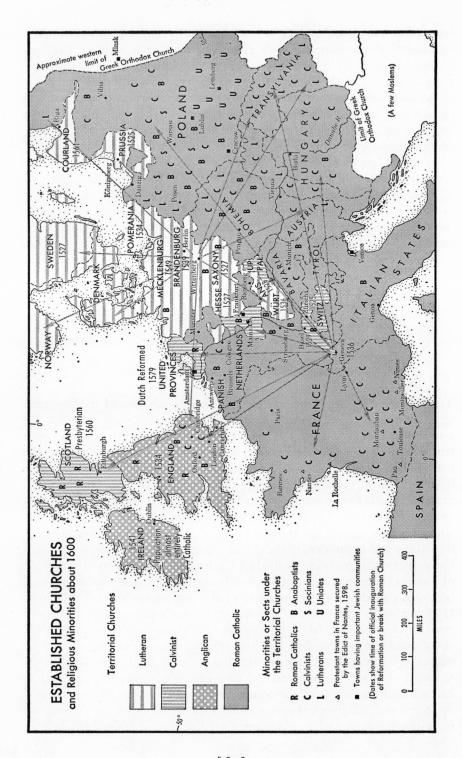

ESTABLISHED CHURCHES
and Religious Minorities about 1600

Territorial Churches

- Lutheran
- Calvinist
- Anglican
- Roman Catholic

Minorities or Sects under
the Territorial Churches

R Roman Catholics   B Anabaptists
C Calvinists   S Socinians
L Lutherans   U Uniates

△ Protestant towns in France secured
   by the Edict of Nantes, 1598.

■ Towns having important Jewish communities

(Dates show time of official inauguration
of Reformation or break with Roman Church)

0   100   200   300   400
         MILES

Approximate western limit of Greek Orthodox Church   ■Minsk

(A few Moslems)

Limit of Greek
Orthodox Church

POLAND
Vilna
Riga
COURLAND 1561
PRUSSIA 1525
Warsaw
Posen
Danzig
Königsberg
Lublin
Cracow
Lemberg
TRANSYLVANIA
HUNGARY
Buda
Danube R.
BOHEMIA
Prague
AUSTRIA
Vienna
TYROL
Venice
ITALIAN STATES
Genoa
SWEDEN 1527
DENMARK
NORWAY
POMERANIA 1534
MECKLENBURG 1549
BRANDENBURG 1539
Berlin
HESSE 1527
SAXONY
Wittenberg
ANSPAL
Bamberg
Frankfurt
Munster
Mainz
WÜRT. 1536
BAVARIA
Munich
Zürich
Basel 1529
Geneva 1536
SWITZ. 1525
Strasbourg
Cologne
Brussels
Antwerp
Amsterdam
NETHERLANDS
SPANISH
Dutch Reformed 1579
UNITED PROVINCES
FRANCE
Paris
Lyon
Rennes
Nantes
La Rochelle
Montauban
Toulouse
Montpellier
△Nimes
Pau
SPAIN
SCOTLAND Presbyterian 1560
Edinburgh
ENGLAND 1534
London
Oxford
Cambridge
Canterbury
IRELAND 1541
Population almost entirely Catholic
Dublin

0°
50°
50°

[82]

lay and in ecclesiastical affairs that was dangerous to Christian society and to the souls of men. Still others, viewing the Reformation from a less subjective religious standpoint, have seen it as a stimulant to the growth of nationalism, democracy, religious toleration, modern science, capitalism, and the materialism of a more secularized society. They consider that it fostered the gradual rise of the middle class—the bourgeoisie—to a position of political, economic, and social predominance at the expense of both the older privileged classes—the clergy and nobility—and the toiling masses—the proletariat.

None of the participants in the Reformation of the sixteenth century was aware of these various—and contradictory—interpretations of his work. Indeed, it appears unlikely that such projections of the forces unloosed by the Reformation could have been anticipated by the reformers themselves, whether Catholic or Protestant. Further, many of the political, social, and economic consequences since attributed to the Reformation would have been stoutly denied at the time. Few men are capable of foreseeing the long-range social consequences of their acts; and, as we have pointed out before, the sixteenth-century reformers on all sides were concerned primarily, if not solely, with religion and ecclesiastical matters. Moreover, post-Reformation polemicists and scholars—the former in an effort to fix blame upon their opponents, and the latter in an attempt to trace the origins of political and social movements—have attributed to the Reformation many things of a highly debatable nature. We cannot settle all of the arguments. But perhaps we can settle upon a few incontrovertible effects of the Reformation and, in passing, review a number of thought-provoking opinions.

SECTS AND SECTARIANISM

It cannot be denied that the Protestant Revolt destroyed the ecclesiastical and spiritual unity of western Christendom or, at least, of the peoples formerly within the Roman Catholic church. Before the end of the sixteenth century Lutheranism had become the state religion of northern Germany and the Scandinavian peoples, with many Lutheran sympathizers in Poland, Bohemia, Hungary, and elsewhere. Similarly, Calvinism had become the established religion in Geneva, in several of the south and west German states, and in Scotland. Calvinist sympathizers divided England (the Puritans) and France (the Huguenots) and were contesting with Lutherans and Jesuits for Bohemia, Poland, Hungary, and Brandenburg. Soon Huguenots would establish temporary Calvinist footholds in the Americas; the English and the Scots would carry Presbyterianism into northern Ireland, the West Indies, and North America; and the Dutch would establish it in South America and New Amsterdam (later New York). At the same time England broke with Rome and set up the Church of England, which soon followed English colonists to Virginia and many other English colonies overseas. To be sure, some of these regions—Poland, Bohemia, Hungary, and a few others—were subsequently regained for the Catholic church, but the basic divisions of the sixteenth century persist throughout the Modern Age, separating western Europe and its overseas possessions into Protestant and Catholic parts.

Nor can it be denied that the Protestant Revolt led to a proliferation of Christian sects in spite of the efforts of Luther, Calvin, and others to prevent it. Many of these sects came to differ from the Roman church and even from legally established churches in some Protestant states about the nature of the church itself, the roles of God and of man, the proper relationships between church and state, and those between the individual Christian and secular society as a whole. They believed in a "gathered church," for which they claimed divine authority from the Scriptures, especially from the words of Jesus to his disciples when he said, "For where two or three are gathered together in my name, there am I in the midst of them" (Matthew 18:20). These sectarians believed that religion is personal, not institutional: that an individual Christian may, by proper behavior and pious faith, receive heavenly grace directly from Christ without the mediation of priest or institutionalized church. Indeed, to them a "church" was merely an assembly of such believers who voluntarily join together in order to strengthen one another's personal means of achieving grace and in order to help others to achieve it. No one was born into such a church; he consciously joined it, usually only after he had reached the age of discretion. Hence they often revealed a strong tendency to reject infant baptism or required rebaptism, as the Anabaptists advocated.

Most of these Christian sects would acknowledge no king, bishop, or Pope save Jesus Christ himself as head of the church. They set up no elaborate hierarchy of church officers and, in fact, they tended to be suspicious of all ecclesiastical hierarchies and betrayed marked anticlerical opinions. Some of the sects would have no priests or ministers at all. They had few sacraments, if any, and no elaborate ceremonies. They laid no claim upon universality and, being small groups, they rarely attempted to dominate the world, or even a nation. As they generally placed heavy stress upon the Sermon on the Mount, they were prone to emphasize the opposition of the true kingdom of Christ to all worldly interests and institutions. To them God appeared more majestic and removed from this world than he did to the more orthodox churchmen; and man in his earthly state was more despicable and weak, without capacity for goodness, and able to be saved only through the tender mercies and infinite grace of God.

As a rule, the sects originated among the poorer people in society. Often they advocated radical social or political methods which the more conservative churches abhorred. They tended toward extreme biblicism, that is, they believed that the Bible supplies a complete rule of life for Christians, politically and economically as well as ecclesiastically and so-

Divisions and Secessions in Western Christendom

The following chart illustrates only the broad outlines of the divisions and sectarian secession which began with the Protestant Revolt and continues to the present day. As time passed, a multitude of new sects emerged, some with only a temporary existence. Many efforts have been made from time to time to reunite Protestants and to bring them and the Roman Catholics together. Actually, little has been accomplished, although current efforts have brought wide Protestant co-operation in such interdenominational organizations as the National Council of Churches in the U.S.A., the World Council of Churches, and the promising world-wide Ecumenical Movement with its periodical conferences of churches of many sects.

THE ROMAN CATHOLIC CHURCH

LUTHERANS
- Several nationalistic churches, as the German Lutheran, Swedish Lutheran, English Lutheran, etc.
- The Pietists of the 17th and 18th centuries (mostly non-separating from the Lutherans)
- Moravians, Dunkers, etc.

CALVINISTS
- Reformed Churches of Europe, as the Dutch Reformed, French Reformed (Huguenots), German Reformed, etc.
- The National Church of Scotland; the Free Church of Scotland; The United Presbyterian Church of Scotland
- The Presbyterian Churches of England, America, and the British Commonwealth of Nations
- The United Brethren Church

"RADICAL SECTS" (Anabaptists, etc.)
- Baptist Churches
- Socinians (Unitarians)
- Mennonites and Amish Mennonites
- Hutterian Brethren (Hutterites)
- Schwenckfelders, etc.

CHURCH OF ENGLAND (Anglican Church)
- English Independents and American Congregationalists
- English Calvinistic (or "Particular") Baptists
- The Society of Friends, or Quakers
- The Methodist Churches
- Universalist Church
- The Protestant Episcopal Church of America
- The Episcopal Church Reformed

cially. In their eyes the laws of God were simple and plain to all who would see, and they had little truck with higher criticism and complicated theology. They aspired to personal perfection in the sight of God, to personal service in the Lord, and to co-operation with their brothers-in-God toward these ends. In such ways, and only in such ways, could they merit God's saving grace and reach eternal salvation. As they were highly individualistic and subjective, they tended toward democratic views and practices, often in contradistinction to the more aristocratically-controlled and conservative churches. And, as the sectarians frequently differed among themselves, they tended to splinter into more and more sects, thus setting the stage for the multitude of Christian churches, sects, and other groups in the Modern Age.

Early in the course of the Protestant Revolt all manner of people began to organize sects. Some of them, such as in the German Peasants' Rebellion, mixed social and economic reforms with religion, and most of them were without the social respectability and scholarly standing of the Lutherans, the Genevans, or the Anglicans. Collectively these groups were known in the sixteenth century as *Anabaptists,* although it was an error to label so many diversified groups with a single denomination. The title derived from their widespread denial of the validity of infant baptism on the grounds that a child could not possibly believe or understand religious doctrines—a clear reflection of both Luther's emphasis upon justification by faith and the new view of the church as a voluntary society of believers. Usually, then, they baptized again, when the believer was old enough to determine his own faith and actions (hence the term Anabaptist, *ana* being a Greek prefix meaning "again"). Later generations were not baptized until they had reached an age of discretion and the prefix was dropped, leaving the name that of the familiar Baptists of today.

The Anabaptists shocked Catholics and more sober Protestants alike in the sixteenth century. Given to the private reading and interpretation of the Bible, they fanned out in all directions and were split even more widely by persecution. Usually they were small groups of common folk beguiled by the smooth oratory or the upright life, or both, of a leader who promised them a better life in this world and eternal salvation in the next. They were often given to Utopian schemes which promised to set up a heaven on earth. Some of them, too, were led into extraordinary and unorthodox practices by the old Christian dilemma posed by Calvin's renewed emphasis upon predestination. If God is all-powerful and all-knowing, he must will and determine everything that happens to all men in this world and in the next. Everyone is predestined by God's inscrutable will to heaven or to hell—that is, he is of the elect or the non-elect and nothing he can do will alter his condition. Why not, then, sin? Indeed, can it not be argued that God *wills* man to sin? Man has no free will in the matter, and if he sins he merely does what God has willed for him to do. By such an argument, a person can always claim to be doing God's will and all moral responsibility of the individual for his acts is destroyed.

The problem of free will versus predestination was very old in the church, and it raised important questions about the nature of God and man. If man is free to choose between good and evil, that is, if he has a free will, then God does not seem to be omniscient and all-powerful; if, on the other hand, man has no such choice, that is, if he is predestined, he is not morally responsible for his acts. Calvin, in keeping with most other theologians, both Catholic and Protestant, argued that the majesty of God and the sinful state of mortal man places a great chasm between God and man which even the most lively faith can only partially bridge. Man should strive to know God, but to claim that he *does* know God to the extent of knowing his will is presumptuous. No man can be certain that he knows God or his will, and moral behavior on the part of a man is one of the best outward signs of his election. The rules of moral behavior are clear in the Scriptures and in the Christian tradition. Man has no choice but to obey them to the best of his ability and to trust to God's free grace for justice and salvation—a grace which transcends human comprehension.

Some of the prophets of Zwickau who plagued Luther after his return from Wartburg Castle displayed unorthodox religious notions, as did some of the leaders of the Peasants' Rebellion. But the shocker came when a Dutch tailor, John of Leyden (1509–1536), became leader of an Anabaptist group that won control of the German city of Münster (1534) and set up a new Zion, or biblical Utopia, with common property, polygamy, and other practices usually looked upon with disfavor by western Christian society. The bishop of Münster imprisoned "King John," as he was called, put him to death in 1536, and suppressed the sect.

Few of the Anabaptists became so wildly fanatic as those of Münster, although they usually tended to "gather" a congregation and to live in communities apart from the rest of the world, working, sharing, and worshiping together as they believed the primitive Christians had done. Though they were violently persecuted on all sides, they clung to their ways with the stubborn faith of martyrs, thus providing the inspiration and institutional ancestry of such present-day sects as the Baptists, the Quakers, the Mennonites, and the Amish.

NATIONALISM

The Reformation also stimulated nationalist sentiments and tended to elevate the power of the state over the church. Both of these effects lay outside the intention of the principal reformers. Yet when Luther appealed to the German nobility in 1521 he aroused German patriotism and called upon the temporal powers to correct the abuses of the spiritual estate. This had the effect of unleashing temporal princes upon the wealth of the church and of establishing state churches. Calvin, too, though he denied the omnipotence of the state over the church, was forced to accede to it in Geneva, at least in point of legality. As we have seen, the principle of *cuius regio eius religio* was practiced long before the Peace of Augsburg, and the English monarchs followed a similar formula in setting up the Church of England. Indeed, Catholic kings, by such treaties with the Papacy as the Spanish Concordat of 1482 and the French Pragmatic Sanction of Bourges of 1438 (reasserted at the Concordat of Bologna in 1516), had already taken broad steps toward the nationalization of their churches. With the dynastic conflicts and religious wars of the sixteenth and seventeenth centuries, nationality and the state religion became increasingly identified. Probably this was nowhere better exemplified than in the struggle between England and Spain in the reign of Elizabeth I, when the Spanish supported the role of "His Most Catholic Majesty," as the kings of Spain were called, against the English "Infidels" with all the enthusiasm they had exhibited against the Moors; and the English repaid in kind, trespassing on many of the rules of Christian decency in their raids upon Spanish towns and colonies. Inevitably, too, Protestant states allied against Catholic powers, and a community of interests arose within each group of powers which welded them together internally while, at the same time, it strengthened the separation of Protestant from Catholic Europe.

THE REFORMATION IN PERSPECTIVE

With regard to other influences attributed to the Reformation there is some doubt. Questions about the true church, the nature of God and man, the role of the sacraments, and other mysteries of the Christian faith are still matters of partisan dispute and opinion. As regards bigotry, intolerance, superstition, witchcraft, and fanaticism, Catholics and Protestants broke about even, although many of these things were more properly attributable to the ignorance of the age than to Reformation developments—and the intensity of religious feeling engendered by the Reformation may have heightened their incidence. The development of religious toleration was largely a product of frustration after the warring parties had reconciled themselves to the fact that they were mutually incapable of destroying one another. It was largely of political, rather than of religious origin, although persecuted sects like the Anabaptists favored toleration by which their own position would have been improved. Sebastian Castellio (1515–1563), a French Protestant, was the author of an early plea for toleration (1554) directed primarily at Calvin; but the theory and the practice of toleration were products of a later period after the fires of religious enthusiasm had burned low. Only in this sense was religious toleration a product of the Reformation—and it was one which neither the Protestant reformers nor their Catholic adversaries envisaged or desired.

Was democracy a product of the Reformation? Certainly none of the major reformers advocated it, although some of the radical sects practiced it in their Christian communities. Luther advocated civil obedience, but he had no high opinion of kings. In his *Treatise on Civil Authority* (1523) he wrote:

> Since the foundation of the world a wise prince has been a rare bird and a just one much more rare. They are generally the biggest fools and worst knaves on earth, wherefore one must always expect the worst of them and not much good, especially in divine matters.

They have no right, Luther added, to decide spiritual things, but only to enforce the decisions of the Christian community. A prince should be resisted if he commanded his subjects to do anything contrary to God's Law, and princes were themselves subject to the fundamental laws of the land. Calvin took a similar stand, but he cautioned his followers that resistance to a prince should never be by private citizens but only by magistrates, or representatives of the people, to whom guardianship of the people's rights was entrusted. Moreover, the government of the Genevan church was republican in form (Presbyterian) and, by analogy with temporal powers, was based upon popular sovereignty—though with a very limited suffrage. Implicit in all this was the notion of a king bound by law and accountable to the people—through their representatives—from whom his authority emanated. In France, Scotland, the Netherlands, and elsewhere Calvinists stood firmly for monarchy limited by law, with representative government to protect the rights of the people. Some went so far as to advocate the deposition or even assassination of kings who trampled upon the rights of the people and the setting up of new kings pledged to observe the laws of the realm. Certainly, though they did not favor democracy as such, the reformers—at least the Calvinists and the radical sects—advocated popular sovereignty and monarchies limited by constitutional laws.

The Calvinist emphasis upon self-discipline, frugality, and hard work, together with Luther's glorification of all vocations as an offering to the Lord of which all men, however humble, are capable, has led some scholars to assert that Protestantism, especially Calvinism, created an ethical climate peculiarly favorable to the rise of modern capitalist society. This thesis was first set forth by a recent German sociologist, Max Weber, and extended and modified by the English economic historian R. H. Tawney. The Weber-Tawney thesis, in much abbreviated form, states that as capital is a means of further production, accumulated by abstention from the immediate consumption of all goods produced, a life of hard work, little play, and much austerity is favorable to capitalism. To be sure, Calvin encouraged such a life. For him, the visible and outward signs of divine grace were moral behavior, a disdain of idleness and frivolous pleasures, and a capacity to serve as a useful and productive instrument of God's will. This productivity included thrift, and the best servant of God was he who, in keeping with the Parable of the Talents (Matthew 25:18–30), multiplies his capital instead of burying it in the ground. Calvin did not imply that poverty is a sin or that wealth is righteousness, but he did emphasize the worth of those qualities which are most typical of bourgeois capitalism. In so doing, he elevated the crafts and commercial pursuits above others, and thus altered the traditional judgment of the relative roles of the social orders as inherited from the Middle Ages—that is, the adulation of knightly chivalry or even of the well-rounded Renaissance gentleman. Advocates of the Weber-Tawney view go on to point out that it was in Calvinist lands that capitalism flourished most after the sixteenth century—in the Netherlands and Scotland, and among the middle-class elements of society in England, Germany, and France.

Yet there are other factors to be considered, and the Weber-Tawney thesis cannot be accepted as the sole explanation of the rise of capitalism in early modern times. Indeed, in the late Middle Ages and during the Renaissance—long before Calvin and Luther—and in areas noted for their firm adherence to Catholicism (Italy, Flanders, and southern Germany) the earliest beginnings of modern capitalistic enterprise are found. Moreover, many Catholic peoples have developed great capitalistic enterprises in more recent times (Belgium, for example), while Calvinists have languished in rural occupations (South Africa, for example). These things suggest that the presence or absence of natural resources suitable for capitalistic exploitation may well explain the presence or the absence of large-scale capitalism. Finally, it should be noted that capitalistic enterprise was primarily the work of the middle class everywhere. The Calvinists were predominantly middle-class folk. Were they capitalistic because they were middle class or because they were Calvinists? To this question we have no satisfactory answer, and until we do the Weber-Tawney thesis cannot be accepted as more than a provocative theory.

Further Reading

Still the best general survey of the Reformation period is Preserved Smith, *The Age of the Reformation* (New York: Holt, 1920), which shows the relationship between the religious, economic, and intellectual revolutions of the sixteenth century. An excellent Catholic treatment is *A Popular History of the Reformation* (Garden City: Doubleday, 1957), by Rev. Fr. Philip Hughes. Three other satisfactory surveys are all available in inexpensive editions: George L. Mosse, *The Reformation* (New York: Holt, 1953), and two books by Roland H. Bainton, *The Reformation of the*

Sixteenth Century (Boston: Beacon, 1952) and *The Age of the Reformation* (Princeton: Van Nostrand, Anvil 13, 1956). Half of the latter is devoted to the documentary sources of the period. The words of the reformers themselves, from Wycliffe to John Wesley, have been collected in *Great Voices of the Reformation* (New York: Modern Library, 1954), ed. by Harry Emerson Fosdick.

The problems of the Papacy, in concise narrative and excerpts from the original sources, are illustrated in James A. Corbett, *The Papacy: A Brief History* (Princeton: Van Nostrand, Anvil 12, 1956). The *Imitation of Christ,* by Thomas à Kempis, is available in numerous inexpensive editions, including Penguin L27, Pocket PL5, and Doubleday Image D17 books. Two biographies of Erasmus are *Erasmus and the Age of Reformation* (New York: Harper, Torchbook TB19, 1957), a realistic account by John Huizinga, and Stefan Zweig's *Erasmus of Rotterdam* (New York: Viking, Compass C13, 1956), a glowing defense of "the first conscious European."

Roland H. Bainton's *Here I Stand: A Life of Martin Luther* (New York: New American Library, Mentor MD127, 1955) is an excellent recent biography by a leading American Reformation scholar. Heinrich Boehmer, *The Road to Reformation: Martin Luther to the Year 1521* (New York: Meridian LA9, 1946), is a straightforward narration by a famous European Protestant scholar. H. Grisar's *Martin Luther, His Life and Work* (St. Louis: Herder, 1930), is a Catholic account which treats Luther as an unstable character. On the immediate political background see Karl Brandi, *The Emperor Charles V: the Growth and Destiny of a Man and of a World Empire* (New York: Knopf, 1940), by far the most scholarly biography of its subject. Another version, sympathetic but critical, is E. A. Armstrong's *The Emperor Charles V,* 2 vols. (New York: Macmillan, 1910). E. Belfort Bax, *The Peasants' War in Germany* (New York: Macmillan, 1899), is the best available work on the subject in English, although unscholarly. For a general view of Calvinism, see John Thomas McNeill, *The History and Character of Calvinism* (New York: Oxford Univ. Press, 1954). Williston Walker's *John Calvin* (New York: Putnam, 1906) is a standard biography of the "organiser of Reformed Protestantism." *The Counter-Reformation, 1550–1600* (New York: Macmillan, 1933) by Beresford J. Kidd is a detailed account of Jesuits, Inquisition, and the Council of Trent. Thomas J. Campbell, *The Jesuits, 1534–1921* (New York: Kennedy, 1921), is a comprehensive history of the Society by one of its members. There are biographies of St. Ignatius Loyola by Paul Dudon (St. Paul: Bruce, 1949), a scholarly Jesuit work; Francis Thompson (New York: Scribner, 1913), not a historical study, but a well-written character portrayal by a famous Catholic poet; and Paul Van Dyke (New York: Scribner, 1926), sympathetic and fair.

S. T. Bindoff's survey of *Tudor England* (Harmondsworth, Eng.: Penguin A212, 1950) is a classic. James Gairdner, *The English Church in the Sixteenth Century* (New York: Macmillan, 1902), describes the years 1509 to 1558. H. Maynard Smith, *Henry VIII and the Reformation* (New York: Macmillan, 1948), covers religious and political aspects of the English Reformation in detail. A handy little volume of the "Teach Yourself History Library" is F. E. Hutchison's *Cranmer and the English Reformation* (New York: Macmillan, 1951). Francis Hackett's vivid and popular *Personal History of Henry the Eighth* (New York: Bantam FC9, 1956) is available as a paperback, as is J. E. Neale's classic biography, *Queen Elizabeth I* (Garden City: Doubleday, Anchor A105, 1957).

On sectarian Protestantism see Franklin H. Littell, *The Anabaptist View of the Church* (Philadelphia: American Soc. of Church Hist., 1952), a detailed analysis; and Rufus M. Jones, *The Spiritual Reformers of the Sixteenth and Seventeenth Centuries* (New York: Macmillan, 1914). On the relation between economic change and religious doctrine see the famous studies by Max Weber, *The Protestant Ethic and the Spirit of Capitalism* (New York: Scribner, 1948), and R. H. Tawney, *Religion and the Rise of Capitalism* (New York: New American Library, Mentor MD163, 1955).

Chapter 18

BEGINNINGS OF
THE MODERN STATES SYSTEM

D URING THE latter half of the fifteenth century a new type of
political organization began to assert itself in the midst of the
waning feudal institutions of western Europe. This was the
absolute monarchy, so called because the kings were more nearly
"absolute" in their centralized authority than their predecessors had been
in the medieval kingdoms. This relative absolutism arose in states in
which monarchs managed to centralize political powers largely in their
own hands by crushing feudal and ecclesiastical opposition. It was generally
effected by daring and imaginative dynasts who took advantage of every
opportunity to enhance their personal powers. It became evident first in
France, England, and Spain, and it gradually spread over nearly all of
Europe. Early efforts to achieve it in the Holy Roman Empire were, as
we shall see, largely thwarted. Nonetheless, it continued to expand, until
by the seventeenth century the greater powers of Europe had become or
were becoming dynastic states.

1 : The Dynastic State

IN THEIR DRIVE for more absolute power, kings everywhere encountered similar sources of opposition and similar means of support. Western Europe
was still medieval in its structure and outlook—a vast complex of individuals
with varying rights and entrenched positions composing a hierarchical framework of interrelationships bound by custom, claiming divine institution,
and blessed with centuries of political and social success. To reconstitute
this society into a series of separate states, each claiming sovereign authority
within its territorial limitations under a monarch with absolute powers,

was to fly in the face of hallowed human relationships, institutions, tra-ditions, and opinions. Inevitably those individuals and institutions with vested interests in the medieval structure opposed such attempts. These were, of course, the Papacy and the Holy Roman Empire—the two-edged sword, spiritual and temporal, of medieval unity—and the estates in every province, especially the nobility. But kings could play upon the divisions and mutual jealousies of their opposition, ranging provincial estates against one an-other, noble faction against noble faction, temporal against ecclesiastical power, and, joining hands now with this faction, prince, king, or Pope and then with that, establish a fluid balance of power which permitted survival. Moreover, national monarchs could appeal, both inside and outside their own domains, to the middle class, the towns, the guilds, and the trading interests. All of these stood to profit from the wider, more orderly domin-ions of spreading monarchies, from the uniformities set up in law and in monetary policies, and from trading monopolies and other privileges which kings offered to them in exchange for their support. National dynasties arose, then, not only because of the ambition of rulers but also because, in the eyes of important new segments of late medieval society, they per-formed a useful function. Absolute monarchy was widely popular, and it performed a service in the emergence of national states analogous to that of representative democracy today.

To add to their dominions and to strengthen themselves against power-ful foes both domestic and foreign, the national monarchs commonly en-tered into dynastic marriages, thus binding together a number of royal or princely houses into a single family faction and, sometimes, into a single dynasty. Whether male or female, the marriageable relatives of dynastic rulers became pawns in the exciting game of international politics, and the dynastic houses of Europe were interlocked. One remarkable series of such marriages was that of the House of Habsburg in the time of Maximilian I (1493-1519). Actually, the series began when Maximilian himself married Mary, daughter of Charles the Bold of Burgundy, and thereby inherited the Low Countries, salvaged from the disastrous war between Charles the Bold and Louis XI of France. Their son, Philip, Duke of Burgundy, mar-ried (1496) Joanna, daughter of Ferdinand and Isabella of Spain. Philip and Joanna had two sons and four daughters, all of whom made dynastic marriages. The eldest son, Charles, inherited the Low Countries from his father and succeeded his maternal grandparents, Ferdinand and Isabella, on the throne of Spain in 1516. Three years later he was elected to suc-ceed his paternal grandfather, Maximilian I, as Emperor Charles V, thus combining huge territories which not only encircled Valois France with hostile Habsburg territories but also terrified the crowned heads lest Charles V dominate the whole of Europe. In Charles V the Burgundian threat to France was revived with even greater danger, and the struggle along the

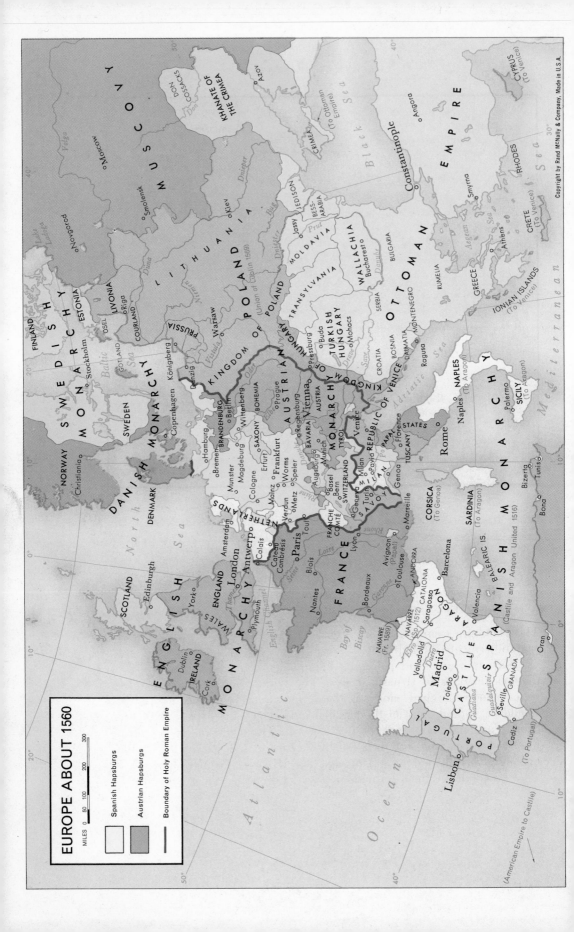

EUROPE ABOUT 1560

MILES 0 50 100 200 300

Spanish Hapsburgs
Austrian Hapsburgs
Boundary of Holy Roman Empire

Copyright by Rand McNally & Company. Made in U.S.A.

MUSCOVY

o Moscow

o Novgorod

Lake Ladoga

o Smolensk

FINLAND

SWEDISH MONARCHY

ESTONIA

LIVONIA

o Riga

OSEL

COURLAND

NORWAY

o Stockholm

GOTLAND

SWEDEN

Baltic Sea

PRUSSIA

o Königsberg

LITHUANIA

o Kiev

KHANATE OF THE CRIMEA

COSSACKS

DON

o Don

AZOV

CRIMEA

(To Ottoman Empire)

Black Sea

Constantinople

o Angora

o Smyrna

OTTOMAN EMPIRE

CYPRUS (To Venice)

RHODES

CRETE (To Venice)

Mediterranean Sea

Aegean Sea

ATHENS

o Athens

GREECE

IONIAN ISLANDS (To Venice)

RUMELIA

BULGARIA

o Bucharest

WALLACHIA

MOLDAVIA

o Jassy

BESS-ARABIA

JEDISON

TRANSYLVANIA

SERBIA

MONTENEGRO

o Ragusa

DALMATIA

BOSNIA

CROATIA

TURKISH HUNGARY

o Buda

o Mohacs

o Pressburg

KINGDOM OF HUNGARY

AUSTRIAN MONARCHY

o Vienna

AUSTRIA

o Prague

BOHEMIA

o Regensburg

BAVARIA

o Munich

TYROL

Venice

REPUBLIC OF VENICE

Adriatic Sea

PAPAL STATES

o Florence

TUSCANY

Rome

NAPLES (To Aragon)

o Naples

SICILY (To Aragon)

o Palermo

CHRISTIANIA

o Christiania

DENMARK

DANISH MONARCHY

o Copenhagen

North Sea

o Hamburg

o Bremen

BRANDENBURG

o Berlin

o Magdeburg

o Wittenberg

SAXONY

o Erfurt

o Frankfurt

o Worms

o Speier

o Augsburg

SWITZERLAND

o Basel

o Bern

SAVOY

MILAN

o Milan

o Turin

o Genoa

Genoa

o Marseille

CORSICA (To Genoa)

SARDINIA (To Aragon)

BALEARIC IS. (To Aragon)

o Barcelona

CATALONIA

ARAGON

o Saragossa

o Valencia

NAVARRE (Fr. 1589)

(Castile and Aragon United 1516)

SPANISH MONARCHY

o Madrid

CASTILE

o Valladolid

o Toledo

GRANADA

o Seville

o Granada

o Cadiz

o Oran

PORTUGAL

o Lisbon

(To Portugal)

ENGLISH MONARCHY

SCOTLAND

o Edinburgh

WALES

o York

ENGLAND

o London

o Plymouth

Thames

English Channel

IRELAND

o Dublin

o Cork

Atlantic Ocean

Bay of Biscay

FRANCE

o Nantes

o Blois

o Paris

o Bordeaux

o Toulouse

o Lyon

Loire

Seine

Rhône

Garonne

ANDORRA

AVIGNON (Papal)

FRANCHE COMTÉ

NETHERLANDS

o Amsterdam

Antwerp

o Calais

o Cateau Cambrésis

o Verdun

o Metz

o Toul

o Cologne

o Mainz

MÜNSTER

o Geneva

o Pavia

MANTUA

o Cateau

o Buda

Ebro

Douro

Guadiana

Guadalquivir

Tagus

(American Empire to Castile)

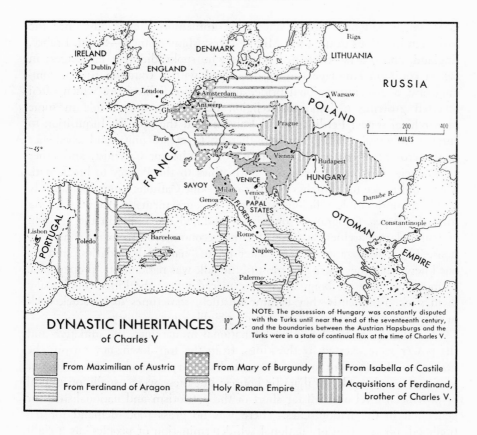

DYNASTIC INHERITANCES
of Charles V

NOTE: The possession of Hungary was constantly disputed with the Turks until near the end of the seventeenth century, and the boundaries between the Austrian Hapsburgs and the Turks were in a state of continual flux at the time of Charles V.

From Maximilian of Austria

From Ferdinand of Aragon

From Mary of Burgundy

Holy Roman Empire

From Isabella of Castile

Acquisitions of Ferdinand, brother of Charles V.

Rhine has continued into the twentieth century. Small wonder that a sarcastic observer wrote of the Austrian Habsburgs:

> *Bella gerant alii, tu, felix Austria, nube;*
> *Nam quae Mars aliis, dat tibi Regna Venus.*
> *(Where others wage wars, you, happy Austria, marry;*
> *For as Mars gives dominion to others, Venus gives it to you.)*

The Habsburg example, though extreme, was only one of many series of aggrandizements through dynastic marriages.

Such territorial and political realignments were effected primarily by the machinations of dynastic rulers. The wishes of the people involved were seldom consulted—nor was there any compelling demand that they should be. Indeed, most of the national monarchies, the prototypes of present-day national states, were products of a long struggle among competing historical forces, guided to their conclusion for the most part by the absolute monarchs. Neither race, nor language, nor religion, nor geography played a *decisive* role in their formation. Every European monarchy contained races which had been mixed since time immemorial, especially since the barbarian invasions of the early Middle Ages. Many of them—Spain, France, England, and others—contained peoples who spoke different languages; in fact, a common language usually developed with a common rule, a common law, a growing national pride, and a national literature which often reflected growing nationalism. Religion played a temporal role in some monarchical states: Ferdinand and Isabella used the Spanish Inquisition to enforce universal Catholicism and thereby to create unity and obedience to the crown; after the Protestant Revolt Lutheran, Calvinist, and other princes seized upon their subjects' antipathies to the Papacy to break with Rome and to set up churches of their own—but Catholic kings had already acquired considerable religious authority by agreements reluctantly wrung from the Popes. Geography sometimes modified the result in the creation of national monarchies, because of either economic or strategic considerations. There was some reference later on to "natural boundaries," but no one knew what they were and most of the talk was nationalistic propaganda. In most instances the boundaries were placed where the kings could make them stick. Frequently they became unstuck, sometimes to be stuck back in the same place, or even farther into neighboring territory.

Constantly, in the formation of national monarchies, the initiative and the power were exerted by the kings, from the top down, never from the people up. There were love of home and country, suspicion and dislike of foreigners, and loyalty to dynastic houses; but these were usually on a local or provincial level and fell far short of the patriotism and nationalism later generated in the nation-states. There was no grass roots demand for nationhood, no assertion of "national self-determination of peoples" as a right of any people claiming separate nationhood, no highly emotional, chauvinistic nationalism such as that which permeates the world today. Most of these troublesome trappings belong to the period since 1776 and the rise of the *nation-state,* where the initiative and the power derive from below, as opposed to the *dynastic state,* where they were imposed from above.

Moreover, paradoxical as it may seem, the so-called absolute monarchs exerted less powerful control directly over the lives, properties, and beliefs of their subjects than most nation-states do today. To some extent, of course, this was because of the lack of rapid communications and the absence of social services. In the main, though, it was because the dynastic state was a loose cluster of provinces formerly independent, sometimes speaking different languages, occasionally separated by foreign territory, usually clinging more or less grimly to local customs and traditions, and held together almost solely by the ruling dynasty. Kings carried on their administration with hand-picked advisers and bureaucrats without consulting the people, who seldom were well informed about what was going on. Wars were far less destructive than they became in the nineteenth century, and armies were relatively small, often made up of hired professional troops not conscripted or "drafted" from the people at large. Unless the subjects were caught in the midst of contending armies they felt wars only in the guise of tax increases. Indeed, most royal subjects felt the king's hand only in terms of taxation and the administration of justice.

Still, the subjects of new dynastic states lived in no bed of roses. It was no easy matter to be like corks tossed on the seas of dynastic politics, having neither knowledge of nor voice in the direction of affairs. Taxes were oppressive, constantly grew greater, and generally fell upon those segments of society which could least afford to pay. There were few governmental services, but these would scarcely be missed for there had been few since the bread and circuses of the Roman Empire. The poor, the sick, the unemployed found succor, if at all, at the hands of the church, not of the state. The absolute monarchies were the products of the political ambitions and activities of kings who, with the support of the middle class, cleared away some of the obsolete customs and institutions of the feudal age, refashioned the structure of the late Middle Ages in the interests of commercial, capitalistic, urbanized society, and for good or ill began a new European system of dynastic states. These reached a remarkable degree of maturity in the sixteenth and early seventeenth centuries, changing the face of Europe into a resemblance of that of today. The remainder of this chapter will be devoted to their successes and failures.

2 : The French Dynasty—from Valois to Bourbon

THE FRENCH monarchy was much more strongly united than the German Empire at the end of the fifteenth century. The Hundred Years' War had assured France of independence from England. The royal domain had been greatly enlarged and Louis XI (the Spider) had laid solid bases for royal absolutism: a royal army paid by royal revenues; royal ascendancy over the Estates-General (in 1469 the Estates-General had asked the king to rule without them in the future and legislation thereafter was by royal decree, although this body was summoned occasionally until 1614); a national church under firm control of the crown; and an administrative structure steadily becoming more centralized under royal control.

Still, this centralization was only a monarchical *administrative* superstructure imposed upon a variety of local bodies. Local autonomy remained strong in France. Beneath the royal panoply was a particularism similar to that of Spain and the German Empire. Provinces like Brittany, Provence, and Languedoc and chartered towns (*bonnes villes*), each had their own local pride and personnel, their own laws, courts, taxes, tariffs, and assemblies (provincial estates). The king and his subordinates worked with and through these local institutions, which preserved their own identities. National unity consisted in their submission to a common king and a common royal administration of things pertaining to foreign relations, war, the royal treasury, and justice in its higher (appellate) levels. As royal absolutism advanced, it contested with local bodies for control over a wider variety of things, usually winning supremacy in coinage, economic policies, and the incidence of law by royal edict.

THE HOUSE OF VALOIS

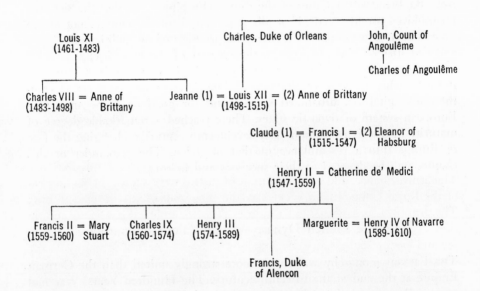

Louis XI's successors became locked in combat with the Habsburgs for almost seventy years. At the outset the French kings appeared to be the aggressors as they dredged up ancestral claims, first to Naples and then to Milan, and invaded Italy in hopes of lining their pockets among the wealthy, disunited Italian city-states. But later, after Charles V's elevation to power, the French monarchs appeared to be struggling to break out of the vise in which Habsburg power had gripped them. In the Italian ventures the French kings added some prestige to French arms, but they also became entangled in a thicket of dynastic intrigues and squirming diplomatic maneuvers from which they were fortunate to emerge without territorial loss. Against Charles V, as we have seen, Francis I and his successor, by a series of brilliant, if ephemeral, alliances with the Turks, with German Protestant princes, and others, managed successfully to defend themselves. Francis even took the offensive against the Habsburgs in the New World, sending

Jacques Cartier on royal voyages of discovery in North America in 1534–35 which established French claims upon the St. Lawrence Valley as a challenge to the Spanish. By the Treaty of Cateau-Cambrésis (1559), the Habsburg-Valois wars ended with no lasting ill effects on France. Indeed, France's demonstrated capacity for survival against great odds enhanced her stature in the growing family of national monarchies.

FRENCH ABSOLUTISM UNDER FRANCIS I

With Charles V of the empire and Henry VIII of England, Francis I was one of a trio of mighty European dynasts in the early sixteenth century. As war provided the circumstances by which his predecessors had managed to enlarge their authority, so Francis I took further advantage of the opportunities offered. In 1516, by the Concordat of Bologna, he made a new settlement with the Pope to supersede the Pragmatic Sanction, which had asserted that the Pope was subordinate to a church council. He won complete control over the selection of bishops and abbots in the French church, thus freeing himself from papal interference in French ecclesiastical affairs and winning papal recognition of the position of royal supremacy in the French ecclesiastical structure.

In governmental administration, Francis enlarged and strengthened the rudimentary bureaucracy which had been constructed by his predecessors. The army, finance, and administration of justice were subject to committees of the Royal Council hand-picked by the king and wholly devoted to him. The army was organized under a series of thirty military governors and, in time of peace, garrisoned in as many districts, thus easing problems of supply and having soldiers at strategic points in case of internal uprisings. Taxes, which were of several kinds, constantly were increased, with no effort to achieve an equitable distribution, and were collected in various ways. The *taille*, a direct tax, was fixed yearly by the Royal Council and collected by royal *financiers* in each of several tax districts; the *aides*, a series of indirect taxes on goods, were farmed; and the *gabelle*, a royal salt monopoly, was collected by corporations chartered for the purpose. The administration of justice in small causes was largely left in seignorial and other local courts, but all appeals went to the *parlements*, and the final court of appeal in all cases was the Royal Council. As rapidly as possible feudal laws were replaced by royal edict, and the king was held above and outside the law according to the formula, "ce qui a été décidé par le prince a force de loi" ("that which has been determined by the king has the force of law"). Legislation was by royal decree, and Francis I prefaced his decrees with the words, "Car tel est notre plaisir . . ." ("as it is our pleasure . . ."). The Estates-General was side-stepped, mostly by not being assembled at all, and lost its capacity (which in France had never been great) to oppose the arbitrary rule of the crown. As one writer declared, it became "compounded of high pretensions and docile submission." It met but five times in the sixteenth century, once in the seventeenth, and not at all from 1614 until 1789.

THE RELIGIOUS WARS

Shortly after the Treaty of Cateau-Cambrésis a series of civil wars broke out in France. In one form or another Protestantism had invaded France, and Calvinism became the predominant Protestant sect. Its followers were known as Huguenots, a name of uncertain origin. In 1559 the Huguenots organized a national synod of the Reformed church in France, with churches in the river towns of southern France, in the centers of trade like Paris and La Rochelle, and in Normandy. Although the majority belonged to the middle class (artisans, merchants, etc.), the Huguenots also embraced many intellectuals and only slightly less than half of the nobility. Most prominent among them were Louis of Bourbon, Prince of Condé, and Gaspard, Admiral de Coligny.

Francis I had little sympathy with Protestants. But in his conflicts with Charles V he found it expedient to ally with German Protestant princes and to wink at Protestantism in his own realm. Upon his death his son, Henry II, became king (1547–1559). Henry looked upon the Protestants with a less lenient eye than his predecessor had done, and while he maintained a firm policy on the whole he was also very fond of hunting, tournaments, and women, and sometimes neglected internal affairs of state. In consequence, political power became contested by ambitious nobles, especially by three powerful families, the Montmorencys, the Guises, and the Bourbons. The Montmorencys, led by Anne of Montmorency and his nephew, Admiral Coligny, rose to prominence by virtue of remarkable military and diplomatic services. The Guises, a powerful ducal family of Lorraine, included Francis, Duke of Lorraine, a great soldier and politician; Charles, his brother, who became Cardinal of Lorraine; and a further political asset, Mary Stuart of Scotland, their niece, whom they contrived to marry to Francis, heir of King Henry II. The third rival was the royal house of Bourbon, the king of Navarre and his brother the prince of Condé. By 1559 Guise supremacy at court seemed assured. In that year, too, Henry II died, the victim of a wound suffered in a joust. When his son, Francis II, a feeble fifteen-year-old boy, succeeded to the throne with his girl queen, Mary Stuart, the Guise faction appeared to be in firm control.

At this point, however, the opposition solidified. The Montmorencys and the Bourbons rallied, and the Huguenots, assured of no further toleration if the Guise faction ruled at court, joined forces with them. In the midst of plots and counter-plots Francis II died, to be succeeded by his ten-year-old brother, Charles IX (1560–1574). At this point, too, the widow of Henry II and mother of the boy kings Francis and Charles assumed the regency. This was Catherine de' Medici, granddaughter of Lorenzo the Magnificent of the famous Florentine family. Never popular at the French court, Catherine was ambitious for her children and anxious to preserve the power of the monarchy from the rapacity of the court factions. Accordingly, she organized the administration around herself, so as to play off the factions against each other in the hope of retaining a balance of power in her own hands. This was no easy task. The Guise faction demanded the destruction of the Huguenots; the Huguenots turned to riots and uprisings; Philip II of Spain encouraged the Catholics and cast a covetous eye upon French territory; Elizabeth I of England aided the Huguenots and hoped to recover Calais which had been lost to the French during the previous reign of Mary Tudor. Concessions to Huguenots alarmed Catholics, and even Anne of Montmorency joined with the Guise to suppress Protestantism. Finally, in 1562, when the Guise faction refused to obey an edict granting restricted toleration to Huguenots, the competing factions came to blows. Between 1562 and 1598 eight civil wars enveloped France, with politics and religion so bound together that it is impossible to disentangle them completely. The wars were relatively local in nature, with small armies, so poorly equipped, especially in artillery, that they rarely could take a well-defended fortification. There were sudden surprise attacks, hasty withdrawals, and few decisive battles. Yet the injection of religious fanaticism into the struggles intensified bitterness on all sides and led to a number of barbarous incidents.

In 1570, after the third war, the queen regent turned to the Huguenots again as a counter to the Guise faction. Admiral Coligny won high favor with the young king, Charles IX, and they arranged a marriage of the king's sister, Margaret, to Henry of Bourbon, King of Navarre, who, after Coligny, was leader of the Huguenots. He was also successor to the throne in the event Catherine's sons left no heirs. The marriage was celebrated August 18, 1572. But the favor won by the Huguenots troubled Catherine and the Guise faction and—without the king's knowledge—they hatched a plot to assassinate Coligny. A hired assassin, however, only wounded the admiral. Whereupon the Huguenots muttered threats against the royal family. At this point Catherine and the Guises, in desperate fear, prevailed upon the king to order a wholesale execution of Huguenots. Charles consented reluctantly, crying, "Well, then, kill them all, that not a single man may be left to reproach me!"

On the morning of St. Bartholomew's Day (August 24, 1572), the Catholics fell upon the Huguenots. Coligny was killed in cold blood and his mutilated body was treated in a shameful fashion. The massacre spread to other parts of France and continued for ten days. Thousands of Huguenots were slain, and Condé and Henry of Navarre (the recent bridegroom) escaped only by pretending conversion to Catholicism. But after Henry had escaped from the court he publicly declared himself a Huguenot and succeeded Coligny as their leader. The Massacre of St. Bartholomew's Day was a horrible blunder. Not only was war renewed but also Protestant opinion everywhere was outraged. English, Dutch, and German aid came to the Huguenots.

Events of the next dozen years gave the wars a new turn. In 1573 Henry, brother of Charles IX, was elected king of Poland, but he had been there only a few months when Charles died (1574) and Henry returned to France to become Henry III (1574–1589). The new king proved to be a pleasure-loving, extravagant fop. In 1576 he concluded a new peace favorable to the Huguenots, and indignant Catholics led by the intense young duke of Guise formed a Catholic League. Convinced that the crown would do nothing for them, the league took matters into its own hands, won aid from Philip of Spain, and set out to free France of Protestantism. Meanwhile, too, since the Massacre of St. Bartholomew's Day there had formed a new party. Moderate Catholics, fired by a patriotic desire to save France from further bloodshed and destruction, urged greater regard for the Estates-General, and questioned both the wisdom and the absolutism of the crown. These were the *Politiques,* to whom Francis, the youngest of Catherine de' Medici's brood, repaired in disgust at the feeble, vacillating measures of his brother the king. But when Francis died in 1584, leaving Henry of Navarre next in line for succession to the throne, the Catholic League could contain itself no longer. It planned to exclude Navarre and to force the king to revoke his concessions to the Huguenots. To do this they made themselves masters of Paris, and Henry III became essentially a prisoner of the duke of Guise.

The last war followed, the "War of the Three Henrys," so called because it began as a triangular contest among the forces of Henry III of Valois, Henry, Duke of Guise (aided by Philip II of Spain and the Papacy), and Henry Bourbon of Navarre (aided by Elizabeth I of England, the Dutch, and several German Protestant princes). Religious issues still glowed fiercely, but in fact the war had become a struggle for the French crown. Henry III, finding no effective support himself, caused the duke of Guise and his brother to be assassinated. When Catherine de' Medici died a few weeks later, Henry exulted, "Now I alone am king." But the reaction of the Catholic League to the murder of the Guise brothers was so violent that Henry III threw himself into the arms of Henry of Navarre. At the Huguenot camp he too was murdered (1589), not by the Huguenots but by a fanatical Catholic monk. Henry of Navarre, the Huguenot leader, became Henry IV, the first Bourbon king of France.

HENRY IV

Henry IV (1589–1610) was indeed at first a "king without a kingdom." All France was ablaze with disorder and intrigue. Paris, controlled by the Catholic League, would not open its gates to a Protestant king. But the new king was a man of great personal charm and courage, quick-witted, and endowed with a realistic outlook. The *Politiques* were soon reconciled to him. Several prominent members of the Catholic League were frankly bribed into accepting him and, in 1593, seeing that France could never be pacified by a Protestant king, Henry renounced his Protestantism and joined the Catholic church. "Paris is well worth a mass," he is reported to have said. The next year he was crowned at Chartres. Then he soon expelled the Spanish, and by a policy of moderation and rehabilitation, together with his amiable spirit and personal appeal, won over the French people. In 1598 he compromised with his old friends, the Huguenots. By the Edict of Nantes, the king granted them political rights equal with Catholics and gave the right to exercise the Reformed Religion (Calvinism) to Huguenot manorial lords, to cities and towns overwhelmingly Huguenot, and to one town in each district (*bailliage*) but not to Paris, its immediate environs, or elsewhere in France. The edict permitted Huguenots to have their own courts including four *parlements* with mixed chambers; and it left them several fortified towns with armed forces to defend them. In short, the Huguenots were recognized as an armed party with legal existence, means of self-defense, and religious toleration with geographical limitations—almost a state within a state. Given less moderate, or less trusted, leadership, the Huguenots were in a good position to strike for independence as the Dutch had done in the Netherlands.

Henry IV's reign was ended by an assassin's knife in 1610, but in the meantime he had founded a new French ruling family, the House of Bourbon, taken measures to heal the wounds of the recent wars, and reasserted a royal absolutism as complete as that of any of his predecessors. His marriage to Margaret of Valois was dissolved after he became king. In 1600 he married Marie de' Medici, daughter of the grand duke of Tuscany, who brought him a large and much-needed dowry and, of even more lasting importance, a son and heir, later Louis XIII of France. Henry kept a tight rein on the kingdom. He never summoned the Estates-General, and he ruled by means of a small council of ministers. He fostered measures to aid France to rebuild its economy after the long destructive wars. His ideal, as he put it, was to put "a chicken in the pot for every peasant on Sunday," and he sought to develop agriculture, manufactures, and commerce. Taxes and other demands upon the peasantry were lowered, marshes were drained, roads improved, canals built, and commercial treaties made to encourage the sale of French produce abroad. Henry introduced the silk industry to France, and he stimulated the expansion of the glass, tapestry, and other enterprises. The first permanent French colony in North America, Quebec, was established in his reign (1608). Thus was resumed the design begun by Jacques Cartier in Francis I's time, and a vast new French overseas empire was founded. Indeed, Henry's policies marked the introduction of mercantilism to France —a system of state regulation of economy designed to foster greater exports and fewer imports, so as to achieve a favorable balance of trade and increase the wealth of the kingdom. As a healer of France's wounds, Henry IV was remarkably successful. His absolutism was tempered with beneficence, and few French kings won as great popularity. The French monarchy had survived the Habsburg menace, weathered the religious wars, and emerged with a new dynasty firmly in control.

3 : England—the Tudor Dynasty

BETWEEN THE END of the Wars of the Roses (1485) and the early years of the seventeenth century (1603) England was ruled by the Tudor Dynasty. During these years England became a national monarchy as unified under royal authority—if, indeed, not more so—as any of the continental states. Yet there were two highly important differences. One was that the English common law, which had been developing since the Norman conquest, supplied the English with a fairly well-rounded, ready-made, customary legal structure. The second difference was that English monarchs were never able successfully to overcome, bypass, or otherwise avoid the continuing power and prestige of the English Parliament as continental dynasts so often managed to do with their inherited feudal assemblies, like the French Estates-General. "He would like to govern England in the French fashion," said the Spanish ambassador of Henry VII, "but he cannot do it." In consequence, the English monarchy was a constitutional, or limited, monarchy, and no Tudor monarch could successfully claim such relatively unfettered absolutism as that of Francis I of France or Philip II of Spain. In fact, the prestige of the English Parliament rose throughout most of the Tudor era, and it emerged at the opening of the seventeenth century with exaggerated notions of its constitutional authority. The survival and growth of the English Parliament during an epoch when similar assemblies on the Continent were being humiliated and destroyed by dynasts preserved in England not only a limited monarchy but also a rudimentary form of representative government destined to become truly the "mother of parliaments" in a later year.

THE ENGLISH PARLIAMENT

"King in Parliament" was the somewhat mystical expression which came to be used to designate the sovereign power of the English monarchy—not "what pleases the king has the force of law," nor act of Parliament alone. The English Parliament emerged from the Middle Ages with the power to make laws or statutes which, when signed by the king, had the force of law. These included tax laws, without which kings were severely limited in what they could do. Moreover, these powers were jealously guarded by Parliaments against royal usurpations of authority and looked to by people of all degrees as a bulwark against royal absolutism. Thus the English Parliament held far more than mere advisory powers such as those of the French Estates-General.

Still, we must not picture the English Parliament as a democratic legislative body elected on the basis of wide suffrage. To be sure, it had become a two-house assembly similar in outward structure to bicameral legislative bodies of today. In this it was unlike the continental assemblies, which, in the case of the French Estates-General, consisted of *three* houses which convened separately: one of the clergy, one of the nobility, and one of the commoners. The Swedish Riksdag consisted of *four* separate estates: clergy, nobles, townsmen, and peasants. The English Parliament had consolidated into two houses: the House of Lords, which included the upper clergy, and the House of Commons. Actually, the House of Lords consisted of titled nobles who in Tudor times were for the most part of Tudor creation and loyal to the Tudor Dynasty. After 1534 the clergy were bishops of the English church, appointed by the king and sworn to uphold him. The English custom of primogeniture kept the number of nobles fairly small as only the eldest son inherited the title of his father, whereas on the Continent all the legitimate sons of nobles became noblemen themselves, often with a variety of titles most confusing to the uninitiated.

The House of Commons was closer to a present-day legislative assembly than any of the continental estates, but it was far from a democratically elected body. Meeting as one body, it represented *both* the townsmen and the rural landed gentry. The *burgesses,* or representatives of boroughs or incorporated towns (but not all towns), were chosen by the local plutocracy, usually the merchant guildsmen of the upper middle class; and the representatives of the rural landed gentry were knights of the shires elected by the freeholders of land. In both instances the apprentices, the tenants, and the property-less workers were excluded from the vote. And in both cases the base of suffrage was sufficiently small that it could be manipulated by the crown. Tudor kings so often found it expedient to accomplish their ends by means of Parliaments which they had to some extent packed or otherwise molded that they found little reason to ignore or destroy them. But they obviously failed to realize that, at the same time, they were exalting Parliament and giving parliamentarians delusions of constitutional power and grandeur.

THE FIRST TUDOR—HENRY VII

The Tudor proclivity for operating by parliamentary means began with the founder of the dynasty, Henry VII (1485–1509). As victor in the Wars of the Roses, Henry could claim the English throne by right of conquest and he could assert hereditary claims. But the latter were tenuous because Henry was descended from a bastard branch of the Lancastrian House, and the former, as it rested upon military might, encouraged military challenge. To strengthen his legal position he appealed to the English Parliament and won assertion of his title by parliamentary act. This, together with Henry's subsequent marriage to Elizabeth of York, niece of his late opponent, Richard III, placed Henry in secure position. Both king and Parliament found the tactic attractive. Henry discovered that it was a peaceful way to make his policies enforceable and to clothe them with a legality peculiarly acceptable in England; Parliament found that the fruits of its deliberations were elevated to something greater than mere advice to the king—that if it had power in *king-making* it might also assume powers in *king-limiting*. Parliamentary authority over money matters provided an effective means. By extraordinary skill in manipulating their Parliaments, the Tudors generally avoided an impasse. Their successors, the Stuarts, were less fortunate, as we shall see.

THE HOUSE OF TUDOR

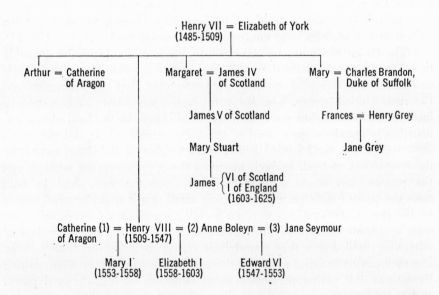

Henry VII was aided further by the fact that few great nobles remained in England to challenge his position, thanks to the slaughter of the Wars of the Roses. Some of these Henry extirpated, and he confiscated their lands when they fomented rebellion by lending support—as they did twice—to pretenders to his throne. Moreover, Henry forbade the English nobles to keep private armies, to make war by themselves, and to interfere in royal justice by attempting to intimidate the litigants. These measures were ably enforced by an administrative court called the Star Chamber, given a new life by act of Parliament in 1487. Actually, the Star Chamber (so called because of the star-studded ceiling of the room in which it met) was a committee of the royal council usually consisting of the ablest legal minds of the kingdom. It employed royal edicts (without juries) to stamp out disorders and to give swift royal justice where local juries and common-law courts were unable to act or were inclined to support local privileges, abuses, or resistance to Tudor demands. In this fashion Henry VII and his successors gradually stamped out feudal resistance to the royal power. Because its proceedings were sometimes arbitrary, occasionally trampled on the rights of defendants, and ignored common-law procedures, the Star Chamber was often reproached with abuse of judicial authority. Its evil reputation, however, stemmed largely from the Stuarts' later inept use of it against political opponents. The Tudors employed it both with success and widely popular acceptance to establish royal authority and to restore the rule of law to England.

Henry VII was one of the ablest rulers of his generation. Highly intelligent, shrewd, and coolheaded, he commanded respect by his capacities and fear by his ruthlessness. Generally he sought to avoid war, and promoted an alliance with Spain which lasted into the reign of his successor—an alliance strengthened by the marriage of Catherine of Aragon, daughter of Ferdinand and Isabella, first to Arthur, Henry's eldest son, and upon his early death to Henry, the king's second son, later Henry VIII of England. He fastened his grip firmly upon Ireland by Poyning's Law (1495), whereby no Irish parliament could meet without Henry's consent, no bill passed by an Irish parliament could become law without Henry's approval, and all Irish acts could be overruled by the English Parliament. In his financial policies Henry was both grasping and parsimonious, and he resorted to extraordinary means of raising money without recourse to the English Parliament. In his administration he generally employed men of the merchant class or others who had worked their way up in the church. Richard Empson, Edmund Dudley, and John Morton were three such men. The first two, both men of the middle class, became known as the king's "ravening wolves" by their ingenious and unscrupulous ways of raising money. With trumped-up charges against the nobility, they seized property to the enrichment of Henry and the impoverishment of nobles; and with forced "loans" they mulcted merchants for the royal coffers. Morton, who became archbishop of Canterbury, was associated (though unjustly) with an exasperating policy called "Morton's Fork," whereby agents sent to collect benevolences from English prelates were instructed to insist upon large sums from both those who appeared prosperous and those who did not on the grounds that the first obviously could afford it and the second, because of their shabbiness, must be feigning poverty in order to avoid their proper payments! By such sharp practices Henry filled his treasury and at the same time avoided having to appeal to Parliament for extraordinary funds.

Henry also promoted English commerce, shipbuilding, and fishing. To win markets abroad for English wool and other products, he negotiated commercial treaties with Denmark and with Florence in 1490 and, more importantly, with Philip of Flanders in 1496. The latter treaty was known as the *Intercursus Magnus* (the Great Interchange) and contributed greatly to the commercial growth and prosperity both of England and the Low Countries. In 1497 and in 1498 Henry promoted voyages of discovery to America. By these, John Cabot laid claim to the coasts of North America in the name of the king of England. English fisherman thereafter frequented the Grand Banks of Newfoundland and, on the basis of Cabot's claim, permanent English colonies were founded later. England, during the reign of Henry VII, became a well-ordered, prosperous kingdom and began to emerge as a dynamic force on the world scene.

THE MIDDLE TUDORS—HENRY VIII, EDWARD VI, AND MARY

Henry VIII (1509–1547) inherited a well-filled treasury and a well-disposed monarchy. The new king was himself greatly admired at the outset for his splendid physique, excellent mind, and fine education. But, unlike his father, Henry VIII loved display and spent lavishly. He hoped to cut a large figure in European affairs, tried to win election as Holy Roman Emperor in 1519 when Charles V was elected, and was gnawingly jealous of Francis I of France. Still, while he toyed with war against France and imitated the Medici in their patronage of literature and the arts, Henry never allowed himself to become too deeply involved in any of these. And, while he spent heavily, he also collected heavily and, as he continued most of the internal political, financial, and commercial policies of his father, his treasury did not become depleted nor did his kingdom suffer in its prosperity. The enclosure of land for sheep-raising and other purposes became a problem in his reign, and he failed to halt it; but while it displaced many persons and, temporarily at least, created a new poor, it also enlarged the English wool trade, which was rapidly becoming a source of considerable national wealth.

At the outset of his reign Henry allowed his father-in-law, Ferdinand of Aragon, to embroil him in a war with France and managed to obtain a nice indemnity. Then, as the Scots had invaded England (they usually did when England warred on France), he turned against them and at Flodden Field (1513) he won the last great border battle between England and Scotland. Soon afterwards Henry's foreign policy became related to the ambitions of his early favorite, Thomas, Cardinal Wolsey of York. Wolsey directed a devious policy of playing the Papacy, the empire, and France off against one another so that England held a balance of power and (as he vainly hoped) so that Wolsey himself could become Pope. From about 1518 to 1530 the cardinal wove English affairs with great dexterity, without committing England irrevocably in the Habsburg-Valois conflicts. But his heavy exactions on the English people made him unpopular, and his failure to win a papal annulment of Henry's marriage to Catherine of Aragon (1529) cost him his political office and nearly cost him his head.

Henry's desire for the annulment sprang from a variety of motives, but a compelling one was his lack of a male heir (see page 73). Soon it became irrevocably entangled with the nationalization of the English church which, from a strictly dynastic and constitutional viewpoint, was the most important single event of Henry's reign. With the aid of Thomas Cranmer, who succeeded Wolsey as Henry's adviser and later was archbishop of Canterbury, he married Anne Boleyn, second in a series of six wives. All this was accomplished, it is important to note, by parliamentary action which, by the Act of Supremacy (1534), declared Henry VIII and his successors to be the "only Supreme Head of the Church and Clergy of England."

Nationalization of the church added greatly to the Tudor dynastic power, combining in the monarch supreme ecclesiastical authority with his temporal power. It also cast England squarely into the conflicts of the Reformation, although Henry, being no Protestant, sought to avoid this as much as possible. The latter years of his reign were given over largely to internal matters related to the nationalization of the church. By a series of parliamentary acts in the late 1530's Henry promoted the dissolution of all monasteries and other religious houses of England. Their properties were for the most part seized by the crown, thereby supplying the king with vast wealth and freeing him further from financial dependence on Parliament.

Henry VIII's immediate successors, the boy king Edward VI (1547–1553) and Mary (1553–1558), had only short reigns. Although they played important roles in the English Reformation (see pages 75–76), they contributed little of permanence to the growth and power of the Tudor Dynasty. In Edward's reign was organized the Company of the Merchant Adventurers "for discoverie of regions, dominions, islands and places unknown" (1551). This enterprise was England's first bid for world commerce, a challenge to the Portuguese and Spanish empires and to the Hanseatic League. Its agents established trading relations with Muscovy and prepared the way for the English Muscovy company chartered by Queen Mary in 1555. It, in turn, soon won from Tsar Ivan IV a monopoly of the White Sea trade, and prepared to tap trade in Persia and India. Aside from these ventures, Mary, by her marriage to Philip II of Spain (1553), temporarily resumed a foreign alignment inaugurated by Henry VII. But it was no longer popular in England, where anti-Spanish sentiment, more or less identified with anti-Catholic feeling, was a factor almost constant in English politics for the rest of the Tudor era.

QUEEN ELIZABETH I

The last Tudor was the first Queen Elizabeth (1558–1603), daughter of Anne Boleyn and Henry VIII. The Age of Elizabeth has become almost hallowed over the years by the glorification of such commanding literary figures as Edmund Spenser, Ben Jonson, and William Shakespeare and by the late flowering of the Renaissance in England in terms of the plastic arts and music, all of which developed high levels of creativity and appreciation. The exploits of Hawkins and Drake, the early attempts of Gilbert and Raleigh to plant colonies in America, and the defeat of the Spanish Armada lend the age a reputation for dramatic achievements. Sir Francis Drake's voyage around the world (1577–80) was a challenge to the Spanish monopoly of trade in the Far East, and before the end of Elizabeth's reign England was well embarked upon the conquest of world trade and overseas colonies. A commercial treaty with the Turks in 1580 was followed by a charter for the English Levant Company in 1581. Other successful voyages to the Far East led to the creation in 1600 of the East India Company, whose vessels returned from their first voyage to the East just in time to mourn the death of Queen Elizabeth in 1603. Already, too, Richard Hakluyt, a geographer and promoter of English trade and navigation, had published his *Principall Navigations, Voyages, and Discoveries of the English Nation,* which went far to fire the enthusiasm of the English for further exploits. Yet in the midst of these exciting and profitable events the grim struggle for dynastic power continued in England and competition with European states was intense.

Elizabeth's early years were devoted principally to the church settlement which was described in the last chapter (see pages 76–77). Although masterly as a middle-of-the-road way between Protestantism and Catholicism, it left two diverse segments dissatisfied, the Puritans and the Catholics. Both were persecuted throughout Elizabeth's reign, both appealed to or sought refuge in foreign lands, and both left a legacy of troubles to the queen's successors. During Elizabeth's time the Catholics appeared the more dangerous of the two. Besides Philip II's Spain, which was always responsive to Catholic appeals for succor, Mary, Queen of Scots, was a thorn in Elizabeth's side. As a granddaughter of Henry VIII's sister Margaret, Mary had solid claims to the English throne. After the death of her first husband, Francis II of France, she returned to Scotland, remarried, challenged Elizabeth's right to the English throne on the grounds of illegitimacy, and became a storm center about which played many of the Catholic forces of Europe. As Catholics under English rule, the Irish, too, lent themselves to intrigues

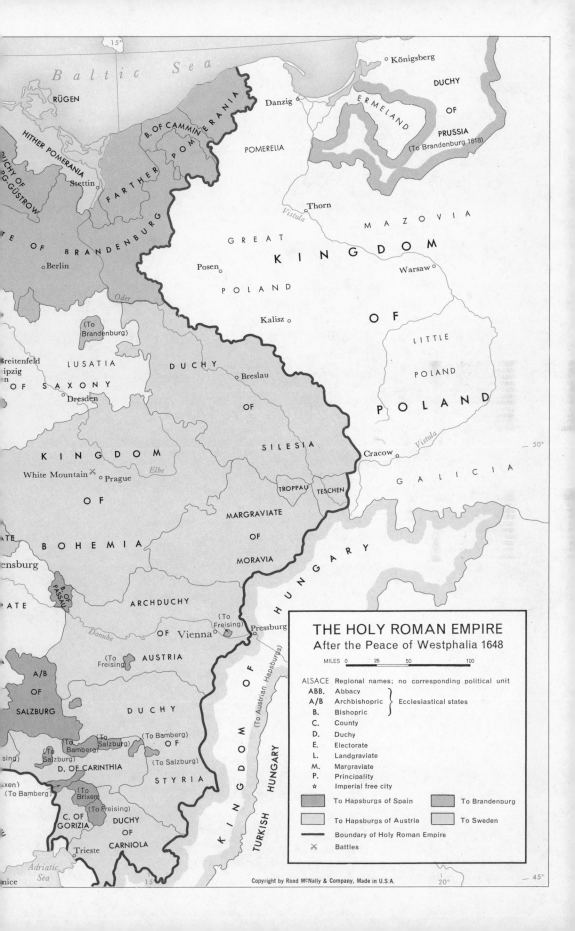

Baltic Sea

RÜGEN

HITHER POMERANIA

DUCHY OF G-GÜSTROW

Stettin

E OF BRANDENBURG

Berlin

B. OF CAMMIN

FARTHER POMERANIA

Danzig

POMERELIA

o Königsberg

DUCHY

OF

PRUSSIA

(To Brandenburg 1618)

ERMELAND

Thorn

Vistula

MAZOVIA

GREAT

Posen

KINGDOM

Warsaw

(To Brandenburg)

POLAND

Kalisz

OF

LITTLE

Breitenfeld
Leipzig

LUSATIA

OF SAXONY

Dresden

DUCHY

OF

Breslau

SILESIA

POLAND

POLAND

White Mountain ✕ o Prague

KINGDOM

Elbe

OF

TROPPAU

TESCHEN

Cracow

Vistula

GALICIA

BOHEMIA

MARGRAVIATE

OF

MORAVIA

ensburg

HUNGARY

B. OF PASSAU

ATE

ARCHDUCHY

Danube

(To Freising)

Pressburg

(To Austrian Hapsburgs)

OF Vienna

AUSTRIA

(To Freising)

A/B

OF

SALZBURG

DUCHY

(To Bamberg)

(To Salzburg)

(To Bamberg)

OF

(To Salzburg)

(To Salzburg)

D. OF CARINTHIA

STYRIA

KINGDOM OF HUNGARY

TURKISH HUNGARY

xen)
(To Bamberg)

(To Brixen)

(To Freising)

C. OF
GORIZIA

DUCHY

OF

CARNIOLA

Trieste

Adriatic Sea

nice

THE HOLY ROMAN EMPIRE
After the Peace of Westphalia 1648

MILES 0   25   50   100

ALSACE   Regional names; no corresponding political unit
ABB.   Abbacy
A/B   Archbishopric ⎫
B.   Bishopric ⎬ Ecclesiastical states
C.   County
D.   Duchy
E.   Electorate
L.   Landgraviate
M.   Margraviate
P.   Principality
☆   Imperial free city

To Hapsburgs of Spain   To Brandenburg
To Hapsburgs of Austria   To Sweden
Boundary of Holy Roman Empire
✕   Battles

Copyright by Rand McNally & Company, Made in U.S.A.

and plots against the English crown. Elizabeth's reign began, then, in the midst of grave dangers. Also, on all sides, as was so often true of the times, defence of the *state* became identified with defence of the *faith,* so that religious enthusiasm blended with patriotism and with dynastic loyalties to create a new nationalism—a nationalism which impelled a solemn Elizabethan scholar and statesman to exclaim on one occasion, "God is English!"

Elizabeth I came to be greatly beloved by the English people, but those who knew her at court found her difficult and fearsome. She was vain, changeable, given to violent temper outbursts, and occasionally shrewish. But she was also highly intelligent, well educated, and so fully in command of affairs that one is led to believe that her lightning shifts in mood were often calculated policy. She was a master of dissimulation and temporizing—a shrewd, realistic dynast worthy of her Tudor forebears and more than a match for her enemies in the dangerous political machinations of the times. She played the dynastic matrimonial game with great finesse, advancing and retreating before a variety of suitors both at home and abroad in a highly complicated political and diplomatic pattern, employing herself as the pawn of dynastic policy and in the end marrying no one. Meanwhile, she long postponed even her own excommunication by the Pope, aided the Huguenots in the French wars, supported the Dutch in their revolt from Spain, winked at the depredations of Drake, Hawkins, and other Elizabethan sea dogs upon Spanish shipping and overseas settlements, and managed to postpone a showdown with Philip II until the sailing of the great Spanish Armada of 1588. Mary, Queen of Scots, occasioned a long battle of wits. The Scottish queen claimed the English throne for a time, but finding herself in trouble with John Knox, under whose leadership Scotland was rapidly becoming a stronghold of Presbyterianism, she temporarily made her peace with Elizabeth. In 1567 Mary was forced to abdicate her Scottish throne, fled to England (1568), and was thereafter held a prisoner of the English queen. In 1587, after many intrigues with foreign princes and complicity in an alleged plot to assassinate Elizabeth, Mary was executed with Elizabeth's consent.

The administration of Elizabeth I was well ordered and the dynasty was kept firmly in control. The queen continued the Tudor policy of operating through Parliaments which she manipulated with great skill. Even so, her last years were marked by a growing restlessness. The Irish rebelled in 1597 and, though the rebellion was put down in 1601, the settlement was temporary and the "Irish problem" had emerged to plague succeeding English governments into the twentieth century. Parliamentary leaders, grown presumptuous with a century of Tudor coddling, were claiming authority over and beyond their historical station, and Puritans were becoming increasingly insistent upon changes in the English church. Only regard for the aging queen, or fear of her retribution, prevented a host of challenges to her policies and authority. Her successor, son of the ill-fated Mary, Queen of

Scots, James VI of Scotland, who founded the Stuart Dynasty in England as James I in 1603, inherited difficult problems from Good Queen Bess.

4 : The Habsburg Dynasties of Germany and Spain

THE HOUSE of Habsburg took its name from the ancestral castle in Aargau, Switzerland. It was a royal German family that included many rulers of Germany. Maximilian I (1493–1519) opened a new era for the house. To the ancestral estates in Austria he added the Netherlands, over which, after the death of Mary of Burgundy in 1482, he ruled as guardian during the minority of his son, Philip the Handsome, Duke of Burgundy; further, in 1493 he succeeded his father, Frederick III, as Holy Roman Emperor. To be sure, his possession of Burgundy was disputed by the kings of France, with whom there arose a hereditary enmity which provoked wars for several generations; his control over Switzerland was lost in 1499 when the Confederated Swiss Cantons rebelled against the emperor's repeated demands for troops and established their independence in fact, though it was not formally recognized until 1648; and his efforts to win the duchy of Brittany by a second marriage with the Duchess Anne (1488 and after) were foiled when Anne married Charles VIII of France in 1491. Still, these failures were well compensated for by his election as Holy Roman Emperor, and he set out to consolidate his power over the German states.

THE HOLY ROMAN EMPIRE UNDER MAXIMILIAN I

The empire consisted of a number of electors and imperial knights and 240 states, each independent of the other and united in a loose confederation by a general Diet under direction of the emperor. The electors and kings considered themselves the equals of the emperor, whom they never hesitated to resist on occasion, while imperial revenues depended upon grants from the Diet and judicial authority rested largely in local hands. The local authorities maintained the right of private warfare, so that "the peace of the empire," while widely desired, was difficult to establish. If the emperor could obtain money to hire well-equipped soldiers, he might subdue the brawling princes, destroy their castle strongholds, and assert centralized control. But this required money, which the Diets were loath to grant. Even when the empire was threatened by outside powers, as it was repeatedly, the Diets refused to vote adequate funds lest the emperor use them for troops to assert his ascendancy over the chaotic divisions within the empire.

These circumstances forced Maximilian to depend largely upon the slender resources of his own domains and whatever loans he could get from banking houses. But the urgent demands for peace within the empire, to-

THE HOUSE OF HABSBURG

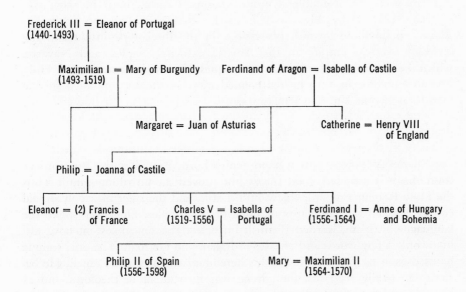

gether with genuine threats from without, enabled him to modernize the internal organization of the empire to some extent. A Diet in 1496 prohibited private warfare within the empire and set up an Imperial Chamber as a supreme tribunal under Maximilian to settle disputes among the German states. Gradually the emperor matured further plans and at the Diet of Cologne (1512) the empire was divided into ten "circles" or districts, each with its own sub-Diet, or assembly, with a director appointed by the emperor and a military leader appointed by the states of the circle. The circles contributed greatly to the better maintenance of public peace, while at the same time they enabled the emperor to assert himself in accordance with the old principle of "divide and rule." At this time there was established under Maximilian an Aulic Council, or supreme court of appeals, by which the emperor won considerable ascendancy over the nobles in judicial matters. Maximilian also strove to create an imperial system of taxation, but German resistance rendered his efforts so ineffectual that he became known as Maximilian the Moneyless.

The emperor's internal reforms strengthened his grasp upon the empire, although it fell far short of centralizing his authority. He added little to his territories by war. His dynasty profited most from the "double marriage" of his children, which brought rewards far beyond what he could have anticipated. To strengthen his house against France, he married his son, Archduke Philip of Burgundy, to Joanna of Castile, and his daughter, Margaret, to John, the only son and heir of Ferdinand and Isabella. John died soon afterwards (1501) without issue, and Philip died in 1506; but the latter had by Joanna two sons, Charles and Ferdinand, who were destined to become illustrious in the House of Habsburg, and four daughters, all of whom were married for profitable dynastic reasons. Charles, born in 1500, was especially noteworthy. He was heir to the Netherlands and to Spain, including, besides the Spanish possessions in the Iberian peninsula and the budding overseas empire in the Americas, Sicily, Naples, and Navarre, which Ferdinand had acquired by conquest. When he was elected Holy Roman Emperor in 1519 he represented more territories combined in one man than anyone since ancient times.

CHARLES V

Charles V (1519–1556) was no genius born. Reared at the Burgundian court, he was assigned good tutors but proved an unwilling pupil. Thus the Holy Roman Emperor knew little Latin, and the ruler of a polylingual empire learned the languages of none of his peoples. He never spoke the languages of Spain, learned Flemish imperfectly as an adolescent boy, and knew only a few words and phrases of Italian and German. The only tongue he used with facility was that of his hereditary enemies, the French. He became fanatically religious, though he was no student of theology, and as he advanced in years he became gluttonous to the extreme, so that Italian critics said the emperor's whole life was summed up in the expression *della messa alla mensa,* "from Mass to mess." Still, his person was pleasing. He was well built save for the "Habsburg jaw," a projecting lower jaw which handicapped both mastication and youthful speech and which he passed on to generations of Spanish Habsburgs—though he himself masked it with a beard in later life and, in consequence, gave a stately, dignified impression as an emperor.

Although he wore the crowns of many lands, Charles was never absolute master of any of them. In fact, from the outset of his career he was put upon the defensive and was never able to take the lead. After he became king of Spain he visited his Iberian dominions (1517–19) with a large and greedy following of Burgundian court favorites. The costliness of his visit, the favors he showed his Burgundian followers by raising them instead of natives to many of the highest offices in Spain, and his obvious contempt for Spanish customs and institutions led to opposition and revolts which were not put down until 1521. Even then, Spaniards felt that Charles' election as Holy Roman Emperor was to their disadvantage in that their king was constantly *in absentia* while he called upon Spain for men and money for imperial purposes. No doubt, these objections would have taken more serious form had not tremendous quantities of gold and silver poured into Spain from the New World, thereby dulling somewhat the effects of the emperor's demands. Even so, Charles avoided his Spanish possessions as much as possible after the visit in 1517–19, though he had learned respect for their native institutions and traditional rights. Later he prepared his son, Philip, especially for the Spanish charge.

In Germany, too, Charles faced difficulties. His vast possessions and potential powers excited jealousy and alarm among the electors and princes, who resolved to regain from the young inexperienced emperor some of the privileges they had lost to Maximilian I. Accordingly, they imposed upon Charles at his coronation a capitulation of thirty-six articles which reaffirmed the privileges and territorial sovereignty of the separate German states, and reasserted the powers of the imperial Diet to declare war, make peace, regulate commerce, control coinage, limit taxation, and supervise the superior judicial tribunals. Moreover, Charles agreed not to prevent the German princes from holding assemblies and forming unions among themselves and not to enter into alliances himself without their consent. All these considerably diminished the modernizing effects of Maximilian's reforms.

If Charles V's vast possessions worried the German estates, they appeared as a positive menace to foreign princes. Francis I of France, especially, found himself encircled by Habsburg territories, and he sought by every means he could to escape. He had a finger in the Spanish uprisings against Charles, he pressed Valois claims in Italy, and by 1521 the two dynasties were at war. The emperor was successful in the first round. At the Battle of Pavia (1525) he overwhelmed Francis, took him prisoner, and held him until he signed a treaty to give up his Italian claims and to cede the duchy of Burgundy (1526). But as soon as Francis was safely back in France he repudiated the treaty, fashioned an alliance with the Pope, Venice, and Francesco Sforza of Milan, and renewed the war. Again the emperor held his advantage, although an incident of the war caused him great remorse. In 1527 imperial troops in Italy, mutinous because of lack of pay, fell upon Rome, sacked the city, and besieged the Pope in the Castle of St. Angelo. By his alliance against Charles, the Medici Pope Clement VII had courted imperial attack, but when imperial troops got out of hand, looted the Holy City, and practically made a prisoner of the Pope, Catholic opinion was outraged and Charles himself was horrified. But his forces won, and in 1529 Francis I signed the Treaty of Cambrai by which he paid an indemnity of two million crowns and once more renounced his claims upon Italy and Habsburg possessions everywhere. The next year Charles was reconciled with the Pope, who formally crowned him emperor at Bologna— the last German emperor to receive his crown at papal hands.

In the meantime the emperor's brother, Ferdinand, had enlarged Habsburg dominions and enhanced Habsburg problems. As Ferdinand had claims upon the Habsburg Austrian territories, Charles ceded them to him in 1522. Four years later Ferdinand was elected king of Bohemia and Hungary. In Hungary, however, a faction of the nobility challenged him and chose John Zápolya as king. A civil war followed, Zápolya was defeated, and he immediately sought Turkish support, which was freely given. Habsburg power and Habsburg interests were brought directly into contact with the terrifying infidel. The situation became more complicated by the growth of Protestantism in Bohemia and Hungary and its toleration by the Turks wherever they managed to win control. Thus the Habsburg borderlands in eastern Europe became a confused, fluid miniature of all the dangers to and follies of Habsburg policy.

The Ottoman menace was not new. The Turks had been in Constantinople for more than half a century. But Suleiman I, the Magnificent (1520–1566), generally rated as the greatest of the Ottoman sultans, gave the Turkish Empire new vitality. In 1521 his forces captured Belgrade and were soon disputing with Ferdinand for possession of Hungary. They laid siege to Vienna in 1529 without success, and by constant military and diplomatic pressure the Turks panicked central and eastern Europe and disrupted Mediterranean commerce throughout the reign of Charles V and beyond.

It was a sign of a new era in European dynastic politics when in 1536 Christian France and Moslem Turkey made a formal alliance against the Holy Roman Emperor. It came in the course of a new war that arose between Francis I and Charles V in 1536, when Francis renewed claims upon Milan. Charles managed a truce after two years, while he vainly strove to stem the tides of Protestantism in his widespread dominions. But the war was resumed in 1542 and, though there were intervals of peace marked by treaties which were only breathers for the contending powers, the conflict continued into the reign of Charles's German successor, his brother Ferdinand. In 1559 Ferdinand concluded the Treaty of Cateau-Cambrésis which marked the end of the Habsburg-Valois wars. The treaty demonstrated the failure of either dynasty to destroy the other. France retained Calais—which she had captured from the English—and three small bishoprics, but confirmed Habsburg control of Milan and Naples, thereby giving up the Valois attempts to gain a foothold in Italy. Turkish pressures on the Habsburg frontiers in east-central Europe continued, however, for many years afterwards.

The events which caused Charles V the greatest exasperation and led him ultimately to abdicate his throne (1556) were troubles within the empire. Even before Maximilian's death the Protestant Revolt had begun in Germany (1517). Martin Luther and his followers quickly and sharply divided the empire into bitter factions. Indeed, Charles V's first meeting with the imperial Diet, at the Diet of Worms in 1521, was devoted, among other things, to the hearing and condemnation of the stubborn monk and, though the emperor had been unimpressed by Luther and outraged by his words, he was also rudely awakened to the divisions which the Lutherans had created within the empire. During the next few years the factions hardened into opposing leagues of princes, opening the empire both to the threat of internecine war and to the diplomatic and military interference of foreign princes.

The lines were drawn by 1530. In 1524 Ferdinand of Austria formed an alliance of Catholic states in southern Germany. The Protestant princes replied with the League of Torgau (1526), which developed into the wider Schmalkaldic League of 1530. But it was 1546, the year of Luther's death, before Charles was able to take forceful action. Then, aided by the Pope, he determined to crush the Schmalkaldic League, destroy the independence of the German states, and restore unity in the church. At first he was successful. In the Schmalkaldic War (1546–1547), and especially at the Battle of Mühlberg (1547), he defeated the league and made prisoners of its leaders. But when Charles sought to reimpose Catholicism in 1548 by an imperial decree called the *Interim* (see page 66) the Lutheran forces re-formed and, aided by Henry II, the successor of Francis I of France, renewed the war (1552) and forced a new settlement which recognized Lutheranism in the empire. This was the Peace of Augsburg (1555) by which the empire became legally divided between Lutheran and Catholic states in accordance with the particularistic (but religiously intolerant) principle of *cuius regio eius religio,* "the ruler shall determine the religion" (see page 66). There-after the ruler in each German state could choose between Lutheranism and Catholicism and enforce the faith selected upon his subjects. No other religion was permissible.

This compromise was more than Charles V could accept and he abdicated, leaving the imperial office and the Habsburg lands in Germany to his brother Ferdinand I (1556–1564). The crown of Spain with its colonies overseas and with Naples, Milan, Franche-Comté, and the Netherlands he left to his son Philip, who became Philip II of Spain (1556–1598). Charles himself retired to a monastery and died there in 1558. His division of his territories led to a separation in the House of Habsburg, Philip II and his successors being known as the Spanish Habsburgs and Ferdinand I becoming the first of a new Austrian line.

THE AGE OF PHILIP II IN SPAIN

The sixteenth century has been called "Spain's golden century," and few countries have risen to such great heights in so short a time and fallen from them so precipitantly. In 1500 Spain was no unified monarchy but rather two major states, Castile and Aragon with their lesser dependencies, held together by the linked crowns of Ferdinand and Isabella. Castile, Isabella's heritage, was the larger, the richer, the more populous of the two, and it was the more centralized under the crown. For years the Castilian monarchs had allied with the towns to humble the nobles, whose fortified castles had been destroyed, their local jurisdictions limited, and their influence in the royal council replaced by civil servants who were steeped in the absolutist tradition. In the Cortes, or assembly of the estates, the nobles had been displaced by town representatives, and the Cortes itself was moribund. In Aragon, however, the situation was different. Here the nobles had defied the crown, asserted feudal privileges to the utmost, proclaimed the right to renounce allegiance to the king and to engage in private war, and had raised the Cortes to a position of authority. Sixteenth-century Spanish dynasts faced the problem of asserting their authority over Aragon and of uniting it with Castile so as to create a united, harmonious, centralized monarchy.

To accomplish these things they found two important aids beyond the usual political intrigues. One of these was control of colonial trade, the royal profits from which enabled Spanish monarchs to develop, independent of the Cortes and in spite of feudal limitations upon their power, the best soldiers of sixteenth-century Europe. The discoveries of Columbus made Castile the pioneer of large, modern colonial empires. Isabella limited all American trade to a single port—at Seville after 1503—with a monopoly controlled by the House of Trade (*Casa de Contratación*) created by a royal ordinance. Ferdinand, who controlled Castile after Isabella's death in 1504, set up an agency to advise the crown and to oversee the government of American colonies. In 1524 Charles V (he was Charles I as king of Spain) reorganized this body as the Council of the Indies which, directly under the crown, served as the supreme governmental agency for the colonies during nearly two centuries thereafter. Thus, as early as the sixteenth century, the kings of Spain could call upon America to redress the balance of power in Europe—in treasure if not in men.

The second instrument of the Spanish monarchs was the Spanish church. Altar and throne were united in Spain as in no other Roman Catholic country. Besides the Inquisition of 1478 as an efficient means to enforce religious conformity in Spain, the king held complete control, after the concordat with the Pope in 1482, over all ecclesiastical appointments in the Spanish hierarchy, thus insuring clerical support for the crown. These means of control were extended to the American colonies and, after 1514, no papal bull could be published in the Spanish dominions without royal approval. Nowhere in Catholic Europe had the Pope so little authority as in Spain, and nowhere was the church used by the state with greater nationalizing effect. Moriscos (Christians of Moorish ancestry), Marranos (Christians of Jewish ancestry), and heretics of all sorts were rooted out of Spanish society, while racial purity, religious orthodoxy, and loyalty to "His Most Catholic Majesty," as the Spanish kings were called, became mutually interdependent and necessary attributes of a loyal Spaniard. Nationalism and national unity grew out of religious enthusiasm as it swept across Spain, with regard for neither political divisions between Aragon and Castile nor the privileges claimed by the nobility. It tended to reduce all men to a common level before the law in a common subjection to the crown.

CHARACTER AND AIMS OF PHILIP II

Philip II was a worthy heir to these developments. Intensely Catholic, he was a serious, hard-working administrator who sought to bind together even more tightly the various parts of his empire, to exa!t the monarchy over the nobility, and to espouse the cause of Catholic orthodoxy everywhere against the heretical, divisive influences of Protestantism. Unlike his father, Philip identified himself with Spain, where he lived most of his life, presiding over his Councils of State and giving painstaking attention to the most minute matters of administrative detail. In his fumbling way, he worked to establish a vast bureaucracy, with every question, great and small, funneled to the king for decision. He rarely employed great nobles except in war, diplomacy, and other affairs in distant places where they would be isolated from Spanish politics and weaken themselves with debts. He would not—and temperamentally could not—delegate authority, even in small things. In consequence, his régime became clogged with paper work, the king laboriously going over every item in rotation and getting farther and farther behind, until the delays of the court became notorious. "If death came from Spain," wrote his viceroy at Naples, "we should live to a very great age."

Philip's determination to defend Catholicism, to stamp out Protestantism, and to uphold Habsburg interests whether in Spain or beyond led him into many areas of conflict: his possessions in Naples and Milan embroiled him in the struggles of divided Italy; his Burgundian inheritance in the Netherlands became infected with Protestantism and rebelled; both dynastic opportunism and anti-Protestantism impelled him to interfere in the affairs of France, where religio-political wars blazed for the last third of the sixteenth century; the Turks in the Mediterranean engaged his attention; and his overseas possessions were raided by both the English and the French, who were on the eve of challenging even more seriously the Spanish-Portuguese monopoly of the New World. Portugal suffered even more after 1580, when Philip succeeded to the Portuguese throne which he claimed through his mother (Isabella, daughter of Manuel I) and backed by a show of force. For sixty years (1580–1640) the entire Iberian peninsula was under the Spanish Habsburgs.

EXPANSION OF THE SPANISH OVERSEAS EMPIRE

In Europe Portugal was Philip's only important addition to Spanish territory, but overseas the Spanish Empire continued to expand. In South America the Viceroyalty of Peru, with its capital at Lima, added parts of Chile and expanded southward into the La Plata region (Uruguay and the Argentine) and, after some fumbling, founded Buenos Aires in 1580. Meanwhile, the Viceroyalty of New Spain, centered about Mexico City as its capital, sprawled from Venezuela northward through Central America and Mexico across the southern portion of western United States from California to the Mississippi River. Westward across the Pacific the Spanish set up a colony in the Philippine Islands in 1565 and founded the city of

Manila in 1570. Eastward across the North American continent St. Augustine was founded in Florida in 1565, and French attempts to colonize in that area were foiled.

Actually, the French had planned to establish a base in Florida from which to launch attacks upon the Spanish plate fleets which annually sailed through the Bahama Straits between Florida and Cuba. These fleets, one from the Isthmus and one from New Spain, sailed under convoy to Havana, where they joined forces in the voyage to Seville. By the opening of Philip's reign they brought to Spain about three hundred million grams of silver and more than forty million grams of gold each year, and by the end of his reign in 1598 the silver had swollen to about two and a half billion grams while the gold had shrunk to about fifteen million annually. This treasure, worth about $30,000,000 in 1556 and $92,000,000 in 1958—with purchasing power many times these sums as compared with that of today—was a prize often sought by foreign powers during the latter half of the sixteenth century and beyond. But it was very seldom won, and its import to Europe, into whose economic bloodstream it poured from Spain, not only aided the Habsburg Dynasty in its struggles but also led to an inflationary rise in prices which historians refer to as "the price revolution of the sixteenth century." Commodity prices, though they varied from place to place, generally rose about 300 per cent during the sixteenth century. No period since has experienced such a century-long upheaval in price structure or found that such a rapid expansion of bullion would buy so little.

THE DUTCH REVOLT

While the empire of Philip II expanded and its treasure poured in, Spain suffered grievous losses in territory and prestige in Europe. One of the most severe blows was the revolt of the Dutch provinces in the Spanish Netherlands. This revolt culminated a long chain of events and circumstances which we may summarize as follows. Philip II, unpopular in the Netherlands, was seldom there after 1559. He became almost wholly preoccupied with Spanish affairs and subjected the interests of the Low Countries to the needs of Spain. These interests were commercial and maritime, and the well-established, wealthy merchants of the Low Countries chafed at Spanish controls and customs. Moreover, Philip assigned the administration of the Low Countries to regents, first his half-sister, Margaret, Duchess of Parma (1559–1567), then to the Spanish duke of Alba (1567–1573), and then to others, all of them supported by garrisons of Spanish soldiers. The regents gave the Netherlandish nobles no voice in affairs, although they had long held considerable powers. They felt their privileges were trampled upon unjustly, grew discontented, and in 1562 they formed a league to defend the interests of the Low Countries against the rapacities, political and economic, of the regents. This league was led by

Lamoral, Count of Egmont, and William of Nassau, Prince of Orange, known as William the Silent. When one of Margaret's advisers sneered at a member of the league and called him a "beggar," the name was quickly appropriated by the league and became both a patriotic cry and the name of the party of opposition—*les Gueux,* "the Beggars."

To these political and economic discontents was added a religious conflict. The Protestant Revolt found wide sympathy in the Low Countries, especially in the northern provinces sometimes called Holland, and the Dutch Protestants, mostly Calvinists, were severely treated. Margaret of Parma introduced the Spanish Inquisition, but the Protestants fought back, sacked Catholic churches, and insurrections occurred on a wide front. In 1567 Margaret resigned and Philip II sent the duke of Alba to the Low Countries with 20,000 soldiers. Alba boasted of the heretics he would slay, and he made good his boast. He set up a Council of Troubles (quickly dubbed the "Council of Blood") which executed many prominent leaders of the opposition, confiscated the properties of others, applied severe taxation to the Netherlands, and won Alba notoriety as a bloody tyrant. In consequence, the league of nobles joined forces with the Protestant commoners to form a united party of *les Gueux* to resist Spain by force of arms. The nobles supplied able leadership, and the heroic stand taken by the Dutch aroused interest and sympathy from abroad. German Protestant princes together with France and England, dynastic rivals of the Habsburgs, supplied money, arms, and soldiers. Alba gave up in 1573, and his successors found all the Spanish provinces determined to drive out the Spaniards.

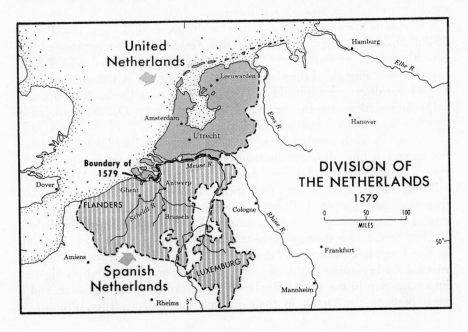

DIVISION OF
THE NETHERLANDS
1579

Gradually, however, the southern provinces (roughly the present-day Belgium) were restored both to Catholicism and to Spain; but seven northern provinces united in the Union of Utrecht in 1579 and declared their independence in 1581 as the United Netherlands. The struggle was a long one. William of Orange was assassinated in 1584, by an assassin possibly in the pay of Spain, and became the first Dutch national hero. In the next year Queen Elizabeth of England came out openly in support of the Dutch and sent them English regiments. Intermittent warfare continued until 1609, when Spain signed a twelve years' truce. Dutch independence, though not formally recognized until 1648, was by then virtually won.

PHILIP II AND ELIZABETH I

English interference on behalf of the Dutch was a factor in Philip II's determination to invade England. In fact, Philip's relations with the English had been difficult since his marriage in 1554 to Mary Tudor, the English queen (1553–1558). Part of a plan to recover England for the Catholic faith (see pages 75–76), it was an unpopular match there, and Philip was ill received. After Mary's death Philip's relations with her successor, Queen Elizabeth I, steadily deteriorated. Religious differences, commercial rivalries, and personal animosities between Philip and Elizabeth all conspired to produce tensions. Determined to bring England back to Catholicism, Philip repeatedly tried to negotiate a marriage with Elizabeth, fostered Jesuit efforts centering around Mary, Queen of Scots, to incite rebellion against the English queen, and let the Inquisition have its way with English merchants caught in Spanish territories.

Elizabeth countered these things with great skill. She toyed with Philip's marriage proposals until he was exasperated; she imprisoned the Scottish queen and finally (1587) had her executed; she allied with Protestants while Philip aided the Catholics, and she winked at the piratical raids of such sea dogs as Sir John Hawkins and Sir Francis Drake upon Spanish ships and settlements in the New World. In 1587 Drake destroyed a Spanish fleet in the home port of Cadiz.

Stung by such provocations, Philip II determined to invade England, put an end to English impudence, and recapture the country for the Roman church. In July, 1588, after long preparations, the "Invincible Armada" set sail with about 120 ships and 24,000 men—far below the 586 ships and 85,000 men originally proposed. Everything went wrong for the Spanish. Their unwieldy men-of-war were outmaneuvered and outgunned by the lighter English fleet, and a strong "Protestant wind" arose which swept them out of the English Channel into the North Sea and to their destruction. It marked the beginning of the end of Spanish preponderance and prestige, an important step in the rise of England's naval prowess and influence; and a great boon to the Dutch in their struggle for independence. Protestants everywhere were heartened, seeing the finger of God aiding them against the foremost champion of Catholicism.

Philip II found little consolation for the blows suffered in the latter part of his reign. The major bright spot in the European scene was the success of his illegitimate half-brother, Don John of Austria, in a naval battle with the Turks in 1571. In this battle a combined fleet of Spanish, Venetian, and papal ships under the command of Don John decisively defeated and almost destroyed a Turkish fleet near Lepanto off the shores of Greece. Thereafter the Turks seldom ventured into the western Mediterranean, but the victory hardly compensated Spain for her losses to the Dutch and to the English. When Philip II died in 1598 the sharp edge of Spanish power had been blunted and Spain's prestige severely shaken. Under his successors Spain fell rapidly into economic decadence and political lethargy.

5 : Conflict Among the Growing States

FERDINAND I (1556–1564), who succeeded his brother, Charles V, upon the latter's abdication, signed the Religious Peace of Augsburg with the Lutheran princes and concluded peace with the French at Cateau-Cambrésis in 1559. Most of the remainder of his reign was devoted to struggles with the Turks in Hungary. His Habsburg successors in the empire were relatively weak emperors, preserved from further losses to the Turks by the death of Sultan Suleiman I (1566), by Turkish preoccupation with a war against the Persians, and by a remarkable decline in Turkish power.

Within the empire the weaknesses of the Peace of Augsburg became increasingly evident. Its failure to recognize Calvinism and more radical Protestant sects was a sore point; its failure to settle the question of the disposition of properties under control of a Catholic prelate who was converted to Protestantism (the "ecclesiastical reservation," see page 66) led to many difficulties, especially as many bishoprics in northern Germany fell into Protestant hands; and after the Catholic Reformation the reformed and revivified Catholic church regained some ground formerly lost to Protestants in Germany. All these things led to new tensions within the empire, with Catholic and Protestant princes and states often cloaking their particularistic political interests and ecclesiastical land-grabbing under the guise of religious reform. By the early 1600's incidents of violence between Catholics and Protestants, especially Calvinists—who captured whole states in Germany in spite of their illegality—were multiplying. In 1608 Christian of Anhalt, a volatile Calvinist prince, formed the Protestant Union open both to Calvinists and Lutherans, although the two were not on good terms. This action impelled Maximilian, Duke of Bavaria, a leading Catholic, to organize the Catholic League (1609). The empire again was divided into

other books say the Elector of the Palatinate Frederick IV.

THE AUSTRIAN HABSBURGS

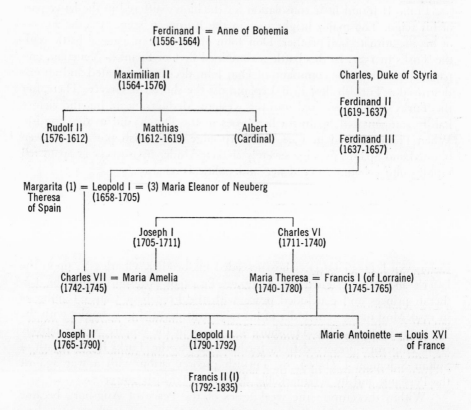

armed camps, its internal peace once more in jeopardy. Out of these conflicting interests within the empire the Thirty Years' War was fashioned. It began as internecine war, primarily religious in origin; but before its end it had become an international dynastic war, with political interests uppermost.

THE THIRTY YEARS' WAR, 1618–1648

The struggle began in Bohemia, a strongly Protestant section of the Austrian Habsburg family domain, and one with increasingly strong nationalist tendencies. When Emperor Matthias, after closing some of the Protestant churches, entrusted the administration of Bohemia to a preponderantly Catholic group of governors, the Protestant princes rebelled. In 1618 they invaded the palace at Prague, threw two of the Catholic governors out the window, and appointed governors of their own. (The victims of the "Defenestration of Prague" were saved by falling into a moat—an escape regarded by many Catholics as miraculous.) Aided by the Protestant Union, the rebels deposed the Habsburg King Ferdinand of Styria from the Bohemian throne, and elected in his stead Elector Frederick of the Palatinate, leader of the Protestant Union and son-in-law to James I of England.

Ferdinand of Styria was elected Holy Roman Emperor in 1619, and with the aid of Spain and of the Catholic League invaded first Bohemia and then the Palatinate. Frederick, who received inadequate support from the mutually jealous and distrustful princes of the Protestant Union, and almost no support from his father-in-law, was defeated by imperial troops under Baron Tilly at the Battle of White Mountain (1620) and fled to Holland. His lands were confiscated and redistributed by the emperor in an unprecedented invasion of German princely sovereignty. Protestantism was extirpated in Bohemia, and the Protestant Union dissolved.

Just when Catholic forces appeared successful, a new champion of Protestantism, Christian IV of Denmark, intervened. Promised belated aid by James I of England and by Holland, and hoping for assistance from the Turks, Christian IV, a Lutheran, hoped both to defend Protestantism and to extend his own domain into northern Germany. But Christian's forces were defeated in 1626 by Tilly and by Wallenstein, a general of the imperial forces whose military policy of plundering and living off the land gave him an evil reputation. Christian's expected assistance from the Turks did not materialize, and the Dutch and English were unable to deliver as much help as they had promised. Imperial forces invaded the Danish king's territory, and in 1629 he signed the Peace of Lübeck, withdrawing from the war in return for restoration of his own lands.

Encouraged by his generals' victories, Emperor Ferdinand II issued the Edict of Restitution as a further blow to the Protestants. The edict demanded the destruction of all Protestant sects except the Lutheran, and the restoration to the Catholic church of all ecclesiastical properties confiscated since 1552; in effect, it restored Germany to the ecclesiastical status of the Peace of Augsburg.

The edict aroused the bitter opposition of both Lutherans and Calvinists; even Wallenstein, created Duke of Mecklenburg by the Treaty of Lübeck, felt that greater religious toleration was a better policy. Wallenstein's criticism of the edict and his growing power and influence caused the Catholic League to secure his dismissal from the emperor's service in 1630.

After the Treaty of Lübeck the French, the Dutch, and the Swedes kept a close watch on the German scene, each nation intent upon its own interests and anxious to reduce Habsburg power. First to intervene was Gustavus Adolphus, Lutheran king of Sweden (1611–1632), who landed his Swedish army on the north German coast in July, 1630. He wanted to add northern Germany to territories already won from Poland and Russia, making the Baltic a Swedish lake and giving Gustavus economic leadership like that of the old Hanseatic League. To accomplish this, he planned a union of north German Protestant states which, under Swedish leadership, would then invade south Germany and restore recognition of Protestantism there, for Gustavus was a sincere Protestant. He negotiated a treaty with Cardinal Richelieu, minister of Louis XIII, whereby Catholic France assisted Protestant Sweden against the Habsburgs. The cardinal had no regard for Protestant Germany, but he had an eye for German territory along the Rhine.

Gustavus' cause was aided when, in May, 1631, Tilly's imperial army captured, sacked, and burned the Protestant city of Magdeburg, killing about 20,000 people. The resulting anti-Catholic sentiment influenced Brandenburg and Saxony to join Gustavus, and the latter moved on to defeat Tilly at Leipzig in 1631 and again in Bavaria in 1632, where Tilly was mortally wounded. Then at Lützen (November, 1632) Gustavus Adolphus was killed, although his army defeated Wallenstein, who had been recalled to service. The loss of Gustavus to the Protestant cause was to some extent offset by the fact that Wallenstein was accused of treason by Ferdinand II and assassinated in 1634. The Protestants were weakened when the emperor negotiated the Treaty of Prague (1635) with the elector of Saxony to impose a settlement only slightly more acceptable to Protestants than that of 1629, and enlisting several states in a common cause against Sweden; but to offset this alliance France intervened openly on behalf of Sweden and carried the war outside the empire.

French affairs were directed by Richelieu until his death in 1642, and then by Cardinal Mazarin. The war became a training ground for French officers, like Marshal Turenne and the prince of Condé, both famous in the great age of Louis XIV, and French arms won a prestige formerly held by the Spanish. The French took Alsace, drove the Spanish out of Italy, and invaded Bavaria. They encouraged Catalonia to revolt against Spain (1640–59), and Portugal took advantage of this revolt to assert her independence from Spain (1640). Spanish fleets fared badly at the hands of the French and Dutch. The French occupied Roussillon, and decisively defeated the Spanish forces at Rocroi in 1643. A brief attempt by Denmark to enter the lists against Sweden in 1643 ended when the Swedes invaded Denmark in 1645. Little by little both Spanish and Austrian Habsburgs were weakened, and after Maximilian of Bavaria was knocked out of the war (1647) Emperor Ferdinand III (1637–1657) had little choice but to accept the Peace of Westphalia in 1648, although Spain continued at war with France until 1659.

THE PEACE OF WESTPHALIA

German princes had pressed for peace as early as 1641, and in 1643 a series of peace conferences began at Münster and at Osnabrück in West-

ISABELLA OF CASTILE AND FERDINAND OF ARAGON

THE EMPEROR MAXIMILIAN I

THE EMPEROR CHARLES V

PHILIP II, KING OF SPAIN

In varying degrees, nearly every dynast patronized the arts; consequently, most of the great artists were commissioned for royal undertakings. Besides furnishing likenesses of closely-related emperors and rulers in Spain, this plate illustrates three separate techniques of Renaissance artists. Maximilian I is shown in an etching by Lucas van Leyden, a Dutch painter and etcher who was a student of Dürer and Italian masters. Ferdinand of Aragon and Isabella of Castile are both represented in woodcuts by unnamed artists. The "Mühlenberg portrait" of Charles V, said to be his favorite, and the painting of Philip II are both by Titian, a Venetian master who lived almost a century (1477–1576) and painted many devotional works as well as royal portraits.

FRANCIS I

CHÂTEAU OF BLOIS,
STAIRCASE OF FRANCIS I's WING

Francis I was a powerful French dynast whose political motto was une foi, une loi, une Roi ("one faith, one law, one king"). Besides being remarkably successful in strengthening royal absolutism, Francis was a great builder and patron of arts and letters. This portrait is by Titian (see Plate IX).

The royal château of Blois was the home of Claude, Francis I's wife. Early in his reign the king added a new wing which, while basically French Gothic in construction, was ornamented in a style characteristic of the exuberance and delicacy of Italian Renaissance artists. It was perhaps the first French construction to reveal Italian influences.

HENRY VII

HENRY VIII

MARY I

ELIZABETH I

Excepting only the boy king, Edward VI (for whom see Plate VII), all of the English rulers of the House of Tudor are represented here. Henry VII, founder of the dynasty, was painted by an unknown Flemish artist in 1505. His son Henry VIII is shown in this portrait by Hans Holbein the Younger, a German who settled in London in 1532 and became court painter. He was one of the great portraitists, with extraordinary capacities for objectivity and details of settings. Mary Tudor ("Bloody Mary"), daughter of Henry VIII and Catherine of Aragon and second wife of Philip II of Spain, posed for this portrait in 1544, several years before her accession to the throne. Elizabeth I, daughter of Henry VIII and Anne Boleyn, was the last of the Tudors. An unknown artist painted her standing over a map of England.

THE ESCORIAL

HAMPTON COURT

"St. Jerome in His Study," by Dürer

FONTAINEBLEAU

This plate illustrates some of the greatest architecture and graphic art of the sixteenth century. The Palace of Fontainebleau in France, built chiefly by Francis I and Henry II, required such a number of Italian artists for its decoration that they formed the "Fontainebleau school" of art. The Escorial, near Madrid, is a huge rectangle (176 x 226 yards), enclosing sixteen courtyards, a monastery, and the royal residence of Philip II of Spain, for whom it was built. "St. Jerome in His Study" is an engraving by Albrecht Dürer, the greatest German artist of the Renaissance (see text, page 130). Hampton Court Palace, near London, built in the time of Henry VIII for Cardinal Wolsey (see Plate VII), is a world-famous example of brickwork.

phalia—the first of a series of general European peace conferences in modern times. The results marked a low point in the political disintegration of Germany and of the Habsburg empire, although some of the separate German states fared well. The demands of the neighboring states were met. Sweden won Western Pomerania and other territories south of the Baltic important to her object of controlling the commerce of the Baltic area; France kept the bishoprics of Metz, Toul, and Verdun and a hold on Alsace; and the sovereign independence of Switzerland and the United Netherlands was at last officially acknowledged. Within the empire there were territorial readjustments. Brandenburg, damaged somewhat by the new Swedish position, was compensated by Eastern Pomerania, the bishoprics of Halberstadt, Camin, and Minden, and most of the diocese of Magdeburg. The Palatinate was divided. Maximilian of Bavaria united the Upper Palatinate to his duchy of Bavaria, and the electorate was confirmed to him and his descendants. The Lower Palatinate was given to Charles Louis, the worthless son of Elector Frederick, and an eighth electorate was set up for him.

Far more important than the territorial changes were the new relationships recognized by the treaty among the states of the empire. After 1648 the states could ally with one another or with foreign princes, although no such alliances were supposed to be directed against the emperor. Thus German particularism was more strongly entrenched than before. Each state possessed its own army, its own foreign service, its own currency system, and its own tolls system. Not only were the weak bonds of the Holy Roman Empire weakened further, but also the new independence of action on the part of German states made clear that the Habsburg efforts to create a unified German state had failed.

Moreover, the weakened internal structure of the empire and its loss of prestige rendered it less able to recover economically and spiritually after the war was over. Germany had suffered the miseries and the losses of life, limb, and property incident to a long and bitterly fought war. To be sure, the incidence of loss in every category was unevenly distributed over the empire, and statistical evidence regarding it is inadequate and unreliable. Even so, it was considerable, and the lessened capacity to recover prolonged the distress. What Germany needed most the Treaty of Westphalia emphatically rejected, a strong *central* government to raise the peasantry from its depressed condition and to eradicate the multiplicity of internal barriers to manufactures and trade in terms of tariffs, coinage restrictions, guild limitations, and other obstacles to economic unity and strength.

Finally, the religious issues were settled, though not so much by the bare terms of the treaty as by their application at the hands of a German people sobered by experience. The principle of *cuius regio eius religio* was reasserted, but at last Calvinists won legal existence along with Lutherans and Catholics, and the right of dissidents to emigrate was recognized. In practice, however, many states, especially Protestant ones, extended toleration to a multiplicity of sects, including Anabaptists and other "radical" groups. On the hitherto explosive question of the ecclesiastical reservation the year 1624 was adopted as the norm: as ecclesiastical properties stood on January 1 of that year so they were to be in the future. This was a singularly happy solution which squared accurately with the divisions in Germany between Catholic and Protestant states. It left the northern German states in Protestant hands and recognized Catholic gains since 1552 in other parts of the empire. Indeed, the divisions between Catholics and non-Catholics in Germany are still similar to those established in 1648. Thirty years of war had dulled the enthusiasms of both parties for trying to exterminate each other. Religious antagonisms continued to exist, but the Thirty Years' War was the last war of religion between Catholics and Protestants.

6 : The States System

By the seventeenth century a centralized dynastic state with a nationalized church had become the model upon which most European leaders attempted to fashion political and social organization. Habsburgs, Bourbons, Tudors, and many lesser families in other states blanketed Europe with a network of dynastic families around whose relationships and rivalries European history turned for nearly three centuries. In this system the sovereign personified the state. In his hands lay law, administration, taxes, army, navy, diplomacy, and economic policy. Such dynastic rule was the mortal enemy of the feudal system, and struggles between crown and nobles went on in every state. But the centralized dynasty, supported by the moneyed middle class, gradually prevailed. The nobility, deprived of troops, castles, taxes, and judicial powers sank into an aristocracy, still wealthy, powerful, and privileged, but dependent on the crown and no longer a dangerous rival to royal authority. Francis I of France, who loved extravagant displays, kept hundreds of lords and ladies at court, giving them positions as attendants upon the royal family. While they elbowed one another for royal preferments, they impoverished themselves with extraordinary expenses, and their estates fell into disorder during their absence. Catherine de' Medici later reported that she had heard Francis I say that "he must keep them amused for two days in the week, for that otherwise they would find themselves more dangerous employment." As the dynastic state became the characteristic feature of European society, political theories were set forth to guide and justify it; an international system of diplomacy arose by which interstate relations were conducted; and national literatures in the vernaculars emerged, often in marked contrast to the literature previously directed to all Christendom, especially by their tendencies toward nationalistic self-adulation.

LITERATURE AND THE ARTS

The cultural expression of the sixteenth century was rich, indeed. Roughly the first quarter of the century, however, was still representative of Renaissance ideals as they developed outside of Italy. In general, the trans-alpine humanists drank from the same classical fountains as their Italian forebears, but they tended to give greater attention to the *content* of ancient works than to their *form* (which had so captivated the Italians). In consequence, they drew inspiration for a new society which would be something more than a revival of antiquity, with a purer Christianity, a deeper learning, and a life cleansed of gross injustices, ignorant superstitions, foolish customs, and senseless wars. In short, they were Christian reformers.

There were many of these men, but we shall note only two, the Englishman Sir (now Saint) Thomas More (1478–1535), and the Dutchman Desiderius Erasmus (1466–1536). More was a scholar and a statesman, who was executed for his opposition to Henry VIII's nationalization of the English church. His principal publication, *Utopia*, or the *Land of Nowhere* (1516), caught the imagination of the world by its description of an ideal, imaginary commonwealth where men lived in peace, health, comfort, and happiness—a perfect society still, unhappily, a "Land of Nowhere." Erasmus, who was a close friend of More, was the most famous of the trans-alpine humanists. He was a cosmopolitan in outlook, and he traveled, studied, and taught in many parts of western Europe. He knew personally nearly all the great men of his day, held a tremendous correspondence almost Europe-wide in scope, and advocated reforms in church and society. His *Colloquies* promoted "the most perfect learning," his *Praise of Folly* was a powerful satire upon the church and contemporary society, and his *Education of a Christian Prince,* written after he was appointed councilor to Charles of Spain (later Charles V), urged the king to treat his public obligations as a moral trust and not from the standpoint of mere political expediency. But, in spite of his criticisms of the church, Erasmus refused to follow Luther and others in breaking with it. And by his cosmopolitan, pacific views, he was out of step with nationalism and the belligerent tendencies of ambitious dynasts.

The national monarchs often patronized literature and the arts after the manner of the Italian merchant-princes and Popes. Indeed, to a considerable extent, they harnessed the forces of the Renaissance and, without stifling them completely, bent them toward the glorification of their courts, themselves, and their peoples. Some of the kings were great builders. The Valois, after their invasions of Italy, employed Italian painters, sculptors, architects, and artisans to work in France "after the Italian manner."

Francis I built the fine palace of Fontainebleau and patronized other works in Paris. François Rabelais (1494?–1553) and Michel de Montaigne (1533–1592) stand out in French literature as extraordinary examples, respectively, of the humorous, biting satire of the French and of their highly nationalist, philosophical, well-written essays. Spain, which had a wonderful legacy of Moorish art and architecture and had developed beautiful Gothic structures, was forced into a cold classical form by Philip II, whose vast, isolated Escorial outside Madrid combined a royal palace, a mausoleum, a church, a college, and a monastery. While it was under construction, Domenico Theotocopuli (1541–1614), better known as El Greco ("the Greek"), settled at Toledo (1576). A Cretan by birth, he had studied with Titian in Italy. At Toledo he became the leading Castilian painter and the foremost representative of Spanish mysticism, with his dark, gaunt, hollow-eyed, elongated figures in majestic settings of landscapes and mystical scenes. Miguel de Cervantes Saavedra (1547–1616), scholar, soldier, playwright, and novelist, is best known for his novel, *Don Quixote de la Mancha* (1605), which was a burlesque of chivalry and knighthood filled with madness, pathos, and the contrasts between the wild knight Don Quixote and his thoroughly sane, matter-of-fact servant Sancho Panza.

Germany produced no literature other than polemics, unless we note Martin Luther's German Bible (1534), which first elevated the German tongue to a literary language. In wood carving, engraving, etching, and painting, however, Germans reached unprecedented heights in craftsmanship. Albrecht Dürer (1472–1528), was court painter to the emperors Maximilian I and Charles V, but his greatest fame stemmed from his etchings (an art which he is said to have invented) and from his engravings and woodcuts. Hans Holbein the Elder (1465?–1524) was a painter of historical and religious scenes, and his son, Hans Holbein the Younger (1497?–1543), was a portrait painter and wood engraver. Lucas Cranach the Elder (1465?–1533), as painter to the elector of Saxony, Luther's protector, became the "official" Lutheran painter and made portraits of Luther and his friends together with religious scenes. Flemish painting, which had reached such high standards of performance under the Van Eycks, was carried on by Pieter Breughel the Elder (1525–1569), who made delightful native scenes, and by Peter Paul Rubens (1577–1640), who painted royal portraits, landscapes, sacred subjects, and classical scenes, all with exuberance and vast expanses of luminous, nude flesh.

In England scores of Tudor manor houses testify to the prosperity of Englishmen and the sturdy construction of nameless architects and builders. The Tudors themselves were not great builders, although Henry VII constructed the lovely Perpendicular chapel in Westminster Abbey that bears his name. Henry VIII's adviser, Wolsey, built the fine brick palace at Hampton Court, and Elizabeth I patronized Inigo Jones (1573–1652), England's first architect of note. Jones constructed stage settings for Elizabethan dramatists and built several public and private buildings. England had no native painters or sculptors worthy of note. Both Henry VII and Henry VIII imported Italians and other foreigners, and supported them in an effort to expand and improve English arts and crafts. Hans Holbein the Younger spent several years as court painter to Henry VIII and most of the portraits of Henry, his wives, and his ministers were done by Holbein. England's greatest forte lay in literature, which blossomed wonderfully during the Tudor Dynasty, especially in Elizabeth I's reign. Henry VII, however, supported humanist scholars, including Thomas Linacre (1460?–1524), onetime teacher of Erasmus and More as well as physician and founder of the Royal College of Physicians (1518). Henry also sponsored Polydore Vergil (1470?–1555?), an Italian who first went to England as papal sub-collector of Peter's pence (1502) but later became a naturalized Englishman (1510). Vergil wrote, among other things, a long Latin history of England which, although not published until 1534, marked a new departure in English historical scholarship by its broad scale and comparative objectivity.

English literature became England's cultural glory in the reign of Elizabeth I. The "Age of Shakespeare," which began about 1580, embraced a galaxy of literary men still well known and widely admired: John Lyly, Edmund Spenser, Francis Bacon, Michael Drayton, William Shakespeare, Sir Philip Sidney, Sir Walter Raleigh, Christopher Marlowe, Ben Jonson—these are but a few of them. To refer to their works is largely unnecessary in the English-speaking world. Their dramas, poems, essays, histories, and other works gave Englishmen a native and common literature of which they could be proud. Moreover, these works, although seldom political in nature were often fiercely patriotic in tone, and they promoted unity of spirit, national solidarity, and national pride. Indeed, English nationalism appears to have been developed beyond that of the continental dynasties in 1600. Was it because of the survival of the English Parliament, which enabled the English people to feel that they had a finger on the rudder of the ship of state?

POLITICAL THOUGHT

In the political thought of the time no one made a more lasting impression than Niccolò Machiavelli (1469–1527)—though the less admirable aspects of his political philosophy have been unjustly castigated by many who appear to have read only part of his works. A Florentine lawyer, Machiavelli served the Republic of Florence in various capacities for fourteen years. His services included diplomatic missions whereby he became familiar with the devious minds and crass motives of many of the leaders of his day. He abhorred the petty jealousies and greed which kept Italy divided into contending city-states, helpless against the superior forces of the Habsburgs and the Valois. Also, he admired the dashing accomplishments of contemporary dynasts and of such freebooting adventurers as Cesare Borgia. He longed for a prince who would unite Italy and free it from internal disorder, papal politicking, and the invasions of its neighbors. In short, Machiavelli was an Italian nationalist. But the end of Italian unity was so important as to justify any means, and Machiavelli's book *The Prince* described those likely to succeed.

He presented a low opinion of his fellow men, and argued that as they are wholly untrustworthy a prudent prince should never keep faith with them "when by so doing it would be against his interest, and when the reasons which made him bind himself no longer exist." By deception, bad faith, and force, a prince may win power, and with power he might later cultivate glory and honor; without power he was lost. Thus Machiavelli set forth a new political realism accurately describing the scene in his own day. He did not pretend that it was upright or moral, but he insisted that it would bring results, and cited illustrations from current events to prove it. In another work entitled *Discourses on the First Ten Books of Titus Livius* (Livy), Machiavelli treated politics from a wholly different angle. Here he was interested, not in the immediate Italian scene, but in the larger question of how to construct a stable, just government. And for this purpose he argued that "The voice of the people is the voice of God," and that as the people are wiser and more constant than princes "governments of the people are better than those of princes." But the arguments in *The Prince* were so shocking to the Christian world that the term "Machiavellian" has come to designate low cunning and unmoral action in many languages. In all his works on politics, too, Machiavelli was wholly secular in his treatment. He envisioned the state as an institution existing for its own ends in this world, not as a servant of the church to prepare men for heaven. His secular approach pushed aside the Christian bases of medieval political thought and prepared the way for the modern study of government.

The theoretical justification of absolute monarchy was widely discussed during the sixteenth century. Continental apologists generally subscribed to the *divine right of kings* theory originally set forth in the high Middle Ages to support the emperor in his contest with the Pope and now adopted by kings against both emperor and Pope. By this it was argued that governments were instituted among men by divine intervention and that kings ruled by the grace of God alone, owing their authority to no earthly superior.

The religious wars provoked much speculation about politics. Both Catholic and Calvinist writers—though for very different reasons—held that governments were man-made; that they originated in a contract or agreement, either tacit or explicit, between the ruler and the ruled; and that the ruler was accountable to the people, who might overthrow him if he exceeded the limits of his authority or ruled unjustly. Francisco Suárez (1548–1617), a Castilian Jesuit scholar, held to this view as did a variety of

Huguenot writers—although the latter would support unfettered absolutism when they were in control and change to limited monarchy when they were not. The French *Politiques* generally subscribed to the contract theory, and Jean Bodin (1530–1596) helped to clarify and strengthen royal authority even though it was of human origin. In *The Six Books of the Republic* (1576), Bodin pioneered in the theory of political sovereignty. Basing his arguments upon reason and human nature, he said that by its very nature and purpose the supreme, or sovereign, power of a state can suffer no limitations, is indivisible, and shares its authority with no other—neither Pope nor emperor, nor Estates-General, nor *parlements*. But neither Bodin nor others who upheld the contract theory explained how, when, and by what means it could be determined when a king became unjust or exceeded the limits of his authority. Some authors, notably Juan de Mariana (1536–1623?), a Spanish Jesuit scholar, upheld tyrannicide, that is, the right of a people to assassinate a king who had become a tyrant. In consequence, monarchs of the time were in constant peril, as the assassinations of William of Orange and the three Henrys of France testified.

INTERNATIONAL RELATIONS

Inevitably, with the rise of independent sovereign states, international relations required new and specialized machinery. Corps of diplomatic agents, protocol, and other features of international usage have been developing since about 1450. Out of a combination of fear, concern for trade and finance, and a desire to be informed about the affairs of their neighbors, Venice began to maintain permanent diplomatic agents in the Italian states in the 1450's. In 1463 Milan began the practice in France, and by the early 1500's it had spread to most European courts and extended even to Turkey. The agents often aroused suspicions, and such monarchs as Louis XI of France, even before Machiavelli's *The Prince* had appeared, began to practice what came to be called *Realpolitik*, that is, placing the practical interests of the state before moral considerations. "If they lie to you, see to it that you lie much more to them," was Louis' instructions to one of his agents. However, if diplomacy was to function at all—if states were to cultivate peaceful relations and avoid a condition of permanent warfare—self-interest necessitated that its processes be regularized and its agents be trained and responsible men. As early as 1558 a Venetian ambassador gave a classic account of an ambassador's role and desirable attributes:

> The office of the ambassador is divided into three parts: to gather information and to advise, a matter in which diligence is important; to negotiate, a matter in which skill is an admirable asset; and to report that which has been seen, a matter in which

judgment must determine those things necessary and significant and lay aside those things of no consequence.[1]

Other "manuals" before 1600 added to these attributes a knowledge of languages, a disarmingly pleasant personality, patience, imperturbability, social grace, and cultured good taste.

Gradually the art of diplomacy acquired form, rules (protocol), and a hierarchy of agents. Ambassadors represented crowned heads in person and held all the privileges and immunities of their royal masters, namely, their persons and goods were inviolate, free from search and arrest in time of peace. Chargés d'affaires, residents, and ministers were charged with particular or limited missions, and as they did not fully represent their kings they held subordinate, but still inviolate, positions. Agents usually engaged in espionage were secret and held no diplomatic immunities. Heralds or messengers were used to communicate in time of war; their purpose was limited and their persons were inviolate. Protocol was formal and pompous in order to impress, befuddle, or even intimidate the respective courts. Questions of precedence—who signs the treaty first, who sits at the head of the table, who leads the procession, etc.—created endless disputes and even today still lead to diplomatic "incidents" occasionally. The Venetians won an early reputation for thoroughness and perspicacity in the new art, but by the seventeenth century the French had overshadowed them.

The *balance of power* principle supplied a fairly successful rule of thumb in European international policy. Originating among the Italian city-states, it was adopted by the Habsburgs and Valois in their conflicts and later by other powers. In essence, it was a defensive policy designed to prevent any single power from dominating Europe. It could be employed for aggressive purposes, but generally, whenever an aggressor succeeded in becoming dangerously powerful and in a position to dominate, his allies deserted and his enemies multiplied. Though informal, this common-sense "system" sufficed to protect the independence of European states and to prevent the domination of any single power until late in the eighteenth century.

Near the beginning of the Thirty Years' War a brilliant Dutch jurist, outraged by the atrocities of the religious wars, became concerned about the knotty question as to whether, among Christian peoples, a war can be just. This was Hugo Grotius (Heug de Groot, 1583-1645), whose *De Jure Belli ac Pacis* (*Concerning the Laws of War and Peace,* 1625) was the earliest basic work on international law. Grotius addressed himself to the problem of what is allowable in war and proper in peace. As his questions concerned secular states and secular affairs, he sought explanations outside of

---

[1] Translated from Léon van der Essen, *La Diplomatie: ses origines et son organisation jusqu'à la fin de l'Ancien Régime* (Brussels, 1953), p. 76.

canon law, scriptural authority, and theology, and he found rational and convincing materials in the Roman Law of Nature and Law of Peoples (*jus gentium*), that is, in the Roman rules regulating relations between Romans and other peoples in the empire. Grotius' lucid, though not original, treatment was the first important work of its kind after the emergence of the states system in Europe. Though no formal body existed to give sanctions to the fledgling international law, its moral effect was considerable, and many of its precepts were, in time, written into international treaties and conventions. Thus by the early seventeenth century the principal elements of the modern states system had been developed.

Further Reading

On the origins and background of state-building sentiment, see Hans Kohn, *The Idea of Nationalism* (New York: Macmillan, 1944), especially Ch. 4, "Renaissance and Reformation." Readable and reliable surveys of this period are R. Trevor Davies, *The Golden Century of Spain, 1501–1621* (New York: Macmillan, 1937), and Edward Dwight Salmon, *Imperial Spain* ("Berkshire Studies in European History") (New York: Holt, 1931). Sources for the reign of Charles V are listed in the bibliography to Chapter 17. M. A. S. Hume's *Life of Philip II of Spain* (New York: Macmillan, 1899) is an old but useful little book. The impact of New World bullion on the European economy is revealingly analyzed by Earl J. Hamilton in his *American Treasure and the Price Revolution in Spain, 1501–1650* (Cambridge: Harvard Univ. Press, 1934). C. V. Wedgwood's laudatory biography of *William the Silent* (New Haven: Yale Univ. Press, 1944) includes a good account of the Dutch wars for independence, 1556–1648, as well. *The Thirty Years War* (New Haven: Yale Univ. Press, 1939), by the same author, is a standard work on the subject. *Gustavus Adolphus: A History of Sweden, 1611–1632* (New York: Longmans, 1953–57), by Michael Roberts, is a recently completed biography in two volumes.

Francis Hackett, *Francis the First* (Garden City: Doubleday, 1935), is a well-known popular treatment. The religious and dynastic strife in sixteenth-century France is sketched by Franklin C. Palm, *Calvinism and the Religious Wars* ("Berkshire Studies") (New York: Holt, 1932). A sympathetic portrayal of the "Fighters for God and Freedom" is given by Otto Zoff in *The Huguenots* (New York: L. B. Fischer, 1942). On Catherine de' Medici see E. Sichel, *Catherine de' Medici and the French Reformation* (New York: Dutton, 1905), and Paul Van Dyke, *Catherine de' Medicis*, 2 vols. (New York: Scribner, 1922), an exhaustive and studiously impartial work. References for the political history of England in this period are included in the bibliography to Chapter 17. On the social and literary temper of the times, excerpts from selected writings are collected in *The Portable Elizabethan Reader* (New York: Viking P27, 1946) and in John Dover Wilson, *Life in Shakespeare's England* (Harmondsworth, Eng.: Penguin A143, 1944). The best popular biography of the Bard is *Shakespeare of London* (New York: Dutton, Everyman Paperback D1, 1957), by Marchette Chute.

The significant political and literary writings of the Renaissance are individually available in a wide variety of inexpensive editions. Useful excerpts are included in such anthologies as *The Portable Renaissance Reader* (New York: Viking P61, 1953) and *The Age of Adventure: The Renaissance Philosophers* (New York: New American Library, Mentor MD184, 1956). Of the modern biographers of Sir Thomas More, Raymond W. Chambers is the most successful. A revealing contemporary *Life* was written by More's son-in-law, William Roper (originally published in 1626; modern edition, New York, Oxford Univ. Press, 1935). Erasmus is discussed in the bibliography to Chapter 17. See also the well-balanced volume of Margaret Mann Philips in the "Teach Yourself History Library," *Erasmus and the Northern Renaissance* (New York: Macmillan, 1950). Herbert Butterfield, *The Statecraft of Machiavelli* (London: Bell, 1940), is an excellent modern restatement of the traditional view of the Florentine. The *Prince* and the *Discourses* have been published together in the Modern Library (New York, 1950). On the origins and early development of diplomacy see especially Garrett Mattingly, *Renaissance Diplomacy* (Boston: Houghton, 1955), a thorough and readable job; also read the introductory chapters in Robert B. Mowat, *The European States System: A Study of International Relations* (New York: Oxford Univ. Press, 1923), and in Harold G. Nicolson, *Diplomacy* ("Home University Library of Modern Knowledge") (London: Oxford Univ. Press, 1939).

PART FIVE

Absolutism and Revolution

Introduction

∽ THE STATES SYSTEM *which had begun in western Europe extended until almost the whole of Europe consisted of dynastic states. Dynastic absolutism reached its apogee during the Age of Louis XIV of France. A splendorous aristocratic culture flowered and was widely imitated. In addition to high accomplishments in the arts, it contained the beginnings of early modern science. Science, with its emphasis upon reason and materialistic realities, revolutionized philosophy and the intellectual outlook of Europe. This in turn gave rise to the Enlightenment and a plethora of reform programs.*

Meanwhile, most of the dynasts had not been absolute enough. They had failed to tidy up the social and institutional debris left over from the feudal ages. Even the "enlightened despots," who hearkened somewhat to reasoned demands for reform, seldom carried their plans to a conclusion. England's American mainland colonies, outraged by plans to tighten the homeland's administrative controls, revolted and employed ideas of the Enlightenment to construct a new nation. The French, more intimately related to these ideas, burst out in violent revolution soon afterwards. The outbreak engulfed Europe and spread to European colonies. Before it was extinguished, the French Revolution had transformed western European society, set up firm constitutional limitations upon absolute monarchies, and witnessed successful struggles for independent statehood on the part of most of the peoples of Central and South America. The states system continued, but national *states had begun to replace* dynastic *states, and Western society had entered upon a new phase.*

The history of the Orient and Near East was quite different. Three empires, built by conquest, rose while the martial vigor of the conquerors remained great and declined as this vigor departed. These were the Mogul Empire in India, the Manchu Empire in China and adjacent parts, and the Ottoman Empire in Asia Minor, north Africa, and the Balkan peninsula. Unlike the European states, these empires were in no sense built upon nationalism, a spirit that had not yet risen in any but Western countries. As they weakened, they became, in varying degrees, a prey to European imperialism.

Chapter 19

THE TRIUMPH
OF ABSOLUTISM

I N THE sixteenth and seventeenth centuries the European states system
expanded geographically to include northern and east-central Europe.
In western Europe, too, at the hands of certain dynasts, it extended in
depth, so as to become even more centralized and more nearly absolute.
In a few states, however, especially in England, the absolute powers of
dynastic rulers were challenged and successfully curbed by parliaments or
other representative bodies. And the parliaments, as conservators of representative institutions, pointed the way toward limited, constitutional monarchies and even toward representative democracy.

1 : The Northlands and the Emergence of Russia

DURING THE high Middle Ages when serfdom was slowly disappearing in
western Europe almost a reverse process was taking place in the regions east
of the Baltic Sea. Here the peasantry was sinking into serfdom (from which
it did not escape until the nineteenth century) while the landed nobility grew
in numbers and in power. A combination of economic and political circumstances appears to have brought about these conditions. The Baltic region
abounded in forest products such as lumber and shipbuilding materials,
and in fish, grain, furs, hides, and other unprocessed raw materials greatly
in demand in western and southern Europe—especially since the latter
regions had become relatively deforested and increasingly urbanized. Ships
of the Spanish Armada and of Don John's fleet at Lepanto were built of
Baltic materials, and the Hanseatic League had grown fat on their monopoly
of the Baltic trade. Moreover, the Teutonic Knights had invaded Poland
and Estonia and temporarily cut off Poland from the Baltic, while to the

east the Muscovites were trying to free themselves from Tartar suzerainty and tribute. Life and property became very insecure for the peasants
and others of small means as the Baltic and Slavic peoples sought to break
the monopoly of the Hanse towns, to contain the Teutonic Knights, and
to cast off the Mongol yoke. As there was no strong monarchy to which to
turn for protection, they turned to the nobles—as had the peasants of
western Europe at the time of the barbarian invasions. The nobles could
employ their services at a profit, both as tillers of the soil and as soldiers,
and gradually they lost their freedom and became bound to the land as
chattels of the nobility. Except in the Scandinavian countries (present-day
Norway, Sweden, and Denmark), serfdom became established in the northlands and no sizable or important bourgeoisie or middle class arose there.
Even that which existed in the Hanse towns tended to diminish in numbers
and importance as the Hanseatic League decayed in competition with new
dynastic states.

In the midst of this vast social transformation the political scene in the
northlands underwent great changes. The Republic of Poland was caught
up among dynamic new neighbors who, as they struggled for territories
and superiority, gave rise to the new kingdoms of Sweden, Prussia, and the
sprawling autocracy of the Russian tsars.

THE "REPUBLIC OF POLAND"

During the high Middle Ages Poland was a considerable kingdom
astride the Vistula River. By a personal union of rulers in 1386, the grand
duchy of Lithuania united with it to form a vast territory extending from
the Black Sea to near the Baltic shores. But the conquests of the Teutonic
Knights denied the Poles access to the Baltic, and in the course of time the
conquests of the Turks in southeastern Europe, of the Russians on the east
and north of Poland, and of Sweden on the Baltic lessened the area of
Poland-Lithuania and placed it in the midst of avaricious neighbors.

The Polish kingdom proved unable to cope with such antagonists.
Throughout the fourteenth and fifteenth centuries Polish kings strove
vainly to strengthen their authority, to set up a more centralized régime,
and to establish an effective standing army. But instead the nobility took
advantage of every crisis, of every foreign threat, to exact new charters to
reaffirm and gradually to enlarge their privileges at royal expense. In 1367
they set up a Diet and, in 1505, by the Constitution of Radom, the Polish
Diet was recognized as the supreme legislative body. In 1572, when Sigismund II died without male heirs, the crown, long elective in theory, became elective in fact. The French Henry of Valois was elected king on
conditions which formally recognized the right of the nobility to elect him
and to limit his authority. Henry himself deserted his new charge in a short
time and, as the nobility were jealous of one another and as interested

foreign powers often sought to influence the elections, few subsequent Polish kings were strong rulers. Indeed, they could not be, and they came to be creatures of factions either of Polish nobles or of foreign powers or, more commonly, a combination of the two. Few of the kings elected were in fact Polish natives.

The weakness of the Polish kings was not compensated by the Polish Diet. Polish nationalists have claimed that the Diet gave Poland a rudimentary form of democracy comparable to that of the English Parliament. But neither the towns nor the small landowners (who practically disappeared) were represented. The Polish Diet represented only the nobility. The nobles met periodically in about sixty regional assemblies of disorderly, warlike gatherings and selected emissaries to the central Diet. To be sure, the Polish nobility became, in proportion to the total population, the largest in Europe, constituting about eight per cent of the Polish people. This jealous, turbulent, particularistic minority was the "democratic base" of the so-called Republic of Poland. Moreover, the nobles' concern for their local "liberties" led to the institution of the *liberum veto,* or "free veto," which paralyzed the Diet as an effective central ruling body because the Diet could take no action against the objection of any single member. The *liberum veto* was a supreme expression of particularism. First employed in 1652, it potentially destroyed the Diet's capacity to take action on any important matter. As parliamentary methods failed, noble factions resorted to force to impose their will upon recalcitrant minorities, and foreign powers fished repeatedly in Polish political waters.

While the Polish nobility protected their freedoms to the gradual destruction of all central order, they also forbade townspeople to acquire land except in small plots, thereby making impossible the rise of any new landed gentry. Moreover, they debased the peasantry, first forbidding them freedom of movement and then subjugating them to servitude, binding them to compulsory labor on huge estates over which the lords ruled as petty autocrats with no effective outside power to which their servants could appeal against exploitation. Thus Poland became a cluster of large estates presided over by noble landlords who ruled their own territories and subjects with an absolute hand and who, through the Diet, gave Poland whatever central authority existed. The population, mostly Polish in the Vistula Valley, included, in the east and south, Germans, White Russians, Ukrainians, and others, presided over by a sprinkling of Polish and Lithuanian landlords. The towns, which gradually lost their commercial importance and prosperity, consisted mostly of Germans and Jews, the latter confined to the ghettos. Between the two groups there was little intercourse, and the towns as a whole existed incongruously in the midst of a vast agrarian society, exerting none of the bourgeois influences prevalent in western and southern Europe.

Only the multiplicity of her enemies, who long tended to neutralize one another, saved Poland from early extinction—and, as we shall see, they learned in time to co-operate and eventually to partition Poland among themselves. The Russians and the Turks began to nibble at Poland's vast territorial expanse in the 1490's. Sweden joined the feast in the mid-sixteenth century, and a new threat, Prussia, arose in the seventeenth. In the midst of these circumstances, while tsarist Russia emerged as a great power and Sweden, Denmark, and Prussia developed as dynastic states, Poland fell, perhaps as much the victim of her own internal weaknesses as of her neighbors' rapacity.

THE SCANDINAVIAN DYNASTIES—
DENMARK AND SWEDEN

The Union of Kalmar (1397), by which Denmark, Norway, and Sweden had been united in a personal union, was challenged in 1520 by Gustavus Vasa (Gustavus I) of Sweden, who defeated the Danes and established the kingdom of Sweden in 1523. Finland had been part of Sweden since the twelfth century. Before Gustavus Vasa none of the Scandinavian monarchs had been able to set up a strong, centralized government. As in Poland, the nobles remained powerful—though the peasants were not debased to serfdom —and the tradition of an elective crown persisted. The Hanseatic League had been a powerful factor in the politics of all the Scandinavian countries, Germans were numerous in the towns, and German princes interfered in Scandinavian affairs. Soon after the Swedish revolt from Denmark, Lutheranism swept into Scandinavia and all three kingdoms adopted the Lutheran faith. During the 1520's and 1530's the kings of Denmark and of Sweden confiscated Catholic church properties, nationalized the churches, whose bishops were dependent upon the crowns, and thereby added materially to the royal power in each country. Norway, however, remained under Danish domination. Moreover, both the Danish and Swedish monarchs soon managed to bury the elective principle and to rule as hereditary monarchs, although factions among the nobility, often encouraged by foreign powers, continued to plague them for many years.

Sweden soon found the commercial monopoly of Lübeck, a leader of the Hanseatic League, intolerable and, led by Gustavus I, set out to break it. In a war ending in 1537 the Swedes succeeded. Immediately thereafter Gustavus I embarked upon a policy of territorial expansion, to carve out a Swedish empire in the Baltic region and to give Sweden commercial supremacy of the region. These objects motivated Vasa policy for more than a century. During this time Sweden created a short-lived Baltic empire and an even shorter-lived Swedish colony in modern Delaware (1638), which was conquered by the Dutch of New Amsterdam in 1655. Sweden's Baltic expansion was gradual and, as might be expected, was contested by her neighbors. Gustavus I's successors took Reval, Estonia, and Narva before 1600 and added eastern Carelia (Karelia) and Ingria soon after, thereby cutting Russia off from the Baltic Sea.

Meanwhile, Sweden had become embroiled in dynastic troubles with Poland. The son of John II, King of Sweden, was elected king of Poland as Sigismund III and, upon his father's death, he was also king of Sweden. But Sigismund was a devout Catholic and his attempts to restore Catholicism in Sweden aroused rebellion. Succeeded in Sweden by Charles IX, youngest son of Gustavus I, Sigismund continued to press claims upon the Swedish throne and thus involved Poland and Sweden in dynastic wars. The first of these was between 1621 and 1629, by which Gustavus Adolphus, son of Charles IX, took Livonia. Soon afterwards he entered the Thirty Years' War, as we have seen above (page 125). By the Treaties of Westphalia at the close of the Thirty Years' War, Sweden won additional territories on the southern shores of the Baltic, a large indemnity, and three votes in the German Diet—not to mention the extreme jealousy of Denmark and growing opposition from other Baltic quarters. Alleged Polish pretensions to the Swedish crown led to a new Swedish attack on Poland in 1655. Brandenburg-Prussia allied with Sweden the next year. But Russia, Denmark, and the German Empire came to Poland's defense in this First Northern War (1655–1660). Brandenburg-Prussia was lured away from Sweden's side when in 1660 Poland recognized the sovereignty of the elector as king in East Prussia, which had long been held as a fief of the Polish crown. But at the Treaty of Oliva in the same year Sweden managed to win Livonia, the last territory she won at Poland's expense.

By this time Sweden had become the dominant power in the Baltic area. Gustavus Adolphus and his successors managed to organize their administration on the French pattern, to outbid the nobles and the Riksdag for power, to centralize administration and control, to command finances and military might, and temporarily to lift Sweden into the rank of the first-class powers. But its attacks upon Poland and its Baltic supremacy aroused the opposition of Brandenburg-Prussia and of Russia, against whom the Swedish empire could not command sufficient resources to compete in the long run. In the Great Northern War (1700–1721) Sweden lost her Baltic preponderance and Russia emerged as a great European power.

RUSSIA BECOMES A GREAT EUROPEAN POWER

West Europeans and Russians have long shared a feeling that a gulf separates them—a gulf that has never been wholly bridged by Russia's "Westernization" in modern times. Insofar as this gulf is real, it stems mostly from the Byzantine origin of early Russian political institutions and practices and of the religion and ecclesiastical organization of Russia. Moreover, for more than two hundred years (1241–1480) the Russians were under the suzerainty of the Tartars, tributaries of the Golden Horde, formerly part of the Great Khan's empire centered at Peiping (Peking) in China. During this time their dress and social customs—whatever they had been before—became more Oriental than European, although as a whole the Russians

GROWTH OF RUSSIA
to 1725

0   200   400
MILES

Principality of Moscow—1300

Principality of Moscow—1462

1462-1505

1505-1670

1670-1725

remained Christians. Consequently, in the late fifteenth century, when Russians began to show nationalistic stirrings, to cast off the Tartars, and to enter into relations with Europeans, they appeared crude, ignorant, and barbarous to Europeans, who in turn appeared strange and intolerable to the Russians. From accounts of merchants and other European emissaries to Russia in the sixteenth and seventeenth centuries, it is clear that European-Russian relationships began in an atmosphere of mutual suspicion, contempt, arrogance, and uncertainty, and that this atmosphere has never wholly been dissipated.

These tensions did not arise principally from racial differences—the Russians are a highly mixed race, though principally Slavic in language—but from differences in public and private values and institutions, in customs and costumes traceable, on the part of the Russians, to Byzantine beginnings with an overlay of Tartar vainglory and cunning patience. Europeans subscribed to the Roman Catholic faith (or derivatives thereof), with the role of the church generally held above that of the state, and a rich tradition of scholarship abiding in the clergy. Russians subscribed to the Greek Orthodox faith, with the church as a department of the state and with clergy often ignorant and untutored. Europeans were moving from an agrarian toward an increasingly urbanized society, with a large and powerful middle class which operated commercial and manufacturing pursuits. But Russians were agrarian still, had no middle class and, in fact, were moving toward a new manorialism with serf labor, while staple manufactures and commerce were carried on in tsar-owned mills, mines, and trading establishments also manned by serf labor. Russia's foreign trade was principally in the hands of foreigners. Europeans were familiar with a rising dynastic absolutism tempered by localism, by the money power of the bourgeoisie, by councils and Diets. While Russians had somewhat the same outward machinery, the tone was different, and they cringed before a tsar who called himself autocrat and who ruled autocratically, more like an Oriental conqueror than like a king bound by laws. There were also superficial differences: Europeans had developed Western fashions in dress and they commonly expected women to mingle with men on social occasions; but Russians wore Oriental-like cloaks or gowns and kept their womenfolk in isolation on all social occasions. And, as in all these matters each side valued its ways above the other's, it is not surprising that their relationships were in a state of almost constant tension.

IVAN THE GREAT

The nucleus of the modern Russian state was the Grand Duchy of Moscow whose grand dukes led the way in freeing Russians from the Tartars. The process began in the fourteenth century and, being at base a military operation, it lent the rising monarchy a militaristic framework. Ivan III

(1462–1505) is usually regarded as the first national monarch of Russia, often called "the Great." A cautious, shrewd negotiator, Ivan skillfully played faction against faction to his own aggrandizement in territory and in power. He claimed succession from the old medieval Russian dynasty at Kiev, the Ruriks, introduced firearms to his military forces—a factor in their successes—and posed as a liberator of the Russians from foreign domination. The movement assumed the nature of a religious crusade as well, for Ivan also laid claim to the protectorship of the Greek Orthodox church. Thus he appealed not only to the Russian nationalist desire to be free of Tartar overlordship but he also assumed the role of leader of a Christian crusade against Islam, the religion of the Tartars. In this fashion Ivan won enthusiastic support from both the old nobility and the church. By a combination of diplomacy and war, he drove a wedge between Moscow's great rivals, Poland-Lithuania and Novgorod, and in 1478 won the vast territory of the latter, which extended eastward to the Ural Mountains. In 1480 he freed Muscovy from further payment of tribute to the Tartars and thus ended the last shred of Tartar overlordship. In 1485 Ivan added Tver, and after two invasions of Poland-Lithuania late in his reign he annexed border territories in White Russia and Little Russia. Already Muscovites had pushed eastward across the Ural Mountains into Asia (1483), heralding Russia's eastward expansion across northern Asia nine years before Columbus' voyage turned the rest of Europe's eyes westward across the Atlantic.

Ivan accompanied his vast expansion of territories with a similar enlargement of his titles and claims to power. In 1472 he married Sophia, niece of the last Byzantine emperor before the Eastern Empire fell to the Turks in 1453. With her arrived Greek Orthodox refugees with whom Ivan con-

THE HOUSE OF RURIK

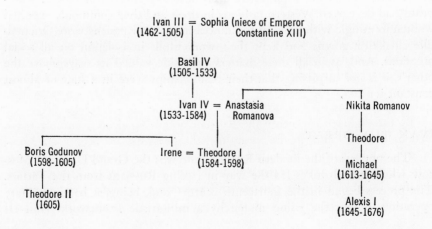

nived to set forth a brave new theory to justify his position. According to this, Moscow became the "Third Rome," successor to the "First," which had fallen because of its heresy, and the "Second" (Constantinople), which, having accepted "union" with the First (at the Council of Florence in 1439), had been punished for its apostasy in its capture by the Infidel. Thus Ivan remained the only faithful Christian prince in the world, the only rightful heir of the Emperor Constantine, and head of the universal Christian Ortho- dox church of the Third Rome. With this new ecclesiastical claim came various Byzantine trappings and assertions of autocracy. Ivan was heralded as the "new Caesar" (*czar* or *tsar*), "autocrat of all the Russias"—although the title was not formally used until Ivan's successor, Ivan IV, was officially crowned tsar in 1547. The Russian church and state became—Byzantine fashion—virtually united in the person of the tsar with the acclaim of the churchmen, although nominally the metropolitan of Moscow, later (1589) recognized as the patriarch, was head of the church under the tsars until the time of Peter the Great. Sometimes called the "Binder of the Russian lands," Ivan the Great gave Russia unity, a centralized, autocratic adminis- tration, and a recognition in Europe hitherto non-existent. He established diplomatic relations with Venice and other European powers which went far to register Russia in the family of European dynastic states.

NOBLES AND PEASANTS

Ivan the Great also inaugurated policies which, as continued by his successors, especially by Ivan IV (1533–1584), placed the nobility at the tsars' command. Using their vast territorial conquests, the tsars endowed a new class of gentry with lands in return for military service. These military fiefs, at first granted for the life of the recipients in return for service, gradually became hereditary, and the new class of service landholders, owing their all to the tsar, became his hereditary servants. At the same time the old nobility, whose titles and estates had long been hereditary, were forced little by little into the service of the tsar and their possession of properties made contingent upon such service. Gradually, both the new and the old forms of landholding became identical, both dependent upon service to the tsar, with a central office of record in Moscow keeping a census of the "service-men" and of their obligations to the tsar in wartime. In his exalted capacity as "autocrat," the tsar referred to these hereditary servants, the landed nobility, as his "slaves."

By the eighteenth century the Russian nobility had been entirely mas- tered by the tsars and, in the meantime, the peasants had been reduced to abject serfdom hardly distinguishable from slavery. During the reign of Ivan III and to a lesser extent that of his immediate successors, many peasants, insecure in their persons and possessions, sought freedom, new lands, and wealth in the Russian borderlands, where retreating Tartars had left opportunities. These became *Cossacks,* a name given to Russian frontiersmen meaning "adventurers." The tsars gave them special privileges to organize frontier settlements, sometimes in return for specific military services but more frequently in a more nebulous fashion. Thus the Cossacks became the Russian equivalent of the American pioneers—the colonizing factors in the expanding tsarist empire. As their settlements grew more populous they set up "republics," temporarily independent of the tsars and somewhat comparable to Texas or California in the growth of the American West. Two of the more important of these were along the Dnieper and the Don rivers, the Ukrainian Cossacks and the Don Cossacks respectively. Others were formed along rivers flowing into the Caspian Sea, especially the Iaik and the Terek.

But those peasants who stayed behind in Russia suffered a different fate. Like their counterparts in Poland, they were forced to seek aid from the large landowners, to whom they generally fell into debt which they could pay only in services. Until their debts were paid they were not permitted to leave their plots of land and, as the new military-service landlords needed farm labor to work their estates, they made it more and more difficult for peasants to discharge their debts. In fact, they promoted legislation forbidding them to leave, and gradually peasants became bound to the soil. In 1649 laws formally fixed their status as hereditary serfs. The landlords held police powers over them, administered justice among them, enrolled them and their children on estates' records for tax purposes, collected taxes from them, bought and sold them like chattels, and, in time, reckoned the wealth of a nobleman's estate by the number of "souls" recorded on the census books. Serfdom remained the lot of the masses of Russian agricultural workers until 1861.

All the above developments were intensified during the reign of Ivan IV (1533–1584), who became known as "the Terrible" because of his insane cruelty in his treatment of the nobility. Ivan was pathologically suspicious of the nobles, whose conspiracies, real or imagined, he sought to counter by calling the first *zemski sobor* (1549), or assembly of nobles, clergy, and town representatives somewhat like the "estates" of western Europe. Then later he persecuted them by confiscating their estates, driving them into exile, and killing them off. During his reign the Cossacks wrested control of the entire Volga Valley to the Caspian Sea from the Tartars and began the conquest of Siberia across the Ural Mountains (1552–56). During these same years, as we have seen, English merchants reached Moscow by way of the White Sea and established trading relations with Russia in spite of the barriers of Poland and Sweden on the west.

BEGINNINGS OF THE ROMANOVS

In 1598 the Rurik Dynasty died out, and a *zemski sobor* chose Boris Godunov as tsar (1598–1605). He proved inadequate in the face of the opposition and jealousy of the old nobles (*boyars*) and died soon after a pretender to the throne came forth supported by Cossacks and Poles. There followed a period of great confusion known as The Time of Troubles (1605–1613). Neighboring powers took advantage of Russia's weakness to regain territories: the Swedes recovered Novgorod, and Sigismund III of Poland invaded Russia in the hope of seating his son, Vladislav, on the tsarist throne. Famine and pestilence added to Russia's disasters. Finally, in 1613, a *zemski sobor* elected to the tsardom Michael Romanov, grand-nephew of Ivan IV. With the aid of his father, a patriotic leader who later (1619) became patriarch of the Russian church, he managed to drive out the Swedes, expel the Poles, regain most of the territories lost, and restore order. Michael Romanov (1613–1645) became the founder of the new Romanov Dynasty, which ruled Russia for three centuries until the revolution of 1917.

THE HOUSE OF ROMANOV

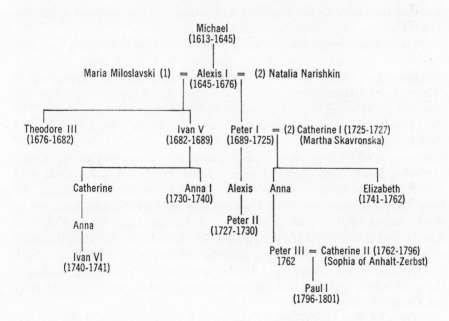

The first Romanov, however, was a weak ruler and without the aid of his more able father it seems doubtful that he could have stemmed the tide of the "Troubles." To check the nobility he relied upon frequent meetings of the national assembly, but the latter failed to develop into a genuine parliament, and local government fell more and more into the hands of the nobles. Indeed, it was many years before the effects of The Time of Troubles were overcome. During the reign of Michael Romanov's son, Alexis (1645–

1676), a national assembly adopted a new code of laws (1649) which legalized and fixed the peasantry as serfs and which tabulated all Russian society into rigid classes according to various kinds of service to the tsar, with fixed obligations according to which "the clergy pray, the gentry serve at war, the merchants collect and supply money, the peasants plow the fields." Thus Russia became a vast, regimented society organized under the tsar to make war upon its neighbors.

Much of Alexis' reign was given over to wars both at home and abroad. A war with Sweden (1655–1660—the First Northern War noted above) yielded nothing. But two wars with Poland (1654–1656 and 1660–1667) won Russia Smolensk and the eastern Ukraine, including Kiev, and placed Russia in contact with the Turks in southeastern Europe. In 1670 the Don Cossacks led a great peasant revolt which was put down with much difficulty the following year. By the end of his reign Alexis had mastered the difficulties which beset Russia during the Troubled Times. He had restored the tsardom and raised it to a new position of autocracy, had regularized the social movements which enslaved the peasants and placed the nobility in positions of service to the tsar, and had abandoned the national assemblies which his restored authority enabled him to ignore.

Alexis strengthened his position in other ways. One of his early favorites, Patriarch Nikon, introduced church reforms which led to many temporary difficulties and, during the tsar's absence at war, Nikon set himself up as "Great Ruler," threatening Alexis' authority. Accordingly, when the tsar returned to Moscow he was forced to banish Nikon to a monastery. The church reforms, however, were long overdue. They refined the Russian church practices of many errors that had crept in because of the crudity and ignorance of the clergy, and made these practices conform to the Greek Orthodox liturgy and ritual. However, many Russians known as the Old Believers clung to the errors, stubbornly and patriotically resisting the reforms as foreign innovations. Thousands of the Old Believers were put to death, and many thousands more were exiled to the lower Volga Valley, to Siberia, and elsewhere. Thus they joined the Cossacks in extending colonization on the Russian borderlands. But the reforms were officially retained, and Nikon, by his unsuccessful challenge to the tsar's position, weakened the patriarchate and prepared the way for its abolition in the reign of Peter the Great.

The Old Believers' views of the church reforms reflected the attitude of many Russians. Both the Romanov tsars had encouraged wider relations with foreigners. To English merchants, who had won trading privileges in the 1550's, were added Dutch, German, and French, while Western physicians, scholars, craftsmen, military officers, and travelers were encouraged to settle in Russia. A "foreign quarter" was set aside in Moscow, and Tsar Alexis employed foreign physicians at court, foreign tutors for his children, and various foreign scholars and scientists. These practices aroused violent protests from those Russians who opposed "Westernization," and opinion became sharply divided on the subject. "You feed the foreigners too well," wrote one brash subject to the tsar, "instead of bidding your folk to cling to the old customs." Nevertheless, Alexis' Westernizing proclivities were only a pale preparation for those to come at the hands of his son.

PETER THE GREAT

Peter I (1689–1725), later known as "the Great" was a son of Tsar Alexis by a second marriage, and his feeble elder brothers kept him from the throne for several years. Actually, Peter succeeded by a coup d'état when he was only seventeen. He was already an extraordinary figure. Though he lacked a formal education, he possessed a quick, inquiring, highly practical mind, and he had picked up all sorts of useful knowledge in Moscow's foreign quarter where he had many friends. He early demonstrated a military and naval bent and unusual qualities of leadership—or, perhaps we should say, "drivership," for he had colossal energy, little patience, a total disregard of conventions, traditions, and the proprieties of human deportment, and a terrifying streak of cruelty. Add to these that he grew into a large, dark-complexioned giant of about six feet eight inches in height and Peter appears as a fascinating but fearsome ruler. His course ran against the grain of the majority of the Russian people: his freethinking approach to life fanned their prejudices and his interest in things foreign aroused their suspicions. Still, Peter managed to ride roughshod over his opponents, to change the face of Russia, and to elevate it to a position among the great powers of Europe.

The tsar's early foreign policy aimed at the expulsion from Europe of the Turks, from whom his half-brother, Theodore III, had already won most of the Turkish Ukraine. Peter launched attacks at Azov at the entrance to the Black Sea. The first, in 1695, was by land and it failed; but the second (1696), supported by naval units constructed under Peter's personal direction, succeeded. Then Peter embarked upon an unusual European journey, traveling incognito with a grand embassy to obtain Western allies for a crusade against the Turks. He visited Prussia, Holland, England, and Austria, worked as a ship carpenter in Holland, observed many aspects of life in the west, especially in science and the crafts, and employed scores of artists, craftsmen, and scientists to work in Russia. His visit was cut short in 1698 by a revolt of the *Streltsi,* the Moscow guard. He rushed to Moscow and put down the revolt with savage cruelty, personally decapitating leaders and disbanding the corps. He had found no Western interest in a crusade against the Turks. But, learning that other northern states objected to Sweden's control of the Baltic, he altered his direction.

He made peace with the Turks in 1700, allied with Poland and Denmark, and advanced against Sweden. At first he proved a poor match for

Charles XII, the brilliant, ill-balanced, boy king of Sweden. Actually, Charles overran Denmark and defeated Peter at Narva within the year (1700). Then, as Peter said, Charles "got stuck in Poland."

While Charles forced Poland from its Russian alliance and sought again to bring it firmly into the Swedish orbit, Peter reorganized his forces, captured Ingria along the Baltic, and began on the delta of the Neva River a new city called St. Petersburg (now Leningrad) to which he later moved the Russian capital (1712). Nearby, at Kronstadt, the tsar also built a naval base and constructed a Baltic fleet. Thus when Charles moved against him afresh, Peter was far better prepared. At Poltava (1709) the tsar decisively defeated the Swedish king, and Charles, unable to get back to Sweden, found refuge with the Turks. There he made an ineffective effort to persuade the Turks to move against Russia, but Peter bought them off with the sacrifice of Azov. Then, after Charles returned to Sweden, which he found in a deplorable condition, Peter raised up such a formidable alliance with Poland, Prussia, Saxony, Denmark, and Hanover, that the Swedes sued for peace. While negotiations went on, however, Charles was killed in an expedition into Norway (1718). Finally, by a series of treaties in 1720-21, the Great Northern War came to an end. For most of the powers involved the *status quo ante bellum* was restored. However, by the Treaty of Nystadt (1721) between Russia and Sweden, Finland was restored to Sweden and Russia obtained Livonia, Estonia, Ingermanland, part of Carelia, and several Baltic islands. Sweden, whose resources were never adequate to maintain a Baltic empire, was reduced to a second-rate power. Russia emerged as a great power with an ice-free port on the western sea—her "window on the Baltic"—and a newly-won role in European affairs.

THE REFORMS OF PETER THE GREAT

Removal of the Russian capital from Moscow to St. Petersburg was a mark of Peter's desire to break with Russia's past and to integrate Russia more closely in the European system of states. While the Great Northern War went on he began changes toward this end. Although he introduced many outward appearances of Westernization such as the Julian calendar, Western dress, cutting off beards, and taking women out of their social isolation, his object was less to imitate western Europe slavishly than to make Russia over into a power able to hold its own in the European theater. More important than these outward signs—which were never more than skin deep with the Russians as a whole—were military, naval, and administrative changes which Peter inaugurated.

Peter created a first-class Russian army and founded the Russian navy. In both instances he was aided materially by western European experts, technicians, and craftsmen whom he hired at state expense. The army was organized along lines copied from the Prussians and the Swedes; the navy was patterned after the Dutch and the English. Both were based on con-scription and supported by new and enlarged ordnance works. Back of these was a more centralized tsarist administration and an enlarged tax structure. Peter ignored the *zemski sobor* and he abolished the *Duma,* or old council of nobles. At the top of his administration, appointed by him and under his direct control, Peter set up a *senate* of nine. This body served as his ad-visory council for the issuance of imperial decrees, as a supreme court of justice, and as supervisor of finances. Under the senate stood nine *colleges* or ministerial departments—bureaucratic central administrative offices like those of western Europe. Beneath them were seventy-two local govern-ments, each with a governor appointed by the senate, assisted by a local council elected by the nobles. Towns had elected town councils under a supreme magistrate appointed by the tsar. Villages were left under the old council of elders, the *mir,* each collectively responsible for the poll tax im-posed by the tsar.

The church became a "spiritual department" of the state. When the patriarch died in 1700 Peter left the office vacant until 1721. Then he created the *Holy Synod,* or committee of bishops. This was headed by a procurator who was, in effect, a bureaucratic officer of state under the tsar, who himself was head of the Russian church. With the capital moved, the Third Rome myth regarding Moscow suffered a heavy blow, and Peter broke completely with the Byzantine tradition when, in 1721, he adopted the title Emperor instead of Tsar. All religious sects were tolerated, but Peter excepted the Jesuits, whom he feared as political intriguers; the Jews, whom he despised as "rascals and cheats"; and the extreme fanatics among the Old Believers.

To enforce his autocratic rule, and to check on his corps of bureaucrats, Peter established a Chancery of Secret Police. But he went farther still. Without destroying the old nobility of birth, he set forth a Table of Ranks in 1722. In this a new nobility of service took precedence over the old nobility. All nobles were forced to serve in the army, the navy, or the civil service, and this official nobility was graduated into fourteen ranks or grades. The upper eight roughly corresponded to the old grades of nobility, but the lowest officer's rank (lieutenant) conferred nobility upon the holder. Thus a nobility of service replaced that of rank. The tsar could reward individual talents without regard to social origin and, further, this service nobility could be recruited from below. Several of Peter's greatest officers were men of lowly origin.

Peter's reforms were carried out with harshness and severity upon a people largely out of sympathy with his policies. The administration was centralized under the emperor, but between the Westernized government and the masses of the people existed a gulf of mutual suspicion and mis-trust—a split between the top and the bottom of society, between the West-ern "intellectuals" and "the people." Moreover, Peter's reign was costly. Taxes multiplied, and as they fell mostly upon the peasants, and as Peter did little to ameliorate their condition, the peasants sank more deeply into penury and servitude. Foreign visitors were likely to be impressed by the new Russia of Peter the Great, more integrated politically, economically, and culturally with western Europe; but Westernization was only a veneer on Russia's top surface, often maintained by foreigners employed by the emperor, but widely disliked. Old Russian or "patriotic" factions arose to counter Westernizing influences, and in the midst of such opposition the emperor's new bureaucracy often weakened under the strain. Subsequent rulers often found the opposition too strong to control. Succession to the throne was many times in dispute, palace revolutions were frequent, selfishness and corruption infected the administration, and the government tended to become an autocracy tempered by assassination.

But, in spite of internal troubles, Russia's emergence as a great power marked a great change in the northlands. In turn, Poland had lost much of its territory and had become paralyzed by its anarchical constitution; Denmark had been reduced by Sweden's separation; Sweden had yielded place to Russia, the new great power of the north. Closely related to these events were alterations in central and eastern Europe.

2 : Central and Southeast Europe—Hohenzollern and Habsburg

To THE SOUTH and east of the Baltic Sea Prussia rose as a kingdom at the expense of Poland, Sweden, and the princes of the German Empire. Its architects were members of the House of Hohenzollern, a German royal family which originated in Swabia (Suabia). Its territorial beginnings date from the union of Brandenburg, a German frontier district which lay between the Elbe and the Oder rivers, and remnants of the state of the Teutonic Knights. Brandenburg was conferred by the German emperor on Frederick of Hohenzollern in 1415, and the latter became founder of the royal Prussian family, Elector and Margrave of Brandenburg.

THE RISE OF PRUSSIA

The Teutonic Knights originated as a military and religious order of knighthood during the crusades (1198). When the crusades failed, the Knights transferred their activities to the east German frontier and became pioneer conquerors in the earliest German *Drang nach Osten* ("pressure toward the East") against the Slavs. They held their conquests as fiefs of the church, with the Pope as their only overlord, and they won great conquests along the Baltic shores. Gradually, they lost their crusading ardor and became a powerful military and commercial corporation of great wealth. They wrested territories from Poland and Lithuania and aroused

IVAN III

IVAN IV

MICHAEL ROMANOV

PETER THE GREAT

The tsars pictured here represent various stages in the emergence of Russia as a European national state. Ivan III, "the Great," Russia's first national monarch, freed Russia from the Tartars, expanded her territories, and strove to make Moscow the "Third Rome." Ivan IV, "the Terrible," placed the nobility in the tsar's service. Michael Romanov was the founder of the Romanov Dynasty, which ruled Russia for three centuries. Peter I, "the Great," the huge, cruel, unconventional tsar who founded the Russian navy, also established St. Petersburg (now Leningrad), won Russia's "Window on the Baltic," and by his prowess during the Great Northern War made Russia a permanent and prominent factor on the European scene.

THE GRABEN, VIENNA

FREDERICK WILLIAM OF HOHENZOLLERN

*Frederick William, the "Great Elector,"
inaugurated policies in Brandenburg-
Prussia which, as applied by him and his
successors, elevated Prussia to the rank of
a great power a century later. Leopold I,
the "Little Emperor in Red Stockings,"
repelled the last Turkish attack upon
Europe, extended Habsburg domains,
and asserted dynastic ascendancy in the
multinational Holy Roman Empire. The
Graben, or moat, was the southwest
boundary of medieval Vienna, the legendary dividing line between East and West.
As the city expanded, the moat was filled
in and became a busy commercial street,
as this eighteenth-century engraving
shows. The monument is the Trinity Column* (Pestsaüle), *erected by Leopold I in
gratitude for the cessation of the plague
in 1679.*

LEOPOLD I OF HABSBURG

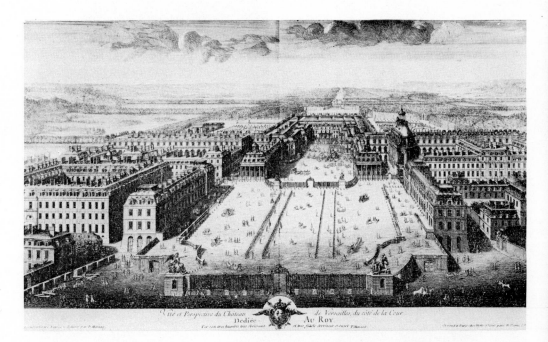

THE PALACE OF VERSAILLES

LOUIS XIV

The heavy impact of Louis XIV stemmed partly from his genuine capacity as a statesman and partly from his ability to act the role of the "Sun King" upon a magnificent stage of his own setting. This painting is by Hyacinthe Rigaud, a favored portraitist who exactly met the taste of the king and the French court. The Palace of Versailles, into which Louis and his court moved in 1682, is outside Paris. The enormous Baroque establishment was overseen during its construction by Louis XIV himself, and it served superbly as a symbol of the magnificence and power of the king both at home and abroad.

CHARLES II

CHARLES I

OLIVER CROMWELL

WILLIAM III

Here are four of the principal figures of the English Revolution of the seventeenth century. Charles I, whose stubborn absolutism and impolitic measures brought his head to the block in 1649, was often painted by Sir Anthony Van Dyke, Flemish-born court artist and a masterful delineator of high society. Oliver Cromwell, the Independents' leader, became Lord Protector during the Interregnum. Charles II always dated his reign from the death of his father, but actually ruled only from the Restoration in 1660. This portrait is by John Michael Wright. William of Orange and his queen Mary II succeeded to the English throne with limited power after the Glorious Revolution of 1688.

such opposition that, finally, in 1466 they were defeated by their enemies and their conquests divided. West Prussia became Polish and East Prussia remained with the Knights as a fief, no longer of the Pope but of the king of Poland. Not long afterwards, in 1525, the grand master of the order, Albert of Hohenzollern—a member of the same family that ruled in Brandenburg—became a Lutheran. With consent of the king of Poland, he proclaimed himself hereditary Duke of Prussia. Less than a century later this ducal house became extinct, and in 1618 John Sigismund, Elector of Brandenburg, inherited the duchy of East Prussia as a fief of the king

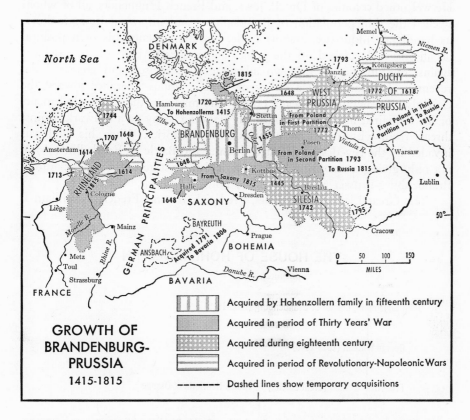

GROWTH OF
BRANDENBURG-
PRUSSIA

1415-1815

|||||| Acquired by Hohenzollern family in fifteenth century

Acquired in period of Thirty Years' War

Acquired during eighteenth century

Acquired in period of Revolutionary-Napoleonic Wars

------ Dashed lines show temporary acquisitions

of Poland. Almost simultaneously he also inherited the principalities of Cleves, Mark, and Ravensberg in west Germany near the Dutch border. Thus the Hohenzollerns of Brandenburg possessed disjointed, widely dispersed territories, part of which they held as electors, margraves, and princes of the Holy Roman Empire and part of which they held in fief from the kings of Poland.

Brandenburg-Prussia was elevated to a new position of importance during the long and constructive reign of Frederick William (1640–1688), "the Great Elector." He took an active part in the latter stages of the

Thirty Years' War and, as we have seen above (page 127), won additional territories by the Treaties of Westphalia. Using the greater freedom of action accorded princes of the empire by the Westphalian settlement, Frederick William organized a permanent army during the 1650's and used his forces with profit in the First Northern War. Joining with Sweden against Poland (1656), he was later persuaded to desert the Swedes and ally with the Poles in return for the Polish king's recognition of his sovereign authority in East Prussia (1660). The Great Elector was an able administrator, and he took pains to strengthen the economy of his domains. He welcomed colonies of Dutch, Jews, and French Huguenots, all of whom swelled the thin population of Brandenburg and improved its agriculture, its handicraft industries, and its trade. He strengthened his own position on all sides. He played off the nobles and estates of his various provinces against one another to his own advantage; he revised and increased the revenues; he maintained a policy of wide religious tolerance toward the Calvinists, Lutherans, Jews, and others who made up the scattered elements of his domains; and he developed his standing army as a bulwark against threats from within and from outside his territories. When his land was invaded by the Swedes he defeated them at the Battle of Fehrbellin (1675), not only giving a smashing blow to Swedish prestige but also proclaiming Brandenburg-Prussia as a new Baltic power of consequence.

The Great Elector's successors, Frederick III and Frederick William I,

THE HOUSE OF HOHENZOLLERN

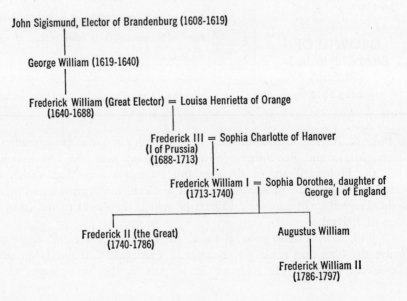

John Sigismund, Elector of Brandenburg (1608-1619)

George William (1619-1640)

Frederick William (Great Elector) = Louisa Henrietta of Orange
(1640-1688)

Frederick III = Sophia Charlotte of Hanover
(I of Prussia)
(1688-1713)

Frederick William I = Sophia Dorothea, daughter of
(1713-1740)　　　George I of England

Frederick II (the Great)
(1740-1786)

Augustus William

Frederick William II
(1786-1797)

were very different from each other, although each in his own way contributed further to the strength and prestige of their dynasty. Frederick III was weak and ill-formed in body, vain and excessively fond of pomp and ceremony, and, like Louis XIV of France (whom he imitated as much as he could), a liberal patron of arts and learning. His second queen, Sophia Charlotte of Hanover, was one of the most cultured and attractive women of her day, and she lent both grace and sincerity to the tinsel court of Frederick. But the latter did found the University of Halle (1694), the Academy of Arts (1696), and the Academy of Sciences (1701), the last being principally the handiwork of the famous mathematician and philosopher, Baron Gottfried Wilhelm von Leibnitz, a close friend of the queen and patronized by the court for many years. Thus the court at Berlin came to be known as the "Versailles of the North," lending prestige to Brandenburg-Prussia and to the House of Hohenzollern. Of even greater political importance, however, was the imperial recognition of the elector as King in Prussia. The Great Elector had freed himself from the overlordship of the Polish crown, but he was unable to win recognition as king from the Habsburgs and the Holy Roman Empire. In 1701, however, a great new war with France threatened the empire and the emperor had serious need of Hohenzollern support. Then the Elector Frederick III won, as the price of his assistance, imperial recognition of his title as Frederick I, King in Prussia. On January 18, 1701, at a typically extravagant ceremony at Königsberg the new king was formally crowned. Thereafter Frederick I and his successors used the new title in preference to their less independent ones as electoral princes in the empire.

Frederick William I, who succeeded his father, Frederick I, as King in Prussia (1713–1740) had no patience with the costly court. Frederick William was a hard-driving, puritanical, irascible, efficient militarist and believer in royal absolutism: "Salvation belongs to the Lord," he said, "everything else is my affair." In most respects, he resumed and broadened the policies of the Great Elector but with an ever more consuming passion for a great standing army, toward whose creation and maintenance he directed his every action. He was not warlike: "My maxim," he said, "is to injure no one, but not to let myself be slighted." His only territorial acquisition was Stettin, at the mouth of the Oder, by the Treaty of Nystadt. His greatest achievements lay in his internal reforms and his efficient, hard-working, disciplined administration. Like the Great Elector, and with a far better eye for detail, he promoted immigration in order to enlarge Prussian population, industry, agriculture, trade—and taxable wealth. He regulated commerce and industry closely in order to reduce imports, encourage exports, and improve the quality of Prussian goods. Though he gave no support to arts and learning as his father had done, he did set up an elementary school system and establish compulsory schooling for children. By the General Directory of 1723 he reorganized the central administration under four departments, or ministries, whose heads reported directly to him. Also, he exercised extreme diligence to insure that each department, down to its local agents, was staffed with honest, capable, and industrious persons. Indeed, he instituted training programs and required examinations to determine the fitness of his servants for office, thereby pioneering in setting up in Prussia a civil service which outperformed that of every other Western state by its integrity, loyalty, and efficiency. The king centralized and improved the administration of justice by creating a royal central court of appeals (*Kammergericht*) at Berlin.

But Frederick William's primary objective was his army. He enlarged it to more than 80,000 men, the third largest in Europe after Russia and France, and far greater than either of these in proportion to the population and resources of his country. The proportions of cavalry and artillery were enlarged, and by elaborate drill and faultless discipline, together with some technical improvements in the arms, the fire power of the infantry was enhanced. As much as possible, the army was conscripted in Prussian territories, although about half was recruited abroad. Frederick William resorted to every device to gain recruits of fine physique, and his famous Potsdam Guard, made up of the tallest men the king could kidnap or otherwise bring into his service, was the military showpiece of Europe. In spite of the enormous cost of his military establishment, the king managed by enlargement of revenues, strict economy in other departments, and careful oversight of all not only to pay the costs, but also to leave a very full treasury at his death. Indeed, Frederick William conscripted, besides his soldiers, the entire resources of his country for the maintenance of his army. And just as he infected the latter with a spit-and-polish discipline of a most exacting sort, so he infected his civilian administration with a militaristic organization and a militaristic efficiency and spirit for which the term "Prussian" has become almost synonymous. Frederick William set up an absolutist rule that left an indelible mark upon the Prussian state. And he alone created the means whereby Prussia became a great power in the hands of his son, Frederick the Great.

THE REVIVAL OF THE AUSTRIAN HABSBURGS

The provisions of the Treaties of Westphalia left the Austrian Habsburgs in a singularly impotent position. Though they remained emperors of the Holy Roman Empire, the office was nominally elective, not hereditary, and the emperor had never been able to effect that centralization of administration and that financial independence from the estates which characterized their rivals in France. They could seldom effectively influence the Diet of the empire, and they were in rivalry with princes whose powers might—as in the case of the kings in Prussia—seriously challenge that of the emperors themselves. Yet, by the end of the seventeenth century the Austrian Habsburgs created a new and powerful dynasty still at the head of the loosely-jointed German Empire, but resting upon new sources of hereditary strength mostly outside the German states themselves. Into the power vacuum of the German Empire they introduced a new authority which proved capable of governing a mass of polyglot states until well into the nineteenth century, and held on until the end of the First World War in 1918.

The story of the creation of this new dynastic power is complicated, and we are compelled to ignore many details. Its broad aspects included a number of more or less constant factors. There was a revitalized Turkish threat, and a community of interests of the Austrians, Poles, Russians, and Venetians in opposing Turkish conquest in Europe. The German states showed a familiar tendency to close ranks in the face of foreign danger. The Polish "republic" continued to decay, with foreign powers winning more and more influence on its internal politics, the selection of its kings, and the direction of its policies. There were complications in Transylvania and Hungary, where Protestants preferred Turkish toleration with tribute to Habsburg rule with Jesuit intolerance, and where local "kings" often played opposing forces against one another to maintain themselves in power. Finally, France's Bourbon king, Louis XIV, who acquired extraordinary prestige in European affairs during the latter half of the seventeenth century, retained his predecessors' rivalry with the Habsburgs, and kept up friendly relations with Turkey as well as an interest in the Polish succession left over from the days of Henry of Valois. Out of the interplay of these factors the Austrian Habsburgs extended their hereditary domains so that they could balance their strength successfully against the divided forces of the German Empire and also play a role in European affairs suitable to a great power.

LEOPOLD I AND THE TURKS

The Habsburg revival began soon after the Thirty Years' War and during the relatively long reign of Emperor Leopold I (1658–1705). Known as the "Little Emperor in Red Stockings," because of his small stature and penchant for Spanish dress, Leopold was Jesuit-trained, pious, virtuous, and devoted to music and book collecting. He was active in the performance of his imperial duties, but he lacked political sharpness and initiative. His court and his policies were Jesuit-ridden and he was especially determined to free his personal domains of Protestantism—as had been accomplished in Bohemia during the latter years of the Thirty Years' War. Leopold I's reign coincided almost exactly with a momentary rejuvenation of Turkish power.

In 1656, as a result of a palace revolution, Mohammed Kiuprili emerged as grand vizier of Turkey and mounted a new attack upon southeastern Europe which lasted, with interruptions, until near the end of Leopold's reign. Mohammed restored discipline to the Turkish army, purged the court of its foppish malingerers, and restored vitality to Turkish finances. The Kiuprilis, including his son Ahmed (1661–1678) and other members of the family, recalled the days of Suleiman the Magnificent, although the Turkish capacities were no longer as great and their arms and armies were no longer technically equal to those of the European powers. Mohammed launched a vigorous attack upon Venice and restored Turkish control over Transylvania, whose deposed "king" appealed to Austria for aid. In 1663 the Turks attacked the German Empire and threatened all of Hungary. The Hungarians, proud, independent, and still Protestant, had not hitherto relished Habsburg rule but they now rallied to Leopold's banner. All Europe was again aroused by the Turks' successes.

The struggle continued with interruptions and shifting European alliances until almost the end of the century. Its most impressive events were the defeat of the Turks at the Battle of St. Gotthard by the imperial commander, Count Montecuccoli, in 1664, and the deliverance of Vienna from a long and terrifying Turkish siege in 1683. The latter was the high point of the Turkish advance into Europe, and the Austrian capital was almost starved into submission before John Sobieski, the king of Poland, with a combined force of Polish and German soldiers routed the besieging Turks and rescued Vienna from the Ottoman's grasp.

The next year Austria, Poland, and Venice joined in a Holy League sponsored by the Pope and began to roll back the Turks. The Austrians bore the brunt of the war and captured the greatest spoils. In 1686 they captured Buda, in 1687 all of Hungary, in 1688 Belgrade. Even when Louis XIV raised up a new war in the west (the War of the League of Augsburg, 1688–1697) and forced Leopold to look to his imperial defences there, the Turks were unable to recoup their losses in southeastern Europe, although they did recapture Belgrade. Russian attacks in the Crimea partially compensated for the Austrian slackening, however, and in 1696, as we have seen, Peter the Great captured Azov. The next year the Austrians, freed in the west, defeated the Turks at Zenta and within two years the Turks sued for peace. By the Treaty of Karlowitz in 1699, Leopold I received almost all of Hungary, Transylvania, Croatia, and Slavonia; Venice acquired the Morea and most of Dalmatia; and Poland obtained Podolia and most of the western Ukraine.

THE TREATY OF KARLOWITZ

The Peace of Karlowitz was a landmark in the development of the Austrian House of Habsburg. Already in 1688 the Hungarian Diet, brought to its knees by the Austrian successes, had declared the Hungarian crown to be hereditary thereafter in the Habsburg family. Later the same year Habsburg suzerainty was acknowledged by the Transylvanians. Thus by 1699 the Austrian House of Habsburg had extended its hereditary lands so that they included three principal possessions with traditional appanages. Leopold I was Archduke of Austria, which included Upper and Lower Austria, Tyrol, Styria, Carinthia, and Carniola; he was King of Bohemia, which included the adjoining territories of Silesia and Moravia; and he was King of Hungary, which included the conquered territories of Croatia and Slavonia, and suzerainty of Transylvania. Simultaneously, of course, Leopold I remained Holy Roman Emperor. After 1699 he and his successors possessed vast hereditary resources outside the empire with which to enforce their policies over German states and maintain an active ascendancy in German affairs.

Over their multinational empire the Habsburgs were the only unifying focal point. No central Diet was created; the several provincial Diets were retained. These were essentially assemblies of great landlords with certain powers over taxation and administration and a satisfying sense of medieval particularism. As long as they supplied taxes and soldiers to the Habsburgs and accepted their leadership in foreign affairs, they were left alone. The peasants were left adrift so far as the Habsburgs were concerned, and they generally sank into serfdom under the rapacious demands of the landlords. The government was of, by, and for the landed aristocracy, and the court at Vienna was a cosmopolitan society of Bohemian (Czech), Hungarian, Croatian, and other noblemen who served the Habsburg monarchy in its army and in the various governmental administrations. However, exclusive favor was given to Roman Catholics, and the Habsburgs used every means to stamp out Protestantism. Jesuit missionaries poured into the newly-acquired possessions, Protestants were persecuted in a variety of ways, and the lands were settled with German Catholics with special privileges in order to loosen the Protestant grip. For the most part, it was destroyed. Just as the Bohemians had been recovered for Catholicism after the Thirty Years' War, so the Hungarians and the Transylvanians were dragged back into the church, forced into exile, or executed on some trumped-up charges of disloyalty. To be considered loyal to the Habsburg crown and free from suspicion of pro-Turkish sympathies, a subject in the new Habsburg lands was forced to forego the Protestant faith. In most instances, the people of the subject states parted with their religion, but they retained a fierce localism which in time developed into intense nationalism. And the Habsburg Dynasty continued to consist of a polylingual, multinational group of peoples never molded into a single national state. Yet it served to raise the Habsburgs into high rank among the dynasties of the eighteenth century. After the Peace of Karlowitz they were able to pursue new designs in the west and to win additional territories. These pertained immediately to the War of Spanish Succession, which in turn directs our attention to the Age of Louis XIV in France.

3 : Western Europe—the Age of Louis XIV

DURING THE LONG REIGN of Louis XIV (1643–1715) France became the very hub of monarchic absolutism and the dominant power of Europe. Her dominance extended into many realms. The French tongue became the language of diplomacy and of polite society. French fashions in dress, in social manners, in the dance, the theater, music, poetry, and other arts became the models imitated everywhere in Europe. In fact, France won an ascendancy which, in some areas, has never been wholly relinquished. In his own day the French king became downright ubiquitous in the eyes of his contemporaries, for he seemed to be everywhere with a finger in the affairs of everybody in Europe, in the Near East, in America, and in the Orient. His court was the most magnificent, his arts and crafts the best in materials and design, his armies the most formidable, and his diplomacy the most far-flung, the most deeply contrived, and the most successful. Behind the extraordinary accomplishments were not only the patient, methodical, hardworking king and his skillful ministers but also preparations and policies which reached back to the first Bourbon king of France, Henry IV.

THE PRECURSORS OF LOUIS XIV

Louis XIII, son of Henry IV, was only nine years old when his father was assassinated in 1610. His mother, Marie de' Medici, became regent, and for several years French affairs were at the mercy of her favorites and conspiring nobles. Happily, in 1624 Louis XIII, who had neither interest nor capacity in public affairs, hit upon Armand Jean du Plessis, Cardinal-Duke of Richelieu (1585–1642), who obtained control and kept it until his death. A practical, loyal, hard-headed man, Richelieu was dedicated to the enlargement of the royal power at home and to an anti-Habsburg policy abroad. In each of three areas he strengthened the monarchy. He reduced the power of the nobles by forcing the destruction of their castle strongholds and forbidding them to build fortified places anew. When the Huguenots revolted (1625) and won naval support from England, the cardinal subjugated them (1628) and revised the Edict of Nantes so that Huguenots no longer could bear arms and hold fortified places, although their toleration as a sect was undisturbed. Thus he corrected a dangerous situation already noted (page 103), and for the most part the Huguenots were content. To deprive the nobles of still more local powers and to centralize royal administration, Richelieu extended the *intendant system*. The royal council had long employed lawyers and others as *masters of petitions* who, armed with royal

THE HOUSE OF BOURBON

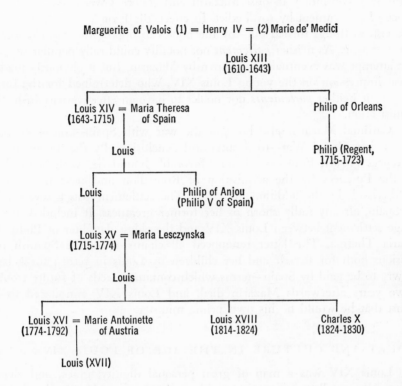

authority, visited the provinces to oversee the local police, justice, and finance. Richelieu made them a regular part of the royal machinery, assigned to fixed districts or intendancies, and acting in the name of the king, to whom they were solely responsible. Thus they supplanted the nobles in many of their local functions and supplied a direct administrative link between the monarchy and local affairs.

Richelieu's foreign policy was even more significant in the long run. As we have seen, he committed France to the Thirty Years' War as an ally of Sweden, and the French role in the last phase of that struggle added new luster to French arms, won an ascendancy over the Habsburgs of both Spain and Germany, and placed France in a position of pre-eminence in military and diplomatic affairs. The war was brought to a conclusion on France's behalf by Richelieu's hand-picked successor, Jules Cardinal Mazarin (1602–1661), an Italian who became a French citizen and diplomatic aide of Richelieu.

Mazarin's position was challenged soon after the end of the Thirty Years' War. His foreign birth and the reckless expenditures incurred by him and by Richelieu during the war led to a series of uprisings in France between 1648 and 1654 known as the *Fronde*. It began when the *parlement* of Paris resisted the registration of tax edicts and the nobility joined it with arms in a conspiracy to oust Mazarin and restore government by law in place of government by royal edict. In effect, the Fronde was an attempt— the last, as things turned out—by the nobles to oppose the royal power by force of arms. As neither *parlement* nor nobility could rally popular support, the attempt was eventually put down by Mazarin. But it obviously made a great impression on the young Louis XIV, who determined for the future to permit neither *parlements* nor nobles to have an effective part in his administration.

Cardinal Mazarin also brought the war with Spain—continued from the Thirty Years' War—to a successful conclusion. By the Treaty of the Pyrenees (1659), France won more favorable boundaries with Spain, both in the Pyrenees by the acquisition of Roussillon and near the Spanish Netherlands by the addition of Artois. The settlement was a severe blow to Spain, already sadly shorn of her former greatness. It included a marriage settlement between Louis XIV and the eldest daughter of Philip IV, Maria Theresa. The latter renounced all claims upon the Spanish possessions both for herself and her children by Louis in return for a large dowry to be paid by Spain—terms which contained seeds of future trouble. Two years afterwards Mazarin died, and Louis XIV announced to his court that he would be his own prime minister.

COURT AND CULTURE IN THE AGE OF LOUIS XIV

Louis XIV was a man of great personal dignity, grace, and charm, marred by equally great egotism, pride, and arrogance. He was hard working and attentive to the "business of being a king," and he subscribed wholeheartedly to the divine-right theory of kingship which he had been taught in his youth. He exalted his authority and his privileges as a king to the utmost. He adopted the rising sun as his emblem and gloried in the title of *le roi soleil* (the Sun King). If he did not make the statement attributed to him, *l'état, c'est moi* ("I am the state"), it was typical of his attitude.

The palace of Versailles epitomized both the political and cultural tone of the reign of Louis XIV, especially in its service to and glorification of the king. On the site of a former hunting lodge a dozen miles from Paris, Louis XIV constructed a huge palace capable of accommodating thousands of guests and with a staff of nearly fifteen thousand household servants, gardeners, grooms, coachmen, and the like. The palace had an extensive park, including lagoons, gardens, and menagerie, together with stables, coach houses, kennels, and other aristocratic trappings. It took thirty years to build and cost at least a billion dollars translated into present-day currency. It was built in the prevailing Baroque style, supposed to have been founded upon the architecture of ancient Rome but far more massive, artificial, and extravagant, adorned with columns, domes, and sculptured scenes based upon classical mythology or the feats of the king. It was a style originating in Italy, and it was widely imitated in seventeenth-century building—in St. Paul's Cathedral in London, the palaces of the Russian tsars at Peterhof near Leningrad, and public buildings in Vienna, Brussels, and elsewhere. For Versailles, Louis employed a succession of architects, chief of whom were Louis le Vau and Nicolas François Mansart, credited with the mansard roof, which has two slopes, the lower and steeper forming a garret. Charles Lebrun, a painter and decorator, worked eighteen years on the interior decorations of the palace and André Le Nôtre designed the gardens. In 1682 Louis moved his court to Versailles, with a host of fawning nobles, minutely regulated with clocklike precision to the daily regimen of the Sun King, and attending his every move. Here the haughty Condé, who had challenged the king during the Fronde, was happy to serve the king his supper—and thus Louis XIV excelled his predecessors in assigning insignificant tasks to noblemen and in depriving them of political power without destroying their social position. The magnificent court of Versailles was both a monument to the greatness of the Sun King and an instrument of policy.

Louis loved beauty in architecture, painting, literature, music, and the dance. But his love for these things was also an instrument of policy, for he felt that their cultivation was becoming to a great king and furnished a means of enhancing his reputation. Accordingly, the arts and letters of France were often directed toward the glorification of the king, who pensioned the artists and literati while he exercised a firm censorship over their works. Little of the painting was impressive either in style or in technique. Nicolas Poussin and Claude Lorrain (professional name of Claude Gellée) produced landscapes and historical scenes in the grand manner but with indifferent ability and largely imitative of decadent Italian masters. Later in the reign a galaxy of court painters such as Hyacinthe Rigaud and Antoine Watteau painted portraits, court scenes, and pastorales with a surer, more original touch. The Sun King loved dancing, and after he had grown too fat to dance himself he favored the ballet, which Catherine de' Medici had previously introduced from Italy and which still employs for most of its techniques the French terms contrived during its heyday at the French court. Jean Baptiste Lully composed ballet music for Louis and, with Philippe Quinault as librettist, Lully also composed and produced operas for the court and became known as the founder of the French opera.

French literature flourished under Louis' patronage and brought high luster to the French language and letters, although the royal taste and the royal censorship limited its scope and led to the exile of some original but non-conforming authors. The standard of literary excellence was defined by Nicolas-Boileau Despréaux, whose *Art of Poetry* (1674) set forth maxims of aesthetic appreciation based upon the criteria of reason and good sense. Some of the literature, however, by its authors' attempts to win royal approval, resembled the Baroque in architecture in its affectation, artificiality, turgidity, and tendency to emphasize form above content. This was well illustrated by the witty aphorisms of François de la Rochefoucauld, who played upon human frailities like vanity, pride, and self-love to set forth scores of short, elegant, pleasing witticisms, such as: "Old people give good advice by way of consoling themselves for no longer being able to give bad examples"; and "We should rather hear evil spoken of us than nothing at all." Of greater and more lasting merit were the gentle, poetic fables of Jean La Fontaine, whose animals, birds, and insects were prototypes of human beings, filled with worldly wisdom and mild satire on contemporary society—with the lion, appropriately, representing the Sun King. La Fontaine's *Novels* and *Tales,* however, were of a different nature, being as licentious as the *Fables* were pure, though couched in delicate language (which suggests that delicacy appertained more to manners than to morals).

Drama was the crowning glory of French literature in the Age of Louis XIV. At least three dramatists won lasting fame: Pierre Corneille, Jean Racine, and Jean Baptiste Poquelin, the last being better known by his pen name Molière. Their style for the most part was classical and, as they wrote almost solely for the court, they were polished, sophisticated, and often artificial. Corneille and Racine wrote tragedies more than anything else. Corneille's plays generally extolled lofty sentiments and taught lessons in morality and patriotism; Racine, whose poetic style was superb, cloyed the court with plays of love and tender sentimentality. Molière, however, was primarily a writer of satirical comedies, with a mocking attitude and a grasp of the subtleties of human nature which elevated him to the first rank of dramatists. The son of a valet of Louis XIII, Molière roamed the country for years with a company of players before he attracted attention of the Sun King. He wrote and produced his own plays at court; most of them poked fun at the vanity, the avarice, the hypocrisy, or the pomposity of the contemporary scene. Indeed, Molière's capacity to make the French courtiers laugh at their own foibles without arousing their anger has often been cited as an extraordinary feature of his career.

Much French prose, if we exclude scholarly works, reserved for later treatment, was anecdotal or polemical in nature. Madame de Sévigné wrote charming *Letters* to her daughter with gossip, occasionally fine pen-portraits of courtiers, and tiring motherly solicitude. The Duc de St.-Simon prepared lengthy, highly descriptive, and sometimes biased *Memoirs* of the latter years of the reign of Louis XIV, whom St.-Simon often criticized severely. Fénelon, who long basked in the favor of Louis XIV as tutor to the king's grandson and as a prelate in the church, was disgraced when his *Télémaque* was interpreted as a satire upon the king and his policies, although *Télémaque* is today looked upon as a classical romance incorporating some of the finest French poetry of the age. Pierre Bayle, a Huguenot who turned sceptic, found it necessary to flee from France, and he migrated to Holland where he became a leading advocate of religious toleration and freedom of thought. His greatest work, the *Historical and Critical Dictionary* (1697), was both a shattering criticism of dogmatic Christianity and an early forerunner of the French encyclopedists of the eighteenth century. Bayle himself was a founder of the French school of rationalism and exerted great influence upon Voltaire and Diderot, both important publicists and promoters of the Enlightenment in the eighteenth century.

LOUIS XIV AND FRENCH ABSOLUTISM

The government of Louis XIV operated through four principal *councils of state*—War, Finance, Foreign Policy, and Interior—whose ministers were responsible only to the king. They had little place in policy making, for while Louis accepted advice, he made all decisions himself—or at least as far as he was able. From the councils down ran a fairly direct chain of command—interrupted at points by special provisions or overlooked feudal institutions—to the intendants, the number of which Louis gradually enlarged until their administrative units included all of France. From the intendants the command ran down to towns, villages, and rural communes. Alongside the royal administration, like disused furniture cluttering up the royal household, existed many local and provincial institutions left over from former ages, feebly operating as and when they could and constantly at hand for those who might dare to reactivate them in case royal authority should falter. Louis never assembled the Estates-General and he ruled by royal edict throughout his reign. The French church co-operated loyally in the union of throne and altar, and the most prominent French churchman, Bishop Jacques Bénique Bossuet (1627–1704), wrote *Politics Drawn from the Words of Holy Scripture* (1678) to justify divine-right absolutism. Louis insisted upon religious unity, however. He intimidated the Huguenots for years, and finally, in 1685, he revoked the Edict of Nantes and required Huguenots to conform to the French Catholic church or leave France. About sixty thousand families fled abroad, to Prussia (where the Great Elector welcomed them), to Holland, to England, and to the British colonies in North America. Many, however, remained in France either to become Catholics or to continue Protestant worship underground. The king's insistence upon religious unity cost France the services of some of its most skilled artisans, scholars, professional men, and merchants.

COLBERT AND MERCANTILISM

The first twenty years of the personal rule of Louis XIV were colored by the policies of Jean Baptiste Colbert (1619–1683), a commoner who rose in the king's service upon the recommendation of Cardinal Mazarin and who became Controller of Finance in 1665. Colbert's views of financial administration embraced not only the tax system but also the entire economic and social structure of the French economy within which the tax structure operated. Colbert subscribed to economic policies often included under the somewhat vague and diffuse denomination of *mercantilism*. Mercantilism was the adaptation by dynastic states of policies practiced earlier by medieval towns and feudal states designed—as circumstances seemed to dictate—to regulate, restrict, and promote economic enterprises toward the ends of self-sufficiency and the enlargement of wealth. Such policies fitted admirably with absolutist government, and the monarchy went far toward state control of the economy by means of tariff manipulations, subsidies, tax exemptions or enlargements, chartered privileges, codes setting forth standards of quality and the like, and state-owned enterprises. Thus the state expanded some enterprises and curtailed others. It carefully regulated the quantities and qualities of goods, especially of those which figured importantly in international trade, and it entered into commercial treaties to extend sales abroad while it curtailed imports as much as possible. It promoted colonial ventures in trade and settlement in order to command raw materials not available at home and to expand markets and the carrying trade of the nation. It encouraged development of a merchant marine with a monopoly of the nation's carrying trade and with a navy to protect and defend it. As basic to its over-all aims, the state sought to promote a favorable balance of trade as widely as possible. Some attention was given to the people's welfare, to wages, and to the quantity, efficiency, and training of labor. But more than a suspicion exists that mercantilists sought to regulate and control the economy mostly to enlarge the people's capacity to bear heavy taxes for support of the royal administration, especially the royal army.

Colbert so perfected his own adaptation of mercantilism to the French economy that his policies are often called "Colbertism." Certainly, he was an indefatigable worker with a broad view of the French economy, a genius for infinite detail, and a surprising grasp of technological and manufacturing processes. His hand was in everything. He set up minute regulations and a corps of inspectors to regulate the kind, the quality, and the quantity of French manufactures. He improved roads, built canals and harbors, rehabilitated the French navy, established (with state funds) trading companies for trade and colonization overseas, and promoted the Academy of Sciences, the Royal Observatory, and other institutions of learning. In reform of the tax structure Colbert abolished local tariffs in a large area of central France called the Five Great Farms, where a tariff union provided one of the largest free-trade areas in Europe; but he was never able to extend it to all of France because vested interests and provincial liberties clung stubbornly to their privileges, and the tolls outside the Five Great Farms remained in the hands of tax farmers.

In all of these things Colbert extended the work begun by Henry IV and continued by Richelieu. Similarly, French overseas colonization was expanded. Cardinal Richelieu had overseen colonizing activities in the West Indies, and French exploration of the Great Lakes region in North America took place in the late 1650's. Colbert stimulated it further by reorganization of the Company of the West Indies, by organization of the Company of the East Indies, and by similar enterprises. Almost simultaneously, French colonies were established in India (Pondicherry, 1674) and Father Marquette and Joliet moved into the Mississippi Valley (1673). La Salle was in the Illinois country before 1680, and by the end of the century French settlements had been set up at New Orleans. Before the close of Louis XIV's reign France had a chain of trading posts and settlements along the St. Lawrence Valley, around the Great Lakes, and down the Mississippi Valley, loosely holding a vast empire in the interior of North America. Yet Colbert's trading companies prospered little. French private capital was not lured into colonial enterprises to any great extent, and the French people failed to respond freely to colonizing plans. Hence the thinly populated settlements in North America; but for state capital and artificial stimulation by the government French colonizing plans would have withered away.

THE WARS OF LOUIS XIV

Colbert's influence went far to fasten upon France a tradition of high-quality products and to strengthen France economically and financially for the demands of the latter part of Louis XIV's reign. In his later years he was eclipsed by the king's war minister, François Michel Le Tellier, Marquis de Louvois (1641–1691), whose aggressive, warlike policies fired the imagination of Louis XIV and encouraged him to undertake belligerent courses far removed from the pacific, constructive polices of Colbert. Indeed,

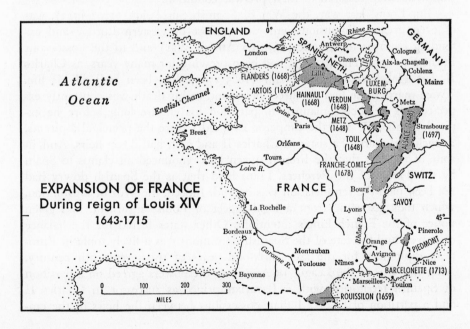

EXPANSION OF FRANCE
During reign of Louis XIV
1643-1715

the king had always nurtured visions of military greatness, and during the course of his personal reign he engaged in four wars of increasing magnitude. Until 1700 these wars were continuations of the policies of Richelieu and Mazarin. They were designed to extend French frontiers to the Rhine River and to the Scheldt at the expense of the Habsburgs, to enlarge the overseas empire, to usurp the emperor's position as temporal leader of the Catholic church and, in fact, to win the imperial title for the Sun King himself. Thus in the War of Devolution (1667–1668) Louis won a series of towns and fortresses of the Spanish Netherlands in Brabant and Flanders. In the Dutch War (1672–1678) Louis undertook to overwhelm the United Netherlands in the one war approved by Colbert, who saw in the Dutch France's greatest rival for control of European trade; but the Dutch built a coalition of the Holy Roman Empire, Spain, Sweden, Denmark, and others so that they defended themselves without loss and Louis' only gains were at Spain's expense, including Franche-Comté and some more fortresses along the Spanish Netherlands frontier. The War of the League of Augsburg (1688–1697) came in consequence of Louis' vigorous attempts to add further German territories to his realm. After Emperor Leopold expelled the Turks from Austria and was free to take a hand in the west, he joined with Louis' inveterate enemy, William of Orange, who had succeeded to the English throne in 1689; together they constructed a mighty league against the French king that carried the war into North America (King William's War) and Asia. Thus Louis lost some of his fortresses along the Dutch border, granted commercial concessions to the Dutch, and reluctantly recognized William III as the rightful king of England. Most of the colonial conquests were restored to their pre-war condition.

But Louis' last war, the War of Spanish Succession (1702–1713), was of even greater dimensions, embracing most of western Europe and extending overseas to America (Queen Anne's War) and to the possessions in the Far East. The struggle had been brewing for many years, as Charles II, last Habsburg king of Spain (1665–1700), had been frail all his life. Twice married, he had no direct heirs, and as his death was constantly expected, his neighbors planned to partition his empire long before he expired. Louis XIV and the Emperor Leopold I were the principal aspirants, as each had married a sister of Charles II and each had direct heirs. And, in spite of the fact that the French queen had renounced all claims to Spain by the Treaty of the Pyrenees, Louis held that as the Spanish dowry had not been paid the renunciation was invalid. Indeed, the War of Devolution, which took its name from a legal aspect of Louis' argument, had given notice of the French king's intentions. Other states feared for the balance of power, and the fate of the Spanish dominions was a lively topic in European diplomacy for the last thirty-odd years of the seventeenth century. After the War of the League of Augsburg the powers agreed on a partition of Spanish territories, with a Bavarian prince as successor to Charles II and a partition of Spain's Italian possessions between the heirs of the em-

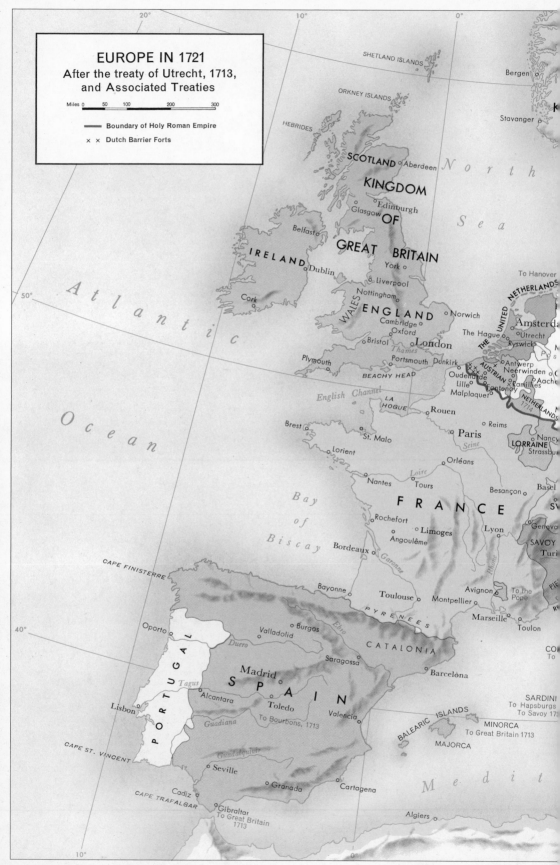

EUROPE IN 1721
After the treaty of Utrecht, 1713,
and Associated Treaties

Miles 0   50   100   200   300

——— Boundary of Holy Roman Empire
× × Dutch Barrier Forts

SHETLAND ISLANDS

Bergen

ORKNEY ISLANDS

North

Stavanger

HEBRIDES

Sea

SCOTLAND   Aberdeen

KINGDOM

Edinburgh
Glasgow

OF

Belfast
IRELAND   GREAT   BRITAIN

Dublin   York

To Hanover

Liverpool   NETHERLANDS
Nottingham   THE UNITED

Norwich   Amsterda

Cork
Cambridge   Utrecht
WALES   ENGLAND   The Hague   Ryswick
Oxford   Pos
Bristol   London   THE
Plymouth   Thames   Antwerp   Neerwinden   Aache
Portsmouth   Dunkirk   AUSTRIAN   Ramillies
BEACHY HEAD   Oudenarde   Fontenoy
Lille   NETHERLANDS
English Channel   LA   Malplaquet   1714
HOGUE   Rouen
Brest   St. Malo   Nancy
Paris   LORRAINE
Reims   Strassbu

Atlantic

Seine

Lorient   Orléans

Nantes   Loire   Besançon   Basel
Tours
Ocean

Bay   Rochefort   FRANCE   Geneva

of   Limoges   Lyon   SAVOY
Angoulême   Turi
Biscay   Bordeaux
Garonne

CAPE FINISTERRE   Avignon   To the   PIE
Bayonne   Pope   R
Toulouse   Montpellier
PYRENEES   Marseille   Toulon

Oporto   Valladolid   Burgos   CATALONIA
Duero   Ebro
Saragossa
Madrid   Barcelona   CO
Tagus   To

LISBON   Alcantara   SPAIN   SARDINI
PORTUGAL   Toledo   To Hapsburgs
Valencia   To Savoy 17
Lisbon   Guadiana   To Bourbons, 1713
MINORCA
BALEARIC ISLANDS   MINORCA
To Great Britain 1713
Seville   Guadalquivir   MAJORCA

Cadiz   Granada   Cartagena   Medit
CAPE ST. VINCENT
CAPE TRAFALGAR
Gibraltar   Algiers
To Great Britain
1713

40°

50°

20°   10°   0°

From R. R. Palmer, *Atlas of World History* (Chicago, 1957), pp. 78-79.

KINGDOM OF SWEDEN

FINLAND

Nystad
Abo
Helsingfors
Vibora
L. Ladoga
KARELIA
St. Petersburg
Uppsala
Stockholm
Narva
INGRIA
Novgorod
Gulf of Finland
ESTONIA
LIVONIA
To Russia
1721
Riga
Dvina
Vitebsk
Smolensk
Moscow

RUSSIAN
EMPIRE

GOTLAND
COURLAND

Baltic

Calmar

Sea

Copenhagen
Lund

Memel
Königsberg
LITHUANIA
Niemen
Vilna
Minsk

To Prussia
1720
Danzig
PRUSSIA
Grodno

Kiev
Kharkov
50°

Hamburg
Stettin
Prussia
Thorn
POLAND

BRANDENBURG
Zorndorf
Berlin
Oder
Posen
Warsaw
Vistula
Lublin
Lemberg
Bar
Targovitza
Poltava

the King

Hanover

SAXONY
Glogau
Leipzig
Dresden
Breslau
SILESIA
Cracow
Dniester

HOLY

ROMAN
Prague
BOHEMIA
MORAVIA
Czernowitz
MOLDAVIA
Cherson

EMPIRE
AUSTRIA
KINGDOM
BESSARABIA
CRIMEA

BAVARIA
Munich
Vienna
Salzburg
Buda
Pest
OF
Pruth
Black

Innsbruck
Danube
HUNGARY
Zenta
Temesvar
TRANSYLVANIA
Sea

TYROL
Drave
Laibach
Agram
BANAT
To Hapsburgs
1718
WALLACHIA
Bucharest

Verona
REPUBLIC
Trieste
CROATIA
SLAVONIA
Karlowitz
Silistria

Venice
Belgrade
Passarowitz
Danube

Modena
Bologna
OF
BOSNIA
To Hapsburgs 1718-1739

Florence
PAPAL
Sarajevo
SERBIA
Nish
BULGARIA

TUSCANY
Tolentino
Ragusa
Sofia
OTTOMAN

Rome
STATES
MONTENEGRO
Adrianople
Constantinople
40°

KINGDOM
Bari
EMPIRE

OF
Salonika

NAPLES
To Hapsburgs
1714-1735
Otranto

Naples
CORFU
(CORCYRA)
Aegean

Tyrrhenian
Athens
Sea
Smyrna

Sea

Palermo
Reggio
MOREA
To
Ottoman
Empire
1718

Syracuse
SICILY
To Savoy 1714
To Hapsburgs
720-35
CRETE

Sea

THE SPANISH HABSBURGS

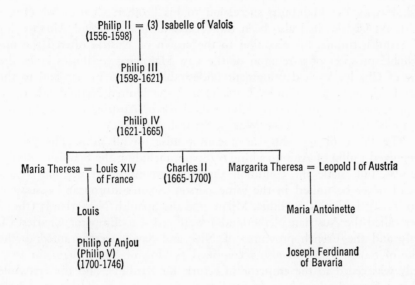

Philip II = (3) Isabelle of Valois
(1556-1598)

Philip III
(1598-1621)

Philip IV
(1621-1665)

Maria Theresa = Louis XIV of France   Charles II (1665-1700)   Margarita Theresa = Leopold I of Austria

Louis

Philip of Anjou
(Philip V)
(1700-1746)

Maria Antoinette

Joseph Ferdinand
of Bavaria

peror of the king of France. But the Bavarian prince died a few months later and new plans were made to partition the Spanish territories between Habsburgs and Bourbons. However, Charles II of Spain, still alive and exasperated by the partition plans, made a will granting his lands intact to Philip of Anjou, grandson of Louis XIV. Soon afterwards Charles II died, and Louis XIV, although he had previously agreed to a partition, was unable to withstand the temptation. Dramatically, he held a full court and formally greeted his grandson as king of Spain. While Philip of Anjou prepared to assume his new duties as Philip V, first Bourbon king of Spain, William III of England with Austria, the United Netherlands, Prussia, most of the German states, Denmark, Sweden, and a few other states joined in opposition.

A bloody war followed, beginning in 1702 and lasting for eleven years. William III died before the war got under way. He was succeeded on the English throne by Queen Anne (1702-1714) and in the military leadership of the Grand Alliance by John Churchill, Duke of Marlborough, an ancestor of Sir Winston Churchill. Marlborough and Prince Eugene of Savoy, a French-born general famed for his leadership of the armies of Leopold I of Austria, gradually wore down the Bourbons. The English captured Minorca and Gibraltar from Spain, and overran the French North American colonies of Newfoundland, Acadia (Nova Scotia), and Hudson's Bay territory. And in four great European battles—Blenheim (1704), Ramillies (1706), Oudenarde (1708), and Malplaquet (1709)—the French were defeated. But the Bourbons still could field an army, and the Grand Alliance

175

was weakening. English Whig ministers who had supported Marlborough and the war were displaced by Tories who favored peace (1710). In 1711 the Habsburg Emperor Joseph I, who had succeeded Leopold I in 1705, died, leaving the Habsburg succession to his brother, Charles VI (1711–1740). As Charles had also been the candidate of the Grand Alliance for the Spanish throne, his accession to the crown of Austria offered the unpalatable prospect of a reunion of the vast Habsburg territories as in the time of Charles V—a development undesirable both to France and to the Grand Alliance. Accordingly, England and the United Netherlands came to an agreement with France behind the back of Austria, and in 1713 the Treaty of Utrecht ended the War of Spanish Succession.

The Peace of Utrecht was a compromise on all sides. The powers recognized Philip of Anjou as king of Spain, including the Spanish colonies overseas, but made the condition that the crowns of France and Spain should never be united in the same person. Spain's European possessions were divided. Naples, Sardinia, Milan, and the Spanish Netherlands (thereafter called the Austrian Netherlands) were ceded to Emperor Charles VI. Sicily and the French provinces of Nice and Savoy were granted to the duke of Savoy who was also recognized as king of Sicily (later, in 1720, Sicily was ceded to the emperor in return for Sardinia, and the erstwhile duke of Savoy became king of Sardinia, a forerunner of the kings of Italy in the nineteenth century). The elector of Brandenburg, who had assumed the title of King in Prussia, was confirmed in his new title and rewarded with Spanish Gelderland for his assistance to the Grand Alliance. The United Netherlands won commercial concessions from France, a monopoly of trade on the Scheldt River, and a series of barrier fortresses against France as well as financial aid from the Austrian Netherlands for their support. England, as it appears in retrospect, won considerable territory and commercial advantages over her rivals. From Spain, England won Gibraltar, which she has kept to this day, and Minorca, which was later handed back. The English also gained trade concessions from Spain, including preferential tariffs for English imports into Spain at Cadiz, the *Asiento* (a contractual monopoly of the slave trade in Spanish colonies, which was given to the English Royal African Company), and the right to send each year one shipload of English goods into the Spanish colonies of America, thereby breaking into the jealously guarded Spanish monopoly of colonial commerce. From France, England won recognition of George I as lawful heir to the English throne after the death of Queen Anne, which occurred soon after (1714). And from the French colonies of North America, England won Newfoundland, Nova Scotia, and the Hudson's Bay territory. These, together with commercial concessions from Spain, sparked the rise of England's commercial and colonial ascendancy in the later eighteenth century.

Louis XIV was an old man of seventy-six when the War of Spanish Succession ended, and he lived only two years afterwards. During his reign

France won an unprecedented ascendancy in European affairs, both politically and culturally. Yet the Sun King's ambitions led him to attempt more than any one man could accomplish, both in his government at home and in the foreign field. His later wars were ruinously costly and wiped out the prosperous days of Colbert. Taxes had multiplied while the government suffered ever larger debts. The peasantry was taxed beyond all reason; the middle class was impoverished; the nobility was emasculated as a political force; and the clergy was subservient to the crown. The Sun King's arrogance, conceit, and unbending pride rendered him impervious to criticism and to advice contrary to his own headstrong courses. Criticisms were voiced, and even printed, but the critics, if found, won only disgrace and imprisonment or exile for their pains. Yet, Louis must have recognized some of the errors of his ways if, as was reported, he called to his bedside his five-year-old great-grandson and successor (Louis XV) and, with the seriousness of a dying man, warned him, "Do not imitate me in my taste for war."

4 : Curbs to Dynastic Absolutism

IN THE MIDST of the tightening dynastic absolutism in the seventeenth century two states staged dramatic rejections of it. One was the Dutch Republic, which would have neither strong monarchy nor centralized administration. The other was England which, while retaining centralization, rejected monarchic absolutism. The first, by its unrivaled commercial prosperity and "golden age" of art and literature, aroused the envy of crowned heads (Peter the Great visited it in person to study it; Louis XIV tried to crush it). The second, after almost a century of intermittent revolution, decapitated one king, exiled another, set up parliamentary supremacy in place of divine-right absolutism, and left a legacy of revolutionary doctrine which has influenced the course of revolutions to this day.

THE DUTCH REPUBLIC

Louis XIV's great minister Colbert wrote a memorial to the king in 1669 in which he declared that

> after a very exact examination it can be stated with certainty that the trade of all Europe is carried on with about 20,000 ships of all sizes; and . . . of this number of 20,000 vessels, the Dutch possess 15,000 to 16,000, the English 3,000 to 4,000, and the French 500 to 600 . . . .

Colbert's statistics may be questioned, but the relative importance of the Dutch carrying trade was correctly estimated. This is the more surprising when it is recalled that the Dutch had only won final recognition of their independence from Spain in 1648, and that between the Treaties of West-phalia and the end of the War of Spanish Succession the Dutch fought two naval wars with England, a colonial war with Portugal, and three wars with France—the Dutch stadtholder William III, serving as architect both of the League of Augsburg and later, as king of England, of the Grand Coalition against Louis XIV.

This "little band of merchants lost on a pile of mud" organized a loose union of states with a republican form of government. They developed a system which resembled that of the later federal union of the United States of America. Each of the several Dutch states had a local legislature and also sent representatives to a federal body called the States-General. The federal executive was called the *stadtholder* and, while this position was held by representatives of the noble House of Orange, all attempts to assert monarchic supremacy and to centralize administration were firmly resisted. Yet the republic was not democratic, for the franchise was limited to the wealthy burghers who, in reality, formed an oligarchic governing class.

These burghers developed an unrivaled commercial power. After Philip II of Spain succeeded to the Portuguese throne (1580) Lisbon, which had hitherto been a major center of Dutch commerce, was closed to the Dutch. Forced to turn elsewhere, they moved into the Far East and the New World. In 1602 the Dutch East India Company was chartered, with unusual authority to establish colonies, maintain armed forces, make war and peace, coin money, and wield full administrative control over its overseas possessions. It became the major instrument for Dutch colonial trade expansion, colonization, and prosperity. It drove the Portuguese and the English out of the Spice Islands, set up a colony at Batavia (1619), at the Cape of Good Hope (1652), and in Sumatra (1667), and established the only continuing link between Japan and the West until the mid-nineteenth century. Its governor-general, Anton van Diemen (1593–1645), and his great mariner and Far Eastern explorer, Abel Janszoon Tasman (1603–1659), both left their names in the South Pacific regions which they explored widely in the early 1640's. In 1621 the Dutch West India Company was chartered with similar powers in the Atlantic trade of Africa and the Americas. But it was somewhat less successful. It set up a Dutch colonial empire in the Caribbean, harassed the Portuguese in Brazil (with whom the Dutch warred from 1657 to 1661), and founded New Amsterdam (now New York), which it lost to the English in 1664. But it never won mastery of the slave trade in Africa nor attained the importance of its sister company in the Far Eastern trade.

This far-flung Dutch empire enabled the Dutch Republic to become the commercial center of Europe in the seventeenth century. Dutch merchants pioneered in new and more efficient methods of building, loading, unloading, and sailing ships, of brokerage, marine insurance, banking, and other commercial pursuits. The Bank of Amsterdam, founded in 1609, was a prime agent in improving methods of international monetary exchange, and Amsterdam was Europe's financial center until the time of Napoleon Bonaparte.

The rich Dutch burghers were lively patrons of scholarship and the arts. Dutch universities, especially Leiden, became renowned in Europe for their work in the fields of law, philosophy, medicine, and the sciences. They were the more attractive because of the broad religious tolerance of the Dutch states, which, though they maintained a state church, the Dutch Reformed church (Calvinist), opened their doors to a wide number of Christian sects and even to some non-Christians, particularly Jews. Leiden developed a reputation in philosophy, law, and medicine which gave it recognition as one of the leading universities in Europe in the seventeenth and early eighteenth centuries, and it attracted foreign students in considerable numbers, including several from the English colonies in America. Its botanical garden was one of the wonders of the age, second only to that of the king of France. Two of Leiden's graduates were among the most renowned scientists of the day, Christian Huygens (1629–1695) and Herman Boorhaave (1668–1738). Huygens was a mathematician, physicist, and astronomer of the first rank. He made many improvements upon optical instruments, devised the first successful pendulum movement for clocks, discovered a satellite of and the rings of Saturn, and was author of the wave theory of light. Boorhaave was a botanist, chemist, physician, and professor of medicine whose renown as a scientist and teacher elevated Leiden to the first rank in medical training.

It was in painting, however, that the Dutch won their greatest cultural prestige. Any observer of seventeenth-century Dutch painting is almost certain to admire the skill with which the Dutch masters portrayed simple, everyday scenes with a reality which make them appear familiar still. Most of the painting was devoted to secular subjects, reflecting the bourgeois tastes of the burgher patrons. Franz Hals and Jan Steen painted portraits, street scenes, and everyday life in the towns and villages with vivacity, humor, high technical skill, and more than a trace of vulgarity. Jan Vermeer, portraying similar subjects with equal, if not greater, skill, displayed somewhat less humor and omitted the vulgar touches. Rembrandt van Rijn was one of the few who did not wholly forsake classical subjects, although he too made portraits and local scenes, surpassing all the others by his arrangement of details and ability to produce dramatic impact by means of lighting effects. These men, with many others of their time, gave the Dutch Renaissance in painting a magnificence recalling that of Florence in the heyday of the Medicis.

The Dutch pre-eminence, however, was of relatively short duration. The British replaced them as masters of the North Sea fisheries, of the African slave trade, and of colonial trade in both America and the Far East. Portugal and Spain, to a lesser degree, did likewise; and Louis XIV launched attacks by land which cost the Dutch sorely. By the time of the Peace of Utrecht (1713) the Dutch commercial ascendancy had begun to wane, and in the eighteenth century it gave way before the English, although Holland continued to be a great colonial, commercial, and financial power until the nineteenth century.

THE ENGLISH REVOLUTION IN THE SEVENTEENTH CENTURY

The internal history of England in the seventeenth century is one of almost constant political and constitutional struggle. It included two civil wars, regicide, and interregnum (1649–1660) with no ruling king, and a bloodless revolution (1688–1689), in which one king fled leaving the throne vacant and another succeeded after accepting limitations upon royal authority at the hands of Parliament. Absolute monarchy, which had never developed in England as it had on the Continent, was further modified until it became limited, constitutional monarchy; and the sovereign powers of the state, hitherto confided to the king in Parliament, passed to Parliament alone. All this proved to be highly significant for the future of representative government, not only in England and her colonies overseas, but also as a blueprint for the establishment of constitutional government with representative bodies in other parts of the world. At the time it took place the English revolution was isolated and did not immediately affect the rest of the world. However, its success in England and England's startling prosperity and pre-eminence in the century that followed catapulted the English constitution and English ways into the limelight in the eighteenth century.

The English revolution unfolded over the space of almost a century, and it roughly coincided with the rule of the House of Stuart (1603–1714), which succeeded the Tudors upon the death of Queen Elizabeth I. Indeed, the Stuarts, by their clumsy and inept management of British crown affairs, contributed heavily to the development of challenges to English royal authority, although, of course, that was far from their intention. Actually, the early Stuarts, James I (1603–1625) and his son, Charles I (1625–1649), were enthusiastic advocates of divine-right absolutism. Both were well-intentioned rulers who, in the midst of difficulties peculiar to England at the time, ran headlong into misunderstandings with Parliaments long since grown heady with a sense of their own importance and authority after more than a century of the Tudors' fawning manipulation. If we lay aside other factors and center attention upon the roles of king and Parliament in the English government as viewed respectively by James I and by parliamentarians, it would seem that a clash was unavoidable. James, who was son of Mary, Queen of Scots, and Henry Stuart, Lord Darnley, had been James VI of Scotland before he succeeded to the English throne. He was author of *The True Law of Free Monarchies* (1598), in which he had expounded the most extravagant claims to divine-right absolutism, and as English king he lectured his first Parliament in 1603 with the words: "I am the husband, and the whole isle is my lawful wife; I am the head, and it is my body." Later he asserted that kings are "God's lieutenants upon earth," and "exer-

THE HOUSE OF STUART

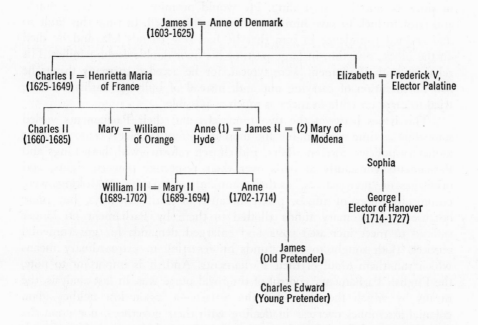

cise a manner or resemblance of divine power upon earth." Compare these words to those of parliamentarians who, for the most part, believed with Sir Thomas Smith's assertion in his *Commonwealth of England* (published in 1589), "The most high and absolute power of the realm of England consisteth in the parliament," which, he said, represented "the whole realm, both the head and body . . . from the prince, be he king or queen, to the lowest person of England!"

Neither James nor Charles understood the English Parliament and neither was capable of manipulating it after the Tudor fashion. Moreover, both exhibited traits of character which further jeopardized their relations with it. James I, an odd, grotesque figure with large rolling eyes, a lolling tongue, and a shuffling gait, was most undignified in appearance; but he possessed a very acute, argumentative mind, was exceedingly well-educated as a scholar, and loved to parade his learning in a pedantic fashion (the "wisest fool in Christendom," said Henry IV of France). Accordingly, he admonished his Parliaments, gave them lessons in king-craft, and warned them that "I must not be taught my office." But his bullying only exasperated parliamentarians. Charles had an even more disastrous effect. Unlike his father, Charles I was a handsome, graceful man with great dignity of bearing and much personal charm. Though well educated, he was less articulate than James and not given to vain pedantry. He possessed an enthusiasm and taste for literature and the arts unsurpassed by his English successors. But he was a poor judge of men, especially of those upon whom he leaned for advice and assistance and, worst of all, he was utterly lacking in sincerity and honest dealing. He would promise anything in a pinch, and trust to luck to save him from keeping his word. In time this fault so undermined confidence in him that he had few friends left, and he died on the block, a victim, in large part, of his own double-dealing follies. His relations with Parliament were typical, for he acceded to many things he had no intention of carrying out and, instead of bullying Parliaments, he tried to carry on without them as much as possible.

The issues between the two monarchs and their Parliaments varied somewhat as time went on, but the most important problems centered about monetary policies, foreign affairs, and church reform—with both kings and Parliaments constantly at odds over their respective powers, rights, and privileges, or "prerogatives," as they commonly called them. Both kings were chronically short of funds, partly because of thriftless ways, but more because the customary funds allotted to them by Parliament no longer sufficed to meet increased costs and enlarged demands for governmental services. Both sought to raise funds by resorting to extraordinary means which ran them afoul of their Parliaments. And, it is important to note, the English Parliaments' control of the royal purse was, in last analysis, the means by which they humbled the Stuarts—a lesson lost neither upon colonial assemblies overseas in dealing with their governors, nor upon the American revolutionists, whose cry, "taxation without representation is tyranny," echoed a long-established principle.

James aroused much opposition because of his foreign policies. James was peace-loving, and his financial troubles fortified his natural bent toward pacific policies. But peace with the Catholic powers, Spain especially, was not popular in England—although the Treaty of London in 1604 established a peace with Spain that made safe (for the moment at least), the Virginia Company's first permanent settlement at Jamestown in 1607. Equally unpopular was James's equivocation when the Thirty Years' War began in 1618. The English people widely supported the king's son-in-law, Frederick, Elector of the Palatinate, after he was chosen king of Bohemia by the Protestants, but James held back and refused to commit England irrevocably in the struggle. Moreover, his attempts to marry his son and heir to the Spanish infanta aroused bitter criticism. When it failed, the English public sighed with relief—but James did little better in their eyes when he arranged a marriage treaty with Richelieu whereby Charles ultimately espoused Henrietta Maria, sister of Louis XIII of France and Roman Catholic to the core. Between Charles and his French consort developed a touching devotion mutually shared, and Henrietta Maria sometimes exhibited better political abilities than the king; but her Catholicism and love of the stage condemned her in the eyes of the Protestant English, especially of the Puritans.

THE PURITANS AND THE EARLY STUARTS

Indeed, the Puritans were the nemesis of both the early Stuarts. Having failed to move Elizabeth I to effect reforms in the English church, they welcomed James I in the belief that, as he had been brought up by the Scottish Presbyterians, he would sympathize with their demands. But James's view of the divine-right monarchy admitted no independence of action on the part of the clergy, and he firmly adhered to English episcopacy, through which the hierarchy was controlled by the crown. "It is my aphorism," he said, "no bishop, no king." Like many absolutist monarchs, he felt that conformity to one state church contributed to the unity of the realm and obedience to the crown. At the Hampton Court Conference of churchmen in 1604, James listened impatiently when Puritan spokesmen pleaded for reform in ceremonies and ecclesiastical government, and finally he cut them off sharply with the words, "If this be all your party have to say, I will make them conform, or I will harry them out of this land, or else worse." English Puritans in Holland, in Caribbean settlements, and in Plymouth Plantation soon knew the sting of the king's words.

After rebuffs from two monarchs the Puritans turned to Parliament. To those parliamentarians who opposed the king on constitutional grounds, hoping to alter the English constitution in favor of greater parliamentary authority, were added others who opposed the king on ecclesiastical grounds, seeking to effect further reforms in the English church by parliamentary action. There was a considerable number of the "political puritans" who were also "religious puritans," but even when the two groups did not coincide they often co-operated against the king. Thus the tensions between king and Parliament mounted. Charles I found his Parliaments even more recalcitrant, critical of royal policy, and unwilling to provide funds. A pattern of opposition emerged: Parliaments drew up remonstrances and grievances to urge ecclesiastical reform, enforcement of laws against Catholics (a slap at Queen Henrietta Maria), protests against unparliamentary taxation, and the like; and they made royal satisfaction of parliamentary grievances the condition upon which royal monetary supplies must depend. Charles, in turn, dissolved Parliament (only to find the next one more demanding), resorted to extraordinary means to raise money without parliamentary action, imprisoned objectors and critics, and packed the courts with his own partisans to insure decisions favorable to the royal cause. Finally, in 1628 Parliament drew up a masterly document known as the Petition of Right, wherein parliamentary grievances were listed in detail and the king was requested to redress them. The petition was remarkable in that it appealed to Magna Carta as if that old document were a constitutional guarantee of the rights of the English *people* against royal prerogative. It was argued that the king could collect no taxes or forced loans without parliamentary consent; that no freeman could be imprisoned or his properties seized without due process of law; that no soldiers could be billeted in private houses; and that no martial law should be proclaimed in time of peace. Charles was forced to give his consent; and the Petition of Right became the first of a series of important constitutional documents defining the rights and liberties of Englishmen against royal absolutism. Less than a year later, after tumultuous scenes, Charles dissolved Parliament and vowed that he would call no more until it would do his bidding.

There followed eleven years (1629–1640) during which Charles tried to rule without Parliament. But, unlike his French contemporaries, he was unsuccessful. His efforts to raise money were unusual, if not illegal, and they raised a storm of popular protest. His favorite churchman, William Laud, whom he made archbishop of Canterbury, so hounded Puritans that about twenty thousand of them went into "involuntary voluntary exile" and founded Massachusetts Bay Colony (1630), Connecticut (1634), and Rhode Island (1636). Still others who weathered the storm in England were embittered, determined the more to oppose the king. Then in 1637 Laud attempted to extend the English church into Presbyterian Scotland. The Scots resisted and drew up a National Solemn League and Covenant for the defense of Presbyterianism. The "Covenanters," as they were called, raised an army and prepared to defend the Scottish Kirk (the national church of Scotland). Soon the king, out of financial necessity, called another Parliament in 1640. But again this Parliament refused to vote money until accumulated grievances were settled, and after about three weeks Charles dissolved it in disgust (the Short Parliament). Soon afterwards the king's forces were defeated by the Covenanters and Charles agreed to pay the Scots £850 a day until a satisfactory settlement could be made. Such financial demands made obligatory the calling of another Parliament, and this one, meeting first in November, 1640, immediately took the reins in its own hands. It impeached the king's favorites, including Laud, and sent them to the Tower of London and, even more ominously, it passed an act declaring that it could not be dissolved without its own consent. By this illegal act, this Parliament prolonged its existence for twenty years (1640–1660) and became known as the Long Parliament—although it was temporarily replaced by other revolutionary governments between 1649 and 1660. With the Scottish army as a convenient ally, it held the king in a most embarrassing position while it proposed to abolish episcopacy in England and further destroy the king's instruments of absolutism, such as the Star Chamber, which it abolished in 1641.

In October, 1641, the Irish, taking advantage of the English divisions, rose up in rebellion and massacred many English people in Ireland. Parliament immediately voted men and money to put down the rebellion and, further to insure the king's tractability, presented Charles with a new list of grievances called the Grand Remonstrance (1641). Among other things, the Grand Remonstrance demanded that the king select only ministers who were approved by Parliament. This the king rejected and, as matters worsened, Parliament passed an ordinance to appoint its own officers to command an army for Ireland, lest one under the king's command be used to subdue Parliament itself. This, of course, was a challenge to the king's authority as commander-in-chief of the armed forces, and before the fall of 1642 both king and Parliament had armed forces under their direct command—not including the Scots, who stood ready to aid Parliament. As no acceptable means of accommodation could be found, the king ultimately retired to Nottingham among his loyal forces, and on August 22, 1642, raised the royal standard which marked the beginning of civil war.

THE ENGLISH CIVIL WARS AND THE INTERREGNUM

Between 1642 and 1649 the English fought two civil wars. The wars released such a flood of reform proposals, pamphlets, parties, and sects that it is easy to overlook the fundamental issues. They remained, however, basically two: the question of parliamentary versus royal prerogative, and the question of revision of the English church. The Puritans, however, had never been in agreement about the forms such revision should take and, with the wars, they divided into a variety of sects. Two groups, however, stood out above the others. The Presbyterians, with Scottish support, proposed to make over the English church upon the Presbyterian model—but still as a state establishment with toleration for no others. The Independents,

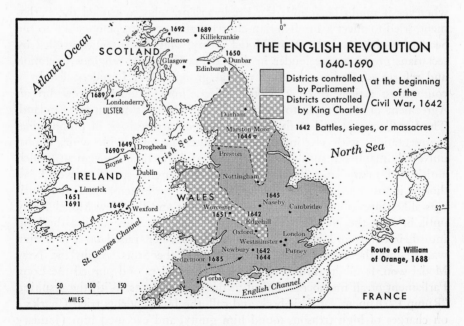

or Independent party, at core Congregationalists, as a minority sect advocated a limited toleration and thus attracted to their side a motley crowd of sectarians. These factions cut across English society socially, economically, and geographically, so that it is inaccurate to view the wars as class struggles. Geographically speaking, northern and western England upheld the king, but there were several pockets of parliamentary support in these areas. Eastern and southern England supported Parliament, but here too were royalist strongholds. Both the nobility and the clergy were divided in their allegiance and, although farm laborers and small farmers generally supported the crown and the urban merchants and workers upheld Parliament, there were numerous exceptions in both cases.

The king carried the day at first, and by the end of 1644 it appeared that the parliamentary cause was lost. Only one parliamentary officer had managed to discipline his forces so that they could withstand the dashing charges of the king's "cavaliers." This was an eastern country squire and obscure member of Parliament, Oliver Cromwell. Cromwell organized his light cavalry after the fashion of Gustavus Adolphus and infused them with a religious will to fight. In consequence, when the parliamentary cause appeared bleak in 1644, Parliament turned to Cromwell and other new officers to "new model" its forces. And with the New Model Army Parliament turned the tide in 1645–46, defeated the king's forces repeatedly, and Charles threw himself into the hands of the Scots. The First Civil War was at an end.

There followed a series of frantic negotiations: the king, as was his wont, promised all things to all sides while he covertly sought foreign aid wherever it might be found; the Presbyterians, who controlled the Parliament, tried to effect a Presbyterian church settlement acceptable alike to the Scots, the king, and the New Model Army; and the latter, controlled by sectarians growing ever louder in their demands, urged religious toleration and reform of Parliament. One radical group, called Levellers, led by a courageous, articulate New Model officer, John Lilburne, drew up an Agreement of the People to submit as a written constitution for England. The Levellers proposed to fix Parliament upon a new basis of proportional representation, with elections at stated intervals, and with wide, almost universal, manhood suffrage. Here was a democratic movement which anticipated many later developments in the English-speaking world, although it was crushed at the time by royalists, parliamentarians, and Puritans alike. Suspicions arose between Parliament and the New Model Army until, in 1647, the New Model tricked the Scots into surrendering the king into their hands and, with Charles as their prisoner, raised up a new civil war against the Presbyterian Parliament and the Scots. Again the New Model won. It subdued the Scots, took over London, and purged the Long Parliament of all members inimical to the Independents. With the resulting "Rump Parliament" at their beck and call, the Independents tried Charles I on charges of high treason, found him guilty, and executed him (January

30, 1649). The queen, with other members of the royal family, had long since found refuge at the court of France.

From 1649 until 1660 England was dominated by the Independents backed by the remarkable New Model Army and guided, insofar as he was able to prevail, by the moderate policies of Oliver Cromwell. These eleven years constituted the Interregnum. Until 1653 the government was a Commonwealth. Both the monarchy and the House of Lords were abolished, and the Rump, of about fifty members of the Long Parliament, governed. The Irish, whose rebellion had never been put down, proclaimed Charles II, the martyred king's eldest son, as king, and the Scots did likewise. Consequently, Cromwell and the New Model were forced to take the field again. They crushed the Irish with great severity, and once more defeated the Scots (1649–52). But once again the army and the Parliament quarrelled, and in April, 1653, Cromwell turned out the Rump and a new government was organized. This was the Protectorate (1653–1660), the only English government to function with a *written* constitution. Cromwell refused to be king, and the Independent faction drew up the Instrument of Government, a constitution which provided a Lord Protector as executive, a Council, and a Parliament elected by a limited number of voters. But the protector (Cromwell) had constant trouble with both Parliament and council and, in fact, the Independent faction (itself a medley of sects) was so small and faced such widespread disaffection, that the protector was forced to resort to a military dictatorship to keep control of the situation. Indeed, this was the tragedy of Oliver Cromwell, who never sought power in the first place, and who hoped to be able to pacify England and to make a settlement in church and state upon a civil foundation without resort to arms. For five years he tried—and failed. When he died in 1658 his son, Richard, succeeded him as lord protector. But Richard Cromwell had no military experience or prestige, and he desired political power even less than his father. New Model officers plotted against him, and after about six months Richard resigned and retired to his country estate. A wild scramble for power among the army officers was ultimately dominated by General George Monck, Oliver's trusted lieutenant in Scotland. Monck led his forces to London, recalled the Long Parliament (insofar as its members still lived), and superintended the establishment of Charles II on the English throne in 1660. With the Stuart Restoration the Interregnum ended and a hardly saddened and little wiser Stuart took command. The civil wars were over, but the principal issues remained unsolved.

THE LATER STUARTS AND THE GLORIOUS REVOLUTION OF 1688

Charles II (1660–1685) was a dashing, handsome, carefree, sensuous prince, whose years of exile had given him the will to survive at any cost. His instincts were those of a divine-right monarch, but circumstances forced him to accept much at the hands of Parliament—to which, after all, he owed his throne. His régime was, perforce, of a limited parliamentary sort, although the king contrived repeatedly to free himself of dependence upon Parliament for his fiscal needs. Perhaps inevitably, there was a widespread reaction against Puritanism, and Restoration England became noted for its gay theaters, its loose morals, its fops, and its frenchified tone. The Church of England was re-established, and a series of acts called the Clarendon Code forbade Puritans the right of public worship, thereby driving them underground. They contrived, however, to exist as Non-conformists, and their common suffering led Presbyterians, Congregationalists, and others to coalesce as they had been unable to do before. The constitutional issues of the Civil War era reappeared in the Restoration Parliaments in the form of party alignments. The Court party, or those who favored a strong monarchy and the Church of England with no quarter to the Non-conformists, came to be known as the "country party" or Tories; those who favored a strong Parliament and toleration to Non-conformist sects were called Whigs. But neither party, as yet, was sufficiently well organized to operate a party system of politics.

The latter years of Charles II's reign were beset with fears about the restoration of Roman Catholicism in England. The king himself was largely responsible. In 1670, in an effort to free himself from dependence upon Parliament for money, Charles II signed secret provisions in the Treaty of Dover with Louis XIV. While the English government sought to check Louis XIV in Holland and elsewhere, the English king agreed that he and his brother, James, Duke of York, would openly espouse the Church of Rome as soon as expediency would allow, and would support the French king in his wars with Spain and Holland. In return, Louis promised Charles £200,000 a year while the wars lasted and military aid in case of an English uprising. The duke of York at once professed the Roman faith, and shortly afterwards the king issued a Declaration of Indulgence (1672), by which he hoped to free English Catholics from restrictions by offering similar freedom to English Non-conformists. Both Anglicans and Non-conformists opposed the move, however, and Parliament forced Charles to withdraw the indulgence in 1673. But the issue was joined. "Popish plots" and rumors of them continued to the end of Charles II's reign—and were the undoing of his successor.

As Charles II died in 1685 leaving no legitimate heirs, his brother James succeeded him. James II, as a Roman Catholic, soon outraged English public opinion by his tactless efforts to obtain for his co-religionists the legal right to worship. When, in June, 1688, his queen gave birth to a son, thereby giving promise of a Catholic succession to the English throne, public hostility to the king rose to a dangerous pitch. A group of English leaders invited William of Orange, the stadtholder of Holland and both son-in-law and nephew of James II, to invade England and seize the throne. William accepted, especially to win England's adherence to the League of Augsburg which he had taken the lead in forming against Louis XIV. Landing in England in early November, 1688, William found almost no resistance, while James, whose slender remaining support melted away, shipped the queen and her infant son to France and soon followed them himself. In January, 1689, a freely elected Convention Parliament, with Whigs in the majority, formally declared the throne vacant and offered the crown to William and Mary, his wife, daughter of James II by his first marriage. They accepted as joint rulers, with actual administration vested in William alone. That the power to decide on succession to the throne should rest in Parliament was a deathblow to the theory and practice of divine-right absolutism. The Declaration of Rights which the new rulers were forced to accept as a condition of their accession rendered the limitation of their authority undoubted. The declaration deprived the crown of the right to suspend laws, to levy money without parliamentary consent, and to maintain a standing army in time of peace. In general, it reasserted all the "true, ancient, and indubitable rights of the people of the realm" which had been catalogued in the Petition of Right, the Grand Remonstrance, and other documents. Later, when the Convention Parliament had been transformed into a regular Parliament, the declaration was enacted as the Bill of Rights (December, 1689), and a Toleration Act earlier in the same year granted freedom of worship to all Non-conformists who took the oaths of allegiance and supremacy to the new king and queen—although Roman Catholics and non-Christians were pointedly omitted. Thus the major issues of the century were at last resolved. Parliamentary supremacy was complete, and the English church was still the established state church, although toleration was extended to Protestant Non-conformists.

The Glorious Revolution finally had achieved without bloodshed what a century of discord and bloody civil wars had failed to accomplish. Yet the final act of the Glorious Revolution took place later, when all Europe was agitated about the Spanish Succession. In 1701, at William's behest, the Parliament passed an Act of Settlement to insure a Protestant succession to the English throne for the future. After William III (Mary had died in 1694 without heirs) the crown was to pass to Anne, Mary's sister, and her heirs; or, in the event that Anne died without issue, it was to pass to the Electress Sophia of Hanover, granddaughter of James I, and her heirs (actually, it passed to Anne, 1702-1714, and to the Electress Sophia's son, George I, 1714-1727, and his heirs, who are still the English monarchs). The act also provided that, to succeed to the crown, the heir must be Protestant, and that none could leave the kingdom without parliamentary consent. Could there exist any longer a shadow of doubt as to where sovereignty lay in England?

Still, England's preoccupation with internal constitutional problems by no means precluded other developments. To the beginnings of permanent overseas colonization were added Jamaica, Carolina, Pennsylvania, and all the other mainland colonies of North America before the American Revolution, save Georgia. England's naval prowess steadily grew and her commercial and financial position was enhanced by the establishment of the Bank of England in 1694.

THE ARTS AND THE ART OF GOVERNMENT

Culturally, England's contributions to philosophy and science were so outstanding in the seventeenth century that we must reserve them for later treatment. In the arts, England still produced little that was indigenous, although Sir Christopher Wren was a notable architect. He proposed plans for rebuilding London after the Great Fire (1666), and redesigned and rebuilt St. Paul's Cathedral and more than fifty churches in London, together with other public and private buildings, including the College of William and Mary in Williamsburg, Virginia. Music began to attract attention in England. William Byrd was an organist and composer of note, and he also founded the English school of madrigal singers that has remained popular to this day. English literature underwent a variety of changes and, with some exceptions, failed to maintain the high performance of the age of Shakespeare. Drama was eclipsed until the Restoration, first by a sharp decline in quality and then by Puritan opposition to stage plays; after the Restoration it was obscene, coarse, and second rate, the plays being mostly imitations or translations of French plays. A vast amount of polemical literature was produced by the civil wars and the partisan strife of Restoration England, much of it scurrilous, with few works of literary merit. If we except the great preacher and metaphysical poet, John Donne, who was much favored by Charles I, the best English literature of the century was by Puritan authors. Towering above all others was John Milton, the Independent. Among his varied works was a treatise in defense of liberty of the press, *Areopagitica* (1644), which has become a classic statement of the case. But his greatest works were his religious epics belonging to Restoration times after Milton had become blind (1652) and after the reaction against Puritanism had set in. *Paradise Lost* (1667), an epic on the fall of man, and *Paradise Regained* (1671), a Calvinistic view of man's redemption, were Milton's masterpieces often compared to Dante's *Divine Comedy* and esteemed high among the greatest literary works in the English language. John Bunyan was another Puritan writer. His *Pilgrim's Progress* (1678), a story of man's tortuous journey through life to the Celestial City, was a most remarkable production for a poor, persecuted, ignorant (but inspired) man such as Bunyan. Of the post-Restoration era, John Dryden was the only seventeenth-century non-Puritan English writer of note. His varied productions included drama, satires, lyric poetry, annals, and many translations from Latin and French. Dryden possessed a fine classical style, but his works lacked originality and his conversion to Catholicism (1687) left him almost an outcast after the Glorious Revolution. England's greatest contributions in the seventeenth century lay, not in literature nor in philosophy and science (great as the latter were), but in the art of government.

For England stood at the crossroads in the seventeenth century, forced to choose between easy acceptance of divine-right absolutism and the hard struggle for constitutionally limited monarchy. Establishment of parliamentary supremacy ran counter to the trends toward more centralized absolutism elsewhere in Europe. More important still, it preserved representative institutions and government by law from the "what-pleases-the-king-has-the-force-of-law" cult of European dynasts who had negated the powers of medieval assemblies and ruled by royal edict alone. Thus the English Revolution of the seventeenth century became of prime importance in pointing the way toward freer institutions of government and in preparing the seedbed of representative democracy.

Further Reading

A good general account of the period is W. F. Reddaway, *A History of Europe from 1610 to 1715* (New York: Barnes & Noble, 1951). In *The Seventeenth Century Background* (Garden City: Doubleday, Anchor A19, 1955), Basil Willey provides useful lectures on the intellectual climate, especially on Descartes, Hobbes, and Locke.

O. Laskowski, *Jan III Sobieski* (London: Faber, 1941), and R. N. Bain, *Charles XII and the Collapse of the Swedish Empire, 1682–1719* ("Heroes of the Nations") (New York: Putnam, 1904), are well-written biographies of the northern kings. The development of Russia into a great European power is outlined in F. Nowak, *Medieval Slavdom and the Rise of Russia* ("Berkshire Studies") (New York: Holt, 1930). Of the numerous works on Peter the Great, the biography by K. Waliszewski (London: Heinemann, 1898) is artfully written and scholarly; Benedict H. Sumner's *Peter the Great and the Emergence of Russia* (New York: Macmillan, 1950) is a recent addition to the "Teach Yourself History Library"; and Harold Lamb's *The City of the Tsar: Peter the Great and the Move to the West, 1648–1762* (Garden City: Doubleday, 1948) is strictly a popular narrative.

The Origins of Prussia (New York: Oxford Univ. Press, 1954), by Francis L. Carsten, traces the development of the classes and institutions that formed the basis of the seventeenth-century Hohenzollern despotism. Sidney B. Fay, *The Rise of Brandenburg-Prussia to 1786* ("Berkshire Studies") (New York: Holt, 1937), is a convenient introduction to the subject in English. The biography of *The Great Elector* (Chicago: Univ. of Chicago Press, 1947), by Ferdinand Schevill, is deeply sympathetic, perhaps too partial. The Habsburgs are well treated in Paul Frischauer's *The Imperial Crown: the Story of the Rise and Fall of the Holy Roman and the Austrian Empires* (London: Cassell, 1939).

On the precursors of the Great King, see C. V. Wedgwood, *Richelieu and the French Monarchy* ("Teach Yourself History Library") (New York: Macmillan, 1950), and Paul R. Doolin, *The Fronde* (Cambridge: Harvard Univ. Press, 1935). Voltaire's eulogistic *Age of Louis XIV* ("Everyman's Library") (New York: Dutton, 1951) is still worth reading as an almost-contemporary appraisal. The following shorter interpretations are an excellent beginning: Lawrence B. Packard, *The Age of Louis XIV* ("Berkshire Studies") (New York: Holt, 1929); Maurice Ashley, *Louis XIV and the Greatness of France* ("Teach Yourself History Library") (New York: Macmillan, 1948); and David Ogg, *Louis XIV* ("Home University Library of Modern Knowledge") (New York: Oxford Univ. Press, 1951). W. H. Lewis, in *The Splendid Century* (Garden City: Doubleday, Anchor A122, 1957), employs a topical analysis to describe the various aspects and levels of life in Louis' France; in *Versailles and the Court under Louis XIV* (New York: Century, 1905) James E. Farmer uses the same technique to sketch the exclusive coterie at the top of the human pyramid. Charles W. Cole, *Colbert and a Century of French Mercantilism,* 2 vols. (New York: Columbia Univ. Press, 1939), is a standard treatise on the development of the French economy and empire. French colonization and exploration are heroically portrayed by Francis Parkman, *Pioneers of France in the New World* (Boston: Little, 1931).

Mary C. Trevelyan, *William III and the Defense of Holland, 1672–1674* (New York: Longmans, 1930), is a political history. For Dutch overseas exploration and colonization see *The Golden Book of the Dutch Navigators* (New York: Century, 1916), a well-illustrated volume by the celebrated artist-historian Hendrik Willem van Loon; and Bernard H. M. Vlekke, *The Story of the Dutch East Indies* (Cambridge: Harvard Univ. Press, 1945). Maurice Ashley, *England in the Seventeenth Century* (Baltimore: Penguin A268, 1956), is an able political survey. George M. Trevelyan, *England under the Stuarts* (New York: Putnam, 1947), and Godfrey Davies, *The Early Stuarts, 1603–1660* (New York: Oxford Univ. Press, 1937), are both high-quality history. Theodore C. Pease, *The Leveller Movement* (American Historical Ass'n., 1916), has long been a classic. Arthur Bryant presents a Tory view of *King Charles II* (New York: Longmans, 1946). G. M. Trevelyan's volume in the "Home University Library," *The English Revolution, 1688–1689* (London: Oxford Univ. Press, 1938), is a careful analysis of the consequences of the Glorious Revolution. H. D. Traill's *William III* (New York: Macmillan, 1903), is old, but still not superseded.

Chapter 20

THE WORLD
OF THE ENLIGHTENMENT

MEN OF every age are likely to consider themselves especially enlightened when compared with generations that have gone before. But in no era have they been so naïvely certain of their own intellectual superiority and perfectibility as the eighteenth-century philosophers who referred to their own times as the *âge des lumières,* the *Aufklärung,* the Age of Reason, and the Enlightenment. Here was an era of superb optimism, when men felt that, by the use of their own earthbound, mortal, human facilities, they could create a perfect society in this world, unfettered by senseless conventions, unjust laws, irrational customs, and blind superstitions. Their object was a secular society with freedom, happiness, and an ever upward-and-onward progress for mankind. Their magic words were "reason," "nature," and "progress"; their high priests were Isaac Newton and John Locke; their method was that of the new sciences (or so they thought); and for their proper appreciation we must turn to the development of early modern science.

1 : The Rise of Early Modern Science

SCIENCE, whether considered as knowledge or as method, is cumulative, each generation standing on the shoulders of its predecessor. Therefore it unfolds gradually. Some historians of science point to the year 1543 as the natal year of modern science, because during that year were published both Andreas Vesalius' *De Humani Corporis Fabrica (Concerning the Anatomy of the Human Body)* and Nicolas Copernicus' *De Revolutionibus Orbium Coelestium (Concerning the Motions of Heavenly Orbs).* The first was a great improvement over prevailing anatomical knowledge, which rested

193

largely upon such ancient works as those of Galen, and it was based upon actual dissections of human bodies and accompanied by marvelous woodcut illustrations. The second set forth a revival of an ancient hypothesis, namely, that the sun and not the earth is the center of the universe, and that the earth revolves around it—a heliocentric theory of the universe. But these works, important as they were, were rather first fruits of a rising new scientific outlook than the dramatic rise of the curtain upon a fully-propped stage of science. The beginnings of modern science stem from the high Middle Ages and, as they relate to changing attitudes and methods inside the minds of men, they are somewhat obscure.

Modern science is far more similar to ancient Greek learning than to that of any other period, although the two are by no means identical in method, organization, or content. For this reason, it seems clear that the rediscovery of ancient learning, from both Arabic and European sources, established a foundation for it. Yet the humanistic scholars who revived and translated ancient classical works exhibited no interest in science and contributed little to its growth. A scattered few of the scholastics, especially those of the ill-reputed nominalists' school, reverted to an ancient doctrine and insisted upon the importance of studying *individual* items of knowledge instead of general, or abstract, knowledge, as the best means to advance learning; and from them stemmed the taproot of modern science. Roger Bacon (1212?–1292), an English Franciscan scholar, was an early advocate of experimental, inductive methods "to test perfectly what can be done by nature." William of Ockham (1300?–1349?), another English scholar, was influential in developing a similar approach into nominalism. But these were relatively isolated events, and they did not, at the time, catch the imagination of a large number of persons.

Probably another factor in the rise of early science was the emergence of the bourgeoisie, the middle class. Here was a group of men whose ambitions in the world of commerce led them to entertain an active interest in the utilitarian values of the new science, especially in the fields of mechanics and navigation. As patrons of humanistic scholars and academies and as practical men of affairs, they combined a knowledge of ancient works and of the folk learning of artisans and craftsmen together with a profit-seeking motive, to find and to employ any new techniques that could be found useful in their business. Indeed, one of the factors in the development of early science was the mingling of the scholarly learning of philosophers with the folk learning of craftsmen and tradesmen. The process was mutually resisted at first because of scholars' snobbish disdain of people who worked with their hands and craftsmen's suspicious fears for the "secrets" of their trade. Usually it took place only after new techniques threatened to destroy craft guilds, or when it had become demonstrable that such exchange of secrets was of mutual benefit. Perhaps one of the earliest examples was in the area of navigation and sailing ships when, as in the case of

Prince Henry's School of Navigation in Portugal, philosophers, astronomers, geographers, and common sailors pooled their knowledge and applied it to remarkable advantage in geographical exploration and discovery. Dynasts and their ministers also combined such groups for military affairs and for the mercantilistic development of manufactures and commerce. Again, overseas discoveries themselves stimulated the new science. Europeans had scarcely become familiar with the science of the ancients before the discovery of the Americas and of other parts of the world confronted them with a host of new flora and fauna to study and classify; new continents, new islands, and new skies to map; new waters to sound; and new peoples with new institutions to study—all fraught with exciting possibilities of great wealth and endless fame.

Yet another factor was the invention and improvement of a variety of instruments by which scientists were enabled to measure scientific data more accurately and to expand their physical powers of observation. Most of these the early scientists developed themselves as means of improving their experimental and observational techniques. Thus Galileo Galilei (1564–1642) first applied (if, indeed, he did not invent) the telescope and the microscope to scientific work (1609), and he experimented with an early type of thermometer (1612). His pupil, Evangelista Torricelli (1608–1647), developed the earliest barometer (1643), although its use in meteorology was not recognized for many years afterwards. Otto von Guericke (1602–1686), the burgomaster of Magdeburg, invented the air pump (1650), which Robert Boyle (1627–1691) later improved and used in experiments to prove the weight of air as well as to develop Boyle's law on the compressibility of gases (1662). Christian Huygens (1629–1695) made many improvements on telescopes and invented (1650) the pendulum movements for clocks (previously suggested by Galileo). And Isaac Newton (1642–1727) constructed the earliest reflecting telescope (1668), the type found most useful for astronomical observations. These instruments, of course, were only a few of those developed for scientific purposes. Their construction and their improvement, however, emphasized the interrelationship between scientific work and technology. From the seventeenth century on science and technology have become increasingly interdependent, with scientific advances sometimes halted by unsolved technological problems of the instrument-makers.

Mathematics became an instrument of science in a somewhat different but even more important sense, and developments in mathematics made possible further achievements in science. Hardly had Euclid's *Elements of Geometry* been translated into vernacular tongues, and the various advances made in trigonometry by the Arabs become familiar to Europeans, when Simon Stevin (1548–1620), a Dutch mathematician and military engineer, published *The Decimal, Teaching with Unheard-of Ease How to Performe All Calculations Necessary Among Men by Whole Numbers without Frac-*

tions (1585), which introduced decimals into common use. Gradually, the use of regularized symbols, such as $+$, $-$, $\times$, and the like, became internationally employed in mathematical works, most of them before 1700. However, π, first introduced in 1706, was not widely used until after 1750. John Napier (1550–1617), a Scot, published his *Marvelous Rule of Logarithms* (1614), which, when accompanied by adequate tables (available a decade later), set forth both the principle of the slide rule and a splendid short cut for a variety of mathematical computations. The French philosopher, René Descartes (1596–1650), developed analytical geometry in an essay published in 1637 and, by showing how to plot an algebraic equation on a graph, demonstrated new methods whereby mathematical precision could be introduced in philosophical discussions. But the climax of achievement in mathematics was the invention of the calculus. A number of seventeenth-century scholars contributed new ways to treat variables and probabilities, but Isaac Newton and Gottfried Wilhelm Leibnitz (1646–1716) almost simultaneously (about 1670), and quite independently, hit upon the calculus—a coincidence which led to mutual charges of plagiarism and ill feelings. Without this mathematical tool, however, Newton's influential and revolutionary hypothesis in physics and astronomy would have been impossible.

THE PHILOSOPHY AND ORGANIZATION OF EARLY SCIENCE

It is hardly oversimplification to say that the philosophy of early science was dominated in the seventeenth century by two schools of thought, represented respectively by Francis, Lord Bacon, and René Descartes. Bacon, like his predecessor of the same surname, emphasized empiricism and inductive reasoning. In the *New Organon: or, True Directions Concerning the Interpretation of Nature* (1620) Bacon proposed "to establish progressive stages of certainty" in discovering the laws of nature. By experiments men could win sensory perceptions which, when patiently repeated and the results compared, would result in an accumulation of data from which an *axiom* could be stated. From these axioms further experiments could be constructed which, in turn, would lead to ever broadening axioms and ultimately to the very laws of nature. Bacon called the process *induction,* although in constructing experiments deductive processes of reasoning also crept in—and, in fact, both induction and deduction are necessary in science. But Bacon's emphasis was a helpful corrective in his time and set science upon a method previously given little systematic use. Bacon rejected all old authorities, philological arguments, superstitions, and ceremonial magic, seeking to formulate natural laws by experiments and induction alone. His emphasis upon free, full, and honest co-operation among scientists, and his advocacy of state-supported academies wherein scientists might work co-operatively with their needs supplied at state expense, helped to set an inexpressibly important standard of free exchange among scientists.

Descartes emphasized reason above experiment. But it was precise reasoning, for Descartes was a mathematician as well as a philosopher, and he felt that the method of analytical geometry leads to a certainty that might be applied to other fields. Reason, said Descartes, is the power to distinguish truth from error, and it is the chief attribute of man which separates him from brutes. Descartes determined to employ reason as the guiding light of his life, and he sought "the Method which each ought to follow for the right conduct of his Reason." The method which he found was described in detail in his autobiographical treatise, *Discourse on the Method of Rightly Conducting the Reason and Seeking Truth in the Sciences* (1637). Descartes sought to order his thoughts in such a manner as to lead to certitude. In order to do this, it was necessary to be very careful about opinions and initial assumptions, for Descartes saw, upon careful self-examination, that he held many false opinions and prejudices. So he set forth four rules for his Method:

> The *first* was never to accept anything for true which I did not clearly know to be such. . . . The *second,* to divide each of the difficulties under examination into as many parts as possible, and as might be necessary for its adequate solution. . . . The *third,* to conduct my thoughts in such order that, by commencing with objects the simplest and easiest to know, I might ascent little by little . . . to the knowledge of the more complex. . . . And the *last,* in every case to make enumerations so complete, and reviews so general, that I might be assured nothing was omitted."

Later, in meditations on the *First Philosophy in Which the Existence of God and the Immortality of the Soul are Demonstrated* (1641), Descartes sought to divest his mind of all false or uncertain opinions, including sensory impressions which he had found to be inaccurate or misleading. He found that he could doubt many things, everything, in fact, except the fact that he doubted. But, he reflected, what is doubting? Is it not a form of thinking? *Cogito, ergo sum,* "I think, therefore I am." This triumphant conclusion furnished a foundation stone from which Descartes finally arrived at God. But, as he wrote to a friend, wherever you find the term "God" you should substitute "the mathematical order of nature."

Descartes deduced laws of nature from the infinite perfections of God, who, he said, "has established the laws of nature just as a king establishes the laws of his kingdom." These laws are understandable by man's reason and they are "eternal and immutable because God is always the same." Thus, Descartes held that a scientific approach to philosophy is the only proper one and that a life of reason is the glory and hope of mankind. His work was complementary to Bacon's emphasis upon experimentation and induction. Although Descartes despised neither of these, he placed science within a broader philosophical framework than Bacon, while his emphasis upon mathematical demonstration went far to establish the pattern whereby scientific discourses were couched in the logic and language of mathematics.

It is important to realize that scientists in the seventeenth century consciously separated science, or "natural philosophy," as they commonly called it from philosophy as a whole. They limited themselves to natural phenomena, and they avoided questions regarding *why* in order to concentrate on those pertaining to *how*. They sought means, not ends; explanations, not justifications. The Royal Society of London stated in 1663 that it had been organized to promote "Physico-Mathematicall Experimental Learning," and it specifically excluded concern for "Divinity, Metaphysics, Moralls, Politicks, Grammar, Rhetorick, or Logick." Thus the new science was wholly secular. But if the limitations tended to advance the natural and physical sciences at a more rapid rate, they may well have been responsible in part for that unhappy, and even dangerous, separation of science and morals which we have come to deplore today.

Many societies, academies, and clubs sprang up in the seventeenth century in an effort to organize scientific endeavors, exchange scientific data, disseminate scientific knowledge, and promote scientific learning over all the world. Two of these organizations of prime importance came into being almost simultaneously. One was the Royal Society of London, chartered in 1662, and the other was the French Academy of Science, founded in 1664. The former, although organized strictly in accord with Francis Bacon's proposals, was chartered by Charles II but given no government support financially; hence, it remained a private enterprise. The latter, sponsored by Colbert and approved by Louis XIV, was a government enterprise in the best mercantilistic sense. Both societies financed experiments, scientific expeditions, and the publication of scientific works. Both published journals, *The Philosophical Transactions,* in London; the *Journal des Sçavans (Savants)*, in Paris. These were imitated widely in Europe and elsewhere. The Academy of Berlin (1700), the St. Petersburg Academy in Russia (1725), and several others arose, including the American Philosophical Society and the American Academy of Science, both of which came into being before the American Revolution had ended. By their promotions and encouragements the societies developed interlocking circles of scientific correspondents on a world-wide scale in the eighteenth century. Their co-operation and exchange of data went far to justify the words of the president of the Royal Society of London in 1753 when he said that

> learned men and Philosophers of all Nations . . . should consider
> themselves and each other as constituent parts and Fellow members of one and the same illustrious Republic, and to look upon
> it as beneath Persons of their character to betray a fond partiality
> for this or that particular district where it happened their lot either
> to be born or to reside. But that their benefactions should be universally diffused and as extensive as the knowledge they profess to

pursue, and should be sensibly felt by all who . . . promote and advance Science and usefull knowledge wherein alone the true interest and welfare of such a Republic consist.[1]

Thus the Republic of the New Science was strictly non-sectarian and international in spirit—to an extent surprising to the more nationalistic sentiments of our own day.

SOME ACHIEVEMENTS OF EARLY SCIENCE

Most early scientists were amateurs. Only physicians and apothecaries (and by no means all of these!) had formal training in their work. Moreover, few scientists were specialists in any one field—indeed, the separate fields or disciplines themselves were seldom distinguished from one another. Not until the late eighteenth century did chemistry, geology, and other separate disciplines begin to emerge from the amorphous mass of knowledge that accumulated regarding natural phenomena. Yet, in spite of amateur status and the lack of prefabricated instruments and laboratory techniques, early scientists accomplished much. Indeed, their failures were sometimes as significant as their successes, as in the pioneer work in which they engaged negative evidence was often as useful as positive discoveries.

In the natural sciences, solid beginnings were made toward the classification and nomenclature of flora and fauna. But because of the magnitude of the task, the multiplicity of workers, and their almost complete dedication to a belief in the fixity of species (which not only denied evolutionary change but also tended to make separate classifications of every hybrid, sport, or other variation), satisfactory systems were not devised until the late eighteenth century. Collections of specimens were gathered from everywhere, museums were begun, botanical gardens multiplied, and considerable work was done in dissection, including even microscopic studies. Anton van Leeuwenhoek (1632–1723), a self-trained Dutch microscopist, made many studies of his "little animals" or protozoa (unicellular organisms) of many kinds, which he first described in 1675. John Harvey (1578–1657), an English physician and close friend of Charles I, made the most amazing discovery in biology when, in 1616, he demonstrated the circular movement of the blood in animals together with the role of the heart as a "central pumping station." His work *On the Movement of the Heart and the Blood* was published in 1628. A host of new drugs was added to the pharmacopoeias of Europe from both the Americas and the Far East. These led to much hopeful testing and considerable quackery, but one, at least, proved

---

[1] Speech of President Macclesfield in presenting the Copley Medal to Benjamin Franklin, Nov. 30, 1753. Royal Society *Journal-Book*, XXII, 413. Quoted by permission of the President and Council of The Royal Society, London.

to be of great value. This was "Jesuit's bark" or "Peruvian bark" (cinchona bark, or quinine). Rumors of inoculation for smallpox as practiced by the Circassians and Georgians in Turkey and by the Chinese were bruited about in Europe in the 1690's. Confirmed in 1714 and put to the test a few years later, the practice of inoculation went far to bring the scourge of smallpox under control in Europe during the eighteenth century, years before vaccination was known (1799).

But it was in astronomy and physics that the most tremendous strides were made. The Copernican theory of the universe attracted great attention, not only because it challenged efforts to confirm or to disprove it but also because the original data were found inadequate and imperfect. A vast amount of new data were discovered. The German Johannes Kepler (1571–1630) discovered that the orbits of planets were elliptical and not circular as Copernicus had assumed. He also found that planets move faster as they approach the sun and more slowly when they are distant from it; and he discovered laws of planetary motion, reduced to mathematical formulas. Galileo made many new discoveries with the telescope. Most convincing, perhaps, were his accounts of the moons of Jupiter, which he found to move around the planet like a miniature solar system. Gradually, as evidence of this sort piled up to strengthen the heliocentric view of the universe, the Copernican theory won general acceptance. In addition, star maps were vastly enlarged and improved; astronomical instruments were greatly perfected; and two new important observatories were erected, one at Paris in 1672 in conjunction with the French Academy of Science and one at Greenwich near London in 1676 under supervision of the English Royal Society. New studies were projected regarding the size and shape of the earth. Popular faith in astronomy was greatly enhanced when Edmond Halley (1656–1742) predicted that the brilliant comet which bears his name, and which he had observed in 1680, would reappear in 1758, which it did—sixteen years after Halley's death.

ISAAC NEWTON AND THE NEWTONIAN SYNTHESIS

Isaac Newton became the most famous scientist of the time, although, inevitably, some of his work was built upon that of his predecessors. This was especially true with regard to Galileo's contributions on the laws of motion. By his studies of pendulums, projectiles, falling bodies, and balls rolled on inclined planes, Galileo went far toward perfecting present-day ideas of acceleration; and he disproved the Aristotelian theory that objects fall with velocities proportional to their weights. Newton carried on from Galileo's beginning to formulate the three classical laws of motion:

1. Every body perseveres in its state of rest, or in uniform motion in a straight line, unless it is impelled to change that state by impressed forces.

2. Change of motion (i.e., rate of change of momentum) is proportional to the impressed force and takes place in the direction in which the force is impressed.
3. To every action there is always opposed an equal reaction.

Beyond these, however, Newton set forth a great theoretical account of the universe based upon the laws of gravitation, which he also described with mathematical precision. All this appeared in his *Philosophiae Naturalis Principia Mathematica* (*Mathematical Principles of Natural Philosophy,* commonly called Newton's *Principia*), published in 1687 by the Royal Society of London. Work on it started at least as early as 1666, when Newton began studies on the force of gravity, traditionally after an apple fell on his head from a tree under which he was sitting. The problem was to explain, not why planets continue to move, but why they move in closed ellipses instead of traveling in straight lines into outer space. Newton found the answer by bringing together Kepler's laws of planetary motion and Galileo's laws of terrestrial motion and showing that they were two aspects of the same laws. Thus Newton enunciated the laws of universal gravitation. The sun, the planets, and their satellites are held in their orbits by the forces of mutual attraction or gravitation. This force of gravitation, according to Newton, is proportional to the product of the masses of two bodies attracted to one another, and inversely proportional to the squares of the distance between them. Thus the whole physical universe is subject to the same laws of gravitation and to the same laws of motion that we experience on earth, and all physical objects in one part of the universe exercise some influence upon all others. All things in the universe form a cosmic system of interconnected parts which operate upon one another by mechanical laws. In a sense, then, the universe operates like a vast cosmic machine.

Newton's work showed that all motion, whether on the earth or in the solar system, could be described by the same mathematical formulas (if they were timed and measured accurately). All matter moved in accordance with the universal law of gravitation. What the *force* of gravitation was in itself, Newton could not explain. But the knowledge of the "natural laws" by which it operated enabled men to predict tides, improve navigation, discover longitude at sea, improve map making, and estimate more accurately the trajectory of artillery shells, whereby to improve the firepower of European armed forces. For more than two hundred years Newton's laws were unshaken. Only in the infinitesimal world of the atom or in the vast regions of outer space have they been found wanting—and the limitations in these areas have been recognized only within the present century.

Although Newton did not claim to be a philosopher, his works had an immediate and profound effect upon both philosophy and metaphysics. Further, Newton enunciated "Four Rules of Reasoning in Philosophy" in his *Principia*. In essence, these provided that: (1) the laws governing the physical world are simple; (2) they are consistent; (3) they are absolute, applicable both to the bodies within reach of our experiment and to all others in the universe beyond our immediate powers to submit to direct experiment; and (4) they can be established by combining inductive and deductive methods of reasoning, that is, by reasoning from observable particular instances to a general rule and then by applying this rule to other instances not observable at first hand. Newton assumed that the entire universe can be explained by his methods and, as his methods yielded brilliant results, he rejected consideration of first causes, or, as he put it, of "occult qualities supposed to be hid in bodies and to be the causes of manifest effects." In short, like other scientists, Newton exhibited no concern for the *why* ("occult qualities") and concentrated on the *how* ("manifest effects") because, as he said, "such occult causes put a stop to improvement" of science. Thus Newton, a devoutly religious man, advocated "Rules of Reasoning in Philosophy" which denounced religious explanations of natural phenomena. These rules separated physics from metaphysics and constructed a materialistic outlook which exhibited nature as a great machine wholly explicable by physical and mathematical laws.

2 : John Locke, Sage of the Enlightenment

THE WORKS of John Locke (1632–1704) held tremendous sway over the ideas of the eighteenth century. Of Puritan parentage, Locke became a scholar, physician, scientist, and philosopher. Exiled to Holland in 1683 because of suspicion of his complicity in Whig plots, he returned to England in 1689 and soon began publication of works which he had had in preparation since the 1670's. He was a gentle, amiable, somewhat shy person, widely liked and highly respected, and he had a tremendous capacity to absorb and interpret in simple language many of the original, revolutionary ideas with which his time was so plentifully endowed. Though not original, he was a great popularizer of ideas and became the source of the central philosophical and political tradition of the Western world, especially in the United States of America. He was an apologist and defender of the Glorious Revolution in England, a champion of Newtonianism, and by his emphasis upon experience as the basis of all knowledge he set empiricism in juxtaposition to rationalism and presented philosophy as a discipline based on average powers of empirical observation and common-sense judgment.

His first work, *Letters on Toleration,* appeared in Latin in 1666 and in English in 1690. Locke subscribed to "equal and impartial liberty," to the view that, as a church is a voluntary organization and as the business of the state is not religion, separation of Church and State was desirable and proper; but he also argued that the State should not tolerate sects which practice immoral rites or plot harm to society. According to Locke, these excluded from toleration all atheists, non-Christians, and Catholics in a manner similar to the provisions of the English Toleration Act.

Locke's second great work, *Two Treatises on Civil Government* (1689), was "to establish the throne of our great restorer, our present King William . . . and to justify to the world the people of England." But it was also to combat opinions set forth earlier by Sir Robert Filmer (? –1653), whose *Patriarchia, or the Natural Power of Kings Asserted,* published posthumously in 1680, had upheld the divine right of kings theory. Also, it reached back to contradict Thomas Hobbes (1588–1679). Hobbes, like Descartes, was a mathematician. His powerful book, *Leviathan* (1651), was the most closely reasoned English political work of the century but, because of the author's ill opinion of human nature and his alleged atheistical views, it was long condemned as a species of Machiavellianism. Locke's first *Treatise* was given over wholly to a refutation of the divine right of kings theory of government. His second was "concerning the true, original, extent and end of civil government." Here Locke set forth a classic statement of the contract theory of the state, together with an assertion of the natural rights of man which went beyond not only the English Bill of Rights but also beyond the radical Levellers of the English Civil War days. "To understand political power right," said Locke, "and derive it from its original, we must consider what state all men are naturally in . . . ." That, he said, was a state of nature, in which all men were perfectly free and equal. Hobbes had also envisioned mankind in a state of nature prior to the formation of civil society. But Hobbes also looked upon natural man as an evil brute, and mankind in the state of nature was in a condition of constant violence, war, and anarchy. Locke, on the other hand, considered natural man to be innately good, and he viewed mankind in the state of nature to be in a condition of wide freedom and complete equality, because "the state of nature has a law of nature to govern it, which obliges every one" to obey. This law is reason, which "teaches all mankind who will but consult it that, being all equal and independent, no one ought to harm another in his life, health, liberty, or possessions." Indeed, these latter are man's "natural rights," which even in a civil state must be held above and outside the power of the law—the rights of life, liberty, and property, as they were usually stated. Hobbes, however, was a defender of absolutism. The only way whereby men can be freed of the horrors of the state of nature is to covenant with one another to observe laws that will terminate the state of war. But, as Hobbes argued,

> Convenants, without the Sword, are but Words, and of no strength to secure a man at all. Therefore . . . if there be no Power erected, or [one] not great enough for our security every man will . . . rely on his own strength. [Those who covenant, then, must] confer all

their power and strength upon one Man, or upon one Assembly of men, that may reduce all their Wills, by plurality of voices, into one Will. [This done, said Hobbes,] the Multitude so united in one Person is called a Common-wealth. . . . This is the Generation of that great Leviathan, or rather (to speake more reverently) of that *Mortall God,* to which we owe under the *Immortal God* our peace and defence.[2]

Hobbes, therefore, placed absolute and undivided sovereignty in the state, and citizens surrendered all their natural rights in order to erect sanctions for maintaining the peace.

LOCKE ON THE ORIGIN OF CIVIL SOCIETY

Locke took a very different view. The state of nature, he said, however idyllic in some respects, had shortcomings. The law of nature, though "plain and intelligible to all rational creatures," was not always clear to biased, ignorant men, who often refused to abide by it; the state of nature lacked an impartial judge "with authority to determine all differences according to the established law"; and lastly, the state of nature provided no power to enforce a judgment and "to give it due execution." For these reasons men preferred to give up their natural liberty and to accept liberty under civil law—"a standing rule to live by, common to every one of that society and made by the legislative power erected in it." Thus, said Locke,

the only way whereby one divests himself of his natural liberty and puts on the bonds of civil society is by agreeing with other men to join and unite into a community for their comfortable, safe, and peaceable living . . . in a secure enjoyment of their properties and a greater security against any that are not of it. . . . When any number of men have so consented to make one community or government, they are presently incorporated and make one body politic wherein the majority have a right to act and conclude the rest.[3]

Yet, as man is by nature free from absolute, arbitrary power, he cannot part with this freedom, nor by his own consent place himself under the absolute, arbitrary power of another. No rational man will consent to alter his condition for the worse, and therefore the power of the state is severely limited to the preservation of the common good and the security of every

---

[2] Thomas Hobbes, *Leviathan* (New York: E. P. Dutton & Co., Everyman's Library No. 691, 1937), pp. xix–xx (Introduction by A. D. Lindsay).

[3] John Locke, *Two Treatises of Civil Government,* in *The Works of John Locke* (10 vols.; London, 1823), V, 394–95.

man's life, liberty, and property—liberty being "a liberty to follow my own will in all things where the rule prescribes not." The supreme power of the state must govern by established laws, known to all, and not by "extemporary decrees." It cannot "take from any man any part of his property without his own consent," and if it tries, its subjects may legally resist it. Thus Locke recognized the right of revolution against arbitrary government whenever the subjects' natural rights were invaded.

Hobbes and Locke, then, though both subscribed to the contract theory of government, gave vastly different interpretations of it, its *raison d'être,* and its operation. For one thing, Locke in reality advocated a double contract whereas Hobbes upheld only one. According to Locke, men emerged from the state of nature by a *social contract* whereby they engaged to form a society after which they negotiated a *political contract* to define and limit the particular government set up. Hobbes created a civil society and a specific government by a single contract. Accordingly, if Locke's political contract were broken the people did not immediately relapse into a state of nature (for the social contract was still in operation), whereas under Hobbes's plan they did. Both men, however, rejected the divine-right theory, and held that governments are man-made and not divinely instituted. Hobbes pointed toward the absolutism of the enlightened despots of the eighteenth century, while Locke expounded constitutional, limited government with majority rule and protection of the "natural rights" of the citizen. Locke was no "democrat"; that is, he did not favor universal suffrage, and he betrayed a bourgeois jealousy for the sanctity of property. Still, he contributed mightily to democratic theory by such statements as that men are by nature "free, equal, and independent," that sovereign power stems only from the people themselves, and that government rests on the consent of the governed. Here were political doctrines that reached beyond the Glorious Revolution toward the republic of the United States, whose Founding Fathers appealed to doctrines strikingly similar to those of John Locke.

LOCKE ON THE ORIGIN OF KNOWLEDGE

Another of Locke's major works was *An Essay Concerning Human Understanding* (1690), which was an early effort in the science now called psychology. In this work Locke was inspired by conversations with friends to try to remove "some of the rubbish that lies in the way of knowledge" and encumbers the understanding of such "master-builders" as Huygens and "the incomparable Mr. Newton"; and he set out to "inquire into the original, certainty, and extent of human knowledge, together with the grounds and degrees of belief, opinion, and assent." He believed that he could solve the problems of how man *knows* by examining the origin of ideas. Unlike Descartes, he rejected belief in ideas innate in the human mind at birth. Instead, he argued, let us then suppose the mind to be, as we say, white paper, void of all characters, without any ideas; how comes it to be furnished? ... To this I answer, in one word, from experience! In that, all our knowledge is founded; and from it ultimately derives itself.[4]

From sensory experiences, then, the human mind, at birth a blank paper, develops impressions which, observed and "processed" by reflection, memory, and judgment (or common sense), "is that which supplies our understandings with all the materials of thinking." Again unlike Descartes, whose rigorous rationalism deduced truth from premises which were self-evident or innate, Locke appealed to empirical observation in the world of nature. Man is himself part of nature, and his mind functions naturally, drawing its primary materials from natural, sensory impulses. Knowledge, then, is open to all who will respond to these impulses, and philosophy is no esoteric discipline dependent upon the quiddities of the scholastics or the linguistics of the humanists. Rather, it is founded upon normal powers of empirical observation and common-sense judgment. Indeed, though Locke did not say so, he made philosophical learning appear so easy as to persuade every man to become his own philosopher—which, during the Age of Enlightenment, can almost be said to have occurred. Locke's influence on popular thought, both in politics and in philosophy, has been widespread in the Western world. In the eighteenth century he was as much the typical philosopher as Newton was the typical scientist. Alexander Pope wrote the oft-quoted lines about Newton, the "first glory of our English race,"

> *Nature and Nature's Laws lay hid in Night:*
> *God said, Let Newton be! and all was Light.*

And Thomas Gray referred to Locke:

> *From whence our knowledge doth begin: how springs*
> *Memory to life, that slender chain of things,*
> *How Reason gains late empire in the heart,*
> *How wrath and fear and care and sorrow start,*
> *All these I sing! Deign thou my song to grace,*
> *O second glory of our English race!*

3 : The Optimism of the Enlightenment

FROM THE WORKS of their seventeenth-century predecessors, especially Bacon, Descartes, Newton, and Locke, a corps of eighteenth-century intel-

---

[4] John Locke, *An Essay Concerning Human Understanding* (17th ed.; 2 vols.; London, 1775), I, 67–68.

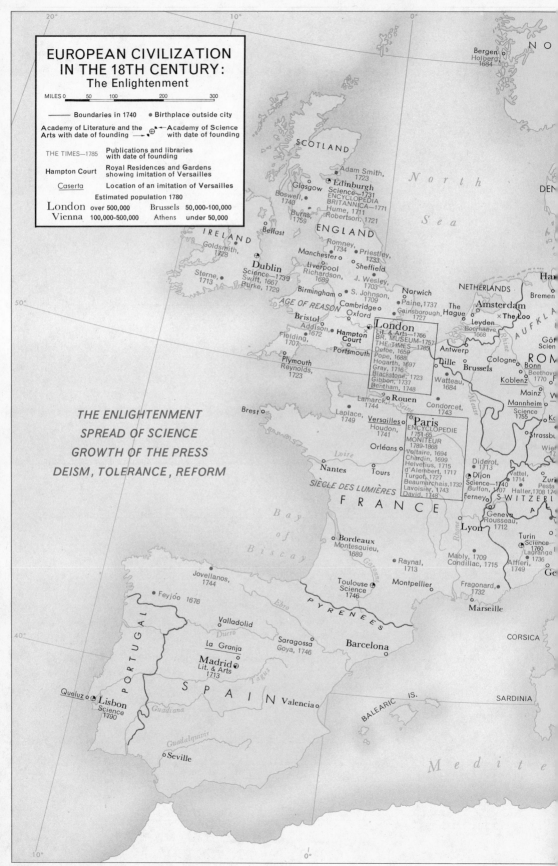

EUROPEAN CIVILIZATION IN THE 18TH CENTURY:
The Enlightenment

MILES 0   50   100   200   300

—— Boundaries in 1740   ● Birthplace outside city

Academy of Literature and the ——●← Academy of Science
Arts with date of founding   ⊕   with date of founding

THE TIMES—1785   Publications and libraries
                   with date of founding

Hampton Court   Royal Residences and Gardens
                 showing imitation of Versailles

<u>Caserta</u>   Location of an imitation of Versailles

Estimated population 1780

London   over 500,000   Brussels   50,000-100,000
Vienna   100,000-500,000   Athens   under 50,000

THE ENLIGHTENMENT

SPREAD OF SCIENCE

GROWTH OF THE PRESS

DEISM, TOLERANCE, REFORM

AGE OF REASON

SIÈCLE DES LUMIÈRES

SCOTLAND

Glasgow   ● Edinburgh
Boswell,   Adam Smith,
1740   1723
Burns,   Science—1731
1759   ENCYCLOPEDIA
           BRITANNICA—1771
● Belfast Hume, 1711
           Robertson, 1721

IRELAND

Goldsmith,
1728

Sterne,   Dublin
1713   Science—1739
           Swift, 1667
           Burke, 1729

ENGLAND

Romney,   ● Priestley,
1734   1733
Manchester○
Liverpool○ Sheffield○
Richardson, J. Wesley,
1689   1703
Birmingham○ S. Johnson, Norwich○
            1709
Cambridge○ Paine, 1737
Oxford○   Gainsborough,
Bristol○   1727
Addison,   The
1672   Hague
Fielding,   Hampton
1707   Court
Plymouth○   **London**
Portsmouth○ Lit. & Arts—1766
Reynolds,   BR. MUSEUM—1757
1723   THE TIMES—1785
            Defoe, 1659
            Pope, 1688
            Hogarth, 1697
            Gray, 1716
            Blackstone, 1723
            Gibbon, 1737
            Bentham, 1748

Brest○

FRANCE

Lamarck●   Rouen○
1744   Condorcet,
                       1743
Laplace,   <u>Versailles</u>○ **Paris**
1749   Houdon,   ENCYCLOPEDIE
            1741   1751-65
Orléans○   MONITEUR
                       1789-1868
Nantes○   Tours○   Voltaire, 1694
                       Chardin, 1699
                       Helvetius, 1715
                       d'Alembert, 1717
                       Turgot, 1727
                       Beaumarchais,1732
                       Lavoisier, 1743
                       David, 1748

Bordeaux●   Dijon●
Montesquieu,   Science—1740
1689   Buffon, 1707
            ● Raynal, Ferney○
              1713
                       Mably, 1709
Toulouse○   Montpellier○ Condillac, 1715
Science
1746   Fragonard● Lyon○
            1732
            Marseille○

Jovellanos,
1744

● Feyjóo 1676

PORTUGAL

SPAIN

Valladolid○

<u>La Granja</u>   Saragossa○
            Goya, 1746
Madrid○   Barcelona○
Lit. & Arts
1713

<u>Queluz</u>○ ○**Lisbon**   Valencia○
       Science
       1790

○Seville

NETHERLANDS

Amsterdam●
× The Loo
Leyden○
Boerhaave,
1668
Antwerp○
Brussels○   Cologne○ Bonn○
                      Beethov
Lille○   1770
Watteau,   Koblenz○
1684   Mainz○
                      Mannheim○
                      Science
                      1755
Condorcet,   Strassb○
1743
                      Wiei○

Diderot,
1713   Vattel, Zuri○
            1714   Pesta○
                     Haller,1708 174
                     SWITZERL
            Geneva○
            Rousseau,
            1712   Turin○
                       Science
                       1760
                       Lagrange,
            Affieri,   1736
            1749   Ge○

CORSICA

SARDINIA

Bergen○
Holberg,
1684

N O

DE○

Ha○

Bremen○

AUFKLÄ

Gö○
Scien

ROM

Bay
of
Biscay

Bay
of
Biscay

PYRENEES

Ebro

Duero

Tagus

Guadiana

Guadalquivir

Garonne

Loire

Seine

Rhine

Rhône

Mediterranean

M e d i t e

North Sea

North
Sea

BALEARIC   IS.

From R. R. Palmer, *Atlas of World History* (Chicago, 1957), pp. 82-83.

SWEDEN

St. Petersburg
Science, 1725 ○ ○ Tsarskoe Selo
Peterhof ○ Slutsk

↑ Lomonosov, 1711
(Near the White Sea)

Upsala
Science
1728 ○

Stockholm
Science—1741
Drottningholm
Swedenborg, 1688

Volga

Moscow
Radischev,
1749

Linnaeus,
1707

Baltic Sea

Dvina

R U S S I A

○ Copenhagen
Science—1743

Niemen

○ Königsberg
Kant, 1724

P O L A N D

—50°

Herder, 1744

Winckelmann,
1717 ● ● Berlin
Potsdam | Science
1700
Lit. & Arts
1703
Charlottenburg

Vistula

Warsaw ○

○ Handel, 1685
○ Weimar ○ Lessing,
1729
rfurt | Breslau
ience | Dresden | Wolff,
1679
MANACH DE
OTHA—1778 ○ Prague
● Gluck, 1714
emberg

Oder

Cracow ○ C A R P A T H I A N S

Dnieper

Dniester

A U S T R I A

Danube

mphenburg
Munich
Science
1759

Vienna
Lit. & Arts
1704
Schönbrunn
Haydn,
1732

Buda ○ ○ Pest

H U N G A R Y

Salzburg
Mozart,
1756

Canova,
e 1757

Adriatic Sea

Venice
Tiepolo, 1696
Goldoni, 1707

Danube

Black Sea

ogna
ience
712
ence

UMINISMO

● Galiani,
1728

○ Constantinople

—40°

I T A L Y

ne ○

Caserta
Naples ○ •. Pompeii
Vico, 1668 Ruins discovered
Filangieri, 1748
1752

O T T O M A N   E M P I R E

_rrhenian
Sea_

_Ionian
Sea_

_Aegean
Sea_

Athens ○

● Palermo

S I C I L Y

_ean
Sea_

CRETE

lectuals and publicists constructed the philosophy of the Enlightenment. Their outlook was conspicuously and consciously affected by the English example—by their admiration of the relatively free, remarkably prosperous society of England after the Glorious Revolution and of the English philosophers and scientists, especially Newton and Locke. Much hinged upon the more or less unconsciously held metaphysics of Newton who, as we have seen, portrayed the universe as a vast machine subject to physical and mathematical laws discoverable by man. Similarly, Locke exhibited the human mind as a machine-like instrument which out of sensory experiences produced knowledge. Both matter and mind, then, were capable of rational explanation without regard for "occult qualities" or "innate ideas," that is, without faith or revealed knowledge (revelation).

The eighteenth century became intoxicated with these notions, carrying them to limits far beyond those acceptable to either Newton or Locke. A host of prophets arose, usually known by their French name of *philosophes*. Only some of them were French and even fewer deserved the name of philosopher. Rather, the *philosophes* were promoters, propagandists, journalists, political scientists, economists, and reformers. They derived their basic principles from the scientists and philosophers of the preceding century; and they envisioned a brave new age in which man, by the use of *reason* would discover the *natural laws* which govern human existence and, by remolding human institutions in accord with nature, create a perfect society, with freedom, equality, justice, and peace. Indeed, if a capsule of the eighteenth-century spirit were compounded, it would consist of concentrated amounts of rationalism, naturalism, secularism, and progress. *Rationalism* was the sense of complete confidence in the unlimited capacities of human reason. *Naturalism* was faith in "natural order"—that is, in a mechanistic universe ordered like a vast machine and operating strictly in accord with the laws of nature. *Secularism* was interpreted as a lively interest in this world as opposed to a relatively small concern about otherworldliness, or the nature of another spiritual existence. *Progress* represented a conviction that man had not only made great advances already but that he also stood on the threshold of even greater achievements whereby, by his own efforts, he would lift himself and his worldly society—figuratively speaking—on a level with the angels and only a little below God himself. Paradoxically, here was a society at once the most secular and the most optimistic since ancient times.

The belief in progress might have been generated out of the entire intellectual complex of the times, but an incident near the close of the seventeenth century focused attention upon it. This was the "War between Ancients and Moderns," sometimes known as the "Battle of the Books." It began in 1687 when a French poet, Charles Perrault (1628–1703), a brother of the architect Claude Perrault, seeking to flatter the Sun King, stated in a poem that antiquity no longer had anything to teach the learned of his day. This statement set off a widespread, long, and sometimes bitter dispute between those who upheld the superiority of ancient classical scholarship and those who argued that the learning of the day was superior. Perrault consulted scientists and proclaimed, "within the last twenty or thirty years more discoveries have been made in natural science than were made throughout the whole period of learned antiquity." The arid dispute continued well into the eighteenth century and spread to many countries. In England Sir William Temple argued that the ancient Greeks "made greater progress in the several empires of science than any of their successors have been able to reach"; and Jonathan Swift's *Battle of the Books* (1704) argued in a similar vein. But gradually the idea gained ground that, while there have been setbacks during eras of war or other hardships, most generations of men have added to the intellectual stores of mankind. Knowledge, then, is cumulative and, accordingly, the moderns are bound to be ahead of the ancients. This view grew into a widely held doctrine of perpetual and inevitable progress extending indefinitely into the future. The evidence, however, was almost wholly drawn from advances in the new science, and almost everyone assumed, without proof, that moral, aesthetic, and political improvements follow upon the enlargement of scientific knowledge. The resultant confusion between *quantitative* and *qualitative* knowledge—between knowledge and wisdom—has plagued the modern world ever since. And the idea of progress also has had continued wide acceptance, especially the notion that material advancement inevitably contributes to intellectual, moral, and spiritual welfare.

THE SPREAD OF THE ENLIGHTENMENT

The hopeful creed of the Enlightenment was developed and broadcast widely by a variety of persons and a variety of media. One highly important person was Voltaire, the pen name of François Marie Arouet (1694–1778), whose life span nearly coincided with the Age of Enlightenment. Indeed, Voltaire above all others epitomized the spirit and thought of the Enlightenment. He subscribed enthusiastically to its tenets, and he spent his entire life explaining and promoting them in satires, plays, essays, histories, romances, scientific treatises, and in thousands of letters to other *philosophes,* to public figures and crowned heads, with many of whom he was on friendly terms. He wielded a sharp pen and was a champion of individual freedom, especially freedom of speech and freedom of opinion. A misconstruction of one of his comments is often cited as the highest standard of intellectual tolerance: "I do not agree with a word you say, but I will defend to the death your right to say it." His early satires got him into trouble with French authorities, and he was imprisoned and later exiled (1726). He spent three years in England, and his *Philosophical Letters on the English* (1733), published after his return to France, were at once a panegyric of English institutions, society, freedom, and learning and a criticism of nearly everything French. Voltaire believed profoundly in the ideas of Newton and Locke, and he wrote many things in their praise. He promoted the belief that the world is governed by natural laws discernible by human reason, and he sought to reform those existing institutions and attitudes of mind that led to oppression, misery, and ignorance. He blasted the intolerance of the church and the cruelties of religious persecutions; and he blasted with equal severity the inequalities and injustices of the courts and penal codes of his day. Indeed, the object of his life was, as he said, "to crush the infamous." This he did with a subjective fervor approaching fanaticism, until the Old Régime cringed at the acid drippings of Voltaire's pen.

Other *philosophes* included Denis Diderot (1713–1784) and Jean le Rond d'Alembert (1717?–1783) who, as editors, headed a considerable body of contributors (which included Voltaire) to the French *Grand Encyclopedia,* published between 1751 and 1765. The "encyclopedists," as they are called, represented a movement typical of the Enlightenment (the still famous *Encyclopaedia Britannica,* which first appeared in 1771, was a product of this movement). Believing themselves living on a new high plateau of learning and in possession of the keys with which to unlock all the secrets of nature, the *philosophes* of many nations set out to prepare compendiums of knowledge for public consumption and reference. Greatest of these was the French *Encyclopedia,* which began as a project to translate an earlier English *Cyclopedia* by Ephraim Chambers. But Diderot, who became the moving spirit behind the French undertaking, grew dissatisfied with a mere translation of a previous work, and set out with the aid of "a society of men of letters and skilled workmen" to prepare an original publication that would "encompass . . . each and every branch of human knowledge," and "to collect all the knowledge that now lies scattered over the face of the earth, to make known its general structure to the men among whom we live, and to transmit it to those who will come after us." The result, after more than twenty years of effort—often interrupted by censors—was a magnificent, illustrated, multivolumed work which still stands as a monument to and an abridgement of the learning of the Enlightenment, with all its naïveté, its faith in the reason and goodness of men, its glorification of science, its materialism, and its reforming zeal.

The French *Encyclopedia,* with English, German, Italian, and other similar publications, went far to popularize the learning and the spirit of the Enlightenment. But a number of other media contributed to the same end. The *salons* of France, Italy, and elsewhere were popular and influential. The salon was a reception room of a large private home where guests assembled at fairly regular intervals for a long afternoon and evening of conversation, usually under the guidance of the hostess who generally was a wealthy woman of the nobility or upper bourgeoisie. Different salons attracted persons of different interests, usually depending upon the tastes of the hostess.

Some discussed language and literature, some science, some politics, and so on, although there was also a measure of interlocking memberships. They were the meeting places of the *philosophes,* welcoming new ideas and new men with little regard for their origins. Impecunious young men were accepted (some appeared practically to have boarded themselves at a succession of weekly salons), and the salons came to have a wide influence on opinion, especially in France.

In England, and to a lesser degree on the Continent, *coffee houses* played a role similar to that of the salons. They lacked the wealthy hostesses and the elegant surroundings, however, and contained fewer patrons of noble lineage. Some of the coffee houses were regular meeting places for men engaged in business enterprises, but many served as the centers of literary, scientific, political, philosophical, and artistic gatherings where from mid-afternoon until late at night learned conversations and discussions went on. The Temple Coffee House in London, for example, was the center of a weekly meeting of botanists and others interested in natural science, just as Child's Coffee House was often the scene of discussions involving such literary and artistic figures as David Garrick, the actor, Thomas Sheridan and Oliver Goldsmith, writers, Dr. Samuel Johnson, of the *English Dictionary* fame, and his indefatigable biographer, James Boswell.

The press disseminated the ideas and the spirit of the Enlightenment yet more widely. The Age of the Enlightenment was a period during which popular books, periodicals, newspapers, and almanacs multiplied as never before. Fontenelles's *Conversations on the Plurality of Worlds,* Algaroth's *Newtonianism for Ladies,* Euler's *Letters to a German Princess,* and Goldsmith's *History of the Earth and of Animated Nature* were all popularizations of science and the new philosophy. Addison and Steele's *Spectator, The Gentleman's Magazine,* the *Année Litteraire,* and many other periodicals published accounts of the latest books and scientific discoveries. The penny press burgeoned in England and her colonies. Franklin's *Poor Richard's Almanac* was only one of the better known vehicles in which summaries of the latest news, spiced with homely gems of wisdom, were disseminated among the people. Most of the periodicals, newspapers, and almanacs regularly reprinted for popular consumption significant articles from the *Philosophical Transactions* of the Royal Society of London or the *Journal des Sçavans* of the French Academy of Science. Thus the learning, the philosophy, and the optimistic spirit of the Enlightenment were spread widely among the peoples of Europe and their overseas colonies.

4 : Religion and the Church

DURING THE Age of the Enlightenment the Christian churches and the Christian religion underwent changes which were more destructive to orthodoxy than those sustained during the Protestant Revolt. However, these alterations were not all of one piece. Some persons drifted away from orthodoxy, substituted a "natural" or a "rational" religion for Christian faith, or embraced atheism outright; others sought to reinforce Christianity by embracing "enthusiasm," that is, an appeal to emotions. And, while enthusiastic new sects multiplied, efforts were made to imbue the old ones with less formalized, more personal emotional fire. Thus arose Jansenism in the Catholic church, Pietism in Lutheran circles, and Methodism in the Church of England. Together, they constituted an impressive evangelistic revival in the seventeenth and eighteenth centuries.

Jansenism, sometimes called Catholic Puritanism, stemmed from the teachings of a Dutch Roman Catholic theologian and onetime bishop of Ypres, Cornelius Jansen (1585–1638). Like Calvin, Jansen greatly admired the teachings of Augustine, and his contentions brought him and his followers into conflict with the Jesuits. The fierce controversies that followed were strictly within the Roman Catholic church, and they tore the church asunder throughout the latter seventeenth and most of the eighteenth centuries, particularly in the Low Countries and in France. Bitterly opposed by Louis XIV and repeatedly condemned by papal bulls, the Jansenists nonetheless survived by virtue of their austere morality, their fervent preaching, their Bible reading, their alleged miracles, and their appeal to those who responded to a religion of the heart rather than to the formalism of the orthodox Mass. Dominant for a time in the Low Countries, they were less successful in France, although they continued strong in country parishes and some provincial towns throughout the eighteenth century. Meanwhile, their bitter foes, the Jesuits, fell upon evil ways. Imprudent leadership, Jansenist charges against them, and reports that Jesuit missionaries compromised Christian orthodoxy with heathen beliefs and practices in the Far East led to their expulsion from Portugal in 1759, their dissolution in France in 1764, and their eviction from Spain (including Spanish colonies overseas) in 1767. Finally, in 1773, the Jesuit Order was formally dissolved, suppressed, and extinguished by a papal bull, not to rise up again until the early nineteenth century. Roman Catholicism was sorely tried by these internal troubles and reached its nadir during the Enlightenment.

Pietism, the Lutheran "enthusiasm," began with the efforts of Philipp Jacob Spener (1635–1705) and his successor in the movement, August Herman Francke (1663–1727), to inject into German Lutheranism a new "piety," a living faith made active by Bible study, individual religious activity, greater communion between the lonely soul and God, hymn singing, mysticism, powerful preaching, and upright conduct. Orthodox Lutheranism, according to the Pietists, had become formal, meaningless, and sterile; it had become "orthodoxy for the sake of orthodoxy," without power to stir the hearts of its communicants. From the University of Halle, where Francke became professor of theology in 1698, went forth a new generation of ministers fired with the ambition to reform and infuse new life into

Lutheranism. But in the long run they failed of their object. Instead of making over Lutheranism, they fell into separatist groups, thus multiplying Protestant sects. The Moravians arose in this fashion, founded by the gentle but energetic Count Nikolaus von Zinzendorf (1700–1760) in Saxony and, in the 1740's, spread into the British colony of Pennsylvania.

Similarly, Methodism began in the Church of England as a result of the efforts of John Wesley (1703–1791) and his brother Charles (1707–1788) to enliven Anglicanism, and to change it from "a lifeless, formal religion" into "a religion of love, joy, peace, having its seat in the heart; in the inmost soul." But the Wesleys ran afoul of English bishops and in time were forced reluctantly to withdraw from the Church of England and to join the ranks of "dissenting" English sects. The Wesleys and their associates were powerful preachers and prolific hymn writers, and they had great success in reviving personal religion "to spread holiness over the land." Their success was especially notable among the working classes of England and on the colonial frontiers of America. They organized hospitals and charitable institutions to mitigate the evils of poverty, drunkenness, and crime; and they founded schools and colleges to combat ignorance and illiteracy. Their social program contributed much toward their success, while the eloquent preaching of the early Methodist leaders moved the hearts of thousands and Methodism became a prominent and important sect in the English-speaking world.

Still, the movements designed to infuse a new spirit into the churches were a negative response to the Enlightenment, an effort to preserve orthodoxy even at the expense of unity. More positively in the path of the Enlightenment were natural religion and deism which insidiously (if often unintentionally) weakened the basic fabric of Christian faith like termites in a building.

NATURAL RELIGION AND DEISM

Natural religion was the refuge of the early scientists. As they examined the remarkable things in nature, they piously exclaimed over the beauty of flowers, the intricacies of anatomy, and the wonders and varieties of God's creation. At the same time they were seeking ways to explain these things in terms of human rationality—to subject God's works and God's laws in nature to rational explanation and to deny "revealed truths" and "miracles." In time most of them argued that the truth of Christianity can be demonstrated by rational proofs, ignoring the spiritual needs to which Christianity had long ministered. Here was an insidious substitution of *rational inquiry* for Christian faith—and faith was (and is) the bulwark of Christian orthodoxy. Obviously, most of the early scientists were drawn into natural religion without suspecting the damage wrought upon orthodox faith, and they loudly proclaimed their "proofs" of Christianity while they swept spiritual questions and orthodox theology under the rug. But there is reason to suspect the sincerity of some who, like Descartes, wrote privately to substitute in his works the expression "the mathematical order of nature," whenever the word "God" occurred; or who, like Newton, wrote voluminously to define the true religion while his unpublished papers reveal that he was an anti-Trinitarian who held "what cannot be understood is no object of belief." If all objects of Christian belief must march under the banner of reason, what becomes of that Christian faith to "believe things incredible"?

Natural religion was a forerunner of the deism, skepticism, and atheism of the Enlightenment. But deism was the product of other factors as well, such as impatience with the multiplicity, intolerance, and cruelty of Christian sects, and it was an attempt to found a religion in harmony with the "natural" religious impulses of all men as divulged by a study of comparative religions. The former left the deist dizzy and exasperated by their conflicting claims and mutual exclusiveness; the latter, a by-product of travelers' accounts of the religions of other lands, including those of primitive folk in America, seemed to demonstrate that man is by nature a religious animal inasmuch as almost all men everywhere exhibit faith in a god (or gods) and have developed more or less elaborate rites and ceremonies of worship.

The taproot of deism sprang from obscure Reformation soil, and the movement reached its height in the seventeenth and eighteenth centuries. Lord Herbert of Cherbury (1583–1648), an English philosopher and diplomat, set forth the most centrally discussed elements of deism. His treatise, *De Veritate (Concerning Truth; 1624)* held that all men are by nature religious, endowed with innate features common to all religions. These elemental articles, five in number, ran as follows: (1) there is one supreme God; (2) he ought to be worshiped; (3) virtue and piety are the chief part of divine worship; (4) men should be sorry for their sins and repent them; and (5) divine goodness dispenses rewards and punishments both in this life and after it. Lord Herbert argued that these articles contained the fundamentals of all religion "according to common reason and universal consent" and that particular faiths should be tested by his code, casting out all principles and practices which "depend not on common reason, but on tradition and authority." All revelation, all miracles were rejected as contrary to reason and nature. Deism prescribed no ceremonies and no specific rites, as each person set his own. Indeed, deism was not a church and had no formal organization; rather, it was an intellectual movement in religious thought—an individual pursuit of spiritual happiness by the practice of reason and truth. Its appeal, at the outset, was principally to intellectuals. In time, it filtered into the ranks of society to become the more or less unconsciously-held position (alongside natural religion) of the "unchurched Christians" of the last two centuries.

Deism had run its course by the end of the eighteenth century, affecting nearly every Western people to some extent. It turned up in the British colonies of North America, where (among others) Benjamin Franklin's "essentials of every religion" as described in his *Autobiography* were almost identical to Lord Herbert's five articles. In France it reached its most extreme forms, more hostile to Christianity, more critical of organized religion than elsewhere. Many French deists held that Christianity was an obstacle which must be removed before the natural morality and goodness of man could find full expression. "Churchmen are interested in keeping the people ignorant," said Montesquieu, and many of the French deists became militantly *anticlerical* without becoming antireligious. In France, too, deism, together with natural religion, became stepping-stones to scepticism and atheism. True deists asserted belief in God—although not the God of orthodox Christianity—even when their belief was as negatively held as in Voltaire's statement, "In the opinion that there is a God there are difficulties; but in the contrary opinion there are absurdities." But others, like Pierre Bayle, the sceptic, declared that knowledge of the ultimate nature of God is impossible for man ("Research into Final Causes, like a virgin dedicated to God, is barren"); or, like Denis Diderot and Baron d'Holbach denied the existence of God and, as the latter said, depended only upon "common sense."

Deism left no sect, but it left permanent marks upon Western thought. Most important among these was the separation of religion and morality. Heretofore it had been believed that to live in accord with the commandments of God and of the church meant to live morally, for to live a moral life it was necessary to live a religious life. But deists held that orthodox religion is unessential to a moral life; indeed, it may imperil morality. Morality, they argued, rests upon principles deduced from man's nature, founded in reason and experience, and in no way necessarily related to religion. Moreover, morality is humanistic in that it is concerned with man's duties to his fellow men. Its basis is the universal desire for human happiness; it is realized by obeying the rules discovered by reason and proved by experience. Moral virtue, then, is doing right by one's neighbor. To extol virtue is to extol social well-being. And at this point deism joined the parade of the *philosophes* in demanding social reforms.

5 : The *Philosophes* and Reform

CHARACTERISTIC of the Enlightenment was the emphasis upon reform. As God, reinterpreted by science and philosophy, ceased to be a personal God who numbered the hairs of every man's head and counted every sparrow's fall and came to be thought of as a master mechanic of a vast machine-like

universe, so man loomed larger on the scene and became the object of a
steadily increasing interest. The oft-quoted lines of Alexander Pope set the
tone:

> *Know then thyself, presume not God to scan;*
> *The proper study of mankind is Man.*

After Newton had converted the universe into a machine, man, as part of
the natural setting, was visualized as being subject to natural law. Studies
regarding man and his institutions were greatly stimulated, the method
being adopted from the natural sciences and the object being to discover
the laws by which man acted as he did. It was assumed that all societies at
all times were governed by the same forces and that human actions could
be reduced to simple formulas analogous to those of physics. Like the laws
of the new experimental philosophy, the laws of human society were natural
laws, discoverable by reason and experience. As experiments are difficult to
construct and even more difficult to carry out, the *philosophes* fell back upon
experience, confident that by deductive reasoning from history processes
now at work can be discovered and analyzed and the laws regulating them
set forth. Thus the idea of science was applied to society and the "social
sciences" were born. History, economics, law, and political science were
elevated to new positions and given new directions.

A NEW HISTORY

History became the great reservoir of "facts" from which the social
scientist deduced the natural laws governing man's proper relations with
man. Indeed, with few exceptions, since ancient times history had been
considered as the gradual fulfillment of divine prophecy, as chronicles of
noble personages, or as a mere register (annals) of events. Inevitably,
of course, much had been called history which had been carefully pruned of
inconveniences to serve as special pleading for specific policies or to justify
the acts of certain great rulers. Now, in the eighteenth century some of the
philosophes had a glimmer of objectivity in history—although most of their
pretensions in this direction far outshone their actual performances.

Voltaire complained bitterly against previous historical accounts for
their concern with supernatural events. He held that history should be the
record of man's progress "from barbarous rusticity" to the "politeness" of
his own day. Moreover, Voltaire sought to broaden history so as to include
all manner of events, not to multiply facts but to assess broad trends, to
comprehend the changing *spirit of man*. He wrote several histories marked
by attention to laws, the arts, manners, and daily life shorn of supernatural
events and with an attempt to record the history of man from a world
view. He consulted archives and other sound authorities. Yet, while Voltaire
did much to improve history and historical scholarship, his own works

were badly infected with his own prejudices, the chief of which was his purpose in writing history. Voltaire wrote history as a proof of progress and as a guide for reforms in society. As such, his histories betray the spirit of the Enlightenment in such a way as to resemble rather tracts for the times than well-balanced, judicious history.

Like Voltaire, Henry St. John, Viscount Bolingbroke (1678–1751), decried the "dry register of useless anecdotes" which had passed for history. But Bolingbroke insisted that history should teach lessons, especially lessons in morality. To him, history properly was philosophy teaching by example, its "true and proper object a constant improvement in private and public virtue." David Hume (1711–1776), a Scottish philosopher and historian, valued history as a means of tracing the rise of human civilization, especially the rise of civil society and the establishment of stable government. He considered history to be instructive about "the constant and universal principles of human nature" which would provide data for the formulation of philosophical principles (laws) of human society. But, like Voltaire, Hume began with philosophical principles already formulated and selected historical data to support them. Only Giambattista Vico (1668–1744), an obscure Neapolitan philosopher and historian, whose works were scarcely noticed in his own day, came up with a philosophy of history that is challenging still today. Like most of his own generation, Vico assumed the similarity and recurrence of human institutions. But instead of viewing history as a record of straight-line progress from barbarism to civilization, Vico postulated a cyclical view wherein, to be sure, history is the record of the development of man from a barbarous state of nature to civilization. Beyond that, however, Vico also saw societies decay and fall prey to others or degenerate into barbarism again—an interesting antecedent of the cyclical theories of Spengler and Toynbee in the twentieth century. Vico emancipated history from the shackles of theology, morality, and politics, and added techniques of a remarkably "modern" sort; his philosophy of history belonged to the Enlightenment only in point of time. His contemporary influence was very slight, and he remained almost unknown until the present century.

A NEW POLITICAL ECONOMY

Beyond alterations in historical scholarship, the *philosophes* also sought to reform the very fabric of existing institutions to bring them into harmony with nature and reason. Mercantilism became one of their objects of attack. Partly they objected to the mercantilists' emphasis upon commerce and industry to the relative exclusion of agriculture as a source of wealth, and partly they felt that the widespread state regulation of economic enterprise artificially (and therefore unnaturally) choked off the free interplay of economic forces in a natural economy. Hence, they recommended reforms

in the interests of freer trade, free enterprise, and greater equality in taxation. One of the early new "schools" of economic thought was that of the
physiocrats, or "advocates of the rule of nature." These consisted of a group
of French "economic philosophers" and publicists centering about François
Quesnay (1694-1774), a physician and surgeon to King Louis XV. The
physiocrats gathered about 1757, held meetings, published the *Journal of
Agriculture* and many other economic tracts, and they strove to translate
their opinions into political action. Soon they attracted wide attention, including that of a Scottish philosopher, Adam Smith (1723-1790), who
visited Quesnay and his physiocratic group in France. Later Smith's book,
An Inquiry Into the Nature and Causes of the Wealth of Nations (1776),
often referred to simply as Smith's *Wealth of Nations,* became the classic
statement of the new economics—indeed, of the "classical economics" which
underlay the capitalistic system of the next century. Smith varied from the
physiocrats at points, especially in giving a greater place to labor and less
to land as a source of wealth. But, like the French school, he denounced
mercantilist regulation and upheld the principles of freer trade and untrammeled private enterprise as those most conducive to prosperity in a state.
Laissez faire et laissez passer (roughly translated as a "let alone policy"
on the part of the state) became the key phrase attributed to Smith's economics. Significantly, it has been left in its French form as befits the physiocrats from whom Smith had borrowed freely—although the *Wealth of
Nations* was a far more rounded and complete system of economic thought
than the physiocrats turned out.

LAW REFORMS AND CODIFICATION

The laws, especially the criminal and penal laws, were another object
of reform by the *philosophes*. They deplored the multiplicity and chaotic
state of the laws and demanded that they be codified into orderly bodies.
Further, they argued that, as many laws originated in tradition, custom,
precedents, or other irrational sources, they should be made conformable to
reason and in accord with nature. Away with customs, mere precedents, and
the like! Laws should be clear, plain, reasonable, and conformable to the
nature of man—which was often to say that they should be utilitarian. A
widespread movement for codification of the laws got under way from the
philosophes' agitation, and it continued well into the nineteenth century,
resulting in the Prussian law codes, projected codes for Russia and Austria,
and others. Perhaps the greatest achievements were the Napoleonic Codes
of the revolutionary epoch a scant half-century later. Voltaire was a mighty
pioneer in advocating law reform, especially for the eradication of the tor-
turing of prisoners to win confessions, the cruel punishments often inflicted
upon persons convicted of relatively petty crimes, the favoritism sometimes
shown to "persons of quality," and the horrible conditions in prisons. The

Marchese di Cesare Bonesana Beccaria (1735-1794), a brilliant young Milanese economist and jurist inspired by Voltaire, published an *Essay on Crimes and Punishments* (1764), which is a landmark in the reform of criminal and penal law. Beccaria's approach was distinctly utilitarian, and it undermined the older Christian views of crimes and punishments. To Beccaria, crime was an injury to society the prevention of which was of greater moment than its punishment. However, he viewed punishment as a deterrent to crime and insisted that it should be made proportional to the seriousness of the injury to society—"to make the punishment fit the crime." Beccaria's book served as the inspiration for nearly all subsequent writings as well as for many practical reforms in criminal law and penal codes to this day.

Most of the *philosophes,* following Voltaire's *Philosophical Letters on the English* (1733), were great admirers of the English political constitution. The English themselves, from John Locke on, wrote glowing tributes to the remarkable political settlement made in the Glorious Revolution, and Voltaire, after his exile in England, praised the harmony of the crown, Lords, and Commons, the liberties of Englishmen as set forth in the Bill of Rights, the religious tolerance effected by the Toleration Act, and the freedom of expression, of movement, and of thought in England. John Locke's *Two Treatises of Civil Government* became identified (though not very accurately) with the English constitutional set-up, and the contract theory of the state was the stock in trade of most *philosophes'* views regarding the origin of civil society. Here was man emerging from the state of nature into civil society. Why did he do it? How can he get back to nature—or at least cast off the shackles of custom and traditional authority in order to enthrone the laws of nature in the civil state?

NEW THEORIES OF THE STATE

Locke had given rational explanations; Montesquieu (1689-1755) sought to explain these questions by reference to history—that is, "scientifically," on the basis of experience. His *Esprit des Lois* (*Spirit of Laws,* 1748) founded political science in its modern sense. Montesquieu had wide knowledge of history and classical political theory. In addition, he searched diligently among the living societies of his own day, from the British colonies in North America to China and Africa, in order to compare and contrast existing institutions and to join fact with theory in testing the validity of legal and constitutional theorists. The *Spirit of Laws* is a long book, and we can only consider its major contributions. "I do not pretend to treat of laws, but of their spirit," said Montesquieu. Like other *philosophes,* the author believed that human nature is unchanging and unchangeable; but Montesquieu maintained that the *forms* of government and the *spirit* of laws are determined by environmental conditions of climate and geography. Laws and governments accord with nature if they correspond to the character of a people, and the character of a people depends heavily upon climate and geography. Montesquieu classified governments according to their fundamental principles: *monarchy,* of which the principle is honor; *republic,* of which the principle is virtue or patriotism; and *despotism,* of which the principle is fear. In each form the institutions were molded by the ruling principle. Moreover, Montesquieu analyzed and clarified (if, indeed, he did not oversimplify) the functions of government which, as applied by the Constitution makers of the United States, became the legislative, executive, and judicial branches familiar to every American schoolboy, together with the system of checks and balances set up to avoid the tyranny of any one branch. "Law in general is human reason," said Montesquieu, and the laws of each nation should be adapted to the people involved, to their ruling principle, and to their environmental conditions. Liberty, so important to human happiness, is not license; rather, "it is the right of doing whatever the laws permit." To achieve it requires laws in harmony with the nature of the people involved, the absence of abuse of power achieved by checks and balances, and moderate, judicious, and humane administration.

Montesquieu exerted a direct and obvious influence on American constitutionalism, especially in his theory of the separation of powers. But in the European scene Jean Jacques Rousseau (1712–1778), the Genevan philosopher, held greater attraction, especially for radical reformers of the French Revolution and even for totalitarian leaders of the twentieth century—although for different reasons. Rousseau has long been recognized as a transitional figure, with one foot in the Enlightenment and the other in the gathering forces of Romanticism, which gradually displaced the Enlightenment. Like the *philosophes,* Rousseau was a worshiper of nature and reason; and like the Romanticists, he displayed occasional flashes of mysticism. His work, *The Social Contract; or, Principles of Political Right* (1762), began with a classic statement of a classic problem of governments everywhere:

> Man is born free; and everywhere he is in chains. One thinks himself the master of others, and still remains a greater slave than they. How did this change come about? I do not know. What can make it legitimate? That question I think I can answer.

Rousseau's answer developed a new and startling version of the contract theory of the state. Unlike Montesquieu, whose essay was based upon a factual survey of the world, Rousseau deduced his doctrines from premises supplied by personal introspection and contemplation. Seized with a "sudden inspiration" in 1749, Rousseau held that "man is naturally good, and that it is only by our own institutions that men become wicked." Nature elevates man; civilization corrupts him. Therefore, if the institutions of civilization would follow nature more closely men would be less corrupt. His *Social Contract* was intended as a blueprint for a civil society designed to follow nature. The answer to his question at the beginning of the treatise is the *social compact*—not a political contract, like Locke's, between ruler and ruled, but a social compact by which a whole society agrees to be governed by its General Will. Sovereignty rests in the whole community and is expressed by the General Will. Formulation of the General Will is everybody's business and cannot be transferred or delegated to representative bodies ("Every law the people has not ratified in person is null and void—is, in fact, not a law"). That this was impractical, especially in large states, Rousseau himself recognized; but he had his eye on an ideal state, "a people of gods," and not a down-to-earth, workable reality. The General Will, however, might be executed by smaller bodies and the size of the body varied inversely with the size of the states—that is, Rousseau preferred democracy in small, poor states, aristocracy in medium-sized states, and monarchy in large, wealthy states. But all, as they were governed by laws expressing the General Will, were republics in Rousseau's eyes, for there the public interest (*res publica*) governed.

Rousseau exalted the state and placed the national welfare above that of the individual's interests. How else can one interpret his description of the essence of the social compact?

> Each of us puts his person and all his power under the supreme direction of the general will, and, in our corporate capacity, we receive each member as an indivisible part of the whole.

Hence, Rousseau's Compact, unlike Locke's Contract, admits no "natural" rights of the individual excepted out of the power of the state. Indeed, in time, Rousseau's social compact became an "authority" by which to justify the collectivism of socialists on the one hand and the totalitarian state on the other. Still, if his own life and deeds be considered in conjunction with his written works as a basis of interpreting Rousseau, it is evident that he was an advocate of democracy and a believer in individualism. The mysticism inherent in the General Will impelled later Romantic writers to equate it with an organic view of the state, and dictators seeking justification for their tyranny claimed, like Hitler, to be the mystical epitomes of the General Will of their peoples.

6 : Enlightened Despotism

THE RUMINATIONS of the *philosophes* about the origin of the state and the structure of law were basic in their concern for reform, their desire to find the way to a more perfect society. On all sides their society cried out for reforms. This was the *ancien régime* (Old Régime), a term applied by French revolutionary writers to the society they swept aside during the

French Revolution, and adopted by later commentators as a vaguely descriptive term for European society and institutions of the eighteenth century. For the most part, the evils of the Old Régime were the result of centuries of accumulation: like a household which, as it acquired new furniture, never had the heart to throw much of the old away. Thus, centralized monarchies had been superimposed upon decentralized feudal states without clearing away many of the now useless remnants of feudalism. The nobles' powers on their manorial estates had been curbed but not destroyed; and they still clung to privileges which, in effect, rendered them relatively tax-free and enabled them to hold a monopoly of lands, of public offices both in church and state, and of social recognition and prestige. Still, the orderly rule of the monarchies had widely replaced the services which the nobility had performed in the feudal age, and nobles as a class had become useless drones in society, clinging to their privileges with a fanatical zeal, often in debt if not impoverished, and proudly striving to keep up appearances.

At the opposite extreme were the serfs and the peasants, many times more numerous than the nobility. Serfdom was declining in western Europe, but it was by no means wholly extinct. Serfs were still bound to the soil, still in that half-slave condition they had been in during the Middle Ages—though no longer with those needs for security which originally had impelled their ancestors to place themselves under protection of the lords. The peasants as a rule did not possess enough land to make a living; and they often added to their meager incomes by renting (share-cropping) land from a noble landowner, working for him as hired help, or by turning their peasant huts into inns—which accounted for many of the wretched inns described by travelers. When times were especially bad, the peasant sometimes deserted his holding, sought employment in the towns, swelled the mobs of the cities, and not infrequently turned to a life of crime. As a peasant on his property, he was still subject to manorial fees and labor services to the lord. He bore a variety of taxes levied by local lords, by the church, and by the royal taxgatherers—and the royal taxes multiplied in number almost constantly. Thus, scattered and poverty-laden, the peasants were too unorganized, too inarticulate, too lacking in leadership to protest effectively. They grumbled, but they seldom rebelled.

Only the middle classes mounted a protest and cried out for reforms. Wealthy bourgeoisie envied the privileged nobility, and merchants found their profits severely reduced by the multiple tariffs and other barriers placed upon their trade. Printers, publishers, and writers constantly had their shops and their works burned or closed by stupid censors. Private enterprise of all kinds was encompassed by restrictions, taxed to death, or paralyzed by endless lawsuits. Accordingly, the bourgeoisie joined their voices with the *philosophes* to demand more equitable taxation, simplified laws, more speedy administration of justice, intellectual freedom, and religious toleration. Theirs was a bourgeois platform; they seldom betrayed concern for the condition of serfs and peasants; but it was a platform of reform for which there was a genuine need—for the sake of efficiency in government if for no other reason. Inefficiency, irrational disorder, and uncertainty had become so widespread that orderly methods and clarity were sorely needed. And it was an orderly method and clarity which the *philosophes* advocated: to reorganize the state and society in accordance with natural laws and to base public policies upon clear reason.

REFORMS BY PHILOSOPHER-KINGS

Yet the *philosophes,* though reformers, were not revolutionaries. They hoped to see reforms effected without violence (which is seldom rational) and in an orderly fashion. Accordingly, they looked toward philosopher-kings—a generation of rulers *wise* enough to recognize rational reform in accord with natural laws and *powerful* enough to bring them about. Their aim was not a ground swell of democratic action but reform imposed from above by enlightened despots. The *philosophes'* ideas about the origin of the state were easily fashioned to support enlightened despotism in spite of the highly regarded English model which, after 1689, was certainly no monarchic despotism. Grotius and Hobbes had supplied the clues, and Baron Samuel von Pufendorf (1632-1694), a German jurist and *philosophe,* supplied the synthesis in his *De Jure Naturae et Gentium* (*Concerning the Laws of Nature and of Peoples*) in 1672. After Grotius (who borrowed it from Cicero), Pufendorf emphasized natural law, which was already being elevated by the new science, as the common basis of reform, a means of establishing peace, order, and common welfare. Natural law as "right reason in agreement with nature" is common to all men, unalterable, eternal, and valid everywhere at all times. Moreover, every man would gladly obey it, as it is in complete harmony with human nature; indeed, anyone who disobeys natural law is "fleeing from himself and denying human nature." After Hobbes and others, Pufendorf held that the state came into being by virtue of a contract in which individuals surrendered all their rights to a single sovereign power so as to obtain order and to secure and promote the general welfare. However, unlike Locke and others we have noted, Pufendorf envisaged the people surrendering all their rights to the sovereign power, who thereby became supreme. Indeed, asks Pufendorf, how can a sovereign power enforce its acts and be sovereign unless it is one undivided, supreme authority? There can be no rights of individuals excepted from it; no right of revolution against it; no recall of authority once vested in it. The sovereign is accountable to none; yet, as his interests are the interests of all, he is the servant as well as the master of all. His interests, his aspirations, his welfare are all inextricably and inescapably bound up with those of his people. As no ruler will act contrary to his own interests, and as his are identical with those of his people, there will

GALILEO GALILEI

SIR FRANCIS BACON

RENÉ DESCARTES

SIR ISAAC NEWTON

These four men contributed mightily to that revolution in thinking which produced modern science and scientific method. Galileo, mathematician, physicist, and astronomer, was the author of the laws of falling bodies and defender of the Copernican view of the universe. Sir Francis Bacon promoted empiricism and inductive reasoning. Descartes, who emphasized deductive reasoning with mathematical precision and established a scientific approach to philosophy, sat for the famous painter Frans Hals. Sir Isaac Newton in his Principia (1687) *leaned upon Galileo, Descartes, and others, and went on to set forth the laws of universal gravitation and a mechanistic view of the universe. This portrait is by Sir Godfrey Kneller, court painter after the Restoration.*

OTTO VON GUERICKE'S EXPERIMENT

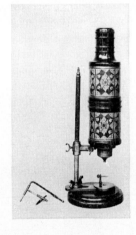

HOOKE'S COMPOUND MICROSCOPE

HUYGENS' AERIAL TELESCOPE

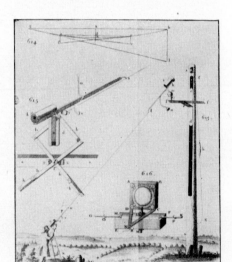

HUYGENS' PENDULUM CLOCK

Instruments are invaluable means to enlarge man's natural powers of observation in scientific work. Early scientists, like those of today, sought their constant improvement. Christian Huygens' aerial telescope was used at the Paris Observatory. Otto von Guericke's experiments at Magdeburg utilized hermetically-sealed hemispheres from which air was expelled by his pump. It was claimed that teams of horses could not pull them apart, so great was the atmospheric pressure. The hemispheres were also used to find the weight of air. Huygens' pendulum clock was the most accurate timepiece of the day. The fourth illustration shows Robert Hooke's own compound (multilensed) microscope.

JOHN LOCKE

VOLTAIRE

JEAN JACQUES ROUSSEAU

CHARLES DE MONTESQUIEU

The men pictured above represent different but interrelated aspects of the Enlightenment. John Locke, English physician, scholar, and popularizer, contributed to philosophy and political science and pioneered in psychology. Voltaire, whose real name was François Marie Arouet, was called "the voice of the Enlightenment." This French philosophe, historian, writer, literary critic, and reformer went far to spread the gospel of reason and to reform criminal and penal laws. Montesquieu was a French social critic, reformer, and early political scientist. Rousseau, a Genevan political philosopher, was an educational reformer as well.

"THE UPHOLSTERER"

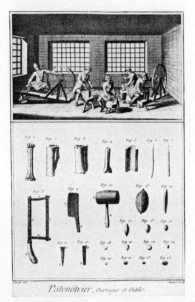

"THE ROSARY MAKER"

DENIS DIDEROT

Co-operative product of the French encyclopedists, the French Encyclopedia *was
a monumental work of many volumes. It
furnishes a many-sided glimpse into the
mind and thought of the Enlightenment,
and its supplementary volumes of illustrations are often unique sources for learning
about the materials and techniques of the
arts and crafts of the times. Denis Diderot, the editor and compiler of the* Encyclopedia, *devoted the latter decades of
his life to assembling and editing the
various authors' contributions, dodging
censors, and bringing the work to completion against great odds. "The Rosary
Maker," "The Pastry Cook," and "The
Upholsterer" are examples of the illustrations mentioned above. Note the materials and tools shown.*

"THE PASTRY COOK"

be complete harmony. Thus the Prussian King Frederick the Great (1740–1786), the foremost enlightened despot, described his role in his "Essay on Forms of Government and the Duties of Sovereigns" (1777):

> Let it be carefully remembered that the preservation of the laws was the sole reason which induced men to allow of, and to elect a superior; because this is the true origin of sovereign power. The magistrate thus appointed was the first servant of the state. . . . Princes and monarchs, therefore, are not invested with supreme authority that they may, with impunity, riot in debauchery and voluptuousness. . . . The sovereign is attached by individual ties to the body of the state; hence it follows that he, by repercussion, is sensible of all the ills which afflict his subjects. . . . There is but one general good, which is that of the state. . . . I once more repeat, the sovereign represents the state; and he and his people form but one body, which can only be happy as far as united by concord. The prince is to the nation he governs, what the head is to the man; it is his duty to see, think, and act for the whole community, that he may procure it every advantage of which it is capable.[5]

The enlightened despot was no less despotic than a divine-right monarch like James I of England; but the theoretical justification of his supreme power was wholly different, and the ends for which he governed were the material welfare and happiness of the people rather than their spiritual purity and eternal salvation. Absolute monarchy had been secularized in its theory, placed within the framework of natural law, dedicated to the methods of political science, and rendered strictly utilitarian in its objects.

Enlightened despotism fired the imagination of most of the rulers of Europe during the middle and later years of the eighteenth century. In varying degrees and with widely different results, almost every king, with his principal ministers, embarked upon programs designed to tidy up the clutter of the Old Régime, and to reform laws, administrations, and policies in conformity with natural law as interpreted by the *philosophes*. The philosopher-king was a close student of the works of the *philosophes,* was often a patron and frequent correspondent of them, and sometimes invited one or more of them to live at his court as a pensioner and adviser. Indeed, some of the enlightened despots, such as Frederick the Great of Prussia and Catherine the Great of Russia, themselves joined the *philosophes* in writing treatises on history, government, and reform proposals. If they sounded very much alike, it was because they drew from the same sources

---

[5] *Posthumous Works of Frederick II,* trans. from the French by Thomas Holcroft (13 vols.; London, 1789), V, 8ff.

and, generally, faced similar problems. Three principal enlightened despots emerged: Frederick II, "the Great," of Prussia (1740–1786), who was the most practical and successful; Catherine II, "the Great," of Russia (1762–1796), who ran into insuperable odds, accomplished very little, and in her later years forsook the path of reform and reverted to despotic conservatism; and Joseph II, Holy Roman Emperor (co-regent in Austria with his mother, Maria Theresa, from 1765 to 1780, and in full control from 1780 to 1790), perhaps the most sincere of the enlightened despots, but one whose impolitic methods led to almost complete failure.

With these three, and with all of the enlightened despots, however, the suspicion lurks that in spite of their fine words they were merely riding the crest of the wave of the Enlightenment as a means to dynastic aggrandizement: they sought reform in order to promote prosperity and content among their peoples who, in turn, would the more willingly bear arms and heavier taxes for larger forces—and the larger armies better enabled the dynast to overawe his neighbors, seize their territories, and place himself in a position of greater power and prestige. The dynastic wars of the mid-eighteenth century, involving most of the enlightened despots, promote such suspicion, and in fact many of the reforms appear as attempts to heal the ravages of these wars. It was as much in the spirit of war as in that of the Enlightenment that enlightened despots persuaded their subjects to accept the identification of the monarchs' objectives with the genuine welfare of the state as a whole, thus contributing to a new spirit of popular nationalism and a rising national patriotism.

THE WARS OF THE MID-EIGHTEENTH CENTURY

Peace did not long prevail after the War of Spanish Succession and the Great Northern War. Spain, annoyed by alleged British abuses of trading privileges in Spanish America granted by the Utrecht settlement of 1713, engaged in desultory maritime conflict which built up to the War of Jenkins' Ear in 1738. But the War of Austrian Succession, beginning in 1740, overshadowed this lesser conflict and set off a major struggle which, with intermissions, lasted until 1763 and engulfed the world.

Two deaths set the stage for the War of Austrian Succession. In May, 1740, Frederick William I of Prussia died. Since his reign had begun in 1713, this crotchety, stubborn, penny-pinching second king in Prussia had built up in Brandenburg-Prussia a thriving economy, a militaristic bureaucracy, a well-filled treasury, and the best-drilled army of Europe. His son and heir, Frederick II, had been given a Spartan training and, in spite of effeminate inclinations toward flute playing and French literature, was anxious to make a mark for himself. His opportunity came when, a few months after his father's death, the Habsburg emperor, Charles VI, also died. Charles VI was the second son of Emperor Leopold I (1658–1705), and he had succeeded his elder brother Joseph I who died in 1711. Neither Joseph nor Charles had male heirs, though both had daughters. It had been the passion of Charles VI to secure the Habsburg succession for his daughters in preference to those of Joseph I, and to this end he had negotiated with the princes of Germany and nearly every European power a series of treaties known as the Habsburg Pragmatic Sanction Treaties. In consequence, when Charles VI died his successor on the Habsburg throne was his daughter, Maria Theresa. However, Habsburg succession in the female line was unprecedented and, in spite of the Pragmatic Sanction Treaties, it was challenged. Taking advantage of Maria Theresa's early position, Frederick II, the young Prussian king, revived old claims upon part of Silesia. When Maria Theresa rejected Frederick's demands the latter attacked, and soon an alliance of France, Bavaria, Spain, Saxony, and Prussia was arrayed against the Habsburg queen.

The War of Austrian Succession lasted for eight years. Frederick II overran Silesia in a quick thrust and in 1742, having won his goal, withdrew from the war. However, Maria Theresa had won enthusiastic Hungarian support and an alliance with England. Soon her military successes so worried Frederick that in 1744 he re-entered the war. But the queen's allies multiplied, and in 1745 her husband, Francis Stephen of Lorraine, won election to the imperial throne as Francis I (1745-1765). In 1748 the war ended and the Treaty of Aix-la-Chapelle confirmed the Habsburg Pragmatic Sanction but left Silesia to Prussia.

Maria Theresa, now empress, could not be reconciled to the Prussian conquest of Silesia, and her intrigues for its recovery led to a new war. But not before a major change took place in the alliances. This change, known as the Diplomatic Revolution of 1756, was primarily the work of the Austrian chancellor, Prince Kaunitz, who induced the French to form an alliance with Austria. Meanwhile, hostilities broke out between France and England in their North American colonies (the French and Indian War), and England concluded a treaty with Prussia. Frederick, knowing of Maria Theresa's alliance both with France and with Russia, launched a surprise attack upon the empire in 1756. The Seven Years' War was on, with the empire, France, and Russia against Prussia and England. The struggle taxed Prussia's powers to the utmost. Frederick's only ally, England, was engaged simultaneously in great naval and colonial struggles with France, extending to North America and India, and her aid to Prussia was principally in the form of subsidies. Thus Prussia faced France, the empire, Russia and, for a time, Sweden; and Frederick was repeatedly in grave danger. Still, by virtue of his military genius and heavy sacrifices on the part of the people of Brandenburg-Prussia, he managed to survive. In 1762, too, the Russian tsarina, Elizabeth, died. Her successor, the depraved Peter III, admired Frederick and at once called off Russian hostilities with Prussia. France had her hands full with England, and French enthusiasm

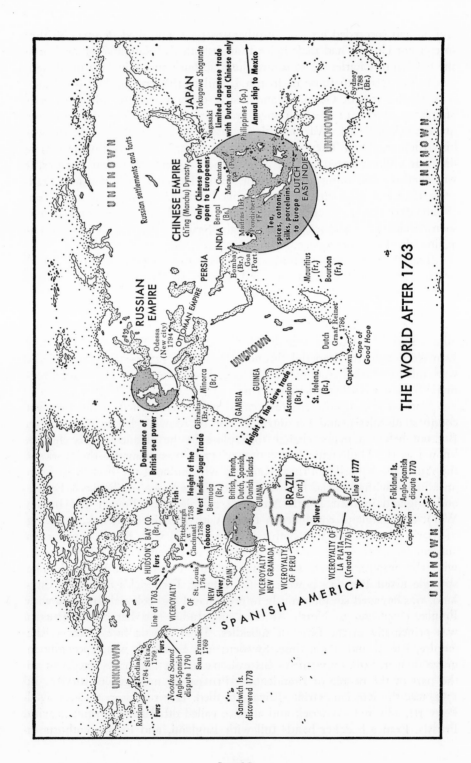

THE WORLD AFTER 1763

UNKNOWN

Russian settlements and forts

JAPAN
Tokugawa Shogunate
Nagasaki
**Limited Japanese trade
with Dutch and Chinese only**
Philippines (Sp.)
Sydney
1788
(Br.)
→ **Annual ship to Mexico**

CHINESE EMPIRE
Ch'ing (Manchu) Dynasty
**Only Chinese port
open to Europeans**
Canton
Macao (Port.)
**Tea,
spices, cottons,
silks, porcelains
to Europe DUTCH
EAST INDIES**
INDIA Bengal
(Br.)
Madras (Br.)
Pondicherri
(Fr.)

RUSSIAN
EMPIRE

Odessa
(New city)
1794
OTTOMAN EMPIRE PERSIA

Bombay
(Br.)
Goa
(Port.)

Mauritius
(Fr.)
Bourbon
(Fr.)

Minorca
(Br.)
GAMBIA
GUINEA
Gibraltar
(Br.)

UNKNOWN

Dutch
Graaf Reinet
1786

**Dominance of
British sea power**

Cape of
Good Hope
Capetown

St. Helena
(Br.)

Fish

**Height of the
West Indies Sugar Trade**
Bermuda
(Br.)

Ascension
(Br.)

Height of the slave trade

HUDSON'S BAY CO.
Furs (Br.)
Pittsburgh
v. 1758
Cincinnati
1788
Tobacco
Silver
SPAIN
NEW
St. Louis
1764
VICEROYALTY
OF
San Francisco
1769
Line of 1763

Nootka Sound
Anglo-Spanish
dispute 1790

Russian
Kodiak
1784 Sitka
1799
Furs

British, French,
Dutch, Spanish,
Danish islands
GUIANA

BRAZIL
(Port.)

Silver

VICEROYALTY OF
NEW GRANADA

VICEROYALTY
OF PERU

VICEROYALTY OF
LA PLATA
(created 1776)

Line of 1777

Falkland Is.
Anglo-Spanish
dispute 1770

Cape Horn

SPANISH AMERICA

Sandwich Is.
discovered 1778

UNKNOWN

[226]

for the unusual alliance with Austria had easily cooled. Frederick was more than a match for Austria. When the European war ended with the Treaty of Hubertusburg in 1763, Frederick kept Silesia and could turn to the task of healing the wounds inflicted upon his kingdom by the war.

Beyond the European scene, also, the Seven Years' War had great significance. It was the last of four colonial struggles between England and France in North America, and it involved India as well. These struggles had coincided more or less with European conflicts. The earliest one, King William's War (1689-1697), was a colonial version of the War of the League of Augsburg and was confined largely to border raids between New France (Canada) and New England and New York. The second, Queen Anne's War (1702-1713), paralleled the War of Spanish Succession, and, besides commercial advantages acquired from Spain by the Treaty of Utrecht, England won from France the Hudson's Bay territory, Nova Scotia (Acadia), and Newfoundland in North America and the Caribbean island of St. Kitts. The third colonial struggle, King George's War, coincided with the War of Austrian Succession and, by the Treaty of Aix-la-Chapelle, England and France made mutual restoration of territories won. The fourth, the French and Indian War, actually began in North America before it merged with the Seven Years' War in Europe. It began in a struggle between the French and the English for control of the upper Ohio Valley and spread to their possessions in India. George Washington's stand with the Virginia militia at Fort Necessity, General William Braddock's defeat near present-day Pittsburgh, the heroic deaths of Generals Montcalm and Wolfe at Quebec—these are events of the French and Indian War familiar to every American schoolboy. Less familiar are the exploits of the Frenchman Joseph François Dupleix and the Englishman Robert Clive in India. Dupleix was one of France's greatest empire-builders, whose efforts to extend French control over India led to conflicts with the English there. Here, too, war arose before the Seven Years' War broke out, with the English led by Robert Clive, a former clerk of the English East India Company. Clive's victory at the Battle of Plassey (1757) was as significant in India as that of Wolfe at Quebec two years later. By 1761 England's supremacy in India was assured. Indeed, England emerged from the Seven Years' War as a dominating colonial power. By the Treaty of Paris (1763) concluding the colonial aspects of the Seven Years' War, France ceded to England Canada and essentially all French possessions in North America east of the Mississippi River. At the same time Spain ceded Florida to England and won the territory west of the Mississippi from France as compensation for her loss. The French colonial empire in both North America and the Far East was reduced to a small fraction of its previous size and importance, and England's greatest colonial gains had been at French expense. The French and Indian War placed England in a new position with regard to her North American colonies, and English efforts to strengthen and perfect colonial policies contributed to the American Revolution.

ENLIGHTENED REFORMS AND DYNASTIC AGGRANDIZEMENT

The period after the Seven Years' War included the most concentrated reform efforts of the enlightened despots. The wars, as usual, had enhanced the powers of their governments; and the enlightened despots, mouthing the reforms of the *philosophes,* employed the state as an instrument of "progress" to enthrone "rational government." Institutions and policies hitherto based on custom and precedent were attacked as contrary to reason. That is, the old system of law and judicial organization, the "feudal" privileges of the church, the towns, the provinces, the estates, and the nobility were swept aside as much as possible to make way for more centralizing agencies of the monarchies, which in turn built more efficient and rational bureaucracies of dynastic power. Thus "Enlightenment" became propaganda for an accelerating centralization of monarchic power. But seldom were the conditions of the masses—the serfs and the peasants—ameliorated, and even the demands of the middle classes were ignored except when they coincided with the state-enlarging ambitions of the philosopher-kings.

PRUSSIA

Before the Seven Years' War Frederick the Great had, with aid of the great Prussian jurist, Baron Samuel Cocceji, promulgated codification of the laws and reform of judicial procedures. Torture was reduced, and access to the courts was made easier, cheaper, and less clogged with corruption. Frederick subscribed wholeheartedly to religious toleration (although he was strongly anti-Semitic) and, while he gave lip service to freedom of speech and freedom of the press these freedoms were distinctly modified by the king's prejudices and pride. After the Seven Years' War he did much to promote and improve agriculture, industry, and trade. No physiocrat did more for agriculture than Frederick, who drained swamps, introduced new crops, imported iron plows, and settled thousands of immigrants on territory previously wasteland. Yet in the affairs of industry and trade Frederick was a mercantilist, who regulated trade, set up stiff tariffs on imports, and promoted state enterprise without regard for the laissez faire policies advocated by the physiocrats. In all his activities the king had a keen eye for means of increasing the state revenues, and while he promoted the prosperity of his people he also replenished his treasury and kept his army in tip-top condition. Moreover, he did nothing to loosen the bonds of serfdom outside his own royal estates; and he clung to a severe caste system in society, seeking to keep everyone in place without social fluidity. He continued to leave the favored Junkers in possession of the chief offices of state, presiding over a militaristic bureaucracy which was the most efficient and dedicated in Europe. Certainly Frederick was "enlightened," as the term was used in his own day, but his enlightenment never stood in the way of his being a Hohenzollern dynast.

THE HABSBURG EMPIRE

Maria Theresa made no pretense of being enlightened. As empress she pursued the age-old dynastic methods of enhancing the power of the crown: she attacked feudal rights and other entrenched privileges, increased taxes, and generally asserted queenly authority at the expense of local aristocratic assemblies—for example, she destroyed the tax power of the Austrian and Bohemian Diets. She would employ force if necessary, or resort to her womanly charm; the anti-German Hungarian nobles were stampeded to her support when as a beautiful young queen, with her infant son in her arms, she appealed to them at the outset of the War of Austrian Succession. Later, as a devoted wife and the mother of sixteen children, she appealed to the solid, conservative tendencies of the empire by her devout Catholicism, her rejection of the Enlightenment, her sensible régime, and her matronly dignity. But her son, Joseph, emperor and co-regent on the death of Francis I in 1765 and emperor after his mother's death in 1780, was a full-fledged disciple of the Enlightenment.

Moreover, Joseph was earnest, sincere, and industrious, anxious, as he said, to make "philosophy the legislator of my empire." But he was also impatient, highhanded, and imprudent in the face of strongly entrenched opposition to his policies in both church and state. The patchwork empire of the Habsburgs, composed of mutually suspicious and locally autonomous Germans, Hungarians, Italians, Romanians, and Slavs was hardly ready for the Enlightenment and for the further centralizing effects of a "rationalized" despotism. Nevertheless, during the ten years of his reign (1780–1790), Joseph II crowded more reforms than any of his contemporaries dared to attempt in twice the time. With supreme disregard for tradition, privilege, and custom, the emperor issued edict after edict, watching with increasing exasperation and frustration the failure or inability of his subordinates to carry them out. He established religious toleration, which included Jews, and extended full civil rights to the sects. He nationalized the Catholic church, appointed the prelates himself, and denied all appeals to the Papacy. He reduced the monasteries and convents by more than a third, using the proceeds of their confiscated lands for educational purposes. Joseph set up a state school system for all children. He completed reform of the laws begun by Maria Theresa, with a new criminal code modeled upon the recommendations of Beccaria, including equality before the law without regard to wealth or class distinctions. He believed in social equality (unlike most of his fellow enlightened despots) and, in spite of loud protests from the nobility, he freed the serfs, abolished most of their obligations to manorial lords, and deprived the latter of their feudal administration of justice to the peasantry. While he retained high tariffs on imports in mercantilist fashion, Joseph adopted a single land-tax system recommended by the physiocrats. He hoped to build a mighty army, lead it to victory over the Turks or Prussia, and acquire territorial additions to the Habsburg lands. Finally, he sought to Germanize the empire by making German the only language of the schools, the courts, and the theaters.

On nearly every side Joseph was resisted. Zealous Catholics resented the religious changes, and the Pope made an unprecedented—but vain—visit to Vienna in person to persuade Joseph to modify his religious edicts. Similarly, the nobility resisted the social, political, and legal changes and the emperor, whose judgment of men was seldom sound, had great difficulty in finding subordinates willing and able to carry out his commands. Shortly before Joseph's death both Belgium (the Austrian Netherlands) and Hungary were in open rebellion against the emperor and he was forced to decree that everything should be restored as it had been at the death of Maria Theresa; only the abolition of serfdom was excepted. His brother, Leopold II, succeeded him and sought to salvage as much of Joseph's reform program as he could, but he, too, died after two years, and Joseph's reforms remained for the most part only a blueprint for the future.

RUSSIA

Catherine II, "the Great" (1762–1796), the third of the principal enlightened despots, was severely handicapped as a reformer both by internal conditions in Russia and by the circumstances of her elevation to the throne. Succession to the Russian throne, often irregular and accompanied by bloodshed, was left uncertain at the death of Peter the Great in 1725. Immediately the officers of the palace guard placed Peter's low-born second wife, Catherine I, on the throne. Five more Romanovs succeeded before Catherine the Great: Peter the Great's grandson, Peter II (1727–1730); his half-brother's daughter, Anne (1730–1740); Anne's sister's grandson, Ivan VI (1740–1741); Peter the Great's youngest daughter, Elizabeth (1741–1762), who, typically, reached the throne by virtue of a military coup; and Elizabeth's nephew, Peter III, who succeeded in 1762. Peter III was weak, incompetent, and mentally retarded. As heir apparent to the Russian throne he had been married to Sophia Augusta Frederica, Princess of Anhalt-Zerbst, a minor German principality. Sophia was a precocious, calculating, ambitious young woman who learned the Russian language, cultivated Russian ways, and joined the Russian church, by which she was rechristened Catherine—later to become Catherine the Great. Her life with Peter III was miserable, but she conspired with the nobility and the army and was herself proclaimed empress six months after Peter III had become tsar.

Peter died (or was murdered) in a drunken brawl, possibly at the insti-
gation of Catherine or of her admirers. Thus the empress, who was neither
Russian nor Romanov by birth, was forced to tread carefully; her position
was never wholly secure on the throne, or, at least, it was constantly subject to challenge. Still, Catherine ruled for thirty-four years and died a
natural death in 1796.

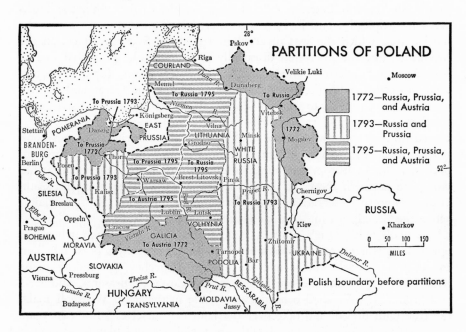

She was a robust, sensuous, highly intelligent, largely self-educated woman and a born politician. She had read the *philosophes'* works, wrote
plays, satires, and essays herself, and, as empress, entered into active correspondence with some of the French *philosophes* and occasionally gave
them pensions. In consequence, she won their admiration and fulsome
praise. Early in her reign she undertook to reform and codify the laws of
Russia on the basis of enlightened principles. With her own hand she
composed the long "Instructions to the Commissioners for Composing a
New Code of Laws" (1767) and assembled a large commission to undertake the work. Catherine's "Instructions" embraced many of the enlightened
views of Montesquieu and Beccaria, but she carefully asserted her absolutism
as sovereign and skirted any reference to Russia's greatest social problem,
the millions of serfs. Moreover, the commission itself was too large to accomplish anything as a body and, actually, Catherine used it principally as
a sounding board of public opinion. When she found no significant expression of dissatisfaction with the autocracy, she dismissed the commission
with no reform or codification of the laws at all. But the empress had

learned much about the Russian temper and made good use of her knowledge in later legislation.

In retrospect, it seems evident that Catherine's real object, like that of Peter the Great, was to enlarge the centralized power of the crown and the territorial possessions of Russia. Her law reform project was interrupted by a war against the Turks (1768–1772) in which the Russians won unprecedented success. Later, in 1783, she annexed the Crimea while the Turks stood by helplessly; and in 1787 she entered into another war against the Turks from which she was diverted in 1792 by a Swedish attack. In the meantime, too, she interfered drastically in Poland. She promoted one of her favorites, Stanislaus Poniatowski, to the Polish throne (1764–1795) and then proceeded, with the connivance of Frederick the Great and the cooperation of Austria, to subject Poland to three successive partitions— 1772, 1793, and 1795, respectively—whereby that hapless "republic" was carved up and swallowed by its neighbors. By these territorial acquisitions, Russia advanced far into central Europe and became an ever more important factor in European affairs. Simultaneously, Russia expanded farther along the northern shores of the Black Sea at Turkish expense, and Catherine promoted explorations into Asia which extended Russian claims across the Bering Sea into Alaska (Kodiak Island, 1783).

Actually, Catherine's reforms were principally undertaken when the opportunity was offered to reorganize local government by a great rebellion in 1773. A Cossack soldier named Emelian Pugachev, pretending to be Tsar Peter III, began the revolt. He rallied Cossacks, peasants, and serfs and promised: "We shall behead every noble in the land. We shall make the true faith prevail and take over the land for ourselves." For two years (1773–1775) the rebellion raged with great violence and bloodshed, and it was suppressed with difficulty only after Pugachev was betrayed by his followers, delivered to Catherine in an iron cage, and drawn and quartered. However, it was clear that the rebellion had been directed primarily at the landed nobility and local officials. Accordingly, Catherine took advantage of the situation to reorganize local government (1775), creating fifty provinces where there had been twenty, and giving most of the local offices to noble landlords under close supervision of the crown. The effect was not only to strengthen the central government but also to bolster the power of the nobility on the principle of divide and rule. The Russian serfs were worse off than before. Indeed, there was little public sentiment in opposition to serfdom; no one loudly and effectively espoused the cause, and Catherine found it expedient to cater to the nobility. In fact, in 1785 she exempted the nobles from taxation and military service and gave them absolute mastery over their serfs.

Still, if the serfs were shackled more tightly, Catherine promoted the Enlightenment among the upper classes. French styles, French books, French ideas, and the French language became so widespread among the aristocracy that Russia was Westernized as never before. In 1785 an Edict of Toleration permitted religious freedom, and Catherine welcomed refugees from other lands. She also promoted schools (for children of the nobility), academies, arts and letters, and, with her own hand, wrote the first volume of the earliest dictionary of the Russian language. All these things contributed to Catherine's reputation as an enlightened despot, while her consistent support of the upper classes, even at the expense of the masses, secured her position on the throne. And her military victories and territorial acquisitions from the Turks and Poland not only added to her prestige but also helped to silence discontent at home.

To some degree, enlightened despotism attracted nearly every crowned head of Europe. France, Sweden, Denmark, Portugal, England, and many of the lesser states of Germany and Italy had kings, princes, and ministers who subscribed to the principles of the Enlightenment and endeavored to enforce reforms in the philosopher-king manner. Most of them managed to improve some of the bad features of the Old Régime. But as a whole, they fell into two categories of failure: those who were really enlightened in most senses but lacked the means to give effect to their reforms (such as Joseph II); and those who had the despotic means but whose enlightenment fell short of genuine social reform (such as Frederick the Great). Taken altogether, the enlightened despots were only plying the old dynastic trade of kings with new justifications for their acts borrowed from the *philosophes*. The partitions of Poland and the further centralization of dynastic power in nearly every state were monuments to their hypocrisy.

7 : The Arts and Literature of the Enlightenment

Two STYLES in architecture dominated the Age of the Enlightenment: the Rococo on the Continent and Georgian in England. Actually, Rococo was less a style of architecture than a system of decoration, with emphasis on slender proportions, easy curves, and light colors supplemented by much gilding and many mirrors. Rococo buildings were occasionally overornate and cluttered, but a few were charming, such as Marie Antoinette's Petit Trianon palace at Versailles and Frederick the Great's Sans Souci palace at Potsdam. The interiors of most Rococo structures showed Chinese influences—Chinese wallpapers, silks, lacquers, and porcelain. Even pagodas were imitated in several structures. Dresden china figurines often added to the bric-a-brac. Georgian architecture, on the other hand, was simple, with straight lines. Georgian structures were usually built with bricks and had many chimneys and chimney pots. It was the style of the English country house of the eighteenth century and is well known in America, where today it is widely employed in college and university buildings.

Painting was largely elegant and sophisticated, designed to please the aristocracy and the wealthy bourgeoisie—although an undercurrent of social criticism was evident as well. In France, Jean Antoine Watteau (1684–1721) painted pastoral scenes with sentimental shepherds and shepherdesses and pictures of fêtes and country dances; Jean Fragonard (1732–1806) depicted amorous nymphs, Venuses, and other monuments to love. Both French painters and many others of their day fitted the Rococo style well—Watteau in the salon and Fragonard in the boudoir. English painting at last had native artists of great skill. Sir Joshua Reynolds (1723–1792), Thomas Gainsborough (1727–1788), and John Constable (1776–1837) produced brilliant portraits and landscapes which surpassed all previous native English painting in technique. Their works were mostly aristocratic in tone, although Constable produced some fine English rustic scenes. William Hogarth (1697–1764) was of a different breed, however. His work was largely satirical, with several series of paintings poking fun at English life and conventions—such as "The Rake's Progress," "Marriage à la Mode," and others. Francisco Goya (1746–1828), almost alone among Spanish painters in his day, painted realistically the bullfights, torture scenes, and customs of the decadent court of Spain, and lent a note of social criticism now and then, especially in the "Disasters of War."

The Age of Enlightenment was an age of musical giants. Italian opera and its imitators dominated the scene; and Italian violin-makers produced instruments of unparalleled beauty of tone, especially Nicolò Amati of Cremona (1596–1684) and his pupil, Antonio Stradivari (1644–1737). Musical theory was considerably advanced by the application of mathematical principles to harmony. But the glory of the age was its constellation of composers: Johann Sebastian Bach (1655–1730); George Frederick Handel (1685–1759); Joseph Haydn (1732–1809); and Wolfgang Amadeus Mozart (1756–1791). Bach's compositions, mostly sacred music, included both vocal and organ music, and he produced some secular music as well. Handel, a German who settled in England and became an English subject, composed, besides his well-known oratorios, more than forty operas together with church music and chamber pieces. Haydn, a Viennese composer, was remarkably versatile, with operas, piano sonatas, overtures, symphonies, oratorios, and many lesser pieces. Mozart, a friend of Haydn and a member of a famous family of musicians of which he became the most renowned, composed over six hundred works, including operas, operettas, symphonies, cantatas, chamber music, dances, and a large number of religious pieces. The works of these composers belong to what is now known as classical music, and productions and recordings of their works are still widely popular among music lovers everywhere.

In literature, the Age of Enlightenment was an age of prose. Poetry ceased to be an instrument of philosophy and became for the most part a means of entertainment. Alexander Pope (1688–1744), the English master of the heroic couplet and the witty epigram, was fairly representative of the poetry of the age. Whether English or continental, the poetry was mediocre, mildly didactic, often mere patter, and no more original than Pope's famous *Essay on Man,* which was an excellent summary of the optimism and rationalism of the times but wholly without originality of thought. However, if it was an age of prose predominantly, the prose took on new forms. At least four literary vehicles assumed new importance for the first time in the eighteenth century: the newspaper, the magazine, the novel, and the almanac. Newspapers began during the Thirty Years' War, but they remained small, irregular, and more like partisan pamphlets than news organs. In the eighteenth century they often retained violent political partisanship but they also became more newsy, regular, and, in many cases, graduated from weeklies or biweeklies to daily papers. They also became cheaper as the volume of their sales and the income from advertisers increased. *The Gentleman's Magazine,* which began in England in 1731, was one of the earliest of its kind—and one of the longest-lived. The magazine catered to a more sophisticated reader than most of the newspapers, whereas the almanac became the news summary and general reference book of the poorest or more remote people. There were scores of them, but Benjamin Franklin's *Poor Richard's Almanac* in America became one of the most famous. The novel, especially the English novel, developed rapidly as a literary form from Samuel Richardson's *Pamela* (1740) and Tobias Smollett's *Roderick Random* (1748) to Henry Fielding's *Tom Jones* (1749) and Laurence Sterne's *Tristram Shandy* (1764).

Many of these developments bespoke a new situation for literature: for the first time in history literary men could make a living, sometimes even a fortune, with their pens. The royal pension, the noble patron, and other forms of support faded from the picture as writers and publishers found markets for their products sufficient to support their enterprises. To some extent, this may have been a result of the nature of much of the literary product, which was often addressed to the reform of abuses, like Montesquieu's *Persian Letters* (1721), Voltaire's novel, *Candide* (1759), and Pierre Augustin Caron de Beaumarchais' comedy, *The Marriage of Figaro* (1784). Didactic writing was also popular, consisting of books of reference, dictionaries, encyclopedias, and other syntheses of learning.

The French language became the arbiter of literary fashion in the eighteenth century. Frederick the Great would use no other language, and Catherine the Great went almost as far. To a great extent, French replaced Latin as the *lingua franca* of learned and literary men everywhere. No doubt, this was partly because of the extraordinary prestige of France in politics, war, diplomacy, and economic affairs; but it was also because, thanks to the French Academy of Language, French had become one of the most precise tongues, especially useful in science, where precision of speech is of first importance. Moreover, the French style was at once elegant and clear, and French literature, especially that of Voltaire and Rousseau, continued to be of a high order. Just as the French *philosophes* dominated the thought of the Enlightenment, so French language and literature were in the vanguard.

Further Reading

The following are able surveys of the period: Ernst Cassirer, *The Philosophy of the Enlightenment* (Boston: Beacon, 1955); John G. Hibben, *The Philosophy of the Enlightenment* (New York: Scribner, 1910); and Preserved Smith, *The Enlightenment,* vol. II of *A History of Modern Culture* (New York: Holt, 1930–34). Carl L. Becker's *The Heavenly City of the Eighteenth-Century Philosophers* (New Haven: Yale Univ. Press, 1932) is an urbane, classic treatment of the ideal of the *philosophes.* In *The Age of Reason* (Princeton: Van Nostrand, Anvil 6, 1955) Louis L. Snyder includes interpretive essays as well as selections from original sources. A fuller collection of source materials is to be found in two paperbacks, *The Age of Reason: The Seventeenth-Century Philosophers,* ed. by Stuart Hampshire (New York: New American Library, Mentor MD158, 1957), and *The Age of Enlightenment: The Eighteenth-Century Philosophers,* ed. by Isaiah Berlin (New York: New American Library, Mentor MD172, 1955). "The Hafner Library of Classics" has an edition of John Locke's *Two Treatises of Government* together with Filmer's *Patriarcha* (New York: Hafner, 1956). The *Essay Concerning Human Understanding,* by John Locke, is available in the "Gateway Series," No. 6016 (Chicago: Regnery, 1956). *The Portable Voltaire* (New York: Viking P41, 1949) includes *Candide* as well as excerpts from the *Philosophical Dictionary* and Voltaire's correspondence with Frederick the Great. Rousseau's *Social Contract* is another of the "Hafner Library of Classics" (New York: Hafner, 1954). Finally, Henry Higgs, *The Physiocrats* (New York: Macmillan, 1897), is an old stand-by.

On the formation of the modern scientific attitude see Herbert Butterfield, *The Origins of Modern Science, 1300–1800* (new rev. ed.; New York: Macmillan, 1957), and Alfred R. Hall, *The Scientific Revolution, 1500–1800* (Boston: Beacon, 1956). Abraham Wolf, *The History of Science, Technology, and Philosophy in the Eighteenth Century* (2d ed.; New York: Macmillan, 1952), is exhaustive; Sir William Dampier's *Shorter History of Science, from Earliest Times to the Present* is lighter and available as a paperback (New York: Meridian M47, 1957). Excerpts from the original sources include: *Discoveries and Opinions of Galileo* (Garden City: Doubleday, Anchor A94, 1951); *Newton's Philosophy of Nature: Selected Writings* ("Hafner Library of Classics") (New York: Hafner, 1953); and *Philosophers Speak for Themselves: From Descartes to Locke* (Chicago: Univ.

of Chicago Press, Phoenix P17, 1957). On Newton George N. Clark's *Science and Social Welfare in the Age of Newton* (New York: Oxford Univ. Press, 1949) is valuable.

A classic study of the *ancien régime* (in France) is Alexis de Tocqueville's *The Old Regime and the French Revolution* (Garden City: Doubleday, Anchor A60, 1955). The despots and their policies are treated in Geoffrey Bruun, *The Enlightened Despots* ("Berkshire Studies") (New York: Holt, 1929), and Arthur H. Johnson, *The Age of the Enlightened Despots, 1660–1789* (New York: Macmillan, 1926). *The Memoirs of Catherine the Great,* trans. by Lowell Bair (New York: Bantam FB410, 1957), provide a peep into the personal diary of the empress. The complex web of war and diplomacy in the eighteenth century receives a clear exposition by Arthur Hassall in *The Balance of Power, 1715-1789* (New York: Macmillan, 1919).

Biographical studies of leaders in early science and the Enlightenment include: Catherine the Great—K. Waliszewski, *The Romance of an Empress* (New York: Appleton, 1929); Gladys S. Thomson ("Teach Yourself History Library") (New York: Macmillan, 1947). Copernicus—Angus Armitage, *The World of Copernicus* (New York: New American Library, Mentor MD65, 1956). Diderot—John Morley, *Diderot and the Encyclopedists* (New York: Macmillan, 1886). Frederick the Great—G. P. Gooch (New York: Knopf, 1947); W. F. Reddaway (New York: Putnam, 1904). Joseph II—Saul Padover (New York: Kemp, 1934). Newton—Sir David Brewster, *Memoirs of the Life, Writings, and Discoveries of Sir Isaac Newton,* 2 vols. (Edinburgh: Constable, 1855); Louis T. More (New York: Scribner, 1934). Rousseau—Matthew Josephson (New York: Harcourt, 1931). Voltaire—John Morley (London: Macmillan, 1872).

Chapter 21

THE FALL OF
THE OLD REGIME

THE HALF-CENTURY between 1775 and 1825 was one of revolutions. By the American Revolution (1775–1783), the United States of America came into being; Great Britain lost her most populous colonies on the mainland of North America, and the rebellious colonies were themselves transformed politically and socially by the upheaval. By the French Revolution (1789–1799), the Old Régime was swept away in France, and an infectious revolutionary spirit went out to threaten the crowned heads of western Europe and the privileged classes of the Old Régime everywhere. In France royal absolutism became constitutional monarchy which, in turn, was overthrown in favor of the First French Republic. As these changes took place, neighboring monarchies, deeply concerned about the security of their crowns, formed coalitions against the French, and the resulting wars only drove the French to greater extremes. In the midst of grave danger from within and without, the French revolutionary government was overthrown in 1799 by a military coup led by Napoleon Bonaparte. The Napoleonic régime followed (1799–1814), during which Napoleon "mastered" the French Revolution and turned it to his own ambitious purposes. By his genius in war, politics, and diplomacy, he extended over Europe a French ascendancy which surpassed the wildest hopes of the Bourbons. As usual, however, the balance-of-power principle operated against Napoleon's conquests, national patriotisms were quickened by the French dominion, and finally Napoleon was brought to bay by a great alliance of European powers.

In the meantime, however, the extension of French power over Spain and Portugal had forced the Portuguese monarchy into temporary exile in Brazil and had led the Spanish colonies in America to challenge the authority of the Bonaparte king of Spain. Later, after the legitimate rulers had been restored to their thrones in Europe they, too, were rejected by their erstwhile American colonies. By the end of the half-century of revolution the whole of the American mainland, excepting Canada, Alaska, and the Guianas, had been organized under new governments independent of European control. And, as new nations were born overseas, the Old Régime in Europe was destroyed beyond recall. New governments, new institutions, a new nationalism, and a new kind of society greeted the new nineteenth century. The society of privilege based upon noble birth gave way to a society of wealth in which the bourgeois power of money, capital, and credit dominated the scene. What follows in this chapter will be devoted to these revolutionary alterations in the Western world.

1 : The American Revolution

ENGLAND FAILED to develop tight administrative controls over her overseas colonies such as those of the Council of the Indies in Spain or the intendant system in France. In consequence, British colonies in America enjoyed a measure of freedom and self-government unknown in their sister colonies. English trading companies, lords proprietors, and colonial "squatters" set up a series of colonies in North America and the West Indies under charters from the crown which granted them wide oversight over their own affairs. In time the colonies developed governments with a governor appointed either by the crown or by the proprietor (though dependent upon the colony for his pay) and colonial assemblies chosen by the people of the colony. Colonial laws and judicial decisions were subject to review by the English government in order to keep them consistent with English law and to protect the royal prerogative. But the review was tedious, time consuming, and, though roughly effective in the letter, it hardly kept the spirit of the colonies in tow. Moreover, as the colonial assemblies exercised considerable control over the purse, they often bent the governors to their will by withholding salaries and other funds necessary for the executive office. In this respect, the colonial assemblies in their relation to the governors were analogous to the English Parliament's dealings with the kings.

The principal oversight of the English colonies lay with the crown, which at first referred it to a series of committees of the Privy Council. In 1696 the Board of Trade and Plantations was set up as a permanent office with a secretary and assistants to gather information, hear grievances, and make recommendations to the Privy Council on all colonial matters. However, neither the early committees of the Privy Council nor the Board of Trade could do more than *advise* the Privy Council and the crown with respect to colonial affairs. Legislation relating to the colonies—mostly devoted to the regulation of colonial trade—was passed by Parliament and enforced by the crown through the offices of the Admiralty, the Treasury, and the bishop of London. The Admiralty took measures for colonial defense, enforced customs laws, and tried offenders. The bishop of London, to whose diocese all the overseas colonies and trading posts were assigned, kept ecclesiastical oversight over the churches and an eye upon the spiritual welfare of the colonies—in both of which he was constantly resented and resisted by the Puritans and other dissenter sects.

In the main, English colonial administration touched the colonies only at two points: the regulation of colonial commerce, and colonial defense. A series of acts known as the Navigation Acts were passed between 1651 and 1664, providing that goods should be transported to the colonies only in English vessels of which the masters and three-fourths of the crews were English subjects. Certain "enumerated" products, such as tobacco and sugar, were to be exported from the colonies only to England. These acts, pushed through Parliament by interested English merchants, were, of course, thoroughly in keeping with the theories and practices of mercantilism and were similar in intent to analogous policies of Spain, France, and others. But as a rule they were far less well enforced in the English colonies than in those of England's competitors in the colonial scene. Moreover, the New England colonies early developed a large shipbuilding and carrying trade themselves; and as the English charters guaranteed to English colonists all the rights and privileges of Englishmen, the Navigation Acts protected their shipping as well as that of the homeland. As regards colonial defense, the colonies went off in all directions, refused to co-operate with one another except on rare occasions, assumed that they could take care of themselves, resented English interference—and cried out shrilly for English protection when they felt real or imaginary threats from a foreign power.

By the mid-eighteenth century, after almost a century and a half of "salutary neglect" by the mother country, the English colonies in mainland America had developed into populous, prosperous, and compact communities extending from Maine to Georgia along the Atlantic coast and inland to the Appalachian Mountains, beyond which they were beginning to penetrate. Their total population approximated one million people. They had several large cities—Philadelphia, the largest, was the second largest English city, next to London itself. Thanks to the English capture of New Amsterdam from the Dutch in 1664 (and to the latter's earlier absorption of Swedish settlements along the Delaware River), together with the immigration of Scottish, Irish, German, French Huguenot, Swiss, and Jewish settlers, and about 200,000 Negroes (mostly slaves), the colonial population in 1750 was no longer wholly of English stock or wholly English-speaking. Large segments of the colonial peoples had no ancestral ties with England or loyalty to the English monarchy. This fact, together with the relative independence of the colonies as a whole from firm English control led foreign observers to remark that the colonies were unlikely much longer to accept a subordinate position in the English system. Still, there was little union among the colonies beyond their general adherence to common institutions of English origin and a vague belief that, somehow, Americans were a new race, free of the shackles of mind and institutions which characterized Europeans. But of independence from England there was, as yet, neither thought nor desire.

Yet, within a single generation after 1750 a Declaration of Independence was issued (1776) by a Continental Congress representing thirteen of the North American colonies, and the American War for Independence had begun. These developments were the unexpected consequences of events on both sides of the Atlantic. In England the first two Hanoverian kings to succeed the Stuart Dynasty (1714) were weak, ineffective rulers. George I (1714–1727) preferred his electorate of Hanover and, as he spoke no English, left much of the oversight of English affairs to English ministers; George II (1727–1760) had similar propensities. Neither monarch was popular in England; both favored Whig ministries and the Whigs were so long in power that, as is commonly the case, the party fell into factions within itself. George III (1760–1820), however, was the first Anglicized Hanoverian monarch, and he was ambitious to assert his royal authority— to rehabilitate the English crown. Accordingly, when he ascended the throne he played the Whig factions off against one another in an effort to be free of the Whig ascendancy, and he skillfully manipulated the royal patronage to establish a firm Tory ministry under his personal direction. After several ministries had fallen, he succeeded in his goal, with Lord North as prime minister from 1770 to 1782. Simultaneously, the king and his ministers pursued colonial policies which precipitated the rebellion in America.

TIGHTENED COLONIAL CONTROLS

Taken altogether, these policies arose from the altered condition of the colonies as the result of the Anglo-French struggle for control of the interior of North America in the French and Indian War (roughly parallel to the Seven Years' War in Europe) and the vast English conquests by the Treaty of Paris in 1763. Simultaneously with the French threat, the English Board of Trade and Plantations was given new life and redirection by Lord Halifax, who became president of the board in 1748. Halifax proposed to reorganize colonial defenses, station British troops in the colonies, and regularize Indian policy and trade, which hitherto had suffered a lack of consistency at the hands of several different colonial administrations pursuing different and often conflicting goals. After the Treaty of Paris (1763) England faced the problems of colonial administration in the former French possessions, roughly equivalent to the St. Lawrence Valley, the Great Lakes area, and the region between the Mississippi River and the Appalachian Mountains, together with Florida won from Spain. At the outset the Indians of the Great Lakes region, led by Pontiac, an able Ottawa chief, and encouraged by French dissidents, rose up against the English (Pontiac's

Rebellion, 1763–1766) and threatened the peaceful English administration of the Old Northwest. The Board of Trade recommended new plans for the English colonial administration, defense, Indian policy, and orderly settlement of the new lands. George III and his ministers sought to apply them.

These policies embraced the following measures: (1) the Proclamation of 1763, which *temporarily* closed to further English settlement the lands west of a line along the Appalachian Mountains from Maine to Florida pending peaceful arrangements with the Indian tribes and orderly organization of trade with the natives. This act outraged both land-hungry settlers and land companies whose speculators in England and the colonies had formulated ambitious land promotions and scented large profits. (2) The establishment of two Indian superintendencies in the colonies, one in the north and one in the south, to oversee Indian affairs, regulate Indian policies, and license and direct Indian trade. To colonists, the English superintendents appeared too "soft" in treating with Indians, and their regulation of Indian trade was almost universally resented and widely evaded. (3) The permanent garrison of English troops in America for colonial defense and a guarantee of the newly-won conquests from France and Spain. To American colonists this seemed wholly unnecessary, especially after the war was over and, ostensibly, the danger had passed. They felt capable of defending themselves in time of peace and, moreover, they resented the English regulars who looked down their noses at the raw, irregularly equipped and poorly disciplined colonial militiamen. (4) The levy of new taxes in the colonies to help pay for the new administration and defense, and the establishment of new imperial agencies for collection of the money in the colonies. To the English, it appeared only just that the colonies should pay a reasonable share of the expenses; to the colonists, who looked upon the entire program with disfavor, the taxes seemed unwarrantable and illegal. Even a considerable segment of English opinion, already aroused by George III's high-handed politics, sympathized with the Americans.

For a decade after 1763 the English attempted by one means after another to raise revenues in the colonies. The Revenue Act of 1764 (also called the Sugar Act and the Grenville Act) prompted colonial lawyers to question its legality: "One single Act of Parliament," wrote James Otis of Massachusetts, "has set people a-thinking, in six months, more than they had done in their whole lives before." The Stamp Act of 1765 led to the Stamp Act Congress, at which representatives of nine colonies met together in New York—the first intercolonial meeting prompted by local initiative—and raised the old English cry, "taxation without representation is tyranny." High-sounding resolves were passed in colonial assemblies, a spate of pamphlets aroused the people further, and colonial opinion was solidified as never before. Royal officials were unable to enforce the Stamp Act and in 1766 it was repealed, although the Declaratory Act of the same year asserted that king and Parliament "have full power and authority to make laws and statutes of sufficient force and validity to bind the colonies . . . in all cases

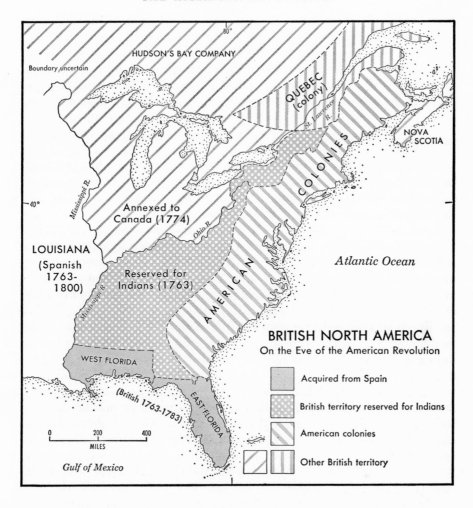

HUDSON'S BAY COMPANY

Boundary uncertain

QUEBEC (colony)

NOVA SCOTIA

Annexed to Canada (1774)

LOUISIANA (Spanish 1763-1800)

Reserved for Indians (1763)

COLONIES

AMERICAN

Atlantic Ocean

WEST FLORIDA

(British 1763-1783)

EAST FLORIDA

0   200   400
MILES

BRITISH NORTH AMERICA
On the Eve of the American Revolution

Acquired from Spain

British territory reserved for Indians

American colonies

Other British territory

Gulf of Mexico

whatsoever." With the taxes repealed, the colonists scarcely noted the Declaratory Act.

The Townshend Acts of 1767 inaugurated new agitation. Again Parliament levied duties on certain British manufactures entering the colonies, together with tea. Moreover, the colonial customs service was reorganized and rendered responsible directly to the English Treasury. The monies collected were to be used to create a colonial civil list, and thus render colonial governors and judges independent of the assemblies. When enforcement proved difficult, especially in Boston, the English government dispatched two regiments of soldiers who were quartered on the Boston people. The assembly responded with the Massachusetts Circular Letter (1768) addressed to the other colonies to urge co-operation in resisting the English. Colonial merchants refused to import English goods, and associations were formed to enforce non-importation agreements. In 1769 the Virginia Assembly passed the Virginia Resolves, sponsored by such prominent Virginians as George Mason, George Washington, and Thomas Jefferson. They declared that the right of taxation in the colonies belonged solely to the colonial assemblies with the consent of the king or his governor. By 1769 colonial opposition to the Townshend duties had reduced English imports by one-half, and the following year all the duties were repealed except that on tea.

THE PATRIOTS UNITE

Repeal of the Townshend duties led to wide reconciliation between England and her colonies, and commercial intercourse returned about to normal. Calm prevailed generally except in Boston, where the English troops were still stationed. In March, 1770, violence broke out between Boston citizens and the soldiers. It was a small incident, largely provoked by the citizens themselves, and the English conducted themselves with admirable restraint. But Sam Adams and his friends, representing extreme views of the situation, made great propaganda value of the "Boston Massacre," and organized intercolonial Committees of Correspondence in more than seventy-five communities. The colonies were on the road to union.

Events of 1773 and 1774 completed the union. Of first importance was the "Boston Tea Party" and the retaliatory measures which followed. The former took place after the English East India Company, being in financial straits, was granted a monopoly of the colonial tea trade free of all duty except the colonial tax left unrepealed in 1770. Its tea imports were widely resisted in the colonies, but in Boston in 1773, a gang of patriots dressed like Indians forced their way upon the company's vessels and dumped their cargos of tea into Boston harbor. This act of violence and destruction determined the new administration of Lord North to take retaliatory measures. A series of acts, known in the colonies as the Coercive, or the Intolerable, Acts (1774), closed the Boston port until the East India Company had been reimbursed for its losses (estimated at £15,000), also established martial law in Massachusetts (setting aside the chartered colonial government), and strengthened the quartering act. All of these acts except the last were aimed at Massachusetts, with the clear intent of bringing that recalcitrant colony to heel. Later in the same year the Quebec Act, long under consideration in London, set up a new government in the French areas north of the Ohio River won by the English in 1763. The Quebec Act enraged the colonists further, partly because of the religious toleration granted to the French Catholics (which was in advance of Catholic toleration in England), and partly because Quebec was expanded to include all the lands north of the Ohio and east of the Mississippi, thus interfering in an area where several of the coastal colonies had ill-defined land claims under their original charter grants.

These acts rallied most of the colonies to Massachusetts' side. In September, 1774, upon invitation of the Virginia House of Burgesses, delegates representing twelve of the colonies met in Philadelphia in the First Continental Congress. Only Georgia failed to send delegates. The congress was assailed by radical demands to declare the colonies entirely outside the legislative power of the British Parliament, tied with Great Britain only through the crown. But more moderate men prevailed, and the "Declaration and Resolves" of the First Continental Congress (October, 1774) were compromising. On the one hand, the congress asserted that the rights of colonists rested upon immutable laws of nature, principles of the English constitution, and their original charters or compacts. These rights included life, liberty, and property (shades of John Locke!) and, as the colonists were not represented in the British Parliament, they were entitled to a free and exclusive legislative power in their several assemblies. On the other hand, the congress "cheerfully" consented "to the operation of such Acts of the British Parliament, as are bona fide restrained to the regulation of our external commerce, for the purpose of securing the commercial advantages of the whole empire to the mother country. . . . " Yet it found "many infringements and violations" of the rights of colonists and, pending removal of these, it proposed to send memorials to the people and the king of England and "to enter into a non-importation, non-consumption, and non-exportation agreement or Association." This agreement, enforced by local committees, led to widespread violence in the colonies as those colonists who dared to challenge the "Association" in a desire to continue in profitable (and legal!) trade were tarred and feathered and their properties destroyed by the "patriots." These economic retaliations injured the colonies more than the British but, while the people within many communities became divided on the issues, the patriots of all the colonies were united.

THE DECLARATION OF INDEPENDENCE

In 1775 war widened the chasm between Great Britain and her American colonies. In Massachusetts the colonial militia (Minute Men) clashed with the British troops on Lexington Green (April 19, 1775), harried the British troops from Concord to Boston, and started a war from which there was no turning back. The word passed swiftly from one Committee of Correspondence to another, and soon all of the colonies were in open rebellion. In May, 1775, the Second Continental Congress met at Philadelphia, representing all aspects of colonial opinion except the Loyalists (soon known as Tories) who, because of the drastic acts of local committees, had become fairly numerous. The congress adopted the militia besieging Boston as the continental army, appointed George Washington, the Virginia planter, as commander-in-chief, and issued a Declaration of Causes of taking up arms. Not all of the radicals yet believed independence from Great Britain to be the only solution. But the sentiment was growing. Before the end of 1775 the congress decided to seek French aid in the war. Thomas Paine's pamphlet *Common Sense* (1776) turned colonial sentiment against George III and presented cogent arguments for independence. Colonial assemblies urged it upon the Continental Congress, and gradually the latter adopted their point of view. In April, 1776, the congress declared American commerce open to the world; in May it instructed the colonies to form state governments of their own making; but it was not until July 2 that a resolution for independence passed the congress. On July 4 the famous Declaration was adopted.

By this time American leaders of the rebellion had advanced far in their acceptance of radical views. Well-grounded in the classics, especially in Roman works, and equally familiar with the French *philosophes,* they fashioned an appealing philosophical justification for their acts which borrowed heavily from the Enlightenment. At the same time, however, they continued in the English revolutionary tradition established in the seventeenth century. They subscribed to the contract theory of government, but theirs was that of John Locke, with its "natural rights" of man, not the "general will" of Rousseau. Even this they tempered to practical politics and spiced with local appeals. Thus, instead of Locke's "life, liberty, and property" as the "unalienable rights" of men, they supplied "life, liberty, and the pursuit of happiness," lest propertyless Americans conceive of the rebellion as one devoted to the protection of the property rights of wealthy seaboard merchants and landowners. Thus, with some modifications, the Declaration of Independence was a model précis of the philosophy of the Enlightenment —turned, however, not in support of monarchy or enlightened despotism, but toward the creation of a representative form of government, a republic:

> We hold these truths to be self-evident, that all men are created equal, that they are endowed by their Creator with certain unalienable rights, that among these are life, liberty, and the pursuit of happiness. That to secure these rights, governments are instituted among men, deriving their just powers from the consent of the governed. That whenever any form of government becomes destructive to these ends, it is the right of the people to deter or to abolish it, and to institute a new government, laying its foundation on such principles and organizing its powers in such form as to them shall seem most likely to effect their safety and happiness.

2 : The Emergence of the United States of America

THE AMERICAN War for Independence was promoted and fought by an organized minority of patriots, while a second group (the Loyalists, or Tories) clung to Great Britain, and a third group was apathetic, seeking to fend off both sides in order to preserve and enlarge its properties and to profiteer in the sale of supplies to both warring parties. Scholars disagree as to the numbers in the factions, but to say that each contained about a third of the population is not far wide of the mark—although they were not equally distributed among the thirteen states. In a dual sense, then, the war was a civil war, with all the bitterness, heartache, and divisions of families and friends that usually attend such conflicts. The properties of Loyalists were ruthlessly confiscated; the neutrals shamelessly profiteered; and, in consequence, a redistribution of land and wealth produced a social revolution within the states even as the war against Great Britain went on. The Second Continental Congress simultaneously served as a central government and a constitutional convention from which the Articles of Confederation were derived (1777, but not ratified until 1781). But it had no legal authority and could only "advise" the states. Consequently, it labored with great difficulty to raise money for the war, equip an army, direct the war and the foreign relations of the rebellious new "nation," and launch a new ship of state. The states gradually organized new governments to replace their old colonial ones. In some instances, as in Virginia and Massachusetts, they devised new constitutions of wide significance for the future. But the states were often jealous of one another and they co-operated poorly, often neglecting or refusing to raise troops or to pay them. Only the halfheartedness of the British (who found many American sympathizers in their midst, anxious to reform Parliament and overthrow the king's party), the aid of foreign powers, the genius of American leadership for compromising differences, the patience and good judgment of Washington, and the knowledge that if they failed they lost all enabled the American revolutionists to win victory, independence, and a united nation.

Sir William Howe succeeded General Thomas Gage as commander-in-chief of the British forces in 1775, and his brother, Admiral Richard, Earl Howe, was in command of the British fleet in North America. The British planned to occupy the chief cities and to send an army from Canada down the Hudson Valley to capture the strategic fort at Ticonderoga on Lake Champlain, and thus to drive a wedge between New England and the other colonies. But the plan misfired. General Howe occupied New York in September, 1776, but Washington held up the British at Trenton and Princeton, and they were unable to take Philadelphia until September, 1777. Meanwhile, a British army under General Burgoyne marched south from Canada; but he did not receive expected reinforcements from Howe and was defeated at Saratoga in October, 1777, and surrendered to the Americans. Saratoga is sometimes considered the turning point of the war. It marked the first significant loss of British troops and it spelled the failure of the British to divide the colonies by isolating New England. Moreover, it strengthened the hand of the Continental Congress, which had long been negotiating for foreign aid. In 1778 the French recognized American independence and signed a treaty of alliance, hoping not so much to help the colonies win independence as to strike a blow at their old enemy and regain some of the colonial empire lost in 1763. French aid was invaluable to the Americans, both because of the money and supplies made available and because of military and naval assistance. A year later Spain, too, entered the war against England in hopes of recovering Gibraltar and Florida. Other European states adopted a more cautious attitude, fearful of the revolutionary ideas set forth by the Americans. But many individuals sought fortunes and glory in America, and a few of them were of considerable value, such as the former Prussian officer, von Steuben, who helped to organize and drill American troops. The Dutch, also, lent great financial aid and, in 1780, Catherine of Russia led the north European states into a League of Armed Neutrality to protect neutral commerce against British naval interference—thereby indirectly giving aid to the American cause.

After the failures of 1778 the British revised their strategy. They abandoned Philadelphia and, while they held New York, their main forces under Lord Charles Cornwallis attempted to subdue the southern colonies. At first the British plan prospered. They took Savannah and Charleston, and commanded Georgia and South Carolina. The American successes of George Rogers Clark in capturing the former French forts at Cahokia and Vincennes in the Illinois country (1778–1779) were in some measure counterbalanced by the treason of Benedict Arnold, who plotted to surrender West Point to the British in 1780. Finally, however, as Cornwallis pushed into Virginia and fortified his position at Yorktown, Washington, with French forces under Lafayette in conjunction with the French fleet in Chesapeake Bay under Rochambeau, closed in on Yorktown. Finding himself bottled up, with no means of escape, Cornwallis surrendered (October 19, 1781). The surrender of Cornwallis at Yorktown ended the severe fighting of the war.

Elsewhere the British were more successful. They defended Gibraltar, and in 1782 they defeated the French fleet which had helped close in on Cornwallis at Yorktown. By this victory they regained command of the seas. But everyone was growing weary of the war. Lord North, severely criticized in Parliament, resigned (1782), and the Whig ministries which followed sought peace. The French found the war more costly than their severely pressed treasury could stand and, moreover, the Americans had become suspicious of French motives, especially as they came to realize that the French coveted the Mississippi Valley for themselves. The British, eager to restore American friendship and trade at the expense of French aspirations, readily agreed to the American demand for the Mississippi as the western boundary and full fishing rights off the Canadian coast. In November, 1782, the British signed a preliminary treaty with the Americans and a general peace was signed at Paris in 1783.

By the general treaty Great Britain recognized the independence of the United States. The Mississippi was accepted as the western boundary of the new nation, but poor definitions of the northwestern and northeastern boundaries led to later difficulties, while the southern boundary led to trouble with Spain. Spain recovered East and West Florida (which gave her entire control of the Gulf of Mexico) and kept Minorca, which had been captured from the British during the war. France got nothing out of the war except a few West Indian islands, a hold on Senegal (from which, subsequently, the huge French West African empire emerged), a bankrupt treasury, and prospects of an ally in America—which failed to develop until the present century.

The American states were ill-prepared to face the problems of nationhood, and the five years after the Peace of Paris are often called the critical period in American history. Treated as a foreign people by England as well as others, the new nation found her ships denied free access to the West Indian trade upon which had depended so much of her prosperity before the war. This loss, together with unstable currency and weak financial condition in America led to severe depression between 1784 and 1787. To many Americans the economic crisis was a consequence of the Articles of Confederation which, having been drawn up during the enthusiasm of the early war years, reflected the weak central government valued by the radicals as a guarantee of liberty. This weakness was demonstrated by the central government's inability to raise adequate revenues and was dramatized in 1786 when state militiamen were needed to protect a federal arsenal during a local uprising in Massachusetts.

THE CONSTITUTION OF THE
UNITED STATES

All these things combined to convince statesmen that a stronger central government was required. After many preliminaries, a convention met in Philadelphia (May, 1787) ostensibly to discuss means of amending the Articles of Confederation. Actually, however, the convention drew up a new federal constitution, which was sent to the states for ratification with the provision that it should become operative upon its acceptance by nine states. After intensive propaganda in its favor—especially in the famous *Federalist Papers* written by Alexander Hamilton, John Jay, and James Madison—the new constitution was ratified (1788). It went into full formal operation on April 30, 1789, when George Washington was inaugurated as the first president of the United States.

The Constitution of the United States was a landmark. It set up a new form of government exciting to the world at large. It was the result on the part of the Constitutional Fathers of a careful study of political organizations from Plato to the writers of the Enlightenment. It was also a product of practical politics, especially in the "great compromise" between large states and small states, whereby a legislative body (Congress) was composed of two houses, one with representation based upon population and the other with representation based upon states. It was a *national* government, not a confederation of states, as demonstrated in its preamble, "We, the *people of the United States . . . .*" It provided that this Constitution, with the laws and treaties made under it, was "the *supreme law* of the land." Yet, while it set up institutions powerful enough to effect the ends of good government, it also provided a system of checks and balances to prevent abuse of that power. This was done by following Montesquieu's notion of the separation of powers. The executive, legislative, and judicial branches were made independent and were provided with checks so as to resist encroachment from one another. The Constitutional Fathers also borrowed from English political experience and from the state constitutions. From the former, they derived the right of habeas corpus and trial by jury and the denial of bills of attainder and ex post facto laws. From the latter they developed many of the democratic sentiments of the early revolution together with some of the social changes effected by the struggle, to wit, formal denial of titles of nobility, primogeniture, entail, and other trappings of privilege. Some of these were included in the first ten amendments, sometimes called the Bill of Rights, which many people, with Lockean concern for natural rights, insisted should be added before ratification. Others were separation of church and state, freedom of religion, freedom of speech, freedom of the press, freedom of assembly, the right of petition, and due process of law. Some of these closely resembled the English Bill of Rights, although their theoretical basis was wholly different: the English Bill of Rights was a grant by Parliament, whereas the American Bill of Rights was based upon natural law, outside and above the legitimate reach of any branch of the government. No government heretofore had so expertly combined the ideals of the *philosophes* with practical politics, the need for centralized political authority with local demands, and the sovereign powers of the state with the rights of individuals.

3 : The French Revolution, 1789–1799

THE FRENCH REVOLUTION began in France, engulfed Europe, and affected the whole world. It destroyed the Old Régime in France, revised the political and social patterns of many other European states, and left a legacy of hates and hopes, ideals and terms, and parties and political methods which have been revived in some measure in almost every reform and revolutionary movement to this day. Its roots struck deeply in the discontents engendered by the Old Régime, watered by the reform programs of the *philosophes*. But its immediate cause sprang from the impending bankruptcy of the Bourbon monarchy. To this, French participation in the American Revolution contributed considerably, while at the same time Frenchmen were fired by American revolutionary sentiments and accomplishments.

BACKGROUNDS OF THE REVOLUTION—
THE OLD RÉGIME IN FRANCE

Many of the discontents engendered by the Old Régime arose from the obsolete structure and the archaic spirit of French society. These were mostly products of inertia—the failure to revise institutions in keeping with changing times and circumstances. Feudalism had long been dead in France as a useful organization, yet French society was permeated with its vestiges. Strangely, in the land of the *philosophes* no enlightened despot had emerged even to attempt reforms. Social, economic, and political institutions were crumbling in decay.

Fundamental to French society were the three estates and their privileges, or lack thereof. The total population of the country was about 25,-000,000. The first estate, the clergy, occupied an important position. Constituting less than one per cent of the population, they controlled about ten per cent of tax-free lands, on which lived the majority of the serfs left in France. They conducted public worship, kept all vital statistics, and controlled such education and poor relief as existed. Between the upper and the lower clergy, however, there was little mutual sympathy. The upper clergy was monopolized by the nobility: they controlled the major wealth of the church and many of them turned over their bishoprics or monasteries to subordinates and resided lavishly (and with doubtful propriety) in Paris or Versailles. The lower clergy, on the other hand, originated mostly from the third estate whose hopes and hatreds they shared. Poorly paid and hard-working, they resented the wealth and aristocratic arrogance of their superiors and, with good Catholics everywhere, deplored the lax discipline of the church. The regular clergy (monks and nuns) declined in numbers and in piety. Land-hungry persons coveted the rich church lands. Although the tithes generally fell far short of the tenth implied, everyone grumbled about them. Moreover, people resented the church's exemption from taxation and felt that the "free gifts" voted by the clergy to the government in lieu of taxes were not only too small, but also constituted a sort of "conscience money" for taxes properly due.

The second estate (the nobility) constituted less than two per cent of the population and they held about one-fourth of the land (a third, if the royal domains be included). They seldom carried out their medieval services of protection and justice on their lands; indeed, those who could afford it lived at court, leaving their estates uncultivated or in the hands of rapacious overseers. Still, they collected feudal dues from those holding lands from them and clung to hunting rights which were often very destructive to peasants' fields. As a class, however, the nobility was sharply divided. At the top were the hereditary nobles, including most of the older nobility, who made up the "nobility of the sword," and looked upon the rest of the nobility as vulgar upstarts. Next were the "nobility of the robe," including those of the *parlements* and other courts and a variety of other offices. They had usually acquired their status originally by buying a hereditary office which, generally, they made lucrative. They were richer than the nobility of the sword—which encouraged intermarriage between the two groups—and they exerted considerable influence by virtue of their firm possession of key governmental offices. At the bottom were the *hobereaux* (sparrow-hawks), the nobles who, being too poor to attend court or purchase an office, vegetated on their estates, exacting with meticulous care whatever manorial dues their peasantry owed them. As a whole, the second estate was widely unpopular, looked upon as snobbish, selfish, worthless drones. But some noblemen demonstrated loftier spirits than the rest, patronized the Enlightenment, and even supported the Revolution.

Nominally, the third estate included everybody else. It made up about ninety-seven per cent of the population, of which about eighty per cent were peasants, the rest being urban workers and bourgeoisie. Compared with those elsewhere in Europe, the French peasants were better off in some respects. Serfdom, though not extinguished, had almost disappeared. Three-fourths of the peasants held land of their own, though as a whole the peasants held only about thirty per cent of the land in France, and only a small number had enough land to support themselves and their families. Moreover, French agriculture suffered heavily throughout the eighteenth century from backward methods of farming, overpopulation, land shortage, heavy taxes, and rising prices for everything the peasant had to buy without commensurate increases for what he had to sell. The peasants paid the bulk of the taxes: tithes to the church, manorial dues to the noble landlords, and multiple payments to the state, including a land tax, an income tax, a poll tax, the *gabelle* (forced purchase of salt from government agents, usually at exorbitant prices), the *corvée* (forced labor on royal highways and other public works), and a variety of less exasperating duties. On the whole, the peasants cared little about the form of government or the reforms of the *philosophes*. They wanted more land, the extinction of manorial dues, and reform of that system of taxation which fell heaviest upon those least able to pay.

The bourgeoisie, though nominally of the third estate, included men of wealth (merchants and bankers), professional men (lawyers and doctors), and craftsmen of all kinds. They totaled less than eight per cent of the population, and all together they owned as much land as the nobility. They were well educated as a whole, much taken with the *philosophes*, and while they suffered less than the peasants and workers, they bitterly resented the abuses of the Old Régime, especially the privileges of the nobility and clergy and the guild monopolies and other restrictions on free enterprise. They demanded the abolition of privilege as a means of winning social and political rights for themselves. And, because of their wealth, experience, and education, they played a leading role in the Revolution.

The government of France deteriorated steadily after the death of Louis XIV in 1715. His great-grandson, Louis XV, a boy of five, succeeded him. While Louis XV reigned until his death in 1774, he did not rule. Ministers and mistresses dominated the scene, while the nobility of the sword scented a fine opportunity to reassert its lost feudal powers, though with little success. The monarchy continued to be highly centralized. Indeed, as one observer noted, it "so thoroughly destroyed all intermediate authorities, and left so wide a vacant space between itself and the public, that it already appeared to be the mainspring of the social machine, the sole source of national life." As there was no widespread system of elective government, even locally, no effective means of communication existed between the people and the royal government. In effect, France was governed by a hierarchy of royal officials, responsible in each province to an intendant who, in turn, was directly responsible to the king. In consequence, the people became accustomed to rely on the central government for everything—and to blame it for every misfortune.

LOUIS XVI

It was Louis XVI, grandson of Louis XV, who succeeded to the French crown in 1774. An affable, well-meaning, but diffident and irresolute man, Louis XVI began his reign well, with able ministers and promising plans for reform. But he was handicapped by his queen, Marie Antoinette, daughter of Maria Theresa of Austria. The queen was beautiful and high-spirited, but also imperious, gossip-loving, extravagant, and ill-educated, given to meddling in state affairs on behalf of her shady court favorites. Thus she was a perfect target for the scandalous stories that grew up around her (most of them untrue), and by the time of the Revolution she had become one of the most hated women in France—"that Austrian bitch," as the unkind phrase went. But Louis XVI was also handicapped by his own mediocrity of mind, his incapacity for leadership, and his tendency to yield when the queen and parasitical courtiers put pressure on him to dismiss able and courageous ministers who were giving him good advice.

France sorely needed strong leadership, able to defy the privileged courtiers. Abroad, French prestige had dwindled since the days of the Sun King, and it was only temporarily revived by participation in the American Revolution. At home, while the nation was outwardly prosperous, it seethed underneath with rising discontent. The most pressing problems, however, were the chronic financial difficulties of the monarchy. Financial disorders evident at the end of Louis XIV's reign had never been corrected. The government debt, already large in 1774, tripled by 1789. Indeed, bookkeeping was so bad that no one could say precisely how much the debt was, though scholars now estimate it at about 4,500,000,000 livres, roughly equivalent to that number of United States dollars as of the post-Second World War era. More than half of the annual budget went for interest on the debt, and every year there was a deficit to pile the debt still higher.

Louis XVI first named as his chief minister Turgot, a prominent physiocrat with a brilliant record as intendant of Limoges. Turgot temporarily reduced the deficit by strict economies, especially at court. Moreover, he introduced reforms to promote freer internal trade and proposed a tax on the nobility. But at this the privileged interests rebelled and, seconded by the queen, obtained Turgot's dismissal (1776) after two years of service. He retired with prophetic words to the king: "Never forget, Sire, that it was weakness which brought the head of Charles I to the block." Subsequent ministers raised new loans until the government's credit was exhausted. In 1786 Calonne, the current finance minister, proposed to revive Turgot's policies—and, indeed, only the removal of the tax exemptions enjoyed by the privileged classes could have averted bankruptcy. To persuade the first two estates to consent to new taxes, Calonne called the Assembly of Notables in 1787, composed of the chief dignitaries of the privileged essates. But they refused. Whereupon the king dissolved the Notables, dismissed Calonne, and himself proposed a land tax to be assessed without regard to the social status of the owners. But the *parlements* refused to register the royal edicts for tax reform and declared, "The nation alone, in Estates-General assembled, can give the necessary consent. . . ," a statement ironically tantamount to the familiar cry of "taxation without representation is tyranny." The king retreated and in August, 1788, issued a call for the Estates-General, that half-forgotten French medieval parliament which had been laid aside by the dynasts since 1614.

FIRST PHASE OF THE REVOLUTION—
THE CONSTITUTIONAL MONARCHY

No one had experience in parliamentary organization and procedure, and the crown had no policies except to dump the financial problem on the Estates-General. In spite of their vast differences in size, the estates had hitherto had equal representation, but this time the king had been persuaded to allow the third estate a double representation so that, in round numbers, each of the privileged orders elected about 300 representatives while the third estate had 600. If separate estates voted independently, as was the past custom (and the intention of the crown), the double representation of

GEORGE WASHINGTON

THOMAS JEFFERSON

JOHN ADAMS

JAMES MADISON

The faces of George Washington, Thomas Jefferson, John Adams, and James Madison are doubtless too familiar to American readers to require identification. However, it is important to place them in the stream of world history. It is even more important to realize that by their leadership, propaganda, and substantial work in politics, both in theory and in practice, they helped to launch a new ship of state. It is a precious part of the American legacy that they dedicated this state to principles of political justice gleaned from wearisome hours of study in the classics of Greece and Rome, a profound awareness of the Enlightenment of their own day, and a practical knowledge of earlier English and American practices and institutions.

"Né pour la peine"

"Sans-culotte de la République Française"

The two-faced priestly aristocracy
(turn upside down)

"Cette fois ci, la justice
est du côté du plus fort"

These cartoons illustrate sentiments held early in the French Revolution. *"Born for punishment"* is the overburdened peasant who receives no recognition in spite of his multitudinous and necessary tasks and for whom all roads lead to the tax collector. The sans-culotte of the Paris Commune in August, 1792, successfully challenged the royal power and soon established the First French Republic. The balance of the three estates is tipped in favor of the Third Estate when Justice is added to the scale. The perfidy of the aristocracy is shown when, looked at one way, the aristocratic priest curses the Revolution and, looked at the other way, he places his faith in the forces of counter-revolution.

LOUIS XVI

MAXIMILIEN ROBESPIERRE

CHARLES MAURICE DE TALLEYRAND-PÉRIGORD

NAPOLEON I

Louis XVI was the well-meaning but blundering king of France who, like Charles I of England years before, was brought to the block for his infirm and impolitic decisions. Robespierre was a country lawyer obsessed by the ideal of a "Republic of Virtue," but, as he was the sole judge of "virtue," his enemies executed him to save themselves. Talleyrand, wily politician and diplomat, survived every overturn and served in every government, including that of Louis XVIII, after Napoleon's downfall. Napoleon Bonaparte was sketched by Girodet-Troison in 1812, a few months before he undertook the ill-fated campaign into Russia.

SIMÓN BOLÍVAR

JOSÉ DE SAN MARTÍN

AUGUSTÍN DE ITURBIDE

PEDRO I OF BRAZIL

Simón Bolívar, the "George Washington of South America," was the cosmopolitan Creole leader of the revolutions in Venezuela, Colombia, and elsewhere. José de San Martín ably led the Army of the Andes in the struggles for independence of Chile, Peru, and the Argentine. Augustín de Iturbide was one of the plotters for Mexican independence and emperor of Mexico in 1822. Pedro I, Portuguese regent for Brazil, proclaimed Brazilian independence in 1822 and served as emperor of Brazil from 1822 to 1831.

the third estate could have no effect, for the consent of only two estates and the crown was all that was necessary to pass an act.

However, the estates assembled amid an unexpectedly turbulent atmosphere. An economic crisis intensified by crop failures in 1788 and an unusually severe winter in 1788-89 had produced widespread unemployment and rapidly rising prices. Thousands of workers were unemployed, and even more thousands of peasants were desperate. It was while these conditions were fastening themselves upon France that the estates chose their deputies and drew up their *cahiers,* or lists of grievances as a guide to the assembled representatives. The third estate chose its deputies by public meetings, and its representatives were dominated by lawyers and other articulate members of the bourgeoisie. As a whole, the *cahiers* demanded far more than merely putting the royal finances in order. In fact, they demanded widespread reforms often reminiscent of the *philosophes'* earlier programs, and almost universally they demanded that France be reconstructed as a *constitutional monarchy.*

Thus the majority of the deputies were prepared to make drastic changes. To effect them, however, they must meet as one body and vote "by head," and not "by order," separately. In this way the third estate, with heavy support from the lower clergy and a few enlightened nobles' votes, could easily control a majority. This procedural question hung fire for several weeks. On June 17, the third estate declared that, as it represented 96 per cent of the nation, it was properly a national assembly representing the general will of the people over which the crown possessed no veto power. Three days later (June 20) barred from its usual meeting place by royal machinations, the third estate met in an enclosed tennis court and vowed they would never disband until they had given France a constitution. A week later the king gave in and ordered the first two estates to join the National Assembly. The Estates-General was replaced by a National Assembly pledged to reform the constitution and society of France. The first act of the French Revolution had been, in effect, to set up a limited monarchy. Thereafter, the National Assembly functioned in a dual capacity: as a legislative body and as a constitution-making body.

Events followed rapidly after the Tennis Court Oath. On July 14 a Paris mob, excited by rumors that the king planned to use troops to overawe the Assembly, attacked the Bastille (a fortress and royal prison), massacred the garrison, and freed the prisoners (who were only five common criminals and two mental cases). It was a shabby affair, but somehow it came to symbolize the beginning of the end of the Old Régime, and Bastille Day has become a great French national holiday of rejoicing. The violence spread to other towns and rural areas. Peasants went berserk over unfounded rumors of brigands on the loose, and overcome by "the Great Fear," as their delusion was called, attacked their landlords, burning many manors and the feudal records upon which the hated manorial dues had been based. On October 5 a mob of Paris women marched the twelve miles to Versailles to demand bread. They interrupted the National Assembly, baffled the king, and terrified the queen, who bore the brunt of their execrations. The next day they returned, taking the royal family, who thereafter resided in the Tuileries Palace, essentially prisoners of Paris. The National Assembly also moved to Paris, where it was increasingly subject to the ever heightening mob pressures and demonstrations.

Meanwhile, however, the National Assembly in piecemeal fashion abolished the Old Régime and set forth a new constitution. Its first important act came in response to the Great Fear. Lest the rural uprisings harden into organized revolt, the Assembly voted (August 11) abolition of all feudal rights and privileges, including the nobles' manorial rights and duties, the clergy's tithes, inequalities of taxation, the sale of offices, and all distinctions of birth for office-holding. About two weeks later (August 26) it set forth "The Declaration of the Rights of Man and the Citizen" with a threefold object: to establish principles upon which the new constitution of France should rest; to abolish additional abuses of the Old Régime; and to serve as a preamble for the constitution in the making. The Declaration was at some points modeled closely after the bills of rights in American state constitutions. It included "the natural, inalienable, and sacred rights of man," such as "men are born and remain free and equal in rights." These rights are "liberty, property, security, and resistance to oppression." "The principle of all sovereignty resides essentially in the nation," and "law is the expression of the general will" in which "all citizens have the right to assist personally, or by their representatives." "Law should be the same for all" and all citizens are "equal in the eyes of the law." Other articles established freedom of religion, freedom of speech, freedom of the press, and separation of powers, and declared that property is "a sacred and inviolable right." Thus the Declaration of the Rights of Man emphasized bourgeois concern for property while it asserted a constitutional liberalism similar to that of the English in 1689 and the Americans in 1789 together with key phrases of the *philosophes*: sovereignty based upon popular consent, natural rights, separation of powers, and the general will.

To meet the mounting financial needs, the Assembly confiscated the lands of the church (November 2) thereby acquiring a national domain which it used as collateral for bonds (*assignats*). The principle was financially sound and the measure would have worked had the government retired the bonds as the lands were sold. Instead, it repeatedly reduced the face value of *assignats,* declared them legal tender, and printed them as paper money until they depreciated to a small fraction of their face value. The result, of course, was more inflation. But in the long run, when subsequent governments repudiated outstanding *assignats,* the burden of much of the public debt was transferred to the hapless possessors of the worthless paper money. Meanwhile, the sale of the church property effected a redistribution of lands. But while bourgeois speculators lined their pockets and the wealthier peasants enlarged their holdings, the poor and landless peasants were unable to buy. Thus, the rich grew richer and the poor poorer. Indeed, the Assembly took little notice of the poor and unemployed. It abolished guilds and internal tariffs and tolls, but it also declared labor unions and strikes illegal.

The confiscation of church lands precipitated a protracted quarrel with the Catholic church. Some members of the Assembly suffered pangs of conscience, but the majority of them, like Voltaire, were eager to "crush the infamous thing" by drastic reforms of the church. In consequence, there followed the Civil Constitution of the Clergy (July 12, 1790), which completely secularized the church and made the clergy a branch of the civil service. The act reduced the number of bishops from 130 to 83, ordered both bishops and priests to be elected by all the voters in their communities (including non-Catholics), fixed the salaries of the clergy (which were paid by the state), dissolved all monasteries and convents, and forbade bishops to apply to the Pope for formal confirmation in office in the usual way. When many Catholics protested against the new settlement, the Assembly ordered all clergy to take oaths to support the new system. Inevitably, of course, the Pope intervened, denouncing the Civil Constitution of the Clergy and the whole French Revolution as well. All but seven of the bishops refused to take the oath and, though about half of the lower clergy complied with the Assembly's order, the French Catholic church was torn apart, with half of its clergy "non-jurors" and half "jurors," the latter under excommunication by the Pope. Good Catholics from the royal family down rallied to the non-juring clergy. Thus the Civil Constitution of the Clergy opened a breach between the Assembly, representing the forces of revolution and reform, and a large segment of the population. In time, the non-jurors became a hard core of counter-revolutionists, plotting with foreign powers to overthrow the revolutionists and restore the absolute monarchy; and, while the quarrel went far to kill Gallicanism in France, as devout Catholics looked more and more to the Pope as their champion, it also gave the church an unenviable reputation among sympathizers with the Revolution as a stubborn foe of all liberty, democracy, and progress.

THE CONSTITUTION OF 1791

The Constitution of 1791, which culminated the principal acts of the National Assembly, sought to place limited monarchy on a permanent footing. It was based upon the principle of separation of powers. Louis XVI headed the executive branch. His actions required approval by his ministers, and his veto on legislation was "suspensive" only; it could, at most, block legislation for four years. Legislative powers resided in a one-chamber body elected for two years. Judicial powers rested in a hierarchy of courts with elected judges. French local government was entirely reorganized. In place of the old bewildering provincial units and intendancies, a tidy local administration was set up. France was divided into eighty-three *départements,* approximately equal in size and corresponding with the eighty-three new bishoprics of the French church; each department was subdivided into *arrondissements* (districts); and each district consisted of a number of *communes* (municipalities) corresponding to the parishes of the church. In each local division the officials were elected and held wide powers of self-government.

Still, the Constitution of 1791 fell short of full democracy. All Frenchmen were citizens, equal before the law; but voting privileges were unequal. The constitution divided all Frenchmen into two classes of citizens: "active citizens" were those who paid annual taxes equal to three days' wages for common labor in their communities, and they alone could vote; "passive citizens" could not vote but held all other civil rights. Only a little over half of the male citizens of France held the franchise. Moreover, members of the legislature were elected indirectly, by a system similar to the American electoral college for the presidency. To be eligible they must belong to the highest tax group. These property qualifications for voting and office-holding emphasized the bourgeois qualities of the new monarchy.

The new constitutional monarchy formally began on October 1, 1791, with the meeting of the new Legislative Assembly elected under the above provisions. But it was doomed to a short life. Aristocrats at home and abroad plotted its overthrow. In the cities of the German Rhineland congregated many prominent French nobles, including the king's brothers. These *émigrés* schemed constantly against the Revolution and sought foreign aid for a counter-stroke. At home, a radical wing of opinion hoped to abolish the monarchy entirely and set up a republic. As the National Assembly had voted to make its members ineligible for election to the new Legislative Assembly, the new deputies were inexperienced, less moderate, and generally less able men. The king, dissatisfied with the suspensive veto and troubled about the Civil Constitution of the Clergy, made a disastrous attempt to flee with the royal family to the *émigrés* (June, 1791). Apprehended at Varennes and taken back to Paris, they were more prisoners than ever; and, while Louis formally accepted the Constitution of 1791, he had forfeited whatever confidence his revolutionary subjects had left in him. Indeed, to many he appeared downright traitorous. Such circumstances did not augur well for the new constitutional régime.

WAR AND PARTY POLITICS

Beyond the borders of France foreign powers assumed a threatening attitude. Edmund Burke, the English statesman, parliamentary reformer, and political writer who had defended the American Revolution, was critical of the French Revolution. He severely attacked the legality and the arbitrary methods of the National Assembly in his *Reflections on the Revolution in France* (1790). In spite of several able replies to him, Burke's views dominated English opinion and cast it irrevocably against the course of events in France. Closer to France, however, Emperor Leopold II, led on by appeals of the *émigrés* and his sister Marie Antoinette, issued to the crowned heads of Europe the Padua Circular (July, 1791) to urge co-operation "in order to restore the liberty and honor" of the French king. Only the king of Prussia responded immediately, and in August, 1791, the two rulers issued a joint Declaration of Pillnitz threatening military intervention in France. Leopold II died in March, 1792, and his son, Francis I, appeared even more dangerous to the French. On April 20, 1792, the Legislative Assembly declared war upon Francis, asserting that he gave "open protection to French rebels" (i.e., *émigrés*) and plotted against French security and independence. From the combined armies of Prussia and Austria on the French borders the commander, the duke of Brunswick, issued a manifesto (July 25, 1792) which declared that they sought no conquests of French territory, that they intended merely to put an end to anarchy in France, to deliver the royal family from captivity, and to restore to Louis XVI "the legitimate authority which is his due." But they also threatened that if "the least violence or outrage" be offered to the royal family by the Parisians, the "liberating" troops would "exact an exemplary and ever memorable vengeance" and hand over the perpetrators of such outrages "to the punishments they shall have deserved."

Instead of terrifying the French, the duke of Brunswick's manifesto stiffened their resistance both to the invaders from without and to the monarchy within. Factional lines, which had been developing since 1789, hardened. These factions, only a few of which became firmly enough organized to be called parties, were new in French political life, but they gave the world a political terminology everywhere familiar. On the right side of the presiding officer in the Legislative Assembly (as he faced the Assembly) clustered together those deputies who were most conservative, that is, those least inclined to support changes from the status quo; on the left sat the most progressive and the radicals, that is, those most inclined to support major changes from the status quo; in the center sat the moderates who sought a course between the two extremes, and with them the indecisive ones, who might be persuaded to the Right or to the Left. From these loose groupings, which first emerged in the Legislative Assembly and became more tightly knit in its successor, the National Convention, have been derived our current terms indicative of political direction, the Right, the Left, and the Center. Yet these terms seldom apply to a static situation. People's sympathies shift constantly with the fortunes of politics and war, sometimes being attracted or repelled by a single personality. So it was during the French Revolution, and the political factions were in a constant state of flux.

Moreover, outside the Assembly arose a variety of political clubs which slowly acquired influence within the Assembly and its successors. Most important of these was the group who first called themselves the "Society of the Friends of the Constitution," although they are better known as the "Jacobins," from the Jacobin monastery in Paris where they met. As a whole, however, the Jacobins were no friends of the Constitution of 1791, for they wanted to destroy the monarchy and set up a republic. One group which broke off from the Jacobins, the Feuillants, with whom Lafayette became associated, did support the Constitution of 1791, but in opposing those who sought its overthrow they were accused of aristocratic sympathies and Lafayette was forced to flee from France (1791). The Jacobins, however, had great organizing ability. They developed a network of Jacobin clubs over all France, the only nation-wide party organization. With this, they captured control of most of the local administrative offices in the election of 1791 and 130 members (of a total of 745) of the new Legislative Assembly. This minority of the Left was skillfully dominated by a group of ambitious deputies from the Gironde, in and about Bordeaux, known as the Girondins. They were led by Brissot and, while they supported a republic, they wanted it to be federal in nature allowing considerable autonomy in local affairs, for they feared the influence of Paris over a completely unified national state. They strongly favored the war in 1792 as they hoped to lead the nation to victory and dominate a new federal republic; but the ill success of French arms under their leadership greatly discredited the Girondins and they soon found themselves outnumbered by more radical Jacobin groups led by an able, intense, country lawyer named Maximilien Robespierre.

The war in 1792 was a turning point in determining the fate of several of the factions. The king and the *émigrés* welcomed it as a means of deliverance from the shackles of constitutional limitations, believing that the new French armies would crumble before the Prussians and Austrians. The Feuillants in the Legislative Assembly also supported the war. The radical Jacobins under Robespierre's leadership hesitated, fearing that the French armies were ill-prepared for war and that their defeat might lead to the re-establishment of absolute monarchy. But the Girondins strongly supported war, hoping to lead French armies to victory and dominate the French scene. They failed on both counts. The French armies were defeated in the spring of 1792 and soon Robespierre was demanding the dismissal of the Girondin leaders. During the summer of 1792 the most radical Jacobins in Paris, aided by the Cordeliers Club, a group of lower middle-class leaders expert in organizing propaganda, mob demonstrations, and riots, plotted an insurrection. They organized armed forces, insinuated themselves into control of the city wards, and on August 9–10, ousted the existing city authorities and set up in Paris an illegal Jacobin commune which quickly challenged the Legislative Assembly itself. On the 10th the commune's forces attacked the Tuileries. The royal family sought refuge with the Legislative Assembly and both king and Assembly sat helplessly while the commune massacred the royal Swiss Guards and palace attendants. The massacre set loose several weeks of extreme violence (the "September Massacres") during which the populace was terrorized by Jacobin-directed mobs. The Legislative Assembly voted to suspend the king, imprison the royal family, and order the election of a new constitutional convention. In the midst of it all the Prussian army broke through the border and appeared able to march on Paris. But a surprising French victory turned them back at Valmy (September 20, 1792). French republicans were delirious with joy and radical Jacobinism rode high. In such an atmosphere the National Convention was elected. Theoretically, the election was democratic, with all the former "passive citizens" enfranchized; actually, it was controlled by Jacobin watchdogs at the polls and only about ten per cent of those eligible actually voted. The result, of course, was an overwhelming victory for republicans. The day after Valmy (September 21, 1792) the National Convention declared France a republic. The Constitution of 1791 had been operative for less than a year. Monarchy was temporarily ended in France. And the most constructive years of the French Revolution were past.

THE FIRST FRENCH REPUBLIC, 1792-1799

To comprehend the strange mixture of violence and idealism of the First French Republic it is necessary to realize that it was born of enthusiasm and nurtured on desperation. Indeed, sometimes it is difficult to dissociate the two. The catchwords of the Revolution, "Liberty, Equality, and Fraternity," were sources of much of the enthusiasm which often approached fanaticism. It took on many forms: the egalitarian titles, *citoyen* and *citoyenne* ("citizen" and "citizeness"), which became mandatory in patriotic republican circles; the red, white, and blue tricolor badge of the republic, without which it became dangerous to appear in public; *sans-culottism,* or the appeal to the common man, who wore trousers instead of the knee breeches (*culottes*) of the gentleman, and was called *sans-culotte* ("without breeches")—the American consul in Paris was badly manhandled by the mob when once he appeared in the streets wearing the usual costume of an eighteenth-century gentleman; the stirring new song, the "Marseillaise," with its patriotic appeal to seek glory by overthrowing tyranny; the revolutionary calendar, which cast aside the Christian way of reckoning time in favor of a new "patriotic" one, with the "Year I" beginning on the first day of the republic, September 22, 1792; the "Constitution of the Year I" (1793), the most democratic instrument of the Revolution, created in

The French Republican Calendar

In their fanatical desire to shed all vestiges of the Old Régime, including the Christian (Gregorian) Calendar, the radical republicans of the National Convention voted (September 22, 1792) that thereafter all public documents were to be dated from "Year I of the French Republic." About a year later (October 5, 1793), they adopted the Republican Calendar amid an atmosphere of neo-pagan enthusiasm. Again, the Convention declared that a new era had begun on September 22, 1792, the day both of the founding of the Republic and of the true autumnal equinox, the latter being an omen that Liberty would soon enlighten both halves of the earth. The new calendar was to be perpetual, not varying from year to year. Each year consisted of four seasons, each season of three "months" of thirty days, each "month" of three ten-day "weeks" called *décades*. To fit the new republican year with the solar year there were added five days (six in leap years), celebrated at the end of the year as national holidays and known as *sans-culottides*. All of the conventional names were altered. The days of the ten-day "week" were called *primidi, duodi, tridi* (i.e., "first day," "second day," "third day," etc.) until *décadi*, which was a holiday in place of Sunday. The twelve months were given names signifying the seasons to which each belonged, as follows:

AUTUMN	*Vendémiaire*	— "Vintage Month"	— Sept. 22-Oct. 21*
	Brumaire	— "Foggy Month"	— Oct. 22-Nov. 20
	Frimaire	— "Frosty Month"	— Nov. 21-Dec. 20
WINTER	*Nivôse*	— "Snowy Month"	— Dec. 21-Jan. 19
	Pluviôse	— "Rainy Month"	— Jan. 20-Feb. 18
	Ventôse	— "Windy Month"	— Feb. 19-March 20
SPRING	*Germinal*	— "Seed Month"	— March 21-April 19
	Floréal	— "Blossom Month"	— April 20-May 19
	Prairial	— "Pasture Month"	— May 20-June 18
SUMMER	*Messidor*	— "Harvest Month"	— June 19-July 18
	Thermidor	— "Heat Month"	— July 19-Aug. 17
	Fructidor	— "Fruit Month"	— Aug. 18-Sept. 16

Because of changes made by law the Republican Calendar did not for every year exactly concur with the Gregorian Calendar as shown. The chart shows concurrences for the Years II and III.

The *sans-culottides* followed on September 17-21, each dedicated to festivals celebrating Virtue, Genius, Labor, Opinion, and Awards, and the sixth day on leap years was known as the *sans-culottide par excellence,* or *Jour de la Révolution,* intended as a gala festival to celebrate the French Revolution as a whole.

The Republican Calendar was not enthusiastically endorsed nor widely adopted in popular usage. It was officially employed until January 1, 1806, when, by a decision of Napoleon I made in September, 1805, it was discontinued.

democratic enthusiasm and laid aside without trial because of desperate circumstances; the bizarre impulses which led Frenchmen to turn Christian churches into "Temples of Reason" and concoct strange rites and ceremonies to worship republican "virtues." In the "Republic of Virtue" itself citizens were called upon to sacrifice all personal interests and merge themselves utterly into the mystical general will of *la patrie* (the fatherland) as defined by Rousseau. There was an element of desperation in it, too, for, as Robespierre said, "It is necessary to stifle the domestic and foreign enemies of the Republic or perish with them." Thus terror was justified, for "the basis of popular government in time of revolution is at once virtue and terror: virtue without which terror is murderous, terror without which virtue is powerless."

The decrees of the National Convention urged peoples everywhere to abolish monarchy and feudalism, proclaim the sovereignty of the people, and join with the French in a brotherly crusade against tyranny. Here was a rampant, jingoistic, new nationalism which seized the imagination of radical French revolutionaries. It infected the armies of the republic, which became downright imperialistic, determined to destroy the bastions of tyranny and to "liberate" peoples whether they wanted to be liberated or not. Savoy and Nice were annexed (November, 1793) and Belgium was liberated and added to the republic the following February. Such actions, of course, aroused a defensive nationalism among the victims of the messianic French, and intensified foreign opposition. Still, these acts of revolutionary enthusiasm were not without some permanent gains: the adoption of the metric system of weights and measures (1795) is a case in point, as was the abolition of slavery in the French colonies (1793); and, while the republic ultimately revealed the cruel force of mass hysteria and the futility of violence as an instrument for promoting brotherhood, it also marked one of the earliest instances when political leaders championed the cause of the poor, albeit without sincerity and for their own political advancement.

The desperation of the First French Republic arose from the fact that it became so besieged on all sides by enemies, both at home and from abroad, that its survival drove republicans to reckless, brutal, and hysterical measures. In France continued food scarcities, depreciated currency, and skyrocketing prices produced constant criticism and disturbance, while non-juring Catholics and monarchists, encouraged by *émigrés* and foreign powers, rose up in open rebellion against the republic until republican supporters were on edge, unable to distinguish between good *citoyens* and enemies of the republic. The trial of Louis XVI for treason and his execution (January 21, 1793)—the queen was similarly dispatched on October 16, 1794—unloosed further internal threats, with a hard core of counterrevolution forming in the Vendée on the west coast of France, supported by outside powers and able to maintain its defiance of the republic for many years. Meanwhile, foreign opposition broadened, and before the end of

1793 an alliance of powers against the republic had formed, consisting of the empire, Prussia, Great Britain, Spain, Portugal, Holland, Sardinia, and Naples. The republic, already torn apart from within, was surrounded by powerful enemies. Small wonder that its leaders were desperate!

The National Convention resorted to extreme measures. An Extraordinary Criminal Tribunal was set up (March 10, 1793) to deal with "every counter-revolutionary enterprise," and a "Revolutionary Committee" was organized in every commune to check on the activities of the populace. These committees set neighbor spying upon neighbor, son upon father, until every community was torn asunder and bitter feuds let loose that have not been wholly resolved to this day. On April 6 the Convention established a Committee of Public Safety "to take, under urgent circumstances, measures of external and internal defense." Its twelve members gradually assumed complete authority of the republic, especially as the factions of the Convention fell into bitter disputes. The Girondins were now on the Right. They showed hesitancy during the king's trial, and demonstrated neither determination nor capacity in leading the republic in the war. Opposed to them was a new faction of radical Jacobins, darlings of the Paris Commune and the *sans-culottes,* known as the "Mountain" (*Montagnards*) because their seats in the Convention, far to the Left, were elevated. Finally, the Mountain leaders charged the Girondins with pro-monarchic sympathies, appealed to force, and purged the Convention of Girondins (May 31–June 2, 1793). A rump Convention, mastered by the Mountain, then reorganized the Committee of Public Safety (July 27). This body fell into the hands of that able country lawyer now grown giddy with the wine of republican revolution, Maximilien Robespierre. The purge of the "enemies of the republic" was heightened everywhere. The Reign of Terror was on.

Most extraordinary measures and events followed. On August 23 the *levée en masse* mobilized both the people and the property of France against the enemies of the republic:

> Young men shall go forth to battle; married men shall forge weapons and transport munitions; women shall make tents and clothing, and shall serve in hospitals; children will make lint from old linen; and old men shall be brought to public places to arouse the courage of soldiers and preach the hatred of kings and the unity of the Republic.

Buildings, horses, and other properties were requisitioned. All France became a vast workshop of war. Under the skillful leadership of Lazare Nicolas Carnot, one of the members of the Committee of Public Safety later hailed as the "Organizer of Victory," fourteen new armies were organized, equipped, and put into the field. Contributing to these accomplishments was the Law of the Maximum (September 29) which was an important part of a series of price- and wage-fixing measures. The prices of most wages and staple commodities were fixed by law to prevent a catastrophic fall in the value of *assignats* and to ration supplies to insure military needs. The republic was newly equipped to deal with its internal economic weaknesses, its counter-revolutionaries at home, and its enemies abroad.

To the shocked surprise of scions of the Old Régime, the armies of the republic were widely successful. They defeated the Vendéans (October 20) and temporarily put to rest an internal threat. They recovered several towns conquered by foreign foes, including Toulon from the British—where a young artillery officer named Napoleon Bonaparte first attracted public notice. They drove the allies across the Rhine and themselves penetrated German territory, "liberating" the people wherever they advanced. With domestic unrest under control and the allies driven from France, the moments of desperation might have passed had not Robespierre become ambitious to purge the republic of unworthy persons and establish a rarified Republic of Virtue. Gradually he came to dominate not only the Committee of Public Safety but also the whole government. In the spring of 1794 he executed his principal rivals and emerged as a dictator (June–July) with a tremendous increase in the intensity of the Terror everywhere. He abolished the Temples of Reason and in an ornate "festival of the Supreme Being" (June 8, 1794) sought to establish deistic worship. But Robespierre's Republic of Virtue was too abstract in ideals, too violent in practice, and too centralized in power to retain popular support. Jealous Jacobin competitors conspired against him, and on July 27 he and his immediate supporters were arrested and executed. The Reign of Terror, which had cost the lives of upwards of 20,000 Frenchmen, was over. The high point of revolutionary fever had passed.

The fall of Robespierre marked the beginning of a movement called the Thermidorean Reaction, from Thermidor, the "Hot Month" of the revolutionary calendar. The new leaders destroyed the institutions of the Terror, deprived the Committee of Public Safety of its independent authority, reduced the power of the Paris Commune, closed the Jacobin Club of Paris, and recalled the surviving Girondins to the Convention. They also repealed the Law of the Maximum (December 24, 1794), releasing a tremendous inflation of prices and depreciation of *assignats* which led to acute economic distress and bread riots. Moreover, in the provinces, especially in the south and west, a new counter-revolutionary White Terror arose against the former supporters of the Mountain and the purchasers of confiscated church and *émigrés'* land. But the tensions of the Republic of Virtue were relaxed, the state permitted a partial restoration of the Catholic Mass, some of the *émigrés* returned, and monarchist agitation was revived, though the dauphin, hailed as Louis XVII, who had been kept prisoner since the execution of his parents, died in June, 1795. Finally, the Convention drew up a new constitution in 1795 (August 22) and on October 26 it dissolved. The republic was retained in name, but the power of *sans-culottism* was broken and the propertied classes—men of wealth but not of birth—dominated the new government.

The Constitution of 1795 established a government known as the Directory, so called because its executive consisted of five directors, an obvious attempt to avoid such centralized executive authority as the monarchy or Robespierre had exercised. Its legislature contained two houses, the Council of Five Hundred and the Council of Ancients. Property qualifications for voting denied the franchise to the poorest quarter of the nation, and eligibility for office-holding was similarly restricted. The bourgeoisie had returned to power.

From all sides the Directory was challenged and its stability imperiled. Monarchist plots threatened from the Right, Jacobin extremists from the Left. The directors and the councils clashed repeatedly, each bent on its own political advantage with little regard for the constitution. The Directory dealt vigorously with economic problems. Its bourgeois supporters deplored the financial weakness of the *assignats;* and the Directory withdrew paper money from circulation, repudiated much of the public debt, instituted various government economies, and gave France the most orderly financial régime it had had since Colbert's time, although at the expense of holders of the old paper money and the creditors of the state. But it failed to establish peace, and among the many plots for the Directory's overthrow were some angling for the political support of the army. Finally, in 1799, one of these plots was successfully carried out. By a military coup d'état of 18–19 Brumaire (November 9–10), Napoleon Bonaparte became First Consul of France and military dictator of the nation. The republic was at an end.

4 : Napoleon and the French Imperium

A VAST and expanding historical literature exists about Napoleon Bonaparte and his régime. In time a Napoleonic cult arose in admiration of his undoubted genius both in war and in politics. His own explanations of his motives were accepted—they were mostly prepared in self-justification years after the events which led to his downfall in 1815—and the little man was cast as a misunderstood hero who sought only to extend the blessings of the French Revolution in the broad interests of European reform, unity, peace, and the brotherhood of men. Indeed, this was Napoleon's early pose: "I am the Revolution," he told the French, and, like the armies of the early republic, his conquests were in the name of the liberation of peoples from tyranny. Still, in the eyes of many, including the "liberated" peoples themselves, the French actions soon appeared more like territorial conquests than liberation. Napoleon emerged as a superb opportunist who employed the catchwords of the Revolution as the enlightened despots had employed those of the *philosophes* to embark upon an ambitious career of conquest and personal power. In many respects he appears now like the greatest of the enlightened despots.

Napoleon Bonaparte was born in Corsica of Italian ancestry. His family belonged to a group of patriots who longed for Corsican independence at the time when that little island fell from Genoese into French hands in the year preceding Napoleon's birth. He left the island when he was nine to study in France, but he never relinquished his loyalty to the Corsican clan into which he was born. Torn between Corsican loyalties and French opportunity, he was a sullen, morose youth, unpopular with his schoolfellows. But he was a brilliant, if ill-balanced, student, and he graduated from military school and became a sublieutenant in the French army. For a time he was an enthusiastic reader of the *philosophes* and was a radical Jacobin sympathizer. But the excesses of the Terror cooled his republican ardor. He rose rapidly in the army, especially after his services at Toulon in 1793. He also advanced rapidly in the estimation of the Directory, first by dispelling a Parisian mob with "a whiff of grapeshot" in 1795 and then by submitting promising plans for the conduct of the war in Italy, where French commanders had failed to meet the Directory's expectation. Finally, he enhanced his opportunities further by marrying Josephine de Beauharnais, a Parisian widow six years his senior and a social belle intimate with the ruling clique of the Directory. Josephine's social and political connections, together with Napoleon's demonstrated military abilities, led to the latter's appointment as commander of the French army in Italy (March, 1796).

The First Coalition, which had formed against France in 1793, was almost destroyed by 1796. Poor leadership, internal disputes, and lack of military success against the French weakened it. Prussia and Spain made peace in 1795, and Holland, conquered by the French, ceased to be independent. Its stadtholder, William V, fled to England, and "patriots" organized the Batavian Republic under French direction and as an ally of France. Only Great Britain and Austria remained at war. In less than two years Napoleon knocked Austria out of the war and only Great Britain remained. He fired the sagging spirits of the army in Italy and led it in a campaign which gradually forced the Austrians out of Italy, while he appealed to the Italians to aid the French in breaking the chains of "the tyrants who oppress you." Posing as a liberator, Napoleon reorganized most of central and northern Italy into a series of republics allied to France. He persuaded the Italians to supply men, money, and supplies to the French, until the Army of Italy was almost independent of support from the Directory and actually filled French coffers with Italian spoils, mostly art treasures. Thus, while Italians were aroused to a nationalist longing for liberty, Napoleon played upon their helpless credulity. He also played fast and loose with his instructions from the Directory, but his military successes, which he was careful to advertise widely in France, soon made him a popular hero and his tendencies toward insubordination were overlooked. He made peace with Austria in defiance of instructions, but the Directory felt constrained to accept it.

This was the Treaty of Campo Formio (October, 1797) by which Austria ceded Belgium (the old Austrian Netherlands) to France in exchange for the Venetian Republic, which Napoleon had conquered; accepted the French annexation of Nice and Savoy; recognized the French-created republics in northern Italy; and ceded the left bank of the Rhine to France. It was further agreed that those German princes who lost territories by the cessions to France were to be indemnified in the empire, thus establishing a principle which began the consolidation of German states and led within a few years to the destruction of the Holy Roman Empire. Thus France had reached the "natural boundaries" long coveted by the Bourbons, with the Batavian Republic (Holland), the Cisalpine Republic (Milan, Modena, Ferrara, Bologna, and Romagna), and the Ligurian Republic (Genoa) as satellites of France. Napoleon had won a masterful peace, and he betrayed increasingly masterful ambitions. Only Great Britain remained at war with France. Against this enemy Napoleon now turned, while other French forces invaded the Papal States, made a prisoner of Pope Pius VI, and organized the Roman Republic under French auspices (February, 1798). In the same month Switzerland fell into the hands of "patriots," Geneva was annexed to France, and the Helvetian Republic was set up. Still later, in January, 1799, when the king of Naples sought to restore the Pope, French forces intervened and, following Napoleon's example, established the classically-named Parthenopean Republic. All of Italy except Venetia was indirectly under French control.

Meanwhile, Napoleon turned his attention to Great Britain. Fear of British naval power dissuaded the French from a direct attack across the English Channel. Accordingly, Napoleon fell in with a grandiose plan to attack India and recover what the French had lost to Robert Clive during the Seven Years' War. The attack, however, would be by land, from Egypt (then a Turkish dependency) across Asia Minor, with plans for a canal at Suez and French control of the Middle East and the lucrative trade of India. The expedition included naturalists, geologists, antiquarians, and other scientists in the best tradition of the Enlightenment. It left Toulon in May, 1798, managed to avoid the British fleet, and put ashore at Alexandria in July, capturing Malta en route. But as a military venture it was a dismal failure. Admiral Nelson and his British fleet found the French vessels in harbor near Alexandria, destroyed them, and cut off Napoleon from France. Plague infected the French troops and on August 24, 1799, Napoleon left his army in Egypt and returned quietly to France, having heard of a Second Coalition forming against France, reverses in Italy, and political intrigues in Paris. His Egyptian forces surrendered two years later to a joint British-Turkish attack. But in the meantime its scholars had laid the foundations of important studies of Egyptian antiquities. A French officer found near the village of Rosetta a stone carved with a trilingual inscription which unlocked the secrets of Egyptian hieroglyphs, opened the door for new studies in Egyptology, and established an Egyptian outpost of French culture which lasted into the present century. The Rosetta stone itself was turned over to the British in 1801, and is still treasured in the British Museum.

Few generals have deserted their armies in the field and made it appear heroic. But Napoleon did, and he was lionized in Paris. He found the capital a hotbed of intrigue, and after a careful scrutiny of the scene he plotted with two of the directors, the Abbé Sieyès and Roger-Ducos, to seize political power. Aided by his brother, Lucien, the rising young president of the Council of Five Hundred, Talleyrand, a canny master of intrigue, and others, Napoleon put his plan to the test on 18–19 Brumaire (November 9–10), 1799. The plot was simple: to force the resignation of the other three directors and, under the pretext of a Jacobin plot against the councils, to set up a provisional government in the hands of the plotters to take measures for the public safety. On the first day the directors were persuaded to resign, the councils moved to St.-Cloud outside Paris to avoid alleged Jacobin interference, and Napoleon was placed in command of the military forces in and about Paris. On the next day at St.-Cloud Napoleon won over the elders, but lost his nerve when he appeared before the Five Hundred, and fainted away. His brother Lucien, aided by Sieyès, saved the situation until Napoleon rallied and troops purged the Council of Five Hundred. A rump gathered by Lucien Bonaparte then deposed the Directory and appointed Sieyès, Roger-Ducos, and Napoleon as provisional consuls entrusted with the government and the preparation of a new constitution for France.

On December 24 the Constitution of the Year VIII (1799) was submitted to popular vote. The work of Sieyès and Napoleon, it preserved republican forms, but it left Napoleon as first consul (of three), elected for ten years, the executive authority. The legislative power was shared by four separate bodies: the Council of State, which proposed laws; the Tribunate, which discussed measures but had no vote; the Legislative Chamber, which voted on measures without discussion; and the Senate, which had a veto power. Both the first and the last bodies were appointed by the first consul, and the other two were elected in such an indirect fashion that Napoleon had ample opportunities to fix the elections. The Council of State, hand-picked by Napoleon, was the mainspring of the system. The Constitution of 1799 was adopted by a vote of 3,011,007 to 1,562, the first of a series of Napoleonic plebiscites which, however rigged they were, demonstrated the plain fact that Napoleon Bonaparte commanded the enthusiastic support of the vast majority of the French people.

If the Constitution of 1799 disguised Napoleon's dictatorship somewhat, he nonetheless showed it openly within a few years. In 1802 he persuaded the legislators to make him first consul for life, with power to name his successor and to amend the constitution when and as he wished. In 1804 he declared himself hereditary Emperor of the French and staged a magnificent coronation ceremony at Notre-Dame in Paris consecrated by the presence of the Pope (December 2). He set up a brilliant court with a new imperial nobility based on achievement (that is, service to the emperor) and not on birth. In the meantime, as a means of solidifying his political position, of pacifying France, and, in some measure, of completing unfinished business of the French Revolution, Napoleon inaugurated a series of reform measures. To a great extent, the success of these measures contributed to the stability and popularity of Napoleon's régime.

NAPOLEON'S REFORMS

1. *Administrative Reforms.* These consisted of both structural and political changes. But the structural changes had more to do with the direction of the flow of political power than with the forms of administration. Actually, the law of February 17, 1800, left the administrative units of local government very much as they had been under the Constitution of 1791, but the officers, instead of being *elected* by the people, were *appointed* by Napoleon —prefects in the 83 departments, subprefects in the arrondissements, and mayors in the communes. Thus France became a highly centralized state in which political power passed from the top down, not from the people up. Another law reorganized the administration of justice (March 18, 1800) along the same lines: a Supreme Court, district courts of appeal in every two or three departments, and a criminal court in every department. The judges of them all were appointed by the first consul. Politically, however, Napoleon proclaimed that he was "not a man of party," and he drew his servants from every political background, including ex-terrorists, old Jacobins, and *émigrés.* This policy gave the new government a broad political basis. Combined with remarkably tolerant policies, including religious freedom, restoration of citizenship to nobles and relatives of *émigrés,* and a general amnesty to all who would lay down their arms against the Consulate, it contributed greatly to the success and stability of the new régime. It supplied order and efficiency at the expense of political liberty and popular government.

2. *Fiscal Reforms.* Gaudin, the finance minister, swept away every vestige of the taxes and even the currency of the Old Régime and the Revolution. Land was resurveyed, new taxes were assessed and collected by a new centralized governmental tax agency, the old paper money was called in and redeemed by the issue of new interest-bearing government bonds, the Bank of France was organized (February, 1800) to manage bond issues and loans, and the currency was reformed (1803) with a decimal coinage system and the now familiar *franc* as its basic unit (replacing the old French pound, the *livre*). By good management and strict economy, the new government

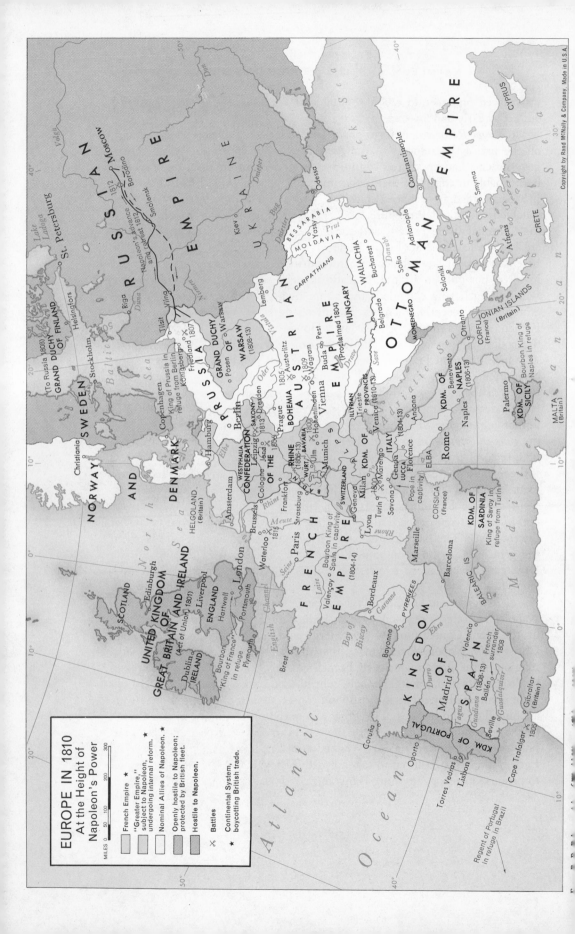

EUROPE IN 1810
At the Height of Napoleon's Power

MILES 0 50 100 200 300

★ French Empire

★ "Greater Empire," subject to Napoleon, undergoing internal reform.

★ Nominal Allies of Napoleon.

Openly hostile to Napoleon; protected by British fleet.

Hostile to Napoleon.

✕ Battles

★ Continental System, boycotting British trade.

Copyright by Rand McNally & Company. Made in U.S.A.

ATLANTIC OCEAN

NORWAY

SWEDEN AND DENMARK

GRAND DUCHY OF FINLAND (To Russia 1808)

St. Petersburg

Lake Ladoga

Helsingfors

Stockholm

Christiania

Riga

Dwina

RUSSIAN EMPIRE

Moscow

Borodino 1812

Smolensk

Napoleon's advance and retreat 1812

Vilna

Niemen

Tilsit

Friedland 1807

Königsberg

GRAND DUCHY OF WARSAW (1808-13)

Posen

WARSAW

Vistula

UKRAINE

Kiev

Dnieper

Bug

Dniester

Odessa

Black Sea

BESSARABIA

MOLDAVIA

Jassy

Prut

WALLACHIA

Bucharest

Danube

Sofia

Adrianople

Constantinople

OTTOMAN EMPIRE

CYPRUS

Smyrna

Athens

CRETE

Aegean Sea

Salonika

MONTENEGRO

Belgrade

Save

HUNGARY

Buda Pest

Drave

AUSTRIAN EMPIRE (Proclaimed 1804)

CARPATHIANS

Lemberg

BOHEMIA

Prague

Wagram 1809

Austerlitz 1805

Vienna

Hohenlinden 1800

ILLYRIAN PROVINCES (1810-13)

Trieste

Venice

KDM. OF ITALY (1804-13)

Ancona

Adriatic Sea

IONIAN ISLANDS (France)

Corfu

Otranto

KDM. OF NAPLES (1806-13)

Benevento

Naples

Palermo

KDM. OF SICILY

Bourbon King of Naples in refuge

MALTA (Britain)

Mediterranean Sea

PRUSSIA

King of Prussia in refuge from Berlin

Berlin

Hamburg

Elbe

Oder

DENMARK

Copenhagen

Baltic Sea

North Sea

HELGOLAND (Britain)

Amsterdam

Brussels

WESTPHALIA

CONFEDERATION OF THE RHINE (1806-13)

Cologne

Leipzig

Jena 1806

Dresden

SAXONY

Frankfort

WÜRT.

BAVARIA

Ulm

Munich

Strassburg

SWITZERLAND

Geneva

Milan

Marengo 1800

Turin

KING OF SARDINIA in refuge from Turin

Genoa

LUCCA

Savona

Pope in Florence captivity

Rome

ELBA

CORSICA (France)

KDM. OF SARDINIA

SCOTLAND

Edinburgh

UNITED KINGDOM OF GREAT BRITAIN AND IRELAND (Act of Union 1801)

IRELAND

Dublin

"Bourbon King of France" in refuge

ENGLAND

Hartwell

Liverpool

London

Portsmouth

Plymouth

Brest

English Channel

Waterloo 1815

FRENCH EMPIRE

Paris

Seine

Loire

Rhine

Meuse

Rhone

Lyon

Bourbon King of Spain in captivity

Valençay (1804-14)

Bordeaux

Bayonne

Garonne

Bay of Biscay

PYRENEES

KINGDOM OF SPAIN

Madrid

Valencia (1808-13)

Bailén French surrender 1808

Barcelona

Ebro

BALEARIC IS.

Duero

Tagus

Guadiana

Guadalquivir

Seville

Gibraltar (Britain)

KDM. OF PORTUGAL

Lisbon

Oporto

Torres Vedras

Coruña

Cape Trafalgar 1805

Regent of Portugal in refuge in Brazil

was placed on a sound credit footing and Gaudin proclaimed a balanced budget as early as 1801–02.

3. *Legal Reforms.* Reform of the law and its codification had been high on the list of the reforms of the *philosophes*. Several of the revolutionary governments had appointed committees to undertake the task, but they had been unable to complete their assignment. Napoleon appointed a committee in August, 1800, to prepare a civil code, which was completed in 1804. Others followed: the Civil Procedure Code (1806), the Commercial Code (1807), the Criminal Code (1808), and the Penal Code (1810). Collectively, these are known as the Napoleonic Code of Laws. It gave France a single, coherent system of law which, with several modifications, remains to this day in force, not only in France, but also in neighboring parts of Europe over which French rule extended, and as far away as Louisiana in the United States. More recently, such revolutionized states as Turkey have used the French code as a model for their laws. However, as framed under Napoleon, the codes did not embrace all the reforms advocated by the *philosophes*. All citizens retained equality before the law, but, while divorce was possible by mutual consent, women and minors were subordinate to husbands and fathers or their nearest adult male relative, and their properties were at the latter's disposal. Property rights were given protection to the exclusion of human rights; the Declaration of the Rights of Man was passed over and the *sans-culottes* were ignored. In practice, Napoleon permitted no freedom of speech, of press, of assembly, of religion, or even of due process of law, if the exercise thereof threatened his power or wishes in any way. His government assumed no responsibility for unemployment or social benefits; workers were forbidden to organize, collective bargaining was outlawed, and in labor disputes the testimony of the employer was preferred to that of the employee. The Napoleonic Code was an ambiguous compromise between the principles of the Enlightenment and the absolutism of the old Roman Law, carefully balanced to preserve authority wherever liberty might challenge it.

4. *Religion and the State.* By a Concordat with Pope Pius VII (1801), Napoleon effected a reconciliation with the church after the break occasioned by the Civil Constitution of the Clergy and the republican attacks upon Christianity. Napoleon recognized that the Roman Catholic religion "is the religion of the great majority of French citizens," tacitly granting toleration to Protestants and Jews. The state continued to pay the clergy, but bishops were nominated by the first consul and consecrated by the Pope. Priests were appointed by the bishops. The Pope renounced all claims upon the church properties confiscated and sold by the state, thereby securing the titles of the purchasers. The state retained vague regulatory powers over the church. Each bishop was required to take an oath of loyalty to the constitution and to promise to report anything being contrived "to the prejudice of the state"

within his diocese. After he became emperor, Napoleon set forth a series of Organic Articles for the Catholic church of France (1806) without even seeking the Pope's approval. They prescribed an imperial liturgy and catechism designed to teach the "duties" of Christians to the emperor. The duties were "love, respect, obedience, fidelity, military service, and the taxes levied for the preservation and defense of the empire and of his [the emperor's] throne." With Napoleon, as his contemporaries said, "all was calculation." In his own words, the church was "a spiritual police force" to maintain obedience to and the security of the emperor.

5. *Education*. The church monopoly of education was challenged by the state during the Revolution. The Constitution of 1791 promised a system of state schools. The Convention began a system of schools for specialized training at the higher levels, such as the Institute of France (1795). Napoleon reorganized and redirected the embryonic state school system. By a decree in 1802, elementary education was left to the communes, and a series of *lycées* was set up by the Consulate and subjected to careful state supervision. Political motives were apparent: the students wore uniforms, were subjected to military discipline, and through their studies were carefully indoctrinated with the "right" propaganda. Heavy emphasis was laid upon the sciences and, to further scientific work, the Institute of France was reorganized in 1803 to carry on the work of the previous academies founded by Richelieu and Colbert. Actually, little was done for elementary education, and higher education in Napoleon's hands was intended to serve the dual purpose of political indoctrination and technical training for the service of the state. Still, he advanced secular education in France, and he furthered the competition of church and state over the control of education that has remained a bitter controversy to our own day.

Napoleon developed a highly centralized state whose every institution was directed toward the maintenance of imperial power. Moreover, it was a police state, with secret police spying on one another and everybody else. Joseph Fouché, the minister of police, was reported to have boasted that "three persons could not meet and speak indiscreetly upon public affairs without its coming the next day to the ears of the minister of police." Yet, within the limits of such a state, it was an efficient and honest government. It preserved equality before the law, and promoted fraternity in the sense of nationalism; but it proscribed liberty. The Revolution was mastered; France was pacified. It was Europe which Napoleon could not bring to heel.

5 : Napoleon and the Coalitions

NAPOLEON faced a series of fluctuating coalitions of powers which ultimately were his undoing. At the center of them all was Great Britain, unwilling to accept French hegemony in Europe. The British were determined to restore Holland and Switzerland to independence, compensate Austria with Italian provinces, reward Prussia with north German annexations, and themselves hold a bag of colonies (mostly the former Dutch possessions) seized for barter purposes. Before the coup d'état of Brumaire a Second Coalition had been formed of Britain, Austria, Russia, Turkey, Portugal, and Naples allied against France. It had overrun Italy and destroyed the French republics there. But then Russia withdrew (October, 1799) and Napoleon defeated the Austrians again in a second Italian campaign (1800) and negotiated the Treaty of Lunéville (February, 1801). This treaty confirmed most of the terms of Campo Formio, ceded the grand duchy of Tuscany to Parma, and further provided not only that German princes who had lost territory west of the Rhine should be indemnified in the empire east of the Rhine, but also that France should have a voice in determining these compensations. In effect, then, France had a voice in the dismemberment of the empire. The Second Coalition fell apart after Lunéville, and even Britain signed the Peace of Amiens (March, 1802). France had its only breathing spell from war since 1792.

But peace lasted little more than a year. Prussia and Austria became alarmed at French machinations in Germany, whereby more than a hundred German states were abolished and their territories given to south German princes who were more and more disposed to follow the leadership of France. England was disturbed by Napoleon's threats from Boulogne, where he concentrated men and ships for a projected invasion, and by French plans for a vast new American colonial empire centering upon Santo Domingo (Haiti) and Louisiana—which Napoleon had acquired from Spain, now his ally. England declared war (May, 1803), and Russia, Austria, and Sweden joined to form the Third Coalition. In trouble in Haiti and scenting danger in Europe, Napoleon hastily dropped his American plans and sold Louisiana to the United States for the bargain price of $11,000,000. He then quickly jettisoned plans to invade England and turned his forces from Boulogne toward Austria.

War against the Third Coalition lasted until 1807, and included some of Napoleon's greatest victories and one serious defeat. The latter was the naval Battle of Trafalgar (1805). Although the British Admiral Nelson died of wounds incurred in the battle, his fleet defeated the combined French and Spanish fleets and established Britain as mistress of the seas. On land, however, Napoleon was uniformly successful. At Austerlitz (December, 1805) he defeated combined Austrian and Russian armies and forced Austria out of the war. By the Treaty of Pressburg (December 26), Austria recognized Napoleon as king of Italy and added Venetia to it; it also gave up Habsburg and imperial lands to Bavaria, Württemberg, and Baden, and recognized the latter two as kingdoms. Six months later the south German states formed the Confederation of the Rhine (the "third Germany") under

Napoleon's protection (July, 1806). On August 1 Napoleon insolently denied the further existence of the Holy Roman Empire. Five days later (August 6, 1806) Emperor Francis II laid down his crown and became merely Francis I, Emperor of Austria. After a thousand years the Holy Roman Empire had expired.

Meanwhile, Prussia joined the coalition and Napoleon advanced against both Prussia and Russia. At Jena and Auerstädt (October, 1806) he routed the Prussians and occupied Berlin; at Friedland (June, 1807) he defeated the Russians; at Tilsit (July 7–9, 1807) he negotiated treaties with both Russia and Prussia. The Third Coalition was broken; only England remained at war with France. The emperor and the tsar (Alexander I) met on a raft in the Niemen River at Tilsit and found unexpected pleasure in each other's company. In consequence, they drew up a treaty which divided Europe between them; the tsar recognized French hegemony over central and western Europe in return for Napoleon's recognition of Russian control over eastern and northern Europe. Moreover, they formed an alliance wherein Russia agreed not to trade with Great Britain and the two powers agreed to join against Britain or any other European power against which it was necessary to make war. Prussia was the principal victim at Tilsit. Deserted by the tsar, the Prussian king, Frederick William III, was treated insolently by Napoleon and was forced to relinquish all Prussian territory west of the Elbe River. He had to give up his Polish provinces for a new puppet state of the French, the grand duchy of Warsaw, to allow French troops to occupy Prussia, and to limit the Prussian army to no more than 42,000 men.

In the three years after Tilsit Napoleon's power blossomed to its fullest extent. Already he had a vision of hierarchical "Grand Empire," based upon a vast array of kingdoms, duchies, principalities, marriage alliances, satellite powers, and allies—all dependent, in one way or another, upon himself as emperor. In consequence, he developed an empire such as Europe had not seen since the days of Rome. Annexed directly to France were Belgium, Holland (after 1810), the German states west of the Rhine, parts of Italy, and the Illyrian provinces east of the Adriatic Sea—a total of 131 departments of which more than a third were non-French. The satellite powers were Switzerland, under Napoleon directly; the grand duchy of Warsaw, under the king of Saxony as Napoleon's agent; the Confederation of the Rhine, under Napoleon's protectorate; the kingdom of Westphalia, under Napoleon's brother, Jerome; the kingdom of Holland, until 1810 under Napoleon's brother, Louis; the kingdom of Italy, under Napoleon's stepson, Eugène de Beauharnais, as viceroy; the kingdom of Naples, under Joseph Bonaparte (1806–1808), then under Napoleon's brother-in-law, Joachim Murat; the kingdom of Spain, of which Joseph Bonaparte became king in 1808. The allies, however unwilling, were Austria, Russia, and Denmark (including Norway). Indeed, only Great Britain, Sweden, and Turkey lay outside the orbit of Napoleon's authority as of 1810.

Still, Napoleon longed for recognition. As a parvenu he lacked the prestige of a Habsburg or a Bourbon. Also he lacked an heir, for his marriage with Josephine had been barren. Accordingly, he divorced Josephine and in April, 1810, married Archduchess Marie Louise, daughter of Emperor Francis I of Austria. Within a year was born a male heir to the throne whom Napoleon promptly made King of Rome—although Napoleon II was destined never to rule in Rome or anywhere else. For already the empire of Napoleon I was beginning to fall apart.

THE DOWNFALL OF NAPOLEON

The reasons for the downfall of Napoleon's edifice were many. We can summarize the principal ones under the following heads: the failure of the Continental System, national regeneration, and the weakening of Napoleon's personal and political powers. In final analysis, however, he was simply defeated in battle by the rejuvenated and overwhelming forces of the coalition of powers against him. To the strength of this coalition the former factors contributed both positively and negatively. Each of them we shall review briefly.

The Continental System was Napoleon's own term for a plan which he inaugurated in 1806 in hopes of ruining England's economic prosperity as a preliminary to the destruction of England's political power. It was a simple extension to the satellites and allies of France's age-old mercantilist policy to build up the export trade of France and to impair that of Great Britain. As such, of course, it was an attempt by France to control the economy of the entire Continent. By the Berlin (1806) and Milan (1807) decrees, Napoleon forbade all trade with England, all commerce in English goods, and the seizure of all neutral ships which complied with Britain's retaliatory order to put in at a British port and pay duties before trading with France. But the Continental System hurt the Continent more than Britain. France's own exports declined rapidly, and unemployment and business failures multiplied. It also antagonized both neutral powers and Napoleon's allies. Seizure of American vessels by both sides led to severely strained relations, and when in 1812 the United States went to war with Britain rather than with France it was partly because the British navy was more effective in interfering with American neutral trade. In Europe the System led to smuggling and various chicaneries until Napoleon's allies, especially the tsar, refused to be bound by the French demands.

To enforce the System, Napoleon attacked Portugal (1807), whose economic ties with England were intolerable to the emperor. The Portuguese royal family fled to Brazil under British convoy (November, 1807). The next year Napoleon lured the Spanish Bourbons from Madrid, persuaded the king and his son to renounce the Spanish throne, and made his brother Joseph king of Spain. Against this extension of French power the Spanish, with

British aid, revolted. The Peninsular War, named after the Iberian peninsula, developed into a fire which Napoleon was unable to extinguish. The Anglo-Spanish forces, commanded by Sir Arthur Wellesley (later Duke of Wellington), were never defeated even though Napoleon hurled more than 300,000 troops against them.

Even the lethargic Germans were aroused against Napoleonic imperialism. Shocked and humiliated by their defeats, both the Prussians and the Austrians underwent a spiritual revolution that generated a fierce nationalism, a rejuvenation of their armies in both organization and morale, and a determination to be free from Napoleonic domination. The popular press broke out with songs, poems, pamphlets, newspaper articles, and plays attacking the French and extolling national heroes. The Prussians evaded the limit set upon the numbers of their troops by assigning recruits to reserves after a period of intensive training and then calling up a new group of recruits. Both Prussia and Austria inaugurated universal military service. A host of patriotic writers fanned German patriotism, including the philosopher Fichte, whose *Addresses to the German Nation* (1807–08) presented the Germans as a veritable "master race." In Prussia General Scharnhorst headed a group of officers who improved the army organization and morale, and Baron vom Stein reorganized local government, abolished hereditary serfdom, and reformed the tax structure. Similar military and political reforms were effected in Austria by Archduke Charles and Count Philip Stadion.

Sentiments against the French were further intensified by Napoleon's exactions. Increasingly, Napoleon bled his satellites by tax demands and conscription of soldiers. To be sure, he built roads, introduced the French law codes, abolished serfdom, and curbed the church; but increasingly these appeared as frenchified policies, by no means wanted by the subject peoples. More and more Napoleon made clear that his satellites and his allies were to be bent to a policy of "France First." Moreover, Napoleon aged rapidly, grew fat, suffered from dyspepsia and sleeplessness, and became increasingly irritable and difficult. Even on the battlefield he delegated to others tasks which he had formerly seen to himself. Thus, when the greatest tests of his military power came, he was less able to meet them.

The first severe test came in Russia. After Tilsit Tsar Alexander gradually lost faith in the intentions of his French ally to leave him a free hand in the Russian sphere of influence. Conversely, Napoleon resented the tsar's refusal to enforce the Continental System. Tension grew, and in 1812 Napoleon massed his Grand Army of about 500,000 men and invaded Russia. But the Russians retreated, followed a scorched-earth policy which left the French without forage for man or beast, refused a pitched battle, and allowed Napoleon to occupy burned-out Moscow, deep in the Russian plains. Meanwhile, the Russians fell upon the French supply trains and destroyed them. Napoleon vainly waited in Moscow for the tsar to negotiate and, as the Russian winter closed in, began a retreat. The Russians immediately fell upon them and, aided by "General Winter," they turned the retreat into a rout. Less than a fourth of the Grand Army survived, and its morale was so shaken that it was useless.

After the Russian success nearly all Europe rallied in 1813 to ally against the French. Napoleon raised a new army, 400,000 strong, but it had neither the equipment, the experience, nor the confidence of the Grand Army that had marched into Russia. At Leipzig, in Saxony, it was defeated in the "Battle of the Nations" (October, 1813), and by the spring of 1814 the allies occupied Paris. Napoleon abdicated (April 11) and accepted the offer of the allies to go into exile as ruler of the island of Elba, near the Italian coast. The last coalition had stood the military test; it remained to be seen if it could weather the problems of a peace settlement.

6 : The Settlement at Vienna and Its Aftermath

ALMOST EVERYONE was exhausted by war in 1814 and desired peace. Even the Parisians greeted their conquerors with apathy. As for the conquerors, peace and security against further French aggression lay uppermost in their minds. To these ends, the allies (Great Britain, Russia, Prussia, and Austria—the Big Four) had agreed on broad policies even before Napoleon's abdication. By the Treaty of Chaumont (March, 1814), they had proposed to remain together for twenty years in order to defeat the French and re-establish "a just equilibrium of the powers." They also proposed to re-establish Holland, Switzerland, and Spain as independent, sovereign states, to reorganize Germany as a federated union of sovereign princes, and to divide Italy into a series of independent states. Actually, the first part of a settlement came with the Treaty of Paris (May 30, 1814) with France. Anxious to propitiate the French in the interests of a permanent settlement, the allies were remarkably lenient. France retained the boundaries she had won in 1792 and recognized the independence of Holland, Switzerland, and the German and Italian states. Louis XVIII, the elder of the two surviving brothers of Louis XVI, became king of France, with a constitutional charter which set up a system similar to the British, with a bicameral legislature, limited suffrage, and guarantees of civil and religious liberty. After this treaty the allies determined to settle the complex problems of the rest of Europe at a general congress at Vienna to meet the following October (1814).

The idea of the Congress of Vienna excited the hopes of everyone. Dispossessed princes turned up at Vienna "like worms after the rain." More than two hundred delegations arrived and were lavishly entertained by Emperor Francis I. Still, the ghosts of Jacobinism and Napoleon were not to be laid to rest by dining and dancing; nor were the Big Four, the victors who had borne the brunt of the wars, likely to forego their commanding position in the settlement. Indeed, their representatives, by previous agreement in the Treaty of Paris, had been in session for weeks before the general congress convened.

The Big Four delegations were led by notable, seasoned men. From Great Britain came the foreign secretary himself, Viscount Castlereagh, anxious to "safeguard Britain's maritime interests and to construct an effective new balance of power in Europe." Representing Austria was Prince Metternich, also foreign minister and an old hand in European diplomacy, likewise determined to set up a new European balance and to establish a strong position for Austria in central Europe and in Italy. From Russia came Tsar Alexander I, difficult not only because he went through changeable moods of romantic liberalism, religious piety, and aggressive realism but also because his territorial demands, especially in Poland, were unacceptable to other powers. And from Prussia there was King Frederick William III, weak and vacillating, much influenced by the tsar, and determined to push Prussian boundaries as far as possible, especially by the addition of Saxony, whose king had been remarkably loyal to Napoleon. To these ambitions of the Big Four were added the greedy claims of every dispossessed princeling and petty state seeking to be restored and enlarged.

Among the conflicting claims the Big Four found most difficult the questions of Saxony and Poland, for each of which the Prussian king and Russian tsar stoutly supported each another, respectively, against the Austrian and British delegations. As the Big Four became deadlocked over these issues, the French representative insinuated himself into the sessions. This was the smooth and oily Talleyrand. Originally a French bishop, he had served in every revolutionary government of France since 1789, and had been Napoleon's foreign secretary until after Tilsit, when he and the emperor disagreed on policies. Thereafter he plotted Napoleon's overthrow, and now he was the foreign secretary of Louis XVIII and French delegate to the Congress of Vienna. Ironically espousing the cause of the lesser powers, Talleyrand won his way into the councils of the Big Four (which, by virtue of the French representative, thereafter became the Big Five) and played a leading role in the congress. It was he who introduced the term "legitimacy" into the congress as a principle of the settlement, meaning the restoration of legitimate rulers to their legitimate governments. Indeed, "legitimacy" and "compensation" (the latter meaning primarily spoils for the victors) became the catchwords of the congress. But they were hardly the bases of settlement in the long run. "Compromise" and "expediency" would serve better to describe the outcome, although, as catchwords they would have held no glamorous appeal.

Most of the points had been settled by the late winter of 1814–15 when news of Napoleon temporarily stopped the proceedings. The erstwhile emperor fled from Elba, landed in Cannes (March 1, 1815), and marched to Paris. Troops sent to oppose him joined with him; Louis XVIII fled without a serious stand; and Napoleon proclaimed himself emperor again and began the short reign known as the Hundred Days (March 20–June 29, 1815). The Big Four renewed their alliance and took the field, with the English duke of Wellington in command. On June 18 at Waterloo, south of Brussels, Napoleon hurled himself upon the allied troops and was defeated. He fled back to France, soon recognized that his cause was hopeless, abdicated again and, having been outlawed by the allies, threw himself into the hands of the British. With the approval of the allies, the British took him to St. Helena, in the south Atlantic, where Napoleon remained as a "guest" until his death in 1821.

By the Hundred Days the allies lost confidence in a repentant France, and France paid the penalty in the Second Treaty of Paris (November, 1815). Her boundaries were pushed back to their position in 1790, she was occupied by allied troops, and she was forced to pay an indemnity for the expenses of the war. Louis XVIII was restored with the Charter of 1814. Meanwhile, the Congress of Vienna had completed its task on June 9, 1815.

The issues of Saxony and Poland were compromised. Russia obtained about three-fifths of Poland, which was set up as a constitutional kingdom under the tsar; Prussia and Austria shared the rest as part of the loot they had won in the earlier partitions. Saxony was divided between Prussia and the king of Saxony, who was restored to his shrunken territory. For the remaining problems the congress made a fairly amicable disposition—and a remarkably stable one, on the whole, for it served for many years without a significant international war. The territorial settlement ran as follows: the legitimate governments were restored in Spain, Portugal, Naples, Holland (to which Belgium was annexed as a barrier against France), Switzerland, Denmark, Sweden (with which Norway was associated), Sardinia (or the kingdom of Piedmont, to which Genoa was added), Tuscany, Modena, Parma, and the Papal States. Russia, besides her Polish possessions, retained Finland (won from Sweden) and Bessarabia (won from Turkey). Austria recovered Tyrol and Salzburg from Bavaria, and received Lombardy and Venetia (including Dalmatia) in Italy. Austria also presided over a new Germanic Confederation of thirty-nine states, set up in place of the Holy Roman Empire, which was not revived, or a unified national German state, which German patriotism wanted. Prussia, however, was placed in a much stronger position, being enlarged not only by parts of Saxony and Poland but also by Swedish Pomerania, the Napoleonic kingdom of Westphalia, and other non-contiguous territories in the Rhineland, including the Saar and Ruhr basins. The object, again, was to establish a bulwark against France; but, as we shall see later, it gave Prussia a fateful finger in southwestern Germany. England's gains were maritime and colonial: Malta, Heligoland, the Cape Colony (Africa), Ceylon, Mauritius, and three West Indian islands—Trinidad, St. Lucia, and Tobago.

To guarantee the settlement, two international alliances were set up. The first, the Holy Alliance (September, 1815) was proposed by Tsar Alexander I and signed by all European rulers except those of Great

Britain, the Papal States, and Turkey. It was an innocuous declaration of Christian principles which were to guide the rulers in their relations with their subjects and with each other. The English dismissed it as mystical and meaningless and, actually, it served very little purpose except as time passed to bind together the three eastern powers (Russia, Austria, and Prussia) in a co-operative pact against liberty and nationalism under the banner of religion. The second, a more realistic and more effective alliance, sponsored by Great Britain especially, was the Quadruple Alliance (the Big Four). An outgrowth of the Treaty of Chaumont, it was signed after the Second Treaty of Paris in the event that treaty should be violated. The members pledged 60,000 men each in the event of trouble, and agreed to hold future meetings to facilitate execution of the treaty. Thus was the basis laid for the future settlement of international troubles by conference, the nucleus of the "Concert of Europe" of the nineteenth century.

Actually, four such congresses were held within the next decade. In 1818 the Congress of Aix-la-Chapelle disposed of the questions regarding the payment of French indemnities, arranged for the withdrawal of allied troops from France, discussed a variety of other problems, and admitted France to a newly-constituted Quintuple Alliance (the Big Five). The harmony among the powers evident at Aix, however, was severely threatened by 1820. In January of that year a revolution began in Spain, and the restored Bourbon king, Ferdinand VII, was forced to accept a constitution which he had rejected in 1814. In June a similar revolt occurred in Naples against the Bourbon king, Ferdinand I, and in August the Portuguese rebelled and demanded a limited, constitutional régime. Meanwhile, the duke of Berry, heir to the French throne, had been assassinated, and a plot to murder the entire Tory cabinet in England had been narrowly averted. To the rulers of Austria, Russia, and Prussia, these events demanded prompt and forceful interference, but at a conference at Troppau (1820) the powers disagreed. England argued that the purposes for which the alliance had been formed did not justify armed interference in the *internal* affairs of European states. Nevertheless, the three eastern states prepared the Troppau Circular, setting forth their reasons for wishing to stamp out the new fires of revolution before they reached serious proportions, and invited France and England to join with them at a new conference at Laibach (1821). England still refused. Meanwhile, Austrian troops interfered in Naples to restore Ferdinand I and keep an uneasy peace. In the same year (1821) the Greeks revolted from Turkish rule, and Ferdinand VII of Spain cried out for aid, especially to restore the Spanish colonies in America, which had been in progressive revolt since 1810. The Congress of Verona met in 1822 to consider Spanish and Greek affairs. Metternich felt that it was impossible to regain the Spanish colonies without British co-operation because the other powers lacked naval power. Moreover, the English were ever more opposed to interference. Legally, they held that it went beyond the legitimate purposes for which the Quadruple Alliance had been created. Politically, they sympathized widely with the aims of the revolutionaries, as they themselves were overcoming their Jacobin-inspired terror of liberal reform. And economically, they were finding it profitable to trade with newly independent Spanish American states and had no desire to see them brought back into the closed colonial system of Spain. Accordingly, the duke of Wellington, who represented the English at the Congress of Verona, was instructed to declare "peremptorily" that if the powers proposed to interfere in the affairs of Greece or Spain, Great Britain "will not be a party." Britain's refusal to co-operate destroyed the congress system for the moment.

French troops crossed the Pyrenees in 1823 and restored the absolutism of Ferdinand VII. In the same year President James Monroe of the United States, mindful of the fact that British policy paralleled his own, warned the conservative powers of Europe that "we should consider any attempt on their part to extend their system to any portion of this hemisphere as dangerous to our peace and safety," and that, while the United States had not interfered in the Latin American revolutions, it would view any attempt to interfere in their affairs with the intent "of oppressing them, or controlling in any other manner their destiny," as "manifestations of an unfriendly disposition toward the United States." This was the Monroe Doctrine, a remarkable assertion of policy and self-confidence by the youthful United States. But it had little effect on the European powers at the time. They were divided in their own councils, and as long as Great Britain refused to co-operate they were incapable of interfering directly in Latin America. Accordingly, the Latin American states became free and independent. To their struggles we now turn.

7 : The Revolutions in Latin America

AT THE BEGINNING of the nineteenth century almost all parts of Central and South America were the colonial possessions of two European powers. The viceroyalties of New Spain (Mexico and Guatemala), New Granada, Peru, and La Plata were under Spanish control; and Brazil was a Portuguese colony. A quarter of a century later all these areas had freed themselves from European control and were exercising some form of independent government. In every case the circumstances which led to their declarations of independence were the direct results of events in the Napoleonic Wars.

It is possible to enumerate several reasons for the colonists' desire for independence. The narrowly restrictive economic policies followed, especially by Spain, and to an only slightly lesser degree by Portugal, certainly contributed. The Spanish government restricted trade in Spain's American colonies to a few ports and to a few privileged companies; imports were heavily taxed, and tolls within Spanish America were heavy and frequent, resulting in fantastically high prices. In the Spanish colonies and in Brazil, the highest governmental posts were reserved for Europeans, and the creoles (Americans of Latin-European ancestry) felt slighted. The intellectual development of the colonies was greatly restricted, both by government and by church, and the Inquisition exercised a close censorship of all printed matter. All these factors contributed to a growing resentment of Peninsular rule by the Latin Americans.

But when one examines more closely these reasons for rebellion, they are found to be at least as much theoretical as factual. They were certainly no worse in 1810 or so than they had been for two centuries before; indeed, the Spanish King Charles III (1759–1788) had made several improvements in the economic lot of his colonial subjects by opening numerous Spanish and American ports to direct trade, and working for the revival of industry and commerce, both in Spain and in the colonies. Furthermore, by the nineteenth century smuggling had become so widespread that it was a commonplace way of life among the Spanish Americans, who circumvented the restrictive policies of their government almost casually. Moreover, although the viceroys and generals in the colonies were, almost without exception, Peninsulars, the secondary (and usually more nearly permanent) posts were very often given to creoles, so that the slights they suffered in that direction were not as important as might at first appear. It seems likely, indeed, that the South Americans simply succumbed to the prevailing revolutionary sentiment, which the wealthy, widely-traveled, and frequently European-educated creoles picked up and carried home with them. They read, and smuggled into their own countries, works by the French *philosophes* and English political writers, which fanned their discontent. They were determined to follow the example of the American Revolution of the English colonies, although their understanding of its causes and of the subsequent governmental organization of the United States was often imperfect. The illegal commercial dealings which the creoles had with other foreign countries had convinced them that Spain and Portugal were no longer world powers of the first magnitude; and when the Peninsular states became involved in the Napoleonic Wars their American colonies took the opportunity to sever their connections with European rule.

When Joseph Bonaparte became king of Spain (1808) Napoleon sent agents to America to require oaths of support from Spanish colonial administrators there; but they were closely followed by other agents from the Spanish local juntas, who insisted that Ferdinand VII, the Bourbon ruler, was still rightful king of Spain. The colonies in general were favorable to Ferdinand, and in 1810 colonial delegates were invited to the Cortes of

Cadiz, representing Ferdinand's committee of regency. In 1812 the Cortes of Cadiz drew up a liberal constitution, promising much in the way of governmental and economic reform for the colonies and making the latter an integral part of Spain, with the right of representation in all governmental assemblies. But Spanish promises of reform did not sound as loudly in the colonies as did the echoes of revolutionary sentiment; the colonials continued to move toward independence. Revolutionary societies were founded, revolutionary journals printed, and such creole writers as Bernardo Monteagudo, "the Thomas Paine of South America," and Friar Camilo Henriquez, editor of the newspaper *Aurora de Chile,* began openly to advocate independence.

THE REVOLT IN THE NORTH

The first step toward separation took place in the area known now as Venezuela. The *cabildo* (municipal council) of Caracas, in April, 1810, deposed and expelled the pro-Bonaparte captain-general and various other officials, and governed in the name of Ferdinand VII. They urged other cabildos to follow suit, and Quito set up a similar government in August, 1810. The committee of regency at Cadiz, however, far from being pleased at the action, declared Venezuela in a state of revolt, and its ports blockaded. Spanish authorities put to death members of the Quito cabildo, and in general acted in a way not calculated to increase the popularity of the Bourbon king in New Granada. Under such treatment, it is not surprising that the Caracas government began to work openly for independence. They placed their forces under the command of Francisco Miranda (1750?–1816), a Venezuelan who had fought under the Spanish flag for the independence of the English colonies in North America. He had tried to secure aid for Venezuelan independence in England and the United States for some years before the Caracas cabildo openly revolted; he had actually invaded Venezuela with a small private army in 1806, but had been forced to withdraw. In December, 1810, he returned to Caracas and took command of the revolutionary army. On July 7, 1811, the cabildo of Caracas formally declared Venezuela independent of Spain, and the following December drew up a federal constitution, markedly modeled upon the Constitution of the United States and upon the Declaration of the Rights of Man.

Unfortunately for the revolutionists, however, the years 1811 and 1812 were marked by military reverses. Venezuelan ports were blockaded by Spanish ships and patriot troops were defeated by royal forces. The misfortunes of the revolutionists were climaxed by an earthquake in March, 1812, which royalist clergy pointed to as a sign of God's displeasure with the Venezuelans. Miranda saw no choice but to sue for peace, and in July, 1812, agreed to hand over the country to the Spanish authorities, providing the lives and properties of the rebels not be harmed. With a short-sightedness which seems typical of the Spanish royalists, their general, Monteverde, treated Venezuela as a conquered country in defiance of the agreement, imprisoning or exiling the rebel leaders and confiscating their property. Miranda himself was captured and sent to a Spanish prison, where he died.

Miranda's successor as revolutionary leader in Venezuela was Simón Bolívar (1783–1830), a wealthy young creole trained in the Spanish army in the Indies, widely traveled in Europe, and greatly influenced by the *philosophes*. He served under Miranda in 1811–12, but escaped after the latter's surrender and went to Bogotá. There he joined the forces of the United Provinces of New Granada, as the former viceroyalty was now called, and raised an army which recaptured Caracas in 1813. For this feat he was given the title, "Liberator of Venezuela!" Unfortunately he lost Caracas again the following year, and withdrew his troops into New Granada territory. In 1815, after the defeat of Napoleon and the restoration of Ferdinand VII, a powerful Spanish army arrived in New Granada, and Bolívar fled with his troops to the West Indies. Spanish troops gradually recaptured most of the rebellious territories, and the end of the dream of independence appeared to be at hand.

Ferdinand VII, who evidently shared with his French Bourbon cousins the distinction of having learned nothing from the French Revolution, withdrew the Constitution of 1812, which had recognized the colonies as an integral part of Spain, and returned virtually to pre-Napoleonic rule in Latin America. In so doing, he alienated the liberals in the colonies who had remained personally loyal to him during the revolt, and effectively recruited new support for the revolutionists. Bolívar, from the West Indies, continued to work for complete freedom of all South America from Spanish control. He sent agents to Europe to raise money and recruit men, and by 1818 he had a force of several thousand, mostly English, Irish, and German, who found time heavy on their hands after the end of the wars in Europe. Bolívar returned to the mainland of South America, entered the Orinoco Valley, gradually added patriots and Indians to his forces, and in October, 1818, a congress of Venezuelan delegates meeting at Angostura chose him president of the country. Bolívar decisively defeated the Spanish near Bogotá in August, 1819, and the Congress of Angostura in December, 1819, proclaimed the union of Venezuela and New Granada as the Republic of Great Colombia.

In 1820 the revolution in Spain forced Ferdinand to make belated efforts to reconcile South America. He offered to make peace if the insurgents would accept the Constitution of 1812, and recognize his sovereignty. But Bolívar stood out for independence, and the war continued. Bolívar and his second in command, General Antonio José de Sucre, invaded the presidency of Quito (Ecuador), captured the city, and added the province to the Great Colombia (May, 1822). A few months later he made contact with the revolutionary forces in the south who, under the leadership of San Martín, had been pursuing a similar struggle for independence.

THE REVOLT IN THE SOUTH

In May, 1810, the cabildo of Buenos Aires set aside a pro-French viceroy and created a provisional junta to govern in the name of Ferdinand VII. Already, however, a strong revolutionary element, led by Mariano Moreno, editor of the *Gaceta de Buenos Aires,* was openly advocating independence. Unfortunately, the Argentinians wasted much of their time at the beginning of their revolution in futile efforts to absorb Paraguay, the Banda Oriental (Uruguay), and Peru, instead of moving consistently against the Spanish in territory nearer home. Paraguay, under the leadership of José Francia, defeated an Argentinian army under Manuel Belgrano in 1811, and established itself as a separate state, loyal to the Bourbons until 1813, when it declared complete independence and set up a permanent national government. The revolt against Spain in the Banda Oriental was led by José Artigas, a gaucho soldier who took up arms against the viceroy, Elío. The viceroy appealed for aid to the Portuguese regent, Prince John, whose wife was a sister of Ferdinand VII. Artigas was willing to unite with the Buenos Aires junta provided the Oriental provinces retained local autonomy. When this was refused, Artigas determined to establish complete independence for his provinces. In the ensuing struggle between Artigas' forces and those of the Buenos Aires junta the Portuguese intervened, and in 1820 the Banda Oriental was annexed to Brazil, where it remained as the Cisplatine Province for several years.

Argentine efforts to invade and annex Peru, still strongly under Spanish control, resulted in the defeat and destruction of Belgrano's army by Spanish forces in 1813, and Belgrano was replaced as Argentina's leader by one of the ablest of all the South American generals of the period, José de San Martín. A creole, San Martín served against the French in the Spanish army for several years before his return to South America to work for independence. He succeeded Belgrano briefly as military leader, then became intendant of Cuyo, a province in the foothills of the Andes, whose chief advantage to him was the fact that it lay directly east of Santiago de Chile. At Cuyo, San Martín gave refuge to the Chilean leader, Bernardo O'Higgins, who had been defeated by the Spaniards and forced to flee. Together they drilled and recruited an army for three years, often enduring great hardship, and producing finally the force known as the Army of the Andes.

In 1816 the restoration of Ferdinand VII in Spain and the success of Spanish armies elsewhere in South America caused the authorities at Buenos Aires to call a congress of delegates, which gave aid and support to San Martín. In February, 1817, the Army of the Andes surprised and defeated Spanish forces guarding the road to Santiago. Chilean independence was proclaimed in 1818, and O'Higgins became president of the country. He and San Martín, making plans for the liberation of Peru, created a small navy, commanded by a former British naval officer named Lord Cochrane, who cruised up and down the coast, heckling the Spaniards in a manner reminiscent of Drake and Hawkins. San Martín landed his troops at a small port in southern Peru and moved northward, adding disaffected Peruvians to his forces as he went. He eventually captured Callao, and the viceroy attempted to negotiate with him on the basis of the 1812 constitution, but San Martín was determined upon complete freedom from Spanish control. In July, 1821, he entered Lima and proclaimed Peru's independence, although much of the country was still under royalist control.

On July 26–27, 1822, at a chance meeting in Guayaquil, San Martín and Simón Bolívar discussed completion of the war and the future government of the South American lands. Much uncertainty exists as to what took place, which probably included the disposition of Guayaquil itself. In any case, they reached no agreement. San Martín favored division of South America into separate monarchies ruled by imported European constitutional monarchs, a policy which Bolívar utterly rejected.

San Martín, unable to secure an agreement, resigned his post in the army and went into voluntary exile in Europe. Bolívar, with aid from General Sucre, continued the work of driving out the Spaniards. In December, 1824, the royalist forces in Peru were defeated, and a short time later Sucre took the province of Charcas, which in August, 1825, was declared independent and renamed Bolivia. Thus ended the South American struggle for freedom from Spanish control.

MEXICO

The war for independence in New Spain was marked as much by trouble between the creoles and the Indians as between Mexicans and Spaniards. In all the Spanish provinces the Indians tended to remain loyal to Spanish rule, which allowed them to keep much of their tribal autocracy, and Mexico was no exception. When the accession of Joseph Bonaparte to the Spanish throne was announced, the cabildo of Mexico City declared its loyalty to Ferdinand. Their action was supported by the viceroy, José de Iturrigaray, who evidently saw himself as a possible future sovereign of an independent Mexico; but he was deposed and imprisoned by the Spanish, and replaced by a series of viceroys of varying degrees of loyalty to the Bourbon kings. At the same time the Indians put up a descendant of the royal Aztec line as a candidate for the Mexican throne, and Dom Pedro of Portugal was suggested as a substitute for his uncle, Ferdinand VII.

Repeated requests for funds to support the Spanish Bourbons became wearisome to the Mexicans and added to separatist sentiment. In September,

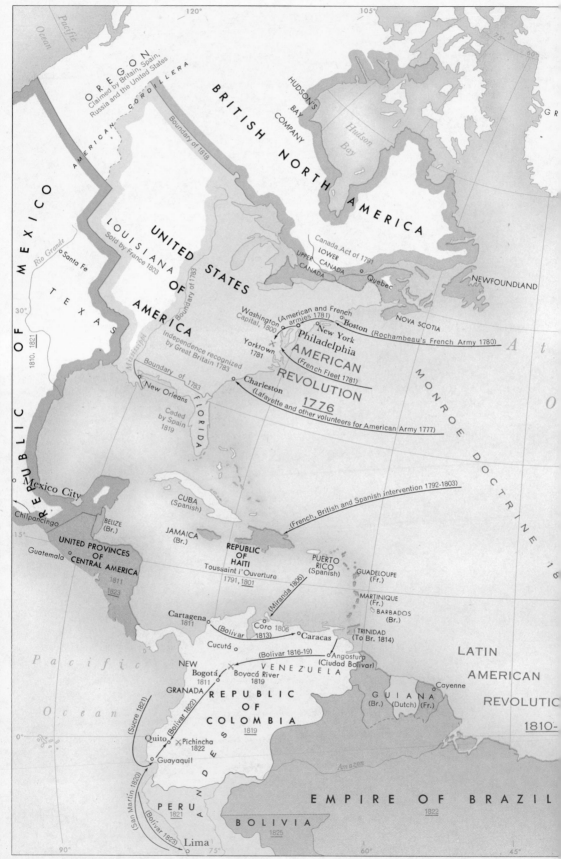

From R. R. Palmer, *Atlas of World History* (Chicago, 1957), pp. 86-87.

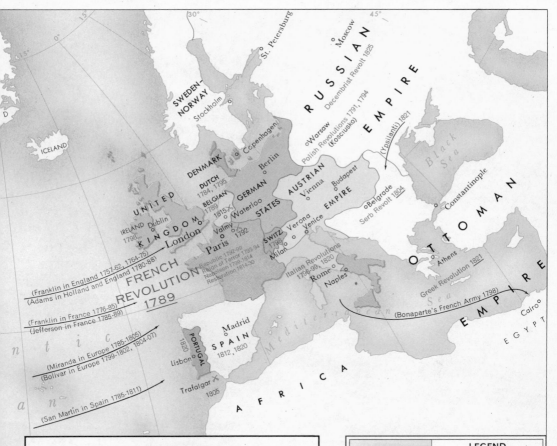

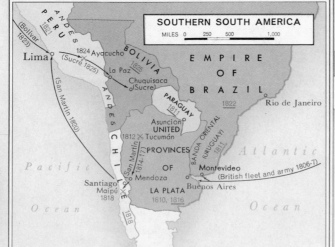

REVOLUTIONS
IN THE ATLANTIC WORLD, 1776-1826

Copyright by Rand McNally & Company, Made in U.S.A.

1810, an open revolt against Spain was led by Miguel Hidalgo, parish priest of the village of Dolores in Guanajuato. He raised a heterogeneous army under the banner of the Virgin of Guadalupe, but its acts of violence and lawlessness alienated many people, and early in 1811 Hidalgo's forces were defeated and he was captured and executed. His work was carried on by one of his *mestizo* (part Indian) followers, another priest named José Morelos. Morelos captured a considerable part of southern Mexico, and actually proclaimed independence in November, 1813; but he was also captured and executed, and his forces scattered.

The remnants of the separatist armies were still carrying on unorganized guerrilla warfare in various parts of the country when, in 1820, Ferdinand VII restored the 1812 constitution in Spain. The conservative royalists in Mexico, particularly the clergy, were dismayed, because their privileged position was threatened, and they began to see much merit in independence. Augustín de Iturbide, a retired officer of the royal army, offered to end the guerrilla warfare. Given authority by the viceroy to do so, he suggested to Vicente Guerrero, the rebel leader, that they join forces for independence. In February, 1821, they agreed upon the Plan of Iguala, based upon a clerical model. Thus Mexican independence was the result of a strange alliance between the revolutionists and the archconservatives.

The Plan of Iguala declared New Spain (Mexico) sovereign and independent, and provided for a constitutional monarchy; the sovereign was to be Ferdinand VII or some other European prince. Of course, full protection was guaranteed to the Catholic church. Features of the plan appealed to both conservatives and revolutionists, and a new viceroy, arriving in the late summer of 1821, signed an endorsement of it, with the added provision that, if no European prince would accept the Mexican throne, the Cortes of the country should elect a ruler.

On September 7, 1821, Iturbide entered Mexico City and created a provisional junta, which swore to support the Plan of Iguala. Until a ruler could be chosen, a committee of regency was appointed, with Iturbide as its president, and a constitutional congress was called. The congress, rather unexpectedly, proved to have strong republican elements, and was less than entirely friendly to Iturbide. The latter, determined to keep his control of the government, staged a military uprising which demanded that he accept the throne. The soldiers' shouts of "Viva Augustín I!" were echoed by the street crowds in Mexico City, and a special session of the constitutional congress (from which some members were barred by Iturbide's army) elected him emperor, and he was crowned on July 25, 1822.

The captaincy-general of Guatemala, to the south of Mexico, had followed the same pattern as the rest of Spanish America, but with much less strife. The local juntas exercised authority in the name of Ferdinand VII until 1821, when the Guatemala City junta proclaimed independence. Soon afterwards Iturbide invited Guatemala to become part of Mexico, but the

Guatemalan provinces as a whole were republican. After Iturbide's coronation he sent troops to force his proclamation as emperor upon the old captaincy-general. The provinces outside Guatemala City were most unwilling to accept Iturbide, and the province of Salvador voted in 1822 to join the United States. The United States government did not open its arms to its new would-be territory, but neither was Mexico able to enforce its domination, since growing republicanism in Mexico itself resulted in Iturbide's resignation as emperor in 1823. A constituent assembly met in Guatemala City, headed, oddly enough, by the former general of the invading Mexican forces; and on July 21, 1823, the United Provinces of Central America declared themselves a united and independent state.

BRAZIL

Quite a different series of events led to the independence of Brazil. Some of the same factors were at work to promote revolution in the Portuguese colony as in Spanish territory; and before the end of the eighteenth century a revolutionary conspiracy under the leadership of Joaquim José da Silva Xavier (known by the nickname of Tiradentes) was formed, but the plot dissolved when its leader was arrested and executed in 1792.

The first real step toward Brazilian independence was taken when Napoleon invaded the Iberian peninsula, aiming at the conquest of Portugal as a long-time ally of England. Prince John, regent of Portugal for his mother, the elderly and insane Queen Maria I, fled Portugal with his family, and established himself at Rio de Janeiro as John I, Emperor of Brazil.

John was quite a successful ruler. He removed old restrictions upon trade and industry, founded the Bank of Brazil, introduced the printing press, established libraries, schools, a botanical garden, and an academy of fine arts. In December, 1815, a royal decree established the United Kingdom of Portugal, Brazil, and Algarve. The advantages to Brazil were somewhat diminished by much heavier taxation and by the emperor's habit of ennobling and enriching his Portuguese, rather than his Brazilian, subjects; but in general the empire marked a great improvement in Brazil's position.

John I encountered difficulties after the end of the Napoleonic Wars. The Portuguese Cortes, in its first session for more than a century, asked the king to return to Portugal; and in the face of increasing demands for a Brazilian constitution and scattered uprisings protesting the heavy expense of the emperor's reign, John returned to Portugal in April, 1821, leaving his son Pedro as regent.

The Cortes in Lisbon, unwilling to grant the Brazilians the constitutional privileges which they were themselves seeking, tried to restore the restrictive policies of Queen Maria's time. Their instructions and letters were unacceptable to Prince Pedro and his Brazilian advisers; and when a particularly infuriating communication from the Cortes reached him one day, while he was riding along the Ypiranga River, he tore his Portuguese colors from his uniform, and proclaimed Brazilian independence on the spot (September 7, 1822). On December 1, 1822, he was crowned Pedro I, Emperor of Brazil; and Portuguese dominion in the New World was ended.

8 : Summary

ONE OBSERVATION stands out immediately: the half-century of revolutions gave birth to many new states, especially in the New World. Moreover, all states, especially those of European origin, were infected with a new species of secular nationalism, a yearning for liberal constitutionalism, a concern for human rights, and a willingness to employ revolutionary tactics to gain these ends. The half-century of revolutions left a legacy to the nineteenth century—one of revolution.

Opposed to this attitude were those who felt that the Enlightenment was bankrupt, that reason had led men to perform most unreasonable deeds, that in the name of natural law men had acted unnaturally and in a beastly, destructive manner. They yearned for the security of tradition, faith, and the *status quo ante bellum*. A "union of the throne and the altar," the rehabilitation of monarchy and the church, was their cure for the ills of society. These were the conservatives, including many who, far from being blindly reactionary, felt that the revolutions had demonstrated the futility of their methods and objectives. Authority grounded in custom and the traditional state was the only means to secure order, decency, and propriety in the world. To them, the revolutions, especially the French Revolution, had been a dismal failure.

Society was altered by the revolutions. The Old Régime was destroyed, and the privileges upon which its inequalities had rested were also destroyed. The bourgeoisie were the principal beneficiaries everywhere. No longer was European society a society of birth; it had become a society of wealth, in which power and prestige depended more and more upon property, money, and credit. The nineteenth century became the century of the middle class.

Further Reading

Evarts B. Greene's *Revolutionary Generation, 1763–90* (New York: Macmillan, 1943) analyzes the economic and cultural developments of the American revolutionary era. A survey of pre-revolutionary period is Lawrence Gipson's *The Coming of the Revolution, 1763–1775* (New York:

Harper, 1954). Edmund Morgan has recently produced a brief and sophisticated summary in his *Birth of the Republic, 1763–89* ("Chicago History of American Civilization" series) (Chicago: Univ. of Chicago Press, 1956). Carl Becker's minor classic, *The Declaration of Independence* (New York: Knopf, Vintage K60, 1958), is an analysis of the document and the ideas which went into it. Another survey for the background of the colonial struggle is John C. Miller, *Origins of the American Revolution* (Boston: Little, Brown, 1943). For the revolution itself, John R. Alden, *American Revolution, 1775–1783* (New York: Harper, 1954), pays considerable attention to the military campaigns. The diplomacy of the period is well defined by Samuel Flagg Bemis, *The Diplomacy of the American Revolution* (Bloomington: Indiana Univ. Press, 1957), although he emphasizes the role of France. A vivid picture of the social background and conditions of the time is John F. Jameson, *The American Revolution Considered as a Social Movement* (Boston: Beacon, 1956). Merrill Jensen in *The New Nation* (New York: Knopf, 1950) re-evaluates the "critical period" of American history. A series of fine essays on the founding fathers and some of the early leaders is Richard Hofstadter, *The American Political Tradition and the Men Who Made It* (New York: Knopf, Vintage K9, 1954).

Adrienne Koch, *Jefferson and Madison; the Great Collaboration* (New York: Knopf, 1950), is a study of the ideas and interrelations of the two minds. *Sam Adams: Pioneer in Propaganda* (Boston: Little, Brown, 1936), by John C. Miller, is a sharp and critical biography of the patriot. Washington's role as commander-in-chief is studied by Thomas Frothingham in *Washington, Commander-in-Chief* (Boston: Houghton, 1930). A study of conflicting ideals between Jefferson and Hamilton is competently presented in Claude Bowers, *Jefferson and Hamilton; The Struggle for Democracy in America* (Boston: Houghton, 1925).

Arthur Young, *Travels in France during the Years 1787, 1788, 1789*, ed. by C. Maxwell (New York: Macmillan, 1929), is a contemporary account of the condition of the French peasantry. Alexis de Tocqueville, *The Old Regime and the French Revolution*, trans. by Stuart Gilbert (Garden City: Doubleday, Anchor A60, 1955), provides a profound analysis of the underlying causes of the Revolution. *From Despotism to Revolution, 1763–1789* (New York: Harper, 1944) is a general survey by the eminent scholar, Leo Gershoy. Georges Lefebvre, *Coming of the French Revolution*, trans. by R. R. Palmer (Princeton: Princeton Univ. Press, 1948), covers the year 1789. A brief and simple treatment of intricate matters is Leo Gershoy's *French Revolution, 1789–1799* ("Berkshire Studies") (New York: Holt, 1932). A study of the social, economic, and religious developments, as well as the political events, is Crane Brinton, *A Decade of Revolution, 1789–1799* (New York: Harper, 1934). An amusing and interesting collection of contemporary caricatures and cartoons is Ernest F. Henderson, *Symbol and Satire in the French Revolution* (New York: Putnam, 1912). *The Jacobins: An Essay in the New History* (New York: Macmillan, 1931), by Crane Brinton, is an able book. James M. Thompson in his *Leaders of the French Revolution* (New York: Appleton, 1929) offers sketches of eleven major leaders. R. R. Palmer studies the Reign of Terror in his *Twelve Who Ruled: The Committee of Public Safety during the Terror* (Princeton: Princeton Univ. Press, 1941).

Geoffrey Bruun, *Europe and the French Imperium, 1799–1814* (New York: Harper, 1938), is a general survey for the period. A recent re-evaluation of Napoleon is James M. Thompson's *Napoleon Bonaparte; His Rise and Fall* (Oxford: Blackwell, 1952). A good study in English of Napoleon and his family is Walter Geer, *Napoleon and His Family; Story of a Corsican Clan,* 3 vols. (New York: Coward-McCann, 1927–29). Harold C. Deutsch in *The Genesis of Napoleonic Imperialism* (Cambridge: Harvard Univ. Press, 1938) discusses the foreign policy from 1801 to 1805, while Robert B. Mowat studies the emperor's aims and methods and his relations with foreign nations in *Diplomacy of Napoleon* (New York: Longmans, 1924). Emile Dard in *Napoleon and Talleyrand,* trans. by C. R. Turner (New York: Appleton-Century, 1937), has produced a study based on original and unpublished sources. A brief study of Napoleon as a man, general, and emperor is Herbert A. Fisher, *Napoleon* ("Home University Library") (New York: Oxford Univ. Press, 1945). Another study of this remarkable man as seen by diverse French historians is Pieter Geyl's *Napoleon: For and Against,* trans. by Olive Renier (New Haven: Yale Univ. Press, 1949).

The best English biography of Talleyrand is by Duff Cooper (New York: Harper, 1932), who gives a sympathetic portrait of the statesman. Algernon Cecil, in his biography, *Metternich, 1773–1859* (New York: Macmillan, 1933), also creates a frank and sympathetic portrait of his subject.

Frederick B. Artz, in *Reaction and Revolution, 1814–1832* (New York: Harper, 1934) presents a broad, sweeping survey of Europe, and in his *France under the Bourbon Restoration* (Cambridge: Harvard Univ. Press, 1931) he emphasizes the social and intellectual developments. A brief summary of the post-war period will be found in Arthur J. May, *The Age of Metternich, 1814–48,* ("Berkshire Studies") (New York: Holt, 1933). The standard work on the Congress of Vienna is Charles K. Webster, *The Congress of Vienna* (Gloucester, Mass.: P. Smith, 1934). Harold Nicolson, a former British diplomat, presents a lucid narrative of the problems at the peace conference in his *The Congress of Vienna, A Study in Allied Unity, 1812–1822* (New York: Harcourt, 1946). Henry Kissinger in *World Restored: Metternich, Castlereagh and the Problems of Peace, 1812–22* (Toronto: Ambassador, 1957) discusses the attempts of the statesmen to bring peace to Europe.

Salvador de Madariaga, *The Fall of the Spanish American Empire* (New York: Macmillan, 1948), is concerned with problems of causation rather than with a narrative of events. In *Rise of the Spanish American Republics As Told in the Lives of Their Liberators* (New York: Appleton, 1918), William S. Robertson surveys the period from 1818 to 1831, and he analyzes the cause of the revolts. John B. Trend in *Bolivar and the Independence of Spanish America* (New York: Macmillan, 1948) offers an interpretation based on new documents and material. The American attitude toward the rebellious colonies is competently presented by Arthur P. Whitaker in *The United States and the Independence of Latin America, 1800–1830* (Baltimore: Johns Hopkins Press, 1941). Joseph F. Thorning, *Miranda: World Citizen* (Gainesville: Univ. of Florida Press, 1952), is a scholarly book, based on new material; Stephen M. Alexis, a Haitian scholar, has produced a sound biography of Toussaint L'Ouverture in *Black Liberator,* trans. by William Stirling (New York: Macmillan, 1949).

Chapter 22

THE ORIENT IN DECLINE

As RECENTLY as the seventeenth century Asia consisted principally of three vast empires, all powerful-appearing and all growing. Across India sprawled the empire of the Great Mogul, founded by Baber but mainly built by his still-abler grandson, Akbar (1556–1605). None of Akbar's successors on the Delhi throne showed intelligence and vigor to match his, but they made additional conquests and kept the great political structure in existence for another hundred years. After 1707 the Mogul Empire crumbled. Mastery of India fell this time not to another conquering wave of Turks or to a native people but to the British.

Since 1644 the Manchus had been lords of China. In the seventeenth and eighteenth centuries this handful of invaders from beyond the Great Wall built an empire that has lasted on the map until the present generation. Besides Manchuria and China Proper, it included Mongolia, Dzungaria, Eastern Turkestan, and Tibet. Nevertheless, by 1800 most of the vigor had departed from the Manchu line. The Chinese had grown restless under the foreign yoke, and the Europeans already showed signs of aggression. The nineteenth century would witness the decline of the once-powerful Manchu monarchy, which collapsed in 1912.

The Ottoman Turkish power, greatly augmented by the capture of Greek Constantinople in 1453, long continued to grow. In the sixteenth century Turkey had been perhaps the foremost military state in Europe, where it held the Balkans, much of Hungary, and a large strip of southern Russia. Western dread of the Ottomans and their ferocious Janissaries continued through the seventeenth century, and in 1683 the Turks gave Europe a final scare by besieging and nearly taking Vienna. With the failure of this attempt, the Ottoman state commenced its disintegration. From then until the First World War its story was one of growing internal decay, accompanied by successive losses of provinces, mostly to European powers.

The causes of this general Oriental decline will be examined as we proceed, but a few important factors can be noted in advance. The Mogul, Manchu, and Ottoman empires were all polyglot states, built by conquering dynasties and aristocracies at the expense of peoples whose independence they destroyed. As long as the ruling castes remained vigorous, they flourished; when they lost military power, direction and drive both vanished and internal corruption began its work. The conquerors never instilled feelings of imperial pride or loyalty in their unwilling subjects, who strove to break away as central control weakened. Moreover, even when Moguls, Manchus, and Ottomans seemed to stand at the very height of power they lagged far behind the European peoples in science and technology. Although occasional Oriental rulers made sporadic efforts to modernize their countries, science and technics had become virtually a Western monopoly. The West left Asia far behind in navigation, seafaring, geographical knowledge, biology, medicine, physical science, and weapon making. Such supremacy spelled decisive military superiority for Europe. It became only a question of time until the Westerners would build empires of their own, partly on the ruins of the older Oriental ones.

1 : India under the Great Moguls

BABER, the founder of the Mogul line, had originally been a petty Turkish chieftain in central Asia. Division and weakness in India rather than his own power had enabled him to conquer the northern Indian provinces between 1526 and 1530. But when he came to feel secure on his newly-won Delhi throne he proved to be a man of different stripe from the ferocious medieval Turkish invaders of India. They had little in mind except to plunder and to force Mohammed's religion down Hindu throats. Although Baber was also a Turk, who could fight with the fury of his race and at times match the cruelty of Tamerlane, he had come to establish a dynasty in India. He meant to construct a permanent empire and to establish a principle of hereditary succession that would keep his family on the throne. Moslem though he was, Baber was no bigot, and we hear little of religious persecution under him or his immediate descendants. His death in 1530 appeared to end hope of a stable Mogul régime, for his handsome, drug-taking son, Humayun (1530–1556), at first proved unable to hold his father's conquests. Humayun, driven out of India, took refuge in Persia, where he gained help at the price of changing his Moslem affiliation from Sunnite to Shi'ite. He then returned to India with a combined Persian-Mogul army, equipped with effective artillery, which had now become familiar to both Persians and Turks. Delhi fell into Mogul hands again, and almost immediately, in 1556, the throne passed to Humayun's son, Akbar, who began reigning when a boy of thirteen.

THE REIGN OF AKBAR

The new Mogul sovereign was far from being emperor of India just then. Of Baber's former empire only the Punjab and the land around Delhi had been reconquered. Because of his extreme youth, the advisers of Akbar regarded him as a puppet fit only to lend his name to the carrying out of their orders. The young ruler at first seemed an unpromising boy. His refusal to study caused his tutors to prophesy a dismal future for him, and to his dying day he remained illiterate and barely able to scrawl a signature. However, the young emperor had redeeming qualities, as he presently showed. He compensated for his inability to read and write by an unbelievable memory which enabled him to absorb what others read to him. His interests included every subject then known in India, and he had an inquiring mind. To mental alertness he joined great bodily strength and utter fearlessness; he is reported to have subdued, singlehanded, rogue elephants that had run amuck and trampled their keepers. Akbar managed early to free himself from his tutors and advisers, and by the second year of his reign he was campaigning at the head of armies. He conquered the remaining Afghan states in India, overcame Rajputana, and marched victoriously eastward. By 1592 he had subdued Bengal, Kashmir, and Sind, and had subjugated the last independent Moslem princes of northern India. His last years were occupied with the southern Deccan, and if he did not dominate the Hindu Brahman states there as completely as he had done the Moslem ones of the north, he did compel them to acknowledge his overlordship.

The conquests of Akbar proved him a great soldier; his administration of India proved him a great man. Lacking patience with the governmental makeshifts of the Turks preceding him, he replaced them with a system inspired in part by the firm law of Genghis Khan and in part by Persian administrative methods. Just as Louis XIV, a century later, eliminated dangerous feudalism in France by turning the rough provincial lords into dainty courtiers dancing attendance on him at Versailles, so Akbar established a court at Delhi where he domesticated the warlike Turkish and Rajput nobles. He meanwhile organized government into bureaus or ministries, headed by a prime minister and including a minister of finance, a general-in-chief, a lord in charge of the court, and a keeper of the great seal. Eighteen viceroys, or subahdars, administered the provinces into which he divided India. The standing army consisted of 140,000 men, at a time when England, the future conqueror of the peninsula, had no army at all.

Akbar realized that he had far more Hindu than Moslem subjects and did not intend the Brahmans to be mistreated. A former zealous lawgiver had written:

If a Moslem wishes to spit in a Hindu's mouth, the latter should open his mouth. These humiliations should mark the inferiority of the infidel, exalt Islam, and bring all false religions low. Allah himself commands us to despise the infidels. He says they are not to be feared, provided you have them beneath your feet. To treat the Hindus with contempt is a religious duty . . . .[1]

Akbar knew that no enduring empire could be built on such a basis. He restored to the Hindus all civil rights that they had lost by the conquest, and ordered tax gatherers to exempt them from heavy payments whenever cases of need could be shown. He also found much in Hindu practices that needed correction. To the best of his ability he stopped the ancient practice of suttee, or widow burning, and even ruled remarriage possible for widowed women. Child marriages he also disliked; his laws forbade Hindus to give their sons in wedlock before the age of sixteen, or their daughters before reaching thirteen.

India had no common language. If only for the convenience of his administration, Akbar saw the necessity for a speech that could be understood by his millions of subjects. He put scholars to work, and they produced a synthetic product called Hindustani, or Urdu, which began as the language spoken in an experimental way at the Mogul court at Delhi. Hindustani spread until today it is used by over a hundred million people. No greater step has ever been taken toward accomplishing the possibly hopeless task of unifying India.

From the best evidence it seems that Akbar, who had started life as a Moslem, had ceased to be one in any real sense before his death. Dogma meant nothing to him. His fundamental outlook was spiritual, yet he was not averse to jesting at the taboos of his religious doctors. Loving beef, pork, and wine—which were all forbidden by the Brahman and Moslem faiths—he once asked those around him which religion would allow him to indulge in these excellent foods and beverages. When told that Christianity, well represented now in India by Portuguese missionaries, did not object to any of them, he suggested with tongue in cheek that they all turn Christian. Akbar will always be remembered in history as a great man of action. Yet between him and such more primitive characters as Genghis Khan and Tamerlane a wide difference existed. He was the most civilized Oriental conqueror ever to come from a nomad line.

LATER MOGULS

Jehangir (1605-1627), who succeeded Akbar on the throne, was a weak man and a wastrel, who nevertheless partly carried on his father's

---

[1] René Grousset, *Histoire de l'Asie* (Paris: G. Crès & Cie, 1922), Vol. III, pp. 222–23.

policies. Though he discarded some of Akbar's enlightened ideas, he showed religious toleration. Could Jehangir have remained mentally and physically fit, he might have been an emperor worth praising. But in view of his inordinate fondness for both drink and drugs, it is a wonder that he lived to reign twenty-two years. He and India were both fortunate in the character of his favorite wife, Nurmahal, whom he allowed to govern the empire when his own dissipation reduced him to physical helplessness. This princess did much better at ruling than her invalid husband even in his better days was ever known to do.

The next Mogul, whose title was Shah Jehan (Sovereign of the World), ruled from 1627 to 1658. Despite a grievance against his stepmother, Nurmahal, he had married her niece, a beautiful girl named Mumtaz Mahall, who became his favorite wife. This princess had but a short life. When she died early in the reign of Shah Jehan her imperial lover built her the most beautiful mausoleum in the world—the series of white marble buildings and minarets at Agra known as the Taj Mahal. The construction of this superb tomb, designed by a Turkish architect from Constantinople, required fourteen years. When Shah Jehan's time came, he too was buried there.

Shah Jehan departed entirely from the tolerant ways of his grandfather. One of his early decrees commanded all Hindu temples, recently built or in course of construction, to be leveled to the ground. It is reported that seventy-two were destroyed in the city of Benares alone. Christian churches, founded by Portuguese Jesuits at Agra and Lahore, were likewise razed. Shah Jehan carried his hatred of the Portuguese to the point of attacking their establishment at Hugli, in Bengal near the modern Calcutta. The Portuguese—the first Europeans who had entered India—enjoyed such a warlike reputation that the Great Mogul dispatched 150,000 men to capture their settlement. The military forces of Hugli consisted of 300 Portuguese soldiers and 700 trained Indian auxiliaries, yet they prolonged the resistance for four months and succumbed only when Shah Jehan's force drained the moat and mined the fortifications. This able defense of Hugli by one of the weaker European peoples demonstrated that the time for Western subjugation of India was drawing near. The forces of Shah Jehan gave the captive Christians, who were mostly civilian natives converted by the Portuguese, a dose of Moslem intolerance. Ten thousand were murdered in various ways, and four thousand were taken to Mogul Agra to undergo whatever tortures seemed adequate for forcing them into Islam.

Shah Jehan aspired to do what his predecessors had never done—to conquer the entire Deccan. He entrusted the conquest to his son, Aurungzeb, who campaigned for several years in southern India. Aurungzeb's bitterest enemy was his older brother, Dara, who considered himself the heir to the throne and did all in his power to curry favor with their elderly father. As Shah Jehan grew old and careless of the burdens of empire, the sons quarreled and fought, paying little attention to the aged ruler. In 1658 Aurungzeb overcame Dara and other brothers and grasped the throne. He imprisoned Shah Jehan and kept him in captivity until his death in 1666. Letters exchanged between the two during this confinement are interesting: Shah Jehan complains of unfilial conduct, while Aurungzeb takes a highly moral tone and lectures his parent on the subject of his undeniably many sins.

AURUNGZEB

Aurungzeb (1658–1707) was the last important Mogul ruler. European knowledge of India had by now grown extensive, and Westerners knew his career in some detail. At the height of his fame the English dramatist John Dryden wrote a play called *Aurengzebe* for the London stage, in which the quarrel between the old emperor, Shah Jehan, and his son is pictured as the result of their rivalry for the love of a princess. It is tempting to wonder what the real Aurungzeb would have thought of this stage counterpart had he ever learned of the drama.

Aurungzeb, who was a last fierce throwback to his central Asian Turkish ancestors, had no tolerance to offer non-Moslem subjects. In retrospect, it can be said that he did everything possible to cause the great Indian empire to disintegrate after his death. He bitterly persecuted Hinduism and destroyed its best temples and palaces. He dismissed all Hindu clerks in government service, although he later had to modify this harsh decree, as it was found impossible to carry on the government without them. His taxes fell more heavily on Hindus than upon Moslems, and one result was the unwilling conversion of many Brahmans who changed faith merely to escape the exactions and insults of the tax collector. When protests from courageous Hindus reached Aurungzeb, he dismissed them with scorn and gave orders to increase the persecutions. When the leader of the Sikh faith refused to embrace Islam, Aurungzeb had him tortured to death. The Rajputs, who had been conquered and then wisely conciliated by the great Akbar, had long been loyal vassals of the Mogul throne. Aurungzeb went out of his way to antagonize these valuable soldiers and goaded them to the point of causing all Rajputana to blaze into rebellion.

Somehow, by a combination of cruelty and cunning, the Mogul managed to quiet his internal enemies and turn his attention to the conquest of southern India, which had never fully accepted Mogul domination. Against the warlike Marathas he is reported to have moved with a huge, unwieldy force that resembled a portable city. In addition to the troops, there went 250 bazaars, half a million camp followers of all kinds, 50,000 camels, and 30,000 baggage-bearing elephants. As the Maratha military specialty was the employment of light guerrilla cavalry tactics, the emperor's massive array proved helpless and had to withdraw. Aurungzeb, however, returned with other better-equipped forces, and by 1690 had overcome most resistance in the Deccan without having ended it for good. He was now an old man in failing health, yet he was compelled to campaign in the south almost until the end of his life in 1707.

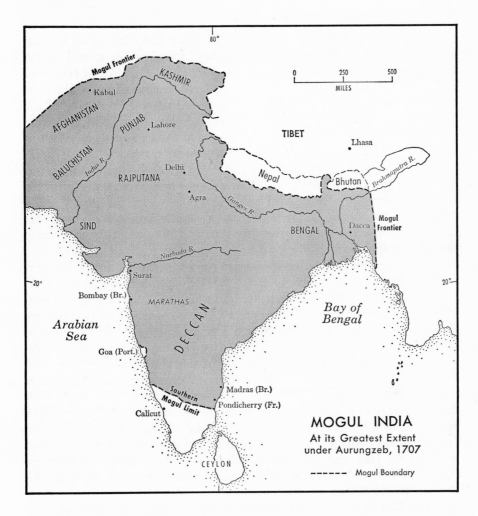

MOGUL INDIA
At its Greatest Extent
under Aurungzeb, 1707

------ Mogul Boundary

This last of the truly great Moguls showed a strange blend of piety and ferocity. Despite his cruelty he fasted, mortified the flesh, dressed like a monk, and spent much time in prayer. To label him a hypocrite is to miss the point, for he considered himself Allah's chosen instrument for Islamizing India. Yet however sincere he may have been, he can be called a destructive force. The Mogul realm, built by the tolerant Baber and Akbar, should have endured for several more generations. Aurungzeb by his blind intolerance made its further survival impossible, and the empire really ended at his death in 1707. The title Great Mogul continued to be held by non-entities descended from him until 1858, when the British put an end to the farce.

THE RISE OF EUROPEAN POWER

Before the middle of the eighteenth century India lay again in frag-ments. The era of Moslem rule had passed, for although several of the new states were Islamic they were weak and had no possibility of becoming the centers of new empires. From the south the zealously-Hindu Marathas raided to the gates of Delhi. The northern Sikhs tore Lahore and all the Punjab from Aurungzeb's weak successors and planned to build an empire of their own. From the west came the forces of the Persian shah, which in 1739 captured Delhi and indulged in a general massacre. The invaders then laid hands on all available gold, jewels, silks, and other treasures, and took them away on the backs of captured horses and elephants. With them to Persia went the gem-studded peacock throne which the luxury-loving Shah Jehan had ordered built for himself a century earlier. India again lay ready to become the prey of the strongest, and the contest for supremacy would be waged between the trading companies of England and France.

As we saw in earlier chapters, the Portuguese were the first Europeans to reach India in ships directly from their homeland. Being interested in trade alone, they did not plan to build an empire. Still, they soon found it necessary to acquire a few bases on the Indian coasts, where Goa became their Eastern capital. Soon the Mogul Empire rose to dominate the bulk of India, and the Portuguese, though they sent a few traders and mis-sionaries to Delhi, otherwise stayed out of the hinterland and contented themselves with controlling trade to Europe. More dangerous Westerners were to follow. Shortly after 1600 the Dutch, French, and English all formed companies for commerce with the East. The Hollanders, who rounded the Cape of Good Hope a little in advance of the other two, largely passed India by and concentrated their commercial and imperial activities in Java and adjacent islands of the East Indian archipelago. There they founded the wealthy Dutch empire that lasted until the Second World War.

The French East India Company at first lagged in its effort, and not until the time of Louis XIV's able minister, Colbert, did it acquire main-land holdings in Hindustan. Then, in the late seventeenth century, the French were allowed by the Mogul to have establishments at Surat on the west coast, Masulipatam on the Bay of Bengal, Chandernagar near Calcutta, and Pondicherry farther south on the east coast. After the death of Aurungzeb and the loss of Indian political unity the French found themselves obliged to mingle in native politics and to take sides in the numerous civil wars and contests between local princes. Though representing a trading company and not the French monarchy, they soon behaved as an imperial power, concluding treaties, making alliances, and maintaining their own armed forces.

The English, who entered India somewhat earlier, did so in a similar manner. Their East India Company, founded shortly before the death of Queen Elizabeth I, existed by a royal charter and consisted of over two hundred London merchants and investors. In its first years the company operated on an individualistic basis and each member had his choice of investing or not investing in a given cargo and voyage to the East. Each time ships returned to England and the Oriental cargos were disposed of, the account books for that particular venture were closed. This proved too loose a way in which to do business, and in 1661 a thorough reorganization took place. The company now became a joint-stock affair, with regular shares that could be bought and sold. The English merchants at first felt more interest in the East Indies than in Hindustan, but the Dutch, who had gained a head start in the islands, proved too strong to be dislodged. A sad experience in the East Indian island of Amboyna, where a colony of English traders was captured and killed in 1623 by the Hollanders, showed that the latter had the upper hand. Thereafter the English concentrated their major commercial efforts in the Indian peninsula. The company acquired Bombay in 1668 from King Charles II, who had recently obtained it as a marriage dowry from his brother-in-law, the king of Portugal. So little did Charles value this island, which is now the site of an enormous Indian city, that he leased it to the company for a yearly rental of £10. Meanwhile the merchants had gained footholds at Madras and in Bengal.

The London merchants had begun operating in India with no thought of territorial acquisition. They wished only toleration from the Moguls and permission to carry on their trade. With this objective, they sent a sea captain named William Hawkins as their ambassador to Jehangir's Delhi court as early as 1609. From his own report, which seems reliable, Hawkins gained favor with the Mogul partly because the bluff English sailor proved an excellent drinking companion. A few years later Sir Thomas Roe, a man of greater personal dignity than the brawling Hawkins, followed as minister to Delhi where Jehangir still reigned. After concluding a commercial treaty with the Mogul emperor he penned this advice to the company merchants:

> By my consent you shall never engage yourselves but at sea . . . .
> The Portuguese, notwithstanding their many rich residencies, are
> beggared by keeping of soldiers . . . . Observe this well. It has also
> been the error of the Dutch, who seek plantations here by the

sword . . . . Let this be received as a rule, that if you will profit seek, seek it at sea and in quiet trade, for without controversies it is an error to affect garrisons and land wars in India.[2]

The advice was excellent as long as the Mogul Empire endured. When it fell both the English and the French found the case far different. They then had to arm for protection against native rulers, and above all against each other. With the Portuguese power ended, and with Holland occupied elsewhere, the contest for India narrowed to the companies of France and Great Britain.

BRITISH DOMINATION IN INDIA

The eighteenth century brought a succession of European wars in which the French and the British were always arrayed on opposite sides. These were in a true sense world wars, for international interests clashed in every part of the earth. In India the companies now had the means for fighting, because, in addition to their European troops, they had hired and equipped as soldiers both Moslems and Hindus of good caste. Such native mercenaries, called sepoys (*sipahi*), soon proved superior to many times their number of poorly-armed soldiers in the service of Indian princes.

In the early stages of international conflict the French held the advantage. Joseph François Dupleix, their leader in India during the War of Austrian Succession (1744–1748), captured most of the English holdings. With adequate backing from France he might well have driven his opponents from the scene forever. But the French government proved less awake to great overseas opportunities than the British, and handed back all Dupleix' conquests on the signing of peace. The mistake could not be rectified, for never again did France have so good a prospect in India. When the next round of the contest, in the form of the Seven Years' War, opened in 1756 Dupleix had been recalled to France and his inferior successor faced the brilliant young English commander, Robert Clive. Clive had gone out to India as a company clerk in 1743, but had soon abandoned his desk in favor of soldiering. Early in the Seven Years' War he won his most noted victory, not over the French but over the nawab of Bengal, while the French stood idly by. The young nawab, long at outs with the English whom he detested, suddenly marched on their Calcutta post, seized 146 of them and thrust them for the night into the small dungeon ever since known as the Black Hole of Calcutta. By morning most of the Englishmen had died of suffocation. News of this brought

---

[2] Sir John A. R. Marriott, *The English in India* (Oxford: Clarendon Press, 1932), p. 44.

Clive from Madras with an army of 1,100 European troops and 2,100 sepoys. By a grove of mango trees known as the field of Plassey, Clive in 1757 routed the nawab's army many times the size of his own and placed a puppet on the Bengal throne. Thereafter the English remained the real lords of the great, heavily-populated province, which became the cornerstone of their Indian empire. Three years later one of Clive's subordinates dealt the French such a crushing defeat that they were eliminated as a threatening power in India. When peace came again in 1763 Great Britain handed back to the French company its cities and factories along the coast, but these now existed on English sufferance and no longer exerted influence beyond their walls and gates. The English East India Company now had no rival capable of blocking its path to the lordship of India. Twice later, during the wars of the American Revolution and the French Revolution, France attempted through agents and intrigue to re-enter the scene and break the British hold on India. Both attempts failed, leaving the Anglo-Saxon grasp tighter than ever. Thereafter it only remained for Britain to eliminate such remaining native powers as the Marathas and the Sikhs. Both were subdued during the first half of the nineteenth century.

INDIAN CULTURE IN THE MOGUL PERIOD

Indian culture in Mogul times took its tone largely from Persia, just as Europe a century later patterned its intellectual life on that of France. Although the use of Hindustani began at the court of Akbar, the Persian language was the principal court speech and was likewise used by the more fashionable and elegant writers of India. The first conqueror, Baber, in composing a book of interesting and poetic *Memoirs,* wrote in his native Turkish, but this autobiography was later translated into Persian. The unlettered Akbar surrounded himself with poets and scholars whose works were read aloud to him. His minister, Abul Fazl, reckoned as the most learned Moslem of the era, wrote an encyclopedic book called the *Institutes of Akbar,* which is our main authority for the life, the laws, and the government of the great emperor. The magnificent work, which took seven years to finish, was of course composed in Persian. Abul Fazl also became interested in the ancient Sanskrit writings, and by translating many of them into Persian he gave the emperor and court a taste of Hindu philosophy in its oldest form. The influence, if not the language, of Persia spread downward to the common people. Many of those who learned to write the new Hindustani used it principally to transmit Persian ideas to their countrymen.

Persian influence in the arts equaled the influence in literature. The architectural monuments left by the Moguls show the Persian style so abundantly that the Indian construction of the period can be classed as a variant of the Persian mode. India, however, yielded stronger building materials than Iran. While the Persians depended on artificial substances such as cement, India possessed abundant marbles and hard stones. For this reason the Indian structures looked more imposing and certainly were destined to endure longer. The Taj Mahal at Agra was built by an Ottoman-Turkish architect who had worked and studied in Persia before coming to India. In style his masterpiece resembles many Persian structures, but whereas these are falling to pieces the marble Taj may last as long as the Egyptian pyramids.

Mohammed's teachings are taken by most Moslems as prohibiting the portrayal of the human form on canvas or in stone. The Persians, however, had never been strict in observing this taboo, and their attitude was shared by the earlier and more tolerant Mogul rulers. We have excellent surviving portraits of all six emperors from Baber to Aurungzeb. European influence was now entering India. Jesuit missionaries brought Western religious paintings, and surviving Indian work shows a resemblance to Italian, Spanish, and Portuguese Renaissance art. Jehangir displayed great pleasure on one occasion when the Englishman Thomas Roe placed a European picture before him and straightway six of the court artists copied it so well that Roe admitted he could not distinguish their work from the original. Sculpture made some beginnings in India during Mogul times, but died a cruel death, as did virtually all the arts, at the hands of Aurungzeb. From his austere court poets, painters, and musicians received a summary dismissal. Architects limited themselves to building a few mosques on the sites of demolished Hindu temples. To Aurungzeb poets were people who told untruths, painters and sculptors were idol makers, and musicians were tricksters who perverted sound to pamper the ear. Historians, too, he thought deserved to be eliminated because they narrated the proud deeds of those who should have been humble. Aurungzeb attempted to keep the events of his own reign from being recorded, but historians eventually had their inning and said what it pleased them to say concerning him.

INDIAN RELIGION

The creative period of Indian religions had long since passed. Great theologians were no more, and religious literature was now of a secondary kind. Sikhism might be called new, but it influenced only a few. Jainism had reached a mummified stage, and Islam had never put forth its finest fruits on Indian soil. With Hinduism the case was somewhat different, as that religion, after centuries under the political heel of the Turkish Moslems, showed signs of revival.

Most of this rebirth took place among the Marathas, who only briefly bent the knee to the Moguls. One of their seventeenth-century prophets, the low-caste grocer, Tukaram, began a revival of spiritual religion accompanied by a revolt against the whole caste system. Many tales are told of his generosity and unworldliness. His less spiritual wife labored and begged to support the family and, when Turkaram gave her clothes away to a passing tramp while she bathed, her indignation is understandable. Tukaram's principal god, Vithoba, had a shrine in the Deccan where an earlier devotee had reportedly once amazed onlookers by causing a she-buffalo to recite the Veda. The saint performed no miracles, but composed simple religious hymns for the people and lived an austere life which has been compared to that of Francis of Assisi. Caring nothing for luxury, he refused an invitation to reside at the Maratha court. The manner in which Tukaram died is obscure; there is still a belief in the Deccan that an ancient hero-god descended to bear him to heaven in his chariot.

Less spiritual but more politically minded was the Maratha Sivaji (1627–1680), who founded the first powerful Hindu state that India had seen for centuries. Though brought up in comparative poverty and illiterate all his days, Sivaji was nevertheless taught the hero tales of the ancient Brahman epics. In childhood he conceived a fierce hatred of the Moslems, whom he regarded as the oppressors of his people and his religion. As a young man he became a warrior, at first a sort of guerrilla bandit leading a small force in the Maratha hills. Moslems learned both to fear and to respect him, for he could make war fiercely and at the same time do so with some of the instincts of a gentleman. They admired his prowess, and admitted that he showed respect for captured women and even for mosques and copies of the Koran. By 1660 Sivaji had founded an important Maratha state, and the Great Mogul Aurungzeb decided it must be blotted out. But Aurungzeb was here facing the foremost Indian soldier of the age, and as long as Sivaji lived no great progress was made by the Mogul. After the hero's death Aurungzeb scored several successes, but none of these eliminated Maratha resistance. When the aged Mogul himself died in 1707 the Marathas took the offensive and helped despoil the fragments of his empire.

The importance of Sivaji is, first, that he started the Indian political balance turning from the Moslems in favor of the Hindus, and second, that he revitalized the Brahman faith. He bore some personal resemblance to his antagonist Aurungzeb, although his was the more attractive character of the two. Like the Mogul, he was devoutly religious, stern as to discipline, and filled with a sense of his own sacred mission. It was he who invited the penniless saint Tukaram to his court, and who took no offense at the latter's courteous refusal. Sivaji is today a well-remembered hero among

Indian peasants, who recount with glee his triumphs over the Moslems. The Maratha power he founded was the last Indian state that could combat the British on anything like even terms.

2 : China to the Manchu Decline

THANKS TO a civil war among generals of the expiring Ming Dynasty, the Manchus crossed the Great Wall and captured Peking in 1644. With little opposition from the demoralized and disorganized Chinese, they enthroned their boy prince as emperor and proclaimed a new dynasty, the Ch'ing, or Pure. By buying off a Chinese general or two and taking care, meanwhile, to effect no violent overturn among officeholders, the Manchus restored order in northern China. They had the sense to realize that no government could rule without concessions to Chinese scholar-bureaucrats, thoroughly saturated with Confucian classics, who had manned the civil service for so many centuries. This was an adjustment the Manchus could easily make; they were warriors who could show Confucius every respect so long as they did not have to study him. The bureaucracy at once swung to their support.

THE CONSOLIDATION OF MANCHU POWER

The conquest of central and south China required several years. A Ming pretender appeared in Nanking and attempted to gain a following, but the Manchus promptly marched against this champion of a lost cause and disposed of him. This victory placed the whole Yangtse River Basin in their hands and opened the way to the far south, where those who still held the Ming standard aloft were wasting their slender energies in quarrels among themselves. The Manchus picked them off one by one, and their conquest of China was practically complete when the city of Canton fell in 1650. The last Ming claimant is principally famous for having been baptized by Jesuits under the Christian name Constantine. "Emperor Constantine" fled as the Manchu army approached, in a shameful contrast to his brave general who fought to the bitter end. The Manchus showed the general every consideration; after beheading him they gave him a funeral with royal honors.

Once in possession of the Chinese throne, the conquerors adopted a double policy. They strove to identify themselves with the great culture, long history, and admirable institutions of China, and tried to avoid being conspicuous as conquering foreigners. At the same time they did not desire to become too Chinese or to lose their identity and be swallowed in the great native mass. They regarded themselves, with good reason, as the more military people of the two. While Chinese soldiers—and even generals—could serve them, the Manchu banner units remained the props of the Ch'ing throne. The conquerors discouraged their people from marrying Chinese and considered it beneath themselves to waste much time studying for bureaucratic examinations. "No bannerman," it was written, "should receive high honors in the civil-service examinations, since he presumably had other opportunities to become an official and at any rate should traditionally devote himself to military affairs." With the higher offices of state open to them by appointment, and with the military service theirs, Manchu aristocrats could afford to leave the grubby routine work to the Chinese.

THE REIGN OF KANG HSI

The second Manchu emperor, Kang Hsi (1662–1722), proved to be one of the great figures in the long imperial history of China. Like his father before him, he came to the throne as a boy. There followed a regency period, during which four Manchurian grandees governed the empire in his name. The regents, though seldom agreeing among themselves and never above beheading one another when opportunity offered, made some conscientious efforts toward good government. In 1669 the maturing Kang Hsi deposed the regency, now reduced by its zeal for decapitation to one member. Resisting the temptation to send his last preceptor's head the way of the rest, he imprisoned him and exercised the power until his own death fifty-three years later. He possessed a fortunate combination of the stronger qualities of the two peoples: the warlike vigor of the Manchus and the intellectual powers of the Chinese. His reign, therefore, saw the empire grow and prosper.

Formosa for some time posed a problem. A Chinese sea captain, driven by the Manchus from the mainland, captured the island from the Dutch and established headquarters there. From Formosa the Chinese resistance movement held off both the Manchus and the Dutch for years, and its leader even attempted a conquest of the Spanish-held Philippines. Kang Hsi considered Formosa a part of his empire, and finally, in 1683, compelled it to surrender to him. It remained subject to the Manchus until ceded to Japan in 1895.

China did not succumb without an expiring effort. The Ming general who had first invited the Manchus to enter had been cajoled by them and rewarded with the governorship of two provinces. In 1672, old and fearing that Kang Hsi meant to make an end of him, the general raised a rebellion in several Chinese provinces and secured the aid of various Inner Mongolian tribes previously forced into submission by the Manchus. The emperor, still young and comparatively untested, showed great ability in coping with the revolt. Striking his geographically-separated enemies one by one, he first subdued the Mongols and then proceeded against the Chinese rebels. These, too, he crushed in detail, and the rebellion virtually collapsed when his chief antagonist, the old general, died of natural causes. By 1685 the Manchu-Chinese Empire was at peace.

A few years later Kang Hsi found himself threatened by a new danger, this time from Outer Mongolia. Since their Yüan Dynasty's expulsion from China in 1368 the Outer Mongols had split into eastern and western groups. The eastern division inhabited the old Genghis Khan territory, and its chiefs all claimed descent from the great conqueror. More powerful now, however, was the western branch, of humbler origin, inhabiting the Altai region and barren Dzungaria. This had a strong and ambitious monarchy, which earlier in the seventeenth century had intervened in Tibetan affairs as protector of the Dalai Lama. For this service to religion the West Mongols had gained a position of moral prestige among Buddhists. As they were also overlords of the Moslems of Eastern Turkestan, they represented a danger on the western frontier of China that Kang Hsi could not tolerate for long. The situation became even more threatening when these West Mongols began an invasion of eastern Mongolia to subdue their own kinsmen and to establish themselves directly north of China. It was known that the West Mongol ruler coveted the Peking throne, and at that moment the danger of a revived Genghis Khan empire seemed a real one. Answering an appeal by the East Mongols for protection, Kang Hsi took the field in person, and by 1697 he had defeated the intruders and driven them in a weakened condition back to their western home. As a barrier against further invasions, he established his rule securely in eastern Mongolia.

One of the last achievements of Kang Hsi's reign was a settlement with the Dalai Lama. This ruler of Tibet, so politically weak and so spiritually mighty, could not be left free to make alliances at will with the enemies of Manchu China. In 1720 Kang Hsi sent to Lhasa a strong army which drove out all opponents of his policies. A new Dalai Lama was then enthroned in a ceremony at which he appeared in public flanked by Manchu officials, two of whom thereafter remained to direct his administration with the support of a garrison from China. In return for the loss of political independence, the Dalai Lama received recognition of his religious authority over the millions of Chinese Buddhists.

THE INTERNAL ADMINISTRATION OF CHINA

The Manchus planned to rule China in the traditional native manner, which meant collection of taxes, suppression of rebellions, and as little interference as possible in the social and economic life of the people. Such loose methods, however, never proved adequate to solve many of the problems that inevitably arose. They could not check the greed of Manchu nobles, who seized the lands of Chinese farmers to build great estates for themselves. Neither could they halt the corruption of Chinese bureaucrats, who often succumbed to the lure of Manchu gold and abandoned their proper work to become propagandistic writers serving the conquerors. Even such passports to public office as the sacrosanct literary degrees were put on the auction block by the undeniably learned Kang Hsi in his frequent periods of need for ready money. Taxes, which are apt to fall most heavily on the backs of those least able to pay, fell mostly that way even in the best days of Manchu administration. The emperor's wars for the suppression of rebellions and the pacification of Mongolia and Tibet required extra expenditures. In the constant search for money, there was a standing temptation to depart from the ethical principles of Chinese administration.

The people of conquered China could not be persuaded that nothing had changed and that they still possessed the stature and dignity they had enjoyed before the conquest. However much the Manchus posed as a native line, the realities of the case invariably revealed themselves. A constant reminder was the queue which each Chinese man wore as a mark of subjection. When times grew especially bad, Chinese peasants formed secret societies, as their ancestors had formed others in past centuries, to remedy conditions by whatever local violence seemed feasible.

The Manchus nevertheless strove to govern China as painlessly as possible. They permitted the country to continue its ancient practice of administration by villages or farm communities. Heads of families or local elder statesmen dominated these simple societies. They took care of litigation and the settlement of neighborhood disputes regardless of written law. If a community could resolve its differences through these home-grown authorities, the government allowed it to do so in its own way. Officials intervened only when appeals reached them or when some governmental interest was involved. The local system rested on a basis of collective culpability. Villages, craft guilds, or families bore responsibility for the conduct of their members. If some unruly or irresponsible resident of the community committed a crime, disturbed the peace, or ran into debt, the others stood implicated until they had punished him or made good his debt. Under such a system, villagers naturally kept a watchful eye on their neighbors and relatives. Taxes must be collected, however, and for this purpose there existed local officials who usually labored harder than the Manchu viceroys, governors, and other dignitaries who bore highly honorific titles.

Chinese history is full of flowery proclamations containing verbose platitudes about the virtues and the desirability of observing lofty moral principles. They come mostly from the imperial throne and the viceroys; few emanate from the local bureaucrats constantly grappling with day-to-day situations. These latter unsung heroes of Chinese administration struggled with village councils and local prejudices, which often ignored Confucius and the higher sages. The local man knew that the sword of his superior hung over him, and that if taxes lagged and all did not go smoothly his head might quickly roll in the dust. Despite the deep philosophical quality of Chinese government, there was a rough-and-ready element about it that made participation in the system a daily challenge.

THE EUROPEANS IN CHINA

China had had a taste of the Europeans during the Mongol period. They had come then as traders and missionaries, the best-known example having been that of the Venetian Polo family. But with the Mongols gone, the Westerners likewise vanished, and China saw no more of them until the late Ming era. Then, led by the Portuguese, they came from the south by way of the Indian Ocean and the Malacca Straits to knock—gently at first—at the Chinese door. Centuries would elapse before the knock lost its gentle quality.

The Russians, in the meantime, were making contact with China by the trans-Asia route. Their advance through Siberia began in 1581, shortly before the death of Tsar Ivan the Terrible. Starting with the capture of the Tartar city of Iskir on the Irtysh River, the Russians, led by fur traders and Cossack adventurers, pushed eastward. The geography of Siberia helped their advance, as the tributaries of the Ob, Yenisey, and Lena rivers flow generally east and west, providing easy waterways. The Muscovites laid the foundations of an empire as they progressed. They made fur-trading agreements with the Tartar and other tribes, and forced or persuaded them to accept the sovereignty of the tsar. As early as 1636 a Russian party learned of a great river called "Mamour," and in the years 1643–46 the exploring pioneer Vasili Poyarkov navigated this Amur River from near the source to its Pacific outlet. As other Russians had already reached the Sea of Okhotsk in the north, the tsar's eastern frontier was now the great ocean. Within a few years the Muscovites had begun probing south of the Amur, meeting only sporadic resistance from the Manchus.

These, of course, were the years during which the Manchu conquest of China went on. The freedom of movement enjoyed for a time by the Russians in the Amur zone is explained by the fact that the emperor at Peking had most of his forces concentrated in the south. When Kang Hsi had consolidated his power in China he presented a stronger face to the Russian encroachers, who at length decided to make a peaceful boundary settlement. Russian plenipotentiaries met those of China at Nerchinsk near the Amur in 1689, and negotiated a treaty with a text in three languages, Russian, Manchu, and Latin—the Latin because two Jesuits had accompanied Kang Hsi's envoys as interpreters. The Treaty of Nerchinsk provided that the boundary should be the Amur River for much of its course, and, east of that, should follow the watershed of the Stanovoi Mountains to the Pacific. This frontier existed until the year 1858. The interest of the Russians in China did not cease with the treaty, and the Manchus did not insist on their total exclusion. Embassies occasionally passed between St. Petersburg and Peking, and the Manchus allowed a Russian Orthodox religious mission to exist in the Chinese capital.

About 1515 a Portuguese trader who came from Malacca landed at Canton. Others followed, over the protests of the Ming emperor's Cantonese officials, and presently a Portuguese ambassador went to the court at Peking. He was treated as a prisoner there and conducted under guard back to Canton, where he died of illness, still incarcerated. During the next forty years the Portuguese made unsuccessful attempts to establish trading posts in China. In 1557 they managed to secure the lease of the small peninsula of Macao near Canton and permission to construct a few buildings there for trade. During the three centuries following its acquisition by Portugal Macao was often the only seaport open for communication between China and the West.

Jesuits, as well as Dominican and Franciscan missionaries, followed the traders into China. The Italian Jesuit, Matteo Ricci, reached Peking in 1601. He gained the favor of the Ming ruler and the imperial scholars, and won for himself and other members of his order the privilege of remaining in Peking and carrying on missionary work in the provinces. As a tactful concession to Chinese love of learning, the Roman Catholic priests wore the costume of Confucian scholars.

Christian influence mounted at Peking under the early Manchus. Through the reign of Kang Hsi, and even after, the Jesuit establishment remained influential. The emperor probably owed his life on one occasion to the priests, because when he fell very ill of fever, they had on hand some Peruvian cinchona bark, which is the source of quinine. Doses of this brought his recovery, and naturally increased the imperial favor toward the Jesuits. Roman Catholicism made a sizable number of converts in China, although for some reason the priests were not allowed to work north of the Great Wall. Jesuit and other missionaries had to acknowledge that, among the Chinese, they were dealing with civilized manners and customs of great antiquity and not with the simple American Indian beliefs that contemporary missionaries were attempting to eradicate in the Spanish New World. For their work in China they developed a particular adaptation of Christianity known as the "Chinese Rites," based on the realization that Catholicism must go hand in hand with customs of the country. The rites made some concessions to ancestor worship and tolerated a limited reverence for Confucius. They permitted perfume and incense burning in certain private kinds of family ceremonial. Celebration of such ancient festivals as the Chinese New Year was also allowed. These departures from the strictest rules of Catholicism, when explained in Rome, drew pronouncements of approval from the Popes.

THE CONQUESTS OF CH'IEN LUNG

The most prosperous of all Manchu reigns was that of Ch'ien Lung (1735-1795). This emperor was born in 1711, came to the throne at the age of twenty-four, abdicated sixty years later in favor of his son, and died in 1799, a little before his eighty-eighth birthday. With his death the star of the Manchus began visibly to set.

Like his grandfather Kang Hsi, Ch'ien Lung was a notable conqueror, a strong administrator, and a cultured man. He left an empire covering more territory than had been ruled from China since Mongol times and containing far more people than Kublai Khan had governed. A census figure for the year 1751 showed a total Chinese population of 181,000,000, and the number grew steadily during the emperor's later years. The growth was no unmixed blessing, for the amount of land under cultivation increased slowly if at all. The provinces of China Proper had to absorb the added numbers, as Manchu policy forbade emigration to sparsely settled Manchuria, Mongolia, and Turkestan, which were in no condition to receive colonists. Whatever hardships may have been caused by overcrowding and the struggle for existence, China, on the surface at least, remained peaceful through most of Ch'ien Lung's reign. No formidable rebellions took place until nearly the end, and the only wars were those of conquest, waged on far-distant frontiers.

Emperor Ch'ien Lung, although he did not lead armies in person, became the arch imperialist of his dynasty. He first found that the West Mongols, with headquarters in Dzungaria, again required attention. Two of their princes disputed the throne, and the losing candidate, Amursana, appealed to Ch'ien Lung for aid. The emperor responded to this plea, and an imperial army made the 2,000-mile march across the Gobi and Dzungaria to Kulja, on the Ili River. There, in 1755, its general installed Amursana as nominal ruler, but principally installed himself as imperial resident and director of the new monarch's affairs. Amursana sulked at this and organized a conspiracy aimed at making himself undisputed ruler of his own country. In 1756 his Dzungar Mongols attacked and slew the imperial garrisons and surprised and murdered the resident in Kulja. The enraged Ch'ien Lung now employed drastic measures against Amursana and his people. Sending a new Manchu general with another army, he gave orders for the extermination of the Dzungars. Amursana, beaten in battle in 1757, fled to Russian Siberia, where he soon succumbed to smallpox. His subjects were slaughtered wholesale, although twenty thousand families escaped to Russia and others were deported to Kansu. Ch'ien Lung later repopulated the empty land with new colonists.

As a by-product of this campaign, there followed the conquest of Moslem Eastern Turkestan. Amursana's West Mongol ancestors had earlier made vassals of the rulers of this country, including the sovereigns of Yarkand and Kashgar. These local princes having assisted Amursana in his rebellion, the imperial army now struck at them, capturing their cities and driving the rulers to refuge farther west in Asia. So great was the prestige of Ch'ien Lung that a western Turkish chieftain obligingly decapitated the Yarkand and Kashgar fugitives and sent their heads to the emperor's general. With the annexation of this new territory in 1760, the Manchu Empire stretched from Korea to a depth of over 3,000 miles in central Asia.

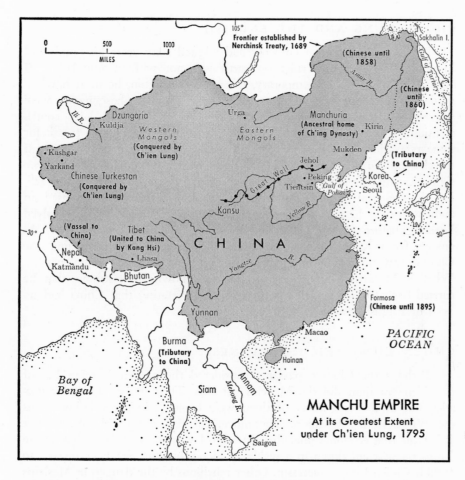

Tibet having grown disorderly again, Ch'ien Lung sent a force to straighten out matters in Lhasa. This move resulted in an enlarged Manchu garrison for the city and the establishment of a new imperial resident, who again acted as overseer for the Dalai Lama and the Tibetan officials. Overlordship of Tibet ultimately involved Ch'ien Lung with the warlike

Gurkhas of Nepal, who completely outclassed the Tibetans as soldiers and continually encroached on their frontiers. At length the emperor sent an army to the assistance of his vassal state. Nepal was invaded in 1792, its capital threatened, and its ruler intimidated into a promise to send a tribute-bearing mission to Peking every five years. Somewhat earlier in Ch'ien Lung's reign a border episode had led to war with Burma and a Manchu-Chinese invasion of that country through Yunnan Province. Although the invaders had been trapped and annihilated by the warlike Burmese, their ruler ultimately found it good policy to acknowledge himself Ch'ien Lung's vassal, which he did in 1790.

CH'IEN LUNG AND THE ENGLISH

By the time the great emperor had reigned sixty years his opinion of himself as the foremost ruler on earth was not without foundation. If he had heard of his contemporary, George Washington, he must have regarded him as one of those petty western chieftains whose names were scarcely worth remembering. He treated George III with lofty condescension. When Lord Macartney arrived from England in 1793 to ask for some relaxation of Chinese trade restrictions, this nobleman and his staff traveled up the Pei River in Chinese boats which, unknown to them, bore signs reading "Tribute Bearers from the Country of England." On reaching the imperial summer residence at Jehol, Macartney was refused an audience unless he agreed to perform the *kotow* ceremony, which involved kneeling before Ch'ien Lung and knocking his head on the floor. As envoys from Korea, Burma, or Siam did this without complaint, the Chinese saw no reason to exempt His Britannic Majesty's representative. Whether Macartney finally kotowed is not known; it is known that he carried back to George III a patronizing letter stating that China had no need of English goods.

CH'IEN LUNG AND THE CHINESE

Perhaps the Chinese peasants considered the emperor's reign less of a golden era than did the Manchu generals. They seemed quiet for decades, but at the end many of them were engaged in a revolt known as the White Lotus Rebellion. The movement had a Buddhist origin, but it is clear that economic maladministration lay at the root. The first White Lotus rising went down in a welter of blood, but the sect later revived to trouble Ch'ien Lung's successor. Other rebellions by the dangerous Moslems of Kansu and the peasants of Formosa kept the imperial troops busy for years.

A clue to the weakness of Manchu administration is furnished by the case of the emperor's favorite, who held twenty offices at a time and stole a fortune estimated at 800,000,000 taels ($600,000,000). Not until Ch'ien Lung's death did this unsavory character undergo investigation, and though he then had to disgorge to the imperial treasury no part of his loot went back to the people he had gouged. Perhaps, too, the tranquillity of China in Ch'ien Lung's earlier years was not as complete as it had been made to seem. Governors and viceroys knew that reports of starvation, banditry, or open rebellion would be unwelcome at imperial headquarters at Peking. Whenever it was possible because of distance to conceal knowledge of such happenings, they omitted mentioning them to the court. The imperial administration most esteemed those governors in whose districts nothing happened; the governors, for their part, made the reports as uninteresting as possible.

THE DECLINE OF CHRISTIANITY IN CHINA

During the reign of Ch'ien Lung the Jesuit Order was suppressed, first by the governments of Portugal, France, and Spain in their dominions, and finally everywhere by a decree of the Pope in 1773. This dealt Christian missionary work in China a blow that proved fatal. Although other Roman Catholic orders had an opportunity to continue the Jesuit effort, they seemed unable to rise to the occasion. Ch'ien Lung does not seem to have understood or paid much attention to the matter. He had never showed the interest in Christianity displayed by Kang Hsi, and he now contributed to its downfall in China by permitting a persecution in 1784. Before the emperor's abdication the French Revolution had paralyzed the activity of the church, and Christian propaganda in China had all but stopped.

THE MANCHU DECADENCE

In 1795 Ch'ien Lung, not wishing to reign more years than his illustrious grandfather Kang Hsi had governed, abdicated in favor of his fifteenth son, Chia Ch'ing (1796–1820). The old monarch took the title Father Emperor and enjoyed the leisure of retirement with books and studies until his death in 1799. Even before Ch'ien Lung's voluntary withdrawal there had been signs of decay in the imperial Manchu structure, although the dignity and enormous prestige of the aged sovereign had served to conceal the symptoms. Now Chia Ch'ing, the first inferior monarch of his line, could do nothing to improve a situation he failed to understand. Unintelligent, cruel, and inclined to drunkenness, he gave a sorry performance as emperor.

The days of Manchu expansion had ended, as the empires of the British and the Russians now largely surrounded China. The time had also passed when a Manchu ruler could govern in utter ignorance of the outside world. Yet when George III of England, through his representatives in India, sent presents to Chia Ch'ing with a suggestion of greater friendship and more trade, the emperor replied:

> Your Majesty's kingdom is at a remote distance beyond the seas, but is observant of its duties and obedient to our laws, beholding from afar the glory of our empire and respectfully admiring the perfection of our Government .... With regard to those of Your Majesty's subjects who for a long course of years have been in the habit of trading with our Empire, we must observe to you that our Celestial Government regards all persons and nations with eyes of charity and benevolence, and always treats and considers your subjects with the utmost indulgence and affection; on their account, therefore, there can be no place or occasion for the exertions of Your Majesty's Government.[3]

Unfortunately, it was not as simple as Chia Ch'ing supposed. Europeans would not stop pressing to end Chinese exclusionism, and at the end of the Napoleonic Wars they redoubled their efforts. The significance of this for China was lost on Chia Ch'ing. When another British delegation, headed by Lord Amherst, arrived in 1816 the emperor's concern was wholly with the question of whether the peer and his staff had first been thoroughly informed as to the number of kotows and genuflections it would be necessary to offer him. The Amherst mission proved wholly uninstructed in Chinese court etiquette and was sent home in disgrace. In all fairness, it should be said that the Manchu attitude rested on more than arrogance. The English, who represented the East India Company rather than their nation, had thus far offered few goods that China needed. Furs, which Chinese merchants most eagerly sought, were obtained either from Russian Siberia or from western North America, whence United States shippers brought them to Macao. The British company, on the other hand, had an interest in building a thriving opium trade. This had given the Manchu government serious alarm and had caused Chia Ch'ing's advisers, in their ignorance, to believe that the solution to their problem lay in shutting off all foreign commerce. They ultimately found that such a radical decision was beyond their power to enforce.

Meanwhile, Manchu administration of China steadily weakened. The White Lotus insurrection, which had been in progress at the start of Chia Ch'ing's reign, was followed by other rebellions, as the government functionaries exhausted Chinese patience by their inefficiency and corruption. Another secret society, called the Triad, spread through the countryside and survived, regardless of how many of its organizers and

---

[3] Herbert H. Gowen and Josef Washington Hall, *An Outline History of China* (New York and London: D. Appleton, 1927), pp. 241–42.

leaders were tracked down and beheaded. Emperor Chia Ch'ing, by the time of his death in 1820, had become a pitiful creature, a virtual prisoner of his own eunuchs, who in their own selfish way determined each important government decision. When the ruler went to join his illustrious ancestors, Manchu China had entered its dying stage, although nearly a hundred years would pass before the dynasty would go the inevitable way of its predecessors.

SOCIETY IN MANCHU CHINA

The Manchu, or Ch'ing, period proved a culturally sterile epoch for China. This was particularly true of literature, philosophy, and religion; science could scarcely be said to exist. Much of the sterility can be explained by the fact that the dominant Manchus had been strangers to culture before their conquest of China. Feeling their inferiority keenly, the new rulers strove to become cultured, and in doing so understandably grasped for everything that was ancient, staid, and revered in Chinese civilization. In their fumbling attempts to maintain the pure tradition, they came closer to creating an ossified cultural pattern, incapable of progress and resistant to all change. Their idea of worthwhile literary activity consisted of making vast compilations of classics thousands of years old. The Manchu position here might be likened to that of a modern wealthy ignoramus who has been persuaded that nothing written since Shakespeare is worth reading. Classics meant Confucian classics to the Manchus, who might have little understanding of Confucius but who nevertheless revered him. Taoism they despised, as the more cultured Chinese had taught them to do, because of its lower-class associations and its connection with alchemy and magic. Western science seemed to fall in the same lowly classification, as to a would-be-cultured Manchu dabbler in learning it seemed to produce only toys unworthy of serious consideration. The visible evidence that the West moved while China stood still caused little worry. No one appeared concerned because a considerable difference existed between the European guns built for China by the Jesuits and those of the Napoleonic era, or because Yankee clippers of the nineteenth century marked a great advance over the ships in which the first Portuguese had entered Canton.

Talented writers existed in China during the Manchu period, but as they sought elegance rather than profundity, they generally limited themselves to exquisite handling of trivial themes. Emperor Ch'ien Lung's own poem, *In Praise of Tea,* is a minor masterpiece, but its title reveals that it could be only minor. Screen painting and ceramic art continued to show at least prettiness. Some technical advance in the making of porcelain took place and new glazes were invented. By Kang Hsi's time the West had grown interested in Chinese pottery, which led to the making of large amounts for export, naturally somewhat altered from traditional Chinese forms to suit the European taste.

Chinese education still consisted mainly of training aspirants for civil-service positions. Manchus furnished about half the bureaucracy, but they did little studying; favoritism governed most of their appointments. Among the Chinese the stiff competition for offices produced several consequences, all unfortunate. Because the course of study and the examinations were extremely rigid, with heavy emphasis upon sheer memory work, the Chinese youths who invariably fared best were of the narrow-minded, mediocre sort, who on achieving comfortable posts became opponents of change and progress. Those with more original minds furnished a good percentage of the failures and they thereafter became disgruntled intellectuals, sullenly disaffected toward the régime. Also, the Manchus trusted northern Chinese more than they did the southerners and saw to it that the civil service was overmanned by the former. In practice, this meant that south China came to be governed largely by northern Chinese, whom the people disliked and associated with the unpopular Manchus. The south was the starting point of most of the rebellions, including the final one of 1911–12 which swept the dynasty away (see page 454).

Like the Arabs during the early caliphate, the Manchus claimed the right to live at the expense of the conquered people. Their own law forbade them to enter business or industry, and those without private means existed on "tribute rice," gathered in the south and transported to Peking and other Manchu garrison towns. The eight banner corps, which statistically included both the soldiers and their families, were stationed in cantonments at the capital and focal points over the country. Originally splendid fighters, they deteriorated in quality because of long spells of idleness. By the nineteenth century they had become almost useless hangers-on, no longer fit for their sole profession of war. The abler commanders and soldiers of the late Ch'ing period were not Manchus but Chinese. The only exceptions to the general story of Manchu decay were a few tribes of the conquering race that never left Manchuria. In the rough homeland they preserved some of the vigor of their ancestors, but remained an isolated backwash with no influence on the course of history.

3 : The Ottoman Turkish Empire

WHEN SULTAN Mohammed II captured Constantinople in 1453 the Ottoman Empire included the northern and western provinces of Asia Minor and European Thrace, Bulgaria, Macedonia, and northern Greece. The empire had already shifted its center of gravity from Asia to Europe, and had a predominately non-Turkish population. Whereas the first sultans

*Akbar, Mogul emperor of India, was a contemporary of Elizabeth I
of England. Although not the first of his line to rule in India, he stabilized
the Mogul realm and left it on such a secure foundation that it lasted
over a century after his death. He is here shown holding court, surrounded
by musicians, falconers, and attendants with tame leopards on the leash.*

*This famous Manchu ruler governed China for sixty years and was a
contemporary of Louis XIV of France and Peter the Great of Russia.
Besides leaving a great name as an administrator, he expanded Manchu
China by the acquisition of Formosa, western Mongolia, and Tibet.*

PLATE DECORATED WITH PICTURE OF EUROPEAN SHIP

*This represents an eighteenth-century Chinese artist's conception of a
European sailing vessel. The ship is accurately drawn according to Western
standards, but the clouds and waves are depicted in a Chinese manner. The
plate was in all probability manufactured for the European trade.*

An eighteenth-century sultan of Turkey, Ahmed III, here fulfills the obligation of every good Moslem to give alms to the poor according to his means. The needy, who scramble eagerly for the coins, seem in this case remarkably well dressed.

had been little more than the chiefs of armies on the march, Mohammed was now ruler of the old Byzantine territory and had to adjust his methods accordingly. To his first epithet "Conqueror" he now added that of "Lawgiver" by sponsoring a codification of Ottoman legislation designed for dealing with the problems of a growing, polyglot empire. He worked out an administrative procedure whereby new provinces could be fitted smoothly into his system as fast as they were annexed. By such measures he put the Ottoman monarchy on an organized basis, very different from the fragile, one-man structures managed by previous Turkish conquerors.

THE FURTHER CONQUESTS OF MOHAMMED II

This busy soldier-sultan rounded out the conquest of Asia Minor by subduing the last independent Moslem principality there. In 1461, by the capture of Christian Trebizond, he eliminated the final vestige of the Byzantine Empire. In Europe he extended his frontiers to the Danube and Save rivers and imposed tribute payment on the Romanian princes of Wallachia and Moldavia lying beyond. The Tartar khanate of the Crimea also became tributary to him. Westward he overran Albania and southward he pushed into the Morea (the ancient Peloponnesus) in lower Greece. In Italy he seemed about to make good his ancestor Bajazet's boast about stabling Turkish horses in St. Peter's Church, for an expedition of his captured the city of Otranto in 1480. This occurred just before the conqueror's death, and the next sultan did not care to push ahead with such a distant adventure. Mohammed II met with only one conspicuous failure. His attack on the island of Rhodes, held by a Christian crusading order, the Knights of St. John, was beaten off in 1480. The Knights retained the island for another forty years, until compelled by the Turks to transfer their headquarters to Malta. Mohammed had for years been a sufferer from gout, a severe attack of which killed him in 1481, as he prepared to set forth on another military expedition whose destination and purpose are not precisely known.

THE ACQUISITION OF THE CALIPHATE

For at least a hundred years it had become customary for an Ottoman sultan to begin his reign by murdering his brothers and all other male relatives from whom he feared competition. This practice, initiated as a matter of policy, had since become a legal right and was expected of each new sultan. However, Prince Bajazet, the oldest son of Mohammed II, got no chance to carry out the policy at the expense of his brother Jem. An ambitious pasha who aspired to be a king-maker suppressed news of the old sultan's death long enough for Jem to gather a following. In the civil war that resulted Bajazet proved victorious. Jem went into exile, first to Rhodes and then to Europe, where he lived several years in France. As he still had an Ottoman party favoring him, his willingness to promise Christian rulers anything in return for aid in gaining the Turkish throne made him a standing menace to his brother and the empire until his death in 1495. It is thought, without definite supporting evidence, that he died of poison and that Pope Alexander VI had a hand in the affair. The Pope certainly attempted to collect a reward Sultan Bajazet had offered for his brother's death.

Bajazet II (1481–1512) did not have the nature of a conqueror, and he preferred study and the arts. The conditions of the times forced an Ottoman ruler to be as much of a warrior as possible, as the military leaders craved further conquests and the soldiers regarded plunder as their due. The sultan strove to satisfy them and at the same time to avoid serious conflicts by limiting military operations to a series of raids beyond his northern frontiers and to the expulsion of the Venetians from fortresses they had long held in the Greek peninsula. At the end of a thirty-one-year reign he left the Ottoman Empire with much the same boundaries it had had at the beginning.

Selim I (1512–1520), the son and successor of Bajazet, was every inch a soldier and resumed the policy of conquest. Turkish relations with Europe being then peaceful, Selim strove not to embitter them while he turned his attention to eastern conquest. As a zealous and orthodox Sunnite, he had a grudge against the shah of Persia, who was an equally devout Shi'ite and who spread religious propaganda in the Ottoman realm. Selim began by ordering a massacre of all Shi'ites in his empire between the ages of seven and seventy. Approximately forty thousand people were slaughtered and their property was confiscated. The sultan then summoned the shah to renounce his errors and embrace the true faith as well as to evacuate some frontier provinces in dispute between the two empires. After several exchanges of interesting Oriental insults between the rulers, Selim invaded Persia in 1514. Thanks largely to his superior artillery, he defeated the shah in a hard-fought battle and took Tabriz, his capital. The Persians, worsted but by no means crushed, ceded Kurdistan and northern Mesopotamia to the Turks.

The next project on Selim's agenda was the conquest of Egypt and its political appendage Syria. Egypt was ruled by the Mamelukes, who were the descendants of foreign slaves converted in past centuries to Islam. They had become a military caste, similar in origin to the Turkish Janissaries, though less disciplined. The Mamelukes exercised the right to choose the sultan of Egypt. They also had dwelling among them a branch of the ancient Abbassid family, whose head they addressed as Caliph, though they gave him more lip service than true veneration. Selim began his campaign in 1516 with a series of victories and conquests that soon placed Syria in his hands. Pushing into Egypt, he defeated the Mameluke sultan in a battle near Cairo. Entering the city, he allowed his followers to indulge in a typical Oriental massacre, particularly directed against the Mamelukes who were slaughtered by thousands in the streets. The defeated sultan, a man of great personal courage, escaped but was presently reduced to hiding in a cave. A local Arab sheik, who had given the fugitive this shelter, presently thought of the reward Selim might pay and handed him over to the Ottomans. The conqueror treated his brave opponent well at first, but soon reconsidered and ordered him hanged.

The Egyptian sultan had exercised a protectorate over the holy cities of Mecca and Medina. Selim now assumed this responsibility and took charge of the keys of the Kaaba. Somewhat earlier he had assumed the title Caliph of Islam and required his name to be used in prayers from the pulpits of mosques. There is a story to the effect that Selim bribed or coerced the last of the Abbassids to transfer the caliphal title to him. This appears to be a legend, for only later did the tale make its appearance. There is, however, no disputing that with Selim the Ottoman rulers became caliphs and held the title until the last member of their line was banished from Turkey in 1924.

The sultan's power could increase even without his direct participation in conquest. In 1516 two Turkish corsairs of Balkan descent, whom the Europeans called Barbarossa because of their red beards, managed to seize the city of Algiers and important neighboring regions along the African coast. Feeling unable to stand alone with the great power of Spain so close, they offered submission to Selim who accepted their allegiance and thereafter numbered Algeria among his provinces. This conquering sultan did not enjoy a long reign. His ferocious disposition doubtless contributed to giving him ulcers, for which his favorite remedy was opium. He expired—possibly of an overdose of the drug—in 1520, and the throne passed to his son Suleiman.

THE CONQUESTS OF SULEIMAN THE MAGNIFICENT

Under Suleiman, or Solomon (1520–1566), the Ottoman Empire reached its peak of power if not quite its maximum size. This sultan is known to Turkish writers as "the Legislator" and to Europeans as "the Magnificent," because of his grandeur and wealth. He would have preferred the former designation, for he was a man of essentially simple tastes who rigorously practiced self-discipline. It is said that he frequently worked at a trade, with which he could have supported himself if necessary. A surviving portrait of Suleiman bears out contemporary descriptions of him as a gloomy-faced man whose cares and burdens of state condemned him to a joyless existence. For all his sad disposition and many conquests, he lacked the cruelty of Selim, and he ordered executions and led armies without passion and solely as a matter of business.

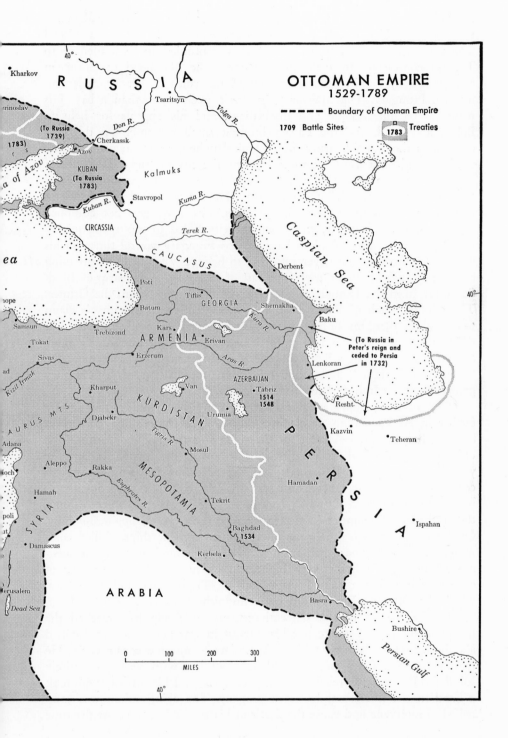

OTTOMAN EMPIRE
1529-1789

▪ ▪ ▪ ▪ ▪ Boundary of Ottoman Empire

1709 Battle Sites   □ 1783 Treaties

Kharkov

R U S S I A

Tsaritsyn

erinoslav

Don R.

Volga R.

(To Russia 1739)

1783)

r s

Cherkassk

Azov

a of Azov

KUBAN (To Russia 1783)

Kalmuks

Kuma R.

Stavropol

Kuban R.

CIRCASSIA

Terek R.

Caspian Sea

ea

C A U C A S U S

Derbent

Poti

Tiflis

GEORGIA

Shemakha

Batum

Baku

ope

Kars

ARMENIA

Erivan

Kura R.

(To Russia in Peter's reign and ceded to Persia in 1732)

Samsun

Trebizond

Tokat

Sivas

Erzerum

Aras R.

Lenkoran

ad

Kizil Irmak

Kharput

Van

AZERBAIJAN

Tabriz
1514
1548

Resht

K U R D I S T A N

Urumia

Kazvin

AURUS MTS.

Djabekr

Tigris R.

Teheran

Adana

Mosul

P E R S I A

Aleppo

Rakka

M E S O P O T A M I A

ioch

Hamadan

Hamah

Euphrates R.

Tekrit

poli

S Y R I A

Baghdad
1534

Ispahan

t

Damascus

Kerbela

erusalem

Dead Sea

A R A B I A

Basra

Bushire

0   100   200   300

MILES

Persian Gulf

40°

40°

[323]

Suleiman began by succeeding where his great-grandfather had failed, and expelled the Knights of St. John from Rhodes. They soon established themselves in Malta, however, where they continued to be a menace to Turkish commerce. In 1526, after lessening the likelihood of European interference by gaining the friendship of the ruler of France, Suleiman invaded Hungary. The Magyar king was scarcely more than a boy. His nobles were quarrelsome and disobedient, and his appeals for help to Bohemia, Poland, and the Papacy brought small response. On the field of Mohacs the Turkish army routed and slaughtered the Magyars, killing the king and presently taking and burning the city of Buda. The bulk of Hungary became a part of the Ottoman Empire and was not liberated until the end of the following century. Three years after his victory at Mohacs Suleiman marched against Vienna. His army was not equipped for a long siege, however, and when the city failed to capitulate quickly he retired. Although the sultan later crossed Hungary several times on his northern campaigns, he never returned to besiege Vienna. His remaining conquests consisted of Transylvania, east of Hungary, and a strip of Black Sea coast from the Danube to the older Ottoman possession, the Crimea. The reigning shah of Persia paid no more attention to Suleiman's claim to be caliph than his father before him had paid to Selim's claim. For this and for the Persian failure to deliver Baghdad to him on demand, Suleiman in 1534 sent a Turkish general against the shah. Once more the Ottomans triumphed, and following another occupation of Tabriz they gained a title to Iraq and much of Armenia.

One of the sultan's greater interests was in expanding the empire farther in Africa and in developing Ottoman sea power. The Barbarossa brothers had acquired Algeria for the sultans in the reign of Selim. The older of the two had since fallen in battle with the Spaniards, but the younger, Khayr-ad-Din Barbarossa, had succeeded him as the most powerful corsair of the Mediterranean and was anxious to help extend Suleiman's power. He broadened Ottoman control further in Algeria, seized Tunis, though he lost it again, and repeatedly raided the coasts of Spain and Italy. On his death in 1546 Suleiman inherited his excellent ships, skilled commanders, and battle-hardened seamen. These kept his banner in the western Mediterranean flying very high, and by means of another pair of corsairs the sultan obtained possession of Tripolitania and Cyrenaica, which the Ottoman Empire did not relinquish until 1912.

By the middle of the sixteenth century Suleiman had reached the height of his power. Thereafter his interest in war and conquest declined and he concerned himself with such matters as mosque construction. He naturally hoped for a peaceful old age, but the wish was not entirely fulfilled. His sons quarreled over the succession, and his favorite wife took a hand in the interest of her own progeny. The aging sultan was compelled to intervene and cause the death of his two ablest sons. At the time

of his death in 1566 there was no one to succeed him save a prince called
Selim, whom Turks have given the unflattering epithet, "the Sot." This
ruler's unsatisfying reign marked the beginning of the Ottoman decline.

THE EMPIRE IN SULEIMAN'S TIME

Suleiman's great historical reputation rests upon more than his conquests. He was an able governor and a famous lawgiver, in whose time
something like a Turkish culture began to exist. Ottoman government
offered an interesting blend of absolutism and Asiatic feudalism. At its
head stood the sultan, now caliph as well, to whom in theory the whole
state belonged and all taxes were paid. The annual Turkish revenue seemed
fabulous to contemporary Europeans, who in Suleiman's time estimated
it as 10,000,000 ducats, or perhaps $22,500,000. This was none too much for
the needs of Turkey, which had more financial demands to satisfy than
Christian countries had as yet. A ducat, moreover, now represented a
lower purchasing power than had been true a century earlier, for the
opening of Spanish mines in the New World had lessened the value of
gold and silver.

The sultan had theoretically absolute power, although in practice he
delegated much of it to his chief minister, or grand wazir. "Standing up
or sitting down, the grand wazir has precedence over all others in rank";
so ran a decree published by Mohammed II. This great official could hold
court by himself in the sultan's absence and be surrounded by a brilliant
retinue when he traveled or went for a promenade. A wazir's opportunities
for misruling the people and accumulating a vast fortune through graft
or bribe taking were innumerable, and all too often he succumbed to
temptation. His was a dangerous office to hold, for jealous officials constantly intrigued against the mighty minister, who always knew that the
sultan might turn against him at any time. An out-of-favor grand wazir
could count himself lucky to retire with his head on his shoulders.

The pashas who governed provinces first bought them for cash and
then repurchased them every year. A pasha of Cairo is said to have bribed
a grand wazir with an annual sum approaching $250,000 in order to enjoy
his lucrative province. Over all the pashas were governors-general: one for
Asia and one for Europe, with a third being ultimately appointed for
Africa. Outside the towns and cities most of the land of European Turkey
and Asia Minor was parceled out in fiefs to Turkish and other Moslem
landlords. These territorial magnates collected revenue and locally enforced the laws in much the manner of European feudal barons. They
had military obligations to the sultan, and had to appear before him in
person when summoned for war. The number of armed followers each
landlord was obliged to bring depended on the size and value of his
holdings. Suleiman, early in his reign, decreed that the central government

alone could grant fiefs above a certain size, and also stipulated that no owner should hold a clear title unless he secured a document from Constantinople confirming his possession. For the government of such a vast empire a new code of laws became necessary, as the old one promulgated by Mohammed II no longer remained adequate. Suleiman had such a code prepared, and it remained the foundation of Ottoman law until the nineteenth century. The sultan's main purpose as a lawgiver was to straighten out and simplify the existing situation, which had grown extremely complicated over the years.

The Janissaries still formed the backbone of the Ottoman army. It will be recalled that these were recruited by taking boys from Christian families, converting them to Islam and training them to be soldiers. For generations the Janissaries remained the shock troops, assigned to the most difficult and dangerous military work. Their number seldom exceeded fifteen thousand, because as they occasionally grew unruly and dangerous, the sultans felt it unwise to have more than that number on hand at a time. When they mutinied and demanded the head of an unpopular general or minister, it was often impossible to refuse them. They were forbidden to marry, at least until late in the history of the corps; and they were expected to reserve their sole devotion and interest for the sultan. Until Suleiman's time the Janissaries, in spite of occasional breaches of discipline, served their original purpose well. Later their discipline slackened, their military effectiveness declined, and they became an unruly group of nuisances with more interest in internal politics than in war. The remainder of the Turkish army consisted of the feudal levies and mercenaries, the latter often hired only for the duration of a single campaign. As late as Suleiman's reign European observers highly praised the discipline of Turkish field forces. The troops, being all Moslems or ostensible Moslems, did without wine and women. Their wars against Christians were still to a considerable extent holy wars, and were looked upon as a religious duty.

Suleiman's empire also possessed a powerful navy. It had plenty of timber for shipbuilding, and the mines of the Romanian provinces produced the needed metals. Only sailcloth was lacking, and this had to be purchased from France. Ships for the Ottoman navy were built chiefly by Greek workers under the direction of experts from Venice or elsewhere in Italy. They went to sea manned largely by Greeks or Italians, as the Turks had no maritime tradition and tended to be landlubbers. Two factors gravely hampered Ottoman naval effort and ultimately put an end to it. Turkey had no important merchant marine, which is customarily the reason for the existence of a navy. Also, naval administration was honeycombed with corruption, which seems to have grown worse with the passage of time. A possible third weakening factor was the Ottoman custom of having the galleys rowed by slave oarsmen, who lacked any interest in the outcome of a campaign and escaped whenever they could. Scarcity of galley rowers caused a draft to be levied in the Christian provinces for rowers. This usually meant that the strongest and best prospects managed to escape or evade service and that those taken for the galleys were often weak and unfit. The Turkish fleet remained powerful during Suleiman's reign but declined soon after.

Because the Turks esteemed military virtue highest and did not care much for education, civil-service posts came to be filled largely by Greeks, Albanians, Italians, Slavs, and even Georgians from the Caucasus. Few of the grand wazirs were of Turkish blood; it is estimated that of the forty-eight holders of this office from 1453 to 1623 only five were genuine Ottomans. Physicians tended to be Jews, and most of the business of the empire involving reading and writing fell into the hands of Armenians, Greeks, and Jews.

For all their fierce zeal for Islam, the Turks did not ordinarily practice religious persecution. If Christians or Jews paid taxes and obeyed the government, they could usually practice their religion in peace. The Patriarch of Constantinople continued to live in state and to carry on his religious functions as freely as in Byzantine times. Janissary guards would severely punish Moslems who attempted to wreck Christian churches or break up religious processions. The Jews multiplied in Constantinople during the sixteenth century largely because religious persecutions had caused many of them to leave the Iberian peninsula. In the provinces, particularly those of the Balkans, Christians did not fare as well as in the cities. Turkish governors subjected them to forced labor and overtaxed them; in this way they built up a heritage of hatred that ultimately ended Turkish rule in the Balkan peninsula.

Although the Ottomans never shone in letters and learning, in the sixteenth century they did make some beginning. The Sublime Porte, as the sultan's government came to be called, encouraged the recording of the national history, and for this purpose appointed state historiographers, who wrote accounts that were naturally tailored to the liking of the authorities. A few Turks wrote popular and religious songs, while others composed prose accounts of the life of the Prophet and of those dervish saints who enjoyed high esteem among the people. Much of the time of Turkish poets was devoted to imitating distinguished examples of Persian and Arabic verse.

LEPANTO

Suleiman at his death left Ottoman power at its very pinnacle, but, as we have seen, the debauched Selim II lacked the ability of earlier sultans. Turkish conquest did not altogether stop in Selim's reign, but much of the vigor went out of the administration. The rapid decline now undergone by once-powerful Turkey is not to be fully explained by the personal deficiencies of one sultan. The causes of decay had been operating unnoticed for years; they were the typical ones undermining Oriental monarchies. The sultans ceased to take a personal interest in state affairs; political corruption increased; favorites replaced able ministers; and harem influence grew too strong.

For the moment, Turkey appeared as dangerous to Europe as ever. An Ottoman expedition attacked Malta, the new western home of the Knights of St. John, and although the assault failed, the Turks seemed likely to conquer the island on their next expedition. In 1570 they invaded Cyprus, then held by the Republic of Venice, and by the next year had captured every Venetian stronghold in the island. The Christian powers saw the need of united action if they were not to be swept from the Mediterranean. In the spring of 1571 the diplomacy of Pope Pius V brought into existence the Holy League among the Papacy, Venice, and Spain. It was directed not only against the Ottomans but also against their north African vassals, Algiers, Tunis, and Tripoli. The allied fleet assembled at Messina in Sicily and consisted of over two hundred galleys plus several heavy merchant ships armed with good-sized cannon. Commanding it was Don John of Austria, the talented, illegitimate half-brother of Philip II of Spain. The Christian armada put to sea eastward and found the Turkish fleet, consisting of ships equal in number but lighter in tonnage, at Lepanto on the Gulf of Corinth in western Greece. After some preliminary scouting, in which the two commanders estimated each other's strength, the Turkish admiral sailed out for battle in October, 1571. In the engagement that followed, the superior weight and armament of the Christian ships inflicted a pulverizing defeat on the Ottoman fleet. Only one wing, commanded by the bey of Algiers, succeeded in fleeing to open water and escaping.

The great defeat at Lepanto did not necessarily mean the end of Turkish sea power. Don John withdrew without exploiting his victory, and by the next year the Ottomans had rebuilt their navy and were at sea again. The Holy League dissolved in 1573, when the Venetians signed a separate peace with the sultan. Nevertheless, Lepanto had a decisive effect. The Turks thereafter kept to their own waters and never again moved into the western Mediterranean in force.

THE OTTOMAN DECLINE

From the accession of Selim II in 1566 to that of his namesake, Selim III, in 1787 seventeen sultans governed Ottoman Turkey. Of all these, three alone showed much aptitude for government. Even the exceptional three practiced extraordinary cruelty and sullied their reputations with senseless murders committed from whim or caprice. The Ottoman story became a dismal record of palace intrigue and misgovernment. Several of the sultans were small boys at the time of their enthronement, and the reigns on the average were short. One ruler, who held the throne for eighteen months in the early seventeenth century, was probably an idiot, or at best no more than an imbecile.

Curiously the Ottoman Empire did not part with any territory for years. There was some weakening of control in Arabia, but except for the holy cities Ottoman sovereignty there had never amounted to much. The allegiance of the Barbary countries, Tripoli, Tunis, and Algiers, gradually slackened, but these had always been tributary states and not real provinces of the empire. Elsewhere the effectiveness of administration declined but Turkish government endured. At first glance, it may seem strange that European powers did not commence the partition of the sultan's territory earlier than they did, but a second glance furnishes the explanation. The old rival Venice decayed faster than the Ottoman Empire, and except for one final spurt of vigor at the end of the seventeenth century, steadily sank to the status of a museum piece. Russia, the future great threat to Turkey, did not become a real menace until the reign of Tsar Peter the Great (1682–1725). The Papacy ceased to be much of a political power during the seventeenth century; and Spain, now a weakening state, found much of its energy required overseas. Habsburg Austria, seldom a foremost military power, was engaged in German and western affairs, while England and France lay too far away to have a firsthand interest. For all these reasons Turkey continued to look like a great power long after it had ceased to be one.

The Ottomans made their last great aggressive effort in 1683. In that year a grand wazir collected a huge, though motley and unwieldy, host and moved northward for a second siege of Vienna. From July to September the Turks encircled the city, whose defending garrison was small. Presently Christian help came in the form of a German army and a Polish detachment led by Poland's last energetic king, John Sobieski. The rescuers defeated the Turks near Vienna and drove them out of Austria. The next year Sobieski and the Austrian Habsburg emperor made an alliance for an offensive war against Turkey, and they were soon joined by Venice, which now put forth its last serious military effort. Presently, too, the Russian Tsar Peter joined the coalition for the sole purpose of wrenching a Black Sea port away from the Ottomans. The Austrians drove the Turks from Hungary, and in 1697 inflicted upon them the worst defeat they had suffered since their beating at the hands of Tamerlane in 1402. The Venetians meanwhile re-entered the Aegean, where they captured some islands and took mainland strongholds in the Morea. The war ended in 1699 with the Treaty of Karlowitz, by which Turkey lost territory to Russia, gave up Hungary and most of Transylvania to Austria, and handed the Greek Morea to Venice.

In the eighteenth century Russia became Turkey's archenemy. Twice the forces of Catherine the Great demonstrated an overwhelming superiority over the Ottoman armies. The Russian fleet entered the Mediterranean, destroyed the Turkish navy in the Aegean, penetrated to the Dardanelles from the south. Catherine proved moderate in her territorial demands, but did secure the opening of the straits to Russian merchant ships and a written pledge of toleration for Christians within the Turkish Empire. Austria, meanwhile, nibbled again at the northern Ottoman frontier. The Russians and the Austrians had further plans for partition of the Ottoman Empire, but the outbreak of the French Revolution, followed in a few years by Bonaparte's rise to power in France, turned their attention westward. The Turks received a respite, which they would have been wise to use in reforming their empire. Such wisdom, however, would scarcely be forthcoming in the Ottoman state as then constituted.

TURKEY AT THE BEGINNING
OF THE NINETEENTH CENTURY

As the new century opened, Selim III (1787–1807), one of Turkey's few intelligent later sultans, waged a lone and hopeless battle to put the empire in order. This despot showed interest in the reforms of the French Revolution and attempted to bring his army up to date and to rejuvenate the outworn Ottoman administrative machinery. Every factor in the situation combined to defeat Selim's well-meant efforts. The Balkan peninsula, which had lost hope of any betterment of Turkish rule, produced repeated revolts. The only Ottoman answer to these was massacre, which shed blood and solved no problems. The sultan made the mistake of looking to Napoleon for protection, which only stimulated the Russian tsar to further aggression. Internally Selim III failed to carry out a reform program, principally because the Janissaries blocked him at every turn.

Turkey still appeared on the map to be a great power, but much of its ostensible territory had become all but independent. Algeria, Tunis, and Tripoli, which had found Ottoman protection convenient in the days of Turkish sea power, resumed full liberty of action now that this power was gone. Egypt made more show of remaining loyal, but even here, where a new band of Mameluke soldiers had taken control, the sultan's power had been reduced to a shadow. In 1798 Napoleon Bonaparte had invaded Egypt and routed the Mamelukes. Following his return to France the British had captured his army and turned Egypt back to the sultan. The latter failed to re-establish Ottoman control because the Albanian-born pasha, Mehemet Ali, installed himself as ruler of the country, exterminated the Mamelukes, and ruled until the end of his long life in 1849. He built Egypt into a stronger military power than Turkey and more than once defeated the sultan's troops in battle.

In Asia too the Ottoman state crumbled. Anatolia was mostly dominated by feudal chieftains called Lords of the Valleys, and the great governors of Syria and Mesopotamia had become almost independent potentates. Southward in Arabia Turkish control had ended in 1803 with the loss of Mecca and Medina to a fierce new religious sect, the Wahabis. Though these fanatics were ultimately routed and their leader sent to Constantinople for decapitation, it was Mehemet Ali of Egypt and not an Ottoman general who won the victory. In Europe the empire had suffered heavy losses and was about to undergo further amputations. Transylvania and Hungary had been lost to Austria, and the area north of the Black Sea to Russia. Turkish hold on the Romanian provinces had grown weak, while the Serbs, Albanians, and Greeks had become ripe for serious revolts and before long did burst into rebellion.

The Janissaries, once the scourge of Turkey's enemies, had entered the final stage of their decadence. No longer recruited from Christian families, no longer properly trained for war, and altogether lacking their old-time morale, they had become a ridiculous crowd of loafers unfit to oppose any half-trained enemy. To get rid of the Janissaries became vitally necessary, yet difficult, because they still surrounded the sultan and retained at least an adeptness in assassination. Mahmud II (1808–1839) finally managed to destroy them in 1826. First quietly building up a modernized artillery corps armed with European cannon, he held this body in readiness while issuing an order canceling all the historic Janissary privileges. As expected, the turbulent ruffians rebelled, to be slaughtered by Mahmud's new artillery. Having broken them, the sultan gave the order for their total extermination, which was carried out to the letter.

The further relations of the Ottomans with their neighbors and subjects will be reviewed in later chapters (pages 405, 481). The nineteenth century, when it opened, promised from all appearances to be the most dismal in Turkish history. As it closed, it was plain that the promise had been amply fulfilled.

Further Reading

Mogul India begins with Baber, and Fernand Grenard, *Baber, First of the Moguls,* trans. by Homer White and Richard Glaenzer (New York: McBride, 1930), furnishes a biography of the interesting founder of the Mogul Empire based in part on his own *Memoirs.* Colonel G. B. Malleson, *Akbar and the Rise of the Mughal Empire* (Oxford: Clarendon Press, 1903), is a short, good biography of the great emperor. Stanley Lane-Poole, *Aurangzíb and the Decay of the Mughal Empire* (Oxford: Oxford Univ. Press, 1908), is a good, brief account of the last famous

Mogul ruler. The rise of the Marathas is covered by C. A. Kincaid and Rao Bahadur D. B. Parasnis, *A History of the Maratha People* (Bombay: Oxford Univ. Press, 1931), which places special emphasis on the hero Sivaji. Early Roman Catholic penetration of India is featured by Pierre du Jarric, *Akbar and the Jesuits,* trans. and ed. by C. H. Payne (New York: Harper, 1926), a work written by a French Jesuit who was a contemporary of Akbar and a visitor at his court. The early age of European empire building in India is well reviewed by Virginia Thompson, *Dupleix and His Letters (1742–1754)* (New York: R. O. Ballou, 1933), a very full account of the man who nearly made India a French possession. A. Mervyn Davies, *Clive of Plassey; A Biography* (New York: Scribner, 1939), is perhaps the best life available of the conqueror of Bengal and real founder of British rule in India.

Good material in English on Manchu China previous to the nineteenth century is scarce, probably because the early Ch'ing period had little connection with the outside world. The best work, though with inevitable limitations, is that edited by Arthur W. Hummel, *Eminent Chinese of the Ch'ing Period,* 2 vols. (Washington: Government Printing Office, 1943–45). It contains about eight hundred brief, scholarly biographies of leading persons of the empire between 1644 and 1912; Mongol, Turkish, and Tibetan, as well as Manchu and Chinese. The Chinese scholar Hu Shih calls it "the most detailed and best history of China of the last three hundred years that one can find anywhere today." John Ross, *The Manchus, or the Reigning Dynasty of China* (Paisley, Scotland: Parlane, 1880), is an older work of reasonable accuracy covering Manchu history from before the conquest until approximately 1880. Eloise Talcott Hibbert, *K'ang Hsi, Emperor of China* (London: Routledge, 1940), is a well-written biography of the great emperor. Captain F. Brinkley, *China, Its History, Arts, and Literature,* 4 vols. (Boston: Millet, 1902), although not a narrative history of China, contains much material valuable for the Manchu period. Sven Hedin, *Jehol, City of Emperors* (New York: Dutton, 1932), provides an account of social life and dramatic incidents in the summer capital of the Manchu Empire. Tieh-Tseng Li, *The Historical Status of Tibet* (New York: Kings Crown Press, 1956), surveys Tibetan history from the beginning to the present and is particularly valuable for Tibetan relations with Manchu China and British India. L. Petech, *China and Tibet in the Early Eighteenth Century; History of the Establishment of the Chinese Protectorate in Tibet* (New York: Heinman, 1950), covers an important and little-known phase of inner-Asian history, namely the relations between the Manchu emperor and the grand lama.

Albert Howe Lybyer, *The Government of the Ottoman Empire in the Time of Suleiman the Magnificent* (Cambridge, Mass: Harvard Univ. Press, 1913), is an old work which still enjoys high standing and, among other merits, includes an excellent study of Suleiman himself. Sir Harry Luke, *The Making of Modern Turkey: From Byzantium to Angora* (London: Macmillan, 1936), is a handy compendium of Turkish history which furnishes useful reading material for the parts covered in the present chapter. George E. Mylonas, *The Balkan States; An Introduction to Their History* (Washington: Public Affairs Press, 1947), furnishes a brief history of the Balkan countries, in considerable part devoted to their long period of subjugation to the Ottomans.

PART SIX

The Golden Age
of the West

Introduction

⚘ THE NINETY-NINE *years which elapsed between the fall of Napoleon and the outbreak of the First World War were the heroic epoch of the Western bourgeoisie. During the nineteenth century manufacturers, bankers, businessmen, and merchants began to exert an influence on society comparable to that which princes and noblemen had enjoyed in the eighteenth century. Behind this fundamental social transformation lay above all the spread of industrialization, shifting economic power from the landed aristocrat to the urban entrepreneur. Once the factory replaced the farm as the major source of wealth, the basis of politics was bound to change accordingly.*

The growth of parliamentarianism accompanied the advance of industrialization. In one country after another representative institutions were established and personal freedoms were recognized, while new libertarian ideals undermined the time-honored theories of royal absolutism. In its hour of triumph the emancipated bourgeoisie extended the suffrage, abolished religious disabilities, ended human bondage, proclaimed freedom of thought, and encouraged a rugged social individualism. Its faith in the beneficent effects of political and economic freedom, moreover, found support in the rising standard of living of the masses. As the advance of technology combined with the progress of science to create an unprecedented physical well-being in the lands of the Occident, the privations and fears which had haunted mankind throughout its history began to recede.

Before long, material preponderance enabled the West to subjugate the world. There were many reasons—political, economic, strategic, and ideological—for the rise of imperialism after the middle of the nineteenth century. Its results, however, were everywhere the same. Native societies, many of them far older than Europe, suddenly found themselves under alien rule. At first the obvious technological superiority of the white man tended to produce bewilderment and demoralization among colonial peoples. But by the beginning of the twentieth century they began to develop a nationalism of their own, which sought to oppose the domination of the foreigner with his own physical and spiritual weapons.

Chapter 23

THE FACTORY SYSTEM
AND THE RISE OF
INDUSTRIAL SOCIETY

D URING THE half-century of revolutions discussed in Chapter 21 another and vastly different kind of revolution began in England and started to spread over the world. This was the Industrial Revolution, a silent revolution in agriculture and manufacturing, involving no military or naval actions, no coalitions, and no peace settlements. It was not a sudden outburst. Rather, it was a process of slow accumulation for a long period. Only a few observers at the time were aware of what was taking place, and their understanding of events lacked deep comprehension. Indeed, the term "industrial revolution" was the invention of Arnold Toynbee (1852–1883), an English economist, sociologist, and historian (uncle of the modern historian Arnold Toynbee), who applied the name a century or so after the events it described had occurred. The term has been challenged, and we should distinguish between "industrial revolution" in the *general* sense of changes in the organization and methods of economic production, which are constantly in revolution or at least in a state of change, and *the* Industrial Revolution in the sense of those *particular* alterations which first took place in England and are still spreading over the world. The former has been taking place since time immemorial and continues to this day; the latter began in the English textile industry in the last quarter of the eighteenth century, spread to other industries in England and abroad, and continues to spread. Thus Toynbee's term, which has become part of the language of historical literature, has utility when properly understood to apply to the Industrial Revolution as opposed to the general fact of unceasing industrial change. And the Industrial Revolution involved alterations of such magnitude in the methods of production, and they took place with such celerity, as to make it stand out above the normal course of events and it still appears to warrant special designation.

People of the Western world today have for the most part become accustomed to sales pressures from the producers of goods or their sales agents, and they have forgotten that once the pressures almost always ran the other way; that is, there were more buyers or would-be buyers of goods than there were goods to buy. Production facilities failed to keep up with demand. In a broad sense, this is still the condition of the so-called backward countries where the pressures originate with the *buyers* of goods, as opposed to the so-called advanced countries where the pressures stem from the *producers* of goods, who wish to sell more. As a whole, the backward countries have not experienced industrial revolution or, as in some cases, they have not yet brought it to maturity. However, the would-be buyers must have capital (purchasing power in some form) or their pressures are slight and, as their number increases, they only fall into greater penury.

In view of the events of the past hundred years or so, it is important to point out that the Industrial Revolution took place in a capitalist society which had not only been in existence for many years (sometimes hampered by the practices of mercantilism and cameralism) but also had already created the basic elements of industrial revolution itself, although conditions did not warrant their widespread application until the eighteenth century. The capitalist system involves always two basic social institutions: private property and the profit motive. It is an economic system wherein capitalists (possessors of wealth in one or more forms) own land and other natural wealth of a society, together with the means of production, distribution, and exchange of goods, including the employment and reward of human labor. Moreover, in this system the organization, operation, and enlargement of the system itself are entrusted to and effected by private enterprise, controlled largely by competitive conditions, although usually with some regulation by the state. Thus, in theory and in practice, capitalism is opposed to mercantilism, cameralism, and socialism, in all of which, in varying degrees, the welfare of the society or state as a whole takes precedence over that of private individuals. As practiced in the eighteenth century and later, capitalism was founded upon the theoretical, liberal assumption that each individual, freely engaged in economic enterprise of his own choice toward the end of individual wealth-getting, with a minimum of state regulation and control (laissez faire), would in the aggregate follow policies conducive to the welfare and enrichment of society as a whole. The French physiocrats of the mid-eighteenth century leaned in this direction, though they did not go the whole way; and the laissez faire principles of Adam Smith and the classical economists of the early nineteenth century elaborated the principle for liberal states. A petition by merchants of London to the English House of Commons in 1820 illustrated the belief. The petitioners begged the House to consider:

That foreign commerce is eminently conducive to the wealth and prosperity of the country, by enabling it to import the commodities for the production of which the soil, climate, capital, and industry of other countries are best calculated, and to export in payment those articles for which its own situation is better adapted; that freedom from restraint is calculated to give the utmost extension to foreign trade, and the best direction to the capital and industry of the country; that the maxim of buying in the cheapest market and selling in the dearest, which regulates every merchant in his individual dealings, is strictly applicable, as the best rule for the trade of the whole nation; that a policy founded on these principles would render the commerce of the world an interchange of mutual advantages, and diffuse an increase of wealth and enjoyments among the inhabitants of each state; that, unfortunately, a policy the very reverse had been, and is, more or less adopted and acted upon by the government of this and every other country; each trying to exclude the productions of other countries, with the specious and well-meant design of encouraging its own productions; . . . [The petitioners are] against every restrictive regulation of trade not essential to the revenue, against all duties merely protective from foreign competition . . . [and they] humbly pray that the House will be pleased to take the subject into consideration, and adopt such measures as may be calculated to give greater freedom of foreign commerce, and thereby to increase the resources of the state.[1]

Actually, few states have found it politically possible or desirable to institute genuine "free trade" and laissez faire policies. Great Britain came nearest to it after the repeal of its Corn Laws in 1846, twenty-six years after the above petition. Accordingly, laissez faire (or "liberal") capitalism has never been widely practiced; it has been only roughly approximated, with free enterprise somewhat limited and free trade largely practiced in the internal commerce of states but not in international trade. Nevertheless, it became an article of faith in liberal capitalistic societies—though not necessarily a fact—that free, untrammeled, competitive enterprise is conducive to the highest material, cultural, and spiritual welfare of a people. This, of course, is a matter of bitter controversy today. Suffice it to say that, for our present purposes, the Industrial Revolution took place in a capitalistic, relatively liberal society. It might have taken place in any one of several states. The fact that it did occur first in England suggests that England's relatively lax mercantilistic controls in the eighteenth century gave greater freedom to individual initiative than was possible with the more rigidly mer-

---

[1] *Hansard* (parliamentary debates), n.s. 1 (1820), cols. 179–82.

341

cantilistic policies of continental European states. Thus the English economic structure, being more flexible, was able to respond to the peculiar conditions that developed in the late seventeenth and eighteenth centuries in such a way as to create the Industrial Revolution.

1 : The Backgrounds of the Industrial Revolution

FUNDAMENTAL TO the coming of the Industrial Revolution was the astonishing growth of population which, beginning about 1650, has continued with only occasional abatement to the present day. The statistics regarding population and population growth are very imperfect, and before 1800 only scattered local data are available and these are mostly limited to western European communities. Since 1800 regular official census reports have been made for most European and American countries. But no census worthy of the name exists before the present century for most parts of Asia, Africa, and the islands of the Pacific (Oceania), excepting Australia and some islands of the British and French empires. There is great uncertainty with regard to the population of China. Nevertheless, demographers have compiled workable statistical information from the data at hand, and the results of their labors are shown in the table below.

Demographers point out that for a thousand years before the beginnings of modern times the population of the world remained relatively constant, rising slowly, to be sure, but at an *average* rate of only about two-thirds of one per cent per year. Since 1650 the population of the world has risen from 545 million to almost two and a half billion, at an *average* rate of about seven per cent per year. Every people increased, but Europeans, including their overseas extensions (colonies before the half-century of revolutions) have grown the most, rising from about 101 million in 1650 to around 780 million in 1950. While Asia increased its population fourfold, Europe increased more than fivefold, and the total number of Europeans, including persons of European stock who settled in other continents, increased more than sevenfold. In 1650 the ratio of non-Europeans to Europeans was well over 4:1; in 1950 it was only slightly more than 2:1. Perhaps the Europeanization of the world in modern times has been, to some extent, a matter of constantly growing quantitative advantages.

Besides the increase in population, an enormous urbanization has taken place in the modern world. As a whole, the world was a vast agrarian community at the beginning of modern times. Cities of considerable size had existed in the ancient world—Rome, the largest ancient European city, may have reached a million inhabitants—but most of them shriveled and fell into decay during the Middle Ages. With the revival of trade in the late Middle Ages, cities regained life and new ones arose until, during the last

Estimates of World Population, 1650–1950*
(in millions)

	1650	1750	1800	1850	1900	1950
Europe	100	140	187	266	401	579
North America	1	1.3	5.7	26	81	168
Latin America	12	11.1	18.9	33	63	162
Asia	330	479	602	749	937	1,335
Africa	100	95	90	95	120	198
Oceania	2	2	2	2	6	13
Totals	545	728.4	905.6	1,171	1,608	2,455

Percentage Distribution

	1650	1750	1800	1850	1900	1950
Europe	18.3	19.2	20.7	22.7	24.9	23.6
North America	0.2	0.1	0.7	2.3	5.1	6.9
Latin America	2.2	1.5	2.1	2.8	3.9	6.6
Asia	60.6	65.8	66.4	63.9	58.3	54.4
Africa	18.3	13.1	9.9	8.1	7.4	8.0
Oceania	0.4	0.3	0.2	0.2	0.4	0.5
Totals	100.0	100.0	100.0	100.0	100.0	100.0

* The estimates for 1650–1900 are taken from A. N. Carr-Saunders, *World Population* (Oxford, 1936), p. 42. For 1950 the figures are from the *Demographic Yearbook, 1954* (6th Issue, United Nations, New York, 1954), p. 111, with European and Asiatic Russia added, respectively, from the *Statistische Jahrbuch fur die Bundesrepublik Deutschland, 1955* (Wiesbaden, 1955), "Internationale Ubersichten," pp. 15–19.

century, urbanization has taken place at a rapidly accelerating pace. Today there are at least twenty cities in the world each with a population of more than two million. There is some dispute over urban populations because of varying practices in counting suburbs. Moreover, the scene changes from year to year. Today, ten of the larger cities of the world will include two not even founded in 1650: Chicago, founded as Fort Dearborn in 1804; and Leningrad, founded as St. Petersburg in 1703. Two others were young villages in 1650: Buenos Aires, founded in 1580; and New York, originally New Amsterdam, founded in 1625. These factors serve to underscore the relative newness of the urbanization of the world.

This rapid increase in the world's population, together with its greater concentration in urban areas, had tremendous effects upon the world's economy. Gradually, of course, the modern world became less and less purely agrarian in nature, that is, relatively fewer people were engaged in agricultural pursuits. More importantly, however, it created a rapidly expanding potential market for goods of all kinds—more people to house, more bodies to clothe, more mouths to feed. However, we must emphasize that the expanding market was only *potential*, not necessarily real: only

Ten of the Larger Cities of the World
With Estimates of their Growth, 1650–1950*
(in thousands)

	1650	1750	1800	1850	1900	1950
London (England)	385	550	900	2,373	6,581	8,346
New York (U.S.A.)	1	12.5	63	515.5	3,437	7,900
Shanghai (China)			527	620	650	5,406
Tokyo (Japan)	350	409	520	672	1,580	5,385
Moscow (U.S.S.R.)	150	200	225	374	1,140	5,400
Chicago (U.S.A.)				30	1,698.5	3,621
Buenos Aires (Argentina)	1	10	40	92	836	3,600
Berlin (Germany)	6.5	114	196	427	2,534	3,488
Leningrad (U.S.S.R.)		75	220	485	1,439	3,300
Paris (France)	536	625	630.5	1,226	2,660	2,850

* In most cases available statistics for the population of cities are no more satisfactory than those for the world in general, and census reports for cities often fail to distinguish between a city and its outlying suburbs. The above figures are compiled from a variety of sources, including Joseph Körösi, *Statistique Internationale des Grandes Villes* (Tome I, Budapest, 1876); Tertius Chandler, *Cities of the World, B.C. 2500–A.D. 1936* (New York, 1940); *Statistique Internationale des Grandes Villes* (The Permanent Office of the Institute of International Statistics, The Hague, 1931); *The Statistical Abstract of the United States, 1955* (Washington, D.C., 1955); and a number of city histories, yearbooks, and general gazetteers.

with a commensurate increase in *capital* (money and credit) in terms of purchasing power would the increase in population create a significant increase in demand for goods and place heavy pressure upon existing facilities of economic production and distribution, Belgium and several of the German states, for instance, increased almost as rapidly as England in population during most of the eighteenth century, but their capital expansion, together with other factors to which we shall presently turn, did not keep pace with England and, therefore, they did not develop a pressure upon existing production and distribution facilities commensurate with that of England.

ENGLAND'S ADVANTAGES

Indeed, England overtook her European neighbors in the eighteenth century and, in so doing, created the peculiar combination of circumstances which led to the Industrial Revolution. A contemporary observer, living in 1700, could hardly have foreseen this development. For, while England in 1700 was a "prosperous agricultural island," it had fewer resources in population and raw materials (in terms of quantity) than many of the larger European states. In fact, as of 1700, France was the largest, richest, most populous state in Europe. Yet in the course of the next century England assumed a firm economic superiority. In 1700 the population of Great Britain was about eight and a half million, compared with France's twenty-three and a half million. Still, England's population, though small, was remarkably versatile, and in the course of the early eighteenth century it grew more rapidly in *rate of increase* than that of any other European state. This expanding population led to an enlarging domestic market for goods and greater productive power; for it was accompanied by rapidly expanding capital and increasing investments based on a sound currency regulated by the Bank of England. This institution, as we have already noted, had been founded in 1694, and by its generally "safe" monetary policies came to be known affectionately as "the old lady of Threadneedle Street."

Besides a rapidly expanding, versatile population and a sound capital structure, England possessed other advantages over her neighbors during the eighteenth century. From 1688 on, throughout the following century, England had domestic peace, broken only by two futile and relatively unimportant Stuart attempts to regain the throne, in 1715 and 1745. The government was stable, controlled throughout most of the first half of the eighteenth century by the Whig party, that combination of landed proprietors and city merchants who took the lead in the Industrial Revolution. The British people enjoyed a liberty which was the envy of their neighbors, including a freedom of enterprise greatly enhanced by the government's lax enforcement of trade regulations and by the powerless condition of the guilds, whose grasp upon the economy had been largely relaxed. British scientific and technological achievements, especially after Newton, were in the ascendancy, with a tradition of individual accomplishment and utilitarian emphasis fostered by the Royal Society of London and the empiricism of Bacon and Locke. The trade of Great Britain, both domestic and foreign, grew rapidly throughout the eighteenth century, in keeping with both domestic advantages and colonial successes. England's insular nature provided many ports easily accessible to the hinterland, often being connected to the interior by navigable waterways. Her geographical position placed her athwart the trade routes between northern and southern Europe and made her more accessible than most of her neighbors to the Far East and the New World.

England's colonial trade grew very rapidly after 1715, partly because of the advantages won by the Treaty of Utrecht (1713), which included both added colonial territory and trading privileges in the Spanish colonies of America. But, in addition to these, England's colonial possessions were enlarged still more by 1763, when she became the dominant colonial power, and in the meantime her American colonies had become the most heavily populated European colonies in the world. Their trade, other than the carrying trade, generally complemented that of England—the colonies sending raw materials to England in return for English manufactured goods of all sorts, thereby adding materially to the pressures which built up around England's domestic production facilities. And lastly, it should be noted that the nature of England's trade, compared with that of France, her closest competitor at the time, also was to England's advantage. France, in the tradition set up by Henry IV, Colbert, and others, concentrated upon the production of luxury goods of highest quality and price for sale abroad, such as fine silks, wines and liqueurs, exquisite china wares, and *objets d'art*. England manufactured and traded primarily in everyday commodities of good to medium quality and medium to cheap price, such as woolen goods, cutlery, kitchenwares, hand tools of all kinds for builders and farmers, and furniture. English goods were staples in wide and constant demand; trade in French goods was considerably limited to the well-to-do, and it suffered with every downward trend in the business cycle. Mostly because of the differences in the nature and prices of their goods, English traders bested the French, even in the latter's territory, in the fur trade with the Indians of North America.

No single European state in the eighteenth century combined all the above advantages that England possessed. And for this reason the Industrial Revolution occurred first in England. At base, it took place in response to such rapidly expanding sales opportunities that persons familiar with the market, scenting larger profits, sought new, faster, and less expensive methods of production in an attempt to meet the market demands. To some extent, similar factors contributed to an agricultural revolution which preceded and accompanied the Industrial Revolution and without which the revolution in industry would have been impossible. To the revolution in agriculture, then, we turn next.

2 : The Agricultural Revolution

BECAUSE OF the interconnectedness of human events, it is difficult to separate the agricultural revolution from other developments. In part, it was a consequence of urbanization. As people moved off the land and produced little or none of their own food, the remaining farmers had to expand production in order that they might feed not only themselves but also the city dwellers. On the other hand, as we shall see, a facet of the agricultural revolution led to the depopulation of agricultural areas, forcing people to leave the land for other occupations in the villages or cities. Indeed, this movement antedated the Industrial Revolution by many years and continued into the nineteenth century. This was the *enclosure* movement, fundamentally the introduction of new techniques in agriculture. Its beginnings date back into the late Middle Ages when landlords, with legal approval, began usurping common wastelands for agricultural purposes. By the fifteenth century the prime object became the enlargement and enclosure of pasture lands for sheep raising, as the English wool trade became increasingly profitable.

This process tended to upset the local self-sufficiency of the manor and, as fewer hands were required, the serfs were allowed to go free. Many of them became free agricultural workers, some swelled the villages and cities, others retained their old plots as leaseholders, becoming free small farmers, or yeomen. The process of enclosure continued with parliamentary approval, although many cried out against it, alleging that it reduced the rural population to beggary and interfered with the age-old rights of feudal tenants. Moreover, as prices rose in the sixteenth century landlords gradually raised the rents on leaseholders, giving rise to indignant protests against "rent raisers." Gradually, however, the medieval open-field system of agriculture disappeared in England, serfdom vanished, and two important new agrarian types arose: the yeoman, and the landlord who introduced new types of agricultural enterprise. Occasionally the yeoman himself experimented with new enterprises but, as it required capital, only the more successful could do it and, in so doing, they themselves often graduated into the large, independent landholder class.

Enclosures for sheep raising persisted until the eighteenth century, but in the early seventeenth century a few landlords began experimenting with new types of agriculture for raising grain and fodder crops. With their success, the enclosure movement continued—but for different reasons—to produce cereals and various kinds of livestock, instead of for sheep raising alone. Most of the new methods were introduced from the Low Countries. Agricultural reformers, like Walter Blith, author of *The English Improver, or a New Survey of Husbandry* (1649), and Sir Richard Weston, who wrote *A Discourse of Husbandrie Used in Brabant and Flanders* about the same time, made a select few of English agriculturalists familiar with new farming methods. The old system of letting land lie fallow for a season after a sequence of wheat and rye gave over to experiments with new crops and new crop rotation with artificial fertilizers, such as chalk, marl, compost, potash, and other substances. Turnips, potatoes, tobacco, clover, flax, madder, hops, and artificial grasses (such as sainfoin) were introduced. Marshlands were drained, and new agricultural implements, especially plows, were perfected. Even the new Royal Society of London set up a "Georgicall Committee" (from Virgil's *Georgics,* an ancient treatise on husbandry) to submit old agricultural methods to empirical tests and to experiment with new methods of soil fertilization and crop rotation.

As the seventeenth century advanced, enclosures and new farming techniques had claimed sufficient new lands and improved the productivity of enough old lands that the fear that the country's food supplies would be inadequate was allayed (this fear coupled with the cry of "overpopulation" had contributed to the beginnings of English overseas colonization at the turn of the century). The farms of yeomen and wealthy landlords increased in size, very small husbandmen were reduced to penury, and many of them joined the landless ones to take to the road, to become beggars or criminals, although many found employment in the cutleries and textile manufactures of the rising towns of Sheffield and Manchester.

During the eighteenth century the innovations of the seventeenth were extended and intensified. A new generation of agricultural reformers arose. Jethro Tull (1674–1741) perfected new methods of pulverizing the soil for planting with horse-drawn implements, and about 1701 he invented a new type of seed drill, which gradually displaced the wasteful method of sowing seed broadcast helter-skelter on top of the soil. Tull's *The Horse-Hoeing Husbandry* (1733) and other works widened familiarity with his methods, but his example also spread far and wide, especially as it was said that he made two blades of grass grow where only one had grown before. Contemporary with Tull was Charles, second Viscount Townshend (1674–1738), grandfather of the Lord Townshend who authored the hated Townshend Acts of the American revolutionary era. After a long career in politics Viscount Townshend retired to his Norfolk estates in 1730 and devoted himself to the perfection of methods of crop rotation which came to be known as the Norfolk System. Usually this was a four-course system of crop rotation, the land being devoted to two crops of grain alternated with turnips and a leguminous crop (clover or beans). The legumes fixed nitrogen in the soil, the turnips and the hay or beans were used as fodder for livestock, and the farmyard manure was used as fertilizer. Thus the fertility of the soil was maintained at a high level, and "Turnip Townshend," as the viscount was called, doubled the yield of grain per acre compared with the older methods, while at the same time none of the land had to lie fallow for a season.

IMPROVED ANIMAL HUSBANDRY

Alongside improvements in grain production and soil conservation went advances in animal husbandry. Hitherto, with livestock running loose in common pastures, there had been little chance of scientific livestock breeding. Moreover, livestock was generally scrawny, rangy, and large-boned. Cattle were valued chiefly for their milk (principally used in cheese making), or for draft purposes (oxen), and their hides were used for leather. Sheep were raised almost solely for their wool. Much pork and fowl was consumed, but little beef or mutton was eaten. The quality of the meat of the kind of animals raised was tough and not very edible. Robert Bakewell (1725–1795) pioneered in scientific livestock breeding, especially to improve cattle and sheep as sources of meat. He developed a new type of sheep, known as Leicesters, which produced good mutton as well as wool. He also created the common longhorn cattle for beef purposes. Others followed Bakewell's methods. Thomas William Coke (1752–1842) developed an improved new breed of pigs, and soon familiar breeds of livestock were developed for specialized purposes: in cattle, the Shorthorns, Herefords, Ayrshires, Devons, and Aberdeen Angus; in sheep, the South Downs, Lintons, and Cheviots; in pigs, the Chester Whites, the Hampshires, and others.

Soon agricultural societies and livestock associations arose. The Society of Arts began in 1754 and offered prizes for improvements in farm machinery; and the Society Instituted at London for the Encouragement of Arts, Manufactures, and Commerce, though more concerned with manufactures, gave rewards for

> Ingenuity in the several branches of the Polite and Liberal Arts, useful discoveries and improvements in Agriculture, Manufactures, Mechanicks, and Chemistry . . . and, in general, all such useful inventions, discoveries, or improvements . . . as may appear to have a tendency to the advantage of trade and commerce.

In 1783 the society began its annual publication of transactions in order to reach a wider audience. In publicizing agricultural reform methods, however, Arthur Young (1741–1820) was unique. A farmer himself, Young traveled widely to observe agricultural practices and to urge forward the new methods. He traveled extensively over Great Britain and published *The Farmer's Letters to the People of England* (1767), the *Annals of Agriculture,* begun in 1784 and published consecutively for forty-seven volumes by 1809, and several other works. His observations made in France during three separate journeys in 1787, 1788, and 1789, are a valuable source of information about conditions there at the beginning of the French Revolution. In 1793 he became secretary of the new Board of Agriculture, set up by the British government to help farmers throughout Britain, and in this capacity Young continued to aid greatly in the spread of new agricultural knowledge.

TENANT AND LANDOWNER

The new methods advanced slowly, however. Apart from endemic rural conservatism, the small leaseholders were difficult to persuade because of economic barriers. The principal problem was that of getting a tenant, who held land on a short lease, to improve land at his own expense. He was always faced with the possibility that, if he invested money for improvements, his lease might not be renewed and he would lose his investment (unless the landowner recompensed him), or, equally likely, the lease would be renewed at a higher rent on the ground that the land was more productive. Thus, a classic drawback to rural tenancy stood in the way of improvement; and until long-term leases could be effected, or tenants' rights to compensation for unexhausted improvements on non-renewal of a lease could be legally enforced, tenants were reluctant to invest much capital in long-term improvements. Still, the pattern for agricultural reform had been set, and the movement continued through the first three quarters of the nineteenth century until overseas competition from the New World forced a readaptation in British agriculture after 1875.

In the meantime British agriculture became capitalistic; that is, larger and improved farms required capital investments, led to greater specialization, and so increased agricultural production that England had become an exporter of cereals before the end of the eighteenth century. Urban investors, including some banks, lent money to "improving" farmers. Yet fewer persons were engaged in agricultural pursuits, and methods of landholding had been revolutionized since the end of the Middle Ages. Although the economic position of the farmers varied from year to year, it improved fairly steadily for the large landholders and for those leaseholders who improved their lands and adopted the new methods. The Napoleonic Wars gave British agriculture a great stimulus and accelerated the spread of improved methods; and the farmers were prosperous throughout the war years. The enclosure movement reached its peak during these years and was essentially completed by 1840. However, many farmers, led on by wartime prosperity, overinvested in their lands, and when the war was over they found themselves overextended. A difficult period of readjustment followed, during which the small leaseholders who were unable to stand the pressures, sold out, and either emigrated or moved to the cities. Thus the total number of agriculturalists was still further reduced, although those who remained gradually stabilized their situation, and from the late 1830's until 1875 British agriculture was prosperous again. Improvements continued, with the gradual disappearance of the small leaseholder.

3 : The Factory System

THE ESSENCE of the Industrial Revolution was the introduction of the factory system of production. This was the classic response of the English merchants to the rapidly expanding market opportunities so peculiarly prevalent in England in the eighteenth century. The exact nature of a factory has been the source of considerable dispute. It requires capital, but is there a minimum amount necessary before a factory emerges, and if so, what is it? It involves a site of some sort, but must this be a building, and if so, how large and what kind? It requires workers, but how many? Is there a minimum number before a factory is established, and if so, what is it? Power machinery is usually involved, but is power machinery the kernel of a factory? Actually, none of these approaches to an understanding of the factory system is satisfactory. The system is, at base, a peculiar form of disciplined, purposeful organization of the elements of production (land, labor, and capital), directed toward the creation of economic goods. It can best be comprehended in terms of those economic and historical forces which pro-

JETHRO TULL

"TURNIP" TOWNSHEND

ROBERT BAKEWELL

ARTHUR YOUNG

Jethro Tull invented a variety of horse-drawn farm implements for tilling the soil and seeding crops. The second Viscount Townshend was known as "Turnip" Townshend for his use of turnips in a new system of crop rotation (the Norfolk System) which avoided the waste of allowing land to lie fallow. Robert Bakewell pioneered in scientific livestock breeding, especially in developing more marketable cattle and sheep. Arthur Young, publicist and indefatigable agricultural reformer, became the first secretary of the English Board of Agriculture in 1793.

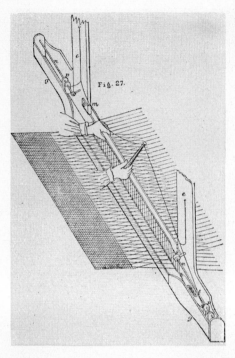

HARGREAVE'S SPINNING JENNY

KAY'S FLYING SHUTTLE

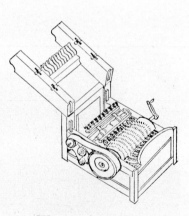

CROMPTON'S MULE

WHITNEY'S COTTON GIN

The flying shuttle, invented by John Kay in 1733, greatly accelerated the process of weaving, although it was still a hand-operated machine. James Hargreave's spinning jenny, perfected in 1764, multiplied an operator's capacity to spin thread many times. Ultimately, it proved adaptable to power-driven methods. Samuel Crompton's mule made possible the production of much finer threads and, therefore, of finer cotton cloth. The cotton gin (here shown open), invented by Eli Whitney in 1793, made possible the machine removal of the seeds from cotton bolls, thereby vastly enlarging the supply of raw cotton for the growing textile industry.

CUGNOT'S "AUTOMOBILE"

OPENING OF THE STOCKTON AND DARLINGTON RAILROAD, SEPT. 27, 1825

TREVITHICK'S LOCOMOTIVE

FITCH'S PADDLE BOAT

Cugnot's "automobile" (1763) was one of many efforts to develop a steam-powered vehicle for road transport. Like others, its excessive weight limited its efficiency and ruined roadbeds. John Fitch experimented with steam-powered boats near Philadelphia in the late 1780's. Despite technical success, he could attract no support and retired in despair. Richard Trevithick was one of several perfecters of the steam locomotive. One of his models, driven about 1800, is shown in the illustration. The opening of the Stockton and Darlington Railroad in England in 1825 was widely celebrated. It marked the beginning of the first railway venture to prove successful.

THE THIRD DUKE OF BRIDGEWATER

JAMES WATT

RICHARD ARKWRIGHT

Francis Egerton, third duke of Bridgewater, was an English coal magnate who
became the prime mover in promoting
canal construction in the latter half of the
eighteenth century. Richard Arkwright,
promoter and successful entrepreneur in
the textile industry, is sometimes called
the "father of the factory system." Matthew Boulton was a Birmingham manufacturer and factory organizer who financed many of the experiments of James
Watt, the Scottish instrument maker who,
in conjunction with others, perfected the
steam engine about 1765 and adapted it
for the transmission of rotary power to
drive other machinery in 1782.

MATTHEW BOULTON

duced it and by comparison with other forms of organization for the production of economic goods.

Four different forms of the organization of production (including the factory system) can be discerned in man's economic experience. These have not necessarily displaced one another in historical sequence. Rather, they often exist side by side at the same time in different industries and sometimes even in the same industry, the transfer from one to another being determined by the circumstances of economic opportunity and individual enterprise. All of them are still present in today's economic society. Thus, the analysis of the forms of organization of production is logical, rather than chronological, consisting of the *household system,* the *handicraft system,* the *putting out* (or *sweatshop*) *system,* and the *factory system.* Let us examine each in turn.

THE HOUSEHOLD SYSTEM

Historically, the household system of production is probably the oldest of the four. It existed widely in primitive societies and continues in some areas of production to the present day. Its essence was, and is, the manufacturing of goods and services for home consumption, with no regularized effort to produce for sale or exchange outside the home. Its workers are the householders themselves, owning their own tools or machines (if any), and working in the home at their own pace. The medieval manor was a classic example of the household system, although pioneer societies in modern times were often forced to employ it in varying degrees. Families still use it in such things as house cleaning, preparation of meals, and, with allowances for individual differences, washing, ironing, mending, processing of foods for storage, and a host of "do-it-yourself" enterprises.

THE HANDICRAFT SYSTEM

The handicraft system preserves many of the organizational features of the household system: the workers work in their homes or in a shop usually attached to their home, own their own tools and equipment, and work according to a schedule of their own making. But it differs from the household system at two important points. First, the handicraft workers usually specialize in the production of some one product or a group of closely related products. Second, they produce for sale in a wide market outside their homes and beyond their own individual uses. Historically, it would appear that the handicraft system originated in some special skill or secret process, or in a monopoly of a particular raw material, carefully guarded by a family or tribe as a means of maintaining a lucrative trade. Like the household system, the handicraft system is very old. It appears among primitive tribesmen in widely scattered parts of the world, wherever a special skill or a secret process (such as cloth weaving or a widely admired dye process) or a monopoly of a specialized raw material (such as flint for arrowheads and axes or red ocher for body paints) made possible a crude monopoly of a product.

The craft guilds which developed in ancient times were built around the handicraft system, and the powerful guilds which developed in the late Middle Ages and persisted into modern times became legalized local monopolies (by means of charters) on a similar basis. By means of the apprentice system, they also developed a regularized system of technical training. The secrets of the trades were controlled and passed on to carefully selected apprentices, who by their apprenticeships were taught the secrets and prepared by intensive training for subsequent introduction into the guild. In every industry where the guilds were still strong, backed by the courts in defense of their monopoly, as in France and many of the German and Italian states, the industrial revolution was retarded in its development. In these places the guilds were able to crush all interlopers (similar to "scabs" at the hands of present-day labor unions), resist the introduction of new industrial processes not adopted by the guilds themselves (an action they were very hesitant and slow to take), and throttle such new organizations of an industry as the factory system involved. Here again England held an advantage over most of her neighbors in the industrial revolution. In England the guilds were generally weak and did not command widespread judicial and parliamentary support. Therefore, they were relatively helpless in combatting new processes, new industrial organization, and interlopers who sought to break their monopolies.

THE PUTTING OUT SYSTEM

As a rule, the putting out system was a kind of organizational superstructure imposed upon the handicraft system—usually by a wholesale merchant with capital and a knowledge of market potentials which he hoped to exploit. It was practiced by the merchant guilds of the late Middle Ages and was an important factor in their ascendancy over the craft guilds. This system continues to the present day, being widely employed in many parts of the world in the manufacture of gloves, knitted footwear, lingerie, and other enterprises for which it is adapted. It is most commonly used in the textile and clothing trade, where it developed at an early date. Indeed, its origin, like that of the factory system, appears to have been a merchants' response to expanding market opportunities—especially markets in distant areas outside the immediate experience of a local craft guild, whose market and chartered monopoly rarely reached outside a particular city or town and its immediate environs. Indeed, craftsmen, whether weavers, tailors, shoemakers, coopers, tinners, or others, rarely kept a large stock of goods on their shelves. Their capital was usually too small to enable them to do so and, as their trade was local, their goods were usually "custom-made," that is, they made up cloth, clothing, shoes, casks, or kitchenwares on the order of and to fit the desires of a particular customer. Large quantities of ready made wares were seldom available. Handicraft workers were, of themselves, ill equipped to meet the demands of a rapidly expanding market and seldom were they able to supply the needs of a distant, unseen market, even in a neighboring county or province.

In consequence, merchants, especially wholesalers, usually became the *entrepreneurs* (that is, "undertakers") who initiated the putting out system. Becoming familiar with market outlets for goods in more distant places, such as overseas trading posts or colonies, they desired to exploit them. A merchant, finding that he could sell a hundred bolts of cloth to sugar planters in Jamaica, would be inclined to take orders for its supply, if he felt reasonably confident that he could command the kind, quality, and quantity of cloth desired at a time necessary to ship it when sailings to Jamaican ports were available. As a man of enterprise and some capital, he would become an entrepreneur of a putting out system. That is, he would buy raw wool in the open market and deliver it to carders who, working in their usual handicraft establishments, would prepare it for spinning into yarn and be paid a fee for their services. The merchant would then pick up the wool and, in turn, deliver it to spinners, weavers, dyers, and the like, each of whom worked in his own shop at home, using his own tools. Each received a fee for his services. When the cloth was ready, the merchant picked it up and delivered it to a vessel bound for Jamaica or stored it in his warehouse pending the ship's departure. This, in brief, was the putting out system, superimposed upon the handicraft system by enterprising entrepreneurs. Multiply such instances many times over, not only in the cloth trade but in nearly every other trade as well, as was done by eager merchants trying to exploit ready markets in Europe, the Levant, and the far-flung British Empire, and one can begin to comprehend the market pressures building up around the handicraft workers of eighteenth-century England.

Moreover, one can also begin to comprehend the exasperation of the entrepreneur who found that his carder had decided to go fishing instead of completing his task at the appointed time; that his spinner had got drunk and had spun the yarn in lumpy, uneven fashion; that his weaver's looms only accommodated materials thirty-four inches wide though the merchant's order specified a yard; that his dyer had dyed different bolts of cloth for the same order in separate batches of dye, which though of the same color were not of the same shade, and that few of his handicraft processors, working in their own shops on their own time, could be depended upon to perform their services on time. And unless they could be reasonably well depended upon, the entrepreneur could not meet the date lines for delivery set by his customers in distant places.

Indeed, although the putting out system had many advantages, especially in that it required comparatively little capital investment on the part of the entrepreneur, scattered the risks of enterprise widely among the handicraftsmen employed, and left the workers free to work in their own shops and at hours of their own choosing, its disadvantages led many entrepreneurs to seek greater direct control over the intermediate processes of manufacture. The principal disadvantages are suggested above, and they may be summarized as follows. (1) Difficulties in meeting delivery date when processors worked at their own pleasure. (2) Unevenness of quality in spinning, weaving, and dyeing, not only because of an individual processor's shortcomings but also because of variations in the quality of the products of different workers in the same process, using different machines and working by uneven standards. Thus a large order of cloth supposedly all of the same width, color, and quality might, at the hands of different weavers and dyers, turn out to be several different widths, different shades of the same color, and woven with widely different degrees of tension. (3) Too much hauling about from place to place. These shortcomings of the putting out system impelled many entrepreneurs to concentrate all the intermediate processes of manufacture in their own warehouses, supplying the tools and all the materials for his workers, who no longer worked in their own shops with their own tools and processing materials but, instead, performed their services in the entrepreneurs' establishments under their immediate direction. This establishment, of course, was a factory, and in a manner similar to this many of the entrepreneurs' putting out enterprises graduated into the factory system.

THE FACTORY SYSTEM

Perhaps now that we have seen how the factory system often came about we can approach its definition with greater understanding. It is, of course, a system for the production of economic goods, and it involves at least four interrelated factors. First, it involves considerable *concentration* of the elements of economic production: land, in the sense of raw materials of many kinds; labor, in the sense of human workers; and capital, in the sense of money and credit in quantities sufficient to build a factory, equip it with necessary tools, and supply it with raw materials and labor (wages) necessary to achieve the productive ends for which the factory was organized.

Second, the factory system involves a *division of labor,* in that workers specialize, or devote themselves to a single task or a closely related group of tasks which, only in their totality, produce the good or goods for which the system is intended. This specialization contributes greatly to efficiency and to standardization of products, and it is a basic factor in modern assembly-line production methods; but it can also become boring to workers, benumb their souls, and demoralize their spirits.

354

Third, the factory system involves a *leadership, direction,* and *control* in any enterprise continuously separate from the laborers themselves. Most factories become a hierarchy of more or less militaristic leadership, however well it may be disguised. The labor crew in each process has its boss and its inspector; each department has its head, who, in turn, is responsible to someone higher up until the whole hierarchy is capped by the board of directors who establish the policies of the enterprise.

Fourth, the factory system is a disciplined organization. This *discipline* is directed toward the efficient and profitable production of economic goods and services. Factory workers work for a specified number of hours, beginning and ending at specified times, and they are under constant supervision and surveillance. They may be disciplined in many ways for their failure to comply with the rules established to maintain the efficiency and standards of accomplishment set up by their employers. Between management and labor in any factory there are generated tensions and certain divergencies of interest which, at base, are the origin of most of the present-day labor problems and management dilemmas.

The factory system was not new in the eighteenth century, although its rise at the hands of private entrepreneurship was. Earlier factories, almost without exception, had been established under the mercantilistic sponsorship of the state and, even when they were managed by private hands they were financed in whole or in part by the state and subjected to state direction. Cloth-making factories had been set up in Flanders and in France in the sixteenth centuries, and the great Gobelin tapestry works and Sèvres china works fostered by Colbert had been organized as national factories. But the organization of factories at *private* hands, with privately-owned capital, was a central feature of the Industrial Revolution in England during the eighteenth century.

4 : The Industrial Revolution

WHEN POWER MACHINERY was combined with the factory system of production in any given industry of a country, the Industrial Revolution occurred in that industry. This took place first in the English textile industry, particularly in cotton textiles. Cotton goods hitherto had been a great luxury in Europe, being imported from India. Consequently, their manufacture was relatively new in England and did not have the deeply entrenched methods and well-established vested interests that characterized woolens.

Let us review the evidence as an example of how the Industrial Revolution first came about. The multiplication of inventions in the eighteenth century, though no essential ingredient of the factory system itself, was closely connected to the association of factories with power machinery.

Indeed, the inventions, like the factory system, formed an interesting set of additional responses to the rapidly expanding market—an effort to increase productivity in order to meet demands and enlarge profit-making opportunities. We have already noted a few of the inventions important in the agricultural revolution of eighteenth-century England. We have also noted the rise of societies to encourage inventions. In the realm of manufacturing the number of inventions was so great that we can give attention to only a few outstanding ones. The British Patent Office, whose records begin with the earliest patent law in 1624, lists 616 patents granted between 1624 and 1760. But within the next thirty years (1760–90) there were registered 976 more—and, in addition, a rather considerable number of inventions are known not to have been patented! Surely, this is a significant index of the technological ferment created by expanded market opportunities. It was also, of course, a magnificent indication of the inventiveness of Englishmen, although, as is the case more often than not, many of the "inventions" were merely successful technological applications of physical and engineering principles discovered by others many years before.

REVOLUTION IN THE TEXTILE INDUSTRY

The earliest eighteenth-century inventions in the textile industry were mere tools for the household and handicraft workers, but they nonetheless aided materially in increasing production. They were usually adaptable for work in various fabrics—wool, flax, silk, and cotton. Such was John Kay's *flying shuttle,* invented in 1733 for the hand loom. The flying shuttle was a mechanically-impelled shuttle carrying the weft by means of cord guides and controlled by a lever or a treadle (see Plate XXX). By its use the speed of weaving was greatly accelerated, and one person could operate a loom which previously had required two. In 1760 Robert Kay improved upon his kinsman's work by inventing the *drop box,* whereby two or three flying shuttles could be used with weft of different colors for making figured patterns of cloth. In the same year the Society Instituted at London for the Encouragement of Arts, Manufactures, and Commerce offered a prize for the "best invention of a machine for spinning six threads of Wool, Cotton, Flax, or Silk, at one time, and that will require only one person to work and attend it." James Hargreaves perfected the most successful device for this purpose in 1764 and patented it in 1770. This was the *spinning jenny,* which actually spun eight threads at once (see Plate XXX). But this number could be increased, and in 1783 the Society reported that "one woman is thereby enabled, with ease, to spin an Hundred Threads of Cotton at one time." Like the previous inventions, the spinning jenny was hand-powered and usually was employed in homes and the shops of handicraftsmen, not in factories.

Already, however, in 1769 Richard Arkwright (1732–1792) had patented the *water frame* or *throstle*. Actually, it had been made by a clockmaker in Arkwright's employ and was similar in principle—though far more successful in practice—to the roller spinning machine invented in 1733 by John Wyatt and Lewis Paul. However, the water frame was driven by water power and its use was one of the earliest examples of the combination of power machinery and the factory system in the textile industry. Indeed, Richard Arkwright was a remarkable organizer, promoter, and entrepreneur. Originally a barber and later a wig-maker, with no direct experience in the textile trade, he combined other men's inventions, other men's money, and other men's labor to establish a series of water-powered cotton mills of a most remarkable sort. Speaking of them, the *Transactions* of the Society for the Encouragement of Art, Manufactures, and Commerce (1783) called them "stupendous works" where

> by the motion of a large water-wheel, the Cotton is corded, roved, and spun into threads, infinitely more expeditiously, and with greater truth [i.e., perfection], than can possibly be done by hand, and better adapted to the general purposes of the manufacturers [for cloth-making].

Arkwright's mills, with constant improvements upon the original water frame, produced cotton thread of high quality, suitable for calico warps, and commercially profitable. Indeed, Arkwright himself prospered and was knighted in 1786. Two years before his death he introduced steam power into one of his mills. The Machine Age had begun.

For even finer cotton fabrics, such as muslins, Samuel Crompton's *mule* (1779) completed the basic inventions for spinning thread (see Plate XXX). Like the water frame, Crompton's mule could be operated by water or steam power, and it produced threads better and more cheaply than those woven in the finest muslins from India. By this time, too, improvements in spinning had outrun those of weaving. This situation was partially corrected in 1785 when Edward Cartwright invented a *power loom*—although, until it was further perfected years later, it hardly bridged the gaps between the two processes. Eight years later (1793) the American Eli Whitney invented the *cotton gin,* a mechanical device for removing the seeds from cotton bolls (see Plate XXX). This helped insure an enlarged supply of raw cotton, for the hand removal of the cotton seeds had been a bottleneck in making a sufficient quantity of raw cotton available for the rapidly expanding industry. The cotton gin also made possible the extensive cultivation of cotton in the southern states of the United States, fastening at the same time "King Cotton" and Negro slavery upon that region. But, excepting the growth of raw cotton, its processing from bale to cloth was now dominated by power-driven machinery increasingly organized under the factory system.

By 1788 there were 143 water-powered spinning factories in England and a few steam-powered ones.

All this was reflected in the increase of the quantities of raw cotton imported to England for processing into cloth of various kinds. For several years prior to 1700 England had imported slightly less than two million pounds of raw cotton per year. This increased at the rate of about 30 per cent per decade to 1750. In the next two decades it increased at the rate of about 60 per cent per decade, but for the decade of the 1780's it increased at the rate of more than 300 per cent, a figure far higher than that for any subsequent decade. By this time England was importing more than eighteen million pounds of raw cotton per year and, while the total imports continued to increase in the future, the *rate* of decennial acceleration never again reached a figure as high as for the 1780's. In other words, the revolution in the English cotton textile industry took place during the decade of the 1780's. It was indicated by a tremendously accelerated productive power created by the association of the factory system and power machinery under the entrepreneurship of Richard Arkwright and his competitors.

Meanwhile, too, the same or similar machinery was invading the manufacture of woolens, linens, and silks in spite of the opposition of handicraft workers, and soon the entire British textile industry was succumbing to power machinery and the factory system. After the discovery of chlorine in 1774 chemical bleaching soon replaced the old laborious methods of the bleaching fields. The invention (1784) of Thomas Bell's cylindrical method of printing calicos and other fabrics multiplied a hundredfold the output, and required less skill than had been required in the old process of hand printing with engraved blocks or copper plates. Later the cylindrical press was adapted for printing books and newspapers as well.

THE STEAM ENGINE

Perhaps no single mechanical invention did more to accelerate the combination of power machinery with the factory system and thus spread the Industrial Revolution than the steam engine. Itself a power machine, it rapidly replaced water power in the textile industry and even more rapidly in the iron industry, where by its own use of metal it stimulated demand even more greatly. The application of the principle of steam expansion as a source of power had been known since ancient times, although no one put it to practical use until the late seventeenth century. The first practical application of steam as a motive power on a commercial scale was the work of Thomas Savery (1650–1715), whose crude engine, perfected in 1698, was successfully employed in pumping water for waterworks and shallow mines. However, it was dangerous and unreliable, and soon it was greatly improved upon by Thomas Newcomen (1663–1729), an ironmonger and blacksmith, assisted by a little-known plumber and glazier named John Cawley (or Colley). Indeed, Newcomen's engine, successfully demonstrated in 1712, was the first steam engine in the technical sense. It won widespread commercial success throughout the eighteenth century as a source of power for pumping water out of mines both in England and abroad. However, because of technological shortcomings, its leaky valves and pistons rendered it very inefficient. John Smeaton (1724–1792), an English civil engineer and instrument-maker, improved upon the Newcomen engine (1769), but the most successful and efficient engine was that perfected by James Watt (1736–1819), an impecunious Scottish instrument-maker, with the advice and assistance of a number of scientific men, notably Dr. Joseph Black of Edinburgh. Watt devised a revolutionary new way to condense the steam from the engine cylinder and increase the efficiency of the engine. He made a working model in 1765 and patented it in 1769. But when he attempted to construct a large engine from the working model he ran into technical difficulties compounded by financial troubles. The former were overcome by the use of new steel cutting tools invented by John Wilkinson (1728–1808), an ironmaster who had created new and more accurate methods of boring out cannon; with Wilkinson's boring device, steam cylinders and valves could be bored true. The financial problems were solved by Matthew Boulton (1728–1809), a prominent Birmingham manufacturer who became Watt's partner in 1775. He supplied the necessary capital, and together they established a plant to build steam engines. Seven years afterwards (1782) Watt perfected a means to transmit the power of the steam engine to *rotary* motion, thereby making possible engines that could be used to drive other machines, and, indeed, he made many other improvements of the steam engine before 1800. By that time 320 of Watt's steam rotary engines were in use in Britain, at work in textile mills, breweries, iron works, and mines. Even a few had been set up on the Continent. They permitted greater flexibility in the location of manufacturing plants, which being hitherto dependent on water power had been forced to locate alongside streams. And they offered a cheap, reliable, and seemingly inexhaustibly expandable source of power. The age of steam power had arrived—and with it the factory system was extended and the Industrial Revolution brought to maturity in England.

IRON AND STEEL

The expansion of industry of all kinds and the increased use of the new inventions were immediately reflected in added demands upon the metallurgical resources of England, especially iron and steel. For a time in the early eighteenth century this became a serious problem. Hitherto iron ore had been smelted by the use of charcoal, but the process was slow and, of greater import, England's forest resources had become so depleted that the supply of charcoal was endangered. The obvious solution was the use of coal instead, of which England had vast resources, especially near New-castle. But repeated attempts failed until, about 1712, Abraham Darby the elder (1677–1717), an ironmaster, succeeded in smelting pig iron by the use of coke, which was easily made from coal at hand in England. Darby's son, also named Abraham, enlarged and improved upon his father's process, and by 1745 the use of coke for iron-smelting was widely employed in England. By this time, also, Benjamin Huntsman (1704–1776), a watchmaker who went in search of a better steel for watch springs, perfected at Sheffield a new method of making steel—Huntsman's steel, as it was first called. It was far harder and better for cutlery and a variety of other purposes than any theretofore made in England. Indeed, Huntsman's steel was the nucleus of the famous Sheffield steel industry.

The use of coal for smelting iron ore led to greater demands for coal, and soon both coal and iron mines, together with the smelting plants, had introduced power machinery and the factory method of organization. In fact, the first of Watt's steam engines sold for rotary power purposes was sold to John Wilkinson, the ironmaster whose new process of boring metal had enabled Watt to perfect his engines. Thus the Industrial Revolution took place in the iron and steel industry almost simultaneously with the revolution in making cotton textiles. Again, production statistics come to our aid. Throughout the first half of the eighteenth century England's production of pig iron remained fairly constant at about seventeen thousand tons a year. But between 1750 and 1788 it increased 400 per cent, the principal increase being in the decade of the 1780's. Thereafter it approximately doubled every decade until 1825. It would appear that the combination of the factory system and power machinery produced the Industrial Revolution in the English iron industry about 1780.

5 : The Revolution in Transportation

THE SPREAD of the Industrial Revolution, both within England and to countries outside England, was stimulated not only by market expansion but also by a revolution in transportation which, like so many aspects of the Industrial Revolution as a whole, snowballed to expand markets still further. The revolution in transportation followed a course determined in large part by inventions and technological improvements, and it progressed from improvements in roads and horse-drawn transport to canals, railroads, and steamboats.

European road construction, as a whole, marked time from the remarkable system of roads laid out in the days of the Roman Empire until the eighteenth century. A few turnpikes were chartered in the mid-seventeenth century in England, but the heyday of the turnpike did not come until the next century. In 1700 roads were poor and coaches, which were few and very uncomfortable, traveled, as they advertised, "on the wings of the wind" —at a scant five miles an hour in good weather! Overland transportation costs were very high almost everywhere. The growth of industry in the eighteenth century led to demands for better, faster, and cheaper means of transport, and it also made possible the capital and technological means of achieving it. In France Pierre Trésaguet (1716–1796), as chief engineer in charge of roads and bridges, constructed the best road system on the Continent. In Britain road building and road-building techniques were advanced almost entirely at the hands of Scots, possibly because Scotland had essentially no roads prior to the eighteenth century. The first was John Metcalf (1717–1810), a blind engineer, who built a remarkably durable 180 miles of road in north-central England and some lesser stretches in southern Scotland. Thomas Telford (1757–1834), the second notable road builder, was a stonemason who turned to bridge construction and road building. He developed a three-stage process, as follows: (1) drain and level the road bed and provide a drain under it at least every 100 yards; (2) form a solid pavement of large stones, seven inches thick, set close with the broader ends downward; and (3) break off the points of the large stones and cover them with seven inches of smaller stones with a finishing coat of gravel. In the course of his career Telford built some 920 miles of roads in Scotland, including 1,200 bridges. With his fellow countryman and successor, John Loudon McAdam (1756–1836), Telford insisted upon the importance of adequate drainage in road making. McAdam, who gave his name to "macadamized" roads, followed Telford's system except that he felt that the large stones at the bottom were unnecessary. Macadamized roads were built up of layers of crushed stones of increasingly smaller size and finished with gravel. By the time of his death Britain had constructed a wide network of durable roads. The fast mail, or stagecoach, carried passengers fairly comfortably at the whirlwind pace of ten miles an hour, and overland transport had diminished in freight costs and improved in service. But already much of the traffic in goods had turned to other, newer media of transport.

Continental European countries, especially Holland and France, excelled in early canal building, the Dutch for drainage and transport, the French for internal trade. In England the first important canals were promoted by Francis Egerton, the third duke of Bridgewater (1736–1803), and constructed by James Brindley (1716–1803), a millwright who became a most skillful engineer in the construction of canals, bridges, and aqueducts. Earlier efforts to construct economical means of water transport, especially for bulky or excessively heavy articles, had concentrated on existing rivers and streams, seeking to canalize them. But they did not always run where transport was desired, they frequently silted up, and their water supply gave out in dry seasons. Accordingly, Brindley abandoned the use of existing streams for the most part, and constructed canals artificially, with careful survey of routes to be followed, aqueducts to carry them over existing streams, and an adequate source of water supply relatively free from seasonal rainfall variations.

It has been said that the canal boom in England came as a result of the duke of Bridgewater's disappointment in love. As a rejected suitor, he left London, retired to his estates in Lancashire, and soon became interested in exploiting his coal properties. But it was expensive and difficult to market his coal overland to Manchester, seven miles away. So he employed James Brindley to build a canal to connect his mines with the city. To do it, Brindley had to construct an aqueduct to carry the canal over a river, a feat which excited much interest. But the canal was a great success, and the duke then employed Brindley to build a canal from Manchester to the mouth of the Mersey River, thus connecting Manchester with the port of Liverpool.

In this way the canal boom began, lasting from the late 1760's until about 1830. Brindley and Telford, the road builder, were the leading canal engineers. The Trent and Mersey (or Grand Trunk) canal was completed in 1766, followed by the Staffordshire and Worcestershire, the Birmingham and Coventry, the Oxford, the Grand Junction (connecting London and the booming Midlands), and others. In all, more than 3,000 miles of canals were built, with another 1,300 miles of improved rivers, and much harbor and lighthouse construction to aid both coastwise and international trade. Most of the canals in the industrial areas of England and Scotland, especially those around Birmingham, Leeds, Sheffield, and Glasgow, proved of enduring economic value. But others proved uneconomic in the long run, or relatively useless because of the lack of commerce to move along them, and these in time fell into decay and disuse. As a whole, however, they served (and some still serve) as a cheap means of bulk transport—usually less than half as costly as overland transportation. They opened up markets for farmers and facilitated greatly the distribution of manufactured wares, in both domestic and foreign trade. They also served as a means of personal travel and recreation. Still, they gave way before railroads and coastal steamboats after 1830, and by 1850 the canal boom was over.

EARLY STEAM TRANSPORT

Curiously, the earliest attempts to employ steam power for transportation were the efforts to construct a steam-powered road vehicle, a kind of early automobile. As early as 1763 a Frenchman, Nicolas Cugnot, constructed a steam-powered vehicle which, in spite of its great weight, ran along the roads very well (see Plate XXXI). But it damaged roads badly, and when it overturned rounding a corner, threatening fire to all about it, it was condemned as a public hazard. Various other attempts, both in France and in England, failed to catch on. Roads and bridges could not accommodate their weight, and the public was unimpressed by their performance. After 1800 no one tried them again for many years, and steam railroads preceded the steam automobile after all.

Railroads—as apart from the steam locomotive—were not new. Coal mines had long employed rails on which to run cars of coal out of the mine, and a few had been constructed across open country for similar purposes, with horsecars somewhat like those that later developed in cities for urban passenger transport. But the steam railroad posed many problems, one of the most important of which was to find rails that would support the tremendous weight of the early, still very inefficient, locomotives. Richard Trevithick (1771–1833), a Cornish engineer, experimented with steam locomotives on both roads and rails for several years around 1800 (see Plate XXXI). In 1801 he carried the first passengers on a steam-powered road carriage, but the project aroused no commercial interest and he abandoned it. He then turned to railroads and in 1803 constructed a successful one for a Welsh mine. But, while he contributed many improvements to the steam engine, especially the locomotive, Trevithick did not succeed in developing a successful railroad for public transportation.

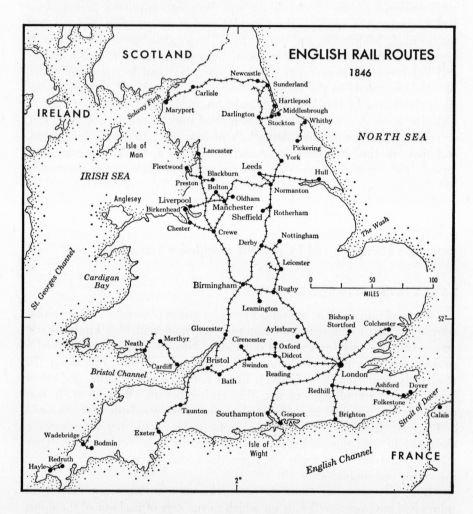

SCOTLAND

ENGLISH RAIL ROUTES
1846

Newcastle
Carlisle
Sunderland
Hartlepool
IRELAND
Maryport
Darlington
Middlesbrough
Stockton
Whitby

NORTH SEA

Isle of Man
Lancaster
Pickering
York
Fleetwood
Leeds
Hull
IRISH SEA
Blackburn
Preston
Bolton
Normanton
Anglesey
Liverpool
Oldham
Birkenhead
Manchester
Sheffield
Rotherham
Chester
Crewe
Nottingham
Derby
The Wash
Leicester

Cardigan Bay
Birmingham
Rugby

0   50   100
MILES

Leamington
Bishop's Stortford
Colchester
52°
Gloucester
Aylesbury
Neath
Merthyr
Cirencester
Oxford
Didcot
Cardiff
Bristol
Swindon
Reading
London
Bristol Channel
Bath
Ashford
Dover
Redhill
Folkestone
Taunton
Southampton
Gosport
Brighton
Calais
Wadebridge
Exeter
Bodmin
Isle of Wight
FRANCE
Redruth
English Channel
Hayle

2°

That honor rests with George Stephenson (1781–1848), who in 1814 made significant improvements on the steam locomotive which lessened its weight and improved its efficiency. In 1825, with Timothy Hackworth and others, Stephenson completed the first successful railroad, the Stockton and Darlington Railroad (see Plate XXXI), originally designed by its promoters as a coal road. Two years later Stephenson enhanced his fame still further when his locomotive, the "Rocket," successfully competed in a race to determine which of several locomotives should be adopted for use on a newly projected railway. This was the Liverpool and Manchester Railway, completed in 1830 with Stephenson as its chief engineer. After 1830 railways became common, gradually being accepted as a means of passenger and general freight transport and not merely as specialized lines for the marketing of coal or other bulky products. The railway age had begun.

The first successful steamboat antedated the railways by a generation. Experimental forerunners were numerous in France, Germany, and the United States. It was in the United States, however, that the first steamboats were perfected at the hands of John Fitch (1743-1798) and Robert Fulton (1765-1815). Fitch was the first to be successful. A veteran of the American Revolution, Fitch had engaged in several unsuccessful ventures before 1785, when he became interested in developing a steamboat and secured financial and legal aid from a group of Philadelphians. His first vessel was successfully launched in 1787 on the Delaware River, and he built two more by 1790 (see Plate XXXI). But his fourth boat was wrecked in a storm (1792) and his financial supporters withdrew their aid. Discouraged, Fitch gave up the project and went as a pioneer to Kentucky, where he died.

Soon afterwards William Symington (1763-1831), an engineer and protégé of the duke of Bridgewater built the *Charlotte Dundas,* a steam-powered paddle-wheel vessel which successfully hauled coal and towed other vessels on the Forth and Clyde Canal for several years after 1802. Robert Fulton, often cited as *the* inventor of the steamboat, saw the *Charlotte Dundas* in operation. Fulton himself began a career as a painter, for which he went to England to study. Later he became interested in mechanics and invention. He was a careful student of canals and canal building, about which he published a very able book (1796). A few years later he tried to interest Napoleon in a submarine which he demonstrated in the Seine River. But Napoleon failed to adopt the device, and in the meantime the American minister to Paris, Robert R. Livingston, commissioned Fulton to build a steamboat (1802). After successful experiments in Paris, Fulton returned to America, and in 1807 sailed his steamboat *Clermont* (powered by an engine made by Boulton and Watt in England) up the Hudson River from New York to Albany. The *Clermont* proved to be the first steamboat which satisfied its promoters financially and, accordingly, it was the first of a long series of steamboats to be commercially successful. Soon steamboats were engaged in coastwise shipping both in Europe and in America. In 1818 the *Savannah* made the first Atlantic crossing, although it had auxiliary sails and ran out of coal before it arrived in port. Actually, the first vessel to cross the ocean entirely by steam power was the Dutch packet *Curaçao,* built at Dover in England and purchased by the Dutch as a mail boat to the West Indies (1827). In 1840 regular transatlantic steamship service began with a fleet of four ships owned by the Cunard Company, founded by Samuel Cunard (1787–1865). By this time steamboats were becoming familiar in most of the rivers and the principal harbors of the world.

6 : Effects of the Industrial Revolution

As THE Industrial Revolution ushered into the world economic, industrial, capitalist, and social movements which have an ever widening and continuing force in our own times, any estimate of its effects must be tentative. Only when the Industrial Revolution has spent is force—if ever it does—its effects may perhaps be assessed with more finality. For it is important to realize that the Industrial Revolution was and is a cumulative affair. It not only engulfed industry after industry in England until, by about 1870, England was almost wholly industrialized and had become the workshop of the world, but also it spread in other countries, similarly moving from industry to industry until it threatened to engulf them all. It had invaded the textile industry of the United States by the 1820's, although its lateral expansion into other industries was not felt until during and after the American Civil War of 1861–1865. It reached Belgium by the 1830's, France by the 1850's, Germany by the 1870's, Russia by the 1890's—although here its full force was not felt until after the Russian Revolution of 1917–18. It continues to spread into India, China, parts of Latin America, Africa, and elsewhere. How can we estimate the effects of such a lively, continuing process?

Still, there have been some interim effects which over the years appear with clarity; others are blurred by the lack of adequate factual information plus conflicting opinions which in some instances have led to bitter dispute.

POPULATION GROWTH AND URBANIZATION

One of the reasonably well-established conclusions is that, as the Industrial Revolution was in some measure the result of population growth and urbanization it also appears to have stimulated further population growth and urbanization—or, at least, it did not retard the movements already under way. The causal relationship between the Industrial Revolution and continued population growth is not established, if indeed it exists; actually, demographers have no satisfactory explanation for the tremendous upsurge in human population during the past three hundred years. But because the Industrial Revolution and the population growth occurred side by side, the normal assumption is that the two phenomena were related.

A glance at the population statistics shown above (page 343) will confirm the fact of continued rapid population expansion, and a glance at the succeeding figures relating to the rise of some of the world's largest cities (page 344) will also confirm the fact of continuing urbanization. In England, and later elsewhere in the world, the Industrial Revolution led to spectacular shifts in population, producing new centers of population density. "The very face of a great country has been remodelled," wrote an English observer in 1833, "various classes of inhabitants [have been] utterly swept away; the habits of all have undergone such vast alterations that they

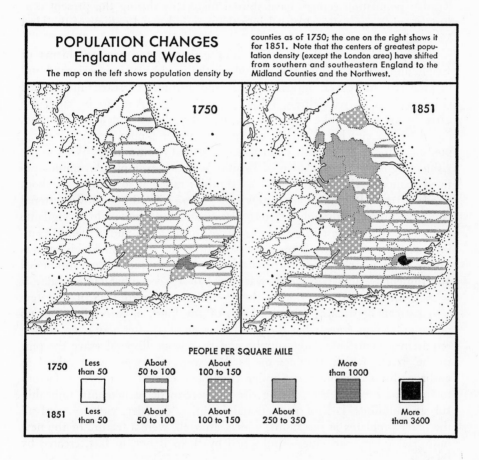

POPULATION CHANGES
England and Wales

The map on the left shows population density by counties as of 1750; the one on the right shows it for 1851. Note that the centers of greatest population density (except the London area) have shifted from southern and southeastern England to the Midland Counties and the Northwest.

1750

1851

PEOPLE PER SQUARE MILE

| 1750 | Less than 50 | About 50 to 100 | About 100 to 150 | | More than 1000 | |
| 1851 | Less than 50 | About 50 to 100 | About 100 to 150 | About 250 to 350 | | More than 3600 |

resemble a people of a different age and generation." In the eighteenth century, when England was still predominantly agrarian, her heaviest population was in the southern and eastern counties; after the Industrial Revolution these population centers changed until today the heaviest population is in the north Midlands and northern England generally, with only a few pockets elsewhere, as London, Bristol, and the coal centers of south Wales. Indeed, as the Industrial Revolution moved into continental Europe and elsewhere, population centers with heavy urbanization grew up around areas in which the raw materials of the new industry, especially iron ore and coal, were concentrated by nature. Thus in France heavy populations have come to concentrate in the valleys of the Seine and the Rhône, as well as in Lorraine; in Germany, in the valleys of the Saar, the Ruhr, and the lower Rhine, with somewhat lesser concentrations in Saxony and Silesia and about Hamburg and Berlin. Other areas in Europe, outside Russia, are Bohemia, northern Italy, and Vienna and Budapest along the Danube. Reputedly, Russian population centers have shifted materially during the present century, moving generally eastward into the new industrial regions of the Ural Mountains.

The sudden growth of large cities gave rise to many problems of supply and urban organization for which the world was inexperienced and ill prepared. Moreover, agrarian values and attitudes persisted and labeled cities as dens of wickedness, iniquity, and disease. And, to be sure, the early boom towns, like their successors today, lacked adequate housing, paved streets, city lights, zoning ordinances, water supply, sewage disposal, police facilities, and the other amenities of settled communities. Witness the rising English industrial town of Birmingham, for example. An unincorporated manorial village originally, its smithies raised it to a town of about 12,000 in 1700. By 1800 it had grown to 70,000—still without any chartered city government, although a Street Commission, a kind of local vigilante committee, did its best to give some order to the town and actually organized a corps of city watchmen in 1801. In 1838, when Birmingham was finally granted a charter of incorporation by which a regularized municipal government became possible, it was a city of 170,000 inhabitants (today it is more than 1,000,000). But in the meantime, prior to 1838, it had few paved streets or squares, few sidewalks of any kind, no street lighting, no police protection (save what the watchmen supplied after 1801), no zoning requirements, no city water supply, and no sewage disposal (save the pigs in the streets, which, troublesome as they were otherwise, were valued as garbage disposal facilities). Similar conditions existed in the new factory towns almost everywhere, giving rise to overcrowded tenements, unhealthful surroundings, lack of recreational facilities, disorder, violence, and all the other problems of the slums, which, after all, were a feature of the new industrial towns and cities—multiplied by them if not, in fact, created by them.

INCREASED WEALTH

The Industrial Revolution, by greatly increasing man's capacities to exploit raw materials and markets, multiplied material wealth rapidly both in terms of capital and of articles for use. By its methods of mass production, clothing, utensils of all kinds, and all manner of consumer goods appeared on the market in unheard-of quantities and, as mass production by machines increased, at lower per unit costs. Lower prices, of course, stimulated consumption and attracted an increasing number of buyers. They also led, in the long-run average, to an increase in the standards of living of almost everyone as measured in the material terms of the per capita consumption of goods. Indeed, had the new wealth been distributed more evenly among the population in the early days of the Industrial Revolution, the material standards of living could have been raised for all to an even greater extent. But this was a problem of social economy about which many disputes have raged and still rage; and it is evident that the world has not yet found a wholly acceptable formula for either "economic justice" or the ideal distribution of wealth. Even so, in most countries where the Industrial Revolution has occurred, the production of goods has caught up with, and sometimes even exceeded, the market needs, a situation the reverse of that which existed in eighteenth-century England. And, as we have noted earlier, in most countries of the Western world today market pressures tend to originate with the producers of goods who seek to sell more rather than with potential buyers who cannot find things to buy.

INTENSIFIED CAPITALISM

As we have already noted, capital and capitalism are ancient features of human society, and the Industrial Revolution took place in a capitalistic society. For the most part, prior to the present century at least, its spread has been at the hands of capitalists operating within a capitalistic framework everywhere. Moreover, the Industrial Revolution magnified and intensified capitalism, and as the revolution spread capitalism seized such a firm grasp upon every economic activity that it tended more and more to bring every aspect of human society within the range of its influence. The factory system required capital in terms of money and credit to construct the factory, equip it with machines, pay the wages of the workers, and operate a business.

Not many early entrepreneurs could personally command enough capital to begin an enterprise without borrowing money from someone else, pooling resources with others (as in partnerships), or organizing stock companies. In most cases, too, they began on a relatively small scale, with little capital and a large financial responsibility in terms of wages, interest to pay on borrowed funds, loans to repay, taxes, and (if a partnership or stock company) profits to share with others whose capital was engaged in the enterprise. In consequence, the number of failures was high, and most of those who managed to survive and remain solvent were operating on a shoestring at the outset. Indeed, the urgent need for capital plagued entrepreneurs for many years as they sought to expand and improve their enterprises in order to exploit a larger market and to seek a larger profit return. Many of them plowed their profits back into their business as a means of plant expansion and improvement, keeping themselves and their families, if not in penury, at least in very modest circumstances. In this fashion, how-ever, they built up industrial capital, a process which, especially in the early days of the Industrial Revolution, was done far more often by a hard-working, thrifty "little fellow" than by a large capitalist who raked in huge profits which he spent in lavish, wasteful living.

As the Industrial Revolution progressed, and as factories and machinery became larger, more complicated, and more costly, the methods of raising capital to finance undertakings altered, and an organized investment system, such as had developed among the bankers and financiers of the late Middle Ages, emerged on a large scale. By this means today entrepreneurs in indus-try and commerce raise the capital they require not only from the opulent few but also from a widely scattered number of small investors whose capital, in the form of savings, stocks, bonds, and life-insurance reserves, is made available through the services of investment banks and bankers, brokers, and the stock exchange. In this fashion, capitalism has extended its influence over an ever increasing number of small investors, for the control of the invested capital that keeps the wheels of industry and commerce turning is exercised by a small body of bankers, brokers, managers, and boards of directors in immediate charge of the various business enterprises. Thus, money supplied by the many becomes employed by the few who establish the policies and manage the enterprise. Whether the few generally manipulate these funds for their own selfish interest, with little or no regard for the many small and widely scattered shareholders and investors who legally constitute the owners of the enterprise, is a moot point. In any case, this form of raising capital slowly replaced the earlier, more direct methods as the necessity for very large capital investments made it impossible for the single entrepreneur, and even the partnership, to command sufficient capital by any other means.

ECONOMIC IMPERIALISM

The Industrial Revolution set the scene for a new outburst of European imperialism. As we shall see in Chapter 25, it did not actually take place until the latter half of the nineteenth century. The events of the half-century of revolutions, especially the revolutions in the Americas, led many Euro-peans to reassess colonial enterprise, with unfavorable conclusions at first. The British in particular soon found that their commerce with the inde-pendent United States of America exceeded that which they had enjoyed when the American states had been colonies in the British Empire and, accordingly, a wide segment of British opinion looked upon colonization with disfavor.

In reality, the new imperialism of the nineteenth century was rather less a matter of settling colonists than a process of economic penetration and capitalistic control, with military and naval forces ready to protect established economic interests. These interests in time were threefold, all of them traceable to the cumulative effects of the Industrial Revolution. In the first place, the Industrial Revolution ultimately enabled European producers to multiply goods beyond the capacity of European markets and their existing overseas outlets to absorb them. Accordingly, about the middle of the nineteenth century European states entered into a savage competitive scramble to stake out market claims, if necessary by direct colonial control, established by military and naval force, in Africa, Asia, the Middle East, and the other "backward" areas of the world. This was, at base, a contest for the control of potential *markets for goods* to supplement those theretofore exploited to the point of saturation. Within a generation, however, a second imperial impulse became evident. This was a matter of seeking imperial controls over backward areas to protect *capital investments* made in the latter regions as a means of developing their economy, that is, to improve harbors, build railroads, and the like. By this time (about 1870 and beyond) surplus capital had developed in Europe and, no longer finding profitable outlets at home, sought investment in other lands. Once investments had been made, or a likely prospect found, the investors demanded from their own government protection and security for their interests. The third form of economic imperialism—and one which had obtained to some extent throughout—was the search for and subsequent control of sources of *raw materials* either wholly unobtainable in the contesting European states or in short supply. This motive became especially evident as new industries arose or new methods developed requiring such things as rubber, aluminum, petroleum, tin, and nickel, most of which were not available in sufficient quantity—if at all—in Europe. All three of these imperialistic impulses operated by the turn of the twentieth century, and later chapters will describe the imperialistic contests which they in part inspired.

SOCIAL CONSEQUENCES

No one is likely to challenge seriously the statement that the Industrial Revolution so fortified the position of the middle class that it became, to all intents and purposes, the aristocracy of the nineteenth century. Just as the French Revolution wiped out the privileged position of the old aristocracy of birth, the Industrial Revolution elevated a new aristocracy of wealth which, because of its wealth and the new structure of society, itself acquired privileges withheld from others. The ascendant bourgeoisie intermarried with the decadent old nobility as the nineteenth century wore on, thereby winning coveted social recognition and prestige for the bourgeoisie and equally coveted capital for the down-at-the-heel nobility. Still, there were tensions between the two groups: the nobility, being for the most part large landowners, had interests which ran counter to those of the bourgeoisie at many points. Usually the landed interests sought high prices for foodstuffs, low taxes on land, and tariffs and tolls on commerce as the chief source of government revenues; whereas the bourgeois industrialists wanted low prices on foodstuffs as a means of justifying the low wages they paid their employees, high taxes on land (lest industrial and commercial sites be over-taxed to make up the difference), and tariffs and tolls on commerce at the lowest point consistent with revenue needs and commercial interests. Increasingly, as the nineteenth century wore on, the middle class dictated the policies of states and, by the end of the century, that old noble aristocracy which remained had so widely identified its interests with the bourgeoisie that those few who had not no longer exerted significant influence. In some respects, those who controlled capital almost controlled the world before the end of the nineteenth century. As the middle class controlled the capital, both their own and, through the investment system, many others', the middle class had become the dominant group in society.

Besides assisting the middle class to become the new aristocracy, the Industrial Revolution gave rise to a new class variously known as the wage-earning class, the working class, the laboring class (laborers or simply "labor"), and later by the Marxian term, the "proletariat." As the factory system arose, most of the agricultural folk dispossessed of their lands by enclosures or other aspects of the agricultural revolution fell into the wage-earning class, together with those household manufacturers and handicraft workers who could no longer compete with the factory system as it invaded their trades. P. Gaskell, writing about *The Manufacturing Population of England* in 1833, stated that both the weavers and the spinners, who, "as they may well be termed during the prosperous days of hand manufacturers, the aristocracy of manufactures," underwent changes during the Industrial Revolution "which modified the whole body and terminated finally in the ruin of the greater portion." In such a fashion was the labor supply drafted for the new factories. Economic forces tore them from their former homes, and forced them to seek employment in the new factory towns where, crowded and ill-housed, they no longer worked in their homes but, "torn from the bosoms of their families," they worked under the disciplined direction of the rising entrepreneurs, often wholly dependent upon wages for a livelihood.

Much has been made of the cruel discipline of the factories, the widespread employment of little children and women, the low wages, and the helpless, hopeless position of the early wage-earners created by the Industrial Revolution. Yet, while there was undoubtedly much to be deplored, if the condition of the new wage-earners in factories be compared with the status of labor before the Industrial Revolution, rather than that which was achieved a century later, the situation appears less indefensible. It is important to remember that the Industrial Revolution effected a social dislocation of wide proportions, that a period of readjustment was necessary, that the hard conditions were part of a transitional period, and that the prevailing social philosophy of laissez faire, together with the fear of the masses generated by radical Jacobin excesses during the French Revolution, left the new wage-earners temporarily stranded at the mercy of their employers.

Moreover, if employers subjected their employees to cruel discipline—and many witnesses attest the fact—it is at least honest to remember that the entrepreneurs were pioneering in an uncharted area of management, that they were often working on a shoestring of capital trying against considerable odds to make a go of a new enterprise; and also that their employees were themselves a dislocated, disgruntled, ignorant lot, even less familiar with what was expected of them than the entrepreneurs themselves. Moreover, although the evidence is not yet all at hand and it is clear that many local differences existed, there is considerable reason to believe that factory workers were better paid than agricultural workers and those who worked in the older centers. Indeed, surveys made in the 1790's stated that rural wages varied conversely with the distance from manufactures. Landlords, farmers, and other employers complained loudly that the wages in factories were higher than elsewhere and the rapid migration of workers to factory towns suggests a similar conclusion. Actually, subsistence wages obtained almost everywhere, and the laboring poor were not expected, even by the social theorists of the day, to earn more. The employment of women and children in the factories was no innovation, for women and children commonly worked in farming and in both domestic and handicraft manufactures. Arthur Young set forth a model family budget for farmers in which he assumed that the farmer's wife would earn a fourth as much as the farmer, a child of ten as much as the mother, and a child of fifteen as much as the father. Nor were the conditions of work in the factories, bad as they undeniably were, worse than those of laborers on farms or in household manufactures. Most of the concern for the wage-earners in the early factories arose from an awakened social conscience of a later age.

Still, within the framework of the times there were factors in the circumstances of early factory workers which led to understandable complaints on their part. Many of them were dislocated families, victims of the agricultural revolution or of the failure of a hand-manufacturing enterprise. Few persons, caught up in such circumstances, are likely to be content with their lot. Moreover, they had left their old homes, which often had included a garden plot (a useful complement to diet and budget), for the raw factory towns, where they seldom found adequate housing and almost never had a garden. Under the factory system, the family worked away from home, usually separately and not as a unit, to both of which circumstances they were unaccustomed. Further, while the hours of work were no longer than those in agriculture or in the hand manufactures, they were regularized, and workers had to operate by the clock, arriving at work at an appointed time, having so much time for lunch, and quitting work on signal. Besides this regimentation, to which many had not been accustomed hitherto, they were constantly supervised, often driven in their work, and disciplined by fines and even corporal punishment if they were careless, indolent, or made honest mistakes. Being unaccustomed to such unremitting discipline (although former handicraft workers must have experienced something like it during their apprenticeship or at the hands of a severe master), they resented it and in some cases exaggerated its severity. Lastly, as has often been pointed out, the wage-earner was insecure, wholly dependent upon his wages for his livelihood and with no cushion to tide him over periods of illness or unemployment. This, of course, was generally true, yet the factory worker was little worse off in this respect than the workers in agriculture or the hand manufactures save, perhaps, his lack of a garden plot. Traditionally, in England, the farm worker, together with the apprentices and journeymen of the handicraft trades, had been protected in some measure against hard times by such laws as the Statute of Apprentices (1563) and the Poor Law of 1601—plus the customary feudal rights such as use of the commons. But the English system of poor relief had broken down long before the factory system became widespread. Especially was it non-operative in the new factory towns. The agricultural revolution had practically abolished all feudal rights, and the machinations of parish officers generally rendered the poor law worthless in order to keep down the poor rates. Obviously, England needed to revise its laws regulating the care of the poor, and in the course of the nineteenth century this was done. Even so, the doctrine of laissez faire, so widely held, was inimical to an active sense of social responsibility. Until such a sense had developed, the poor were dependent upon whatever compassion their condition generated in the hearts of their more fortunate fellows and upon the vicissitudes of the market which their employers sought to supply.

However, by their concentration in ever enlarging numbers in the factory towns, wage-earners were enabled to make beginnings of organized self-help. They suffered, of course, from the lack of experienced, or even adequate leadership, and everywhere labor unions, as we understand the word today, were held strictly illegal, condemned by law and innumerable court decisions as unjustifiable "combinations in restraint of trade." Similarly, the weapons of a later labor movement were denied to them: collective bargaining, strikes, and the like were held illegal and severely punishable. Nonetheless, wage-earners were able, within the law, to organize friendly societies for charitable, co-operative self-help. Some churches, especially the new Methodists, espoused their cause, and gradually the need for labor legislation with a sense of greater realism and social responsibility was driven into peoples' consciousness. However, the labor movement, with its labor laws and court decisions, belongs to a later chapter. Suffice it to say for the present that the nucleus of the movement was born before 1800, its membership and the urgencies of its demands being largely among the effects of the Industrial Revolution.

Considered as a whole, the Industrial Revolution created and set in motion most of the aspects of modern industrial society. Subsequent revolutions in industry, commerce, and financing have taken place—such as the mechanization of agriculture, the new revolution in transportation effected by the automobile and aircraft, the revolution in communications following upon the telegraph, the telephone, radio, and television, and the revolution in business methods characterized by the enlargement of business capitalization and enterprise by means of trusts, cartels, and other combinations. Still, these are mostly differences in degree, not in kind, and they serve merely to emphasize the continuing incidence of the Industrial Revolution.

Further Reading

Arnold Toynbee, *The Industrial Revolution* (Boston: Beacon, 1956), is the reprint of the noted lectures. A scholarly survey of England for the period is Thomas S. Ashton, *An Economic History of England: the Eighteenth Century* (London: Methuen, 1955). The same author's *The Industrial Revolution, 1760–1830* ("Home University Library") (New York: Oxford Univ. Press, 1954), is a short, general picture of the new changes. A more extended study is Arthur Redford, *The Economic History of England, 1760–1860* (New York: Longmans, 1931). *Studies in the Development of Capitalism* (New York: International Publishers, 1947), by Maurice Dobb, is a competent work.

Alexander Carr-Saunders, *World Population; Past Growth and Present Trends* (New York: Oxford Univ. Press, 1937), discusses the causes and consequences of the expansion of population over the last three hundred years, while Mabel Buer in *Health, Wealth and Population in the Early Days of the Industrial Revolution* (London: Routledge, 1926) studies the growth and expansion of the population between 1760 and 1815. *The Village Laborer, 1760–1832* (New York: Longmans, 1920), by J. L. and Barbara Hammond, is an excellent study of the life of the poor prior to the reforms of 1830. Lord Ernle, *English Farming, Past and Present* (5th ed.; New York: Longmans, 1936), is a standard work. The enclosure movement of the eighteenth and nineteenth centuries is evaluated by Gilbert Slater in *The English Peasantry and the Enclosure of Common Fields* (London: Constable, 1907). There is a large amount of interesting material in Edward C. Gonner, *Common Land and Enclosure* (London: Macmillan, 1912). George Fussell traces the history of the farmer's implements before the advent of the tractor in *The Farmer's Tools, 1500–1900* (London: Melrose, 1952).

Paul Mantoux, *The Industrial Revolution in the Eighteenth Century* (rev. ed.; New York: Harcourt, 1929), trans. by Marjorie Vernon, is essential to any study. Witt Bowden, *Industrial Society Towards the End of the Eighteenth Century* (New York: Macmillan, 1925), deals with forces which brought about the transition and social changes. *The Rise of Modern Industry* (8th ed.; London: Methuen, 1948), by J. L. and Barbara Hammond, gives an idea of the causes and significance of the revolution. A brief introduction to the cotton industry is George W. Daniels, *The Early English Cotton Industry* (New York: Longmans, 1920). A broadly conceived study of the same industry is Alfred P. Wadsworth, *The Cotton Trade and Industrial Lancashire, 1600–1780* (Manchester: Manchester Univ. Press, 1931). Erich Roll, *An Early Experiment in Industrial Organization, Being a History of the Firm of Boulton and Watt, 1775–1805* (New York: Longmans, 1930), is a lucid account of all the details of the organization; G. D. H. Cole, *Life of Robert Owen* (2d ed.; New York: Macmillan, 1930), is a brief history of the early years of Owen's labors at the New Lanark mills. A sense of reality is achieved by George Unwin in *Samuel Oldknow and the Arkwrights; the Industrial Revolution in Stockport and Marple* (New York: Longmans, 1924).

Abbott P. Usher, *History of Mechanical Inventions* (Cambridge, Mass.: Harvard Univ. Press, 1954), presents some of the developments from the time of the Greeks to the present. S. T. McCloy, *French Inventions of the Eighteenth Century* (Lexington: Univ. of Kentucky Press, 1954), discusses the French contributions. John Nef, *Rise of the British Coal Industry,* 2 vols. (London: Routledge, 1932), is a lucid, detailed study of developments between 1550 and 1700. Another important work, and indispensable for an adequate appreciation, is Thomas S. Ashton, *The Coal Industry of the Eighteenth Century* (Manchester: Manchester Univ. Press, 1929). The same author's *Iron and Steel in the Industrial Revolution* (2d. ed.; Manchester: Manchester Univ. Press, 1951) is based on original sources and provides interesting reading.

Lillian C. Knowles, *Industrial and Commercial Revolutions in Great Britain during the Nineteenth Century* (4th ed.; New York: Dutton, 1921), is a sound general survey. J. H. Clapham, *Economic History of Modern Britain: the Early Railway Age, 1820–1850* (New York: Macmillan, 1927), is a veritable encyclopedia for the period. An important contribution to the record of industry and transport is Henry W. Dickinson, *A Short History of the Steam Engine* (New York: Macmillan, 1939). John Lord, *Capital and Steam-Power, 1750–1800* (London: King, 1923), is largely based on the papers of the pioneer engineering firm of Boulton and Watt. An interesting study, complete with illustrations, is Charles Hadfield, *British Canals* (London: Phoenix House, 1950). *Poor John Fitch; Inventor of the Steamboat* (New York: Putnam, 1935), by Thomas Boyd, is a biography of the unsuccessful and eccentric inventor. Margaret Rose (McAdam) Pember-Devereux has written a short and fascinating biography of her ancestor, *The Colossus of Roads; a Life of John Loudon McAdam* (New York: Oxford Univ.

Press, 1936). *From Trackway to Turnpike* (New York: Oxford Univ. Press, 1928), by Gilbert Sheldon, is a study of roads in Devon.

Lillian C. Knowles, *Economic Development in the Nineteenth Century* (London: Routledge, 1932), discusses the spread of the Revolution in France, Germany, and the United States. A fairly compact outline of the economic developments in France and Germany is J. H. Clapham, *Economic Development of France and Germany, 1815–1914* (4th ed.; New York: Macmillan, 1936). Henri E. Sée, *Economic and Social Conditions in France During the Eighteenth Century,* trans. by E. Zeydel (New York: Knopf, 1927), is a readable, well-balanced study. A sweeping survey of the rise and development of "security capitalism" is George W. Edwards, *The Evolution of Finance Capitalism* (New York: Longmans, 1938). Gilbert Hubbard and D. Baring offer a careful account of the rise of industrialization in Japan, China, and India and its repercussions on England in *Eastern Industrialization and the Effect on the West* (New York: Oxford Univ. Press, 1935). The activity of British merchants in China is studied by Michael Greenberg, *British Trade and the Opening of China, 1800–42* (London: Cambridge Univ. Press, 1951). Alfred Krupp, *Krupp, a Great Business Man Seen Through His Letters,* ed. by William Berdrow, trans. by E. W. Dickes (New York: Dial, 1930), depicts the career and character of the German steel magnate between 1826 and 1887. Egon Corti, *Rise of the House of Rothschild,* trans. by Brian and Beatrix Lunn (New York: Cosmopolitan, 1928), traces the rise and development of this great international banking family.

Chapter 24

THE LIBERAL ERA

1815-1871

A DIFFERENT Europe emerged from the fires of the French Revolution and the Napoleonic era. More than twenty years of war had destroyed the political structure of enlightened despotism, intensified the economic effects of industrialism, and altered the traditional class structure of continental life. The conservative statesmen who gathered in Vienna in 1814 might dream of a return to the stable civic order which European society had known under the *ancien régime,* but there could be no turning back the clock. The eighteenth century was over, and the legitimists of Metternich's school soon discovered that a new age had opened which pursued its own goals by its own methods.

1 : The Conflict of Ideologies

THE CHANGED social environment in which men found themselves after the restoration of peace was bound to alter their civic faith. In the benign atmosphere of the Enlightenment it was easy to believe that some day a philosopher-king would exercise his absolute authority to inaugurate a humanitarian millennium on earth. But after the terrible ordeal of revolution and warfare which ended at Waterloo such a hope began to seem naïve. The great doctrinal need of the new age was a statement of belief voicing its distinctive political ideals and aspirations.

LIBERALISM

The ideology which best expressed the dominant mood of this new age was liberalism. To the middle class of Europe it brought a view of man and society which harmonized with its own experiences and interests. It condemned the aristocratic bias of the benevolent absolutism of the preceding century without embracing the egalitarian principle of Jacobinism. While it sought to deprive the landed nobility of its monopoly of political influence, it did not flirt with the great unwashed who respected neither life nor property. It followed the path of what the French called the *justemilieu,* the straight and narrow path between despotism on the right and radicalism on the left. Wherever the factory system went, the industrial bourgeoisie followed, and behind the industrial bourgeoisie came liberalism.

Theoretically, liberalism relied on the political teachings of the Age of Enlightenment which justified opposition to royal tyranny—the teachings of Locke, Voltaire, and Montesquieu (see pages 202, 208, and 218). Practically, it drew on the experiences of the revolutions of the seventeenth century in England and the eighteenth century in America and France. It maintained that government was based on a social contract between governor and governed, by which the latter agreed to obey the former in return for protection of the inalienable rights of the individual. Among these rights—guaranteed by God and nature alike—were life, liberty, property, and the freedom of speech, press, petition, assembly, and religion. The state was limited in its power over the citizen, for it could not deprive him of fundamental privileges which were his birthright. One of the most famous liberal documents, the American Declaration of Independence, argued that "all men are created equal," equal in the sense that they all possess as their natural heritage lifelong personal rights. It therefore followed that instruments of political repression and censorship, laws conferring special privileges on hereditary aristocracies, and legal discriminations because of race or religion were unjustifiable in theory and evil in effect. Individual freedom was the hallmark of liberalism.

Yet if all men were equal in the protection which they enjoyed against oppression, that did not mean that they were equal in the right to direct state policy. It was self-evident that the ignorant, the stupid, the reckless, and the subversive could not be entrusted with the determination of the fate of a nation. Only those who had proved their ability and intelligence ought to have a voice in government, and the best way to prove ability and intelligence was to accumulate property. In a speech before the French legislature the eminent liberal statesman François Guizot described his formula for social progress with disarming simplicity: *"Enrichissez-vous!"* [get rich!]. For Guizot, as for most liberals, the best of all governments was a constitutional monarchy, in which the king reigned without ruling and in which the masses obeyed without controlling. The state should retain the trappings of royalty, because they gave the nation a sense of tradition and stability. But the real power behind the throne ought to be a parliament elected by a highly propertied suffrage. The ruler might perform the executive functions of government: he might appoint civil and military officials; he might conduct foreign affairs; he might even declare war and conclude peace. All legislative enactments, however, especially the adoption of budgets, must have the approval of a parliamentary assembly representing the well-to-do elements of society. Ideally, moreover, the functions of the crown should be exercised by a ministry appointed by the monarch but responsible to the legislature. Since the crown was to enjoy the shadow but not the substance of authority, and since the masses were to be carefully excluded from a voice in government, the dominant role in the state would fall to the main beneficiary of industrialism, the educated and propertied bourgeoisie.

In economics as well as in politics, liberalism preached an individualistic freedom and reflected middle-class interests. Rejecting the mercantilistic theories of the preceding age, it advanced the principles of laissez faire propounded by the classical school of English economists. From Adam Smith's *The Wealth of Nations,* published in 1776 (see page 217), it borrowed the view that the free competition of nations and individuals, unrestrained by protective duties and monopolistic practices, must in the long run result in the greatest possible economic well-being of society. For the enlightened self-interest of millions of individuals engaged in the pursuit of profit would lead each to seek gain in that branch of industry or agriculture for which he was best fitted, and the consumer would be the beneficiary of this natural economic specialization. From Thomas Malthus' *Essay on the Principles of Population* (1798) liberalism learned that the unemployment, hunger, and suffering which followed in the wake of the Industrial Revolution were not the result of economic dislocation caused by the factory system, but the natural and inevitable outcome of the laws of population growth. Since men tended to multiply at a faster rate than their food supply, providence itself arranged for the re-establishment of a balance between population and nourishment by such means as wars, epidemics, and famines. Finally, the dismal science of laissez faire economics accepted the doctrine advanced by David Ricardo in his *Principles of Political Economy* (1817) that the wages of labor are governed by a natural "iron law" with which man cannot tamper. They will not fall below the subsistence level, for then the worker will be unable or unwilling to perform his job. But neither can they rise above that point of remuneration at which the laboring population increases so rapidly that a shortage of work develops and wages fall once again:

> There is no means of improving the lot of the worker except by limiting the number of his children. His destiny is in his own hands. Every suggestion which does not tend to the reduction in number of the working people is useless, to say the least of it. All legislative interference must be pernicious.

DEMOCRACY

Armed with a consistent philosophy of state and society, liberalism marched forth into the nineteenth century to remake the world in its own image. But its outlook was too narrow and its interest too exclusive to win the support of all opponents of royal absolutism. Among the lower middle class, among small businessmen, petty shopowners, independent tradesmen, lawyers, journalists, and intellectuals, there arose an ideology known variously as radicalism in England, republicanism in France, and democracy in Germany. It, too, condemned the teachings of divine-right monarchism, but it sought to replace them with the tenets of the Jacobin Republic of Virtue (see pages 261–65). Its heroes were not Locke and Washington, but Rousseau and Robespierre. It spoke of the sovereignty of the general will, it approved manhood suffrage, it favored a republican form of government, and it advocated governmental measures to improve the lot of the masses through the supervision and regulation of economic life. It believed in the freedom of the individual and in the sanctity of private property no less firmly than liberalism, but it also argued that a stable government must be based on the consent of that "rabble" which middle-of-the-road bourgeois statesmen regarded with contempt. In the final analysis, it was prepared to subordinate property rights and even personal rights to the ideal of the greatest good of the greatest number.

Throughout the early nineteenth century the democrats remained a persecuted political faction opposed by both conservatives and liberals. In Great Britain William Cobbett spent two years in jail and Jeremy Bentham found himself under attack as a dangerous subverter of society. In France Godefroy Cavaignac and A. A. Ledru-Rollin were subjected to police surveillance and bureaucratic harassment. In Italy the views of the exiled radical Giuseppe Mazzini were propagated by a small band of his devoted followers who often paid for their convictions with imprisonment. In Germany Gustav von Struve and Friedrich Hecker were forced to disguise their republican leanings behind a façade of subtle innuendoes. Only after 1870 did democracy become a respectable political faith in Europe capable of exerting a significant influence over national parliaments and over the voting public.

SOCIALISM

At first the industrial worker was in sympathy with the teachings of democracy. The conservatives preached to him only the virtues of obedience and piety, while the liberals made little effort to disguise their distaste for the lower classes. The urban proletariat, therefore, was favorably disposed toward a radicalism which advocated manhood suffrage and social equality. Before long, however, its attention was attracted to another political doctrine. If liberalism was essentially the ideology of the mill owner, socialism became the ideology of the mill hand. By the end of the nineteenth century it had emerged as the secular faith of the European worker, who often sacrificed for its sake his religious belief and his dynastic loyalty. In return, it provided him with a purpose and an ideal; it explained his sorrows and resentments;

it assured him of a final judgment which would avenge his years of oppression. In the meantime he could attend socialist party meetings, relax at socialist party dances, find a wife in the socialist party women's auxiliary, take his family to the socialist party picnics, pay his medical bills through the socialist party sickness insurance, and be sure that eventually the expenses of his burial would be paid through the socialist party funeral fund. Socialism was more than an ideology, more than a movement; it was a way of life.

The basic notion of socialism—the notion that the government ought to destroy the profit motive as the driving force of economic life by assuming ownership of the means of production and transportation—had its roots in antiquity. But only since the advent of industrialism had it been able to acquire a consistent theoretical foundation. The factory system had given birth to a new class in Western society, the industrial proletariat. Torn from its roots in the village and unassimilated by the older urban population, it was in need of a social philosophy to define its position in the community. Socialism satisfied that need. It brought a measure of hope and a sense of security to those millions who had abandoned a rural way of life followed by their ancestors for centuries to find a new existence in the slums of London or Paris or Berlin or Vienna. Its successes must be explained in terms not of its economic teachings, which were as a matter of fact open to serious criticism, but of the emotional satisfactions which it provided for the uprooted and the dispossessed who were the spiritual victims of the Industrial Revolution.

The earliest exponents of modern socialism were usually men of upper or middle-class origin, who for humanitarian reasons sought to eliminate the economic hardships which accompanied the factory system. They shunned mob violence and class conflict; they were even ready under certain circumstances to tolerate a degree of capitalism. What they wanted was the creation of a system of voluntary co-operative ownership of industrial enterprises, in which the advantages of communal proprietorship would soon become self-evident. Count Henri de Saint-Simon and Étienne Cabet described imaginary societies in which men lived and worked not for selfish profit but for the common good. Charles Fourier and Louis Blanc presented detailed blueprints of socialistic communities and undertakings which could offer the individual economic security and personal satisfaction. Robert Owen tried to translate these plans into reality by founding an experimental colony in New Harmony, Indiana (1825–28). But the pioneer socialists relied almost invariably on methods of popular education and appeals to philanthropic sentiment for the realization of their schemes. Only occasionally would some hard-bitten conspirator like "Gracchus" Babeuf or Filippo Buonarotti secretly plot for the violent overthrow of existing society and the establishment of a communistic social order.

It was Karl Marx (1818–1883) who molded the diffuse visions of the early socialists into a disciplined system of thought. Member of a scholarly

At the time of this photograph Marx was leading the drab existence of a political exile in London. Ignored and embittered, he managed to support his family only through the generosity of friends. Yet the gentleman with the formidable beard, who spent his days in the British Museum studying economics and philosophy, was one of the intellectual architects of the modern world. After he died his apocalyptic vision of a future society free from human exploitation became the basis of a secular religion which millions embraced.

Until his empire collapsed in 1870 Napoleon III was the great enigma of Europe. Always planning some sensational political coup, he mystified the diplomats of other countries and sometimes of his own as well. Queen Victoria thought him too clever to be trusted, but fascinating. Tsar Nicholas I made little effort to disguise his dislike of a ruler whom he considered an upstart. But perhaps the shrewdest characterization of the French emperor came from Bismarck: "a great unrecognized incapacity."

Even the physical appearance of the enigmatic tsar has been a subject of controversy among historians. According to Leonid I. Strakhovsky, "his noble, tall and majestic figure, often inclined in graceful posture reminiscent of ancient statues, was . . . exceptionally well built." Harold Nicolson, on the other hand, maintains that "above the high gold collar, below the vast green hat worn sideways under its cascade of cock feathers, [was] the face of a pale benignant calf." This portrait, painted by the eminent artist Sir Thomas Lawrence, suggests that Nicolson is perhaps closer to the truth.

A self-made man who rose from frontiersman to president, Jackson is one of the folk heroes of the American West. The brand of democracy which he preached emphasized the political primacy of the majority and the economic freedom of the individual. These key doctrines did not originate with him, but he became their champion and symbol. As for his stand on the sectional controversy, he summed it up in the toast which he proposed at a dinner in 1830: "Our Federal Union—it must be preserved!"

Jewish family in the Rhineland, eloquent, brilliant, and supremely self-confident, the radical publicist was contemptuous of the ideological fuzziness of "utopian" theorists like Saint-Simon or Fourier. They had spent their lives composing pleas, exhortations, sermons, and lectures. He based his views on rigidly logical argumentation, on what he himself called "science." Socialism, he maintained, was not only desirable; it was inevitable. It would be achieved not by dignified appeals to benevolent sentiments, but through the process of history itself. For history was determined by the conflict of economic forces which shaped the character of human society. In ancient times the class struggle between slave and master had settled the fate of Greece and Rome. In the Middle Ages serf and lord became the protagonists in a titanic battle which gave birth to the Modern Age. At present, it was the capitalist and the proletarian who were locked in combat for the mastery of the world. But the outcome was not in doubt. The laboring masses had to conquer; the entire course of the economic development of the West guaranteed that. As for the individual, he could enlist on the side of destiny and help hasten its progress, or resist it and be crushed. In any case, the capitalistic order would be overthrown to make way for the classless society of economic and social justice.

As a matter of fact, Marx maintained, capitalism was already digging its own grave. Through ruthless competition, through periodic financial crises, through merciless exploitation, the rich were becoming richer and fewer, the poor poorer and more numerous. The process of bourgeois self-destruction would culminate in a revolution toppling established governments which represented only the interests of the capitalists, and preparing the ground for a new economy free from oppression. In the *Communist Manifesto,* which Marx and his friend Friedrich Engels published in 1848, the new "scientific" socialism threw down the gauntlet to the bourgeoisie of Europe: "Let the ruling classes tremble at a Communistic revolution. The proletarians have nothing to lose but their chains. They have a world to win. Workingmen of all countries, unite!" While for men of property Marxism preached only eternal warfare, to the proletariat it brought a gospel, a messiah, and a promise of a socialist paradise. Countless workers in all countries embraced the new faith, followed it, practiced it, and sometimes died for it.

CONSERVATISM

While liberal, democrat, and socialist vied for the allegiance of the new forces in European life, conservatism was vainly trying to protect the old order. But in grappling with the political and social effects of the French Revolution and the Industrial Revolution it was forced to seek a new ideological foundation. The familiar arguments of divine-right absolutism made less and less sense in an age which had seen anointed monarchs fleeing before republican armies and libertarian ideals. Something different was

Rulers and Régimes of
The Leading States of Europe Since 1815

AUSTRIA
Francis I, 1792–1835
Ferdinand I, 1835–1848
Francis Joseph, 1848–1916
Charles I, 1916–1918
Republican Régime, 1918–1938
Union with Germany, 1938–1945
Republican Régime, since 1945

ENGLAND
George III, 1760–1820
George IV, 1820–1830
William IV, 1830–1837
Victoria, 1837–1901
Edward VII, 1901–1910
George V, 1910–1936
Edward VIII, 1936
George VI, 1936–1952
Elizabeth II, since 1952

FRANCE
Louis XVIII, 1814–1824
Charles X, 1824–1830
Louis Philippe, 1830–1848
  (Orléanist Monarchy)
The Second Republic, 1848–1852
Napoleon III, 1852–1870
  (the Second Empire)
The Third Republic, 1870–1940
Pétain Régime, 1940–1944
Provisional Government, 1944–1946
The Fourth Republic, 1946–1958
The Fifth Republic, since 1958

GERMANY
William I, 1871–1888
Frederick III, 1888
William II, 1888–1918
The Weimar Republic, 1918–1933
The Third Reich, 1933–1945
Military Government, 1945–1949
The Federal Republic (West) and the
  Democratic Republic (East),
  since 1949

ITALY
Victor Emmanuel II, 1861–1878
Humbert I, 1878–1900
Victor Emmanuel III, 1900–1946
  (Mussolini Régime, 1922-1943)
Humbert II, 1946
Republican Régime, since 1946

PRUSSIA
Frederick William III, 1797–1840
Frederick William IV, 1840–1861
William I, 1861–1888
Part of United Germany, since 1871

RUSSIA
Alexander I, 1801–1825
Nicholas I, 1825–1855
Alexander II, 1855–1881
Alexander III, 1881–1894
Nicholas II, 1894–1917
Provisional Government, 1917
Communist Régime, since 1917

SARDINIA
Victor Emmanuel I, 1802–1821
Charles Felix, 1821–1831
Charles Albert, 1831–1849
Victor Emmanuel II, 1849–1878
Part of United Italy, since 1861

needed to defend established institutions like the throne and the altar, and that something was the doctrine of political romanticism. To the teachings of individual freedom which attracted the bourgeoisie, to the visions of a classless society which were held out before the proletariat the Restoration replied with a new emphasis on history and tradition. The individual, it argued, cannot live by the paper schemes and perfectionist plans which the doctrinaire theorist never tires of spinning. He must have his roots in his country and in the unique national heritage of which he is a part. The proposition that all men are equal is meaningless, because as a matter of fact men differ in speech, in culture, in religion, in nationality, in property, in education, and in outlook. To pretend that these differences do not exist is to destroy the foundations of society and invite anarchy. The historic institutions of a people—its monarchy, its church, its aristocracy, its government—are living bonds between past and present. They cannot be uprooted with impunity, for on them depends the spiritual and physical well-being of the individual and the nation.

These views sounded eminently sensible to those who had a vested interest in the status quo. The landed nobility, the military caste, the aristocratic bureaucracy, and the established church agreed with the new conservatism, which differed from the old in its language but not in its objective. They found, moreover, important intellectual allies among romanticist political thinkers who sought a refuge from war and revolution in traditional institutions. The most important of them was Edmund Burke (1729–1797), who as early as 1790 had warned the world in his *Reflections on the Revolution in France* that a nation which destroyed its roots in the past in order to attempt to achieve some impossible ideal of constitutional perfection would end by drifting into chaos and then dictatorship. Under the Restoration this argument was repeated over and over again by Louis de Bonald in France, Karl Ludwig von Haller in Switzerland, Adam Müller in Germany, and Friedrich Gentz in Austria. Yet although kings endorsed it, clergymen propounded it, and aristocrats defended it, romanticist conservatism failed to change history. As the years wore on, it grew progressively weaker, expiring at last, quietly, some time before 1914. Even afterwards coteries of intellectual reactionaries continued to dabble in its philosophy, and some of its spirit and vocabulary was taken over by the fascist movement. But by the early twentieth century it had ceased to exist as a vital political force in its own right.

2 : Western Europe

IF THE nineteenth century was the heroic age of liberalism, western Europe was its land of promise. There, nature and history had collaborated to create those conditions which are particularly conducive to the development of representative government. The factory system was raising the standard of living and improving the level of education. The political and social domination of the landed aristocracy had been weakened by revolution and industrialization. And a vigorous and courageous middle class was prepared to lead the struggle against absolutism. It was thus understandable that liberal institutions should find an especially favorable environment on the northeastern and northwestern shores of the Atlantic.

GREAT BRITAIN

In the years after Waterloo Great Britain succeeded in gradually transforming itself from an oligarchy governed by the well-to-do into a democracy ruled by the people. What is more, it effected this change without bloodshed and without lasting bitterness. In the seventeenth century it had affirmed the principle that Parliament is supreme in the field of legislation. In the eighteenth century it had invented the device of responsible cabinet government, by which Parliament was also able to control the executive branch of government. In the nineteenth century it democratized its political institutions and achieved a new sense of social responsibility.

Even before the French Revolution a group of young reformers—Tories as well as Whigs—had begun to agitate for a thoroughgoing change in governmental policy. The younger William Pitt, Edmund Burke, and Charles James Fox among others were urging an expansion of the suffrage, a reduction of tariff rates, and the extension of full political rights to Catholics. But the war with France which broke out in 1793 put an end to the reform movement by enlisting all national energies in the defense effort and causing every demand for change to seem like the first step to revolution. In 1815 England emerged from its ordeal victorious and strong, but completely dominated by the spirit of unbending conservatism which held sway among the Tory statesmen in control of Parliament.

The immediate post-war years were a period of bitter conflict between the masses, clamoring for political and economic reform, and the government, determined to resist all innovation. A revolution led by the radicals and supported by the lower classes remained a distinct possibility, even after some of the more moderate Tories succeeded in lowering the import duties on grain, revising the harsh criminal code, and emancipating Roman Catholics and Non-conformists. It was only after the Whigs came to power in 1830 that the opposition to reform was finally forced back. In 1832 the most important English parliamentary enactment of the nineteenth century gave the vote and the political balance of power to the industrial middle class. The following year slavery was abolished throughout the British Empire, and the agitation of Christian humanitarians like William Wilberforce was crowned with success. At the same time the government began to reduce illiteracy and combat radicalism among the masses by extending financial assistance to church schools. In 1834 the poor laws were revised; in 1835 municipal government was liberalized; and in 1836 the right of counsel in court proceedings was extended.

While the urban bourgeoisie was the chief beneficiary of this decade of reform, the industrial proletariat also won important concessions from a government anxious to maintain social stability. In 1833 the first measure to regulate successfully the employment of children in factories was adopted with the aid of conservative landowners and over the opposition of liberal industrialists. And in 1846 the corn laws—the tariff duties on imported grain which tended to inflate the cost of living—were finally repealed. Thereafter, Great Britain was a stronghold of free trade for almost a century. Yet the demands of the worker for the right to vote remained unfulfilled another twenty years. Neither the Liberals nor the Conservatives, as the Whigs and Tories were now called, were ready to entrust their fortunes to the masses. In vain did the radicals during the 1840's present to Parliament the People's Charter, a petition calling for universal manhood suffrage, secret ballot, and equal electoral districts. Only after the middle of the century did the notion of admitting the lower classes to the franchise come to be seriously considered in well-to-do circles. The Liberals were the first to make a cautious effort in this direction. But it was the Conservatives who, refusing to be outdone by their rivals, took the leap in the dark. In 1867 they promulgated another great suffrage bill enfranchising the workers of the cities, and Great Britain crossed the dividing line between liberalism and democracy.

The years of reform at home were also years of prestige abroad. With a full treasury, a powerful navy, and a natural defense against invasion, the English government could play a vital role in the colonial affairs of the world and even on the European continent itself. After the collapse of the Quintuple Alliance in 1822, it managed to prevent an attempt to reconquer the Spanish colonies in the New World. In the 1830's England won a guarantee of the independence and neutrality of Belgium. It intervened time and time again in the Near East to protect Turkey against the ambitious designs of the Russians. It actively participated in diplomatic conflicts and settlements involving Spain, Portugal, Denmark, Germany, and Italy. The man who was most influential in the conduct of the foreign policy of Great Britain was Lord Palmerston (1784-1865), a Liberal statesman who personified those qualities of aggressive confidence and moral self-righteousness characteristic of the English public in the nineteenth century. The masses cheered "Old Pam," as he assured them that he would make the name of Briton mean in the modern world what the name of Roman had meant in the ancient. On the Continent, however, among princes and statesmen tired of the posturing and swaggering in London, there was a less complimentary view of the United Kingdom's leading diplomat:

And if the devil have a son,
Then his name is surely Palmerston.

Towering over this age of British progress and prosperity was the figure of Queen Victoria. A woman of narrow outlook and limited understanding, she yet reflected perfectly the mood of the self-satisfied bourgeoisie which dominated her reign. In her middle-class respectability and simple piety the public recognized itself, and in singing the praises of the monarch it was extolling its own virtues. Ruler and people harmonized so completely that her name became permanently associated with her era. Her husband, the German Prince Albert, was less fortunate. The English always looked upon him with a jaundiced eye, because he was more interested in practical politics than seemed proper in a member of royalty, because he hoped to reassert a measure of monarchic influence over parliamentary life, and worst of all, because he was a foreigner. But he died in 1861, and thereafter nothing stood between the ruler and her subjects. By the end of the long reign—which extended from 1837 to 1901—she had become a national institution, a motherly symbol to a people which could remember no other sovereign. For most Britons, the Victorian Era was a golden age in which their country advanced steadily toward greater economic well-being and diplomatic influence.

FRANCE

Across the English Channel in France political development was not as placid. The French Revolution had left physical and psychological wounds which even a century of national progress could not heal. It had made the aristocracy more reactionary, the lower classes more radical, the bourgeoisie more ambitious. Whereas behind Great Britain lay a long tradition of peaceful compromise, in France there were bitter memories of a profligate court and the revolutionary guillotine. Social antagonisms were greater and sharper, and a readiness to use force in order to achieve change was more widespread than in Great Britain. Yet France also had more verve, more reckless idealism than her neighbor. English political writers were always ready to sermonize about Gallic instability and lack of serious purpose, but they tended to overlook the profound belief of the French in political principle.

In 1814, however, many Frenchmen had been ready to compromise their principle and accept a restoration of the Bourbons. Exhausted by revolutions and wars, they saw in the stodgy Louis XVIII (1814–1824) a welcome change from the extravagant ambitions of Napoleon. The new king, brother of the unhappy Louis XVI and uncle of the uncrowned "Louis XVII" who had died in 1795 in a republican prison, had learned something from the misfortunes of his family. Behind an unimpressive exterior was a sharp mind which recognized that the past could not be brought back to life. He granted his subjects a constitutional charter establishing a legislature dominated by the well-to-do; he refused to revoke the legal equality of all citizens introduced by the Code Napoléon; he made no effort to restore the lands of the aristocracy which the peasantry had acquired after 1789; and he tacitly resolved to rule in the spirit of moderate constitutionalism. But his brother who succeeded him in 1824 as Charles X was made of sterner stuff. Determined to resurrect the France which he had known in his youth, he increased the authority of the church in education, dissolved the middle-class National Guard, generously compensated the nobility for its lost lands, and finally, in July, 1830, attempted to silence the opposition by modifying the suffrage requirements so as to disfranchise the bourgeoisie. The result was a three-day uprising in Paris engineered by the liberals and executed by the mob, an uprising which led to the downfall of the king. In his place, the triumphant bourgeoisie selected as ruler Louis Philippe, duke of Orléans, and cousin of the Bourbons. As for the peasantry of the countryside, it shrugged its shoulders and went on cultivating its fields.

The new king knew how to repay his political debts. His reign, which lasted until 1848, has been appropriately called the era of the bourgeois monarchy. He spoke, behaved, dressed, and looked like a prosperous merchant, banker, or certified public accountant. The Constitutional Charter of 1814 (see page 277) was retained in a slightly modified form, which extended the competence of the legislature yet still restricted the suffrage to men of property. In François Guizot (1787–1874), moreover, Louis Philippe found a minister highly sensitive to the wishes of the middle class. At home the government encouraged the growth of factories, the construction of railroads, and the flow of investments. Abroad it followed a safe and sound policy of befriending everyone and antagonizing no one. And in dealing with the opposition in the parliament it displayed a "fatal dexterity," manipulating elections and corrupting voters in a fashion which would have warmed the heart of an American ward politician. The outcome of its efforts was an industrial bourgeoisie fat and sleek, but also a growing discontent among the other classes of the population. On the Right were the legitimists, especially strong in the aristocracy, the army, and the church, who were still faithful to the memory of Charles X and who could not forgive Louis Philippe for his disloyalty to the Bourbons. On the Left were the republicans and Utopian socialists supported by the urban proletariat, who dreamed of a democratic commonwealth and a controlled economy. And everywhere there was a growing nationalism, a dissatisfaction with the uninspiring foreign policy pursued by the king, and a yearning for the revival of Napoleonic glories.

The storm broke in February, 1848, following a course which had become traditional in French politics. The Parisian mob rose in insurrection, built barricades, fought troops, forced Louis Philippe to abdicate, and proclaimed a republic. A National Assembly chosen by manhood suffrage was to prepare a constitution, but in the meantime a provisional government composed of republicans and socialists held the reins of power. The elections revealed, however, that the country as a whole was much more conservative than the capital, and in June hostility between the cautious bourgeoisie and peasantry on the one hand and the radical proletariat on the other led to another bloody conflict. The workers of Paris were defeated by the army, and the representatives of the nation then proceeded to publish a middle-of-the-road constitution. Yet civic chaos played into the hands of the nephew and heir of the great Napoleon, Louis Napoleon Bonaparte (1848–1870), who was elected president of the republic on a platform promising law and order to the upper classes, work and bread to the lower classes, and military and diplomatic prestige to all. Immediately after his inauguration he began to plot the overthrow of the republic, and three years later—on December 2, 1851—the president executed a coup d'état which left him master of the state. One year more, and he crowned his triumph by announcing a revival of the empire and proclaiming himself Napoleon III.

The emperor had spent most of his life in exile, dreaming and scheming for a victory of the Bonapartist cause, often only one step ahead of the police, sometimes actually arrested and imprisoned. Now that he was in power he remained a political opportunist, living by expedients rather than principles. Among his contemporaries he soon won a reputation as a clever and unpredictable statesman, but behind the enigmatic expression and the strange blue eyes there was only an overwhelming desire to remain ruler. This desire led the country from one adventure to the next, until emperor and empire went down in tragic defeat. For the time being, however, the unscrupulous, the upstart, the corrupt gathered at the court, where they found a ready welcome. France speculated on the stock exchange, gambled in commercial ventures, invested in industrial enterprises, danced the cancan, hummed the tunes of Offenbach, and transformed Paris into the world capital of fashion, luxury, and the arts sacred and profane. Over this carnival which lasted twenty years presided the monarch, smiling, genial, devious.

Although the empire always claimed to represent the will of the people, it was actually for the first half of its existence a thinly disguised dictatorship. The press was muzzled, the opposition suppressed, the vote rigged, the legislature intimidated. Yet as long as the government subsidized economic expansion and won military glory, the nation was ready to accept it as the only alternative to political anarchy. When after 1860, however, France began to suffer diplomatic reverses and to sink deeper into debt, the mood of the country changed ominously. Sensing his loss of popularity, the emperor attempted to recover lost ground by becoming the champion of liberal reform. The censorship was relaxed, the legislature received greater authority, parliamentary criticism became permissible, and finally, in 1869, the empire was transformed into a constitutional monarchy on the English model. Since he was obviously unable to fill the shoes of his illustrious uncle, Napoleon III decided to play Queen Victoria. But he could not escape his nemesis. In May, 1870, the nation voted 7,358,000 to 1,571,000 in favor of the new policy of parliamentarianism. Four months later the emperor was a prisoner and the empire a shambles. The carnival had come to an end.

To a Bonaparte who had no legitimate historical claim to power success was the indispensable condition of survival. As long as he could parade victories before the people, all was well. But once the magic of his name failed to produce results, his only claim to allegiance vanished. During the 1850's he still managed to win wars which brought France prestige, if little else. Between 1854 and 1856 his armies, allied with Great Britain, defeated the Russians in the Crimea, and in 1859 he overcame the Austrians in Italy. Then came a succession of disasters. In 1863 a Polish revolution which he had supported diplomatically was crushed by Russia. His plan to create a satellite state in Mexico ruled by the Austrian Archduke Maximilian failed miserably when the United States forced the French to withdraw from the New World and Maximilian himself was executed by his enemies. And the defeat of Austria by Prussia in 1866 established a powerful new state on the eastern frontier of the French Empire.

Feeling the scepter slipping from his grasp, Napoleon liberalized the government. But then in July, 1870, he blundered into a war with the Prussians. His hope was that a victory would bring the dynasty new prestige. Instead, German armies defeated the imperial troops in one battle after another, until on September 2 at Sedan 104,000 Frenchmen, including the emperor himself, were captured. On the following day Paris read the telegram sent by Napoleon: "The army has been defeated and taken prisoner; I myself am a prisoner." It was the death knell of the empire. On September 4 an insurrection in the capital deposed the Bonaparte Dynasty, and a defeated France returned to its republican tradition.

THE LOW COUNTRIES AND SCANDINAVIA

The Low Countries, strategically situated between France and England, followed the liberal example of their powerful neighbors. Both Belgium and Holland, with their high standard of living, their developing industrialism, their energetic bourgeoisie, and their tradition of sturdy self-government, were favorably disposed toward theories of constitutionalism. Yet their union in 1815 under the House of Orange had not been happy. The two peoples were separated by the religious antagonisms of Protestant and Catholic, by the cultural differences between Dutch and French, and by the economic conflicts of commercial and industrial interests. In 1830 there was a revolution in Belgium, which led to its political independence, confirmed by an international guarantee of its perpetual neutrality. As their first ruler the Belgians chose a German prince, Leopold of Saxe-Coburg (1831-1865). The uncle of Queen Victoria and the son-in-law of Louis Philippe, he governed his small state in a spirit of sober bourgeois parliamentarianism, winning the respect of the great powers and the support of his subjects. As for Holland, King William I (1815-1840) had issued a cautious constitution in 1815, which was amended and democratized during the great revolution which overwhelmed Europe in 1848. Possessing valuable colonies in the Far East, important mercantile and marine establishments, prosperous factories and banks, and a well-to-do peasantry, the Dutch, like the Belgians, were naturally inclined to accept liberal theory and practice.

So were the Scandinavians. Among the mariners, fishermen, and independent farmers of the north there had developed a strong opposition to the political and economic claims of the nobility. Even in the age of enlightened despotism royal ambitions had met with hostility, and in the nineteenth century this tradition of independence led to the victory of constitutionalism. Denmark, reduced in size and importance by the Napoleonic Wars, adopted on June 5, 1849, a liberal constitution which was the first step in a farreaching program of parliamentary and social reform. In Norway, bound by a personal union to Sweden, a representative assembly enjoyed extensive powers of government and constituted a check on the pretensions of the crown. In Sweden, on the other hand, King Charles XIV, formerly General Bernadotte, a friend of Napoleon, and his successor Oscar I exercised an authoritarian and militaristic rule supported by the aristocracy. Even after 1864, when a modern parliament replaced the antiquated Riksdag with its four estates, the monarch and the nobility retained extensive power. It was to be expected that the political union of Swedes and Norwegians would be turbulent, and before long a strong movement for separation developed among the latter.

3 : Central and Southern Europe

BEYOND THE frontiers of France industrialism was slower and absolutism stronger. Liberal doctrines encountered the resistance of a powerful landed aristocracy, while nationalist slogans had to overcome a deep-seated tradition of localism. Yet although the armies of Napoleon had been expelled from central and southern Europe after only a few years of occupation, the revolutionary ideas they had brought with them could not be entirely suppressed. Throughout the nineteenth century Germans, Italians, Spaniards, and

Portuguese sought with varying degrees of success to adapt their native political institutions to the new ideals of parliamentarianism and nationalism.

GERMANY

In Germany there was a brief reform movement in the period which followed the Napoleonic Wars, when a number of idealistic academicians, publicists, and intellectuals dreamed of transforming the German Confederation into a united fatherland governed in accordance with parliamentary practice. But by 1819 the conservatives led by Metternich (1773–1859) managed to suppress their opponents, and for the next thirty years Teutonic kings and princes ruled by divine right over submissive subjects. Some of the smaller states adopted more or less liberal constitutions, but the two giants of Germany, Austria and Prussia, remained opposed to any compromise with reformism. The only comfort liberal patriots could find in those years was the creation of the Zollverein, a customs union established in 1834 under Prussian auspices, which embraced most of Germany. Efforts to achieve political change, however, were answered by the censor and the jailer. "No power on earth," announced Frederick William IV of Prussia (1840–1861) in 1847, "will ever succeed in prevailing upon me to transform the natural relationship between prince and people, the relationship which by its inward truth has made us so powerful, into a contractual, constitutional one."

One year later he was eating his words. The revolution which broke out in France in February, 1848, swept eastward across the Rhine, overthrew established authority in Germany, put in power men who for more than a generation had been clamoring for change, and gave central Europe a taste of liberal reform and national unification. In the spring, demonstrations and riots in almost all the states forced the rulers of the German Confederation to agree to reform and led to the meeting of a representative national assembly in Frankfurt am Main to prepare a constitution for a united fatherland. But the Frankfurt Parliament was too preoccupied with transforming the country politically and economically into a liberal bourgeois state to retain the support of the masses who had made the spring uprising possible. Instead of helping the peasant become an independent farmer and protecting the artisan against the competition of the factory system, the parliamentarians prepared to create a new nation of mills and banks, dominated by the educated and the propertied. The result was a gradual decline in popular enthusiasm for the revolution.

By the time the Frankfurt Parliament completed its constitution in the spring of 1849, it stood isolated before a revived conservatism. Desperately seeking to save the national cause, it invited the ruler of Prussia to become the emperor of a united, liberal Germany. But Frederick William IV had

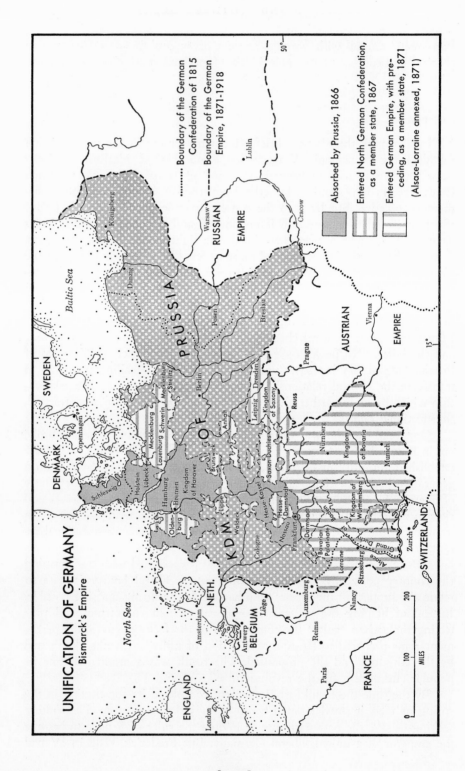

UNIFICATION OF GERMANY
Bismarck's Empire

Boundary of the German
Confederation of 1815

Boundary of the German
Empire, 1871-1918

Absorbed by Prussia, 1866

Entered North German Confederation,
as a member state, 1867

Entered German Empire, with preceding, as a member state, 1871
(Alsace-Lorraine annexed, 1871)

ENGLAND

London

North Sea

NETH.

Amsterdam

Antwerp
BELGIUM
Liège

Luxemburg

FRANCE

Paris

Reims

Nancy

Lorraine

Strassburg

Alsace

SWITZERLAND

Zurich

Baltic Sea

SWEDEN

DENMARK

Copenhagen

Schleswig

Holstein

Lübeck

Lauenburg

Mecklenburg
Schwerin

Mecklenburg
Strelitz

Hamburg

Bremen

Oldenburg

Kingdom
of Hanover

Brunswick

Waldeck

Lippe

Cologne

Hesse-Kassel

Nassau

Frankfurt

Hesse-Darmstadt

Darmstadt

Bavarian
Palatinate

Grand Duchy

Kingdom of
Württemberg

K D M

O F

P R U S S I A

Königsberg

Danzig

Berlin

Posen

Breslau

Anhalt

Leipzig

Dresden

Kingdom
of Saxony

Saxon-Duchies

Reuss

Prague

Nürnberg

Kingdom
of Bavaria

Munich

RUSSIAN
EMPIRE

Warsaw

Lublin

Cracow

AUSTRIAN
EMPIRE

Vienna

50°

15°

0   100   200
MILES

[394]

had enough of parliaments, constitutions, and reforms. Rejecting what he called "the crown from the gutter," he helped disperse the Frankfurt Parliament. By the end of 1850 the old order had been completely re-established, while thousands of liberals were languishing in prison or building new lives on the plains of Wisconsin and Missouri.

The effect of the failure of the revolution was a profound disillusionment with constitutionalism. German patriots increasingly came to favor a policy of *Realpolitik,* a policy of letting the ends justify the means and emphasizing success at the expense of principle. By the early 1860's they had found one of the greatest of all practitioners of *Realpolitik* in the person of a hard-bitten Prussian landed aristocrat, Otto von Bismarck (1815–1898). Always a conservative in his political philosophy, and at first violently opposed to national unification, he had gradually come to the conclusion that the triumph of nationalism was inevitable. It was therefore better that the Prussian monarchy rather than parliamentary politicians or Habsburg bureaucrats should receive the credit for what was bound to happen anyway. In 1862 he received an opportunity to put his ideas into practice when he was named prime minister of Prussia in the midst of a constitutional crisis.

Soon after the outbreak of the revolution Frederick William IV had reluctantly promulgated a constitution for his kingdom, and now some ten years later the liberals had managed to win a majority in the legislature. King William I, who had recently ascended the throne (1861), entrusted Bismarck with the task of taming the parliament, a task which the latter found congenial. For four years he governed in defiance of the chamber and in violation of the constitution. The policy he pursued was dangerous, but there was a method in his madness. By creating a united German fatherland he hoped to conciliate the bourgeoisie and reconcile it to continued conservative influence in government. On September 30, 1862, he boldly described his theory of statecraft: "The great questions of the time are not decided by speeches and majority resolutions—that was the great mistake of 1848 and 1849—but by blood and iron."

The chance to use blood and iron came soon enough. Bismarck had long realized that Prussia could reorganize central Europe only after crushing its rival Austria, and as prime minister he worked tirelessly to arrange a day of reckoning with the Habsburgs. In 1864 he persuaded Vienna to join him in a war against Denmark for the possession of the two German duchies of Schleswig and Holstein. Immediately after their victory the recent allies found themselves involved in a bitter quarrel over the disposition of their conquest, a quarrel carefully fostered by the wily Prussian statesman. In 1866 it came to open hostilities. The Austrians could boast the best marching bands in Europe, but the Prussians had the very effective needle gun and a military genius in Field Marshal Helmuth von Moltke. The Seven Weeks' War was a glorious triumph for Bismarck, who became the hero of all Prussia. He forced Austria to withdraw from German affairs, and then proceeded to organize the states north of the Main River into the North German Confederation, dominated by the Hohenzollerns. As for his parliamentary opponents, he managed to compose his differences with them by promulgating a moderately liberal constitution for the new national union. He completed his mission four years later by skillfully provoking the Franco-Prussian War which proved to be a succession of German victories. On January 18,1871, while the siege guns were booming around Paris, the princes of Germany met in Versailles to proclaim the formation of a united state and to acknowledge William I as their chief. The German Empire was born.

ITALY

If the creation of a unified Germany under Prussian auspices was the most momentous diplomatic development in Europe in the nineteenth century, the establishment of a united and liberal kingdom in Italy was not far behind in political significance. The French Revolution had awakened sentiments of nationalism and liberalism among the Italians in opposition to the prevailing provincialism and absolutism. But during the Restoration, Austria, in possession of the two northeastern provinces of Lombardy and Venetia, took the lead in maintaining the status quo. At first, resistance to the policies of Metternich was the work of secret associations like the Carbonari, which were organized throughout the peninsula by the patriotic and the discontented. Yet, after Carbonarist revolts failed in 1820–21 and 1830–31, three new schools of national thought arose to direct the revival of Italian political consciousness, known as the *Risorgimento*. Young Italy, founded by the enthusiastic but visionary Giuseppe Mazzini (1805–1872), urged an uprising of the masses led by the youth to establish a democratic, centralized republic. The Neoguelph movement was inspired by the gentle priest Vincenzo Gioberti, who hoped that the Papacy would help create a loose confederation of Italian states, thus fulfilling national hopes without violence and bloodshed. Finally, the party around Marquis Massimo d'Azeglio maintained that the rulers of the kingdom of Sardinia should strive to organize a constitutional national monarchy with their dynasty at its head.

The revolution of 1848 put each of these solutions of the Italian problem to the test. Each failed, but one managed to survive defeat and achieve its purpose a decade later. At first, during the "springtime of nations" in 1848, the forces of Mazzini, of Pope Pius IX, and of King Charles Albert of Sardinia co-operated in a national war against Austria. But the tenacity of the Habsburg armies and the growing rivalry of republicans, monarchists, and clericals weakened the common effort. Pius IX, alarmed by the antipapal resentment of the Austrians—who were as loyal Catholics as the

UNIFICATION OF ITALY

MILES 0   50   100   150

TUSCANY	Independent states in 1815
---------	Northern boundary of Kingdom of Italy, 1866-1919
1859	Joined by plebiscite with Sardinia
1860	Joined by revolution and plebiscite with Sardinia, to form Kingdom of Italy, proclaimed 1861
1866, 1870	Joined with Kingdom of Italy

Italians—decided to avoid too close identification with the nationalist ideology. Thereupon, Mazzini succeeded in establishing briefly a democratic republic in Rome in defiance of the Pope. The latter, however, soon regained control over his capital with the aid of troops dispatched by the new French president Louis Napoleon, who was seeking the support of the church for his political ambitions. Charles Albert attempted to continue the struggle with his own resources, risking his political future on the slim chance of a victory over the Austrians. But at the Battle of Novara in March, 1849, that chance vanished, and even the royal plan to fall on the field of battle rather than endure defeat failed. Brokenhearted, the king abdicated in favor of his son who became Victor Emmanuel II, and then withdrew into a humiliating retirement from which he was delivered before long by his premature death. The only lasting achievement of the movement on which he had gambled so heavily was the liberal constitution, the *Statuto,* which he had promulgated in Sardinia early in the revolution.

Within a decade, however, the national cause managed to recover from its defeat and to open a new campaign for unification. The author of this remarkable transformation was Count Camillo di Cavour (1810–1861), the new prime minister of Sardinia. A grand aristocrat with the outlook and appearance of a bourgeois, Cavour recognized that only with the assistance of the liberal Western powers could the Austrians be expelled from Italy. During the 1850's, therefore, he labored tirelessly to make his small mountainous state politically liberal and economically progressive. Carefully cultivating friendly diplomatic relations in the courts of Europe, he finally succeeded in concluding a treaty with Napoleon III which in 1859 led to a joint war against Austria. The outcome was Sardinian acquisition of Lombardy and of the small principalities of Tuscany, Modena, and Parma.

No sooner had Cavour completed this expansion in northern and central Italy than an unexpected stroke of good luck brought his work within sight of complete success. In 1860 the gallant adventurer Giuseppe Garibaldi with about a thousand followers organized a private expedition against the corrupt rule of the Neapolitan Bourbons in the south. Invading Sicily, he seized the island in a campaign of only a few weeks, and then crossed to the mainland and promptly made himself master of the rest of the kingdom of the Two Sicilies. In a remarkable display of selflessness he handed over his conquests to Victor Emmanuel II and retired to his farm to lead the life of a private citizen. Now only the Austrian province of Venetia and the papal possessions around Rome were lacking to complete the process of unification. The former was acquired when Italy allied herself with Prussia in the Seven Weeks' War. The latter required even less exertion, for when the French garrison in the Eternal City was withdrawn for service in the Franco-Prussian War it was promptly replaced by the troops of the new Italian kingdom. By 1870 the Sardinian government had consummated

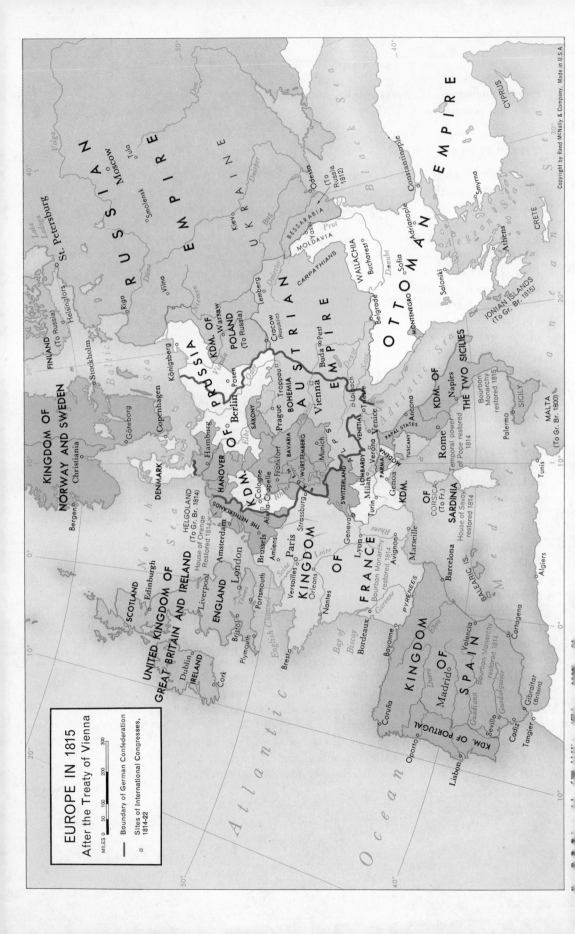

EUROPE IN 1815
After the Treaty of Vienna

MILES 0 50 100 200 300

—— Boundary of German Confederation
▫ Sites of International Congresses, 1814-22

Copyright by Rand McNally & Company. Made in U.S.A.

the amalgamation of the peninsula, and, a new nation joined the ranks of the great powers.

THE IBERIAN PENINSULA

While Italians were rejoicing in the revival of the political glories of their land, Spanish patriots could only mourn the contrast between a splendid past and the tragic present. Poor, backward, proud, deprived of its colonies, exploited by its aristocracy, dominated by its church, Spain struggled vainly throughout the nineteenth century to find a system of government appropriate to its needs and circumstances. The liberals sought to uphold the constitution of 1812 and the more moderate charter of 1845, while the conservatives found their champions in unscrupulous royal intriguers like King Ferdinand VII and his brother Don Carlos. The accession in 1833 of Queen Isabella II merely meant that the inefficient oppressiveness of the previous reign was replaced by the inefficient immorality of the new.

A revolution in 1868 resulted in the deposition of the queen whose private life had scandalized her pious subjects, but once again the new order was not much of an improvement over the old. For two years the Spaniards tried to find someone willing to risk becoming their king. When an Italian prince finally agreed in 1870 to ascend the throne as Amadeo I, they lived up to their reputation for political instability by forcing him to abdicate three years later. A brief experiment in a republican form of government proved even more disastrous, and in 1875 the son of Queen Isabella II was unenthusiastically invited to wear the crown as Alfonso XII. But the sham constitutionalism of the new régime could not deal effectively with the fundamental problems of Spanish political insecurity and social discontent.

Similarly, in neighboring Portugal declining economic fortunes and bitter class antagonisms made a satisfactory adjustment to the liberal era difficult. True, there was the constitution of 1821, which had introduced a measure of individual freedom and parliamentary government, but there was also a strong conservative party which stanchly adhered to the traditions of the past. Its leader Dom Miguel plunged the country into a civil war which raged from 1828 to 1834, but even his defeat and the moderate reigns of Queen Maria II and her two sons, Pedro V and Luiz I, failed to end the widespread corruption in public life, the heavy burden of taxation, the low state of popular education, and the steady migration of thousands of persons to Brazil. Besides, the huge colonial empire of some 800,000 square miles, which Portugal proudly insisted on retaining, was an expensive luxury for a state which financially had enough difficulty keeping its own head above water. While Western liberals sometimes spoke optimistically of Portugal as an Iberian Belgium or Holland, as a matter of fact deep-seated social ills and economic weaknesses were undermining the political structure of the country.

4 : Eastern Europe

THE HEART of conservatism lay on the other side of Europe among the great estates and ancient castles of the east, where proud aristocrats lorded over a cowed peasantry. The lands of the Habsburgs and the Romanovs were still governed in the spirit of royal absolutism which had been destroyed in western Europe by the French Revolution. On the plains which extend beyond the Vistula and the Alps factories and railroads were few and middle-class entrepreneurs and politicians timid. Faint echoes of the liberal ideas which were on the march elsewhere did manage to penetrate the walls of censorship surrounding the eastern autocracies, but their effect was limited. Theories of divine-right monarchism, on the other hand, found a favorable reception in Vienna and St. Petersburg, and the poverty-stricken populace of village and town remained respectfully obedient to the throne. For what did high-flown talk about individual rights and representative government mean to the masses which barely managed to keep body and soul together?

THE AUSTRIAN EMPIRE

The Austrian Empire remained essentially a conservative anachronism throughout the nineteenth century. Its social structure made it conservative, its political organization made it anachronistic. Not only did the governing aristocracy oppose constitutional reform, but the irreconcilable demands of opposing nationalities within the state engendered a mounting civic tension. Throughout the Habsburg crownlands peoples of different languages and traditions began to clamor for recognition and self-determination. In Bohemia it was Czech against German, in Galicia Ukrainian against Pole, in Hungary Slovak, Romanian, and Croat against Magyar, and in Istria Italian and Slovene against German.

At first the claims of the oppressed peoples did not go beyond a defense of the local culture against the prevalent Germanism, but gradually this linguistic nationalism changed into a political consciousness seeking autonomy within the empire. The Bohemian historian Francis Palacky sang the past greatness of the Czech nation and demanded administrative freedom for his nation. In Hungary the Magyars, hard pressed by the Habsburg authorities in Vienna, bullied in turn the minorities in their midst and embarked on a loud campaign for cultural and governmental autonomy. Among the Croats, Slovenes, and Serbs of the south there developed an

Illyrian nationalism which maintained that they all had a common political and linguistic tradition. Even some of the dominant Germans, attracted to their brothers farther north, began to advocate a united Teutonic fatherland in which the Germanic Austrians could take their place. Despite the most strenuous efforts of the bureaucracy, these conflicting patriotisms continued to gain strength in the years after the Congress of Vienna.

Habsburg fortunes reached their nadir in 1848. The news of the downfall of Louis Philippe in France led to the outbreak of revolutions throughout the Austrian Empire. In Vienna itself the aging Metternich was forced to resign and escape incognito to England, while a national assembly went to work to prepare a liberal constitution. In Hungary the radical politician Louis Kossuth forced the government to accept the March Laws establishing a parliamentary and autonomous Magyar state. In Bohemia the Czechs won a promise of self-government; in Lombardy-Venetia the Austrian garrisons were driven out of Milan and Venice; and in Galicia the Poles demanded political concessions. But the proverbial luck of the Habsburgs did not desert them in the hour of their greatest need. The army and the bureaucracy, still loyal to the dynasty, were able to exploit the differences which arose among the revolutionaries on the morrow of their triumph. Moreover, in the reactionary new emperor, Francis Joseph (1848–1916), and his reactionary new prime minister, Felix zu Schwarzenberg, they found leaders with determination and nerve. In the summer of 1848 Prince Alfred zu Windischgrätz suppressed the uprising in Bohemia by playing off German against Czech, while Field Marshal Joseph Radetzky was able to defeat the Italians torn by the rivalry between liberals and democrats. Revolutionary Vienna was captured by the imperial forces in the fall; and the Hungarians, fighting with stubborn courage, were finally crushed the following summer by the armies of the Austrians, the Croatians, and the Russians, who were sent by the tsar to help his fellow autocrat. Within less than two years the Habsburg Empire was restored in all its uncompromising conservatism.

The 1850's were years of reaction in Austria. Revolutionaries were imprisoned, voices of criticism were silenced, local rights of self-government were abolished. The administration was completely centralized in Vienna. Yet the Bach System, as this iron régime was called after Minister of the Interior Alexander Bach, did not eliminate national dissatisfactions. It merely sat on them. At the first sign of weakness in the government they were bound to rise to the surface again. When the Austrian armies were defeated in 1859 by the combined forces of France and Sardinia, the myth of the military invincibility of the state was shattered, and the subject peoples immediately began to revive their demands for political concession. The ministry tried to satisfy them by promulgating the October Diploma of 1860 and the February Patent of 1861, constitutional decrees establishing a halfhearted parliamentarianism in the empire. But the Hungarians, the most vigorous of the oppressed nationalities, refused to settle for anything less than the March Laws of 1848. Francis Joseph was at first inclined to engage in a test of strength with Magyar nationalism, but when his troops were defeated once again in the Seven Weeks' War (1866) he realized that he could not risk a new revolution. In 1867, therefore, he concluded the *Ausgleich,* a constitutional compromise between Austria and Hungary which remained the political foundation of the state until 1918.

The Habsburg lands were divided into two distinct national entities, the Austrian Empire and the Kingdom of Hungary. The former was to be ruled by a constitution based on the February Patent of 1861, the latter by the March Laws of 1848. A few functions of government such as military affairs and foreign policy were to be exercised by common ministries, but in most cases the partners in the Dual Monarchy acted as entirely separate and independent countries. They were held together, however, by a common fear of the other nationalities, for even in combination the Germans in Austria and the Magyars in Hungary constituted less than half of the total population of the state. Surrounded by a Slavic sea, they were willy-nilly obliged to maintain their alliance against the subject peoples whom they were jointly dominating. Of course, they might have been able to solve the problem of the national minorities by a federalist reorganization of the government giving autonomy to the oppressed. But then they would have had to surrender their monopoly of political and economic influence. Neither the bureaucrats in Vienna nor the magnates in Budapest were capable of such magnanimity. They preferred instead to delude themselves that the grumblings about them were only the work of a few malcontents who refused to accept their proper station in life. "The situation is critical but not serious" became the credo of a ruling class marching blithely to destruction.

RUSSIA

Russia, too, had its national minorities. Within its borders lived millions of Poles, Lithuanians, Latvians, Estonians, Finns, Ukrainians, and Jews, as well as a bewildering variety of Caucasian and Asiatic peoples, all restive under tsarist oppression. But whereas in Austria the dominant national elements were a minority of the total population, in the possessions of the Romanovs the Russians proper included about half of all inhabitants, and the state could therefore better afford to ignore the wishes of the subject peoples. Still, it had to wrestle with the equally serious difficulties created by a rapid transformation in the social and economic structure of the country. Russia in the nineteenth century was a land bewildered and frightened by the sudden transition from an age of serfdom and autocracy to one of industrialism and liberalism. Confronted by the political strains arising out of the need to adjust to swiftly changing material conditions, its rulers introduced alternately policies of stern repression and moderate reform, failing to stem popular discontent with either. Revolutionary ideas could not be exiled to

Siberia, and imperial concessions were too little and too late to prevent the collapse of the monarchy. The final act of the tragedy of Russian absolutism was played out on a terrible July day in 1918 when the last of the tsars and his entire family were slaughtered by the soldiery of a new and even more pitiless régime.

At the time of the Congress of Vienna, however, it looked as if a new era of civic progress were opening for the colossus of the north. Tsar Alexander I (1801–1825), a well-intentioned neurotic who had been educated in the political theories of the French *philosophes,* acceded to the throne determined to win a place in history as a philosopher-king. In conversation with his intimates over a cup of tea in some luxurious salon he could discourse tirelessly about the need for reform, but he somehow always managed to find a reason for postponing the execution of his philanthropic plans. Perhaps the poet Lord Byron was not far from the truth, when he portrayed the emperor

> *With no objection to true liberty,*
> *Except that it would make the nations free.*

In any case, the Russian peasant continued to groan in serfdom, and the Russian nobleman continued to play God, while Alexander fought first against Napoleon, then for Napoleon, and then against Napoleon again. In 1813 he became the liberator of Europe, and two years later the end of the war with France freed his hands for the work of domestic reform. He appeared, however, to be in no hurry to renounce his prerogatives. True, he gave Poland an autonomous status and a liberal constitution; he maintained friendly relations with parliamentarians in England and France; he even gave a measure of encouragement to revolutionaries in Greece plotting an uprising against the Turks. Yet the reforms which he granted to the Russians themselves were few and unimportant, and after the Congress of Troppau in 1820 he listened with growing interest to the conservative theories of Metternich. By the time of his death in December, 1825, he had turned into an out-and-out reactionary—moody, restless, resentful, haunted by visions of the murder of his father in which he himself had been implicated.

His brother and successor, Nicholas I (1825–1855), was cast in a different mold. He was blessed with a simple and unquestioning faith in royal absolutism which was never troubled by the doubts which had assailed his predecessor. Trained as a soldier, he approached the problems of statecraft with a drill sergeant's insistence on blind obedience. His natural inclination toward conservatism, moreover, was intensified by the unsuccessful uprising organized upon the death of Alexander I by a handful of liberal army officers and Francophile aristocratic intellectuals. This Decembrist Revolt of 1825 was easily suppressed, but the tsar never forgot that the reformers had planned to introduce a constitutional régime by replacing him with his brother Constantine. Throughout the thirty years of his reign he remained the foremost opponent in Europe of the principle of popular sovereignty. In 1830–31 he crushed an uprising of the Poles and revoked their right of self-government; in 1849 he helped the Austrians defeat the rebellion in Hungary; and in 1852–53 he opposed Napoleon III because of the revolutionary origin of the authority of the Bonapartes. The autocrat who was prepared to help destroy liberalism abroad was certainly not going to tolerate it at home. Critics of the government were jailed, the press was censored, schools were supervised, and radical agitation was stifled by the Third Section, an early example of that long series of secret police organizations which have become a tradition in Russia. Autocracy, orthodoxy, and nationalism were the articles of faith of a militant tsarism.

Most Russians seemed to look upon the unbending conservatism of their monarch with fatalistic resignation. There were a few opponents of the established order like Michael Bakunin and Alexander Herzen, who from a safe distance beyond the Russian frontier continued to condemn the political and economic institutions of their native land. But their denunciations made a deeper impression on radicals in London and Paris than on the benighted muzhiks of the eastern steppes. Even the educated classes learned to accept what they could not change, consoling themselves with the thought that while Nicholas I ruled his possessions with an iron hand he also inspired great respect in foreign countries. If liberalism suffered under his rule, national pride flourished. Tsarist troops invaded the Balkans and terrorized the sultan in Constantinople; they defeated Polish and Hungarian revolutionaries; they threatened to intervene in Germany in defense of the Habsburgs; they subjugated tribal princes and nomad chieftains in the Caucasus and in Siberia. Russia loomed over the European horizon like a giant bestriding the world.

Yet the giant had feet of clay. In 1853 the tsar overplayed his diplomatic hand by provoking hostilities with Turkey, which promptly received assistance from France and England. The Crimean War resulted in a resounding defeat for Russia, a defeat seriously weakening the autocratic principle. The state was shown to be corrupt and backward, and public opinion, which for more than a generation had venerated an unconquerable absolutism, turned against the fallen idol.

Nicholas I died in the midst of the war, a disappointed and broken man, so that his son Alexander II (1855–1881) was left to reap the whirlwind. Like his uncle Alexander I, he was eager to conciliate his subjects without relaxing his hold over them. Although in 1861 he finally decreed the abolition of serfdom, the aristocrats retained the most fertile fields, while the peasants were obliged to pay a heavy price for the modest allotments of land which they acquired. Three years later the emperor established district and provincial *zemstvos,* elective councils enjoying jurisdiction over schools, roads, hospitals, and orphanages; but he would not even hear of the creation of a national representative legislature. In 1864 he promulgated a progressive judicial system; in 1870 he reformed municipal government; and in 1874 he modernized the army. Having shown himself so magnanimous to his subjects, he confidently expected to be hailed as the Solon of the age. Instead, the Poles rose in revolution, the peasants clamored for more land, and the newspapers demanded further political concessions. Once the tsar realized that nothing less than a parliamentary system of government would satisfy the liberal opposition, his enthusiasm for change left him. By the early 1870's he showed himself to be a true son of Nicholas I by abandoning the policy of reform and setting out on the familiar road to reaction.

THE OTTOMAN EMPIRE

South of Russia lay the sick and dying Ottoman Empire. The religious fervor and military zeal which once made the Turks invincible had long since evaporated, leaving behind them sultans who won their victories in the harem rather than on the battlefield, and pashas who plotted against their own government more than they prepared for war with foreign enemies. What is more, with the rise of nationalism throughout Europe, the subject Orthodox Christian peoples in the Balkans grew increasingly restless under the corrupt rule of Constantinople. Greeks, Bulgarians, Serbs, and Romanians began first to develop pride in their cultural tradition, then to remember a great historical past, then to form secret patriotic societies, and then to raise the banner of rebellion. Finally, the great powers found themselves more and more attracted by diplomatic complications in the Balkans. Whereas elsewhere in Europe firmly established states had become the rule, in the southeast political conditions were fluid enough to tempt diplomats to fish in troubled waters. Economically the region was backward, but its strategic location at the crossroads of three continents gave it major importance. Two powers especially found themselves deeply involved in the complexities of the Near Eastern question. Russia, convinced that the disintegration of Turkey was inevitable, had resolved to gain the vital straits connecting the Black Sea with the Aegean, and to assert her influence over the Christian nationalities in the Balkan peninsula. England, on the other hand, unwilling to see Russian naval might established in the eastern Mediterranean and anxious to retain the rich Turkish markets, became the champion of the Sublime Porte. The conflicting influences and policies of St. Petersburg and London with regard to the Ottoman Empire made of it an international problem of the first magnitude.

At first, the Russians seemed to be gaining the upper hand. Revolutions in Serbia in 1804–13 and 1815–17 and in Greece in 1821–29 weakened the Turkish government and provided the tsar with an excellent pretext for an invasion of the Balkans. Although the British cabinet was forced by public opinion at home to intervene halfheartedly in the Near East in order to persuade the sultan to make concessions to his Christian subjects, it was Russia which by the brief war of 1828–29 against the Ottoman Empire won independence for Greece and autonomy for Serbia. The Turks, deciding that resistance against their powerful neighbor was useless, entered into a close alliance with Russia by the Treaty of Unkiar Skelessi of 1833.

For a few years Romanov influence was paramount in Constantinople, but then the balance began to shift in favor of the British. In 1841 Britain encouraged the sultan to replace the unwelcome alliance with the tsar by an international convention barring all foreign warships from the Straits. And before long the English ambassador, Stratford Canning, had managed to persuade the Sublime Porte to resist the demands of St. Petersburg by promising the Ottoman Empire the support of Queen Victoria's navy. Nicholas I confidently decided in 1853 to call the Turkish bluff, only to end up much to his chagrin with a war on his hands against England, France, and Sardinia, as well as Turkey. Hostilities were largely confined to the siege of the great naval base of Sevastopol in the Crimea. Upon its fall, Alexander II was forced to sign the Peace of Paris in 1856, promising to abstain from any intervention in Ottoman affairs and to destroy all Russian military installations on the Black Sea as a pledge of good behavior. Great Britain and Palmerston had won a splendid victory.

The Crimean War proved only a temporary check to Russian designs. No sooner were hostilities over than Alexander II began to plan for a revision of the Peace of Paris. His opportunity arrived in 1870. While the rest of Europe was absorbed in the Franco-Prussian War, the tsar repudiated the demilitarization clauses of the treaty and proceeded to rebuild naval installations on the Black Sea. In the meantime one more autonomous Christian nation had been established in the Balkans. A political union of the two Danubian principalities of Moldavia and Wallachia took place in 1858; and the new state of Romania chose as its ruler first a native aristocrat, Alexander Cuza, and then the Hohenzollern Prince Charles. The Sublime Porte during the 1850's and 1860's made a determined effort to strengthen its position by a policy of liberal modernization. Early in 1856 the *Hatt-i Humayun,* a reform edict inspired by English and French influence, granted the Christian subjects of the sultan security of life and property and equality of legal and political status. Five years later, with the accession of the enlightened Abdul Aziz (1861–1876), Turkey entered on a period of rapid Westernization designed to protect the empire against rebellion within and aggression without.

The most important development in the Orient, however, was the completion in 1869 of the Suez Canal connecting the Mediterranean with the Red Sea. The work of the French diplomat and promoter Ferdinand de Lesseps, the canal gave a new economic and strategic importance to the lands of the Ottoman Empire. By intensifying the rivalries of the great powers, it helped set off a new round of plotting, scheming, intriguing, manipulating, and wirepulling in the Balkans which culminated in the summer of 1914 in the outbreak of a world war.

5 : The New World

IF THE BALKANS were the easternmost frontier of European civilization, the Americas were its western boundary. On the other side of the Atlantic in the New World the great states of the Occident had established islands of cultural influence which survived political separation. With a few exceptions here and there, England, France, Spain, and Portugal had lost their colonial possessions in the Western Hemisphere in the late eighteenth and early nineteenth century, but their languages, their religions, and their ideologies continued to flourish on the banks of the Mississippi and the Amazon. American ways of life were no mere copies of the European, for changes in environment and experience had produced changes in outlook and character. Yet the culture of the New World was unmistakably derived from the Old. The Canadian habitant, the New England Yankee, and the Argentine Gaucho were obviously different from the Norman, the Yorkshireman, and the Castilian three thousand miles away. But they were all part of a common tradition in a sense in which no Chinese, Indian, or Arab was. The term "Atlantic Civilization" expressed this community of thought and feeling.

THE UNITED STATES

Nevertheless, in the years which followed the War of 1812 most Americans would probably have insisted that their ties to an effete Old World were finally severed. The recent hostilities with Great Britain had brought the United States little military renown and less territorial gain, so that the Monroe Doctrine of 1823, proclaiming a policy of mutual non-interference between the Western and the Eastern Hemispheres, met with the general approval of the young nation. The ambitious and the restless could find an outlet for their energies in the settling of a virgin continent. The Louisiana Purchase of 1803 had carried the Stars and Stripes from the Mississippi to the Rockies, but for the next fifty years manifest destiny and insatiable acquisitiveness kept adding new possessions. In 1819 Florida was obtained more or less peacefully from Spain. In 1845 the recently established Republic of Texas was annexed. A two-year war with Mexico, costing but few lives and little money, was ended in 1848 by the Treaty of Guadalupe Hidalgo, which ceded New Mexico and California to the United States for fifteen million dollars, a bargain even in those days. The long and

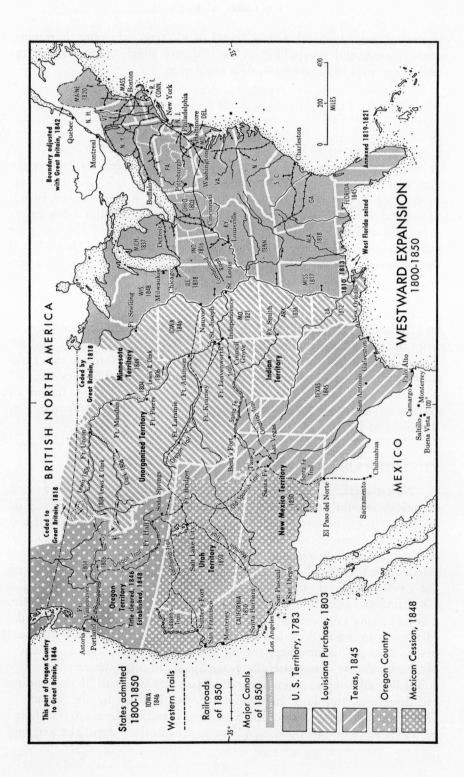

WESTWARD EXPANSION
1800-1850

This part of Oregon Country
to Great Britain, 1846

States admitted
1800-1850
IOWA
1846

Western Trails

Railroads
of 1850

Major Canals
of 1850

U. S. Territory, 1783

Louisiana Purchase, 1803

Texas, 1845

Oregon Country

Mexican Cession, 1848

BRITISH NORTH AMERICA

Boundary adjusted
with Great Britain, 1842

Ceded to
Great Britain, 1818

Ceded by
Great Britain, 1818

Annexed 1819-1821

West Florida seized

MEXICO

disputed boundary with Canada was adjusted by a series of conventions in 1818, 1842, and 1846. By the middle of the century a lusty republic stretched from ocean to ocean, confident of its rising star.

The experience of the Western frontier had a profound influence on political life in the settled and established East. Certainly the democratization of state and federal government and the attack on economic and social privilege drew strength from the backwoods, where each man was as good as the next and where birth and background counted for little. The most valiant champion of this aggressive lower-class democracy was President Andrew Jackson (1829–1837), soldier, statesman, farmer, and adventurer, who throughout his life remained the enemy of too much wealth and too much education. His civic philosophy breathed the air of uncompromising egalitarianism: "The duties of all public offices are . . . so plain and simple that men of intelligence may readily qualify themselves for their performance; and I cannot but believe that more is lost by the long continuance of men in office than is generally to be gained by their experience. . . . No one man has any more intrinsic right to official station than another." Out of the spirit of frontier fraternalism arose a powerful reform movement which gradually led to the establishment of virtually complete white manhood suffrage and the defeat of important financial interests represented by the Second Bank of the United States. In the cities political and economic organizations of labor, like the Workingmen's party and the General Trades' Union, began to agitate for factory regulation, social progress, educational improvement, and banking control. Even the feminist convention which met in Seneca Falls, New York, in 1848 to demand the legal emancipation of women reflected the generous faith in the fundamental equality of all mankind which was becoming a part of the American attitude toward life.

There was one kind of equality, however, about which there was an irreconcilable difference of opinion in the United States. More and more the slavery question divided the citizens of the republic, until a fratricidal war finally resolved it at terrible cost. What was at stake was not only human bondage, not only the oppression of the black man by the white, but the struggle of two societies and two economies. For the Southerner the enslavement of the Negro was indissolubly bound up with a system of agriculture built about the cultivation of cotton; it determined the low tariff policy advocated below Mason and Dixon's line; it emphasized the aristocratic organization of society in Virginia or Alabama or Mississippi. In the North freedom of labor aided industrialization; it led to a need for economic protectionism; it encouraged the democratization of social life.

From time to time attempts were made to adjust sectional differences, as by the Missouri Compromise of 1820, the Tariff of 1833, the Compromise of 1850, and the Kansas-Nebraska Act of 1854. But on both sides tempers were growing shorter. Southerners, feeling themselves surrounded by a ring of enemies, were increasingly determined to resist restrictions on slavery

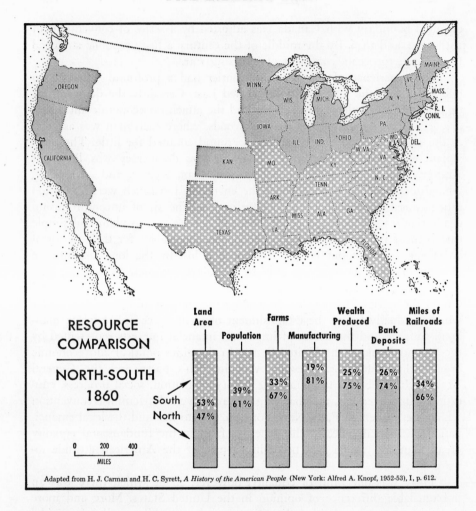

RESOURCE COMPARISON

NORTH-SOUTH 1860

	Land Area	Population	Farms	Manufacturing	Wealth Produced	Bank Deposits	Miles of Railroads
South	53%	39%	33%	19%	25%	26%	34%
North	47%	61%	67%	81%	75%	74%	66%

0   200   400
MILES

Adapted from H. J. Carman and H. C. Syrett, *A History of the American People* (New York: Alfred A. Knopf, 1952-53), I, p. 612.

in the newly settled territories. The Northerners, while usually willing to tolerate Negro bondage where it already existed, opposed its extension elsewhere. By the late 1850's the political unity of the nation was reaching the breaking point. "'A house divided against itself cannot stand,'" asserted the rising Illinois politician Abraham Lincoln (1809-1865) in 1858. "I do not expect the Union to be dissolved—I do not expect the house to fall—but I do expect it will cease to be divided. It will become all one thing, or all the other."

In 1860 Lincoln was elected as president on a platform demanding a halt to any further extension of slavery. The result was the secession of the Southern states and the outbreak of a civil war which raged for four years. Almost two million men, brothers in speech and culture, were engaged in a desperate struggle. Little by little the superior resources of the North supported by the West wore down the valor and militancy of the

Southerners, until by 1865 the exhausted Confederate States of America had been defeated and occupied. For a hundred years many of the wounds inflicted at that awful time remained unhealed. But the Civil War was also a great turning point in the development of the United States, a national ordeal out of which emerged a stronger and greater country. It marked the triumph of industrialism in American life and the rise of an economic colossus in the New World. It gave added strength to the federal union, placing it on a new foundation of constitutional and political stability. Most important of all, it ended human bondage which had belied the promise of democracy, bringing closer to realization the hope of the great wartime president that "government of the people, by the people, for the people, shall not perish from the earth."

CANADA

In British North America the half-century following the War of 1812 was also one of conflict. True, there was no slavery question to disturb the politics of Canada, but there were the cultural and religious differences between French Catholics and English Protestants, and there was growing friction between the elected legislature, representing the interests of the local population, and an appointed executive, attempting to carry out the wishes of the royal cabinet in Great Britain. In 1837 hostility between rulers and ruled led to armed uprisings, which were easily suppressed, but which brought back to the government in London unpleasant memories of 1776. Lord John Durham, a prominent statesman with radical leanings, was sent to the New World to make a firsthand examination of political conditions. In 1839 he published his *Report on the Affairs of British North America,* the most important document in the history of English imperial administration. Essentially what he proposed was the establishment of complete self-government for the colony except in foreign affairs, commercial policy, public lands, and constitutional system. Canada was to become another Great Britain, with its own freely chosen parliament, its own royal governor who reigned but did not rule, and its own laws, courts, and traditions.

At first the government in England hesitated to embark upon what seemed to many a dangerous experiment inviting separation. But during the governorship of Lord James Elgin from 1847 to 1854 the principle of local autonomy was introduced in the province of Canada, and was then promptly extended to other British possessions in North America, namely, Nova Scotia, New Brunswick, Prince Edward Island, Newfoundland, and British Columbia. Without fully realizing it, the United Kingdom had stumbled upon a method of colonial rule which guaranteed political freedom for the overseas territory without endangering the economic and military interests of the mother country.

As for the deep-seated conflicts between French Canadian and English Canadian, a method for settling them peacefully was created by the British

North America Act of 1867, which established a federal union composed at first of the four provinces of Quebec or Lower Canada, Ontario or Upper Canada, New Brunswick, and Nova Scotia. In the years which followed they were joined by Manitoba, British Columbia, Prince Edward Island, Alberta, Saskatchewan, and finally Newfoundland. In their stronghold of Quebec the French were free to follow their cultural tradition and religious faith without fear of outside interference, while in the national parliament in Ottawa they met with their English neighbors to agree upon common policies for dealing with common problems. In an age of increasingly intolerant nationalism the Dominion of Canada provided an example of peaceful adjustment of historical differences between two diverse peoples.

LATIN AMERICA

If North America was blessed with Anglo-Saxon constitutional experience, Central and South America were heir to the decaying despotism of the Iberian peninsula. South of the Rio Grande the struggle for independence, which had come to an end during the early 1820's, was followed by an endless succession of wars, revolutions, uprisings, coups, and assassinations, highly complex in detail but monotonously similar in outcome. The overthrow of Spanish rule had created a political vacuum in the New World which the colonists seemed unable to fill. They lacked the governmental experience and financial security on which sound administration is built. To make matters worse, all the succession states except Brazil had chosen the republican form of government, which in the hands of the backward or unscrupulous easily degenerated into anarchy. San Martín, foreseeing the dangers which would face the continent after liberation, favored a limited monarchy, and even Bolívar, who had strong democratic convictions, was willing to accept for the time being some sort of moderate royalism to bridge the gap between autocratic and popular rule. Most of their followers, however, were impractical doctrinaires or scheming politicians, who for a variety of idealistic and selfish reasons advocated republicanism. The result was an aggravation of what would under the best of circumstances have been an extremely difficult political situation.

The United States and Canada were inclined to look upon their neighbors to the south as a people suffering from congenital instability. Yet in all justice, Spanish America had to wrestle with almost insurmountable obstacles to peaceful development created by God as well as man. Only about 20 per cent of its population was white, while 31 per cent was mestizo, 45 per cent Indian, and 4 per cent Negro. What is more, the racial differentiation had come to reflect a social division, with the aristocratic white minority maintaining a politically and economically oppressive rule over the backward colored majority. The church, which because of its extensive landed property and powerful political influence tended to ally itself with the upper classes, was another important force opposed to social reform. And finally, nature had not been kind to the Latin Americans. The French *coureur de bois* and the English frontiersman had a rich continent to conquer and exploit. The Spanish and the Portuguese, on the other hand, often found in the New World impenetrable jungles and barren plateaus inhabited by native tribes which stubbornly resisted subjugation. Even the great gold and silver mines of the Incas and the Aztecs had long since ceased to produce much wealth. As far as the oppressed and ignorant masses were concerned, politics became little more than the favorite sport of a handful of ambitious, influential men seeking power for prestige or profit.

Although it had been the hope of the leaders in the struggle against Spain that Latin America would be able to maintain some form of political union based on an identity of culture and religion, the liberated states promptly developed a jealous particularism which led to a series of devastating wars. From 1825 to 1828 Argentina was engaged in hostilities with Brazil for the possession of Uruguay. Chile, still remembering the military glory won by O'Higgins and San Martín, fought the Peruvian-Bolivian Confederation from 1836 to 1839. On the Caribbean island of Hispaniola relations between the two neighboring pygmy republics, French Haiti and Spanish Santo Domingo, were always strained. No sooner had the latter proclaimed its independence from Spain in 1821, than the former marched in and established a union based on naked force. In 1844 Santo Domingo revolted and managed to form a government of its own, but feelings toward Haiti remained bitter for a century and more. Between 1865 and 1870 the half-mad Paraguayan president, Francisco Solano López, was involved in a struggle with Brazil, Argentina, and Uruguay, which won a melancholy distinction in the annals of military barbarism by destroying 80 per cent of the inhabitants of Paraguay and leaving the country with a population of some 28,000 men and 200,000 women. For that matter, all the wars waged in Latin America had a distressing tendency to degenerate into organized banditry, arson, rapine, and murder.

Far from achieving political unity, the successor states of the Spanish Empire tended to divide and subdivide into new nations. When the wars of independence ended, there were ten new governments in the New World, namely, Mexico, Central America, Colombia, Peru, Bolivia, Paraguay, Argentina, Chile, Brazil, and Haiti. Then the political and economic forces of separatism went to work, and within a generation the number had risen to eighteen. In 1825 Uruguay rose in revolution against Brazil and with foreign aid succeeded in winning an independent status. The Great Colombia established by Bolívar disintegrated after a few years, when Venezuela seceded in 1829 and Ecuador in 1830. The union of Bolivia and Peru proclaimed in 1835 was short-lived, for Argentina and Chile were determined to prevent the rise of a potential rival, and their opposition was enough to destroy the confederation after four years. As for the United Provinces of

Central America, which had withdrawn from their unhappy association with Mexico in 1823, by 1840 they too had dissolved into their component political units, Guatemala, El Salvador, Honduras, Nicaragua, and Costa Rica. Sporadic efforts to re-establish unity continued throughout the 1840's, but they were unable to overcome jealousy and resentment. Finally, a confusion of comic opera plots and counterplots on Hispaniola brought about the independence of Santo Domingo and created one more state playing the endless game of Latin American politics.

The internal development of the Iberian nations of the Western Hemisphere was characterized by the same instability which their foreign policy displayed. On the surface there was the familiar division between liberals and conservatives, the former preaching political reform, economic progress, and religious freedom, the latter defending the interests of the aristocracy, the military, and the clergy. The conflict between centralism and federalism in the system of administration was another divisive issue in public affairs. Finally, personal ambition, financial greed, and bureaucratic corruption added fuel to the flames. Yet the fundamental problems of Latin American society remained unsolved. The oppressed peon continued to lead a precarious existence one step ahead of starvation; the great landowner continued to live a life of baronial splendor; and in the meantime reactionary fought progressive, federalist assassinated centralist, one dictator followed another. In 1845 Tomás Cipriano de Mosquera became president of Colombia as the candidate of the conservatives, and sixteen years later he returned to power after the customary revolution as a liberal. In Venezuela the moderates under José Páez were in the saddle from 1830 to 1846; then from 1846 to 1861 it was the turn of the conservatives, led by the brothers José Tadeo and José Gregorio Monagas, until Páez returned from exile to become once again the strong man of the country. In Guatemala the liberals under Francisco Morazán enjoyed ten years of political prosperity from 1829 to 1839, when the clericals under Rafael Carrera got the keys to the presidential palace. In Mexico the colorful Antonio López de Santa Anna became president in 1833 as a convinced federalist, and after suffering a series of unhappy reverses, returned to power in 1853 as an equally convinced centralist.

Despite poverty, war, and revolution, however, Latin America managed to make some progress toward political and economic stability. The larger states in particular enjoyed a measure of success in coping with the cumulative effects of centuries of exploitation. Brazil, having retained the monarchic form of government under the House of Braganza, was able to avoid much of the civil unrest which plagued its neighbors. Because of his authoritarian inclinations and his involvement in Portuguese politics, Pedro I was forced to abdicate in 1831 in favor of his infant son. After reaching his majority, Pedro II (1840–1889) proved to be an enlightened ruler who fostered the growth of agriculture, the introduction of industry, and the improvement of

UNITED STATES

Columbia

Ohio

Mississippi

Missouri

Arkansas

42nd Parallel

Parallel

Ceded to U.S. 1848

120°

100°

90°

80°

70°

60°

50°

40°

30°

20°

10°

0°

A t l a n t i c

O c e a n

Tropic of Cancer

Red

Sabine

Gila

Mesilla Strip. Sold to U.S. 1853

Gila

CALIFORNIA

LOWER
CALIFORNIA

Santa Fé

Chihuahua

San Francisco

Monterey

San Diego

M E X I C O
Independent 1821
Monarchy 1822-23
Republic 1824

Monterrey

Rio Grande

Rio Grande de Santiago

Mexico
City

Puebla

Acapulco

Vera Cruz

Jalapa

Tampico

New
Orleans

Gulf of Mexico

Habana

CUBA
Sp. until 1898

JAMAICA
(British)

Caribbean Sea

BRITISH
HONDURAS
Belice

YUCATAN
Independent
1839-43

CHIAPAS
To Mexico 1823

Guatemala
GUATEMALA

San Salvador
SALVADOR

HONDURAS
Tegucigalpa

NICARAGUA
Managua

MOSQUITO COAST
British Protectorate
1841-50

San José
COSTA RICA

TEXAS
Independent 1836
Annexed to U.S. 1845

CENTRAL AMERICA
Independent 1821
United with Mexico 1821
Independent Confederation 1823
Divided into five states 1838

HAITI
Independent with Haiti
until 1844

Santiago

Port au
Prince

DOMINICAN REPUBLIC
(SANTO DOMINGO)

Santo
Domingo

PUERTO
RICO
Sp. until 1898

VIRGIN
ISLANDS
(Den.)

TRINIDAD
(British)

CURACAO (Dutch)

La Guaira

Caracas

VENEZUELA
(1829)

Orinoco

Maracaibo

PANAMA ISTHMUS
To Colombia 1821-1903

Panama

GALAPAGOS IS.
Ecuador since 1832

Quito
ECUADOR
State of the Equator 1830

Bogotá

GREAT
COLOMBIA
(1819-1830)

New Granada 1831
Granadine Confederation 1853
United States of Colombia 1863
Republic of COLOMBIA 1886

BRITISH
GUIANA

DUTCH
GUIANA

FRENCH
GUIANA

Ceded by
Colombia to
Brazil 1907

Ceded by Ecuador to
Venezuela to
Brazil 1859

Ceded by Ecuador
to Brazil 1904

Mosquitia

Magdalena

MARAJO I.

Belem

Amazon

P a c i f i c

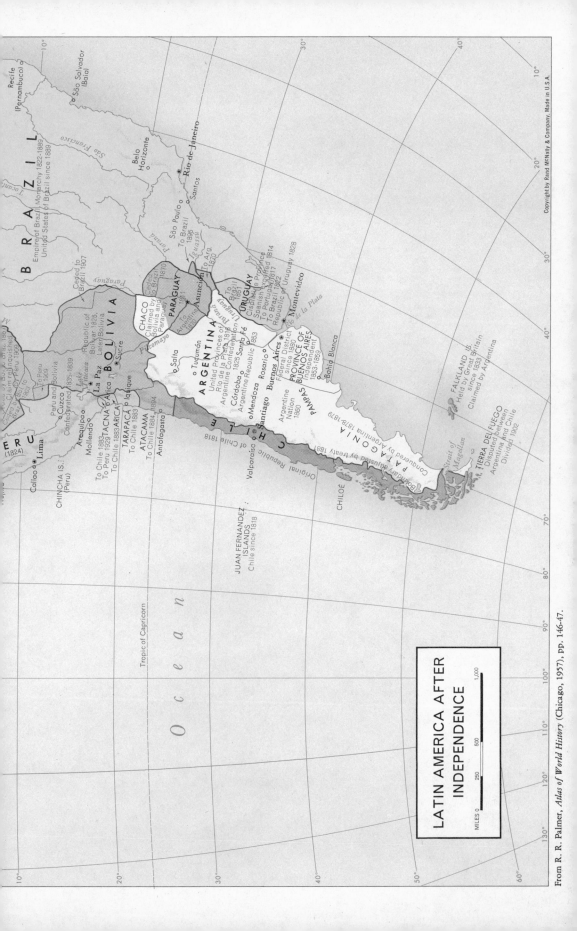

LATIN AMERICA AFTER
INDEPENDENCE

MILES 0   250   500   1,000

From R. R. Palmer, *Atlas of World History* (Chicago, 1957), pp. 146-47.

transportation. Argentina during the 1830's and 1840's was governed by the ruthless Juan Manuel de Rosas, but after his overthrow in 1852 the country progressed rapidly under a succession of gifted presidents such as Bartolomé Mitre and Domingo Sarmiento. By 1840 Chile had also emerged from the period of political insecurity which followed the end of Spanish rule, and during the administrations of Manuel Bulnes, Manuel Montt, José Joaquín Pérez, and Domingo Santa María it expanded toward the Straits of Magellan, subjugated the Araucanian Indians, promoted popular education, and extended democracy in government. In Mexico, the most important Iberian state of North America, the fall of Santa Anna in 1855 opened an era of radical reform in church and state led by Benito Juárez. The attempt of the French to establish an empire in the New World disrupted these efforts, but after the defeat of Maximilian in 1867 (see page 391) the task of political and social modernization was resumed.

Optimistic liberals in both hemispheres were convinced that Latin America was preparing at last to shake off the yoke of oligarchy and clericalism. For wherever they turned they could see their ideas on the march; they could see the growth of parliamentarianism, the expansion of industrialism, the rise of middle-class influence, the unfolding of freedom. Human bondage was being abolished along the Volga and the Mississippi; representative institutions were being introduced in Vienna and Berlin; freedom of worship was being proclaimed in Constantinople and Mexico City; factories were rising in St. Petersburg and Buenos Aires. Hereditary class privileges were being abolished, arbitrary governmental practices were being abandoned, religious discriminations were disappearing, protective tariff walls were falling, man's inhumanity to man was abating. It was good to be a bourgeois liberal around the middle of the nineteenth century. The enlightened and benevolent man of property was on the side of the angels; he fought for a cause that was invincible. As he contemplated the forces of injustice and oppression in flight before his righteousness, he sang with the poet Alfred Tennyson:

> The old order changeth, yielding place to new,
> And God fulfills himself in many ways,
> Lest one good custom should corrupt the world.

Further Reading

Among the many general accounts of the political development of Europe in the years between Metternich and Bismarck two deserve special mention: Frederick B. Artz, *Reaction and Revolution, 1814-1832* (New York: Harper, 1934), and Robert C. Binkley, *Realism and Nationalism,*

1852–1871 (New York: Harper, 1935). Arthur J. May, *The Age of Metternich, 1814–1848* (New York: Holt, 1933), is more modest in scope, but still sound and readable. For the dominant ideologies of the early nineteenth century see Guido De Ruggiero, *The History of European Liberalism* (New York: Oxford Univ. Press, 1927); H. A. L. Fisher, *The Republican Tradition in Europe* (New York: Putnam, 1911); and Hugh Cecil, *Conservatism* (New York: Holt, 1913). Harry W. Laidler, *Social-Economic Movements* (New York: Crowell, 1949), is a convenient survey of socialist thought. It should be supplemented, however, with more penetrating accounts of revolutionary theoreticians and traditions like Isaiah Berlin, *Karl Marx* (New York: Oxford Univ. Press, 1948), and Edmund Wilson, *To the Finland Station* (Garden City: Doubleday, Anchor A6, 1953).

Elie Halévy, *A History of the English People in the Nineteenth Century*, 5 vols. (Gloucester, Mass.: P. Smith, 1949–52), has become a classic. Less comprehensive yet equally sound are E. L. Woodward, *The Age of Reform, 1815–1870* (New York: Oxford Univ. Press, 1938), and David Thomson, *England in the Nineteenth Century* (Baltimore: Penguin A197, 1950). For sheer biographical brilliance nothing surpasses Lytton Strachey, *Queen Victoria* (New York: Harcourt, 1921) and *Eminent Victorians* (Cape Town: M. Miller, 1947), or David Cecil, *Melbourne* (New York: Grosset, Universal Library 7, 1956). E. Bourgeois, *History of Modern France, 1815–1913,* 2 vols. (New York: Macmillan, 1919), is reliable but plodding. Equally learned and much livelier are Frederick B. Artz, *France Under the Bourbon Restoration, 1814–1830* (Cambridge, Mass.: Harvard Univ. Press, 1931), and J. M. Thompson, *Louis Napoleon and the Second Empire* (Oxford: Blackwell, 1954). Napoleon III is portrayed as a picturesque adventurer in Philip Guedalla, *Second Empire* (London: Hodder, 1937), and as a statesman of vision in Albert Guérard, *Napoleon III* (Cambridge, Mass.: Harvard Univ. Press, 1943).

J. G. Legge, *Rhyme and Revolution in Germany* (London: Constable, 1919), is a collection of source materials illustrating the rise of liberalism and nationalism in central Europe. For the events of 1848 there is Veit Valentin, *1848: Chapters of German History* (New York: Norton, 1940), a drastically abridged translation of a major work in German. Perhaps less profound but certainly more readable are P. Robertson, *Revolutions of 1848* (Princeton: Princeton Univ. Press, 1952), and Raymond Postgate, *Story of a Year: 1848* (New York: Oxford Univ. Press, 1956). C. G. Robertson, *Bismarck* (New York: Holt, 1919), still presents the best portrait of the Iron Chancellor available in English, for Adolphus W. Ward, *Germany, 1815–1890,* 3 vols. (New York: Macmillan, 1916–18), suffers from an excess of detail, while A. J. P. Taylor, *Bismarck: The Man and the Statesman* (New York: Knopf, 1955), often sacrifices good judgment for the sake of an aphorism. B. King, *History of Italian Unity,* 2 vols. (New York: Scribner, 1912), and Arthur J. B. Whyte, *The Evolution of Modern Italy, 1715–*

1920 (Oxford: Blackwell, 1944), describes the *Risorgimento*. Among the noteworthy biographies of the political leaders of Italy are W. R. Thayer, *The Life and Times of Cavour,* 2 vols. (Boston: Houghton, 1914); Arthur J. B. Whyte, *The Political Life and Letters of Cavour, 1848–1861* (New York: Oxford, 1930); Gwilym O. Griffith, *Mazzini: Prophet of Modern Europe* (London: Hodder, 1932); Stringfellow Barr, *Mazzini: Portrait of an Exile* (New York: Holt, 1935); and the two studies by George M. Trevelyan, *Garibaldi and the Thousand* (New York: Longmans, 1920), and *Garibaldi and the Making of Italy* (New York: Longmans, 1920).

Helene du Coudray, *Metternich* (New Haven: Yale Univ. Press, 1936), and Josef Redlich, *Emperor Francis Joseph of Austria* (New York: Macmillan, 1929), deal with the Austrian Empire through the lives of two outstanding public figures. A. J. P. Taylor, *The Habsburg Monarchy, 1809–1918* (New York: Macmillan, 1949), is lively but sometimes also frivolous. Michael Karpovich, *Imperial Russia, 1801–1917* (New York: Holt, 1932), provides a useful introduction to more specialized works like Leonid I. Strakhovsky, *Alexander I of Russia* (New York: Norton, 1947); Anatole G. Mazour, *The First Russian Revolution, 1825* (Berkeley: Univ. of California Press, 1937); and Stephen Graham, *Tsar of Freedom: The Life and Reign of Alexander II* (New Haven: Yale Univ. Press, 1935). For economic conditions in Russia see G. Pavlovsky, *Agricultural Russia on the Eve of the Revolution* (London: Routledge, 1930), and Geroid T. Robinson, *Rural Russia under the Old Regime* (London: Macmillan, 1949). R. W. Seton-Watson, *The Rise of Nationality in the Balkans* (London: Constable, 1917), and Wesley M. Gewehr, *The Rise of Nationalism in the Balkans, 1800–1930* (New York: Holt, 1931), examine political developments in the Ottoman Empire, while Vernon J. Puryear, *England, Russia, and the Straits Question, 1844–1856* (Berkeley: Univ. of California Press, 1931), is the best account of the origin and course of the Crimean War.

F. J. Turner, *The Frontier in American History* (New York: Holt, 1920), is a standard work on the westward movement in the United States. The rise of popular democracy forms the theme of a brilliant, provocative book by Arthur M. Schlesinger, Jr., *The Age of Jackson* (Boston: Little, Brown, 1945). On the sectional struggle there is Allan Nevins, *Ordeal of the Union,* 2 vols. (New York: Scribner, 1947), while A. C. Cole, *The Irrepressible Conflict, 1850–1865* (New York: Macmillan, 1934), and J. G. Randall, *The Civil War and Reconstruction* (Boston: Heath, 1937), are among the best examples of the vast historical literature dealing with the Civil War. R. G. Trotter, *Canadian Federation* (London: Dent, 1924), and C. F. Wittke, *History of Canada* (New York: Crofts, 1933), deal with the formation of the federal union in British North America. André Siegfried, *The Race Question in Canada* (New York: Appleton, 1907), is a perceptive study of the relationship between English and French Canadians. The history and society of the Iberian states of the New World are described by

F. García Calderón, *Latin America* (New York: Scribner, 1913); Robert E. Speer, *South American Problems* (New York: Student Volunteer Movement for Foreign Missions, 1912); and A. C. Wilgus (ed.), *South American Dictators during the First Century of Independence* (Washington: George Washington Univ. Press, 1937).

Chapter 25

THE EUROPEANIZATION
OF THE EARTH

B Y THE CLOSE of the nineteenth century Europe unquestionably dominated the earth. It had acquired this dominance partly by empire
building and partly by infiltrating the rest of the world with its
industrial techniques, manufactured products, and political, scientific, and religious ideas. By 1880 the powers of Europe, which had earlier
been disillusioned with imperialism, were again growing consciously imperialistic. Some proceeded to add, greatly or moderately, to empires whose
foundations they had laid much earlier. And as the search for colonies
became competitive and developed into a race, powers with no previous
territorial ambitions outside Europe felt the economic, military, or psychological need for expansion and founded wholly new empires.

England and France, which had been colonial powers since the seventeenth century, took advantage of long experience and the strategic location
of older possessions to expand their overseas holdings enormously. Holland,
already the possessor of rich footholds in Indonesia, annexed additional
parts of the East Indies. Spain and Portugal, the first European colonizing
states, which had long since lost most of their original empires, felt the
expansionist fever again and increased their territories in Africa. Russia, a
land colossus stretching from the Baltic to North America, avoided the
seaways, gladly parted with Alaska to the United States, and expanded at
the expense of Turkey in the Caucasus, the Moslem principalities in central
Asia, and Manchu China along the Amur River and the Pacific. Belgium,
Italy, and Germany, which as nations were creations of the nineteenth century, became imperialistic for economic and patriotic reasons and built new
empires, Belgium and Italy in Africa, and Germany in Africa, the Far East,
and Oceania. Some European states took no part in the race for colonies.
Austria-Hungary and the Scandinavian kingdoms remained aloof, although
Denmark clung to its old West Indian possessions and took precautions to
bolster its half-recognized sovereignty over Greenland. Turkey, a semi-

European state, was declining and on the defensive, and the newly-liberated Balkan countries thought only of expanding their immediate frontiers. Neutralized, landlocked Switzerland refrained from any form of overseas competition. Two non-European powers, the United States and Japan, began acquiring colonies late in the nineteenth century. Their expansion was largely a part of the movement originating in Europe. The United States had now reached substantially the stage of industrialization and commercial ambition that Great Britain and Germany had attained. Superficially Westernized Japan had come to resemble a European power in ambition and world outlook, and though the Japanese remained spiritually Oriental they could expand only by acquiring the arms and using the methods of the West.

What is meant by Europeanization? European domination of the globe meant more than the building of empires. Western inventions, gadgets, and physical comforts penetrated to the remotest parts. The network of rails built by the British in India altered that country more than did the work of all the empire builders from Robert Clive in the eighteenth century to George Curzon in the twentieth. Chinese provinces that seldom saw a European were ultimately pierced by rails and telegraph wires. Afghan tribesmen owned European rifles, Abyssinian statesmen regulated their days by watches from Zurich, and nervous Persian grandees sought remedies for insomnia or constipation in patent medicines from Berlin or Bordeaux. Mongol tribesmen doctored their camels' saddle sores with American salves—or even tooth powders—while inhabitants of Río de Oro and Río Muni received smoking pleasure from cheap Spanish cigarettes. Scholars in Moslem mosques and Brahman temples reinforced their dimming vision with European spectacles. Native physicians trained in Western methods took temperatures and cured or killed patients in Manila, and similarly-trained dentists filled teeth in Port Arthur and Port Said. Steam locomotives built in Warwickshire chugged between Tientsin and Peking, while steamboats constructed on the Clyde bore dark-skinned passengers over Lake Nyassa. More than one British trooper campaigning beyond the Khyber Pass was knifed with steel bearing a Leeds or Sheffield trademark, and in far Mozambique the heads of one party of Portuguese were impaled on steel points made in Europe.

The impact of the West on the outside world was not limited to science and industry. Protestant and Catholic missionaries in the nineteenth century spread the gospel as never before. The optimism which Protestant England felt regarding conversion opportunities was expressed early in the century in the well-remembered lines of Anglican Bishop Reginald Heber, known in churches as the "Missionary Hymn":

> *From Greenland's icy mountains,*
> *From India's coral strand;*

Where Afric's sunny fountains
Roll down their golden sand:
From many an ancient river,
From many a palmy plain,
They call us to deliver
Their land from error's chain.

Perhaps Heber and like-minded churchmen exaggerated the strength of the "call" being sent them from benighted, dark-skinned heathen, but their work did bear fruit. In the islands of the Pacific and in Africa south of the Moslem belt they made millions of converts, though they had less success in Asia. Wherever they founded missions they endeavored to introduce the only way of life they knew, the Western way. By use of medicines and all other means within their limited power, they strove to cure the sick, feed the hungry, and make the miserable lives of the natives more bearable. If they acted as forerunners of imperialism, they did so for the most part innocently and unknowingly.

Non-Europeans could not help being impressed with the prowess of the Westerners, who seemed to have the civilization that succeeded where others failed. Because the white man could make a superior gun, build a ship that crossed the ocean rapidly, construct iron monsters that ran swiftly on rails, and prevent or cure diseases that had previously meant certain death, it appeared to follow that his views on other matters must likewise be superior. The black, brown, or yellow man proved often willing to give these other ideas a test. There was, for example, the white man's theory of government. By the late nineteenth century all Occidental states except Russia had some form of representative institution, and this fact was noted in Africa and Asia. It is true that by 1900 only Japan, the most Occidentalized of the Asiatic countries, had in any way succeeded in conforming to the European patterns of government. Yet in both China and the Spanish-held Philippines, agitation for republics had begun years before the turn of the century.

Africans and Orientals also were impressed by European nationalism, that intangible yet mighty force which made the Western states such solid entities. From great Asiatic cities to tiny African villages natives could hear "Rule Britannia," "La Marseillaise," "Deutschland über Alles," "La Brabançonne," and "Inno di Garibaldi," accompanied by elaborate rites and salutes to the flag. Those who visited Europe witnessed even greater patriotic pomp. Nationalistic writings by Rudyard Kipling or Heinrich von Treitschke could be read by Ceylonese, Siamese, and Madagascans, whose form of nationalism in the past had been devotion to a tribe, a religion, a caste, or a dynasty. The Western idea proved contagious, and non-Europeans learned to think in nationalistic terms, although different peoples made the transition in different ways. In Japan earlier feudal loyalties were merged into the worship of an emperor, a hitherto secondary figure who now became sacred. Chinese nationalism was equated with the ancient objection to all foreigners, though with a growing realization that the "foreign devil" must be somewhat emulated. The Indian movement's objective came to be expulsion of the British, although the multitude of races, creeds, and languages made any other basis of agreement difficult to find. In the Philippines it began in 1889 with the formation of the nationalistic and secret Katipunan Society, whose first objective was the murder of all Spanish officials and priests and its second the expulsion of Spain from the islands. Yet by 1900, or even by 1914, militant Asian nationalism had not progressed to the point of seriously threatening Europe's domination, and the African brand gained ground even more slowly. As the present century opened, the statesmen and citizens of Europe had small reason to think that their world dominion would pass away within the lifetime of a generation already born.

1 : The Extension of the European Empires

IN 1815 the statesmen at the Congress of Vienna had redrawn the map of Europe, while paying much less attention to the rest of the globe. The only colonial gainer had been Great Britain; the losers had been France, Spain, and the Netherlands. And even the British had made their gains more as the by-product of the recent wars than as the result of genuine expansionism. Europe had small interest in overseas possessions just then. The English throne was still held by the aged George III, in whose reign the thirteen American colonies had been lost under circumstances humiliating to the British people. Elderly Frenchmen could remember 1763, when France had surrendered Canada and the Mississippi Valley, and comparatively young ones recalled the recent loss of Haiti. The wars for Spanish American independence were well under way by 1815, and astute European statesmen, notably Talleyrand, foresaw the early liquidation of Spain's New World empire. Brazil still hung to Portugal by a slender thread, though many could predict the early snapping of that thread, which, in fact, did occur in 1822.

The present and the recent past combined to make Europeans consider the acquisition of colonies wasted effort and unprofitable experience, and the growth of industrialism had not yet produced a new drive for colonial possessions (see page 370). Jeremy Bentham, the English utilitarian philosopher, insisted that the British colonial empire merely drained the national treasury, because it provided no tax revenue and needed expensive protection by the Royal Navy. Bentham was also fond of pointing out that the United States as an independent republic furnished the United Kingdom a far more profitable market than it had ever furnished as a group of colonies. Another opinion was that colonies remained loyal to a mother country only as long as they needed protection. The eighteenth-century French finance minister Anne Robert Turgot had said, "Colonies are like fruits which cling to the tree only until they ripen." In the decades of growing liberalism and free trade following the Congress of Vienna the original purpose of colonies, which had been to supply the mother country with raw materials and a monopolized market, appeared to have grown obsolete.

The unfavorable attitude toward possessions persisted in many minds into the second half of the century. Some English statesmen regarded their colonies as burdens to be dispensed with as soon as possible. At the outbreak of the American Civil War in 1861 William Ewart Gladstone hopefully suggested that his country might avoid the fearful impending conflict by ceding Canada to the North as compensation for the loss of the slaveholding states. Prussian Otto von Bismarck said in 1868, "I will have no colonies. They are only valuable for creating office holders. A colonial history will be about as useful to us as sable robes for a Polish noble family that has no shirts." Later, at the Congress of Berlin, he declared that Tunisia was not worth a bad cigar. In 1889, in one of his last speeches to the German Reichstag, he said, "To this day I am not a 'colonies man' and I entertain the gravest apprehensions on the subject; but I was compelled to decide upon yielding to the general demand of the nation. . . . If the locomotive of empire has struck out on a track by itself, I shall not be the one to throw stones in its way." Other opinions could be cited to show that European statesmen often moved reluctantly toward imperialism. Move they did, but often only after their hands had been forced by empire-minded agents in colonial areas.

BRITISH IMPERIAL EXPANSION—ASIA

The British Empire in 1815 looked small on the map when compared with its size a century later. Its center of gravity, however, was already visibly shifting from the New World to the Old, where it included about half of India, the Australian colonies of New South Wales and Tasmania, and the Cape of Good Hope. In the Western Hemisphere it consisted of eastern Canada, Guiana, and a number of West Indian islands.

Although the British were in no imperialistic frame of mind in 1815, they valued India as the foundation stone of their empire. The huge subcontinent represented lucrative commerce, and Britain lived by trade. Although the government of British Hindustan still rested with the East India Company, the crown steadily encroached upon its sovereignty, and as recently as 1813 had deprived the company of its trading monopoly. Lancashire cotton goods woven on power looms steadily captured the Indian market. The company, unable to compete by offering its own cotton, hand-woven by native labor, had turned to opium selling as a revenue producer. Opium had first been grown exclusively in the company's Bengal territory. When independent Indian states began contesting this monopoly by growing the poppy themselves, the company made treaties with their princes to restrict the competition. China was a market for company opium, and the amount annually entering the Manchu Empire through Macao and Canton soon reached sixteen thousand chests.

In addition to enriching traders and manufacturers, India furnished careers to thousands of civil servants and soldiers. Englishmen now spent their entire active lives in the Indian bureaucracy, which was being re-organized in favor of trained officials in place of the plunderers and spoils-men who had disgraced it in the past century. And at a time when the rest of the empire was at peace, the frequent Indian wars gave promising officers opportunity to obtain the combat seasoning they needed.

Between the fall of Napoleon and the outbreak of the Sepoy Mutiny in 1857 British India grew rapidly. A campaign against the warlike Gur-khas of Nepal converted those sturdy mountaineers from enemies to friendly allies of the English, in whose Indian armies they thereafter en-listed in considerable numbers. Equally successful campaigns against the Maratha confederacy of central India caused its chiefs in 1819 to accept British overlordship, with the understanding that their foreign relations should be handled in future by the raj (British régime). When Burma gave trouble in 1826 a company army invaded that country, which ceded most of its sea frontage. Later Anglo-Burmese wars in 1852 and 1886 brought about the annexation of the rest of Burma.

The company received a setback when it invaded Afghanistan in 1839 to prevent possible Russian domination of that frontier country. A British army, attempting to retreat from Kabul, was caught in mountain snows and wiped out by the attacks of Afghans and frontier tribesmen. As the Com-pany's raj had always rested largely on prestige and a tradition of invinci-bility, this costly debacle weakened discipline among its native and sepoy soldiers. It also caused the warlike Sikhs of the Punjab to prepare for war in the belief that they could defeat the company. Before dealing with the Sikhs the British annexed the territory of Sind at the mouths of the Indus. General Sir Charles Napier performed this seizure in 1843, without orders and without particular provocation from the people of Sind. *"Peccavi"* ("I have sinned") was his one-word Latin report to Governor-General Lord Ellenborough, and he described the action in his diary as "a very advanta-geous, useful, humane piece of rascality." Two wars with the Sikhs then fol-lowed, and though the British sepoys did not fight with their old-time discipline and vigor, the result was the annexation of the Punjab in 1849. The company reorganized the province and treated it well, providing encouragement to the warlike Sikhs to enlist in its armies, where they made excellent soldiers.

THE SEPOY MUTINY

The next major event in Indian history was the Sepoy Mutiny, in which the British were threatened with the loss of the empire they had been building for a century. Reasons for the mutiny were numerous. Prophecies predicted the early fall of the British raj, and the Afghan disaster had not been forgotten. In connection with the recent Crimean War (1854–1856), sepoys had been warned that they must cross the ocean if so ordered, and the caste-conscious soldiers feared that in a foreign environment their caste status would be injured. Indians had been alarmed by the aggressiveness of Lord Dalhousie, governor-general from 1849 to 1856. He had annexed native states on the least provocation, and had built railways and telegraph lines across the country until some suspected that he meant to make India a replica of Europe. A horrifying report also ran to the effect that paper cartridges for the new Enfield rifles being issued to the troops were greased with the fat of the cow, which Hindus worshiped, and of the pig, which Moslems abhorred. Since the paper containers must be opened with the teeth, the most sacred religious taboos were threatened. The rumor had a factual basis, and although the government quickly realized and corrected its blunder, the damage to morale could not be repaired. More important than any of the Indian beliefs was the fact that numerous British regiments had been sent to the Crimea and had not been returned to Hindustan by 1857. This left the percentage of white troops to sepoys dangerously low.

The mutiny began at Meerut near Delhi in May, 1857, when several regiments rioted and slew their English officers. Other units followed suit, and a throng of mutineers marched to Delhi, where a descendant of the old Mogul line still lived. Moslem sepoys gave an Islamic touch to the revolt by proclaiming that obscure person Emperor of India. This rash step cooled relations between Moslem and Hindu mutineers and guaranteed that the newly-recruited Sikh sepoys, with their centuries-old tradition of hatred for the Moguls, would never co-operate. The Sikhs in fact now assisted the British to suppress the very sepoys who a decade earlier had been used to conquer them. For the time, however, north-central India was in the hands of the mutineers, who held Delhi, massacred all the English at Cawnpore, and besieged a small garrison and numerous white families in Lucknow. In small towns and outlying districts Britishers had small chance of escape. Energetic measures in central India kept the mutiny from spreading southward, and Bengal, where Calcutta was the capital of British India, remained fairly quiet. Before the first reinforcements from England landed in November, 1857, the British forces already present, aided by Sikhs and Gurkhas, had broken the back of the mutiny. Delhi had been retaken and Lucknow relieved. The raj was saved, largely because the rebellion had been a soldiers' revolt, without substantial backing from the Indian people. The year 1858 was spent in stamping out the embers of the mutiny, and by the opening of 1859 India was again at peace.

The principal casualty in this bloody episode was the East India Company. In 1858 an act of Parliament abolished the venerable organization, transferring its jurisdiction and holdings to the crown. A minister for India entered the British cabinet, and the governor-general at Calcutta became the queen's viceroy. Her Majesty undertook to fulfill all treaties with the native Indian princes just as they had been guaranteed by the company. From 1858 to 1919 British India was ruled by the minister and the viceroy, the latter being aided by a civil bureaucracy with headquarters first at Calcutta and then at New Delhi following the transfer of the capital there in the twentieth century. Most of India's population now lived directly subject to the crown, though a number of princes continued to have internal jurisdiction over their states and to possess small armies. At each princely court dwelt a British resident to advise the sovereign and to direct his foreign policy, and the fact that this advice amounted to a command was played down as much as possible. The princes felt secure on their thrones and became powerful supporters of the British raj.

The main era of expansion had ended, but in the second half of the nineteenth century the British acquired what remained of Burma and advanced on the northwest frontier. They invaded Afghanistan again in 1878–79, this time successfully, and although they did not permanently occupy the country they accomplished their purpose of checking Russian influence. In 1904 Viceroy George Curzon, alarmed by the growth of Muscovite prestige in Tibet, sent a British-commanded Sikh expedition to the Dalai Lama's hitherto isolated city of Lhasa. Tibet continued nominally subject to Manchu China, but British influence became paramount there and remained so for years. In 1876 Prime Minister Disraeli devised a new honor for the queen by having her proclaimed "Kaisar-i-Hind," meaning Empress of India, though the words are a synthetic creation taken from no one language living or dead. This new title for Victoria, though in a sense meaningless, had symbolic value because it raised the dignity of Indian princes and people by giving their ruler a title which specifically named their country. Victoria became Queen-Empress and her successors King-Emperors until the independence of India in 1947.

Through the nineteenth century the British conscientiously worked to improve India. The Charter Act, passed by Parliament in 1833, practically ended the company's commercial career, provided for reform of Indian law, and made English the language of future higher education. It also said, "No native of India, or any natural-born subject of His Majesty, shall be disabled from holding any place, office, or employment by reason of his religion, place of birth, descent or colour." Slavery, which flourished until 1843 in India, was abolished in that year by the British. Suttee (*sati*), the custom of burning widows by their husbands' tombs, had been forbidden, despite many Hindu objections, in 1829. Thuggee (*thagi*), the occupation of a fraternity of hereditary religious murderers who infested the Indian roads, was stamped out, with many thugs being caught and punished by hanging, imprisonment, or transportation.

India developed rapidly under the company and more rapidly under the crown. The American Civil War and the Union blockade of Southern ports created a heavy demand for Indian cotton, whose price increased in four years by 450 per cent. Although this inflated cost dropped after the war, by 1875 there were thirty-eight cotton mills in the Bombay Presidency alone, financed mostly by Indian capital and employing Indian labor. With local cheap workers operating British-made machines, coarse cotton cloth from England, which had once captured the Indian market, could now be undercut and undersold. Indian jute experienced a rapid development, mostly in the Calcutta vicinity. Iron smelting had begun well back in the nineteenth century but progressed slowly until 1886, when Jamshedi Tata, of the rich Parsi Tata family of Bombay, entered the industry. He purchased an old steel mill which previous owners had found unprofitable, and with imported machinery began the manufacture of steel. The center of the industry became Jamshedpur in western Bengal near the center of India's richest iron and coal deposits. Large-scale steel production dates from 1911, the year in which the Jamshedpur mills entered the export business.

India has always suffered periodic droughts and famines. The British government first adopted a system of money relief, which helped little when there was no rice to be purchased. The need was for a series of extensive irrigation developments to prevent drought and for an adequate railway and road system to aid distribution. Initial steps toward increasing agricultural acreage were taken in the administration of Sir John Lawrence (1864–1869). Within a dozen years the land irrigated by government works had risen to 10,500 acres, and by 1931 to 31,000,000 acres. A factor partly defeating the purpose of this expansion was the high Indian birth rate, which, with the comparative security brought by the British raj, caused the already-overburdening population of India to grow at increased speed.

The native intelligentsia in the late nineteenth century began thinking in nationalistic terms despite the great barriers to unity posed by religious and caste differences and the absence of a common language other than English and the synthetic Hindustani. The first Indian National Congress, of Hindu, Parsi, and Moslem delegates, met at Bombay in 1885. The Congress made several mild demands and suggestions, concerned largely with equal opportunities for Indians in the civil service. Friction developed as the Moslems, with a smaller professional and literary class than the others, doubted their ability to compete successfully for positions and opposed the

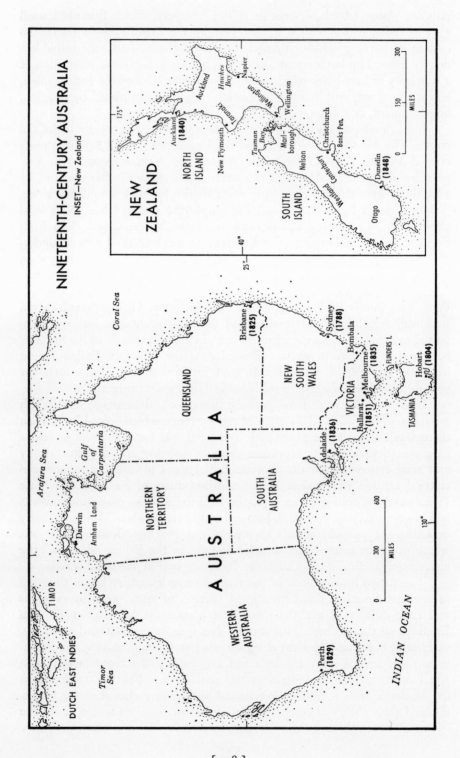

NINETEENTH-CENTURY AUSTRALIA

INSET—New Zealand

Hindu-Parsi demands. Later Congresses proved more vehement in requesting reforms, but to the outbreak of the First World War Indian nationalism had not assumed menacing proportions.

Elsewhere in Asia the British confined their acquisitions to strategic points or favorable trading centers. Singapore was purchased from the sultan of Johore in 1824; and Aden, guarding the Red Sea entrance, was seized by force in 1839. Following the Opium War with China, the British in 1842 annexed the island of Hong Kong, where they soon constructed a thriving city.

BRITISH IMPERIAL EXPANSION—AUSTRALASIA

England's Australian colonies originated in 1788 when Captain Arthur Philip of the Royal Navy brought a fleet loaded with convicts to establish a penal settlement at Sydney on Botany Bay in New South Wales. This was a direct result of the loss of the thirteen American colonies, to which the British had long shipped the overflow from their jails. The Australian prisoners were petty offenders and debtors rather than hardened criminals. As there was no place to which they could escape, strict confinement for them was unnecessary. Some took a jocular view of their situation and within a few years could sing:

> *True patriots we, for be it understood,*
> *We left our country for our country's good.*[1]

Australia's only previous inhabitants had been a sparse race of "Blackfellows," who may have come in remote ages from south India. They were among the most primitive human beings in the world, and offered no opposition to white exploration and colonization of Australia.

New South Wales stagnated during its first few years, as the colonists could not gain a living from the country and depended on supplies shipped from England. The situation of this "rural slum" improved with the discovery of nearby coal deposits. Then John Macarthur, a captain in the Sydney garrison, learned that sheep from nearly all quarters could thrive in Australia. Meanwhile, another convict settlement had been made in Tasmania, which existed by the production of whale oil and sealskins. By 1820 the combined population of the two colonies had risen to 34,000 and by 1840 Australia had 190,000 white inhabitants. Free immigrants now outnumbered convicts and a movement existed to ban future forced migrations. Tasmanian numbers had grown too great for the island, and colonists from there had crossed to the mainland where, with the help of immigrants from New South Wales, they founded Melbourne, the future capital of Victoria, in

---

[1] G. W. Rusden, *History of Australia* (Melbourne: Melville, Mullen & Slade, 1897), Vol. I, p. 51.

1836. Steps toward colonizing Queensland in the north were taken in 1841, and a number of Melbourne sheep and cattle men drove their livestock westward and made a beginning of Adelaide, the first settlement in South Australia. Distant Western Australia had been colonized since 1829, the year of the founding of Perth, a sheep-raising settlement on the Swan River. The attractive name of this stream had been used as a lure to draw settlers from the mother country, who felt some disappointment when they saw that all the swans were black. By mid-century the importation of convicts had almost ceased, both because free settlers did not like to associate with the "old lags" and because the preponderance of males among them increased the already high percentage of men to women in Australia. Tasmania continued to receive a few convicts until 1853, and Western Australia obtained a cargo by request of its local labor employers as late as 1867.

Australia experienced its first major gold strike in 1851. The lucky prospector, Edward Hammond Hargraves, had just returned from the '49 rush to California and noticed the resemblance between the Sierra rock formations and those behind the Blue Mountains west of Sydney. Before the year ended still richer deposits had been found in Victoria. The gold rush furnished the principal reason for Australia's population increase from 405,000 in 1851 to 1,145,000 in 1861. Gold also explains why the last vestige of penal-colony government was now abandoned in most of the colonies in favor of responsible self-government. The exception was Western Australia, where convict transportation had continued longest and where the propertied classes preferred continuing under crown control to sharing authority with ex-convicts. Not until 1890 did Western Australia care to accept the democratic status of responsible government. Little enthusiasm for federation existed in the Australian colonies, which showed their fierce independence of each other by refusing to adopt a standard gauge for their railways. Much localism and provincialism remained to be overcome before the unified and federalized Commonwealth of Australia could be proclaimed on the first day of the twentieth century.

The New Zealand islands had been discovered by the Dutchman Abel Janszoon Tasman in 1642 and carefully coasted by the Englishman James Cook in 1770. North Island had as inhabitants the handsome Polynesian Maoris; South Island contained a handful of these people but was otherwise empty. Though highly intelligent, the Maoris had a stone-age culture and a primitive religion. They fought fiercely when angry and practiced cannibalism, more from vindictiveness than a desire for human flesh. They lived under the rule of tribal chieftains and held land on a communal basis.

Led by the Church of England in 1814, both Protestants and Catholics opened missions on North Island. Within thirty years the missionaries had converted most of the Maoris, at least nominally, to Christianity; had stopped cannibalism; and had modified the wild ways of the people. The preponderance of English missionary work, the fear that France might

The Suez Canal, which required ten years to construct, was the work of a private corporation headed by the French promoter Ferdinand de Lesseps, who had the aid of Khedive Ismail of Egypt. The grand opening, on November 17, 1869, was a gala event attended by sovereigns and illustrious persons from all over the earth. Linking the Mediterranean with the Red Sea, the canal greatly shortened the voyage between Europe and the Orient.

Cecil John Rhodes was a multimillionaire and British empire builder in southern Africa. His dream was a solid stretch of British territory extending from Cape Colony to Egypt. Although failing to realize this, he was largely responsible for the annexation of Rhodesia and Nyasaland. A lifelong enemy of the Boer republics of the Transvaal and Orange Free State, he was primarily responsible for the Boer War of 1899–1902. This picture shows Rhodes relaxing during one of his many journeys through wild country.

On the overthrow of the Manchus in 1912, the presidency of China was taken by Yüan Shih Kai, a veteran Chinese soldier who had served the Manchus and had only turned against them at the last when their cause became hopeless. Yüan, who found the task of governing the new republic very difficult, remained president until his death in 1916. He made an unsuccessful effort to restore the monarchy with himself as emperor.

Here is a scene in Manchuria during the Russo-Japanese War of 1904–1905. The Russian soldiers and Red Cross workers in the picture appear to have interrupted their duties to attend the hurried funeral. Neither the name of the officer in the coffin nor the town where the burial took place can now be known.

attempt annexation, and the efforts of a colonization society in which the Colonial Office lacked confidence, stimulated Great Britain to take official action in New Zealand in 1840. In that year Captain William Hobson of the Royal Navy and many of the North Island chieftains made the Treaty of Waitangi, by which England obtained sovereignty and the queen promised the natives her protection. The latter received assurance that their land right would be protected.

English emigration to New Zealand moved slowly at first and for a time was confined to North Island. Relations with the Maoris became tense and the colonization company got on badly with the settlers, most of whom were not farmers by occupation. Yet by 1850 several settlements had been established, with Auckland as the largest, and the Australian gold discoveries soon increased New Zealand prosperity by creating a demand for foodstuffs. New Zealand then had its own gold rush, beginning in 1861 with a strike in Otago in South Island. This drew many settlers southward at a time when North Island was being plagued by a series of Maori wars which dragged on spasmodically from 1860 to 1870. The natives, though beaten, won general respect because of their gallantry in war, and when peace came they received decent treatment. They regained some of their lost land and obtained representation in the New Zealand parliament. The destiny of this race appears to be absorption by the whites, as no barrier to intermarriage exists and race mixture goes on rapidly.

After 1870 New Zealand began a policy of governmental borrowing and spending to build railways and stimulate prosperity. Although this created severe financial problems, it at least brought immigration, and by 1880 the population of the two islands had reached 485,000, inclusive of 45,000 Maoris. The islands had meanwhile acquired democratic self-government. Local subdivisions were wiped out and all important decisions were henceforth made by the New Zealand parliament, although a royal governor still represented the crown.

BRITISH IMPERIAL EXPANSION—SOUTH AFRICA

In 1806, as a by-product of the Napoleonic Wars, a British expedition seized Cape Colony from the Dutch, and England kept this region on the conclusion of peace. Although the original settlers were Dutch Boers, called Afrikaners, with a sprinkling of French Huguenots, English immigrants now arrived in considerable numbers. Relations between the British government and the Boers became strained, especially after the abolition of slavery throughout the empire in 1833. Four years later many slaveholding Boers trekked northward with their families in wagons to avoid British jurisdiction. Some crossed the Orange River to establish the Orange Free State, and other more venturesome ones crossed the Vaal to found the Transvaal Republic. The British, meanwhile, occupied the Natal region in 1842.

Through the nineteenth century the crown government and the British-held districts were generally on bad terms with the two independent Boer communities, as the Afrikaners remained slaveholders and insisted on their right to exploit the Negroes. Ill feeling was intensified in 1869 by a diamond strike and rush of prospectors to the borderlands of the Orange and Transvaal republics. Many of the diamond-seekers were British who wished the crown to annex the Boer communities, but the Colonial Office for the time decided not to yield to the demands of the prospectors.

The situation changed in 1877 when the Transvaal Boers seemed on the verge of destruction at the hands of Cetshwayo, the powerful king of the neighboring Zulus. Prime Minister Benjamin Disraeli, thinking that the Boers now wished union with the empire, allowed the annexation of the Transvaal to be proclaimed. There followed the Zulu War, in which the British, after an initial setback, defeated Cetshwayo and virtually annexed his country. It was then seen that Disraeli had been mistaken and that the Boers had wished to remain independent. An outbreak in 1881, in which small bodies of British troops received rough handling from the embattled Dutch farmers, caused the ministry to reassess the situation. Headed now by the Liberal Prime Minister Gladstone, it decided not to press the issue but to restore the Transvaal's independence. This decision, though probably a wise one, had an unfortunate repercussion, as it led the Afrikaners to think they had defeated the British Empire and forced Mr. Gladstone to yield. Imperial-minded Englishmen, who disliked the prime minister, regarded his action as a disgraceful sacrifice of the national honor. From 1881 until the outbreak of the Boer War eighteen years later, the two British possessions Natal and the Cape existed as self-governing colonies, and the Boer states Transvaal and Orange as fully-independent republics.

BRITISH IMPERIAL EXPANSION—AMERICA

The internal history of Canada until the formation of the united dominion in 1867, has been told in another chapter (see page 411). Several boundary questions with the United States arose in the first half of the century, although each was adjusted peacefully. A convention in 1818 agreed upon the 49th parallel as the frontier from the Lake of the Woods westward to the "Stoney" (Rocky) Mountains. Border rivalry between New Brunswick and Maine was settled by a boundary compromise in 1842. Four years later the 49th parallel frontier was extended from the Rockies to the Pacific Coast, with all Vancouver Island being left in British hands.

In the 1850's the era of railway building began, and as most of the lines ran in an east-west direction they gave an impetus to interprovincial trade. Their existence revealed the possibilities of tapping the resources of the great Canadian west. The principal early line, called the Grand Trunk, connected the western frontier of Ontario with eastern railways extending to the Atlantic. Although a financial failure and bankrupt by 1861, the Grand Trunk drew the loose parts of Canada closer together and stimulated thoughts of union between the provinces.

West of the settled provinces to the Arctic and the Pacific, British North America remained under Hudson's Bay Company jurisdiction. As long as this vast preserve remained a sparsely-settled land of trappers, the company's jurisdiction proved adequate. But in 1856 a gold discovery along the Fraser River on the Pacific coast brought such a rush of settlers that the province of British Columbia was created in 1858. Simultaneously, a heavy influx of population into the Red River region of present Manitoba placed British Columbia a step closer to eastern Canada. British Columbia joined the dominion in 1871, on the condition that within a decade a railway should link it with the east. Sir John Macdonald, the dominion prime minister, gave the charter for the line to a group of Canadian financiers. Although not completed within the stipulated time the Canadian Pacific began operating in 1885. Its financial problems, like those of many a United States line, merely began with its completion. It was so thoroughly associated with the Macdonald political Conservatives that a party member said, "the day that the Canadian Pacific busts, the Conservative Party busts the day after." Fortunately for both party and railway, a rebellion soon occurred in the Canadian west, and the part played by the line in its suppression restored it to popular favor.

The railway provided a needed stimulus to Canadian development. Immigrants bound west, who had previously traveled through the United States, could now use it to go directly to their new homes. Assorted racial groups—Ukrainians, Czechs, Poles, Magyars, German Mennonites, and Jews—settled beside other newcomers from the old provinces and from Britain and the United States. They naturally raised many new problems, some of them religious, and these problems became connected with the question of church teachings in the public schools. From 1867 to 1914 Canada developed along lines familiar in the United States. Empty areas filled up, young towns and cities dotted the prairies, and more railways were built. Agriculture remained the dominion's mainstay, but industry appeared, financed by British loans and encouraged by bounties and tax exemptions from the dominion and provincial governments.

The British Empire held its Caribbean colonies during the nineteenth century without expanding them. Abolition of slavery in 1833 struck the economies of the West Indian and British Guiana plantations a heavy blow and especially injured those of Jamaica. Freed Negroes often preferred idleness to any form of labor for wages, and chose to roam at will and live by whatever means seemed ready to hand. After a formidable black uprising in 1865, the white Jamaicans felt unsafe and abandoned the self-government they had enjoyed for two centuries. They voluntarily became a crown colony, governed and protected from London.

FRENCH IMPERIAL EXPANSION

Compared with the complicated history of the British Empire in the nineteenth century, the colonial story of France until the partition of Africa is a simple one, quickly told. One point of resemblance exists, however, for the British Empire is often said to have been built in a fit of absent minded-ness, meaning that the expansion went on without attracting much attention in England. With France, until the closing decades of the century, the case was much the same.

The restored French monarchy emerged from the Congress of Vienna with no non-European possessions other than Senegal, French Guiana, a few West Indian and Indian Ocean islands, and a scattering of ports in India. During the next fifteen years France did little in the colonial line, but in 1830 its king, Charles X, decided to chastise Algeria. The Algerines, who were little more than a nest of pirates, had given ample provocation, and Charles announced that "satisfaction of the honor of France, with the aid of the Omnipotent, would redound to the benefit of Christianity." French troops began the seizure of Algeria in June, 1830, but the subjects of Charles showed either indifference or hostility to the enterprise and a month later displayed more interest in his dethronement than in his African ven-ture. The July Monarchy of Louis Philippe found itself burdened with the embarrassing heritage of Algeria. The new government decided against aban-doning the project and undertook to complete the conquest, but thorough pacification required over twenty years. By then Louis Philippe had been replaced by a republican régime in Paris, and one of the new government's first acts in 1848 was the abolition of slavery not only in Algeria but every-where in the French Empire.

When Napoleon III became emperor in 1853 he turned to imperialistic schemes as a way of drumming up popularity at home, but did not notice-ably convert the French people to such a policy. He extended the frontiers of Algeria southward, pushed French authority farther up the Senegal River, increased his country's influence in Madagascar, commenced the oc-cupation of French Somaliland, and acquired a foothold in Indo-China. Any gains in public favor these advances may have won the emperor were more than eclipsed by his tragic blunder in undertaking the Mexico ad-venture in 1862. Napoleon's troops overran most of that republic, and Archduke Maximilian, brother of the Austrian emperor, was persuaded to go there to reign as emperor. When the United States ended the Civil War the Andrew Johnson government forced Napoleon by threats to withdraw his forces, leaving Maximilian to die in 1867 before a Mexican firing squad. The prestige of imperial France, greatly lowered by this tragedy, was shattered in 1870 at the Battle of Sedan, in which the emperor and his defeated soldiers remained prisoners in Prussian hands.

The Third French Republic that followed proved more imperialistic than any of its monarchic predecessors. It occupied Tunisia in 1881 to forestall the Italians, vigorously engaged in the scramble for Equatorial Africa, annexed Madagascar and Indo-China, and acquired territory from Manchu China. By then, imperialism had again grown popular and the French public vigorously supported this expansion.

Although the construction of the Suez Canal ultimately aided British imperialism, the work itself was largely French. Ferdinand de Lesseps, the son of an agent who had served the first Napoleon in Egypt, was more of a diplomat and promoter than an engineer, but credit for the canal is mainly his. He gained a concession from Saïd Pasha, viceroy of Egypt, and to finance construction he sold bonds, mostly in France. De Lesseps had opposition from Great Britain, which disapproved of the canal and preferred to solve the problem of transportation between the Mediterranean and the Indian Ocean by railway from Syria to the Persian Gulf. Lord Palmerston, the English prime minister, ridiculed de Lesseps' project, saying, "There are three authorities adverse to the execution of this scheme. The English Government, the Turkish Government and Nature. The first two are not likely to change their views, but the third will be found inflexible." De Lesseps was often hard pressed for capital, but received Egyptian aid in the form of near slave labor and French aid in the form of diplomatic support from Napoleon III. On November 17, 1869, he had the satisfaction of seeing the canal opened for traffic, while a distinguished group, including the empress of France and the prince and princess of Wales, looked on. In 1875 the Egyptian Viceroy Ismail became nearly bankrupt, and he placed his large block of Suez Canal shares on the market. British Prime Minister Disraeli seized the opportunity this offered England, and at a time when Parliament was not in session bought the shares with money borrowed from the Rothschild firm. These, although less than a majority, gave Britain substantial voting control of the canal, a control exercised until its seizure by Egypt in the summer of 1956.

DUTCH IMPERIAL EXPANSION

The Hollanders, because they had been allies, however unwilling, of Revolutionary France and Napoleon, lost Ceylon and the Cape in 1815 but were allowed to retain Dutch Guiana and Curaçao in the New World and to repossess their substantial foothold in the East Indies. Nothing important happened in the Western Hemisphere colonies in the nineteenth century, but in the Eastern colonies major changes took place. The previous Dutch relationship with the East Indies had been primarily economic, involving tribute collection more than administration. This relationship changed

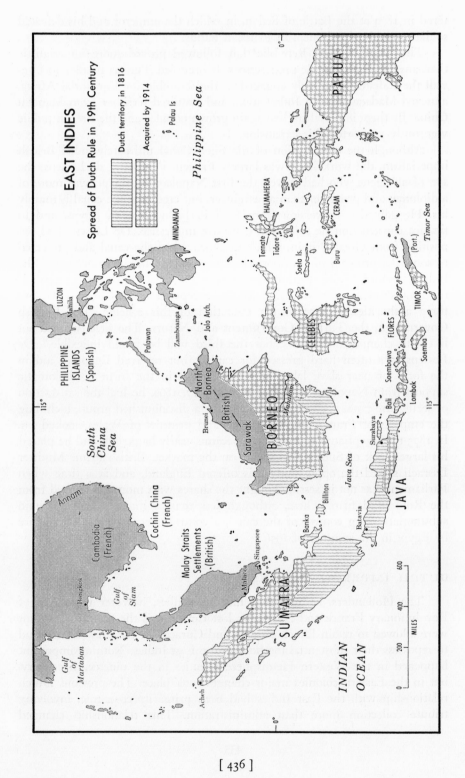

EAST INDIES

Spread of Dutch Rule in 19th Century

Dutch territory in 1816

Acquired by 1914

during the century, as Holland fastened its political rule on the whole archipelago except North Borneo and the eastern half of New Guinea. The occupation became complete with the subjugation of Acheh in western Sumatra in 1899 and the surrender of the last Moslem sultanates of Celebes in 1910.

From the end of the Napoleonic Wars, when the islands were restored to Dutch control following British occupation, to 1848 Netherlands India was ruled by the kings of Holland (William I and William II) and their ministers. The grasping severity of these profit-hungry monarchs brought back memories of the Dutch East India Company and its greedy directors. But in 1848 the Dutch constitution was amended to give the national parliament, the States General, an important voice in colonial government. As this body was responsive to public opinion, reforms in the administration and in the treatment of the native population became possible.

The institution most in need of reform was the *Cultuur-Stelsel* (Culture System), by which Javanese and other East Indian peasants were required to labor ostensibly one-fifth of their time raising such crops for the government as could be sold in Europe. When introduced, about 1830, the system had seemed a great improvement over the old tribute-taxation practice, by which the peasants had labored without regulation as to time but had in fact needed two-thirds of their working days to produce what the Dutch demanded. But the new method became subject to endless abuse. Native laborers were so exploited under it that they lacked time to grow the rice they needed to live with any security. The greed of both Dutch and Indonesian officials caused rapid deterioration of much of the soil, which was worked to the limit without regard to the future. Around mid-century Dutch public opinion began to turn against the *Cultuur-Stelsel,* and long before its total abolition the lot of the natives had somewhat improved. A new agricultural law in 1870 paved the way for the termination of the *Stelsel,* although it continued to be used in a few places for sugar-raising until 1890, and in others for coffee until 1915. It was succeeded by a system of private capitalism and hired labor.

RUSSIAN IMPERIAL EXPANSION

In 1815 the Russian tsar ruled the largest single territory in the world, and he and his successors materially added to it within the following century. The Russians were the one nation of European imperialists who did not need to cross water to build an empire. Russian America, as Alaska was then called, had been acquired through the accident of its discovery by Vitus Bering for Russia in 1741, and occupied because of the later ephemeral value of the Pacific fur trade. In two wars with Turkey—in 1828 and 1877—Russia acquired those parts of the Caucasus still remaining in Ottoman hands. Year by year the Muscovites drove southward through central Asia toward the borders of Persia and Afghanistan. With the occupation of Merv in 1884, Kokand in 1876, and Pamir in 1895, the Russian frontier reached its present location.

Between the great northern bend of the Amur River and the Pacific Ocean, the Chino-Russian boundary had been established along the Stanovoi Mountains by the Treaty of Nerchinsk in 1689 (see page 310). There it might have remained indefinitely had not Nikolai Muraviev come from St. Petersburg as governor of eastern Siberia in 1848. He bore orders from Tsar Nicholas I to make recommendations about revictualing the Pacific outposts, to develop trade with China, and to seek a better outlet to the Pacific than the Amur. The tsar had said, "The Amur is a useless river. It does not assure us of access to the ocean. At its mouth the channel has only a three-foot depth. What could we do with such a river?"

No voyager along the Pacific coast had ever located the Amur mouth, and a widespread belief existed that it did not flow into the ocean. Even had Nicholas been correct in his estimate of the river, its use was forbidden to the Russians by the former establishment of the boundary at the Stanovoi Mountains well to the north. The energetic Muraviev made the necessary investigation, and learned that the river was navigable to the ocean and that Sakhalin was an island and not a peninsula as had been generally thought. The Crimean War postponed his project for annexing the Amur territory to Russia, but in 1858 he persuaded the new tsar, Alexander II, to put pressure on Manchu China, then engaged in a losing war with England and France. China first agreed to cede all its claims north of the river, and two years later, in response to more pressure inspired by Muraviev, it abandoned to Russia the area between the Amur and Korea known as the Maritime Province. In 1861 the Russians founded Vladivostok as their new "window" on the Pacific. Muraviev had always insisted that Russia should dispose of its North American holdings, as they would be defenseless if attacked and had ceased to produce any worth-while revenue. When the United States purchased Russian America in 1867 for $7,200,000, the transaction was regarded as a favor to Russia, which gladly bowed out of the New World. Within ten years the tsar, in his own opinion, more than compensated himself for the loss by the acquisition of Sakhalin.

2 : The Partition of Africa

IN 1815 most of Africa was as unknown to Europeans as it had been to the ancient Greeks and Romans. The coastal contours were mapped, and recently the two Scotsmen James Bruce and Mungo Park had explored the Blue Nile and the Niger, but elsewhere tropical Africa remained a mystery. Europeans in their imaginations arranged its geography to suit themselves and committed great errors in the process. They placed the headwaters of the Nile in various strange locations and imagined impossible tributaries for the great river. Some thought that the Niger, whose existence was known, entered the Nile; and others, before Park's explorations, had believed that it flowed westward and entered the Atlantic as two streams, the Senegal and the Gambia. European map makers generally erred in making the Congo a small river with no considerable basin, and no one had a correct idea of where the Zambezi originated. The large lakes of inner Africa were unknown, and the mountains either unknown or misplaced.

Europe's general ignorance of Africa did not apply to its northern extremities. The Barbary states—Morocco, Algeria, Tunis, and Tripoli—as well as Egypt, were hostile to Europeans, but their geography had been known from Roman times or earlier. And, as we previously saw, the Dutch Boers inhabited the Cape of Good Hope region and would soon be ready to undertake their "Great Trek" northward across the Orange and Vaal rivers. The Sahara Desert and equatorial Africa, which made up the bulk of the continent, furnished the real geographical puzzle.

THE FIRST STAGE—EXPLORATION

Europe's eagerness to possess African territory, which became fully aroused about 1880, was preceded by several generations of exploration. Mungo Park solved part of the mystery of the Niger by the time of his death there in 1806, and by 1830 Richard Lander had traced the remaining course of this river. A party of Englishmen traversed the Sahara and discovered Lake Chad in 1822, and by 1827 an Englishman and a Frenchman had visited the mysterious Tombouctu. The Germans Heinrich Barth and Gustav Nachtigal added further to knowledge of the Sahara, and eastward the Englishmen John Hanning Speke and Richard Burton discovered lakes Tanganyika and Victoria. Samuel Baker as good as solved the riddle of the Nile and its tributaries in 1864.

There is no doubt that the greatest of all African explorers was the Scottish medical missionary, Dr. David Livingstone. Born in 1813 and ordained a minister of the (Presbyterian) Church of Scotland, he went to South Africa for missionary work in 1841. He labored with some success near the Kalahari Desert, which he was the first white man to cross. Feeling the call to further exploration, he pushed northward to the Zambezi and discovered Victoria Falls in 1851. On a later expedition he ascended the Zambezi and turned westward to visit Luanda in Portuguese Angola. From there he returned to the great river and followed it to its mouth near Quelimane in Portuguese East Africa.

Desire for further knowledge now dominated Livingstone. In 1859 he ascended the Zambezi to the Shiré, flowing from Lake Nyassa, and followed this tributary to the great lake itself. Here he saw at its worst the pernicious slave trade dominated by Arab traffickers, and made a fierce resolve to suppress it and to improve the lot of the helpless Negroes. He became in the best sense an agent of imperialism, because he correctly believed British rule the surest remedy for the evils he daily saw. Livingstone made his final entry into Africa in 1866. He marched with a company of Negroes to Lake Tanganyika, where he fell ill and remained for several years, although he managed in intervals of health to make various important explorations. To the outside world he seemed lost until James Gordon Bennett, publisher of the New York *Herald,* undertook the discovery of the greatest living discoverer. Bennett sent his best reporter, the Welsh-born Henry Morton Stanley, to Africa in 1869, with orders to spend as much money as necessary and to "find Livingstone!" Stanley did so early in 1871, when he encountered the famous Scotsman by the shore of Lake Tanganyika and greeted him with the words, now immortal, "Dr. Livingstone, I presume." The two spent months together and undertook explorations in common, although Livingstone declined to accompany Stanley on his return march to the coast. After the return of the young reporter-explorer to civilization through Zanzibar, news came by Negroes of Livingstone's death, while on another expedition in 1873. Stanley, now thoroughly interested in Africa, became the greatest of the later explorers. Financed by the *Herald* and an English paper on his next expedition, he marched from Zanzibar to the Upper Congo and descended the great river to its mouth. He later became associated with King Leopold II of Belgium and was the monarch's chief agent in founding the Congo Free State, later the Belgian Congo.

Governments now sponsored explorers for national purposes. Carl Peters penetrated east Africa for Germany; Savorgnan de Brazza, an Italian in the service of France, explored the present French Congo. Portugal, which had never forgotten its old-time supremacy in Africa, sent Alexandre Serpa Pinto, Hermenegildo Capelo, and Roberto Ivens eastward from Angola to cross the continent and if possible to create a Portuguese corridor connecting Angola with Indian Ocean Mozambique. Italians explored Somaliland and Abyssinia, in which their country had the greatest interest. By 1900 Africa had ceased to be the Dark Continent. Although sundry dim spots remained to be explored, the courses of the great rivers had been traced, the mountains had been discovered, and maps of substantial accuracy could be made.

THE SECOND STAGE—IMPERIALISM

By the late 1870's several great European powers and a few lesser ones thought of Africa as a ground for imperialism. The early nineteenth-century prejudice against colonies had largely disappeared, and two new powers, Germany and Italy, had entered the scene, both with strong interests at home favoring overseas expansion. With the Industrial Revolution creating its inevitable demand for raw materials and markets, with problems of overpopulation facing Europe, and with national prestige a greater item than ever before, the idea of empire became popular. The untutored African millions and the vast resources their continent supposedly possessed offered what seemed the perfect scene for imperialistic growth.

Great Britain and France gained the lion's shares of Africa. In the south the Cape Town multimillionaire Cecil Rhodes was mostly responsible for the British advance. He engineered the northward push, by which England bypassed the Boer republics and annexed Bechuanaland and his namesake and creation Rhodesia. On the west coast, where it had long possessed several minor colonies, Great Britain added huge Nigeria and smaller Ashanti to the list. In eastern Africa English acquisitions included Kenya, Uganda, British Somaliland, and Zanzibar.

France moved south and east from Algeria and the Senegal to absorb the whole Sahara Desert, and entered equatorial Africa by annexing the French Congo. On the east side France gained a tract of Somaliland and in 1896 completed the conquest of Madagascar. The French African empire exceeded all others in area, but consisted too largely of the Sahara to become the most lucrative.

The new states Belgium, Italy, and Germany all succumbed to the African temptation. King Leopold of Belgium was elected head of an international corporation for the development of the interior of the continent. He soon turned this into a private preserve, known as the Congo Free State because of its lack of tariff barriers. In his hunger for rubber profits, Leopold initiated a system of forced labor in the Congo which made the Dutch East Indian *Cultuur-Stelsel* seem mild. His emissaries held women as hostages to make their husbands produce rubber, and it is even rumored that cannibal tribesmen were sometimes given a free hand with recalcitrant villages. In 1908, just before his death, Leopold deeded the huge Free State to his nation, in whose hands it became the Belgian Congo.

Italy entered Africa largely to gain prestige and play the role of a great power. In the 1880's it acquired title to Eritrea and Italian Somaliland, partly because these barren regions were not coveted by other European states. In the 1890's, under the premiership of the aged Francesco Crispi, Italy extended its protectorate over the old Christian realm of Abyssinia. But in 1896, when the Italians attempted to occupy the country, their army was met and annihilated by the Abyssinians under the stouthearted ruler Menelik. This was the one major reverse suffered by Europeans in Africa, and it caused the abandonment of all Italian claims to Abyssinia until Mussolini revived them forty years later.

Germany entered the African race still under the chancellorship of Bismarck, who had small personal interest in an overseas empire. The Iron

Chancellor in his last years of power found his hand forced, and consented to the occupation of German East Africa, German South-West Africa, and Togoland, all of which his country held until World War I.

Portugal, though a poverty-stricken little kingdom, resolved not to be left out of the competition and for a time resumed an active career of empire building. Portuguese ambitions chiefly involved establishing sovereignty over the Lake Nyassa region—English-dominated since Livingstone's time— and of running a transcontinental corridor between Angola and Mozambique. Part of the ambition could have been realized in 1887, when the British government offered Portugal a free hand north of the Zambezi in return for abandonment of the Nyassa claim. The Portuguese refused the offer which was not repeated, for in 1889 Cecil Rhodes formed the Chartered Company with the intention of pushing English territorial claims northward between the two Portuguese coastal possessions. A clash of interests in Nyasaland caused Great Britain to threaten war in 1890, and helpless Portugal consented to the present boundaries of its two major colonies. The Portuguese seemed threatened with the loss of both possessions at the turn of the century, when Great Britain and Germany made treaties looking forward to their future partition. Bad Anglo-German relations in the ensuing years kept the treaties from going into effect.

Spain, whose imperial days were also largely past, took some interest in the African partition. Spanish expeditions explored inland from Río de Oro, in which their country had an interest, and Spain emerged with a clear title to this worthless territory, whose only assets were valuable coastal fisheries. Río Muni, a small enclave just north of the French Congo, also went to Spain.

THREATS OF WAR

African boundaries were usually arranged by treaties signed before the territories involved were fully occupied. A Berlin Congress of 1884–85 laid down general rules, agreed to by all, as to how claims should be made valid. More than simple priority of discovery was required; claimants needed to perform positive acts leading toward development. Nevertheless, there were times when war between European states over Africa seemed close. Had the Anglo-Portuguese crisis of 1890 led to war, it might have been too one-sided to disturb the world greatly. But if the English and French had fought in 1898, as they seemed about to do, the case would have been different.

For reasons not connected with the general African partition the British in 1882 had occupied Egypt. In the 1890's they undertook the conquest of Egypt's historic tributary, the Sudan. Sir Herbert Kitchener, who commanded the expedition, defeated the Sudanese in a major battle in 1898 and occupied Khartoum, their leading city. He then received the disturbing news that an unidentified European expedition was on the Nile above him, apparently determined to contest possession of the upper river. The fact was that the governor of the French Congo had sent Major Jean-Baptiste Marchand with an oversize exploring expedition across Africa, with orders to raise the tricolor on the Upper Nile. Kitchener hastened with a few Egyptian and Scottish troops to Fashoda, where Marchand welcomed him "in the name of France." Anxious weeks followed, as the expeditions faced each other and statesmen in London and Paris, informed by cable of the events, argued the matter bitterly and newspapers thundered for war. France finally yielded and Marchand withdrew, removing the greatest war threat between the two nations since Napoleon's time. Later crises between great powers also ended bloodlessly, and the Italian conquest of Turkish Libya in 1911 and the French occupation of Morocco a year later came as the result of compromise agreements.

THE RESULTS OF THE PARTITION

Boundaries of European African possessions, as established by 1900, endured substantially until the First World War eliminated Germany from the continent. In revised form they endured until the Second World War, when Italy was expelled. Although Africa has now turned nationalistic and seems bent on eliminating all European control, the verdict of history will probably be that the partition mainly benefited the natives. It is nonsense to speak of them as living idyllically before the Europeans stepped in; those disposed to do so should read Livingstone's accounts of the life he saw before the partition years. Most Africans in the old days lived in misery, filth, and disease, ground down by their rulers and witch doctors, and subject to the constant raids of slave runners. The Europeans, selfish though many may have been, and hypocritical as their governments surely were, generally raised African living standards and brought civilization to millions. Leopold of Belgium and many of his employees certainly gave European occupation a bad name, but on the other hand there is the case of Savorgnan de Brazza, who said to his subordinates, "Make yourselves understand not only the words the blacks pronounce but also their minds. . . . No arms, no escorts. Don't forget that you are intruders who haven't been invited."

Christianity certainly exercised a beneficial influence. In this day, when it is fashionable to ridicule missionaries, it is easily forgotten that men like Livingstone literally gave their lives for the advancement of Africa. Protestants led the way into most of Africa, but Catholics did not lag far behind. Cardinal Lavigerie, originally bishop of Algiers, in 1868 founded the "White Fathers," whose principal mission was the evangelization of central Africa. Some years elapsed before their work could begin, yet the program started by Lavigerie ultimately exceeded the Protestant effort in number of converts gained.

To the benefits just enumerated may be added the railroads, the river steamers, the roads, the industries, the increased opportunities for gainful employment, and the higher standards of health and sanitation. Now that

Africa is casting off European rule, its people will be unwise and unrealistic if they choose to minimize "the innumerable benefits procured unto them by the same."

THE BOER WAR

At the turn of the century there occurred an unfortunate episode whose effects are still much in evidence. This was the Boer War (1899–1902) between Great Britain and the Orange and Transvaal republics. Its causes may be traced partly to the hostility between Briton and Boer that had existed since England's annexation of the Cape in 1806, but more particularly to bad Anglo-Transvaal relations since 1881. During the Transvaal revolt of that year Prime Minister Gladstone had conceded the Boer state its independence, with some understanding that the crown should manage its foreign affairs. The Boers soon repudiated this part of the agreement and the British did not press matters. There now arose in the Cape the towering figure of Cecil Rhodes, the arch English imperialist of his time, who once declared that if he could find a way to the moon he would annex it. Rhodes dreamed of a British empire in Africa stretching from "the Cape to Cairo," to be held together by a railway of his own building. He saw the Boer republics as obstacles, and partially surrounded them by the annexation of Bechuanaland and Rhodesia. An almost equally commanding figure had arisen in Paul Kruger, the Transvaal president. "Oom Paul" (Uncle Paul) as he was called, was a stubborn, narrow-minded old rustic, a member of the most hard-shelled religious denomination among the Boers, the "Doppers." He was also one of the ablest statesmen of the time and could match Rhodes in all but financial resources. Between these two a long-distance contest for control of South Africa continued for years. Racial friction grew following the discovery of gold at Witwatersrand in the Transvaal and the resulting inrush of miners, mostly British. Kruger made citizenship in his republic almost impossible for outsiders to acquire. When the *Uitlanders* (foreigners) appealed to him, he would only say, "This is my country and these are my laws. Those who come here must obey them." His uncompromising attitude made even the non-British *Uitlanders* look to the queen's government as their main hope.

At the end of 1895 Rhodes' assistant, Dr. Leander Starr Jameson, invaded the Transvaal with a force of Bechuanaland Rangers, with the intention of overthrowing its government. The attempt at surprise failed, with Jameson and his entire command being captured by Kruger's forces. Rhodes denied complicity, but as his usual instructions to Jameson were known to be, "Take what you can get and ask me afterwards," few believed his denial. He now lost political authority in the Cape Colony, though he remained a great financial figure. Jameson's raid had made the Boer War inevitable. It came late in 1899, when the British authorities presented Kruger with a list of demands that he met in part but not in full. When fighting began the Orange Free State joined the Transvaal, and for the rest of the year the efficient Boer armies inflicted humiliating defeats on the ill-prepared, inadequate British forces in South Africa. Stung by the early reverses, the English people, who had entered the conflict without enthusiasm, prepared to fight a major war. By the start of 1900 the arrival of reinforcements from England and elsewhere in the empire had turned the tide. By midyear the regular armies of the Boers had been defeated and much of their territory overrun. Some of the Afrikaners refused to admit defeat and resorted to guerrilla tactics; their name for raiding parties added the word "commandos" to our language. Their stout resistance postponed a final British victory until 1902, when the last Boer leaders accepted the Treaty of Vereeniging and laid down their arms.

Following its victory the British government behaved rather well toward the Boers and spent large sums for their rehabilitation. No such generosity could efface the ill feeling, and although some Boer leaders, notably Louis Botha and Jan Smuts, became reconciled and pro-British, others have continued to nourish a grudge until the present. In 1910 the Cape, Natal, the Transvaal Colony, and the Orange River Colony united as a self-governing dominion with the blessing of Great Britain. Rhodesia, preferring to go its own way, remained outside the Union of South Africa and later was divided into the separate colonies of Southern and Northern Rhodesia.

3 : The Far East

CHINA, Japan, and Korea entered the nineteenth century still desiring to have as little to do with the outside world as possible. The Manchu monarchy, whose rise and early history have been already related (see page 306), had begun to decay but seemed determined to make up in supercilious haughtiness for whatever it lacked in power. Japan continued the exclusionism that had commenced with the first Tokugawa shoguns in the early seventeenth century. Korea, the "Hermit Kingdom," also felt self-sufficient, though it rendered a nominal allegiance to China. Indo-China consisted of a group of independent states. Siam (now Thailand) was united though weak. The Philippines continued under a rather listless Spanish rule that would not be seriously threatened by the revolutions about to begin in the American colonies of Spain.

CHINA TO THE END OF THE TAI PING REBELLION

Manchu China asked only to be left alone to ignore and be ignored by the rest of the world, particularly the West. But while this had been to some extent possible in the eighteenth century, it was not at all possible in the nineteenth. The West, more powerful than ever and in search of every profitable market that existed, refused to allow China the seclusion it craved.

Chinese resistance power steadily weakened as the century passed. In the reign of Chia Ch'ing the empire fell into confusion and suffered from numerous rebellions. In the next reign, that of Tao Kuang (1820–1850), the bad situation grew worse. The eight Manchu Banner Companies lost all semblance of efficiency, and for the suppression of the revolts their place had to be taken by locally-trained provincial militias. The new military policy created additional hazards for the government, as it involved putting arms in the hands of the subjugated Chinese, who, once armed, had a tendency to turn rebels and bandits. Neither Manchus nor Chinese proved any match for European forces during the nineteenth century.

The activities of the British East India Company brought about the Opium War (1839–1842), the first armed clash between Great Britain and Manchu China. In the eighteenth century the company had begun the export of opium to China through Canton and Portuguese-held Macao. Manchu administrators objected to this, and the friction had grown greater by the refusal of emperors Ch'ien Lung and Chia Ch'ing to treat British envoys as representatives of an equal power. When Parliament ended the trading activities of the company in 1833, it made an exception of Chinese commerce and thus allowed the opium trade to continue.

There is some exaggeration in the frequent assertion that England forced the Opium War on China solely because it desired to continue selling the harmful though profitable drug. A Chinese historian writes, ". . . it seems clear that England did not wish to open hostilities on account of the infamous trade." What counted most was the British desire to establish regular and legitimate commerce with China, a commerce which the Manchu officials refused to allow. Matters had already reached the crisis point around Canton when the emperor sent Lin Tse-hsü, an energetic mandarin from the court, to deal with the foreigners. In the strict performance of his duty, Lin ordered all opium either ashore or aboard ship at Canton to be handed over to him. He secured the shore supply but lacked means of boarding the ships. When a Chinese villager was killed in a brawl with some British seamen, Lin ordered the offender delivered to him for punishment. The English commercial superintendent evaded compliance because he did not know the identity of the guilty person, whereupon Lin put an end to all British commerce in the Canton area, and his officers destroyed what opium they could seize.

A desultory war followed in which the British blockaded the mouth of the Pearl River and seized points along the coast. The Chinese, lacking a navy, could make no effective resistance and finally signed the Treaty of Nanking in 1842. The Manchu government promised payment for the

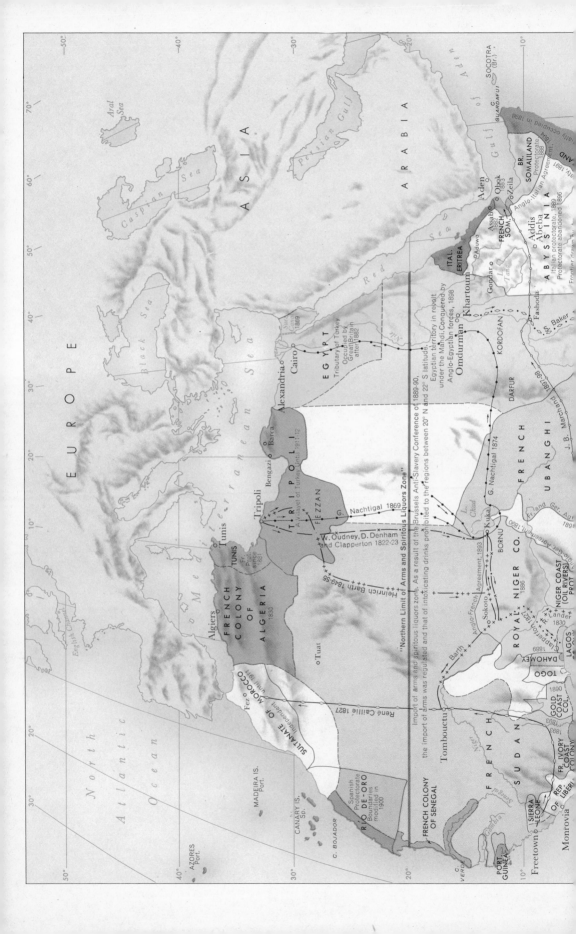

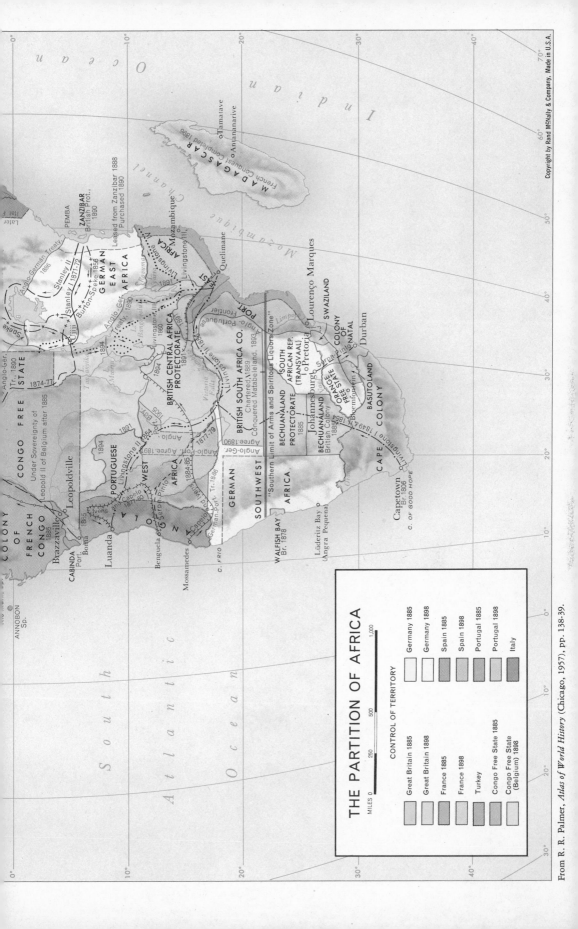

THE PARTITION OF AFRICA

CONTROL OF TERRITORY

Great Britain 1885	Germany 1885
Great Britain 1898	Germany 1898
France 1885	Spain 1885
France 1898	Spain 1898
Turkey 1885	Portugal 1885
Congo Free State 1885	Portugal 1898
Congo Free State (Belgium) 1898	Italy 1898

MILES 0   250   500   1,000

From R. R. Palmer, *Atlas of World History* (Chicago, 1957), pp. 138-39.

opium and other destroyed British property, ceded the island of Hong Kong, opened the ports of Canton, Foochow, Amoy, Ningpo, and Shanghai to British trade, and consented to a uniform and moderate tariff rate on both imports and exports. The Nanking Treaty marked the real opening of China to foreign goods and influence. Other Western nations, with the United States and France in the lead, eagerly followed the British in demanding concessions. China again yielded, and soon foreign colonies lived in the "Treaty Ports," perilously at first and amid a population that held them in hatred. Chinese complacence was not greatly jarred by the defeat at British hands. Citizens of the Manchu Empire still considered themselves the sole source of enlightenment, and took the reverse as a minor setback similar to many others in their history. England and the Western powers learned the real lesson, namely, that China was an easy victim for any modern state with an adequate navy.

Another conflict, often miscalled the Second Opium War, broke out between England and China in 1857. This time aided by France, the British, whose Indian Sepoy Mutiny for a time prevented their sending many troops to China, again defeated the Manchu forces. By the Treaty of Tientsin in 1858, the Western allies forced the Chinese to open more ports, to admit a British ambassador to Peking, and to permit travel, trade, and increased missionary activity in the hinterland. When the terms of the treaty seemed likely to go unenforced, an Anglo-French army forced a way from Tientsin to Peking and drove the emperor and court to take refuge in Manchurian Jehol.

The tide of British-Chinese relations next turned favorable. The great Tai Ping Rebellion broke out in south China in 1850, led by a convert to Christianity who styled himself the "Heavenly King." The motives of the rebels, in addition to the distorted Christian aims of the Heavenly King, were the ancient and customary ones caused by agrarian abuse, unjust taxes, and corrupt officials. The direct purpose was to overthrow the Manchus and substitute a Chinese dynasty founded by the Heavenly King. Although this person proved to be a figurehead with no talent for leadership, his generals and soldiers for a time seemed likely to destroy Manchu rule. The British and other Westerners remained mere observers for some years, but presently saw the Tai Ping movement degenerating and threatening to reduce China to chaos in which the hard-won gains of the recent wars might be lost. The English government, after having earlier helped weaken the Manchus by the capture of Peking, now turned to their support, being followed in this attitude by the West in general, including the United States. A volunteer corps, consisting largely of foreigners and called the "Ever-Victorious Army," was raised to fight for the Manchus. On the death of its American organizer, this élite body was reorganized, and, with the full approval of the British authorities, placed under the command of the English soldier Charles ("Chinese") Gordon. At the same time some improvement took

447

place in the regular Manchu troops commanded by the famous viceroy Li Hung-chang. The Ever-Victorious Army and the revitalized Manchu forces broke the back of the Tai Ping Rebellion in 1864 and captured Nanking which had become the insurgent capital. The Heavenly King died a suicide and his son, who briefly attempted to carry on the revolt, fled to Kiangsi where he was taken and executed. The suppression of the rebellion permitted the wavering dynasty to survive for another forty-eight years. Great Britain, which had helped to sustain the Manchus, profited by gaining increased ascendancy at the imperial court.

THE OPENING OF JAPAN

The early Tokugawa shoguns had sealed Japan off from the outside world in the first half of the seventeenth century. This seemed for a time the best solution to the country's problems, as prosperity increased and the Japanese experienced a considerable cultural revival. Yet by the middle of the nineteenth century some change seemed in the offing. The quality of the shoguns had declined, and outlying clan chieftains had become almost independent. Moreover, Japan showed signs of tiring of its isolation. Interest in Western ideas increased, as through the Dutch establishment in Nagasaki a small trickle of European books entered Japan. Some Japanese scholars learned to read Dutch and found, among other things, that Western authors described the human anatomy more accurately than did the ancient Chinese sages whom they had studied until then.

The first Western move to open Japan came from the United States. In 1853 Commodore Matthew Calbraith Perry arrived with a fleet in Edo Bay near Tokyo, made a show of force, and handed the authorities a letter from the President. He then sailed away but returned the following year and obtained a treaty by which an American consul was stationed in the country, two ports were opened to trade, and provisions were made for future commerce. England, Russia, and Holland quickly secured similar concessions for themselves, and all gained extraterritorial rights for their people residing in Japan, meaning that these would be governed by their own consuls instead of living subject to Japanese law. More treaties followed, as other Western countries made their own demands and as the original four extended the privileges already acquired.

Japan nevertheless had its traditional, conservative element that would not permit such concessions without a fight. The reigning shogun was weak and inefficient, and the secluded emperor had the unusual experience of being appealed to by all schools of Japanese thought. Clashes took place between reactionary Japanese and foreigners. Early in 1867 the emperor died, to be succeeded by his fourteen-year-old son Mutsuhito, better known as Meiji (enlightened). A growing party in Japan, inspired by thoughtful historians, had for years insisted that the shogun was a usurper and that power legally belonged to the emperor. An armed conflict now settled the matter, as war clans acting in Meiji's name defeated the shogun and forced him to abdicate. The imperial residence was moved from Kyoto to Edo (Yedo), now renamed Tokyo. The feudal lords surrendered their land rights to the government, and an imperial edict abolished feudalism.

Japan spent the years until 1894 rapidly modernizing itself. Emperor Meiji believed in progress and gave full support to ministers engaged in the reforming work. The new army, based on universal conscription, was modeled on the Prussian system. A navy, at first under the supervision of European advisers, came into existence. A constitution, largely the work of Prince Ito Hirobumi, who became Japan's first notable premier, went into effect in 1869. Ito had taken as his model the German imperial system established by Bismarck. His constitution, besides assuring the authority of the emperor, provided for a cabinet and a two-house legislature consisting of a Chamber of Peers and a House of Representatives elected by Japanese males of suitable property qualifications.

Domestically, Japan forged ahead. As internal and foreign commerce increased, banks developed, headed by the Bank of Japan and the Yokohama Specie Bank. The islands were connected by fast steamers. Railroads, at first state-constructed and later privately built, spread their network across Honshu. A manufacturing revolution began, as steam factories rapidly forced out the old handicraft industries. The nation established a universal education system, with elementary schools for all children, high schools for a more limited group, and universities for the talented and wealthy. Although Catholic and Protestant missions made headway, most Japanese preferred their ancestral religious ways. Buddhism, while still the faith of millions, was supplanted in government favor by the ancient Shinto, which had a more nationalistic tone.

The Japanese learned that representative government brought party rivalry. It likewise brought intimidation, bribery, and other forms of corruption. Factional strife became hot, and the meetings of the first three legislatures proved singularly sterile in spite of Ito's strenuous efforts to secure agreement on a program. It required the pressure of a war with China in 1894–1895 to bring the parties together. That war had been looming for years. Japan and China had resumed their old rivalry for the control of weak Korea, a contest that became critical as Russia showed signs of interest there. When a rebellion broke out in Korea, both the Manchu government and Japanese government sent forces for its suppression, which straightway attacked each other in July, 1894. The Chinese counted heavily on the divisions in the Japanese parliament (Diet) and were startled at the speed with which all factions swung to the support of their emperor.

The war proved a quick and easy victory for Japan, whose fleet sank the recently-modernized but improperly-trained Chinese navy, and whose armies captured Port Arthur and Wei-hai-wei, facing each other from the neighboring Liaotung and Shantung peninsulas. The Japanese did not encounter a united China, for as Li Hung-chang said, "The one province, Chihli, is facing the whole nation of Japan." The Manchus sued for peace, and by the Treaty of Shimonoseki in 1895 agreed to pay a large indemnity and to cede the Liaotung peninsula, Formosa, and the Pescadores Islands to Japan. Russia, France, and Germany objected to Japan's having a foothold on the Asiatic mainland, and presented what amounted to a joint ultimatum at Tokyo in which they demanded the return of Liaotung to China. As Japan in 1895 could not hope to resist three major European powers its government yielded, handed back the peninsula, and accepted an increased indemnity instead. This humiliation made the Japanese feel gravely disappointed over the outcome of the war and convinced them that they must one day fight Russia, a task for which they now made serious preparations.

THE CLOSING YEARS OF THE MANCHUS

Since the close of the Tai Ping Rebellion China had been less isolated than before but had continued to resist Western culture. The Manchus had shown strength enough to suppress a Moslem rebellion in central Asian Kashgaria following that of the Tai Pings, but had been helpless to prevent the French conquest of Indo-China, which they had long considered a vassal region.

When the Sino-Japanese War revealed to the European world the utter helplessness of the tottering Manchu régime, the huge, inert empire appeared to be as much a field for future imperialism as Africa. Western powers lost no time in staking out their claims. Germany, now thoroughly imperialistic under its ambitious young Kaiser William II, found a pretext for interference after the murder of two German Catholic missionaries in Shantung in 1897. It seized Kiaochow Bay, demanded and gained a heavy indemnity, and forced China to concede mining and railroad-building rights in the surrounding province of Shantung. Russia had posed as the friend of China by keeping Japan out of Liaotung, but now proved the extent of this friendship by demanding and gaining for itself the peninsula with its valuable Port Arthur. "Here is why I have taken this step," said Tsar Nicholas II, who never took a step without the prodding of his ministers, "After the conference the Foreign Minister reported to me that, according to his information, British warships were cruising off the ports in question and if we did not occupy them England would do so." The information was false, but Li Hung-chang, now China's leading diplomat, acquiesced in the seizure, "to use one barbarian to check another barbarian." Russia, meanwhile, had advanced China the capital to pay the first installment of the indemnity to

Japan, and in return secured the privilege of building its Trans-Siberian Railway, then under construction, across Manchuria to Vladivostok. The British had had no designs on Port Arthur, but grew alarmed at its seizure by Russia and in 1898 obtained the lease of nearby Wei-hai-wei for as long as Russia should hold Port Arthur. France stepped in to demand and receive the port of Kwang-chow-wan in south China, and some rectification in its own favor of the Cochin Chinese frontier. Italy attempted to enter the partition race by demanding a base on the coast of Chekiang province; but the Chinese, who had yielded to the greater powers through fear, this time found the strength to refuse. All these concessions promised to grow into greater spheres of influence, as each was accompanied by promises regarding railroad construction and other economic developments in adjacent Chinese provinces.

China appeared to have learned its lesson at last, and made hasty attempts at change and modernization. Young Emperor Kuang-hsü issued many decrees for military reform, extension of education, improvements in the bureaucracy, and railroad building. But intelligent though he was, Kuang-hsü lacked experience, political sagacity, and stamina. He proved no match for his aged aunt Yehonala, the widow of the deceased emperor, who was strong and determined as well as the head of the reaction party. This empress dowager, who was likewise known as Tz'u-hsi and "Venerable Buddha," suddenly seized control of the government in 1898, made the emperor a virtual prisoner, annulled his reforms, and executed several of the reformers.

This strong-willed woman, though possessing ability, knew nothing of the West, believed what she wished to believe, and thought that China could still go its way despite the foreigners. She gave secret support to a society for the slaughter of Westerners and Chinese Christians, called the "Righteous Harmony Fists," better known as "Boxers." They were a north China group, with little support in the south. In 1899 and early 1900 they began terrorizing northern provinces, killing Christians and burning missions. The empress, when appealed to by foreign diplomats in Peking, ordered the Boxers' arrest but gave secret orders for their encouragement and assistance.

An open break between the Manchu régime and the foreigners came in June, 1900, when the dowager, pressed by her reactionary advisers, declared war on the rest of the world. She commanded all foreigners in her realm to be killed, though cautious officials took the liberty of rewording her order to make it sound less ferocious. The high point of the Boxer movement came with the beleaguering of Western and Japanese diplomatic officials and a number of their guards in the legations at Peking, which fortunately were adjacent and could be so barricaded as to stand a siege. Reinforcements arrived from the coast as soon as possible. They consisted of European detachments plus Japanese, and an American contingent sent hastily from the newly-occupied Philippines. Before their arrival the empress and a remnant of her court had fled to the remote interior. The relief column fought its way into Peking on August 15, 1900, and ended the danger.

It now remained to be seen how much of a price the powers would exact from China. As for the Russians, one of their officials declared, ". . . from the very beginning of the campaign it was the desire of the military party not only to punish the Boxers but also permanently to annex Manchuria." The United States desired to save China from further loss of territory, not from altruistic motives but simply because American trade might have been banned from regions dominated too closely by other powers. Secretary of State John Hay, originally on the advice of a British adviser, proposed the "Open Door" policy, which in effect meant that Chinese territorial integrity should be preserved and that opportunities be kept equal for all. Partly because the main attention of several European powers was now turned in another direction than China, they all willingly or grudgingly accepted Hay's proposal. China nevertheless had to pay for its Boxer indiscretion. Payment took the form of a total indemnity of $333,-900,000, punishment of the officials most involved, concession to the foreign powers of a legation compound in Peking to be guarded with their own soldiers and inaccessible to Chinese, and other humiliations. For years thereafter foreigners resident in China had the right to behave as a privileged caste.

THE RUSSO-JAPANESE WAR

When Russia, after depriving Japan of Port Arthur and the Liaotung peninsula, seized these places herself, the Japanese felt that there must one day be a reckoning. When Russia used the Boxer outbreak as a pretext for filling Manchuria with soldiers and later declined to withdraw them, the reckoning seemed closer. When Russia displayed unmistakable designs on Korea, it became evident that it could not be postponed much longer. A Japanese of the time remarked that Korea is an arrow pointed at the heart of Japan. With the arrow in the bow of an unfriendly power, it must at all costs be parried.

Japan pushed preparations for war, and in 1902 strengthened its position by an alliance with England that assured British support in case any other European power came to Russia's aid. The Japanese then made a last-minute bid for peaceful compromise, in which they offered to recognize a Russian sphere of influence in Manchuria provided their own prior rights in Korea were respected. Russia, feeling certain that an Oriental nation as small as Japan would never fight a European state as large as itself, refused in a contemptuous manner. Too late the tsar's ministers learned their mistake, for in February, 1904, Japan attacked their fleets at Chemulpo (Inchon) in Korea and at Port Arthur. In this initial surprise Japan so crippled the Russian Far Eastern naval units that they could take little further part in the war. Immediately, the Japanese laid siege to Port Arthur and attacked and drove northward the main Russian forces in Manchuria. Port Arthur held out until January, 1905; and a month after its fall Field Marshal Oyama drove the Russians with heavy loss from Mukden, the Manchurian capital, though failing to flank and destroy them. The Russian Baltic Fleet, after sailing around the Cape of Good Hope and through the Indian Ocean, reached Tsushima Strait in May, 1905, to be intercepted and destroyed there by the main Japanese naval force under Admiral Togo.

Russia was still not a defeated power. Although its sea power was gone, it had poured reinforcements into Manchuria and was ready to launch an offensive. Japan, on the other hand, had almost reached the end of its financial resources. But serious revolutionary outbreaks in European Russia compelled the tsar to make peace. The treaty was signed in September, 1905, at Portsmouth, New Hampshire, following mediation by President Roosevelt. Japan secured paramount interest in Korea and the cession of Port Arthur and the Liaotung peninsula, while taking the southern half of Sakhalin. Each power agreed to evacuate Manchuria except for certain armed railway guards. Japan had clearly emerged the winner; Asia had beaten Europe for the first time in centuries. Not only did the Japanese thrill, but a flush of triumph ran through the whole non-European world from Morocco to the Philippines. Nine years earlier a small Italian army had been destroyed in Abyssinia, but no one had thought of that event as a turning point. The downfall of the Russian colossus was an altogether different matter, even though the extent of Japan's victory, which did not eliminate Russia as a major factor in the Far East, was somewhat exaggerated. Five years after the war Japan did what had been inevitable from the moment of victory. Somewhat brutally, considering the good impression it desired to make on the Asiatic world, it annexed Korea and turned the old Hermit Kingdom into an ill-treated possession.

THE PASSING OF THE MANCHUS

Following the Boxer outbreak and the ensuing humiliation for China the Manchu Dynasty lived on borrowed time for twelve years. The old dowager empress reigned until her death in 1908, and during her last years she made some attempt to move abreast of the times. She decreed a new military system along Western lines, and made some show of modernizing the education of the imperial bureaucrats. A further reform permitted intermarriage between Manchus and Chinese, but this could not turn Manchus from their three-centuries habit of regarding Chinese as inferiors.

A republican movement had been in existence for years. Its chief spokesman was Dr. Sun Yat-sen, the educated son of a poor Chinese family from near Canton. His known rebellious tendencies compelled him to reside much of the time outside China. Dr. Sun was the especial hero of Chinese students educated abroad. He had read much Western history and believed that Europe and America had evolved on three leading principles: nationalism, democracy, and socialism, which he called "people's livelihood." Nationalism and democracy he desired for China; socialism he favored at a later time with its defects removed.

The empress and her puppet nephew died a few hours apart in November, 1908. A child of three was placed on the throne and in his name further reforms were attempted. A written constitution was promised and a Chinese commission went abroad to study Western governments. Before any results could be obtained the Chinese Revolution had started in Canton in April, 1911, partly as a reaction against a government decree nationalizing the railroads. The first movement subsided but the second, beginning at Wuchang, was rapidly joined by the provinces, and a republic was proclaimed. Dr. Sun Yat-sen, then in the United States, hurried to Nanking, the new revolutionary headquarters, to be inaugurated provisional president of China on January 1, 1912. Manchus were slaughtered and Chinese queues, symbolizing loyalty to the existing dynasty, were clipped, by force if necessary.

In Peking helpless Manchus spent the first weeks of 1912 in futile debates while seeking some alternative to abdication. But the hour of the Ch'ing Dynasty had struck, as Dr. Sun would accept nothing less than the sweeping away of all imperial authority. The nobles yielded on February 12, when their little emperor gave up his throne. The line that had begun with the accession of a boy in 1644 ended with the resignation of another boy in 1912. The presidency of the new republic went not to Sun Yat-sen but to General Yüan Shih-kai, who had been appointed acting director by the emperor's abdication decree. Yüan's task would be to bring democracy, if possible, to the world's oldest despotism.

4 : Oceania

IN THE nineteenth century the British Empire, Germany, and France, with help from the United States and Japan, partitioned the Pacific islands. It is impossible to describe the whole lengthy process here, so a few annexations will be described, followed by a summary of the remainder.

The Hawaiian Islands, whose Polynesian inhabitants resemble the New Zealand Maoris, were discovered in 1778 by the English explorer James

Cook, who called them the Sandwich Islands in honor of his friend the Earl of Sandwich, First Lord of the Admiralty. A few years after Cook's discovery Chief Kamehameha of Hawaii, the largest island of the group, trained his warriors and received firearms from the whites. He conquered the entire archipelago, becoming its king and founding a dynasty. The kingdom rapidly took on Western trappings, adopting a national flag and generally welcoming foreigners. Even before the first missionaries arrived, Kamehameha II, the son of the founder, overthrew the native idols and established an atmosphere favorable to Christianity. Protestant missionaries from the United States who came in 1820 began the conversion of the islands, and were soon followed by others of various denominations. Within a few years Hawaii had become substantially Christian.

Whalers and trading ships of many flags now made Honolulu a port of call. White influence constantly mounted as the kings used principally foreign advisers. A British protectorate proclaimed in 1843 was quickly terminated, but the Hawaiian government remained weak, and annexation by a major power was only a question of time. The native population declined in numbers, principally from the introduction of foreign diseases, which between 1832 and 1860 reduced the total from 130,000 to 63,000. Ultimately, the gaps were more than filled by immigrants from China, Portugal, and Japan. By the 1880's Hawaiian independence had become a mere polite fiction, as Americans dominated the judiciary, the ministry and privy council, and even married into the royal family. In 1884 the kingdom granted the United States the exclusive right to use Pearl Harbor in Oahu as a naval base.

The last Hawaiian monarch was Queen Lydia Liliuokalani ("The salt air of Heaven"), composer of the song "Aloha Oe," who took the throne in 1891. Unfortunately for her future prospects, she was a strong-willed woman who hoped to make the royal sovereignty again effective. Her reign began just when American sugar interests in the islands desired annexation to the United States because the recent McKinley tariff had destroyed the Hawaiian sugar supremacy in the American market. When Liliuokalani proved difficult to manage, a group of notables deposed her in 1893 and set up a provisional government to ask for annexation. Unexpected opposition from President Grover Cleveland blocked the annexation treaty, whereupon Hawaii became a republic under the presidency of Sanford B. Dole. The republic lasted until 1898, when military needs caused by the Spanish-American War finally brought annexation. Other United States acquisitions in the Pacific included Midway, Wake, Howland, and Baker islands.

The Samoan Islands, also Polynesian, became the scene of rivalry between Great Britain, the United States, and Germany, with the first two powers generally standing together against the Germans. The most valuable member of the group is Tutuila, with its splendid harbor of Pago Pago.

Fleets of Germany and the United States were prepared to fight each other off Apia in Samoa in 1889, when a tropical hurricane destroyed both squadrons and reopened the matter for arbitration. As a result, the Samoans remained independent for another ten years under a native king. When he died bankrupt the British withdrew from competition and allowed the Germans and the Americans to divide the islands. The United States received Tutuila and turned Pago Pago into a naval base.

Germany also gained a share of Papua, or New Guinea, dividing possession with Holland and the British Empire. After the Spanish-American War had expelled Spain from the Philippines and Guam the Kaiser's government bought the Spanish title to the Marshalls, Carolines, and Palau, and the Marianas north of American-held Guam.

The oldest French Pacific possession is Tahiti, over which France proclaimed a protectorate in 1842, as self-compensation for the British annexation of New Zealand. The second oldest is New Caledonia, acquired in 1853, followed at considerable intervals by the annexation of the Society Islands, the Marquesas, the Tuamotus, and a part of the New Hebrides.

Great Britain annexed the largest number of Pacific islands, beginning with Fiji in 1874. Some British acquisitions were made with the purpose of stopping "blackbirding," the white practice of kidnaping South Sea islanders for service as shepherds and herdsmen in Australia. Although the natives sometimes signed or put their marks to contracts supposed to guarantee them reasonable lengths of service, pay, and living conditions, promises meant nothing after the "blackbirds" had been taken from home.

> Of the voluntary recruits, not a few were runaways who, for reasons of their own, left without the knowledge or permission of their elders. This weakening of their fighting power angered the chiefs, who blamed the ships for stealing their men, and greeted the next boat that touched their coast with flights of arrows.[2]

Others were as good as kidnaped, as the lawless men who conducted the traffic considered themselves beyond the reach of any civilized power. The British government, with the assistance of other governments, eventually stopped blackbirding, but the sordid commerce continued into the twentieth century.

In other parts of the Pacific the British acquired North Borneo and a share of New Guinea besides numerous small islands including the Solomons, the Tongas, the Gilberts, Fanning, and Ellice. Prior to the First World War the Japanese limited their expansion in Oceania to the Bonins (Ogasawaras) and Marcus, both fairly close to Japan.

---

[2] R. A. Derrick, *A History of Fiji* (Suva: Government Press, 1957), Vol. I, p. 171.

The twentieth century has thus far witnessed no anti-European nationalistic reactions among the Pacific islanders. Their numbers are small and in many places growing smaller. The isolation in which the natives have lived, and to some extent still live, makes a Pan-Polynesian or Pan-Melanesian movement unlikely in the near future. To these factors may be added the easygoing ways of the people, who seem comfortable and content with being looked after by others.

5 : Results of Global Europeanization

THIS CHAPTER has pointed out many of the changes that came to the world through Europeanization. We must now point to a few not previously mentioned. The most noticeable change was the revolution in communications. In 1800 messages between London and Canton required almost a year to send; in 1900, thanks to cables and telegraphs, they required a matter of hours. The British expedition that captured Cape Town in 1806 needed months to reach its destination and more months to send its victory report to England; in 1899 the outcome of each Boer War battle became known in London almost before the firing ended. Whereas it had taken Muraviev months to cross Siberia in 1848, the same distance in 1904 could be covered in a little over a week, thanks to the recently-completed Trans-Siberian Railway.

The second half of the nineteenth century saw the sailing ship pass virtually into oblivion and the steamer take its place. One reason for the change was the steadily increasing speed of steamships, but also important was the fact that steam brought release from the dependence on winds and currents. A sailing ship, even the fastest, had to follow routine paths; a steamer could sail where its navigator wished. Part of the early English contempt for the Suez Canal arose from failure to realize that the age of sails had nearly ended. And if steam had not been ready to dominate navigation the canal might truly have been a costly fiasco, as the wind and tide conditions of the Red Sea would have caused most sailing-vessel seamen to prefer the old Cape of Good Hope route between the Atlantic and Indian oceans. The revolution in navigation through steam changed the face of the earth, causing new ports and cities to grow and old ones to lose former importance.

Precision and location-finding instruments, all Western in origin, changed the cartographic, if not the actual, face of the globe. By 1900 natives of remote regions could see accurate maps of their homelands, such as they could never have made by themselves. The heights of mountains—Everest, Kilimanjaro, Aconcagua, Ararat, and McKinley—had been accurately determined; the depths of oceans, estuaries, and bays were known. Between 1900 and the First World War the poles themselves had been reached, the North Pole by the American Robert Peary in 1909 and the South Pole by the Norwegian Roald Amundsen in 1911. While both these discoveries were sporting events rather than scientific achievements, they would not have been possible without the advances in science the previous century had brought. It is difficult to determine the extent to which non-European living standards rose as a result of the new industries, increased trade, and advanced forms of agriculture brought by the Westerners. In Africa the rise was easily perceptible; in Asia, except for Japan, the trend was more difficult to perceive. But it is certain that huge fortunes were accumulated by Asiatics, and some of the wealth must have trickled down to the peasants and laborers. Much of the potential gain, however, may have been offset by the enormous population increase that Western rule or methods made possible.

Better communications and travel facilities caused considerable population displacement throughout the world, which perhaps throws some light on the question of which peoples will inherit the earth. The existence of the British and Portuguese empires made possible a substantial migration to east Africa of Indians who in the previous two thousand years had shown no noticeable desire to go there. Australia, which for ages had lain empty at Asia's doorstep, suddenly became desirable to would-be immigrants from the Orient, once the British had performed the pioneer work. Thwarted by the white Australian immigration laws, the Chinese moved instead into Malaya and the South Pacific islands, where the long-term future may belong to them. The existence of the British Empire accounts for the arrival of Hindu colonists in the West Indies and Caribbean, where again they will have much to say concerning the future. The work of the Russians and Japanese in developing Manchuria seems to have had, as its major effect, the migration of Chinese millions there. And if one may hazard a prophecy, the nomad peoples of central Asia appear doomed in the face of a constantly-advancing Chinese wave, which may fill those areas, insofar as they are habitable, faster than Russians can fill adjacent Siberia.

European science and technology finally ceased to be the monopoly of the white man, and with a few possible reservations, became the common property of mankind. Today a Chinese, an Indian, an Arab, or an Indonesian can become a scientist, a technician, or a mechanic. The very important question is whether the Oriental will himself materially add to the body of scientific information that has come to him from an alien culture. If he proves unable to do so, the white man, for all his political decline, will remain in a sense the world leader. The Frenchman Paul Valéry asks a question that can well serve as our conclusion here: "Will Europe remain what it still seems to be, namely the most valuable part of the universe, the pearl of the sphere, the brain of a vast body?" It has been all those things for a long time, and the world is certainly in no condition to dispense with Europe now.

Further Reading

Charles Frederic Mullett, *The British Empire* (New York: Holt, 1938), offers a history of the British Empire extending from the beginnings of overseas enterprise until shortly before the Second World War. Arthur Percival Newton, *A Hundred Years of the British Empire* (New York: Macmillan, 1940), covers the period from the accession of Queen Victoria in 1837 to the outbreak of the Second World War. Herbert I. Priestley, *France Overseas; A Study of Modern Imperialism* (New York: Appleton-Century, 1938), reviews French colonialism from the time of the Bourbon restoration in 1815. Harry R. Rudin, *Germans in the Cameroons, 1884–1914* (New Haven: Yale Univ. Press, 1938), is a case study in German imperialism, examining all phases of German administration. A very handy short history of Canada is Alfred Leroy Burt, *A Short History of Canada for Americans* (Minneapolis: Univ. of Minnesota Press, 1942), a valuable description of Canada as well as a narrative of its past. Useful for Australia is Brian Fitzpatrick, *The Australian People, 1788–1945* (Melbourne: Melbourne Univ. Press, 1946), which is likewise analytical as well as narrative.

In the long *Cambridge History of India*, 6 vols. (New York: Macmillan, 1922–32), vol. V, *British India*, and vol. VI, *The Indian Empire*, trace the history of the British raj from the arrival of the first Europeans to the year 1918. George Dunbar, *A History of India; From the Earliest Times to the Present Day*, 2 vols. (3d ed.; London: Nicholson, 1943), has much material in the second volume that is valuable for the present chapter. Li Chien-nung, *The Political History of China, 1840–1928*, trans. by Ssu-yu Teng and Jeremy Ingalls (Princeton: Van Nostrand, 1956), is an objective work by one of China's leading historians. William James Hall, *Tsêng Kuo-fan and the Taiping Rebellion* (New Haven: Yale Univ. Press, 1927), provides not only a good account of the rebellion but a detailed description of Chinese administration under the Manchus. Bernard M. Allen, *Gordon in China* (London: Macmillan, 1933), tells of Gordon's share in crushing the Tai Ping Rebellion. Arthur N. Holcombe, *The Chinese Revolution; A Phase in the Regeneration of a World Power* (Cambridge, Mass.: Harvard Univ. Press, 1930), deals with the overthrow of the Manchus and with later Chinese politics. Robert B. Porter, *Japan, the Rise of a Modern Power* (New York: Oxford Univ. Press, 1918), is principally concerned with the opening of the country, its modernization, the Sino-Japanese War, and the Russo-Japanese War. Frederick McCormick, *The Tragedy of Russia in Pacific Asia*, 2 vols.

(New York: Macmillan, 1907), is principally an account of the Russo-Japanese War preceded by some background material concerning the causes.

John Scott Keltie, *The Partition of Africa* (2d ed.; London: Stanford, 1895), though old, is still as complete a survey as can be found regarding the partition. Harry Hamilton Johnston, *A History of the Colonization of Africa by Alien Races* (Cambridge: Cambridge Univ. Press, 1899), also deals mainly with the partition. Reginald Ivan Lovell, *The Struggle for South Africa, 1875–1899* (New York: Macmillan, 1934), outlines the four-cornered rivalry between the British Empire, the Germans, the Portuguese, and the independent Boer republics for control of South African territories. G. B. Pyrah, *Imperial Policy and South Africa, 1902–10* (New York: Oxford Univ. Press, 1955), extends from the conclusion of the Boer War to the formation of the Union of South Africa in 1910. Ralph S. Kuykendall, *The Hawaiian Kingdom, 1778–1854, Foundation and Transformation* (Honolulu: Univ. of Hawaii Press, 1947), and *The Hawaiian Kingdom, 1854–1874, Twenty Critical Years* (Honolulu: Univ. of Hawaii Press, 1953), furnishes the best history of the long-extinct kingdom of Hawaii.

Chapter 26

NATIONALISM
AND DEMOCRACY
1871-1914

NEVER DID the sun shine more brightly over Europe than in the years from 1871 to 1914. For almost half a century no war among the great powers disturbed the tranquillity of the West. For almost half a century there was a swift increase in population and a steady expansion of industrial production. Seeking new fields to conquer, the leading states embarked on a course of imperialism. They colonized and modernized; they carried the blessings of technological progress to the four corners of the earth. Among colored peoples, restless under the white man's domination, there was bitter resentment, but before the Occidentals stretched an endless vista of political strength and economic prosperity. To be sure, bright young men who gathered in arty drawing rooms suffered from a feeling of cynicism and boredom, the feeling of *fin de siècle*. And in far-off native quarters dark-skinned agitators were beginning to denounce the cupidity of the foreign master. But to the average citizen of England or France or Germany these were the views of the lunatic fringe.

1 : The Indian Summer of the European Age

SUCH OPTIMISM was not unjustified. European society had created a better life for its growing population; and it had developed a civic philosophy which came to grips with the problems created by the Industrial Revolution. After 1871 laissez faire liberalism, with its emphasis on the rights of property, slowly gave way before a popular democracy preaching

461

the primacy of the general welfare over individual prerogative. Middle-class constitutionalists had at first been so determined to destroy the power of royal despotism that they refused to consider any compromise with personal freedom. But once the battle against absolutism was won, they were in a better position to adapt their social theories to proletarian needs. Recognizing factory labor as a political force, which in the hands of radicalism could turn against established authority, they gradually began to strengthen the civic and economic position of the masses.

BOURGEOIS REFORMISM

Libertarian doctrines which in 1815 had reflected only the narrow self-interest of an ambitious social class became by 1914 instruments for the advancement of society as a whole. A new humanitarian impulse broadened the outlook of bourgeois parliamentarianism. John Stuart Mill (1806–1873), a political theorist who in his intellectual development had progressed from individualistic liberalism to egalitarian democracy, spoke for militant reform in his *Principles of Political Economy* (1848):

> Each person should have power to dispose by will of his or her whole property; but not to lavish it in enriching some one individual, beyond a certain maximum, which should be fixed sufficiently high to afford the means of comfortable independence. The inequalities of property which arise from unequal industry, frugality, perseverance, talents, and to a certain extent even opportunities, are inseparable from the principle of private property, and if we accept the principle, we must bear with these consequences of it: but I see nothing objectionable in fixing a limit to what any one may acquire by the mere favor of others, without any exercise of his faculties, and in requiring that if he desires any further accession of fortune, he shall work for it.

The achievements of middle-class democracy were considerable. Everywhere in Europe there was an extension of the franchise to the masses. The Third French Republic and the German Empire introduced universal manhood suffrage at the time of their formation during the Franco-Prussian War. The United Kingdom admitted virtually every adult male to the polls by the parliamentary reform bill of 1884. In 1905 the Russian government agreed to give the proletariat the right to vote. Austria followed in 1907, and Italy in 1912. Some of the smaller states were even more daring, and by the time of the First World War Norway and Denmark had introduced female suffrage.

The problems of industrial labor were also attracting sympathetic attention in governmental circles. During the 1880's Germany pioneered in the establishment of social insurance against sickness, disability, and old

For sheer satirical brilliance in caricaturing nineteenth-century bourgeois Philistinism nothing surpasses the cartoons of Daumier. Here he depicts a session of the legislature of France, ridiculing the middle-class politicians who came to power under the parliamentary régime. The gentlemen whom he so unflatteringly portrays are all prominent lawmakers. The crabbed, hook-nosed figure on the far left in the front row is François Guizot, while his jovial colleague wearing eyeglasses who is engaged in conversation with him is Adolphe Thiers.

PUNCH, OR THE LONDON CHARIVARI.—December 11, 1875.

"MOSÉ IN EGITTO!!!"

"Moses in Egypt," the title of this cartoon which appeared in the well-known English magazine Punch, is actually the name of an opera by Gioacchino Rossini. It is a latter-day Moses, however, that the artist is portraying here. The pleased Disraeli, having just acquired control of the lifeline of the British Empire, is exchanging meaningful glances with an amused sphinx. For the next eighty-one years the government of Great Britain remained the major stockholder in the Suez Canal Company, until Egypt nationalized the strategic waterway in 1956.

On public occasions the Iron Chancellor usually appeared in uniform. He liked to affect an air of bold determination, and a military costume strengthened the impression of resoluteness he was trying to create. But, as a matter of fact, his was an exceedingly complex personality, often troubled by doubts and fears which he took pains to disguise. This photograph of him taken in middle age suggests better than most pictures the shrewd, subtle mind of the man.

The French diplomat Camille Barrère described the ostentation with which the last emperor of Germany liked to surround himself in the following dispatch: "I have never seen around a sovereign more plumes, helmets, marshals, ministers in boots, . . . princes, gigantic cuirassiers, gilded carriages transported from Berlin, and caparisoned horses." This photograph taken in 1913 illustrates what he meant. William II, wearing a hussar's uniform, is shown on the left reviewing his troops, while behind him marches an impressive array of plumes, helmets, marshals, and ministers in boots.

age. In 1911 England went still further by protecting its working population against unemployment as well as illness. Italy prescribed a weekly day of rest for labor and nationalized private insurance companies. Austria experimented with the municipal ownership of public utilities. In America, states like Massachusetts and Illinois were adopting minimum-wage schedules and assisting mothers with dependent children. Opportunities for academic training and social advancement also improved, as one government after another hastened to educate its masses through free and compulsory elementary schooling. The result was a decline of proletarian illiteracy and an increasing influence of the lower classes in public life.

PROLETARIAN RADICALISM

The improvement in the lot of the proletariat took the wind out of the sails of radicalism. Since social progress under an enlightened capitalism was becoming a reality, political extremism lost much of its appeal. In the first half of the nineteenth century the ruling classes of Europe had lived in constant fear of revolution. They could remember the widespread popular uprisings of 1820–21, 1830–31, and 1848–49. But after 1871 the only serious insurrection to affect a major state outside chronically unstable Turkey occurred in Russia in 1905. There, moreover, it merely re-emphasized the lesson that sedition was the alternative to reform. Similarly, the rise of Marxian parties on the Continent was not a symptom of the aggravation of class conflicts, but rather a sign of the growing political consciousness of the masses. The workers joining the socialist movement did so in order to attain a higher standard of living, to win a higher wage and a shorter workday. They emphasized more and more bread-and-butter objectives, immediate gains in daily economic life. Almost imperceptibly, the proletarian had ceased to be a civic outcast. He was becoming part of an organized social force capable of achieving an important position within the capitalistic system.

The great European federation of socialist parties reflected this decline of revolutionary militancy. In 1864 Marx had founded the First International Workingmen's Association, a radical organization established to direct the struggle against private property in all countries and on all continents. Yet despite its grandiose pretensions, it was never more than a feeble hodgepodge of diverse political tendencies. Torn by factionalism and persecuted by the police, it collapsed after twelve years of futile conspiring. The Second International, founded in 1889, had better luck. Less concerned with doctrinal subtleties, even prepared at times to sacrifice dogma for practical advantage, it grew and prospered. By the time of the First World War its following ran into the millions. It still continued to deliver blood-and-thunder sermons about the evils of capitalism, but in spirit it was steadily drawing closer to middle-class democracy. As it acquired offices, newspapers, housing developments, clinics, administrators, bureaucrats, and employees of its own, it became less violently opposed to the established order. At times it was actually prepared to enter into an alliance with democratic parliamentarianism. In England the socialist James Keir Hardie helped organize the middle-of-the-road Labor party. In France Alexandre Millerand agreed to enter a cabinet composed of representatives of the progressive bourgeoisie. In Germany Gustav Noske came out in favor of colonial expansion and against a reduction in armaments. It was becoming obvious that socialism's bite was not nearly as bad as its bark.

Some socialists even argued that the theory of the class struggle should be modified in accordance with changing economic conditions. In the 1890's Eduard Bernstein in Germany began to preach revisionism, maintaining that the teachings of Marx must be interpreted in the light of practical experience. Specifically, he stressed the improvement of the conditions of labor under capitalism, and urged the abandonment of the doctrine of the irreconcilability of social conflicts:

> Socialism will come . . . not as the result of the ever increasing oppression, misery, and degradation of the workers, but as the result of their growing social influence and the relative improvements, of an economic, political, and general social (ethical) nature, which they have achieved. I see socialist society arising not out of chaos, but out of the union of the organizational accomplishments of workers in the realm of the free economy with the accomplishments of militant democracy in state and community. Despite all the convulsions and the flailing about of the forces of reaction, I still see the class struggle itself assuming more and more civilized forms. And it is precisely in this civilizing of political and economic struggles that I perceive the best guarantee for the realization of socialism.[1]

At its congress in Amsterdam in 1904, the Second International condemned revisionism as heresy. Most of the great Marxian theoreticians—such as August Bebel, Karl Kautsky, and Jules Guesde—declared that it represented an unacceptable departure from ideological orthodoxy. But no amount of dialectical sleight of hand could overcome the mood of gradualism which had become dominant among their followers. When 1914 came each socialist party urged the worker to support his government against his fellow worker across the frontier. The great crisis of bourgeois society thus created an irreparable breach in the ranks of socialism.

For those who did not want their radicalism diluted there was anarchism. Convinced that all government was based on oppression, it insisted that all government was evil. Society should ideally be built on voluntary

---

[1] Eduard Bernstein, *Von der Sekte zur Partei* (Jena: Eugen Diederichs, 1911), p. 76. Trans. by Theodore S. Hamerow.

co-operation, on the free consent of men and women ready to subordinate their private interests to the common good. Not the policeman on the street corner, not the bureaucrat behind his desk, but the natural human impulse to work for the welfare of mankind should become the bulwark of a new social order. Yet how could the existing coercive system of rule be overthrown? Some anarchists agreed with the gentle Prince Peter Kropotkin, who taught that a moral regeneration of the individual must precede the establishment of a better society. Others, acting on the advice of Michael Bakunin, waged a war of terror against the representatives of established authority. They threw bombs and fired revolvers, assassinating Empress Elizabeth of Austria, King Humbert I of Italy, President Sadi-Carnot of France, and President William McKinley of the United States. Still others, accepting the anarchosyndicalism of Georges Sorel's *Reflections on Violence* (1908), believed that trade-unions would become the shock troops of revolution and destroy capitalism through a general strike.

Despite its promises of Utopia, however, anarchism did not prove a serious threat to the ruling classes of the West. In the popular mind, it always remained the familiar caricature that peered out of the pages of the newspapers, wild-eyed and black-bearded, hurling dynamite at the world.

Here and there in France, Italy, and Spain anarchosyndicalism did manage to win a following in militant proletarian circles, but generally it could not compete successfully with the socialists for the support of the masses. The anarchist movement attracted the intellectual and the Bohemian, not the rank and file of labor, and in the early years of the twentieth century it entered a period of decline.

THE RISE OF NATIONALISM

Since socialism was growing more powerful but less aggressive, and anarchism more aggressive but less powerful, bourgeois society was safe against its critics. The danger which it faced came from its avowed defenders. The great crisis of 1914 was not the work of a proletariat rising against the middle class, but of forces which established authority had created and nourished. It was the product of an irresponsible, aggressive nationalism.

In its simplest form, nationalism preached that all men of common culture and common history properly constituted a single political organism. Its origins could be traced back to antiquity, to the Hebrew notion of the chosen people and the Roman concept of municipal citizenship. In the Middle Ages there had been vague stirrings of a national feeling among the states of Europe. The Renaissance and the Reformation weakened the unifying force of religious life and encouraged the rise of national monarchies. In his *Defense and Illustration of the French Language,* published in 1550, the Frenchman Joachim du Bellay proclaimed "my natural affection toward my fatherland," and thirty years later the Englishman John Lyly was assuring his countrymen that they held a special place in the sight of God: "So tender a care hath He alwaies had of that England, as of a new Israel, His chosen and peculiar people."

But it was a German clergyman educated in the enlightened teachings of the eighteenth century who first advanced a systematic theory of nationalism. For Johann Gottfried Herder (1744–1803) each people possessed a historic heritage in the form of a distinct culture which separated it from every other people. By identifying himself with his national culture the individual became a link in the spiritual bond which connected the present with the past and the future. Yet he also belonged to humanity, within which each nation had its unique mission:

> Nature has distributed its gifts differently according to climate and culture. How could they be compared to one another? Rather we should rejoice, like Sultan Suleiman, that there are such varied flowers and peoples on the gay meadow of this earth, that such different blossoms can bloom on both sides of the Alps, and that such varied fruits can ripen.

The cultural nationalism of Herder became political in the course of the French Revolution and the Napoleonic era. During the Restoration nationalism continued to grow, especially among those peoples which were politically disunited. The Germans recalled the glory of the Holy Roman Empire, the Italians remembered the grandeur that was Rome, the Magyars sang the deeds of Janos Hunyadi, the Czechs of Johann Ziska, the Poles of Vladislav Jagiello, the Greeks of Pericles, the Irish of Hugh O'Neill. Everywhere enthusiastic young men were joining patriotic organizations like the Burschenschaften, the Carbonari, the Young Ireland party, and the Hetairia Philike. Their purpose was to reconstruct Europe on the principle of nationalism. Once each people was free to determine its own form of government, they maintained, men would live peacefully in mutual respect. Giuseppe Mazzini was their most eloquent spokesman:

> Nationalities are sacred, and providentially constituted to represent, within Humanity, the division or distribution of labor for the advantage of the peoples, as the division and distribution of labor within the limits of the state should be organized for the greatest benefit of all citizens. If they do not look to that end, they are useless and fall.

Yet there were also indications that nationalism might in the end prove to be a Frankenstein monster. During the revolution of 1848 John Stuart Mill noted sadly: "In the backward parts of Europe and even (where better things might have been expected) in Germany, the sentiment of nationality so far outweighs the love of liberty that the people are willing to abet their rulers in crushing the liberty and independence of any people not of their race and language." In the hands of the practitioners of *Realpolitik* who governed Europe after 1871 nationalism became a weapon in the struggle for diplomatic hegemony. There was less and less regard for the aspirations of other states, less and less concern for the welfare of humanity. Nationalism turned into an obsession, stimulating the spread of militarism and racialism. In that poisonous atmosphere the German General Friedrich von Bernhardi asserted in all earnestness that war "is not only a necessary element in the life of people, but also an indispensable factor in culture, indeed the highest expression of the strength and life of truly cultured peoples." The London *Saturday Review* stated bluntly, "England has awakened to what is alike inevitable and her best hope of prosperity. *Germaniam esse delendam* [Germany must be destroyed]." The Russian diplomat Alexander Izvolski exulted, when the shooting finally began: *"C'est ma petite guerre* [This is my little war]." The age which had begun with the great voyages of discovery in the fifteenth century came to an end in 1914 in the trenches of Flanders.

2 : Western Europe

GREAT BRITAIN

For England the closing decades of the reign of Victoria were a golden sunset. Never before had the country been so prosperous, never again was it to be so self-confident. As the indestructible queen grew older, the ministers who had guarded the throne in the early years of her rule—Melbourne, Russell, Palmerston, Peel, Derby—began to pass from the scene. Their place was taken by the second generation of Victorian statesmen. After 1870 the Liberal party was guided by the sincere, long-winded William Ewart Gladstone (1809–1898). His great opponent was Benjamin Disraeli (1804–1881) —intellectual, dilettante, and fop—of Jewish birth, who emerged as the dominant figure in a party which had come to represent the interests of the proudest aristocratic families. The landed nobility willy-nilly accepted his leadership, for he alone seemed capable of saving it from defeat. Convinced that the old shibboleths of throne and altar had lost their meaning in an age of industrialism, he transformed the Conservative party into the champion of imperialism. To middle-class insistence upon domestic reform he replied with the call for a bold foreign policy.

It was fitting that the two great Gladstone ministries of 1868 to 1874 and 1880 to 1885 should be devoted to an improvement of political and social institutions. In 1870 a new education law laid the foundation of a system of universal elementary schooling, and an order in council introduced the merit principle into the civil service. In 1871 the practice of purchasing commissions in the armed forces was ended; in 1872 the ballot was made secret; in 1883 corruption at the polls was suppressed; and in 1884 the extension of the suffrage to agricultural laborers established virtually universal manhood suffrage. During the Disraeli ministry from 1874 to 1880, on the other hand, the British lion roared. In 1875 the prime minister cleverly engineered the purchase by his government of a controlling share in the management of the Suez Canal Company. In 1876 he fired the imagination of the country by sponsoring a bill conferring upon the queen the title Empress of India. In 1878 he checked Russian expansion in the Near East, obtaining Cyprus from Turkey in return for promises of military assistance which did not cost a single pound. Even after his death Conservative statesmen like Lord Robert Salisbury, Arthur Balfour, and Joseph Chamberlain remained exponents of an energetic diplomacy. In the years from 1885 to 1905, when the Conservatives were usually in power, Downing Street continued to acquire overseas possessions and wave the Union Jack.

The Liberals finally managed to win a major parliamentary victory as a result of economic difficulties at home. By the early twentieth century British industry was encountering growing competition from Germany, America, and Japan. At first the urban proletariat sought to improve its position through unionization and strike activity. But then in 1900 the Labor Representation Committee, which soon became the Labor party, began to attract the working class by its advocacy of democratic socialism. A growing demand for protective tariffs added to the difficulties of the Conservative party, and in 1905 King Edward VII (1901–1910) called on the leader of the opposition, Sir Henry Campbell-Bannerman, to form a new ministry.

For the next ten years the Liberals were at the helm, introducing innovations which would have shocked such earlier stalwarts of the party as Lord Russell and John Bright. The moving spirit behind this reform movement was David Lloyd George (1863–1945), a fiery Welshman of lower-class background who attacked the rich with a hatred nurtured by his early poverty. In 1906 labor unions were declared immune against the damage suits of employers; in 1909 pensions were granted to workers over seventy; in 1911 the masses were insured against sickness and unemployment; and in 1912 a minimum-wage law for the coal industry was promulgated. Moreover, when the conservative aristocrats who dominated the House of Lords protested against new taxes on wealth by rejecting the budget of 1909, the ministry took the issue to the country, won two bitter electoral campaigns, and with the Parliament Bill of 1911 deprived the upper chamber of the right to veto measures approved by the House of Commons.

The colonial possessions of Great Britain were the indirect beneficiaries of the growth of democracy in the mother country. The dominion status obtained by Canada in 1867 proved so successful an instrument of imperial administration that it was soon extended to other overseas territories inhabited by a European population. In 1901 New South Wales, Victoria, Queensland, South Australia, Western Australia, and Tasmania were united in the Commonwealth of Australia. In 1907 New Zealand was elevated from a colony to a dominion. And in 1910 Cape Colony, Natal, Transvaal, and Orange River Colony formed a federal state in which Briton and Boer ruled jointly over the native Negro masses.

But what England managed to accomplish in distant lands she failed to do only a few miles from her shores. For Ireland remained an insoluble problem throughout the nineteenth century. Separated by religion, by occupation, and by political sentiment from their Anglo-Saxon masters, the Irish rebelled time and time again against their position within the United Kingdom. In London one cabinet after another attempted in vain to end sedition on the Emerald Isle. In 1829 Catholics were given the right to hold public office, and in 1869 the Irish Episcopal Church was disestablished. Between 1870 and 1903 a series of land-purchase laws enabled the tenant to buy his farm from the landowner and transformed Ireland into a country of independent peasant proprietors. Finally, in 1914 a bill giving the island political autonomy was adopted, only to create the danger of a civil war between the Protestant minority concentrated in the north and the Catholic majority of the south. But a national tragedy in Ireland was temporarily averted by the international tragedy of Europe. When hostilities began on the Continent, both sides in the Irish dispute agreed to conclude an armistice and support the government in its hour of need.

FRANCE

In France, in the meantime, democratic republicanism was helping a defeated country recover from military disaster. Yet when the Third French Republic was born in 1870, it looked as if it would not last even as long as the ill-fated Second French Republic of 1848. The war continued to go badly, Paris was forced to surrender early in 1871, and the general elections held a few days later produced a national assembly dominated by monarchists. That spring an insurrection of the Parisian radicals was suppressed only with the help of the army; and the harsh peace treaty surrendering Alsace-Lorraine to Germany and providing for an indemnity of five billion francs weakened the position of the government still further.

If the royalists had been able to compose their differences, they would have had little difficulty in destroying this republic without republicans. The champions of the grandson of Charles X, however, were at loggerheads with the supporters of the grandson of Louis Philippe, and in the meantime republicanism was gaining strength. President Adolphe Thiers, a lifelong monarchist, finally came out in favor of it. Although he was forced out of office for this temerity, his countrymen increasingly tended to agree with him that a republic was "the government which divides us least." In

1875 a series of constitutional laws created a republican form of political organization based on a chamber of deputies elected by universal manhood suffrage, a senate chosen by a complicated system of indirect elections, and a president appointed by the legislature. When four years later the royalist president M. E. P. M. de MacMahon resigned in the face of a hostile parliamentary majority, the victory of the republicans was complete.

Aided by a swift political recovery and steady economic expansion, the republic was now in a position to settle old scores. In France the Catholic church, never forgetting the bitter days of Jacobin persecution in the French Revolution, was traditionally opposed to democracy. During the 1880's it paid the price of defeat. In 1880 the Jesuit Order was ordered dissolved; in 1882 a system of free, secular education was established to train a generation of loyal republicans; in 1884 divorce—prohibited under the Restoration—once again became permissible. At the same time the government attempted to reconcile proletarian and bourgeois by issuing an amnesty to the participants in the Parisian uprising of 1871 and by legalizing labor unions. It even made an effort to enlist nationalist sentiment through a policy of colonial expansion in Africa and Asia.

Nevertheless, the enemies of the republic refused to give up hope. The monarchists, the clericals, the aristocrats, the chauvinists continued to dream of a royalist restoration. By chronic venality, moreover, democratic politicians played into their hands. In 1887 a shocked country learned that the son-in-law of President Jules Grévy was selling membership in the Legion of Honor, and in 1893 the failure of the Panama Company led to the revelation that legislators had been in the habit of receiving lavish gifts from the managers of the unlucky enterprise. The result was a sudden rise of political discontent on the Left as well as the Right. Radical doctrines gained new strength as the trade unions formed the General Confederation of Labor to work for the overthrow of capitalism. And conservative malcontents found their hero in the dashing General Georges Boulanger, who preached a war of revenge against Germany and issued thundering pronouncements about the need for political change. Had his nerve been as strong as his language, he might perhaps have made himself master of France. But when in 1889 the government prepared to try him for treason, his courage evaporated. The brave soldier fled abroad, and in a supremely Gallic gesture committed suicide on the grave of his mistress.

The great crisis in the history of the republic, however, was still to come. In 1894 Captain Alfred Dreyfus, a Jewish army officer serving on the general staff, was convicted by a court-martial of selling military secrets to Germany and was sentenced to lifelong imprisonment on Devil's Island. Yet when two years later a re-examination of the evidence suggested that not Dreyfus but a Major M. C. Esterhazy was the traitor, the military authorities decided to suppress the new findings. Why compromise the army's reputation for infallibility for the sake of a confirmed republican and a Jew at that? Still, the news that an innocent man had been unjustly imprisoned leaked out. Before long the nation was involved in a bitter struggle during which the fate of one individual became a symbol of the conflict of political ideologies. Against him were the enemies of the government who saw in him the personification of all the evils of democracy. For him were intellectuals like Émile Zola, republicans like Georges Clemenceau, and socialists like Jean Jaurès.

The scales of public opinion slowly shifted in his favor, and by 1906 the affair had reached a denouement which not even a Hollywood scenario could have improved. Of his foes, General Le Mouton de Boisdeffre resigned, Esterhazy went into exile, and Colonel Hubert Henry killed himself. Dreyfus, on the other hand, was exonerated and promoted to major, and his champion, Colonel Georges Picquart, became minister of war. As for Zola, he died too soon to enjoy all the spoils of victory, but his spirit must have rejoiced at the splendid state funeral and the ceremonial interment in the Pantheon. The government could now also insist on a strict reckoning with the opposition. The armed forces were purged of conservative extremists, known monarchists were dismissed from the civil service, most religious orders were suppressed, and in 1905 church and state were separated. France continued to be plagued by proletarian discontent and labor unrest, and inefficiency and corruption remained the incubus of public life. Yet the republic had at last crushed its enemies.

THE LOW COUNTRIES AND SCANDINAVIA

The Low Countries were also exposed to the economic and social consequences of industrialization and democratization. In Belgium the reigns of Leopold II and Albert I witnessed the rise of socialism and a wave of labor unrest. Proletarian demands for an extension of the franchise to the lower classes led to the establishment of universal manhood suffrage in 1893, but the urban masses were still resentful of the system of plural voting which clearly favored the aristocracy and the bourgeoisie. Finally, the school problem remained a source of contention between the Liberals and the Clericals, the former in favor of a public and secular organization of education, the latter demanding financial support from the government for church institutions of learning.

In Holland political developments under King William III and Queen Wilhelmina followed a similar pattern. Radical influence among the masses resulted in the adoption of social legislation. Lower-class agitation led to extensions of the right to vote in 1887 and 1896, although universal manhood suffrage was not achieved until 1917. And differences of opinion regarding religious instruction divided the freethinking Liberals from the Calvinist Conservatives and the Catholic Clericals.

The Scandinavian countries, too, pursued a policy of democratic reform. Denmark succeeded in improving its agricultural system by fostering rural co-operatives, encouraging dairy farming for the British market, and creating a class of peasant proprietors. During the 1890's an old-age pension law and a health insurance measure were promulgated. Early in the twentieth century universal manhood suffrage was introduced, the right to vote was given to most women, and the cabinet became responsible to the lower chamber of the legislature. At the same time Sweden was undergoing an industrialization accompanied by the usual effects: the rise of radicalism, the introduction of social legislation, the adoption of protective tariffs, and finally in 1907 the establishment of practically universal manhood suffrage. Yet political and economic progress was not enough to reconcile the Norwegians to the union with their eastern neighbors. Traditional grievances troubling relations between the two peoples were further aggravated by the development of a cultural nationalism in Norway. Impatience with the slow pace of constitutional reform in Stockholm and the feeling that Norwegian commercial interests were ineffectively represented by the consular service of Sweden strained political ties to the breaking point. In 1905 the parliament in Oslo declared the union dissolved, and upon its invitation Prince Charles of Denmark became King Haakon VII of Norway.

3 : Central and Southern Europe

GERMANY

From 1871 to 1918 the German Empire remained the most powerful of the states of Europe. Militarily, it possessed an efficiently organized army which conscripted its soldiers from a population of some sixty million, second only to Russia. Politically, it formed a federal union of twenty-five states, governed with the consent of a parliament elected by universal manhood suffrage, but dominated by an energetic, conservative Prussia. Economically, it prospered in the struggle for international markets. Its factories and mines in the Ruhr constituted one of the greatest concentrations of industrial might in the world. Its optical goods, chemical products, electrical appliances, and precision instruments enjoyed an international reputation. In the hunt for profits it pursued tactics which envious competitors called "ungentlemanly," meaning that they were imaginative and successful. German salesmen traveled to Asia and Africa, they learned Turkish and Arabic, they adjusted the designs of their wares to the tastes of the Chinese and the Persians. By the time of the First World War the industrial output of Germany had left France far behind, and it was slowly but surely passing Great Britain.

As long as Bismarck was master in Berlin, the political resources of the state were employed to maintain the diplomatic equilibrium. Convinced that with the achievement of national unification the legitimate aspirations of Germany had been satisfied, he practiced his statecraft for the benefit of the status quo. But in his domestic policies he was less moderate. Throughout the 1870's he was engaged in the futile *Kulturkampf,* a struggle against the political influence of Catholicism. His motive was the desire to stimulate patriotic sentiment and please his liberal allies. Yet the effort to supervise the religious education and the secular activity of the clergy resulted only in the rise of the Catholic Center party which fought the Iron Chancellor to a standstill. Realizing at last that a victory was impossible, he arranged an orderly retreat, and in the 1880's he turned against an even more dangerous foe, Marxism. His new campaign was a skillful blend of blandishment and repression. To win the loyalty of the workingman, Germany became the world's pioneer in social legislation, insuring the urban masses against illness in 1883, accident in 1884, and old age in 1889. To overcome the threat of revolution, socialist newspapers were suppressed and socialist leaders imprisoned. But neither the velvet glove nor the mailed fist could destroy radicalism. The Social Democratic party continued to grow, until Bismarck in despair began to think about the abrogation of the liberal constitution which provided the enemies of the government with a measure of protection.

His opportunity to put these plans into effect never arrived. After 1888 there developed a growing coolness between him and the young new emperor, William II (1888–1918). Both were ambitious, both were unbending. There simply was not enough room in public life for two such colossal egoists. In 1890 the grand old man of Germany was curtly dismissed and the country prepared to follow a new course. The Iron Chancellor had made bombastic speeches as well as any superpatriot; he had boasted on one occasion that "we Germans fear God and nothing else in the world." But as a matter of fact there were many things of which he was afraid, and caution had become a habit with him. The emperor, on the other hand, actually believed with all his heart such nationalistic nonsense as "our Lord God would not have taken such great pains with our German fatherland and people, if He did not have still greater things in store for us." The result was a reign of tub-thumping and saber rattling which antagonized the world.

Bismarck had practiced colonialism with reserve; William II became a loud and aggressive imperialist. Bismarck had carefully avoided any challenge to British supremacy on the seas; William II, influenced by the jingoistic Admiral Alfred von Tirpitz, launched a naval race which drove England into alliance with his enemies. Bismarck had consistently avoided involvement in the Near East, which he considered of little importance for central Europe; William II actively fostered German influence in the Ottoman Empire, arousing resentment in St. Petersburg and London. The emperor's disastrous foreign policy led to an international isolation of his government which provoked political discontent at home. In 1912 the last general election held before the outbreak of hostilities gave a third of all votes to the socialists and strongly endorsed the parties in opposition to the régime. Demands for a restriction of the prerogatives of the crown became more insistent, until the coming of the war put a halt to the rising movement for constitutional reform.

ITALY

Italy was the weakest of the great powers. A country without the natural resources essential to industrial greatness, rich only in classical ruins and bumper crops of babies, it had achieved national unification against heavy diplomatic odds. Once this goal was reached, however, there was a violent reaction against the idealistic mood of the *Risorgimento*. Many who had sacrificed all in the struggle against the foreign enemy were now determined to enjoy the material benefits of victory. And since there were not enough benefits to go around, too often those with the sharpest elbows rose to the top.

The masses continued to live amid a poverty which was bearable in the progressive north, total and appalling in the barren south. Politics became a game of musical chairs played by a small minority of the well-to-do who alone possessed the right to vote. Now the Right would be in power, wrestling with chronic deficits, imposing new taxes, distributing patronage, manipulating elections. Then the Left would profit from the delinquencies of its rivals, win a parliamentary majority, form a cabinet, and proceed to commit precisely the same sins.

Civic and economic shortcomings were intensified by the Italian ambition to play the role of a major power. Statesmen eager for re-election could always make political capital with rabble-rousing speeches about the imperative need to acquire overseas colonies and to conquer regions like the Trentino and Istria, which were inhabited by Italians but ruled by Austria. While they fired the public with patriotic oratory, the taxpayer was forced to support an army and a navy out of all proportion to the size of his pocketbook. Lastly, the church problem complicated national affairs still further. The Papacy, refusing to accept the loss of its temporal possessions, persisted in urging the faithful to adopt a policy of passive resistance toward their government. Thereby it created a crisis of conscience for millions of Italians torn between piety and patriotism.

From the establishment of the Italian kingdom in 1861 until 1876 the politicians of the Right dominated the national government. Cautious bourgeois liberals from the north, they ruled in the spirit of Cavour. They encouraged industrialism and strengthened the army, but also levied taxes right and left. Managing at last to balance the budget, they were voted out of office by a financially exhausted electorate. For the next twenty years the country was in the hands of the parties of the Left, composed largely of underpaid professionals and small businessmen from the south. These were radical and anticlerical in speech, cynical and rapacious in deed. Their leaders, Agostino Depretis and Francesco Crispi, attacked the church, condemned poverty, and insisted that only an aggressive foreign policy could win for the nation its rightful place. Yet despite their promises the standard of living remained miserably low. Moreover, corruption in high places came to be accepted as normal, and political criticism was met with stuffed ballot boxes and with the panacea of "transformism," a high-flown euphemism for the practice of buying off dangerous opponents. As for colonial aspirations, Tunis was snatched from under Italian noses by France in 1881, and Ethiopia inflicted a humiliating defeat on Italian arms in the war of 1895-96. Only the hot and unhealthy wastes on the east coast of Africa known as Eritrea and Somaliland were left to salve national pride.

By the beginning of the twentieth century political ineffectualness had led to the rise of socialism and anarchism. While liberals, democrats, and nationalists followed each other in office, the peninsula was swept by an epidemic of labor strikes and political assassinations which took the life of King Humbert I himself. The government's answer was to try to reach an understanding with the church, to promulgate a modest program of social legislation, to introduce universal manhood suffrage, and to wage a successful war against Turkey in 1911-12 which brought the country another half-million square miles of desert sand in Tripoli. Yet civic and social antagonisms continued to mount. By 1914 Italy was a frightened country, disillusioned with parliamentarianism and haunted by the specter of revolution. The coming of a world war seemed to its leaders to offer a way out of a hopeless impasse.

THE IBERIAN PENINSULA

Economic and social weaknesses also blocked civic progress in the Iberian peninsula. In Spain the moderate constitution of 1876 maintained a parliamentary system of government in which the conservatives, under Antonio Cánovas del Castillo, and the liberals, under Práxedes Mateo Sagasta, rotated in office without significant differences in policy. While they were alternately enjoying the spoils of bureaucratic power, the endemic political discontent of the country mounted. The Carlist reactionaries and Catholic ultraroyalists accused the authorities of doctrinaire liberalism. The republicans and the socialists charged them with blind conservatism. The anarchists were opposed to all government as a matter of principle. And the particularists in Catalonia demanded cultural and administrative autonomy for their region. The war with America in 1898 which cost the Spaniards Cuba and the Philippines turned an outraged patriotism against the national leadership, while the hatred between clerical and anticlerical added to the embitterment of public life. Under the circumstances there was noth-

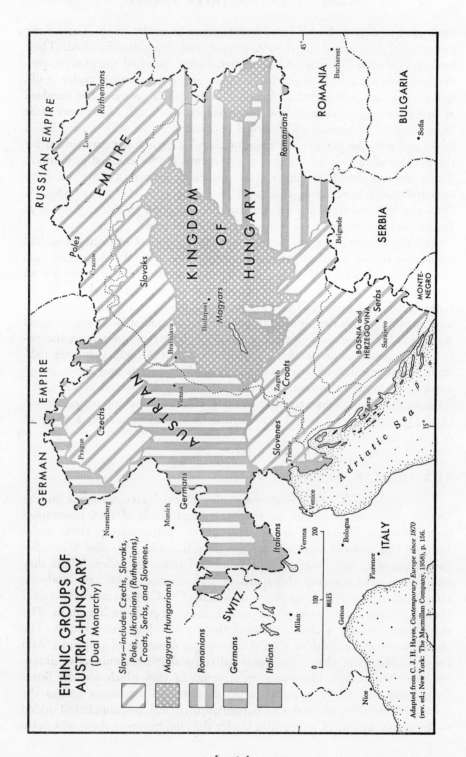

ETHNIC GROUPS OF AUSTRIA-HUNGARY
(Dual Monarchy)

Slavs—includes Czechs, Slovaks, Poles, Ukrainians (Ruthenians), Croats, Serbs, and Slovenes.

Magyars (Hungarians)

Romanians

Germans

Italians

Adapted from C. J. H. Hayes, *Contemporary Europe since 1870* (rev. ed.; New York: The Macmillan Company, 1968), p. 156.

ing for the crown to do but steer a middle course amid conflicting ideologies.

The Braganzas in Portugal, like the Bourbons in Spain, tried to follow a policy of political opportunism. But they were less successful. As long as Luiz I was on the throne, the government was by turns in the hands of two cliques of professional politicians—the Regenerators and the Progressives —about as different as tweedledum and tweedledee. Such an artificial parliamentarianism was open to the attacks of the republicans. Still, with the support of the army and the bureaucracy, the king managed to keep the opposition in check. The scandals and extravagances surrounding his successor, Carlos I, however, played into the hands of the enemies of the monarchy. The new ruler, moreover, had no patience with the intricacies of party politics, preferring to govern with an iron hand through his prime minister, João Franco. Yet the Portuguese were in no mood for a game of divine-right absolutism. In 1908 their sovereign was assassinated in broad daylight while driving through the streets of Lisbon. Two years later his son, Manuel II, was deposed and a republic was proclaimed. Turning against the church, which was considered a stronghold of royalism, the new order adopted a series of anticlerical decrees. Monastic orders were suppressed, religious instruction in elementary schools was prohibited, and church and state were separated. A national assembly in the meantime promulgated a constitution designed to transform the country into a model democracy. But more than a sheet of paper was needed to overcome the civic tradition of a people. The conservatives continued to plot for a monarchist restoration, and the socialists went on organizing strikes, until the nation finally sought relief from strife in a succession of gingerbread dictators.

4 : Eastern Europe

THE AUSTRIAN EMPIRE

As the nineteenth century drew to a close the three great autocracies of the east still presented the appearance of substantial solidity. In the Austrian capital there was a superficial gaiety which disguised the fact that the state was suffering from serious weaknesses. For the *Ausgleich* of 1867 had failed to solve the problem of nationalism which was destroying the unity of the Habsburg crownlands. The Czechs, the Slovaks, the Poles, the Ukrainians, the Italians, the Romanians, the Croats, and the Slovenes grew more insistent in their demands for regional autonomy, while the Germans and the Hungarians were more determined than ever to maintain their dominant position. Emperor Francis Joseph was a fitting symbol of the tragedy of his realm. Morose, lonely, and tired, his brother Maximilian executed in Mexico, his wife Elizabeth assassinated in Switzerland, his son

477

Rudolf a victim of his own suicidal impulse, his nephew Francis Ferdinand a sacrifice to Serbian fanaticism, the old man silently carried the heavy burden of dynastic responsibility.

In the western half of the Dual Monarchy public affairs at first followed the familiar pattern of bourgeois constitutionalism. Conservatives, liberals, democrats, and socialists competed for the favor of a propertied electorate. But with the intensification of particularist sentiment political parties came to represent more and more national groups rather than civic ideologies. Ultimately the legislature degenerated into a bedlam of ethnic factions screaming epithets and hurling inkwells. The adoption of universal manhood suffrage in 1907 failed to relieve the tension, and in view of the irresponsible conduct of the parliamentary representatives the government was forced to rule by bureaucratic decree.

In Budapest, on the other hand, all was decorum. The Liberals and the Independents deliberated in a dignified fashion, although the apparent stability of Hungarian politics was built on a policy of repression. Only Magyars could sit in parliament, and while they were promulgating laws which served their special interests, the oppressed nationalities encouraged by their brothers across the border conspired against the state. By 1914 the inward disintegration of the empire had advanced so far that a group of influential government leaders, among them Foreign Minister Leopold von Berchtold and Chief of Staff Conrad von Hötzendorff, decided that only a successful war against Slavic nationalism could save their country from ruin.

RUSSIA

The Russian monarchy was also entering a critical period. Pursued with determination, the reform program of Alexander II might have prepared the country for the transition from agrarian feudalism to industrial capitalism. But the Tsar Liberator was not a man to compromise and conciliate. Since his subjects failed to display proper appreciation of the favors conferred on them, he would show them that he was still the Autocrat of all the Russias. The policy of reaction pursued after 1870, however, only drove the opposition underground. At first the radicals organized a populist movement to arouse revolutionary ardor among the peasantry. Yet when the muzhik remained deaf to slogans of civic justice and economic emancipation, they turned to terror. In a state in which the public expression of political dissatisfaction was prohibited, violence was the only weapon at the disposal of the critics of the established order. Alarmed by the campaign of assassination against prominent officials, the emperor finally resolved to adopt once more a program of moderate concession. In 1881, acting on the advice of Minister of the Interior Michael Loris-Melikov, he agreed to establish a representative council to advise the government in the adoption of needed legislation. But it was too late for a reconciliation with the enemies of autoc-

EXPANSION OF RUSSIA IN EUROPE

Russia 1533

Acquired to 1598

Acquired to 1914

Held at other times

Dates indicate time area held or gained by Russia

0   200   400
MILES

racy. On March 13, the day he gave his assent to the reform plan, the tsar fell before a terrorist bomb.

If Alexander II resembled Alexander I in his good intentions and weak will, his son Alexander III (1881–1894) seemed to inherit the inflexible conservatism of Nicholas I. All projects of constitutional reform were tossed into the wastepaper basket, all thoughts of compromise with the opposition were suppressed. For thirteen years Russia was ruled with an iron hand. Terrorism was crushed by the ruthless Viacheslav Plehve, who commanded the secret police, while ideological warfare against subversion was directed by Constantine Pobiedonostsev, the chief administrative officer of the national church. Bureaucratic controls over education, research, and writing multiplied, and the government organized a systematic persecution of religious and ethnic minorities. The Protestants in the Baltic provinces and the Catholics in Poland were exposed to official harassment, but the harshest treatment was reserved for the Jews. They became the scapegoats for all the ills besetting the nation. The economic and social disabilities under which they lived were made more rigorous, and the authorities encouraged the oppressed peasantry to vent its resentments in pogroms directed against a frightened and helpless people. At the same time, however, the state was unwittingly preparing the ground for a revival of radical thought. Not only did the reign of injustice win recruits for the opponents of tsarism, but in order to maintain the political and military strength of the country the emperor—under the influence of his minister of finance, Sergei Witte—fostered the growth of industrialism. And with industrialism came a factory proletariat and the socialist ideology.

The storm finally broke over the last of the Romanovs. The handsome Nicholas II (1894–1917) was an overbearing but weak man, governing his possessions with a stubbornness born of fundamental insecurity. Determined to maintain his father's policy of unbending autocracy, he lacked his father's iron will. While he continued to imprison political malcontents and to oppress national minorities, the opposition was secretly winning new strength. In 1898 the Russian Marxists, inspired by the teachings of George Plekhanov, organized the Social Democratic party. Five years later it divided into the militant Bolsheviks under the leadership of V. I. Lenin and the moderate Mensheviks whose spokesman was Julius Martov. In 1901 the radical agrarians founded the Social Revolutionary party, which preached a rural socialism adapted to the needs of the peasant masses. Finally in 1903 the democratic bourgeoisie formed the Union of Liberation, a party of moderate constitutionalists.

At first the enemies of tsarism made little progress in the face of official persecution, but the military fiasco of the government in the Russo-Japanese War opened the way for insurrection. Having come into conflict with the Land of the Rising Sun over Manchuria and Korea, Nicholas II in 1904 provoked a war with the Nipponese. The outcome was a succession of dis-

asters on land and sea which forced the Russians to sign the Treaty of Portsmouth on September 5, 1905, establishing Japan as the dominant power on
the eastern coast of Asia.

By this time Russia was in the throes of revolution. The news of military reverses combined with an accumulation of economic grievances to
produce a wave of political murders, demonstrations, and strikes. Hoping
to stem the tide, the tsar in the fall of 1905 issued the October Manifesto,
promising to promulgate a democratic constitution, to restrict the prerogatives of the crown, to set up a representative assembly or Duma elected by
a generous franchise, and to guarantee civil rights and liberties. His strategy
was successful, because to bourgeois moderates these concessions were
enough, while to proletarian radicals they were only the beginning. Having
split the opposition, the government further strengthened its hand by recalling the army from the Far East and floating a huge loan in France.

The first Duma, which assembled in 1906, was under the influence of
the liberals, but by now the authorities felt confident enough to order its
dissolution. When in the following year the second Duma proved even more
hostile toward absolutism, it met a similar fate. The reactionary prime
minister, Peter Stolypin, won the support of the peasantry by introducing
rural reform legislation. At the same time he published a new electoral law
increasing the representation of the propertied classes. Hence the third
Duma, elected in 1907, and the fourth, meeting in 1912, were submissive,
and conservative statesmen at court began to rub their hands in satisfaction
at the clever way in which they had tamed subversion. But they were mistaken. The day of reckoning had only been postponed. The outbreak of
hostilities in 1914 was the first step toward another and even more terrible
revolution.

THE OTTOMAN EMPIRE

The forces of democracy and nationalism were also undermining the
political structure of the Balkans. For one thing, the oppressed Orthodox
peoples of the peninsula—the Greeks, the Serbs, the Romanians, and the
Bulgarians—worked ceaselessly for the dismemberment of the Ottoman
Empire. Yet each in turn regarded the ambitions of its neighboring co-
religionists with suspicion. Secondly, among educated patriotic Turks there
was a growing realization that their country faced the alternative of reform
or collapse. In an age of parliamentary government and industrial production, they argued, there was no place for theocratic absolutism. Thus a
struggle between traditionalists and modernizers complicated by the antagonism between Christian separatism and Ottoman centralism divided the
empire. Even more important, the roles which the great powers had customarily assumed at the Sublime Porte began to change. Toward the end
of the nineteenth century Great Britain, long the defender of Constanti-

GERMANY

RUSSIA

AUSTRIAN EMPIRE

Crakow

Galicia

Austro-Hungarian
Empire, 1867

Vienna

Ruthenia

Budapest

Bucovina

Bessarabia
To Russia 1812

Jassy

KINGDOM
OF
HUNGARY

Moldavia

Odessa

Zagreb
(Agram)

Transylvania

To Moldavia 1856
Returned to
Russia 1878

Croatia-Slavonia

Banat
To Serbia 1833

To Romania 1878

Dalmatia

Bosnia-
Herzegovina
Occupied 1878
Annexed 1908

Belgrade

ROMANIA
Independent 1878

Wallachia
United with Moldavia 1858

Bucharest

Black Sea

Split

Sarajevo

SERBIA
1804
Independent
1878

Dobrudja

Ceded to
Romania 1913

To Montenegro
1913
To
Montenegro
1878

To Serbia 1878

BULGARIA
Independent 1908

Varna

Limit of
Ottoman
Empire,
1815

Sofia

Eastern Rumelia
United to Bulgaria 1885

MONTENEGRO
Independent 1878

Antivari

To Serbia 1913

Philippopolis
(Plovdiv)

Adrianople
(Edirne)

Adriatic
Sea

To Montenegro
1878

Bulgaria
1913

Macedonia

To Bulgaria
1913

Constantinople
San
Stefano

Unkiar-
Skellesi

Durazzo

ITALY

ALBANIA
Independent 1912-13

To Greece 1913

Salonika

TURKEY

Ionian Islands

To Greece 1881

Aegean Sea
Islands to
Greece 1913

Anatolia

Smyrna

Br. Protectorate 1815-1863
To Greece 1863

GREECE

Euboea

Athens

Independent 1830

Morea

Dodecanese
Islands

Rhodes

BALKAN PENINSULA
TO 1914

States shown as national units of 1914

To Italy 1912

Crete

Autonomous 1898
United to Greece 1908-1913

—·—·—·— Boundary established by
Congress of Berlin, 1878

————— Boundary established by
Treaty of San Stefano, 1878

nople, resolved to reduce its commitments in the Balkans. Control of the Suez Canal and possession of Egypt provided sufficient protection for its lifeline to India. The German Empire under William II, on the other hand, developed a growing interest in the Near East. It advised the Turkish government, reorganized the Turkish army, bolstered the Turkish economy, and planned direct rail communication between Berlin and Baghdad. Austria, driven out of Italy and Germany, also turned southward, partly to recoup its political losses, partly to counter the appeal of Serbian nationalism. And Russia never ceased to dream of the conquest of the Straits.

The 1870's opened in the Balkans on a familiar note. Christian nationalism and Moslem maladministration provoked an uprising against Ottoman rule first in Bosnia and Herzegovina and then in Bulgaria. Both sides conducted their military operations to the accompaniment of the customary atrocities. Europe as usual closed its eyes to Slavic excesses and grew indignant at Turkish barbarity. Once again the Russians had a perfect pretext for intervention in the peninsula. Charging in from the north like St. George about to slay the dragon, Alexander II defeated the armies of the sultan in 1877, and early the following year he forced the Sublime Porte to sign the Treaty of San Stefano. The tsar won full possession of Bessarabia in Europe and Ardahan, Kars, and Batum in Asia; Serbia and Romania gained recognition as independent states; Montenegro acquired the port of Antivari; and a large autonomous Bulgarian state was established, nominally under the suzerainty of the Sublime Porte, actually as an outpost of Russian influence.

But the congratulations which the diplomats in St. Petersburg were exchanging proved a little premature. The great powers had no intention of leaving the sultan at the mercy of his ambitious neighbor. Once again a coalition of major states led by Great Britain stepped in between Russia and Turkey. Remembering the unpleasant outcome of the Crimean War, Alexander II reluctantly agreed to a new settlement of the Near Eastern question. The Berlin Congress, meeting from June 13 to July 13, 1878, allowed the English to occupy Cyprus, authorized the Austrians to administer Bosnia and Herzegovina, encouraged the French to seize Tunis, and made vague suggestions to the Italians about expansion into Albania. As for the minor states in the Balkans, most of them were delighted to see tsarism's pet Bulgaria reduced in size, but their satisfaction turned to chagrin when their own claims were also largely ignored.

The Berlin Congress introduced a period of relative stability in the Near East. Tsarist hopes of expansion into the Ottoman Empire had been frustrated twice within twenty-five years, and Russia therefore turned eastward to the Pacific. Without the support of the big brother of all the Slavs the Balkan peoples could do little more than cast poisonous glances in the direction of Constantinople. Security from foreign attack, moreover, relieved the Sublime Porte of the need to adopt domestic reform. In 1876, confronted by the danger of revolution, Sultan Abdul Hamid II had accepted a constitution granting political equality, religious freedom, and parliamentary representation. Within a year, however, he decided that there was no longer any reason to play the liberal. Dismissing his progressive advisers, he returned to the tradition of absolutism.

In the decades which followed the sultan ruled by cruelty and deception, living up to the popular view of how an Oriental despot behaved. By the beginning of the twentieth century his tyranny had led to the rise of a secret opposition party, the Young Turks, composed of Westernized bureaucrats and officers. Convinced that only a modernization of the political institutions of the state could save it from destruction, they prepared for the overthrow of the authoritarian régime. In 1908 the banner of revolution rose in Macedonia, and when the troops sent to suppress the insurrection joined it, Abdul Hamid II decided that once again the time had come to be enlightened. The constitution of 1876 was dusted off and reissued, and for a few weeks there was wild jubilation throughout the empire, as Moslem and Christian celebrated the arrival of the millennium.

Then the first outburst of enthusiasm began to subside. The Young Turks made the discovery that good intentions and eloquent speeches were not enough to solve the complexities of the Near Eastern question. To begin with, the emancipated minorities within the country preferred to seek union with their brothers beyond the frontier rather than become good Ottomans. Secondly, imperialistic foreign governments closed in around Turkey. In 1908 Austria annexed Bosnia and Herzegovina which it had been administering for thirty years. In 1911–12 Italy made war on the Ottoman Empire, seizing Tripoli in northern Africa and occupying the Dodecanese Islands off the coast of Asia Minor. And late in 1912 a Balkan coalition composed of Bulgaria, Greece, Serbia, and Montenegro attacked the armies of Sultan Mohammed V, and within a few months conquered all of his remaining European possessions except the region around Constantinople.

Embittered by this succession of disasters, the Young Turks decided to forget the fine words about civic equality and save what they could from the general debacle by a suppression of political discontent. Reviving the same dictatorial methods of government against which they had recently rebelled, they employed the army to oppose all demands for local autonomy. In Enver Pasha they found a leader who in 1914 took them into war on the side of Germany, hoping that a military victory would restore the vitality of the state.

5 : The New World

THE OCEAN separating the Old World from the New was a geographical boundary between two ways of life. North America, only recently explored and settled, was largely free from the dissatisfactions which held Europe in their grip. Its society had not yet stratified into hereditary castes separated from each other by exploitation and resentment. Its economy was still shaped by the opportunities which the taming of a continent continued to offer. Beyond the western limits of the civilized community, rich unpopulated lands beckoned to the restless. Socialism had little appeal to a working class which could escape from oppression by starting a new life a few hundred miles away. Since the Atlantic formed an impregnable defense against the great powers of the Eastern Hemisphere, the Americans never knew the curse of militarism. Far from the injustices of older civilizations, they pursued their destiny with an artless confidence that all would turn out for the best.

THE UNITED STATES

The Civil War had decided the outcome of the struggle between liberal industrialism and aristocratic agrarianism in the United States. After a decade the efforts of the victorious Union to reconstruct society below Mason and Dixon's line through a preferential political treatment of emancipated Negroes and poor whites failed. Yet the South remained a land tormented by economic poverty and racial hatred for a long time. The plains and mountains of the West were swiftly divided among farmer, rancher, and miner, so that by the beginning of the twentieth century the frontier had ceased to exist. The country beyond the Mississippi, however, remained dependent on the corporate wealth which had its stronghold in the East. A dominant influence in American life came to be exerted by the "robber barons" of high finance, who planned railroads, built steel mills, mined coal, slaughtered cattle, and founded banks. From their offices in New York, Pittsburgh, or Chicago, John D. Rockefeller, J. P. Morgan, Andrew Carnegie, H. C. Frick, Philip D. Armour, and E. H. Harriman were making themselves masters of all creation. To resist them was futile. Social critics like Henry George and Henry Demarest Lloyd vainly sermonized about economic injustice, while labor associations like the National Labor Union and the Knights of Labor were no match for the captains of industry. Such farm organizations as the Patrons of Husbandry in the 1870's and the People's party in the 1890's, which sought safety in government regulation or in currency manipulation, were equally unsuccessful in resisting the business community. A youthful capitalism, creative and ambitious, ruled over the land.

The acquisitive instinct of the stock exchange cast its shadow over government. Never before and never again did financial self-seeking direct national policy so completely. The brilliant statesmen who had debated the great issues of human bondage and constitutional freedom in the years before the Civil War were succeeded by a race of pygmies, obedient to the

485

call of party expediency and private advantage. Presidents Ulysses S. Grant, Rutherford B. Hayes, James A. Garfield, Chester A. Arthur, Benjamin Harrison, and William McKinley were only political mediocrities. And while they were at least personally honest, the same could not be said of many of their followers for whom they provided a respectable front in the White House. Senator James G. Blaine accepted a sizable bribe for his favors to railroad interests; Secretary of War William W. Belknap sold an appointment to a trading post in Oklahoma; Secretary of the Treasury William A. Richardson permitted one of his agents to keep a few hundred thousand dollars he had collected in taxes; Ambassador Robert Schenck sold fraudulent stock to foreign investors while representing his country abroad; Congressman Oakes Ames offered shares at half price to his colleagues in Washington to keep them from looking too closely at a construction company which he headed. Senator Roscoe Conkling expressed the creed of a cynical, hard-boiled bossism in the assertion: "When Dr. Johnson defined patriotism as the last refuge of a scoundrel, he ignored the enormous possibilities of the word *reform*."

Before the nineteenth century came to an end the growing republic began to seek new worlds to conquer. The same faith in manifest destiny which had guided the nation in the march from sea to sea inspired an imperialistic agitation for overseas possessions. Senator Albert J. Beveridge, one of the most ardent of the expansionists, argued that the acquisition of colonial dependencies was inevitable, because the "American Republic is part of the movement of a race—the most masterful race of history—and race movements are not to be stayed by the hand of man." To a people getting tired of provincial tranquillity his words were an exciting call to adventure. Finding in hapless Spain an ideal victim, the United States in 1898 waged a "splendid little war" which left it in possession of Cuba, Puerto Rico, Guam, and the Philippines.

In the course of the next twenty years America extended its influence throughout the Caribbean. It encouraged the secession of Panama from Colombia and then constructed an interoceanic canal across the new state. It sent troops to Santo Domingo, Haiti, Nicaragua, and Mexico. It announced its intention of assuming the role of an international police force in order to put a halt to chronic wrongdoing in the Western Hemisphere. The apostle of the expansionist gospel was the irrepressible Theodore Roosevelt—cowboy, writer, naturalist, President—all teeth and pince-nez, warning the world against "the loss of the virile fighting virtues, of the fighting edge."

Even more important than imperialism in the long run was the growth of a spirit of civic reform. The Progressive movement, which arose early in the twentieth century, differed from socialist radicalism in its acceptance of the institution of private property, and from agrarian populism in its urban flavor and outlook. Fundamentally, it was a middle-class effort to return to a golden age of self-sufficient simplicity, before the individual had been overwhelmed by monopolistic finance and party bossism. It demanded political responsibility, economic freedom, and social justice. Not the destruction of capitalism but its purification became the goal of the enthusiastic young men and women who joined in the great moral crusade against the forces of corruption. President Woodrow Wilson expressed its passion for righteousness in his first inaugural address:

> The evil has come with the good, and much fine gold has been corroded. With riches has come inexcusable waste. . . . We have been proud of our industrial achievements, but we have not hitherto stopped thoughtfully enough to count the cost, the cost of lives snuffed out, of energies overtaxed and broken, the fearful physical and spiritual cost to the men and women and children upon whom the dead weight and burden of it all has fallen pitilessly the years through. The groans and agony of it all had not yet reached our ears, the solemn, moving undertone of our life, coming up out of the mines and factories and out of every home where the struggle had its intimate and familiar seat. With the great Government went many deep secret things which we too long delayed to look into and scrutinize with candid, fearless eyes. The great Government we loved has too often been made use of for private and selfish purposes, and those who used it had forgotten the people.

The Progressives went to work in a spirit of dedication. Publicists like Upton Sinclair, Ray Stannard Baker, Ida Tarbell, and Lincoln Steffens attacked wickedness in industry and politics. Mayors like "Golden Rule" Jones in Toledo, Tom Johnson in Cleveland, and John Purroy Mitchel in New York fought municipal corruption. Governors like Robert M. La Follette of Wisconsin, Albert B. Cummins of Iowa, and "Alfalfa Bill" Murray of Oklahoma opposed state bossism. Senators and congressmen like Hiram S. Johnson, Moses Clapp, and George W. Norris fought the good fight in Washington. They forced the dissolution of a few of the big trusts, outlawed some of the monopolistic practices of big business, strengthened public regulation of railroads, and introduced the income tax. To reduce the influence of party machines they instituted direct primaries in about two-thirds of the states, adopted the initiative and the referendum in almost half of them, and by the seventeenth amendment to the federal Constitution provided for the direct election of senators. In one state after another, reform laws restricted the labor of children, protected women employed in factories, and limited the working hours of men. The impulse to do good also led to a vigorous agitation for the elimination of slums, the construction of settlement houses, the building of playgrounds, and the suppression of John

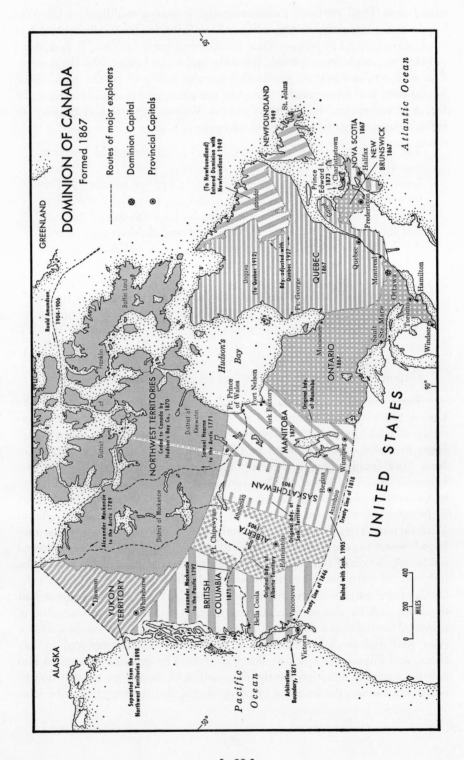

DOMINION OF CANADA
Formed 1867

- - - - Routes of major explorers
⊛ Dominion Capital
⊙ Provincial Capitals

GREENLAND

Atlantic Ocean

NEWFOUNDLAND
1949
St. Johns

(To Newfoundland)
Entered Dominion with
Newfoundland 1949

Labrador

Prince
Edward I.
1873

NOVA SCOTIA
1867

NEW
BRUNSWICK
1867

Charlottetown
Halifax

Fredericton

Ungava (1912)

(To Quebec 1912)

Bdy. adjusted with
Quebec 1927

Ft. George

QUEBEC
1867

Quebec

Montreal

Ottawa

Hamilton

Roald Amundsen,
1904-1906

Baffin Land

District
of
Franklin

*Hudson's
Bay*

District
of
Keewatin

Samuel Hearne
to the Arctic 1771

Ft. Prince
of Wales

Port Nelson

York Factory

Moosonee

ONTARIO
1867

Sault
Ste. Marie

Toronto

Windsor

Toronto

90°

UNITED STATES

NORTHWEST TERRITORIES
Ceded to Canada by
Hudson's Bay Co., 1870

District of Mackenzie

Alexander Mackenzie
to the Arctic 1789

MANITOBA
1870

Original bdy.
of Manitoba

Winnipeg

Regina

Assiniboia

SASKATCHEWAN
1905

Treaty Line of 1818

Original bdy. of
Sask. Territory

Athabaska

ALBERTA
1905

Ft. Chipewyan

Original Bdy. of
Alberta Territory

Edmonton

United with Sask. 1905

ALASKA

Separated from the
Northwest Territories 1898

Dawson

YUKON
TERRITORY

Whitehorse

Alexander Mackenzie
to the Pacific 1792

BRITISH
COLUMBIA
1871

Bella Coola

Vancouver

Victoria

Treaty Line of 1846

Arbitration
Boundary, 1871

*Pacific
Ocean*

0   200   400
MILES

Barleycorn. The great campaign for civic morality continued until the United States entered the First World War.

CANADA

Canadians did not display the same passion for reform. Their progress was slower than that of the great neighboring republic, but they did not suffer as much from adolescent growing pains. The achievement of dominion status in the 1860's marked the beginning of a period of unspectacular though steady advance. Until 1891 the country was governed almost without interruption by the Conservatives under Sir John A. Macdonald, and then until 1911 by the Liberals under Sir Wilfrid Laurier. The former statesman was English, Protestant, and protectionist; the latter French, Catholic, and free-trade. Both, however, proved equally loyal to the British crown and equally opposed to separatist provincial tendencies.

Canada formed its own army and police, its own administration and civil service, and its own financial and postal system. But the ties to the mother country were not weakened. As a matter of fact, when England found itself involved in the Boer War, a Canadian expeditionary force was sent to South Africa as evidence of imperial solidarity. To the original four provinces joined in 1867 under the British North America Act were added by 1905 five additional ones extending from ocean to ocean, although the total population of the dominion still remained less than ten million. The completion of a transcontinental railroad in 1885 fostered an expansion of agriculture and a boom in mining. And the large-scale introduction of farm machinery made possible an intensive cultivation of the western plains, so that before long Canada could take its place beside the United States, Argentina, Australia, and Russia as one of the granaries of the world. Dyed-in-the-wool Yankee imperialists continued to hope that some day the dominion would join the American union, but neither the French nor the English Canadians gave much encouragement to such ambitions. While maintaining cordial relations with Washington as well as London, they preferred to seek their destiny as the citizens of a free and sovereign nation.

LATIN AMERICA

South of the Rio Grande an uneasy stability followed the chaos of the first years of independence. To be sure, even after 1870 there was always bound to be a war, a revolution, or at least a conspiracy in progress somewhere in Latin America, but these were generally not as violent as in the wild and woolly days earlier in the century. The larger states in particular were developing political and economic strength. In Brazil Emperor Pedro II was deposed more or less peacefully in 1889, after alienating the armed forces by a cautious foreign policy and the landed aristocrats by the abolition of slavery. The establishment of a federal republic coincided with the opening of an era of agricultural and industrial progress. The coffee crop virtually monopolized the world market, while animal husbandry, forestry, mining, rubber, and cotton helped support a population second only to the United States in the Western Hemisphere. In Argentina the economy was based on the beef, wheat, wool, corn, and flax exported to feed and clothe the masses of Europe. In Chile the rich nitrate deposits seized from Peru and Bolivia during the War of the Pacific—between 1879 and 1884—gave the country a new economic importance and confirmed its position as the dominant power on the west coast of South America. And in Mexico money from the United States helped to expand the output of mining and the production of petroleum.

But the unaccustomed peace which Latin America began to experience was enforced by the firing squad. Security had been purchased at the price of freedom. While some foreign observers, deceived by appearances, waxed eloquent about the new respect for law and order developing in the Iberian countries of the Western Hemisphere, the masses remained hagridden by political dictatorship and economic exploitation. In Venezuela a new constitution was promulgated in 1874, then another in 1881, then a third in 1894. Yet the proliferation of state charters could not disguise the fact that power was actually in the hands of a succession of strong men of whom the most successful was Antonio Guzmán Blanco. In Colombia the dictators José Marroquín and Rafael Reyes were in power during the first decade of the twentieth century. But the secession of Panama aroused widespread resentment against the government, and after 1909 President Carlos Restrepo introduced a program of moderate political and social reform. In Mexico Porfirio Díaz, the perfect example of a Latin *caudillo,* governed with the help of bayonets from 1876 to 1911. And the revolution which at last drove him into luxurious exile on the Champs Élysées in Paris only substituted anarchy for tyranny. Francisco Madero, who defeated Díaz, was in turn overthrown by Victoriano Huerta; Huerta was deposed by Venustiano Carranza; Carranza was attacked by Francisco Villa; and Villa finally provoked the United States into sending a punitive expedition south of the border under General John J. Pershing. As for the lands of Central America and the West Indies, there Yankee admonitions and Yankee marines helped maintain an appearance of stability. Unfortunately, as soon as Washington relaxed its grip, the old tradition of political discord would reassert itself. The truth was that mass poverty and social antagonism had created in Latin America an environment unfavorable to democratic government.

6 : The Coming of the War

IN 1914 the nineteenth century came to an end. A strong, prosperous Europe entered into a ruinous war which weakened conquered and conqueror alike.

As they took the fatal step, the participants tried to persuade themselves that they were at Armageddon, engaging in a battle between the forces of right and wrong. But, as a matter of fact, the antagonists were brothers, children of the same culture and the same history. Nothing demonstrated their fundamental identity of interest more clearly than the military struggle itself which, in defeating some, crushed them all.

In the long run the only victors in that struggle were some businessmen who profited from the economic boom of the war years, the communists who came to power amid the ruins of tsarism, and colonial peoples who began to press their demands for political concession against the exhausted states of the West. The ultimate irony was that with greater wisdom the outbreak of hostilities might have been avoided altogether. The conflict of political objectives arising out of nationalism, imperialism, and capitalism was not irreconcilable. The great imperialistic powers like England and France fought not against but for each other. The captains of industry in Germany and Italy had no valid motive for disrupting the international business community. Even national interests were injured rather than served by the military contest. It was essentially human pride and human weakness which caused the First World War.

EUROPEAN ALLIANCES AND ALIGNMENTS

Throughout the nineteenth century there had been international conflicts in Europe, but these had been of short duration and for limited objectives. The Russians had fought the Turks in 1828–29 to help liberate Greece; the English and the French had taken up arms against Russia in 1854–56 to defend the Ottoman Empire; the French had defeated the Austrians in 1859 to further Italian unification; the Prussians had attacked the Austrians in 1866 to gain domination over Germany. Yet the alliances which had preceded these wars did not persist after the return of peace, because until 1870 the European balance of power established by the Congress of Vienna was not seriously threatened. A new era in diplomatic relations opened, however, with the outbreak of the Franco-Prussian War. First of all, the German Empire emerged out of that struggle as the greatest political and military state of the West. Secondly, France refused to accept the loss of Alsace and Lorraine as permanent and continued to dream of retaliation upon the Teutons. As long as Bismarck stood at the helm in Berlin the international equilibrium remained undisturbed. The Iron Chancellor was convinced that his country had reached its logical dimensions and that the maintenance of peace was therefore the best guarantee of its national security. He knew well enough that the French would welcome a war of revenge, but by their own unaided efforts they could hardly hope for success. Consequently, his objective became to keep his western neighbor isolated and therefore peaceful. England would follow its traditional policy of splendid isolation unless its vital interests were imperiled. Italy was too

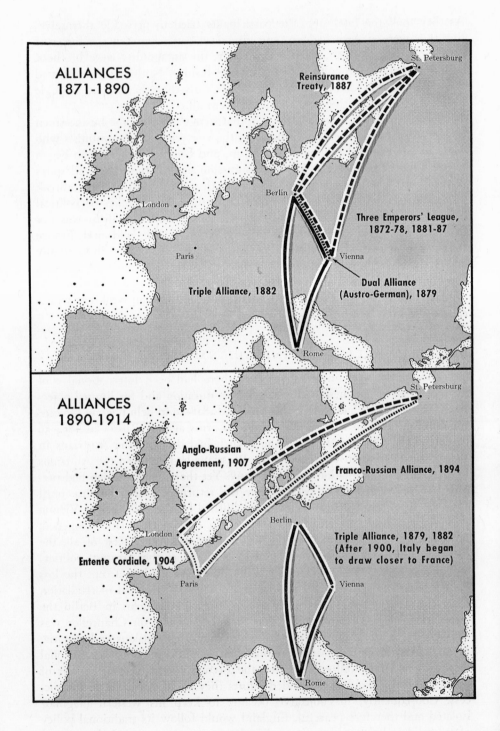

ALLIANCES
1871-1890

Reinsurance
Treaty, 1887

St. Petersburg

London

Berlin

Paris

Three Emperors' League,
1872-78, 1881-87

Vienna

Dual Alliance
(Austro-German), 1879

Triple Alliance, 1882

Rome

ALLIANCES
1890-1914

St. Petersburg

Anglo-Russian
Agreement, 1907

Franco-Russian Alliance, 1894

Berlin

Triple Alliance, 1879, 1882
(After 1900, Italy began
to draw closer to France)

London

Vienna

Entente Cordiale, 1904

Paris

Rome

busy trying to pull itself up by its bootstraps into the ranks of the great powers to risk involvement in a dangerous military adventure. Autocratic Russia and Austria would normally be reluctant to enter into a partnership with republican France. The political outlook was thus distinctly favorable to Germany.

The greatest asset of Germany was the brilliant statecraft of Bismarck, who patiently built one diplomatic dike after another to maintain the status quo by segregating France. A meeting of William I, Francis Joseph, and Alexander II held in Berlin in September, 1872, led to the formation of the Three Emperors' League, an informal agreement among the conservative monarchies of the east to work together for the preservation of peace. Unfortunately, the conflicting aims of St. Petersburg and Vienna in the Balkans made lasting co-operation between them impossible, and during the crisis of 1878 which culminated in the Berlin Congress the two courts fell out. One year later Bismarck concluded a defensive treaty with Austria directed against Russia and France. In 1882 this Dual Alliance became a Triple Alliance, as the Italians, outraged by the French seizure of Tunisia which they themselves had long planned to occupy, decided to seek revenge with the assistance of the Teutonic powers.

Still, the Iron Chancellor had too much respect for the armed might of Russia to accept a permanent estrangement between the Romanovs and the Hohenzollerns. In 1881 he revived the Three Emperors' League, and when six years later tension in the Near East disrupted once again this uneasy collaboration, he executed one of his most daring maneuvers. By the secret Reinsurance Treaty of 1887, William I and Alexander III each agreed to maintain neutrality if the other were attacked by a third power. Had this arrangement become known in Vienna, there would have been bitter recriminations among the members of the Triple Alliance. But the sorcerer of the Wilhelmstrasse in Berlin spun his fine web of international intrigue with consummate skill.

Bismarck's successors were less deft. Arguing that the German government had entered into too many incompatible commitments, William II refused to renew the Reinsurance Treaty in 1890. He was confident that the Autocrat of all the Russias would never agree to an association with the ideological heirs of the Jacobins. He underestimated, however, the force of national self-interest. Early in 1894 Russia and France concluded a defensive pact directed against the Triple Alliance. All the major powers of Europe except Great Britain were thus members of one or the other of two great alliance systems, and the Court of St. James's did not straddle the fence long either. The reckless policies pursued by the Kaiser drove England into the arms of his enemies. From the point of view of the British, it was bad enough that their markets were gradually being conquered by German businessmen. But then the aggressive imperialism practiced by Berlin, the growing Teutonic influence in the Near East, and the ambitious program of naval construction advocated by Admiral Tirpitz intensified the feeling of alarm on Downing Street. In 1904 the United Kingdom and France signed a colonial agreement settling their differences regarding Egypt, Siam, Newfoundland, and Madagascar which had embittered the relations·of the two countries in the past. On paper it seemed to have only a remote bearing on the continental diplomatic situation, but in practice it introduced a period of close political and military co-operation between London and Paris, popularly known as the *Entente Cordiale,* the friendly understanding.

The treaties of 1894 between France and Russia and of 1904 between France and England led logically to the completion of the triangle by a treaty between England and Russia. In 1907 their governments agreed to adjust conflicting claims in Persia, Afghanistan, and Tibet, thereby clearing the way for a new policy of collaboration between these traditional enemies. The Triple Alliance and the Triple Entente now became mutually opposed armed camps. Their role in bringing on the war was accurately described by the German diplomat Arthur Zimmermann on August 1, 1914, when he realized that the bullets were about to start flying: "It all came from this damned system of alliances, which was the curse of modern times."

A DECADE OF CRISES

Like gamblers playing for such high stakes that they cannot afford to withdraw from the game, the great powers clashed in a series of crises which gradually prepared Europe for the idea of a recourse to arms. Neither side wanted a test of strength, but pride, ambition, and resentment made compromise ever more difficult. Before they fully realized what was happening, they had passed the point of no return.

The first encounter took place in 1905, when France prepared to end, and Germany to defend, the independence of Morocco. William II won an early tactical victory by forcing Paris to submit the issue to an international conference meeting in Algeciras in Spain. Yet his jubilation soon turned to chagrin, as all the major states except Austria voted to give France a dominant voice in the internal affairs of the sultanate. In 1908 the decision of Vienna to annex Bosnia and Herzegovina, which it had been administering since the Berlin Congress, brought the Continent once again to the brink of disaster. Russia, the champion of Slavic Orthodox nationalism, was supporting Serbian claims to the two provinces, when to the assistance of the Austrians came Germany "in shining armor"—to use the Kaiser's exuberant figure of speech. With bitterness in its heart the court of St. Petersburg was forced to back down. In 1911 there was another crisis, as France moved to complete its conquest of Morocco, and Germany once more began to rattle the saber. England rushed to support its ally, but the danger of an open clash was averted when Berlin agreed to settle for two bits of French Equatorial Africa. Finally, in 1913 the outcome of the hostilities between the Ottoman Empire and the Balkan coalition of Bulgaria, Greece, Serbia, and Montenegro again threatened to involve the major countries in a world war. The Serbians backed by the Russians were determined to acquire the Turkish province of Albania, while the Austrians were resolved to keep their sworn enemies from the Adriatic shore. Moreover, the Italians, who had their own designs on the coastland, seconded the efforts of Francis Joseph. Only the readiness of Vienna to employ military means to decide the question compelled the government of the tsar to agree to the creation of an independent Albanian state. It secretly vowed, however, that this would be its last retreat.

THE OUTBREAK OF HOSTILITIES

By the summer of 1914 Europe had run out of diplomatic miracles. On June 28 Archduke Francis Ferdinand, the heir to the Austrian throne, was assassinated in Sarajevo, the capital of Bosnia and Herzegovina, by the fanatical Serbian nationalist Gavrilo Princip. For weeks important officials in Belgrade had known of his intentions and had even given him material assistance, although the police authorities in Vienna could only guess at such connivance. For the statesmen of Austria the murderous deed provided an opportunity to settle accounts with Serbia, which had long fanned political unrest among the Slavic subjects of the Habsburgs. On July 23 the imperial government dispatched an ultimatum made deliberately so harsh as to be unacceptable. Five days later, after the expected rejection, Austria declared war. The advisers of Francis Joseph felt sure that they would be left free to crush their weak opponent while the great powers growled at each other without daring to risk involvement in hostilities.

But they had not reckoned with Russia's determination to avoid another political defeat. On July 30 the tsar after some hesitation ordered the general mobilization of his armies, thereby unintentionally forcing the hand of the diplomats in Berlin. For the German strategic plan, prepared nine years before by General Alfred von Schlieffen, provided that in the event of a Russian mobilization the Kaiser's forces were to engage at once in war with Russia and France. They were to turn first against the latter in overwhelming strength and achieve a swift victory in the west by an unexpected thrust through neutral Belgium. Then a strong, united front could be established against the slowly assembling tsarist forces. The decision of Nicholas II to call up the army reserves thus panicked the Germans, forced them to declare war against Russia on August 1, drove them to commence hostilities against France on August 3, and a day later drew Great Britain into the struggle. The English cabinet had thus far been unable to decide on neutrality or participation, but the invasion of Belgium tipped the scale in favor of the advocates of aiding France. On August 4 the United Kingdom entered the conflict, and the First World War was under way.

Yet far from seeking hostilities, most of the leaders of Europe had been desperately anxious to avoid them. Certainly among the crowned heads there was little pugnacity. George V wrung his hands; Francis Joseph shrank from a struggle in which he saw little chance of victory; William II sent pleading telegrams to St. Petersburg; Nicholas II worried about the "thousands and thousands of men who will be sent to their death." The mood of the diplomats was even more despairing. The German chancellor, Theobald von Bethmann-Hollweg, broke down; the English ambassador in Berlin, Sir Edward Goschen, cried; the foreign secretary of Great Britain, Sir Edward Grey, lamented; the Austrian ambassador to the United King-dom, Albert von Mensdorff, was crushed by sorrow; the German ambas-sador in London, Prince Karl Max Lichnowsky, was on the verge of a collapse; the Russian minister of foreign affairs, Sergei Sazonov, and the German ambassador in St. Petersburg, Friedrich von Pourtalès, embraced in tears before separating; the German ambassador in Paris, Wilhelm von Schön, sobbed as he delivered the declaration of war to the French govern-ment. There was not a dry eye in the government offices of the great powers during those early days of August. Not even the military men displayed much enthusiasm at the prospect of taking the field. The German chief of staff, General Helmuth von Moltke, became ill; the German secretary of the navy, Admiral Alfred von Tirpitz, was frightened; the Russian minister of war, General Vladimir Sukhomlinov, appeared nervous and depressed.

Only the sheep being led to the slaughter found it all very exciting. While bands played and girls waved their handkerchiefs, countless young men paraded gaily through towns and villages away from humdrum routine to a glorious adventure. Before long, millions of them would lie beneath a vast field of white crosses stretching from the English Channel to the Black Sea. And on the evening of August 4, as his world was coming to an end, Sir Edward Grey in London addressed the approaching darkness: "The lamps are going out all over Europe; we shall not see them lit again in our lifetime."

Further Reading

Carlton J. H. Hayes, *A Generation of Materialism, 1871–1900* (New York: Harper, 1941), is a thoughtful account of the last decades of the nine-teenth century, criticizing the secular outlook of the period. For a less tendentious approach see E. Fueter, *World History, 1815–1920* (New York: Harper, 1920). The development of political radicalism is analyzed in Bert-

rand Russell, *Proposed Roads to Freedom* (New York: Holt, 1919), and
G. D. H. Cole, *Socialist Thought: Marxism and Anarchism* (New York:
St. Martins, 1954). W. A. McConagha, *The Development of the Labor
Movement in Great Britain, France, and Germany* (Chapel Hill: Univ. of
North Carolina Press, 1942), J. Joll, *The Second International, 1889–1914*
(London: Weidenfeld, 1955), and P. Gay, *The Dilemma of Democratic
Socialism: Eduard Bernstein's Challenge to Marx* (New York: Columbia
Univ. Press, 1952), are important studies of the socialist movement. Of the
numerous works dealing with nationalism the following merit special
attention: Carlton J. H. Hayes, *Essays on Nationalism* (New York: Mac-
millan, 1926) and *The Historical Evolution of Modern Nationalism* (New
York: Macmillan, 1948); Hans Kohn, *The Idea of Nationalism: A Study
in Its Origins and Background* (New York: Macmillan, 1944); Louis L.
Snyder, *The Meaning of Nationalism* (New Brunswick: Rutgers Univ.
Press, 1954); and B. C. Shafer, *Nationalism: Myth and Reality* (New York:
Harcourt, 1955).

R. C. K. Ensor, *England, 1870–1914* (New York: Oxford Univ. Press,
1936), and G. M. Young, *Victorian England* (Garden City: Doubleday,
Anchor A35, 1954), depict the golden age of Great Britain. George Danger-
field, *The Strange Death of Liberal England* (New York: Random, 1935),
deals with the decline of laissez faire before the First World War. The
standard biography of Gladstone is John Morley, *The Life of William
Ewart Gladstone*, 3 vols. (New York: Macmillan, 1903), but there is also
the less strenuous P. Magnus, *Gladstone* (New York: Dutton, 1954). Similarly, Hesketh Pearson, *Dizzy: The Life and Personality of Benjamin Disraeli* (New York: Harper, 1951), is sprightlier than the magisterial W. F.
Monypenny and G. E. Buckle, *The Life of Benjamin Disraeli*, 6 vols. (New
York: Macmillan, 1910–20). James O'Connor, *History of Ireland, 1798–
1924*, 2 vols. (Garden City: Doran, 1926), describes the Irish struggle for
self-government. For a brilliant account of the Third French Republic, see
D. W. Brogan, *The Development of Modern France, 1870–1939* (London:
Hamilton, 1940). Other sound introductions are R. W. Hale, *Democratic
France: The Third Republic from Sedan to Vichy* (New York: Coward-
McCann, 1941), and David Thomson, *Democracy in France* (New York:
Oxford Univ. Press, 1952). Matthew Josephson, *Zola and His Time* (New
York: Macaulay, 1928), and Geoffrey Bruun, *Clemenceau* (Cambridge,
Mass.: Harvard Univ. Press, 1943), portray two republican heroes of France.

William H. Dawson, *The German Empire, 1867–1914*, 2 vols. (New
York: Macmillan, 1919), is a work of substantial scholarship, although on
social and cultural developments it should be supplemented with Koppel S.
Pinson, *Modern Germany* (New York: Macmillan, 1954). The economic
growth of Germany has been examined in such books as Thorstein Veblen,
Imperial Germany and the Industrial Revolution (New York: Viking,
1939); W. F. Bruck, *Social and Economic History of Germany, 1888–1938*

(New York: Oxford Univ. Press, 1938); G. Stolper, *German Economy, 1870–1940* (New York: Reynal, 1940); and Alexander Gerschenkron, *Bread and Democracy in Germany* (Berkeley: Univ. of California Press, 1943). For military developments see Gordon A. Craig, *The Politics of the Prussian Army, 1640–1945* (New York: Oxford Univ. Press, 1955). Benedetto Croce, *A History of Italy, 1871–1915* (New York: Oxford Univ. Press, 1929), written by an eminent philosopher, is critical of the policies of the Italian kingdom. Arthur J. B. Whyte, *The Evolution of Modern Italy, 1715–1920* (Oxford: Blackwell, 1944), and René Albrecht-Carrié, *Italy from Napoleon to Mussolini* (New York: Columbia Univ. Press, 1950), are solid histories. S. William Halperin, *Italy and the Vatican at War* (Chicago: Univ. of Chicago Press, 1939), and A. William Salomone, *Italian Democracy in the Making* (Philadelphia: Univ. of Pennsylvania Press, 1945), deal with religious and political questions.

Oscar Jaszi, *The Dissolution of the Habsburg Monarchy* (Chicago: Univ. of Chicago Press, 1929), and Arthur J. May, *The Hapsburg Monarchy, 1867–1914* (Cambridge, Mass.: Harvard Univ. Press, 1951), present the best accounts of the Dual Monarchy. On the nationality problem in Austria-Hungary, see R. W. Seton-Watson, *Racial Problems in Hungary* (London: Constable, 1908), *The Southern Slav Question in the Habsburg Monarchy* (London: Constable, 1911), and *German, Slav, and Magyar*, (London: Constable, 1916). Hugh Seton-Watson, *The Decline of Imperial Russia, 1855–1914* (London: Methuen, 1952), is a first-rate work describing the last years of tsarism. Bertram D. Wolfe, *Three Who Made a Revolution* (Boston: Beacon BP6, 1955), vividly portrays Lenin, Trotsky, and Stalin before their rise to power. The diplomacy of Russia is treated in F. H. Skrine, *The Expansion of Russia, 1815–1900* (New York: Macmillan, 1903); A. Lobanov-Rostovsky, *Russia and Asia* (Ann Arbor: Wahr, 1951); and B. H. Sumner, *Tsardom and Imperialism in the Far East and the Middle East, 1880–1914* (New York: Oxford Univ. Press, 1942). For the Near East see William Miller, *The Ottoman Empire and Its Successors, 1801–1927* (New York: Macmillan, 1936); J. A. R. Marriott, *The Eastern Question* (New York: Oxford Univ. Press, 1940); Donald C. Blaisdell, *European Financial Control in the Ottoman Empire* (New York: Columbia Univ. Press, 1929); Hans Kohn, *A History of Nationalism in the East* (New York: Harcourt, 1929); William N. Medlicott, *The Congress of Berlin and After* (London: Methuen, 1938); and Edward M. Earle, *Turkey, the Great Powers, and the Bagdad Railway* (New York: Macmillan, 1923).

There are two fine works dealing with the aftermath of the American Civil War: W. L. Fleming, *The Sequel of Appomatox* (New Haven: Yale Univ. Press, 1919), and Allan Nevins, *The Emergence of Modern America, 1865–1878* (New York: Macmillan, 1927). Lewis Mumford, *Technics and Civilization* (New York: Harcourt, 1934), and L. M. Hacker, *The Triumph of American Capitalism* (New York: Simon & Schuster, 1940), consider the growth of industrialism in the United States. On politics between Lincoln and McKinley see Matthew Josephson, *The Politicos, 1865–1896* (New York: Harcourt, 1938), while an interesting treatment of expansionism may be found in Julius W. Pratt, *America's Colonial Experiment* (New York: Prentice-Hall, 1950). The best study of the Progressive movement is J. Chamberlain, *Farewell to Reform* (New York: Liveright, 1932). George Glazebrook, *Canadian External Relations* (New York: Oxford Univ. Press, 1942); John B. Brebner, *North Atlantic Triangle* (New Haven: Yale Univ. Press, 1945); and O. D. Skelton, *Life and Letters of Sir Wilfrid Laurier,* 2 vols. (New York: Century, 1921), describe the diplomatic and civic development of Canada. J. Fred Rippy, *Latin America and the Industrial Age* (New York: Putnam, 1947), is a useful general history. For the leading states of Latin America there are J. P. Calogeras, *History of Brazil* (Chapel Hill: Univ. of North Carolina Press, 1939); F. A. Kirkpatrick, *A History of the Argentine Republic* (New York: Macmillan, 1931); L. Galdames, *A History of Chile* (Chapel Hill: Univ. of North Carolina Press, 1941); and Henry B. Parkes, *A History of Mexico* (Boston: Houghton, 1938).

Raymond J. Sontag, *European Diplomatic History, 1871–1932* (New York: Appleton-Century, 1933), is less smooth but more judicious than A. J. P. Taylor, *The Struggle for Mastery in Europe, 1848–1918* (New York: Oxford Univ. Press, 1954). William L. Langer, *European Alliances and Alignments, 1871–1890* (New York: Knopf, 1950), and *The Diplomacy of Imperialism, 1890–1902,* 2 vols. (New York: Knopf, 1935), are model diplomatic histories. Of the major works dealing with the outbreak of the First World War Sidney B. Fay, *The Origins of the World War,* 2 vols. in 1 (New York: Macmillan, 1928), defends the Triple Alliance; Bernadotte E. Schmitt, *The Coming of the War, 1914,* 2 vols. (New York: Scribner, 1930), champions the Triple Entente; and Luigi Albertini, *The Origins of the War of 1914,* 2 vols. (New York: Oxford Univ. Press, 1952–53), occupies a middle position. Briefer accounts are to be found in Bernadotte E. Schmitt, *Triple Alliance and Triple Entente* (New York: Holt, 1934), and Nicholas Mansergh, *The Coming of the First World War* (New York: Longmans, 1949). Among studies of the underlying causes of the crisis of 1914 are E. M. Carroll, *French Public Opinion and Foreign Affairs, 1870–1914* (New York: Century, 1931), and *Germany and the Great Powers, 1866–1914* (New York: Prentice-Hall, 1938); Ross J. S. Hoffman, *Great Britain and the German Trade Rivalry, 1875–1914* (Philadelphia: Univ. of Pennsylvania Press, 1933); and E. L. Woodward, *Great Britain and the German Navy* (New York: Oxford Univ. Press, 1935).

PART SEVEN

The Contemporary World

Introduction

꿍 To SPEAK of the twentieth century as a period of transition may seem platitudinous, for history never stands still. In every age a process of metamorphosis is at work. Nevertheless, it is true that the progress of technology has vastly increased the speed at which political institutions and social beliefs are changing. The First World War, by inflicting terrible devastation on the belligerents, put an end to the dominant position of the Continent. And the Second World War, an outcome of the tensions which gripped European society during the interwar years, hastened the course of its decline.

For colonial peoples, however, the collapse of the Continent was a political blessing. Taking advantage of the growing weakness of the imperialistic powers, native patriotism enjoyed increasing success in shaking off alien rule. The emancipation of the Orient is not yet complete, but there can be no doubt that colonialism is a thing of the past. The question now is what will take its place. Not only is it still undecided whether democracy or communism will win the allegiance of the newly-liberated native masses, but there is also a danger that an uncompromising nationalism may make impossible the co-operation between East and West which is so obviously in the best interest of both.

Under the circumstances it is not surprising that the culture of the twentieth century should reflect the uncertainty and malaise of a world in crisis. Out of the debacle of old values the writer and the artist are trying to fashion some new universal standard of aesthetics. And when the task proves too much for them, they turn inward to stream-of-consciousness literature, to non-representational art, to atonal music, often erecting a barrier between themselves and the layman. Yet their work, even when it is most puzzling, must be understood as part of a quest for artistic forms which can express the underlying spiritual impulses of our age.

Chapter 27

THE PASSING OF
THE EUROPEAN AGE

1914-1945

THE INTERNATIONAL conflict which began in 1914 was not really a world war. It was essentially a contest among European states, by European means, for European objectives. That some of the campaigns were fought on other continents did not alter the fact that it was first and last Europe which was going through a crisis. Lands overseas were concerned with the hostilities, to be sure, but only to the extent that their national development depended on the political and economic condition of the great powers. They did not sacrifice their population; they did not waste their wealth. It was European society alone which destroyed the foundations of its stability.

When the twentieth century began, the Continent was still a going concern, suffering perhaps from some of the early symptoms of middle age, but still basically vigorous. True, its industrial supremacy was no longer beyond challenge, and its grip on colonial possessions was weakening. Yet these changes were gradual enough to be tolerable. In a period of peace and prosperity the West would in all likelihood have been able to adjust to them with relatively little social tension. What the First World War did was to hasten and intensify a process of decline which was probably unavoidable, but not necessarily catastrophic. As it was, in the course of a few years a sound civic order was bled white and left spiritually exhausted. The European Age had passed.

1 : The First World War

THE OUTCOME of the war was in a sense determined within a few weeks after its beginning. Given the human and the material resources of the opponents, the only chance of a Teutonic victory lay in a sudden success. The Schlieffen plan had recognized this truth, and that is why immediately following the declaration of hostilities the armed might of Germany turned westward to achieve a swift conquest of France. At first all went on schedule, and on August 25 General Moltke informed the Kaiser: "In six weeks the whole story will be concluded." But his optimism was premature. The French finally took a stand along the Marne River from which they could not be dislodged, and on September 9 the German commander confessed: "It goes badly—the first hopes have been utterly belied. . . . Bitter disillusionment is already upon us." Both forces now tried to outflank the enemy by moving to the west, and both succeeded in reaching the sea at about the same time. By the end of 1914 the war of maneuver had become a war of attrition, as millions of men faced each other across no man's land from two long lines of trenches extending six hundred miles from the English Channel to Switzerland.

THE PERIOD OF STALEMATE

For the next three years there was a complete stalemate on the western front. The Entente Powers vainly tried to break the deadlock by such desperate offensive actions as the Battle of Champagne in 1915, the Battle of the Somme in 1916, and the Battle of Ypres in 1917. The Germans, on the other hand, sought to save their manpower by confining themselves by and large to defensive operations, especially after the attack against Verdun, which they launched in 1916, proved a costly failure. But time was on the side of France and England, for they had greater access to raw materials and neutral trade than the Central Powers. The limited success of the German navy at the Battle of Jutland in 1916 was not enough to break the British blockade, while the effort to starve the United Kingdom into submission in 1917 by the unrestricted use of the submarine only provided the United States with one more reason for joining the Entente Powers. The bleak outlook for the Teutonic cause eventually brought Italy, Japan, and more than twenty other states into the war on the side of the western allies, while Berlin and Vienna could find comfort only in the accession of weak Turkey and weaker Bulgaria.

Yet the high command of the Central Powers was convinced that there was still an alternative to defeat. When the war began it had expected a quick victory in the west and a test of endurance in the east. Instead, there was a total impasse on the western front and a succession of brilliant German victories in the eastern theater of operations. The common soldier serving in the armies of the tsar faced the enemy with courage, but his leadership was usually unintelligent and sometimes corrupt, while his equipment was totally inadequate. Even so, the Russian forces succeeded in inflicting serious reverses upon the Austrians, although they were no match

The Belligerents in the First World War*
(In the order of their participation)

I. The Central Powers

Austria-Hungary: July 28, 1914   Turkey: November 3, 1914

Germany: August 1, 1914   Bulgaria: October 11, 1915

II. The Allied and Associated Powers

Serbia: July 28, 1914   United States: April 6, 1917

Russia: August 1, 1914   Cuba: April 7, 1917

Luxemburg: August 2, 1914   Siam: July 22, 1917

France: August 3, 1914   Liberia: August 4, 1917

Belgium: August 4, 1914   China: August 14, 1917

British Empire: August 4, 1914   Brazil: October 26, 1917

Montenegro: August 9, 1914   Panama: November 10, 1917

Japan: August 23, 1914   Guatemala: April 22, 1918

Italy: May 25, 1915   Nicaragua: May 6, 1918

San Marino: June 1, 1915   Costa Rica: May 24, 1918

Portugal: March 9, 1916   Haiti: July 15, 1918

Romania: August 27, 1916   Honduras: July 19, 1918

Greece: November 24, 1916

III. New States recognized by the Allies which became involved in the war and signed some of the peace treaties

Hejaz: March 19, 1917

Czechoslovakia: June 30, 1918

Poland: November 2, 1918

IV. States which broke relations with some of the Central Powers and signed some of the peace treaties

Bolivia: April 14, 1917   Uruguay: October 17, 1917

Peru: October 6, 1917   Ecuador: December 17, 1917

*Not all Allied and Associated Powers were at war with all of the Central Powers, and declarations of war by one member of a coalition against different members of the other coalition did not occur at the same time. For example, Italy declared war against Austria-Hungary on May 24, 1915, Turkey August 21, 1915, Bulgaria October 19, 1915, and Germany August 28, 1916. Reference is made only to the first declaration of war in this table, which is reprinted by permission from C. E. Black and E. C. Helmreich, *Twentieth Century Europe* (New York: Alfred A. Knopf, 1950), p. 838, adapted from Quincy Wright, *A Study of War* (Chicago: Univ. of Chicago Press, 1942), vol. I, p. 646, Table 42.

for the best military organization in Europe. Skillfully directed by General Paul von Hindenburg and General Erich von Ludendorff, the Kaiser's forces won impressive successes in 1914 at the battles of Tannenberg and the Masurian Lakes, and in 1915 they occupied Poland and Lithuania.

The Entente Powers, anxious to bolster the tottering tsarist régime, made determined efforts to open a direct line of communication between east and west through Turkish territory. But the surprisingly strong resistance of Ottoman troops trained by German officers proved too much for them. In 1915 a campaign against the Straits, designed to secure free passage from the Mediterranean to the Black Sea, failed miserably, and in 1916 an attempt to establish contact between England and Russia in the Middle East resulted in the capitulation of a British garrison at Kut-el-Amara. The dismissal of Grand Duke Nicholas Nikolaievich as supreme commander of the Russian armies and the assumption of direct leadership by Nicholas II himself in September, 1915, only made matters worse. The Central Powers were by now gambling on a decisive victory against the tsar's forces, which would enable them to dictate a peace settlement in the east and then organize an offensive by their combined armies against the weary Entente Powers in the west.

THE TURNING POINT OF THE WAR

The year 1917 was the turning point of the war, for new political and military developments enabled the belligerents to break the deadlock which had prevailed on the western front for more than three years. For one thing, Russian resistance finally began to collapse, as a revolution in March forced the tsarist order to give way to a provisional government dominated by democratic reformers. The new régime tried for a few months to continue hostilities against the Central Powers, but in November it in turn fell before an insurrection led by the Bolsheviks. The latter agreed at once to the conclusion of an armistice with the enemy, and on March 3, 1918, Russia signed under protest the Treaty of Brest-Litovsk. It was forced to surrender virtually all its European acquisitions since the days of Peter the Great, leaving Germany free to transform the eastern borderlands into a Teutonic sphere of influence. The Kaiser's high command could at last plan for a major attack in the west, which would complete its triumph by defeating the French and English armies.

But in the meantime the Entente Powers had found a new ally whose enormous resources proved in the long run decisive. From the beginning of the war public opinion in the United States had favored their cause, as cultural ties, economic interests, and military considerations made a victory of the western democracies seem desirable. Early in 1917 the opening of a submarine campaign against neutral trade with Great Britain supplied the immediate justification for American participation in the conflict, and on April 6 Congress voted for a declaration of war on Germany.

By the time General Ludendorff opened his great offensive in the west in March, 1918, the last chance of a German success had vanished. Although at first he made important gains, the tide slowly began to turn, and by July the initiative had passed to the other side. The Kaiser's armies were forced into an orderly but uninterrupted retreat, and on October 2 the high command admitted, "we can carry on the struggle for an appreciable time yet and can cause severe losses to the enemy; we can, however, no longer win." Military operations came to an end at last on November 11, after William II had abdicated in the face of insurrection and disorder. The new republican government of Germany accepted an armistice under conditions which in effect precluded a resumption of hostilities.

BEHIND THE LINES

The First World War opened a new period in the conduct of armed conflict among states, the period of total national effort. Its significance lay not only in the magnitude of the struggle: the thirty odd governments involved; the sixty-five million men in uniform; the twenty-nine million wounded, captured, or missing; the eight and a half million dead; the direct costs of two hundred billion dollars; and the indirect costs of a hundred and fifty billion more. It was the complete subordination of every aspect of public and private life to the demands of the struggle which distinguished this new mode of warfare. Gone were the days when campaigns were fought by professional soldiers under universally respected rules, while the civilian went about his usual business. After 1914 the difference between soldier and civilian became one of degree rather than kind, as both were subjected to the rigid discipline made necessary by the conditions of modern war.

For the first time in the history of Great Britain the government of Prime Minister Herbert Asquith introduced military conscription, which Englishmen had traditionally considered incompatible with personal freedom. In the United States Bernard Baruch regulated factory production in violation of the sacred principles of free enterprise. In Germany Secretary of the Interior Karl Helfferich prepared the National Service Law, which put into operation a system of forced labor and provided for the compulsory arbitration of industrial disputes. In France Premier Georges Clemenceau was merciless toward those suspected of defeatism, imprisoning some like Joseph Caillaux, exiling others like Louis Malvy. The rights for which liberals had fought for more than a hundred years were sacrificed to Mars. Worst of all, the belief in the fundamental decency of man which Western society in its better moments had upheld was drowned in a sea of hatred fed by governments seeking to counteract war-weariness. Frenchmen and

Americans were told that "the Huns" amused themselves by impaling babies with their bayonets, while the Germans bolstered up their morale with such pieces of "poetry" as:

> Hate by water and hate by land;
> Hate of heart and hate of the hand;
> We love as one and hate as one;
> We have but one foe alone—England.

Unlimited means of warfare led logically to unlimited objectives of warfare. In the course of the hostilities each side sought to convince public opinion that it wanted nothing more than international justice. The English writer H. G. Wells coined the phrase "the war to make the world safe for democracy," which became the unofficial slogan of the western allies. A more systematic statement of political aims came from President Wilson of the United States, who in his Fourteen Points spoke of the freedom of trade and navigation, the reduction of armaments, the adjustment of colonial claims, the right of oppressed peoples to national self-determination, and the formation of a league of nations. In the Teutonic camp the lower chamber of the German legislature announced: "The Reichstag strives for a peace of understanding and lasting reconciliation of nations. Such a peace is not in keeping with forcible annexations of territory or forcible measures of political, economic, or financial character." And Emperor Charles, who in 1916 succeeded Francis Joseph as ruler of the Dual Monarchy, made known his longing for a peace of compromise and moderation.

Yet it was too much to expect that nations which were sacrificing their bravest sons on the battlefield should renounce all thought of compensation. While publicly parading their virtue, they were privately preparing for a division of the booty. In a series of secret treaties the Entente Powers agreed on a partition of enemy territories, England claiming Mesopotamia and Palestine, France the Rhineland and Syria, Russia the Straits and East Prussia, and Italy the Trentino and Istria. Nor were the Central Powers less grasping. In December, 1917, General Hindenburg declared: "Belgium will continue to exist and will be taken under German military control until it is ripe politically and economically for a defensive and offensive alliance with Germany. . . . Nevertheless, for reasons of military strategy, Liège and the Flemish coast, including Bruges, will remain permanently in Germany's possession." A few weeks later Count Ottokar Czernin, the Austrian foreign minister, was on his way to Brest-Litovsk to participate in the spoliation of Russia. Whichever side won the war, the peace settlement was bound to be based on coercion.

THE PEACEMAKERS AND THE PEACE

The statesmen who gathered in Paris in January, 1919, to draft the treaties to be imposed on the defeated enemy acted by and large as might

Adapted from R. R. Palmer, *Atlas of World History* (Chicago, 1957), pp. 178-79.

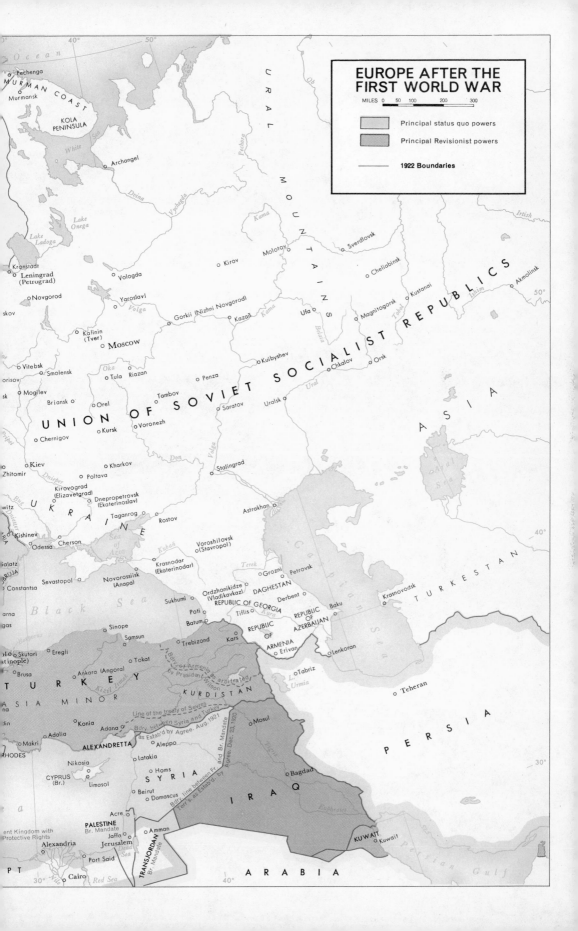

EUROPE AFTER THE
FIRST WORLD WAR

MILES 0 50 100   200   300

Principal status quo powers

Principal Revisionist powers

1922 Boundaries

have been expected under the circumstances. Although they represented thirty-two "allied and associated" states, the task of peacemaking became essentially the responsibility of the leaders of the victorious great powers, the Big Four. President Wilson was there, with the mind of a university professor and the soul of a Presbyterian elder, lecturing, preaching, exhorting. He could be an inspiring idealist at his best, a tiresome phrasemonger at his worst. And during the conference, unfortunately, he was not at his best. The economist John Maynard Keynes said about him: "He had no plan, no scheme, no constructive ideas whatever for clothing with the flesh of life the commandments which he had thundered from the White House. He could have preached a sermon on any of them or have addressed a stately prayer to the Almighty for their fulfilment; but he could not frame their concrete application to the actual state of Europe." Prime Minister Lloyd George of England, on the other hand, was a clever politician anxious to maintain himself in power by any expedient. The radical firebrand of pre-war years had become a shrewd demagogue. Having won an election in December, 1918, by flaunting slogans like "Hang the Kaiser!" "Make Germany pay!" and "Squeeze the German lemon until the pips squeak!" he now found himself embarrassed by promises which he knew could not be kept. Georges Clemenceau of France was a hardheaded, hard-bitten old man, determined to make his nation secure against its traditional enemy. Instinctively distrustful of political sentimentality and verbal posturing, he thought in terms of nineteenth-century *Realpolitik*: "Mr. Wilson bores me with his Fourteen Points; why, God Almighty has only ten!" The least influential member of this diplomatic quartet, the Italian prime minister Vittorio Orlando, was also the least complicated. His purpose was simply to defend his country's "sacred egoism" by getting as much Austrian territory as possible.

Given the temper of the western allies, given the wishes of their voters and the illusions of their taxpayers, the Central Powers could expect nothing but a Carthaginian peace. The Treaty of Versailles, signed on June 28, 1919, deprived Germany of Alsace and Lorraine in the west, of Posen and part of West Prussia in the east, and of all its colonies in Africa and Asia. Its army was reduced to one hundred thousand professional soldiers, and its armaments and fortifications were rigidly restricted. For damage done to the civilian population of the victors it was to make financial reparations which were eventually fixed at thirty-two billion dollars. And it was to support an allied army of occupation in the Rhineland for fifteen years. To rub salt into its wounds, Article 231 asserted: "The Allied and Associated Governments affirm and Germany accepts the responsibility of Germany and her allies for causing all the loss and damage to which the Allied and Associated Governments and their nationals have been subjected as a consequence of the war imposed upon them by the aggression of Germany and her allies." Of the idealistic Fourteen Points little was left except the Covenant of the League of Nations, which became a constituent part of the treaty with Germany. As for the Dual Monarchy, immediately after the defeat of the Central Powers it disintegrated into its component national elements. Most of the Habsburg possessions were divided among new countries like Czechoslovakia, Poland, and Yugoslavia, or among old ones like Italy and Romania. Only the two diminutive states of Austria and Hungary remained. Their union of four hundred years was now dissolved, and they had to adjust to new humble circumstances formalized by the treaties of St.-Germain and Trianon. Finally, the Treaty of Neuilly made small Bulgaria even smaller, while the Treaty of Sèvres deprived the Ottoman Empire of all its territories except the interior of Asia Minor and the city of Constantinople.

The diplomats responsible for these settlements were tired men wrestling with problems of the greatest complexity under conditions which made constructive statesmanship exceedingly difficult. Their mistakes were

TERRITORIAL DIVISION
of the
AUSTRO-HUNGARIAN EMPIRE
after the First World War

Based on Saucerman, *International Transfers of Territory in Europe*, U.S. Government Printing Office, 1937.

Austrian territory prior to division.

Hungarian territory prior to division.

In addition, Fiume and its immediate environs, formerly Hungarian, became a free city in 1920; it was ceded to Italy in 1924.

understandable and perhaps excusable, but it would be hard to argue that they produced a good peace. To begin with, the terms which they imposed upon the defeated enemy were such that he could not reconcile himself to their permanent acceptance. The conservative statesmen who met in Paris at the beginning of the nineteenth century had made it possible for their foe to retain his self-respect by negotiating a treaty which was stern but not unfair. The democratic statesmen who met in Paris a hundred years later were less generous. True, self-interest rather than generosity is the dominant principle in international relations, but when the world desperately needed a period of peaceful reconstruction, self-interest demanded generosity. The humiliating conditions dictated to the Central Powers sowed the seeds of future wars by breeding bitterness and defiance.

To make matters worse, the western allies intensified the effects of their ill-advised harshness by an even more ill-advised weakness. Having decided on a settlement sure to arouse the opposition of the vanquished, they should have upheld it with sufficient resolution to overcome that opposition. For to adopt a policy of repression without the means for its enforcement was to invite disaster. As it turned out, the democracies demanded strict observance of the peace treaties only while there was no determined resistance to them. As soon as the losers found themselves in a position to take a strong stand, the resoluteness of the victors vanished. They hastened to concede under threats of violence what they had denied to pleas for justice. Appeasement, however, only invited aggression. By their exclusive concern with narrow partisan advantage, the peacemakers of 1919 gained no more than a breathing spell of twenty years. Then the West plunged once again into a catastrophic world war.

2 : The Rise of Communism

THE FIRST WORLD WAR marked the end of the European Age. Throughout the nineteenth century Occidental society had lived in a mood of optimism inspired by a succession of scientific discoveries and imperialistic conquests. Hence it could afford the luxury of benevolence. It abolished personal servitudes, ended religious discriminations, eliminated economic evils, and composed political differences. The tragedy of 1914 closed the heroic era of the middle class of the West. Politically, it fostered an extremism of the Right as well as the Left; economically, it destroyed the popular belief in the efficacy of a laissez faire capitalism; socially, it aggravated traditional class differences; ideologically, it encouraged attitudes hostile to the fundamental assumptions of liberalism.

Whereas before the war experience seemed to indicate that in the long run liberty contributed to the welfare of mankind, after the war it began to teach that individualism led to an anarchic struggle of all against all.

Forced to decide between freedom and security, many chose security. Until Sarajevo the masses of Europe did not have to make the choice. Thereafter they could no longer escape it. Especially in countries where economic hardship was greatest and national resentment profoundest there arose out of the military ordeal a reaction against the doctrines of bourgeois liberalism and a search for new authoritarian means of achieving political objectives.

THE RUSSIAN REVOLUTION

Communism was one form of this reaction. Ideologically, it was the offspring of the left wing of the pre-war socialist movement, but its growth was made possible by the experiences of the war itself. It won its first victories in Russia, a land which had suffered more than any other from the effects of the military conflict. After the Revolution of 1905 the Romanov state had taken the first hesitant steps toward parliamentary government, but at the time of the First World War representative institutions were still only a thin veneer over a tradition of authoritarianism. Reverses at the front and privations at home destroyed the remnants of popular loyalty to tsarism, and in March, 1917, there was a bloodless insurrection which forced the abdication of Nicholas II.

He was replaced by a provisional government representing cautious liberals like Paul Miliukov and moderate socialists like Alexander Kerensky. It immediately proceeded to democratize the political institutions of the country, but by its failure to make peace and to introduce economic reform it played into the hands of the Bolsheviks. The latter, directed by V. I. Lenin and Leon Trotsky, began to agitate for a conclusion of the war, a division of the land among the peasantry, and a seizure of the factories by the workers. They soon won the support of the soviets, labor councils representing the organized industrial proletariat. Though at no time more than a minority, they made up in disciplined militancy what they lacked in numbers. Like the Jacobins in 1792, they were the only ones who in the face of confusion and despair had a clear program of action. On November 6, 1917, they led an insurrection against the provisional government, seized the reins of power, and formed a radical régime resolved to destroy the capitalistic order.

The communist victory opened a period of civil and foreign wars which continued for more than four years. First, conservative groups in opposition to the new government took up arms under such leaders as General Anton Denikin, General Nikolai Yudenitch, and Admiral Alexander Kolchak. Secondly, the western allies, frightened by the specter of radicalism, offered military and financial assistance to the counter-revolutionary forces. Finally, a secession movement developed in the borderlands,

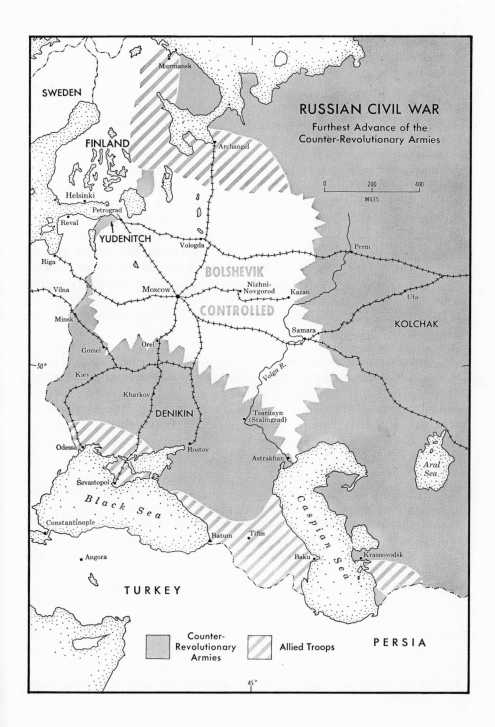

RUSSIAN CIVIL WAR

Furthest Advance of the
Counter-Revolutionary Armies

0   200   400
MILES

SWEDEN

FINLAND

Murmansk

Archangel

Helsinki

Reval

Petrograd

YUDENITCH

Vologda

Riga

BOLSHEVIK

Vilna

Moscow

Nizhni-
Novgorod

Kazan

CONTROLLED

Minsk

Gomel

Orel

Samara

50°

Kiev

Kharkov

Volga R.

DENIKIN

Tsaritsyn
(Stalingrad)

Odessa

Rostov

Astrakhan

Sevastopol

Perm

Ufa

KOLCHAK

Aral
Sea

Black Sea

Caspian Sea

Constantinople

Batum

Tiflis

Angora

Baku

Krasnovodsk

TURKEY

Counter-
Revolutionary
Armies

Allied Troops

PERSIA

45°

where Poland, Finland, Lithuania, Latvia, Estonia, the Ukraine, Georgia, Armenia, and Azerbaijan declared their independence from Russia.

Assailed by a thousand dangers, the Bolsheviks acted with a ruthless determination. Against civilian enemies they introduced a reign of terror under the Cheka, a political police organization headed by Felix Dzerzhinsky, which boasted of its role as the "unsheathed avenging sword of the Revolution." Against armed opponents they formed the Red Army, commanded with unexpected skill by Commissar of War Trotsky. To retain the support of the masses they partitioned large estates among the peasants and gave workingmen control over industrial plants, although at the same time they ordered the forcible requisitioning of grain and prohibited strikes in the nationalized factories. The struggle between the Reds and the Whites dragged on, with neither side asking or receiving quarter. But through sheer will power the Soviet government succeeded in defeating its enemies one by one, until by 1922 it had overcome all the forces of the opposition. The critics at home had been silenced; the armies of the monarchists had been dispersed; the halfhearted intervention of the western allies had come to an end. The communist régime had survived the first great test of its claim to power.

ECONOMIC RECOVERY

The price of this triumph was enormous. War, revolution, terror, hunger, and disease had created a population deficit of more than 20,000,000 persons. The value of imports fell from $400,000,000 in 1917 to $30,000,000 in 1918 to less than $2,000,000 in 1919. Between 1913 and 1920 the output of agricultural products declined 50 per cent, of manufactured consumer articles 87 per cent, of cotton wares 95 per cent, of pig iron 97.6 per cent, and of iron ore 98.4 per cent. Economic recovery became essential for the survival of the Bolsheviks. In order to achieve it they prepared to end the system of complete governmental direction of production known as War Communism. In characteristically blunt fashion, Lenin admitted the failure of the wholesale adoption of socialistic practices: "We have eighteen People's Commissariats. Of these at least fifteen are absolutely no good."

In 1921, therefore, came the New Economic Policy, a compromise with capitalism which permitted the establishment under close official supervision of private commercial and industrial enterprises, and which legalized the sale of a part of the farmer's crop for profit. This "temporary retreat" from Marxian orthodoxy was followed in 1928 by the First Five-Year Plan and in 1933 by the Second Five-Year Plan, carefully organized national campaigns to increase productive capacity, especially in heavy industry. At the same time the authorities introduced a program of rural socialization, forcing the peasants to give up their individual holdings and form huge collective farms. The result of these strenuous efforts was a remarkable revival of Russian economic strength, although in comparison with most capitalistic states the standard of living remained low. In its haste to carry out industrialization and collectivization, the government ignored the interests of the consumer, insisting that advances in production which the bourgeois democracies had needed a hundred years to achieve must be attained in the Soviet Union in ten. By the time of the Second World War the country had became a major manufacturing power, but it had paid for its accomplishments with the physical privation of an overworked, impoverished people.

THE STALIN DICTATORSHIP

Meanwhile, an autocracy more despotic than tsarism had fastened its grip on Russia. From its beginning the Soviet régime had preached the rule of the proletariat, but at first it had tolerated such socialistic opposition groups as the Mensheviks and the Social Revolutionaries. Even when it turned the weapon of terror against them, it continued to permit freedom of discussion within the Communist party. After the death of Lenin in 1924, however, the march to complete authoritarianism became inexorable. For a few years the state was torn by the contest for leadership between Leon Trotsky and Joseph Stalin. The former urged an unceasing emphasis on revolutionary uprisings throughout the world; the latter maintained that for the time being communism must concentrate on consolidating its hold on the Soviet Union. By 1927 Stalin had won control of the party and, through the party, of the government. An ambitious, unscrupulous bureaucrat, he began to transform the political structure of the country into an out-and-out personal dictatorship.

By 1929 Trotsky had been expelled from the land he had helped win for the Bolsheviks, but before long a more tragic fate befell other communist officials prominent enough to constitute a possible threat to the autocrat. Between 1935 and 1938 such famous leaders of the revolution as Gregory Zinoviev, Leo Kamenev, Karl Radek, and Nikolai Bukharin were tried on fantastic charges of treason, conspiracy, and sabotage. Even more fantastic, they confessed without a word of defense to crimes of which they were obviously innocent. The purge trials presented a mystery which will probably remain unsolved until the secret archives of the Kremlin are opened, but their effect was clear. The last potential sources of opposition in the government, the army, and the party had been suppressed. It was a piece of irony that in 1936, while the judicial murder of the most brilliant sons of Russian Marxism was in progress, a new constitution was promulgated providing for universal suffrage, secret voting, and freedom of speech, assembly, and the press. An obsequious assembly of communist delegates heard from Stalin that "the constitution of U.S.S.R. is the only thoroughly democratic constitution in the world." In fact, he had forced on his country a tyrannical cult of the leader.

THE DIPLOMACY OF THE SOVIET UNION

The diplomatic position of the Soviet government had gained strength since those days following the revolution when it was an outcast among nations. After the failure of the allied intervention in Russia the statesmen of the western democracies had sought to encircle the Bolsheviks with a "sanitary cordon" of hostile countries consisting of Romania, Poland, the Baltic States, and Finland. The communists, confident that their revolution was only the first in a series of imminent anticapitalistic uprisings, responded with a propaganda campaign directed at the proletarian masses of Europe. Their agitation did inspire futile insurrections in Hungary, Germany, and Finland. But by 1920 it had become obvious that bourgeois society had regained its equilibrium and that a world upheaval was not around the corner after all. That was when Lenin turned to the East. Perhaps colonial peoples struggling against bourgeois imperialism would prove to be natural allies of the working class of the West. In the early 1920's the Soviet Union began to pay court to Turkey, Persia, and China. Still, while these countries welcomed Russian military and economic support, they stubbornly refused to accept the doctrines of Marxism.

Admitting reluctantly, therefore, that for the time being neither could destroy the other, communism and capitalism prepared to re-establish the commercial and diplomatic connections severed by the revolution. In 1924 and 1925 Great Britain, Italy, France, and Japan recognized the Soviet Union, although resentments and suspicions continued to trouble their relations. With the rise of fascism in the 1930's, however, middle-class democracy and proletarian dictatorship were willy-nilly forced into closer collaboration. Both feared the totalitarianism of the Right; both wanted to reinforce their political position. In 1933 Russia exchanged ambassadors with the United States; in 1934 it entered the League of Nations; in 1935 it concluded a defensive alliance with France. Right up to the eve of the Second World War Stalin went on frantically seeking security for his régime in the popular-front policy, advocating co-operation between bourgeois parliamentarianism and Soviet radicalism against fascist aggression.

Yet despite Russian protestations of good will there could be no lasting reconciliation between communism and democracy. For the ideology by which the leaders of the Soviet Union justified their policy assumed a fundamental conflict of interest between the bourgeoisie and the proletariat. The revolution of 1917, they believed, was only the initial victory in a struggle which would not end until capitalism had been extirpated. That was why the Bolsheviks established the Third International to encourage and direct communist organizations throughout the world. In 1921 they boldly proclaimed their plan of action:

> The working class and the Communist Parties of all countries prepare themselves not for a period of quiet agitation and organization, but for prolonged struggle which capital will now force upon the proletariat, in order to beat it into submitting to all the burdens of capitalist policy. In this fight the Communist Parties must develop the highest militant discipline. Its Party leaders must coolly and deliberately consider all the lessons of the fight, they must prudently review the battlefield, uniting enthusiasm with the greatest deliberation. They must forge their militant plans and their tactical course in the spirit of collective thinking of the entire Party, giving due consideration to all criticism by comrades of the Party. But all the Party organizations must unhesitatingly carry out the course adopted by the Party. Every word and every step of every Party organization must be subordinated to this purpose. The Parliamentary factions, the press of the Party, the Party organizations must unwaveringly obey the order given by the Party leadership.[1]

3 : Fascism on the March

FASCISM, like communism, was a twentieth-century reaction against the nineteenth-century libertarian ideal. But whereas communism had its roots in the socialist thought of the pre-war days, fascism was an expression of the ideological chaos created by the war itself. To nations exhausted by military sacrifices and economic exactions it offered an alternative to revolution. It promised to save the traditional institutions of property and status, but only within a framework of dictatorial control. While democracy had insisted that the freedom of the citizen was essentially in harmony with the welfare of society, the new authoritarianism taught that the individual had to submit to a bureaucratic regulation of his activity to protect the vital interests of the state. Such submission meant the suppression of the instrumentalities of popular representation and the surrender of the freedom of speech, religion, and assembly. In place of these liberties were to come obedience and discipline. For only by sacrificing his independence to social stability and national might could the citizen defend himself against anarchy. In 1923 the

---

[1] Third (Communist) International, *Theses and Resolutions Adopted at the Third World Congress of the Communist International, June 22nd–July 12th, 1921* (New York: Contemporary Publishing Association, 1921), p. 198.

German political theorist Artur Moeller van den Bruck voiced the mood of bitter disillusionment with the liberal faith: "It is the disintegrating atmosphere of liberalism which spreads moral disease amongst nations and ruins the nation whom it dominates."

FASCIST ITALY

Nowhere was this disillusionment deeper than in Italy, where the war had aggravated all the ills of the country. At the peace conference its government got only 9,000 square miles of territory and 1,600,000 new subjects, not much of a compensation for some 460,000 dead and nearly 1,000,000 wounded. Moreover, the demobilization of the armed forces and the end of the war boom led to spreading unemployment. The result was a radicalization of the masses. In 1919 the socialists became the largest single party in parliament; in 1920 a wave of strikes and lockouts resulted in the seizure of many factories by workers; in 1921 a communist party was formed with the blessings of the Third International.

As for the authorities, they seemed incapable of coping with the danger of a political upheaval. One prime minister followed another in rapid succession, first Vittorio Orlando, then Francesco Nitti, then Giovanni Giolitti, then Ivanoe Bonomi, and then Luigi Facta, none of them able to win public confidence. Out of this confusion of ideologies and factions arose Benito Mussolini and his Fascist party. Originally an ardent socialist, he had become during the war an even more ardent nationalist. After hostilities came to an end he began to preach the subordination of all party differences to the cause of Italian greatness. Around his banner rallied frightened businessmen, unemployed veterans, disgruntled superpatriots, restless adventurers, all who saw in the black shirt of fascism the only defense against the communist hammer and sickle. Although its representation in parliament did not exceed thirty-five deputies, the party demanded full executive power. In October, 1922, a march on Rome by some thirty thousand of its members frightened King Victor Emmanuel III into forcing the resignation of the Facta cabinet and appointing Mussolini as prime minister.

Once in a position of authority, the fascists proceeded to assume autocratic power. The parties of the opposition were dissolved, and their leaders imprisoned or even murdered, as was the Socialist deputy Giacomo Matteotti. No one was surprised when in 1924 the supporters of Mussolini increased their representation in parliament to 375 seats, more than ten times the number they had won in the last free election three years before. After all, who wanted to risk a beating by a strong-arm squad for criticizing the actions of the government?

Having manufactured a popular endorsement of its policies, fascism went to work reorganizing the constitutional and social structure of the state. The prime minister was authorized to rule by decree, and the electorate was reduced from ten million to three million persons. The ruling party was given the right to name official candidates for the legislature. At the same time labor unions and trade associations were replaced by syndicates and corporations, organizations in theory representing the interests of employers and employees, in fact subservient to the bureaucracy. Thereafter strikes and lockouts became illegal.

The Duce also did his best to encourage patriotic enthusiasm. Resplendent in black shirt and military tunic, he harangued wildly cheering crowds from the balcony of his palace in Rome, proclaiming the birth of a new Italy, disciplined and aggressive. Young men were enrolled in the ranks of the fascist militia, where they received training in the arts of war. Boys between the ages of eight and fourteen learned obedience and combativeness in the *Balilla*. For that matter, children from six to eight were not considered too young to learn how to stand at attention in the Sons of the Wolf. Mussolini meant it when he thundered: "Above all fascism . . . believes neither in the possibility nor the utility of perpetual peace. It thus repudiates the doctrine of pacifism—born of a renunciation of the struggle and an act of cowardice in the face of sacrifice. War alone brings up to its highest tension all human energy and puts the stamp of nobility upon the peoples who have the courage to meet it."

Then there were the ambitious programs of land reclamation, industrial expansion, military modernization, and naval improvement. The government practiced aggrandizement in Europe and colonialism in Africa. Its talent for dealing with political opponents, moreover, improved with time. In 1924 the dictator won 4,800,000 votes and his foes 2,250,000; in 1929 the figures were 8,500,000 and 136,000. Even the Papacy seemed to fall in step. By the Lateran Treaties of 1929, church and state composed the differences which had troubled their relations for more than fifty years. The former received sovereign rights in Vatican City and financial compensation for its territorial claims; the latter won recognition as the legal source of political authority in the country. Many foreigners, impressed by the ostentatious vigor of the new régime, conceded that at least "the trains are running on time." Only the Second World War revealed the moral bankruptcy behind the achievements of the sawdust Caesar.

NAZI GERMANY

In Germany parliamentarianism held out a little longer before it too succumbed to the combined effects of military collapse and economic privation. The fall of the empire had brought to the helm the parties of moderate socialism, bourgeois democracy, and progressive Catholicism, which before the war had advocated civic reform. Yet the tasks facing them after 1918 proved beyond their strength. The republic proclaimed by the national assembly meeting in Weimar had to cope first with widespread communist uprisings inspired by economic hardship. No sooner were these suppressed, than the reactionaries attempted to seize power and establish an authoritarian form of rule. While engaged in the struggle against its enemies on the Left and the Right, the government was forced to sign the Treaty of Versailles, a millstone around the neck of German liberalism. And as if all this were not enough, the precarious financial situation led to a catastrophic inflation, which in November, 1923, reduced the value of the currency to the point where one dollar was worth two and a half trillion marks.

The middle class, traditionally the backbone of constitutionalism, was thus impoverished and demoralized. The economic recovery which began a year later proved no more than a brief respite. By 1929 the great depression which descended on the entire capitalistic world brought new unemployment and despair to the masses of central Europe. The end of the Weimar Republic was at hand. President Paul von Hindenburg, the hero of the war years, was a bewildered, tired old man. Chancellor Heinrich Brüning fought frantically but vainly to stem the rising tide of totalitarianism. The democratic parties in parliament, paralyzed by indecision, debated endlessly whether to support the cabinet because of its good intentions or criticize it for its lack of accomplishment. In this atmosphere of confusion, amid rumors, fears, plots, and counter-plots, the senile president was persuaded by his conservative advisers to dismiss Brüning. A few months later in January, 1933, Adolf Hitler, the leader of the National Socialist party, was invited to become head of the government.

The new chancellor was the embodiment of all the demonic forces which the ordeal of war and depression had unleashed. He had grown up in the Dual Monarchy during the years of its political decline before 1914, and had fallen under the spell of the virulent chauvinism which seemed to infect everything it touched in that doomed empire. The disasters which followed the First World War created a favorable environment for his gospel of hate. In the 1920's he began to preach in Germany a doctrine of national regeneration through the overthrow of parliamentarianism and the persecution of the historic scapegoat of political reaction, the Jews. At first the undisguised brutality of his views repelled all but a handful of fanatics, so that as late as the election of 1928 his party won only 12 seats in parliament out of 491. The economic crisis which began a year later, however, destroyed popular confidence in liberalism. In their bewilderment millions began to clutch at ideological straws. The one worker out of every three who was unemployed, the small businessman sinking into bankruptcy, the wealthy industrialist afraid of a communist revolution, the patriot seeking to avenge the humiliating defeat, the aristocratic landowner contemptuous of democratic government—each for his own reasons was ready to acclaim the messiah in the brown shirt. Yet at no time was Hitler able to win a popular majority through a free vote. Only the control over the state apparatus which he acquired as chief minister made possible his establishment of a dictatorship.

Within a year after taking office he had transformed the republic into an autocracy by methods which Mussolini had used with success in Italy. The chancellor received the right to rule by decree; adverse opinions were suppressed; rival parties were dissolved; political opponents were packed off to concentration camps. Every enterprise and every interest was brought under the supervision of the state. The Labor Front directed the activities of the worker; the Hitler Youth provided patriotic recreation for the young; the Evangelical church amalgamated the independent Protestant communities under the leadership of so-called "German Christians"; the Ministry of Church Affairs kept a sharp eye on the doings of Catholic clergymen; and the Strength through Joy supplied cheap vacations to the lower classes There were National Socialist associations of writers, actors, motorcyclists, athletes, housewives, aviators, students, and scientists. And looking down on this vast system of totalitarian regimentation from a million posters was the stern face of the Führer.

Most Germans accepted the authoritarian régime gladly, even enthusiastically. Under the new order the economic depression came to an end, as the government program of military rearmament and industrial expansion solved the problem of unemployment. Trade unions were abolished, but at the same time production was stimulated by public works and secret remilitarization. The establishment of youth labor camps, the reintroduction of conscription, and the world-wide economic recovery of the middle 1930's also helped restore social stability in central Europe.

Why then should the man in the street have opposed National Socialism? True, he had to be careful about what he said, but in return he got bread and circuses. The former he earned in factories manufacturing airplanes and tanks; the latter were provided by the splendid congresses of the party and the parades of its special armed units, the S.A. and the S.S. Everywhere flags were flying and drums were rolling; everywhere arms were raised in the Nazi salute; everywhere could be heard the greeting "Heil Hitler!" The Western democracies which had been deaf to the pleas of the republic now listened attentively to the wishes of the Third Reich. As for the masses, they would read now and again about some socialist "shot while trying to escape," or see a Jew beaten by a uniformed bully. Usually they turned the other way and tried not to notice what was happening.

THE SPREAD OF FASCISM

The successes of fascism in two of the major powers encouraged autocratic tendencies among those secondary states which had never wholeheartedly accepted liberalism. In Spain King Alfonso XIII tried to deal with political discontent by conferring dictatorial powers on General Miguel Primo de Rivera. But in 1930 the prime minister resigned in the face of mounting popular unrest, and the following year a republic was proclaimed. Then came a confused period of conflict between the radicals and the conservatives, until the election of 1936 resulted in a decisive victory for the parties of the Left advocating land redistribution, industrial regulation, labor welfare measures, and anticlerical legislation. Defeated at the polls, the forces of the Right representing the army, the aristocracy, and the church resorted to arms. Led by General Francisco Franco and assisted by Germany and Italy, they defeated the republican government after a savage civil war which raged until 1939. In its place they established a régime based on the principles of fascism. The dictatorship in Spain was warmly welcomed by the dictatorship in Portugal formed early in the 1930's under the leader of the National Union party, Antonio de Oliveira Salazar. By the time of the Second World War the Iberian peninsula was completely dominated by a traditionalist, clerical authoritarianism.

In eastern Europe, amid the Balkan nations carved out of former Turkish possessions and the succession states built on the ruins of Russia and Austria, the rule of force was an ancient tradition. The teachings of parliamentarianism were meaningless to the exploited peasant masses, and authority passed easily into the hands of the propertied classes. Most of the countries in this region boasted liberal constitutions promising representative government and personal freedom. But they were politically too inexperienced and economically too backward to translate democratic words into democratic deeds. Some were simply old-fashioned dictatorships ruled by strong men with the support of the army and the bureaucracy, like Poland under Marshal Joseph Pilsudski and Yugoslavia under King Alexander I. Others flirted with the theories of reactionary totalitarianism without succumbing to them entirely, like Romania under King Carol II and Hungary under Admiral Nicholas Horthy. And a few openly announced their adherence to fascist policies, like Austria under Chancellor Engelbert Dollfuss and Lithuania under President Antanas Smetona.

For fascism seemed strong and confident. While democratic nations were torn by doubts, the Italian political theorist Alfredo Rocco preached that only the authoritarian principle of statecraft could save the world from class war:

Fascism therefore not only rejects the dogma of popular sovereignty and substitutes for it that of state sovereignty, but it also proclaims that the great mass of citizens is not a suitable advocate of social interests, for the reason that the capacity to ignore individual private interests in favor of the higher demands of society and of history is a very rare gift and the privilege of the chosen few. Natural intelligence and cultural preparation are of great service in all such tasks. Still more valuable perhaps is the intuitiveness of rare great minds, their traditionalism and their inherited qualities.[2]

4 : Democracy on the Defensive

FOR THE liberal states the interwar years were a time of ordeal. The conflict which was supposed to make the world safe for democracy had instead weakened the foundations on which European democracy had rested. It had encouraged the growth of industrialism on other continents; it had destroyed the dream of free trade by intensifying economic nationalism; it had stimu- lated the opposition to imperialism among colonial peoples; it had led to the establishment of overseas barriers to immigration; it had shaken popular be- lief in bourgeois parliamentarianism; it had aggravated social insecurities and resentments. Worst of all, it had caused liberalism to lose faith in itself. Not only the masses of the West but its leaders as well were seized by a moral panic. Teachers and writers, convinced that war was the work of munitions manufacturers and international financiers, "the merchants of death," urged the young never again to bear arms for their country. Economists and sociologists, shocked by the widespread sufferings which accompanied the economic depression of 1929, began to condemn capitalism as an exploitative system of production. Even those statesmen and businessmen who attempted to defend established institutions did so with little conviction. The bourgeois political order faced a terrible crisis.

FRANCE

After struggling against the enemy for four ruinous years, France emerged from the First World War a broken, sick nation. More than half of its male inhabitants who were between the ages of twenty and thirty-two when hostilities began had fallen on the battlefield. The hundreds of de- stroyed towns and thousands of wrecked factories were eventually restored by the expenditure of eighty billion francs. But the one and a half million dead could not be brought back to life, nor could the half a million maimed be made whole again. The hope that Germany would be forced to pay the costs of the war proved to be no more than wishful thinking, for not even the seizure of the rich Ruhr by French troops in 1923 succeeded

---

[2] Alfredo Rocco, "The Political Doctrine of Fascism," *International Conciliation*, No. 223 (October, 1926), p. 405.

in squeezing much money out of the impoverished Weimar Republic. The loss of investments in Russia and the high price of reconstruction produced a financial crisis which did not come to an end until 1928, when Prime Minister Raymond Poincaré devalued the franc from nineteen cents to four. This repudiation of almost eighty per cent of the liabilities of the state, the spread of communism among the lower classes, the chronic instability of the post-war cabinets, and the involvement of important politicians in the peculations of the shady financial manipulator Sergei Stavisky produced an outburst of antirepublican sentiment. Royalist and fascist organizations like the *Action Française,* the *Solidarité Française,* the *Front Paysan,* and the *Croix de Feu* proliferated, and in February, 1934, a wave of political disorder swept over the country threatening to topple the government. A hastily-formed coalition cabinet under Gaston Doumergue representing the middle-of-the-road parties managed to weather the storm, but not before the republic had come closer to collapse than at any time since the Dreyfus affair.

To counter the danger of a reactionary coup, the parties of the Center and the Left, the Radical Socialists, the Socialists, and the Communists, formed in 1935 a parliamentary alliance known as the Popular Front. The following year they won a major electoral victory on a platform urging the defense of political democracy and the advancement of social welfare. The new cabinet headed by the socialist intellectual Léon Blum went to work at once to revive the confidence of the proletariat in the republic. The forty-hour work week was proclaimed, paid vacations were guaranteed to all factory employees, labor disputes were subjected to compulsory arbitration, the munitions industry was nationalized, the Bank of France was placed under public control, and fascist organizations were dissolved or at least restrained.

Yet measures which conciliated the worker alienated the businessman, and before long the coalition of bourgeois liberalism and proletarian radicalism began to encounter serious financial difficulties. Anxious to halt the continuing decline in the value of the franc, the government announced a temporary suspension of further plans for social reform. But differences of opinion among the parties supporting it grew steadily, and in 1938 the Popular Front came to an end. The cabinet of Edouard Daladier which followed moved farther and farther to the Right. Labor attempted to resist this conservative tendency by organizing a strike campaign, but its opposition only led to stern government action against trade unions. While important industrialists were muttering among themselves that Hitler was better than Blum, while millions of workers were announcing that their allegiance belonged not to Daladier but to Stalin, France marched to disaster.

GREAT BRITAIN

In England political differences were less intense, but economic difficulties were even greater. The most serious effect of the First World War

Orlando, Lloyd George, Clemenceau, and Wilson posed for this picture in 1919 during the peace conference in Paris. The four victorious leaders exude an air of statesmanlike calmness, which is subtly enhanced by such details as the handsome rug on the floor, the paintings on the wall, and the books in the background. Actually, serious political differences among them had already begun to appear, and the treaty which they were soon to complete was marred by vindictiveness and weakness.

Trotsky was the most colorful figure among the Bolsheviks, a rare combination of intellectual and man of action. He could compose revolutionary pamphlets and lead armies, write literary criticism and address a mob, lecture on
socialist doctrine and help run a government, speak half a dozen languages
and even win a reputation as a ladies' man. Colonel Raymond Robins, head
of the American Red Cross in Russia, called him "the greatest Jew since Jesus
Christ." Here he is shown in the center reviewing the Red Army.

Only an air of self-conscious solemnity suggests that the statesmen in this picture have just avoided the outbreak of war. Chamberlain and Daladier, soberly dressed in civilian clothes, pose with Hitler and Mussolini, to whom they sacrificed the Czechs as the price of peace. The two dictators, however, seem strangely unelated by the triumph which their aggressive diplomacy has won. The handsome young man on the right is Count Galeazzo Ciano, Mussolini's son-in-law and foreign minister.

The civilian and military representatives of Japan wait aboard the U.S.S. "Missouri" in Tokyo Bay on September 2, 1945, to sign the surrender documents. In the foreground on the right is General Douglas MacArthur, commander of the allied forces in the Pacific. Saluting him is General Jonathan M. Wainwright of the United States, who spent more than three years in Japanese captivity. The act of capitulation depicted here marked the conclusion of the Second World War.

was not the loss of two million casualties nor the expenditure of eight billion pounds, but the increased industrial rivalry of other states which had expanded their productive capacity during the hostilities. Trade was a matter of life and death to a country which had to purchase almost two-thirds of its food supply abroad. Yet between 1913 and 1929 Great Britain's share of the world's exports fell from almost fourteen per cent to less than eleven while its population was steadily growing. The result was chronic unemployment and social unrest, which culminated in 1926 in an unsuccessful general strike involving some two and a half million workers.

Hard times also brought mounting criticism of the theories of freedom of trade and freedom of enterprise which had been unquestioningly accepted in the nineteenth century. The Liberal party, traditionally identified with economic and political individualism, was especially vulnerable to attacks on the teachings of laissez faire. In 1922 it was replaced by the Labor party as the chief parliamentary opponent of the Conservatives. While on the American stock exchange investors were engaging in wild speculation, while even among the defeated Germans there was an appearance of confidence after the stabilization of the currency in 1923, in the United Kingdom newspapers were full of stories about strikes and lockouts, about workers without work and families on the dole.

The depression beginning with the Wall Street crash of 1929 was the climax of a series of economic reverses which staggered Great Britain. The number of unemployed, never less than a million throughout the 1920's, rose to two and a half million in 1930. At the same time exports were shrinking and profits falling. Faced by a national emergency, Prime Minister J. Ramsay MacDonald decided to introduce a program of recovery which would have scandalized the statesmen of the pre-war years. On September 21, 1931, the country went off the gold standard, and the expression "sound as sterling" lost its historic meaning. In the following year a century of free trade came to an end, when protective duties of ten per cent ad valorem were imposed on most imports. Before long the government adopted almost all of the other practices of economic nationalism which the hard times were encouraging everywhere in Europe. It controlled foreign exchange, manipulated paper currencies, made public appeals to "buy British," and established a system of preferential tariffs within the empire at the Ottawa Imperial Economic Conference of 1932.

These measures succeeded little by little in alleviating the worst effects of the depression. But they also represented an abandonment of cherished economic beliefs. Fascism and communism made little headway among the masses, yet the exuberant self-confidence of the days of Palmerston and Disraeli had vanished. The prime ministers of the 1930's, MacDonald, Stanley Baldwin, and Neville Chamberlain, expressed the subdued mood of the nation in their policies. Honest, sincere, hard-working, and well-meaning, they labored in an unimaginative, plodding way to restore financial prosperity and maintain diplomatic influence. They lived in times, however, which demanded more than the sober virtues of the certified public accountant. For opposed to them were ruthless fanatics. The silk umbrella and the black Homburg reflected the middle-class respectability of one side, just as the steel helmet and hobnailed boot expressed the militant authoritarianism of the other. Only in 1939 did the English government recognize at last the serious danger to its position as a major power. By then it was almost too late.

The decline in the authority of Downing Street encouraged greater independence on the part of the dominions. Their contribution to the war effort of the Entente Powers had been considerable, and with the coming of victory they received their reward in the form of a new freedom of action in international affairs. Represented at the peace conference by their own statesmen rather than those of the mother country, they succeeded in vindicating their claims to the spoils of conquest. The Union of South Africa gained control of German South-West Africa, Australia acquired most of the German Pacific colonies south of the equator, and New Zealand was entrusted with the administration of German Samoa. As befitted the dignity of full-fledged states, moreover, they obtained admission to the League of Nations as sovereign members. Before long they were establishing diplomatic relations with foreign countries and concluding political and commercial treaties. The English government agreed at the imperial conference of 1926 that dominions "are autonomous Communities within the British Empire, equal in status, in no way subordinate one to another in any respect of their domestic or external affairs, though united by a common allegiance to the Crown, and freely associated as members of the British Commonwealth of Nations." This view was given formal sanction in the Statute of Westminster of 1931, which substituted free co-operation for historic right as the basis of the imperial union.

Under this arrangement, relations between the crown and the dominion governments were harmonious everywhere except in Ireland. The end of the First World War opened a period of civil war in the island which continued until the signing of a treaty in 1921 establishing the Irish Free State. Even then the uncompromising nationalists under Eamon de Valera would not accept the exemption of Protestant Ulster in the north from the jurisdiction of the new state. In 1937, a few years after winning a parliamentary majority, they promulgated a new constitution severing virtually all remaining ties between Dublin and London. Yet neither diplomatic negotiations, nor financial inducements, nor deeds of terrorism succeeded in overcoming the obstacles to a reunification of the Emerald Isle.

THE UNITED STATES

During the First World War the United States emerged as the greatest power in the world. Its industrialists won new markets; its bankers became the creditors of the West; its farmers fed hungry millions; its soldiers decided the outcome of the hostilities. But the great crusade for world democracy was followed by a mood of isolationism which rejected the Treaty of Versailles and refused membership in the League of Nations. During the 1920's a people enjoying the highest standard of living on earth turned from the Old World with its endless and insoluble problems. "We are so snug here," announced President Calvin Coolidge. "Nothing they do can touch us."

Having shut the gates of immigration and liquidated their wartime commitments, millions of Americans applied themselves to the task of getting rich. True, the farmer was in serious financial distress through most of the post-war decade, and Congressional efforts to revive rural prosperity by protective tariffs were futile in a nation which was an exporter of agricultural products. Gangsters and bootleggers flourished amid the speak-easies which mushroomed in the wake of prohibition, "an experiment noble in motive." And a series of sensational disclosures of corruption in government proved that even members of the cabinet were not immune to the attraction of a few hundred thousand dollars. Yet as long as the value of shares on Wall Street continued to climb, God was in his heaven, all was right with the world.

It was the collapse of the stock exchange in October, 1929, which revealed how hollow the optimism of the twenties had been. Almost overnight proud fortunes became worthless, as investors lost their life savings and factories began to close their doors. President Herbert Hoover, who only a year before had confidently predicted the day "when poverty will be banished from this nation," believed that ultimately recovery would come about through the operation of the impersonal forces of the free market. While waiting for nature to take her course, however, he helped raise the high import duties still higher by the Smoot-Hawley Tariff, and organized the Reconstruction Finance Corporation to make loans to hard-pressed financial establishments. Unfortunately for him, the election of 1932 arrived before prosperity did. After nominating Franklin D. Roosevelt for the presidency, the jubilant Democrats went on to an overwhelming victory at the polls, although the outcome would probably not have been much different if they had named Tom, Dick, or Harry. For the United States was going through its blackest hour since the Civil War. The inaugural address of the new president did not exaggerate in its description of the grave problems which the country faced:

> Values have shrunk to fantastic levels; taxes have risen; our ability to pay has fallen; government of all kinds is faced by serious curtailment of income; the means of exchange are frozen in the currents of trade; the withered leaves of industrial enterprise lie on every side; farmers find no markets for their produce; the savings

of many years in thousands of families are gone. More important, a host of unemployed citizens face the grim problem of existence and an equally great number toil with little return. Only a foolish optimist can deny the dark realities of the moment.

No sooner had Roosevelt moved into the presidential mansion than he began putting into effect his program of recovery. The New Deal was not a consistent system of economic thought; much less was it a scheme for the gradual introduction of socialism. Essentially, it proved to be a technique of improvisation on a grand scale, a process of tinkering with the mechanism of production to see what would make the wheels start turning once more. To reduce agricultural surpluses, the government under the Agricultural Adjustment Act and the Soil Conservation Act paid the farmer to curtail output. To stabilize conditions in industry, the National Industrial Recovery Act allowed businessmen to reduce competition, until the Supreme Court in 1935 declared the measure unconstitutional. The worker won recognition of his right to unionize through the National Labor Relations Act; he gained financial protection against unemployment and old age through the Social Security Act; and he achieved an improvement in the conditions of labor through the Wages and Hours Law. The hungry found employment in government projects under the Public Works Administration and the Works Progress Administration. The exporter profited from the devaluation of the dollar and the negotiation of favorable tariff agreements with several foreign states. For the small investor there was regulation of the stock exchange; for the small depositor there was insurance of savings banks.

A new America was being fashioned by the jaunty president. To millions he was a warm voice on the radio assuring the nation that it had nothing to fear but fear itself. Others saw in him "that man in the White House," who was undermining the foundation of the republic. His accomplishments were considerable, and the New Deal unquestionably mitigated the worst consequences of the depression. But it failed to destroy the cause. Unemployment, hunger, demoralization, and insecurity continued throughout the thirties, until a new world war put an end to hard times.

THE SMALL DEMOCRACIES

The small democracies had even less success in coping with the political and economic problems of the interwar period. In the Low Countries neither the policy of neutrality followed by Holland nor the alliance with France concluded by Belgium achieved security against the German menace. And neither the introduction of protective tariffs in the former nor the adoption of labor welfare laws in the latter provided a cure for unemployment. The Scandinavian states, after more than a century of almost uninterrupted peace, were confident that any future military contest would leave them untouched. While the war clouds were beginning to gather on the horizon, Sweden, Norway, and Denmark under the auspices of a moderate socialism proceeded with ambitious programs of mass welfare. Yet not far away Hitler's airplane factories were working twenty-four hours a day and millions of young men were receiving instruction in the use of the rifle.

In the east Finland and Czechoslovakia were two small islands of democracy threatened by a rising tide of authoritarianism—communist in one case, fascist in the other. The government in Prague was in a particularly vulnerable position. Opposed by unfriendly German and Hungarian minorities, it was further troubled by the rivalry between the two dominant nationalities, the Czechs and the Slovaks. During the presidency of the astute Thomas G. Masaryk the state still managed to defend its political interests. But with the rise of National Socialism in the 1930's a period of mounting danger opened for the little Slavic republic.

LATIN AMERICA

Last among the defenders of democracy were the states of Latin America. To them theories of representative government were not a standard of public conduct but a justification of diplomatic policy. In 1933, on taking office as president, Franklin D. Roosevelt announced his determination to "dedicate this Nation to the policy of the good neighbor." In other words, Washington promised to abandon imperialism in favor of a free collaboration between Latin and Anglo-Saxon in the Western Hemisphere. In the years which followed, the United States withdrew its marines from Haiti and abrogated its rights of intervention in Cuba. Tariff concessions and government loans also won friends south of the Rio Grande.

At the Pan-American conference held in Lima in 1938 the nations of the New World expressed their resolve to defend themselves against "all foreign intervention or activities that may threaten them." The warning was meant primarily for fascist ears, and yet in their treatment of political opponents the governments of South America employed methods familiar in Germany and Italy. True, theirs was the old-fashioned despotism of the *caudillo* which avoided the ideology and vocabulary of the European authoritarians. But in their violation of personal freedom and parliamentary authority there was little to choose between Hitler or Mussolini on the one hand and such dictators as Getulio Vargas of Brazil, Rafael Franco of Paraguay, Federico Páez of Ecuador, or Óscar Benavides of Peru on the other. In some of the larger states like Argentina, Chile, and especially Mexico there were signs of resistance to the tradition of rule by the strong man. But even there party bossism rather than popular democracy was the arbiter of politics.

5 : The Pipe Dream of Peace

NOT ONLY DID the First World War betray the promise "to make the world safe for democracy"; it also failed to live up to the expectation that it was "the war to end war." While hostilities were still in progress, the problem of peacemaking seemed simple enough. Justice would be done, no more and no less; and justice meant the punishment of the warmongers on the other side and the rewarding of the peace-loving states on this side. Translated into diplomatic practice in Paris in 1919, this view led to the imposition of a punitive peace upon the vanquished which was bound to arouse resentment among them. But their protests were ignored as long as they lacked the military means to obtain redress.

The statecraft of the western allies proved in the long run to be self-defeating. No major power could fashion permanent security for itself out of the permanent insecurity of another major power. The victims of an international diplomatic order based on the lasting subordination of some of its members were sure to work with all means at their disposal for the overthrow of that system. It did no good to charge them with bad faith and call them aggressors. Having been compelled by force to accept what they considered a manifestly unfair arrangement, they had no hesitation about using force to compel its revision. The treaties on whose sanctity the victor states insisted throughout the interwar period were for the defeated states nothing more than a piece of legalized extortion to be denounced at the earliest possible moment. In 1815 the duke of Wellington had warned the conquerors of that day that "if peace and tranquillity for a few years is their object, they must make an arrangement which will suit the interests of all the parties to it, and of which the justice and expediency will be so evident that they will tend to carry it into execution." The wisdom of his views was demonstrated a hundred years later.

A DECADE OF INTERNATIONAL STABILITY

At first there was nothing to make the victors doubt the correctness of their policy. Before them was the prospect of an enduring peace based on their preponderance of power. The League of Nations provided an instrument for the pacific settlement of international differences and for the prompt defeat of all unilateral attempts to alter the peace treaties. The desire to avoid future armed conflicts, moreover, led to the Washington

Conference of 1922 and the London Conference of 1930 limiting naval armaments. The Permanent Court of International Justice was established at The Hague in 1922 to adjudicate diplomatic disputes, and by the Kellogg-Briand Pact of 1928 sixty-three states solemnly announced that "they condemn recourse to war for the solution of international controversies, and renounce it as an instrument of national policy in their relations with one another."

Not content with pacific declarations, the Quai d'Orsay in Paris also succeeded in creating a system of defensive alliances designed to guarantee its dominant position on the Continent. The re-establishment of the pre-war connection with Russia was out of the question, for to the bourgeoisie of the Third Republic communism was the work of Satan. But might not the succession states of eastern Europe prove a satisfactory substitute for the tsarist régime? After signing a military convention with Belgium in 1920, France proceeded to negotiate political agreements with Poland in 1921, with Czechoslovakia in 1924, with Romania in 1926, and with Yugoslavia in 1927. Finally, the French and the German foreign ministers, Aristide Briand and Gustav Stresemann, initiated a policy of reconciliation between their governments which led to the Locarno Pact of 1925. Berlin renounced all efforts to obtain a revision of its western frontier, and the following year it was rewarded with an admission to the League of Nations.

THE DISINTEGRATION OF THE PEACE

The coming of the depression destroyed the illusion that the danger of war had vanished, because the fears and tensions which accompanied hard times played into the hands of political extremists. Among nations with authoritarian leanings the belief grew that armed might could rectify long-standing civic and economic grievances. The first major break with the system of security established at Paris came in 1931–32, when the Japanese seized Manchuria and organized it as a vassal state. The attempts of the League of Nations to mediate in the conflict were met by Japan's withdrawal from the world organization. The weakness of the post-war diplomatic structure was now revealed, convincing a bold opportunist like Hitler that the moment was ripe for a one-sided revision of the Treaty of Versailles. In 1935 Germany announced the reintroduction of military conscription, and the following year it remilitarized the Rhineland. As for England and France, they sent protest notes which the Führer promptly buried in the files of the foreign office.

At the same time Mussolini was avenging the defeat of Italian arms forty years before by conquering Ethiopia. Emperor Haile Selassie appeared in Geneva to plead before the great powers for assistance against fascist tyranny, but the weary democracies were in no mood to become involved in a war over the wastes of east Africa. They went through the motions of introducing economic sanctions against the attacker, yet when to no one's surprise these failed to stop the armies of the Duce, they acquiesced in his aggression. In 1936 the two triumphant dictators formed an alliance which came to be known as the Rome-Berlin Axis, and soon thereafter they were joined by Japan in the Anti-Comintern Pact directed ostensibly against communism.

The diplomats of the western democracies sought to counter totalitarian expansionism with a policy of appeasement. Struggling against unemployment and poverty, they were ready to make almost any sacrifice in order to avoid another world war. They had an uneasy feeling, moreover, that the Treaty of Versailles had not really been fair, and that demands for its revision were in principle reasonable. Finally, at least some of them hoped that after a few concessions from London and Paris the Rome-Berlin Axis would turn eastward against Russia, and the authoritarians of the Right and the Left would destroy each other to the advantage of the liberal states.

During the Spanish civil war, while Germany and Italy were giving assistance to the insurgent forces and the Soviet Union was providing supplies for the republican government, England and France followed a course of non-intervention, seeing no evil, hearing no evil, doing no evil. They looked hard the other way when in 1937 Japan embarked on a new campaign against China. They contented themselves with halfhearted reproofs when in the spring of 1938 the Third Reich engineered the incorporation of Austria, a step which enjoyed popular support among the Germans and the Austrians, but which was also a clear violation of the Treaty of Versailles. Six months later, when the Führer began to press Czechoslovakia for the cession of the Sudetenland, a region inhabited largely by a German population, Chamberlain and Daladier prepared to sell out their democratic friends in Prague. Chamberlain in particular was pathetically anxious to find a peaceful settlement of the dispute. His airplane trips to confer with the Nazi dictator finally inspired one wit to comment: "If at first you don't concede, fly, fly again." On September 29, 1938, the two chief statesmen of liberal Europe met in Munich with Hitler and Mussolini to accept all the demands of the totalitarian powers, thereby averting the danger of an international conflict through the sacrifice of the Czechs. Great Britain was now "the lion of least resistance," its authority as a victor in the First World War undermined, its prestige as a founder of the League of Nations dissipated. Yet so great was the prime minister's relief that hostilities had been avoided, so great was his faith in the sanctity of a tyrant's signature, that after returning to London with one of the most humiliating treaties in his country's history he triumphantly announced to a crowd of well-wishers: "There has come back from Germany to Downing Street peace with honour." And his listeners interrupted their singing of "For He's a Jolly Good Fellow" to cheer this colossal piece of self-deception.

534

THE OUTBREAK OF THE SECOND WORLD WAR

They were disabused soon enough. Less than a month after he had made his promises to the western statesmen Hitler issued a secret directive to his military advisers informing them that "the armed forces must be prepared at all times for . . . the liquidation of the remainder of Czechoslovakia." The blow fell in March, 1939, when the Czech state which had been rendered defenseless by the Munich Agreement was completely dismembered by Germany. Even Chamberlain, no longer able to delude himself regarding the ambitions of National Socialism, admitted that "public opinion in the world has received a sharper shock than has ever yet been administered to it, even by the present regime in Germany." Recognizing at last that the policy of appeasement was a costly failure, the democracies resolved to take a strong stand in the next international crisis, regardless of the consequences. They announced this intention through a pact of mutual assistance with Poland, and sought to strengthen their military position by a program of rapid rearmament.

As the Führer began to send threatening notes to Warsaw regarding the Polish Corridor which separated East Prussia from the rest of the fatherland, England and France entered into negotiations with Russia for the establishment of a united front against fascist encroachment. Stalin, however, had just decided that nothing was to be gained from a policy of collaboration with the liberal states. Instead, on August 23, 1939, he executed a complete about-face by concluding a non-aggression treaty with Germany. The Führer was thus freed from the danger of a war on two fronts. "The Soviet Union has joined the Anti-Comintern Pact" was a quip circulating in the capitals of Europe. But there was nothing amusing about the consequences of the Kremlin's astounding reversal of diplomacy, because the outbreak of hostilities had now become inevitable. For about a week the Third Reich played a game of cat-and-mouse with Poland, until on September 1 the German armies crossed the frontier to attack a weak, isolated opponent. Two days later, grimly resolved to stand up to the fascist menace, London and Paris dispatched declarations of war to Berlin. Another world conflict was under way.

6 : The Second World War

IN PREPARING for the Second World War the military leaders of the western democracies had relied on the experiences of the First World War, just as in planning for the First World War they had studied the lessons of the Franco-Prussian War. In both cases the actual course of events caught them

The Belligerents in the Second World War*

(In the order of their participation)

I. The Axis and Satellite States

Germany: September 1, 1939

Italy: June 11, 1940

Hungary: April 10, 1941

Bulgaria: April 24, 1941

Romania: June 22, 1941

Finland: June 25, 1941 (Previously at war with the U.S.S.R. Nov. 30, 1939 to March 12, 1940)

Japan: December 7, 1941

Manchukuo: December 8, 1941

Slovakia: December 12, 1941

Croatia: December 14, 1941

Albania: December 17, 1941

Thailand: January 25, 1942

Nanking government of China: January 9, 1943

II. The Coalition Against the Axis

Poland: September 1, 1939

United Kingdom: September 3, 1939

France: September 3, 1939

India: September 3, 1939 (Action taken by government in London)

Australia: September 3, 1939

New Zealand: September 3, 1939

Union of South Africa: September 6, 1939

Canada: September 10, 1939

Norway: April 8-9, 1940

Belgium: May 10, 1940

Luxemburg: May 10, 1940

Netherlands: May 10, 1940

Greece: October 28, 1940

Yugoslavia: April 6, 1941

Union of Soviet Socialist Republics: June 22, 1941 (Previously invaded Poland Sept. 17, 1939; at war with Finland Nov. 30, 1939 to March 12, 1940; declared war on Japan August 8, 1945)

United States: December 7, 1941

Philippine Commonwealth: December 7, 1941

Panama: December 7, 1941

Costa Rica: December 8, 1941

Dominican Republic: December 8, 1941

Nicaragua: December 8, 1941

El Salvador: December 8, 1941

Haiti: December 8, 1941

Honduras: December 8, 1941

Guatemala: December 9, 1941

Cuba: December 9, 1941

China: December 9, 1941 (Chinese-Japanese incident had begun July 7, 1937)

Czechoslovakia: December 9, 1941 (Government-in-Exile)

Brazil: May 2, 1942

Mexico: May 22, 1942

Ethiopia: December 1, 1942

Iraq: January 16, 1943

Bolivia: April 7, 1943

Iran: September 9, 1943

Colombia: November 26, 1943 (State of Belligerency with Germany)

Liberia: January 27, 1944

Ecuador: February 2, 1945

Paraguay: February 8, 1945

Peru: February 11, 1945 (State of Belligerency with Germany and Japan)

Chile: February 12, 1945 (State of Belligerency with Japan)

Venezuela: February 14, 1945 (State of Belligerency with Germany and Japan)

Uruguay: February 22, 1945

Turkey: February 23, 1945

Egypt: February 26, 1945

Syria: February 26, 1945

Lebanon: February 27, 1945

Saudi Arabia: March 1, 1945

Argentina: March 27, 1945 (Declared war against Germany and Japan, but not a signatory to Declaration by United Nations)

Mongolian People's Republic: August 9, 1945 (Declared war against Japan, but not a signatory to Declaration by United Nations)

III. Axis satellites which subsequently declared war against the Axis

Italy: October 13, 1943

Romania: August 24, 1944

Bulgaria: September 8, 1944

Finland: September 15, 1944

San Marino: September 21, 1944

Hungary: January 20, 1945

*Reprinted by permission from C. E. Black and E. C. Helmreich, *Twentieth Century Europe* (New York: Alfred A. Knopf, 1950), pp. 843-44. Compiled from Katherine E. Crane, "Status of Countries in Relation to the War, August 12, 1945," *Department of State Bulletin* (1945), 13:230-241; Royal Institute of International Affairs, *Chronology of the Second World War* (London, 1947).

by surprise. In 1914 what had been expected to be a contest of maneuver turned out to be a trial of endurance, and in 1939 what had been expected to be a trial of endurance turned out to be a contest of maneuver.

The French army, still reputed to be the strongest on the Continent, had defeated the enemy once by means of trench warfare, and it proposed to defeat him again with the same technique. During the 1930's it had constructed a chain of powerful fortifications along the eastern frontier known as the Maginot Line, complete with running water, electric light, and central heating, and there it expected to sit out any future war until victory arrived. This emphasis on defense, both as a concept of strategy and as a state of mind, reflected the effects of the terrible ordeal which the country had undergone twenty years before. The Germans, on the other hand, having been on the losing side in 1918, applied themselves thereafter to the invention of new tactics designed to counter the process of attrition which had been the undoing of the Kaiser. They found what they were looking for in the application of armored force closely supported by air power in sufficient strength to break through a fixed entrenched position. Bold and original methods of attack developed by a group of capable general officers and executed by well-trained troops made the Wehrmacht the best military organization in the world when hostilities began in 1939.

THE AXIS IN THE ASCENDANT

The first weeks of the war provided an impressive display of its offensive power. Throughout the summer which preceded the outbreak of the conflict there had been optimistic comment in western newspapers about Poland's capacity to resist attack, about the bravery of its army and the impenetrability of its mud. Yet within a month the Germans had overrun the country and divided it with the Russians in accordance with a secret protocol appended to their non-aggression treaty. There followed half a year of deceptive inactivity, and then in the spring of 1940 the Wehrmacht marched forth to its greatest triumphs. In April it seized neutral Denmark and Norway in order to safeguard its flank in the north, easily defeating an Anglo-French expeditionary force sent to the defense of Scandinavia. One month later it invaded the Low Countries, and then broke through the French position at Sedan. Fanning out to the west and the south, it took the Maginot Line from the rear against little opposition, for the guns of the fortifications had been constructed to face immovably toward the Rhine. On June 10 Mussolini, anxious to participate in the division of the spoils, declared war against the democracies. Four days later Paris fell, and on June 22 the new head of the government of France, Marshal Henri-Philippe Pétain, agreed to an armistice which left most of his country occupied by the enemy. Early the following month the Third Republic came to an end,

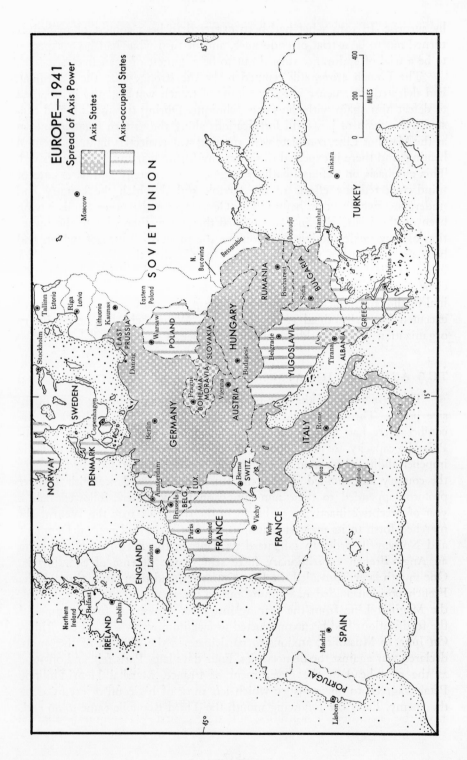

EUROPE—1941
Spread of Axis Power

Axis States

Axis-occupied States

SOVIET UNION

Moscow

TURKEY
Ankara

Istanbul
Dobrudja
Bessarabia
N.
Bucovina

RUMANIA
Bucharest
BULGARIA
Sofia

GREECE
Athens

Eastern
Poland

Tallinn
Estonia
Riga
Latvia
Lithuania
Kaunas

Stockholm

SWEDEN

EAST
PRUSSIA
Danzig
Warsaw
POLAND

Prague
BOHEMIA
MORAVIA
SLOVAKIA
Vienna
HUNGARY
Budapest
AUSTRIA

Belgrade
YUGOSLAVIA
Tirana
ALBANIA

Sicily

NORWAY

DENMARK
Copenhagen

Berlin

GERMANY

Amsterdam

ITALY
Rome

Corsica
Sardinia

Northern
Ireland
Belfast
Dublin
IRELAND

ENGLAND
London

Brussels
BELG.
LUX.

Berne
SWITZ.

Paris
Occupied
FRANCE

Vichy
FRANCE
Vichy

SPAIN
Madrid

PORTUGAL
Lisbon

45°

15°

45°

0   200   400
MILES

[538]

as the legislature voted by an overwhelming majority to establish an authoritarian régime.

Meanwhile, the British by heroic efforts managed to evacuate more than three hundred thousand men from the beaches of Dunkirk, men who were later used in better planned and more successful operations against the fascist powers. For the time being, however, western Europe lay prostrate before the jubilant Führer. Winston Churchill, who on May 11 had replaced Chamberlain as prime minister of England, was facing up to the hard truth when he warned his countrymen that "I have nothing to offer but blood and toil and tears and sweat."

For an entire year the government in London stood alone against the totalitarian assault. Since Britain's navy still controlled the seas, Hitler decided to prepare the way for an invasion of England by massive air raids which would destroy the opponent's will to resist. From August, 1940, until May, 1941, the Royal Air Force and the Luftwaffe met day after day in weird roaring battles in the sky, until the German high command decided to abandon temporarily the plan for a landing in England. For one thing, its losses in airplanes and in airmen were heavy enough to make the outcome of an amphibious military operation uncertain. Secondly, the Führer was once again beginning to look to the east. Hungary, Romania, and Bulgaria had been bribed or bullied into joining the Axis, but Greece and Yugoslavia stubbornly clung to their political independence. In April, 1941, therefore, the last lightning campaign of the Wehrmacht completed the subjugation of the Balkans.

THE TURNING OF THE TIDE

Two months later, on June 22, Germany attacked Russia in one of the fateful developments of the war. The ideological differences between the two dictatorships had been aggravated to the breaking point by conflicts of interest in the Baltic Sea and in the Balkan peninsula. Convinced that the Red Army could be crushed before the onset of winter, Hitler dispatched a force of more than three million Germans, Italians, Romanians, Hungarians, and Finns against the Soviet Union. It was 1812 all over again. Again the invaders won important early successes; again they advanced deeper and deeper into hostile territory; again they encountered burned villages and guerrilla bands. Yet, unlike the emperor of France, the leader of the Third Reich was never to enjoy a triumphal entry into the Kremlin. The swastikas came within forty miles of Moscow, but on December 6 a Russian counter-attack over the frozen plains drove them back for the first time. The following day came the electrifying news that the Japanese had bombed Pearl Harbor, and that the United States was finally in the war.

The American attitude had been sympathetic to the democratic cause from the beginning of hostilities, although at first Washington would not

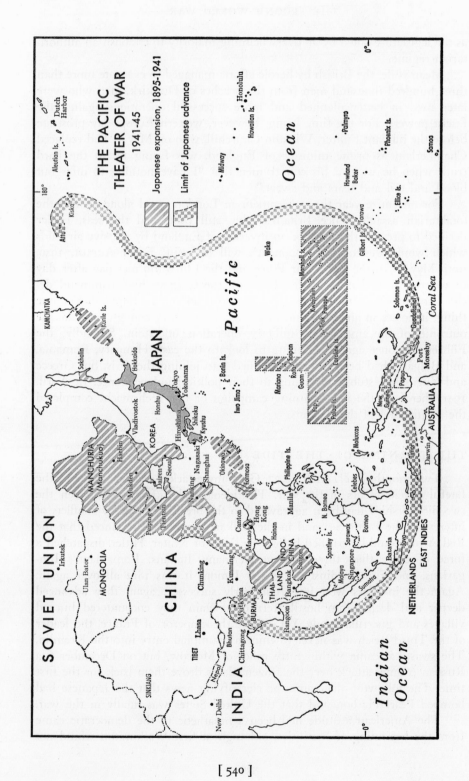

THE PACIFIC
THEATER OF WAR
1941-45

Japanese expansion, 1895-1941

Limit of Japanese advance

go beyond moral encouragement to England and France. After the great German victories in western Europe, however, it began to extend military and economic aid to the British. Indeed, in order to insure the uninterrupted flow of supplies across the Atlantic, it sent troops to Greenland, Iceland, and Ireland and provided merchantmen with naval protection against submarines. The difference between antifascist neutrality and antifascist belligerency was rapidly melting away when developments in the Far East created the immediate occasion for the final transition from one to the other.

Japan, engaged since 1937 in military operations against China, had taken advantage of the defeat of France to win control over Indo-China. Its war machine, however, depended heavily on imports from the New World of strategic materials, mainly oil, steel, scrap iron, copper, and lead. In the summer of 1941 President Roosevelt cut off the shipment of goods to the Japanese in order to curb their imperialistic ambitions, leaving them no choice but to abandon their colonial conquests or to acquire new economic resources. Their answer came on December 7, "a date which will live in infamy," when a surprise air raid on the Hawaiian Islands crippled the United States navy and exposed the western Pacific to the attack of the expansionists in Tokyo. Four days later Germany and Italy declared war on America, and the campaign in eastern Europe, in the Mediterranean, and in Asia merged in one great global conflict.

The spring and summer of 1942 were the high-water mark of Axis success. In the Soviet Union a new offensive was swiftly carrying the Germans toward the rich oil fields of Caucasia; in North Africa General Erwin Rommel, "the desert fox," was leading the fascist forces deep into Egypt to within seventy miles of Alexandria; in the Far East the Japanese were seizing the Netherlands East Indies, the Philippines, Hong Kong, Malaya, and Burma. Then the tide began to turn. The Red Army succeeded in pushing back the Wehrmacht in a series of savage battles, of which the most important took place at Stalingrad. In the Pacific the mikado's warships were stopped in the Coral Sea and at Midway Island, while his troops got their first taste of defeat when the United States marines landed on Guadalcanal in the Solomon Islands. And in the Mediterranean theater of operations a concerted advance by the British from the east and the Americans from the west closed in on the German Afrika Korps, capturing its last strongholds of Tunis and Bizerte in May, 1943.

The next campaign against the Axis was an invasion of Italy, designed to topple the shaky régime of Mussolini. The swift conquest of Sicily did lead to the resignation of the Duce, but Hitler rushed enough troops south to gain control of most of the peninsula. For nearly another two years hard fighting continued amid the Apennines. By the beginning of 1944, however, the grand coalition against fascism was winning the upper hand on all fronts. In eastern Europe the Russians were crossing their pre-war frontiers, carrying the war to the enemy. In the Italian boot the Allied armies were slowly advancing northward toward Rome. In the Far East the forces of General Douglas MacArthur, having occupied strategic points in the Gilbert and the Marshall islands, were sending their bombers closer and closer to the Japanese homeland. Everywhere the struggle was financed by America, which was producing vast quantities of war materials and shipping them to the four corners of the earth. The New World, protected by its oceans against air attack and military invasion, had become the arsenal of democracy.

THE VICTORY OF THE GRAND COALITION

The last phase of the war opened on June 6, 1944, with the invasion of western Europe by Allied troops under General Dwight D. Eisenhower. They succeeded by the end of the summer in driving the enemy out of France and Belgium, while the Red Army was making itself master of eastern Europe and approaching the frontiers of East Prussia. Recognizing the hopelessness of the military situation, a group of German officers attempted to assassinate Hitler in order to facilitate peace negotiations. But their effort failed, and the struggle went on to the bitter end. Late in 1944 the Wehrmacht launched a last desperate offensive against the western Allies in the Forest of Ardennes. When that failed, the Third Reich was left incapable of further effective resistance.

In the spring of 1945 a co-ordinated attack by the Russians in the east and the Americans in the west culminated in the meeting of their forces along the Elbe on April 25. Five days later, as his capital was falling to the troops of the Soviet Union, the Führer committed suicide, and on May 7 in Reims General Alfred Jodl accepted the instrument of unconditional surrender for Germany. Japan continued to fight alone for another few months, although the Allies had in the meantime retaken the Philippines and were now in a position to raid Japanese cities from air bases on Iwo Jima and Okinawa only a thousand miles from Yokohama and Nagasaki. What finally forced the mikado's government to agree to lay down its arms was first the destruction of the city of Hiroshima by an atomic bomb on August 6, and then two days later the entry of Russia into the conflict in the Far East. In the middle of the month Japan announced its readiness to meet the demands of the grand coalition, and on September 2 its civilian and military leaders signed the terms of capitulation on board the U.S.S. *Missouri*. Hostilities which had begun in the summer of 1939 on the road to Danzig came to an end six years later on the other side of the world in Tokyo Bay.

The agony of total conflict made familiar by the First World War recurred on an even more tragic scale in the Second World War. Those killed on the battlefield numbered some fifteen million men, while civilian losses were at least equally great. One out of every twenty-two Russians, one out of every twenty-five Germans, one out of every forty-six Japanese was dead or missing. The bitter quip that during hostilities the safest place is the front proved to be almost literally true. In England 20 per cent of all homes were damaged or destroyed; in Germany close to 25 per cent of the buildings were reduced to rubble; entire cities like Stalingrad, Warsaw, Kassel, and Rotterdam were desolate ruins; in Hiroshima a single atomic explosion took the lives of fifty thousand people and leveled four square miles. The financial costs of the conflict were estimated at from two to four trillion dollars, but what currency could express human suffering and sorrow? The Axis treated conquered countries with a ruthless brutality. It even organized a systematic, cold-blooded extermination of ethnic minorities which brought death to six million Jews. Yet the democracies were not entirely above reproach either. Their mass bombing of enemy countries drew no distinction between the good and the bad, the innocent and the guilty. How many Americans felt uneasy in March, 1945, about the great air raid on Tokyo which caused 185,000 civilian casualties? How many Britons protested two months later against the sack of Berlin by the Red Army? Amid the hatred and cruelty which had become instruments of modern warfare there was little room for such unpatriotic sentiments as compassion for the other side.

Seen in historical perspective the Second World War was part of a vast political process, the passing of the European Age. It weakened still further the civic and material bases on which the Old World had built its greatness. For it intensified the reaction of the Orient against imperialism, strengthened the economic position of America, and established the military preponderance of Russia. But for those who in 1945 had to face the future from the ruins of their civilization it was also a crushing personal tragedy. Now their only source of strength was an instinctive faith in the ultimate value of life, like that of the fifteen-year-old Jewish girl, Anne Frank, who wrote in her diary shortly before she was deported to her death in a wartime concentration camp:

> That's the difficulty in these times: ideals, dreams, and cherished hopes rise within us, only to meet the horrible truth and be shattered. . . . Yet I keep them, because in spite of everything I still believe that people are really good at heart. I simply can't build up my hopes on a foundation consisting of confusion, misery, and death. I see the world gradually being turned into a wilderness, I hear the ever approaching thunder, which will destroy us too, I can feel the sufferings of millions and yet, if I look up into the heavens, I think that it will all come right, that this cruelty too will end, and that peace and tranquillity will return again.[3]

---

[3] From *The Diary of a Young Girl* by Anne Frank, p. 278. Copyright 1952 by Otto H. Frank. Copyright 1952 by the American Jewish Committee. Reprinted by permission of Doubleday & Co., Inc.

Further Reading

The best military histories of the First World War are C. R. M. Crutt-
well, *History of the Great War, 1914–1918* (New York: Oxford Univ. Press,
1934); B. H. Liddell Hart, *A History of the World War, 1914–1918* (Boston: Little, Brown, 1935), and *The War in Outline, 1914–1918* (New York:
Random, 1936); and G. G. Aston, *The Great War of 1914–1918* (London:
Butterworth, 1930). For events behind the lines see F. P. Chambers, *The
War Behind the War, 1914–1918* (New York: Harcourt, 1939); H. D. Lass-
well, *Propaganda Technique in the World War* (New York: P. Smith,
1938); and M. Dickson, *The Food Front in World War I* (Washington:
Public Affairs Press, 1944). John W. Wheeler-Bennett, *The Forgotten
Peace: Brest-Litovsk* (New York: Morrow, 1939), is a brilliant treatment
of Russia's withdrawal from the war. On the surrender of the Central
Powers there are Frederick Maurice, *The Armistices of 1918* (New York:
Oxford Univ. Press, 1943); Harry R. Rudin, *Armistice, 1918* (New Haven:
Yale Univ. Press, 1944); and Karl F. Nowak, *The Collapse of Central
Europe* (New York: Dutton, 1924). The standard account of the peace con-
ference is Harold W. V. Temperley (ed.), *A History of the Peace Conference of Paris,* 6 vols. (New York: Oxford Univ. Press, 1920–24). Harold
Nicolson, *Peacemaking, 1919* (New York: Harcourt, 1939), and Paul
Birdsall, *Versailles Twenty Years After* (New York: Reynal, 1941), are important briefer works, while John M. Keynes, *The Economic Consequences
of the Peace* (New York: Harcourt, 1920), presents a shrewd estimate by
a well-known economist.

William H. Chamberlin, *The Russian Revolution, 1917–1921,* 2 vols.
(New York: Macmillan, 1935), is a balanced history of the Bolshevik seizure
of power. Sympathetic eyewitness accounts may be found in Leon Trotsky,
The History of the Russian Revolution, 3 vols. in 1 (New York: Simon &
Schuster, 1936), and John Reed, *Ten Days That Shook the World* (New
York: International Publishers, 1926). Edward H. Carr, *A History of Soviet
Russia,* 4 vols. (New York: Macmillan, 1950–54), is favorable to the revo-
lutionary cause, while George Vernadsky, *The Russian Revolution, 1917–
1931* (New York: Holt, 1932), offers a critical interpretation. The develop-
ment of Russia under communism is described in John Maynard, *Russia in
Flux* (New York: Macmillan, 1948); Alexander Baykov, *The Development
of the Soviet Economic System* (New York: Macmillan, 1947); and Harry
Schwartz, *Russia's Soviet Economy* (Englewood Cliffs, N.J.: Prentice-Hall,
1954). Merle Fainsod, *How Russia is Ruled* (Cambridge, Mass.: Harvard
Univ. Press, 1953), is a solid work, but it has not superseded such studies as
Samuel N. Harper, *The Government of the Soviet Union* (New York:

Van Nostrand, 1949), or Julian Towster, *Political Power in the U.S.S.R., 1917-1947* (New York: Oxford Univ. Press, 1948). The best biography of Stalin is Isaac Deutscher, *Stalin* (New York: Oxford Univ. Press, 1949). Max Beloff, *The Foreign Policy of Soviet Russia, 1929-1941,* 2 vols. (New York: Oxford Univ. Press, 1947-48); Frederick L. Schuman, *Soviet Politics at Home and Abroad* (New York: Knopf, 1946); and Louis Fischer, *The Soviets in World Affairs* (Princeton: Princeton Univ. Press, 1951), deal with the diplomacy of the Kremlin. For the ideology of the Soviet Union see Rudolf Schlesinger, *The Spirit of Post-War Russia* (New York: Universal Distributors, 1947); John Somerville, *Soviet Philosophy* (New York: Philosophical Library, 1946); Michael T. Florinsky, *World Revolution and the U.S.S.R.* (New York: Macmillan, 1933); Franz Borkenau, *The Communist International* (New York: Norton, 1939); and Martin Ebon, *World Communism Today* (New York: McGraw-Hill, 1948).

H. Holborn, *The Political Collapse of Europe* (New York: Knopf, 1951), is a penetrating analysis of the interwar period. On the development of fascism there are A. Rossi, *The Rise of Italian Fascism, 1918-1922* (London: Methuen, 1938), and Herbert W. Schneider, *Making the Fascist State* (New York: Oxford Univ. Press, 1928). B. King, *Fascism in Italy* (London: Williams, 1931); Gaetano Salvemini, *The Fascist Dictatorship In Italy* (New York: Holt, 1927), and *Under the Axe of Fascism* (New York: Viking, 1936); Herbert W. Schneider, *The Fascist Government of Italy* (New York: Van Nostrand, 1936); and Giuseppe A. Borgese, *Goliath: The March of Fascism* (New York: Viking, 1937), describe the régime of Mussolini. The soundest treatment of the Weimar Republic is S. William Halperin, *Germany Tried Democracy* (New York: Crowell, 1946). Arthur Rosenberg, *The Birth of the German Republic, 1871-1918* (New York: Oxford Univ. Press, 1931), examines its origin, while Arnold Brecht, *Prelude to Silence* (New York: Oxford Univ. Press, 1944), deals with its fall. A thoughtful account of National Socialism is presented in Franz L. Neumann, *Behemoth: The Structure and Practice of National Socialism* (New York: Oxford Univ. Press, 1942). John W. Wheeler-Bennett, *Wooden Titan: Hindenburg in Twenty Years of German History, 1914-1934* (New York: Morrow, 1936); K. Heiden, *Der Fuehrer* (Boston: Houghton, 1944); and Alan L. C. Bullock, *Hitler: A Study in Tyranny* (New York: Bantam F1896, 1958), are important biographical works. John W. Wheeler-Bennett, *Nemesis of Power* (New York: St. Martins, 1954), traces the relationship between militarism and totalitarianism in Germany. The background and course of the civil war in Spain are treated in Gerald Brenan, *The Spanish Labyrinth* (New York: Macmillan, 1943), and A. Ramos Oliveira, *Politics, Economics, and Men of Modern Spain, 1808-1946* (London: Gollancz, 1946). Hugh Seton-Watson, *Eastern Europe between the Wars, 1918-1941* (New York: Macmillan, 1945), is an outstanding study of authoritarianism in eastern Europe.

Harold J. Laski, *Democracy in Crisis* (Chapel Hill: Univ. of North Carolina Press, 1933); Walter Lippmann, *The Good Society* (New York: Grosset, Universal Library 3, 1956); Carl Becker, *New Liberties for Old* (New Haven: Yale Univ. Press, 1941); and Friedrich A. Hayek, *The Road to Serfdom* (Chicago: Univ. of Chicago Press, Phoenix P4, 1955), describe and illustrate ideological differences in the liberal camp between the wars. The effects of the great depression are discussed by Paul Einzig, *The World Economic Crisis, 1929–1931* (New York: Macmillan, 1931); H. V. Hodson, *Slump and Recovery, 1929–1937* (New York: Oxford Univ. Press, 1938); and H. W. Arndt, *The Economic Lessons of the Nineteen Thirties* (London: Oxford Univ. Press, 1944). E. J. Knapton, *France since Versailles* (New York: Holt, 1952), and Alexander Werth, *The Twilight of France, 1933–1940* (New York: Harper, 1942), deal with the last years of the Third French Republic. See also W. R. Sharp, *The Government of the French Republic* (New York: Van Nostrand, 1938); Charles A. Micaud, *The French Right and Nazi Germany, 1933–1939* (Durham: Duke Univ. Press, 1943); André Géraud, *The Gravediggers of France* (Garden City: Doubleday, 1944); and André Maurois, *Tragedy of France* (New York: Harper, 1940). Robert Graves and Alan Hodge, *The Long Week End: A Social History of Great Britain, 1918–1939* (New York: Macmillan, 1941), depicts the decline of England. G. E. Elton, *The Life of James Ramsay MacDonald* (New York: Collins, 1939), and Keith Feiling, *The Life of Neville Chamberlain* (New York: Macmillan, 1946), are significant biographies. For imperial problems there are Eric A. Walker, *The British Empire* (New York: Oxford Univ. Press, 1943), and R. G. Trotter, *The British Empire-Commonwealth* (New York: Holt, 1932). Frederick L. Allen, *Only Yesterday* (New York: Harper, 1931), is a colorful history of the twenties in America. More sober but also more substantial is H. U. Faulkner, *From Versailles to the New Deal* (New Haven: Yale Univ. Press, 1950). Arthur M. Schlesinger, Jr., *The Age of Roosevelt: The Crisis of the Old Order, 1919–1933* (Boston: Houghton, 1957), presents a vivid account of the economic crisis. Robert E. Sherwood, *Roosevelt and Hopkins* (New York: Harper, 1948), is a prize-winning book by an eminent writer. The New Deal has been described with understanding and discrimination by B. Rauch, *History of the New Deal, 1933–1938* (New York: Creative Age, 1944), and D. W. Brogan, *The Era of Franklin D. Roosevelt* (New Haven: Yale Univ. Press, 1950).

G. M. Gathorne-Hardy, *A Short History of International Affairs, 1920–1939* (New York: Oxford Univ. Press, 1942), is a useful introduction to interwar diplomacy. For a challenging interpretation see Edward H. Carr, *The Twenty Years' Crisis, 1919–1939* (London: Macmillan, 1939). F. P. Walters, *A History of the League of Nations,* 2 vols. (New York: Oxford Univ. Press, 1952), and Felix Gilbert and Gordon A. Craig (eds.), *The Diplomats, 1919–1939* (Princeton: Princeton Univ. Press, 1953), are valuable for an understanding of international affairs in the twenties and thirties. The weaknesses of the democratic powers become apparent from a reading of Arnold Wolfers, *Britain and France Between Two Wars* (New York: Harcourt, 1940), and W. M. Jordan, *Great Britain, France, and the German Problem, 1918-1939* (New York: Oxford Univ. Press, 1943), while the alliance of the authoritarian states is scrutinized by Elizabeth Wiskemann, *The Rome-Berlin Axis* (New York: Oxford Univ. Press, 1949). On the policy of appeasement the following works are of major importance: Frederick L. Schuman, *Europe on the Eve: The Crisis of Diplomacy, 1933-1939* (New York: Knopf, 1939); John W. Wheeler-Bennett, *Munich: Prologue to Tragedy* (New York: Duell, 1948); and Lewis B. Namier, *Diplomatic Prelude, 1938-1939* (New York: Macmillan, 1948), and *Europe in Decay: A Study in Disintegration, 1936-1940* (London: Macmillan, 1950). For the Second World War see Walter P. Hall, *Iron out of Calvary: An Interpretative History of the Second World War* (New York: Appleton-Century, 1946); J. F. C. Fuller, *The Second World War, 1939-1945* (London: Eyre, 1948); and Chester Wilmot, *The Struggle for Europe* (New York: Harper, 1952). Winston S. Churchill, *The Second World War*, 6 vols. (Boston: Houghton, 1948-53), is a vast, stirring narrative by a leading statesman.

Chapter 28

THE WANING
OF COLONIALISM

T HE PASSING of the European Age was in part a result of the awakening of the Orient. For more than four hundred years the West had maintained domination over distant races with colored skins. In the fifteenth century a small continent, still emerging from medieval provincialism, had embarked on a course of world conquest during which it easily subjugated the older civilizations of the East. The voyages of exploration were only one instance of the growing technological superiority of Europe. It soon became apparent that the bow and arrow were no match for firearms; that the steam engine was more efficient than all the slave labor of the potentates of Asia. The consequence was the establishment of vast colonial empires by the leading states of the Occident.

The motive behind the imperialism of the mercantilistic age was essentially commercial, although Spain also supported important missionary enterprises among native peoples, while England encouraged the emigration of religious and economic malcontents to her overseas possessions. Those who saw their independence threatened by the coming of the white man soon learned that the choice before them was submission or destruction. Some, like the Caribs of the West Indies, perished from the diseases and physical exactions which accompanied Spanish colonization. Others, like the Hottentots of South Africa, were enslaved by Dutch settlers. And still others, like the Bengalis of India, came under the indirect rule of Great Britain.

1 : Europe and the World

EARLY IN the nineteenth century there was a reaction in Europe against imperialism. The successful revolutions of the English colonies in North

America and of the Spanish colonies in South America apparently demonstrated that the acquisition of overseas dependencies was in the long run a fruitless enterprise. While the mother country fought wars and incurred debts to win colonial possessions, as soon as these acquired sufficient political experience they seceded and formed their own states. Moreover, once the nations of the West began to industrialize their economies, their interest in overseas acquisitions waned. The conquest of new lands in Asia and Africa seemed less attractive when there were factories and railroads to build at home. Finally, since economic liberalism and free trade were on the march, there appeared to be no advantage in the possession of colonial sources of raw materials or captive markets for manufactured goods. Even Benjamin Disraeli maintained in 1852: "These wretched colonies will all be independent too in a few years and are a millstone around our necks."

THE WHITE MAN'S BURDEN

In the second half of the nineteenth century the attitude toward imperialism changed once more. Industrial capitalism began to seek new fields to conquer, as the demand for raw materials and customers continued to grow. And since after 1870 the movement for free trade gave way before protectionist policies, colonies again assumed commercial importance. The advocates of expansionism armed themselves with the economic theories of scholars like Paul Leroy-Beaulieu, who maintained that colonial dependencies were essential to national might. They seized on the military theories of writers like Alfred T. Mahan to prove that national greatness was impossible without overseas possessions. They employed the language of scientists like Charles Darwin to assert that the laws of nature made inevitable the domination of the earth by the white man. They even made God himself an imperialist, arguing that colonialism meant the Christianization of the heathen.

Karl Pearson, a professor of mathematics at University College, London, expressed a widespread attitude in his evaluation of imperialistic policies:

> History shows me one way, and one way only, in which a high state of civilization has been produced, namely, the struggle of race with race, and the survival of the physically and mentally fitter race . . . . This dependence of progress on the survival of the fitter race, terribly black as it may seem to some of you, gives the struggle for existence its redeeming features; it is the fiery crucible out of which comes the finer metal. You may hope for a time when the sword shall be turned into the ploughshare, when American and German and English traders shall no longer compete in the markets of the world for their raw materials and for their food supply, when the white man and the dark shall share the soil between them, and

each till it as he lists. But believe me, when that day comes mankind will no longer progress.[1]

THE INTERACTION OF EAST AND WEST

Who could resist the common appeal of profit, patriotism, and religion? Once the process of national unification in Europe was completed during the Franco-Prussian War, a new imperialism began to conquer the rest of the world. By the time of the First World War Africa had been explored and partitioned by the great powers; Asia had been divided into spheres of influence which retained the shadow of native independence without its substance; Oceania had become a conglomeration of naval bases, coaling stations, and trading posts. The economy of the West entered a period of rapid expansion based on the exploitation of overseas resources. Rubber from the Belgian Congo, oil from Persia, tin from Malaya, jute from India, all contributed to the increasing well-being of the Occidental. Not only the industrialist and the financier, but also the factory worker and the farm hand profited from the creation of a complex international financial structure controlled by the stock exchanges of the West. True, even without colonialism there would in all probability have developed a close economic interdependence among the various regions of the earth. For scientific technology and rational production tended to establish a single global market regardless of diplomatic developments. Yet the fact that the leading states of Europe gained political control over distant sources of raw materials meant that the formation of the universal economy took place under conditions highly advantageous to them. The Occidentals became the beneficiaries of the armed authority which their governments exercised over alien peoples in distant lands. Their high standard of living was made possible because the Chinese, the Indians, and the Egyptians were not free to tax the profits of foreign companies or interfere with their export policies. In effect the West was acting in accordance with the old Scottish maxim: "Thou shalt starve ere I want."

Exploitation, to be sure, had been familiar among colonial peoples long before the European came. The colored masses which in the nineteenth century began to serve the needs of the Occident were as a rule exchanging one master for another. The government bureaucrat and plantation overseer simply replaced the tribal chieftain and provincial aristocrat. What is more, the white man brought with him standards of official conduct which represented a significant improvement over native institutions. He suppressed cannibalism, murder, slavery, and brigandage. He improved medical care, public sanitation, agricultural methods, manufacturing techniques. He built schools and orphanages, factories and railroads.

---

[1] Karl Pearson, *National Life from the Standpoint of Science* (London: Adam and Charles Black, 1901), pp. 19, 24.

Still, the material benefits which followed Westernization were purchased with the political subjection and social subordination of colonial peoples. The Occidental was willing to educate them, but he was resolutely opposed to their admission to a status of equality within his own community. The apologists of imperialism tended to overlook the psychological effect which the domination of an alien civilization had on the indigenous population. With the technological and cultural advances introduced by Europeans came spiritual bewilderment for the natives. While the Spaniards were establishing the first universities in the Western Hemisphere, the Aztecs became bondsmen. Under the rule of Great Britain the Kaffir, the terror of the African veld, settled in the slums of Durban. Materially, his position was probably better than before, for the colonial authorities transplanted to the tropics humanitarian ideals which had slowly matured in the more favorable environment of the Temperate Zone. Yet although they did much for the physical improvement of the colored man, they failed to realize that he also needed a sense of dignity and worth. Hence, what to him was a natural desire to make his own decisions seemed to the imperialist evidence of rank ingratitude.

THE REACTION AGAINST COLONIALISM

The reaction against colonialism assumed several forms. The first was a resolve to use sheer force in order to drive out the foreigners. Throughout the nineteenth century there was a struggle between native traditionalism and European imperialism. The Sepoy Mutiny in India in 1857–58 was one example; the Zulu War of Cetshwayo in South Africa in 1879 was another; the Boxer Rebellion in China in 1900–01 was a third. Rallying behind their ancestral gods, the colored masses of the world fought the white man time and again. But the end was always the same. He was simply too strong for them. He had cannon, railways, steamships, and factories. More important, he had civic discipline and a rational view of nature. There could be no question about who would emerge victorious in a contest of force.

The obvious futility of armed resistance encouraged the growth of an assimilationist tendency among the subject peoples. Since the old gods had failed, the new ones must be better. Important groups in the indigenous community, especially the educated and propertied, succumbed to the impulse for cultural identification with the conqueror. In every major colonial city of Asia and Africa could be found a class of native inhabitants assiduously cultivating Occidental manners. Politicians, lawyers, doctors, and clerks worked tirelessly at being Anglo-Saxon or Gallic. They imitated the English spoken at Oxford or the French heard at the Sorbonne. They wanted to have nothing to do with the traditional ceremonies and beliefs of their forefathers. Their one consuming ambition was to win acceptance as completely Westernized. Their tragedy was that they could not escape from themselves. The Occidental treated them with a show of cordiality to encourage their conforming zeal, but behind their backs he often poked fun at their efforts to show themselves better than their fellows. As for inviting them to his club or his home, that was out of the question. Alienated from their countrymen, patronized by the Westerners, the assimilated natives usually found themselves in a world of make-believe which offered them neither peace of mind nor sense of belonging.

Finally, out of the interaction of Orient and Occident arose a political movement which sought to oppose the imperialism of the West with the weapons of the West. Recognizing that uncritical imitation was as self-deluding as blind rejection, it advocated a program of civic reform which would enable native society to put an end to foreign rule without destroying its cultural tradition. Its point was that an adjustment of convention to progress was necessary, but that adjustment must not restrict the political independence or debase the social dignity of the colored man. The ideas of Herder, exported from central Europe to the banks of the Yangtze and the Nile, proved a powerful weapon in the struggle against colonialism. The language of the Indian patriot Chitta Ranjan Das had an unmistakably Mazzinian ring:

> What is the ideal which we must set before us? The first and fore-most is the ideal of nationalism. Now what is nationalism? It is, I conceive, a process through which a nation expresses itself and finds itself, not in isolation from other nations, not in opposition to other nations, but as part of a great scheme by which, in seeking its own expression and therefore its own identity, it materially assists the self-expression and self-realization of other nations as well: Diversity is as real as unity. And in order that the unity of the world may be established it is essential that each nationality should proceed on its own line and find fulfilment in self-expression and self-reali-zation . . . . I contend that each nationality constitutes a particular stream of the great unity, but no nation can fulfil itself unless and until it becomes itself and at the same time realizes its identity with Humanity. The whole problem of nationalism is therefore to find that stream and to face that destiny. If you find the current and establish a continuity with the past, then the process of self-expres-sion has begun, and nothing can stop the growth of nationality.[2]

International developments in the years following the First World War hastened the decline of imperialism. Once native peoples became acquainted with the traditions of the West, they began to apply that knowledge to the solution of their own national problems. The struggle against colonialism was thus in a sense not the struggle of Orient against Occident, but of one complex of Occidental theories and practices against another. The white

---

[2] P. C. Ray, *The Life and Times of C. R. Das* (London: Oxford University Press, 1927), p. 265.

man's political domination of the earth was drawing to a close, yet his ideological influence was stronger than ever. The question was no longer whether the hegemony of Europe was finished, but what would take its place.

After they were freed from the control of the imperialistic states, the subject peoples sometimes turned to democracy as a form of government suited to their needs. The father of the Chinese Republic, Sun Yat-sen, for example, announced in the declaration of aims of his party that "the Kuomintang's Doctrine of Democracy includes direct democracy and indirect democracy." Sometimes the colonial administrator was replaced by the party boss, closer to the local population in race and speech, but no more selfless and probably less efficient. Thus in Latin America political independence often merely substituted one form of exploitation for another. Finally, communism made a determined effort to win a following among the intellectual leaders of the colored races, preaching that the war of the Western proletarian against bourgeois exploitation and of the Eastern coolie against colonial oppression were part of the same crusade against capitalism. In his *Imperialism: The Highest Stage of Capitalism* Lenin gave the classic Marxian exposition of imperialism:

> If it were necessary to give the briefest possible definition of imperialism we should have to say that imperialism is the monopoly stage of capitalism. . . . Monopolies, oligarchy, the striving for domination instead of striving for liberty, the exploitation of an increasing number of small or weak nations by an extremely small group of the richest or most powerful nations—all these have given birth to those distinctive characteristics of imperialism which compel us to define it as parasitic or decaying capitalism. More and more prominently there emerges, as one of the tendencies of imperialism, the creation of the "bondholding" (rentier) state, the usurer state, in which the bourgeoisie lives on the proceeds of capital exports and by "clipping coupons."[3]

As the Orient continued to emerge from alien rule the struggle for its ideological allegiance assumed major importance.

2 : The Far East

CHINA

For China the years between the two world wars were a period of difficult adjustment to new civic ideals. Once the popular enthusiasm

---

[3] V. I. Lenin, *Imperialism: The Highest Stage of Capitalism* (New York: International Publishers, 1939), pp. 88, 124–25.

aroused by the fall of the Manchu Dynasty subsided, three political groups began to compete for the authority which the old order had relinquished. There was first Sun Yat-sen and his Kuomintang or Nationalist party, advocating the transformation of the country into a parliamentary state. Those still devoted to the authoritarian tradition of the past found their champion in Yüan Shih-kai, who had favored the deposition of the boy emperor, but who wanted to replace the monarchy with a strong man, preferably himself. Lastly, military governors and political bosses, the *tuchuns,* made themselves masters of the outlying provinces.

Japan was thus presented with an opportunity to satisfy the expansionist ambitions which the great powers had thwarted for twenty years. In 1915, while the Europeans were busy fighting each other on the other side of the world, the government of the mikado extorted from Peking special economic concessions in southern Manchuria and Inner Mongolia. Far from protesting against this policy of aggression, the Entente Powers promised to assign the special rights which Germany had enjoyed in Shantung to the Japanese in return for military assistance in the prosecution of the war. At the peace conference, moreover, they kept their promises to Tokyo. The Chinese cabinet, on the other hand, met with a rejection of its demands for the abolition of extraterritoriality, the renunciation of spheres of influence, and the withdrawal of foreign troops.

Then in the early 1920's came new hope for the unhappy republic. After settling the most pressing international problems arising out of the First World War, the great powers were once again in a position to oppose Japanese designs on the mainland of Asia. Early in 1922 the representatives of China, Japan, the United States, Great Britain, France, Italy, Holland, Belgium, and Portugal, meeting in Washington, bound themselves to respect the independence and integrity of China, and even permitted it to increase its tariff rates. What is more, Japan responded to the prodding of the West by agreeing to the withdrawal of its troops from Shantung.

Meanwhile the Kuomintang had succeeded in winning popular support for its civic program. Soon after the death of Yüan Shih-kai in 1916 it broke with his reactionary successors and established a government of its own in Canton. From there it directed a vigorous military offensive against the conservatives in the north and the provincial war lords allied with them. In 1926 its forces captured Hankow and Wuchang. Early the following year it took Shanghai and Nanking, proclaiming the latter city the new national capital of China. Finally, on June 8, 1928, Peking, the last major stronghold of the conservative opposition, fell into its hands. Confident that the ordeal of civil war was now over, the triumphant nationalists renamed the city Peiping, "Northern Peace."

Yet the peace won by the Kuomintang was short-lived. Its struggle against the heritage of the past had encouraged extremist tendencies which soon turned against its moderate outlook. In the years after the First World

War Marxism became an important ideological force in China by exploiting patriotic resentment against foreign imperialism and economic discontent fed by mass poverty. Since the policy of the Kremlin was to ally itself with native peoples against bourgeois colonialism, political agents of the Soviet Union like Michael Borodin worked tirelessly in the republican camp to arrange a marriage of convenience between nationalism and radicalism. Sun Yat-sen was willing to accept the friendship of a government which was providing him with military advice and financial assistance. And in 1924 he even persuaded a congress of his party to approve the admission to membership of all communists ready to subscribe to its principles. With his death a year later, however, the uneasy alliance which he had helped create began to dissolve. Although the right wing of his following had long been opposed to any hobnobbing with Bolshevism, it had hesitated to disobey the orders of the founder of the republic. Now it was free to express openly its antiradical sentiments. In Chiang Kai-shek, moreover, it found a leader who was not afraid to break with the leftists. The struggle between Stalin and Trotsky made impossible any effective intervention by the Soviet Union in behalf of Chinese communism, so that the conservative purge of the Kuomintang could proceed undisturbed. Late in the 1920's the radicals were expelled from the party, and shortly afterwards they were driven out of their fastnesses in the provinces of Fukien, Kiangsi, and Hunan south of the Yangtze River. But they managed to survive these reverses by effecting a long march northwestward and establishing themselves in Shensi province in 1935. There they held out for ten long years under Mao Tse-tung and Chou En-lai, until the end of the Second World War presented them with new political opportunities.

For the time being, however, the Kuomintang seemed to be victorious over the radicals as well as the reactionaries. It therefore attempted to consolidate its hold on power. An organic law promulgated in 1928 was designed to guide the state in the transition from authoritarianism to democracy. It provided in essence for a benevolent dictatorship of the party under the leadership of Chiang Kai-shek. China also resolved to play a more effective role on the international stage. By 1930 nine nations, among them Germany, Russia, Belgium, Italy, Denmark, and Portugal, had agreed to surrender their rights of extraterritoriality, and the others were being urged by the authorities in Nanking "to enable China, now unified and with a strong central government, to rightfully assume jurisdiction over all nationals within her domain."

But the fact was that the country was not unified, and that its central government was not strong. True, the communists had been driven into the borderlands of the north, yet famine and disease kept winning new recruits for them in every province. The prevalence of political bossism, cultivated by ambitious war lords, further undermined the prestige of established authority. Finally, within the Kuomintang itself there arose a disillusionment with the opportunism of its leadership. Chiang was not blind to the dangers threatening his rule, but the drain on his resources created by a succession of military campaigns made the work of reform exceedingly difficult. Even so, he might eventually have succeeded in overcoming the forces of disunion, had not the Japanese decided to take advantage of his embarrassment by reviving their program of imperialism.

JAPAN

After the First World War Tokyo had seemed to be willing to renounce the expansionist schemes inspired by disorders in China and Russia. Thus at the Washington Conference of 1922 it surrendered its privileged position in Shantung. This renunciation clearly represented a victory for moderate diplomats like Baron Kijuro Shidehara, who hoped to harmonize the interests of the two great nations of the Far East. Japan's intervention in the Soviet Union, which had begun during the Bolshevik Revolution, also came to an end when it agreed to withdraw its troops from Siberia in 1922 and from northern Sakhalin in 1925.

At the same time problems of political reform and economic welfare were becoming increasingly important for the nation. The masses, no longer meekly subservient toward those in authority, began to agitate for an extension of the franchise. Their demands were met in 1925 by a law granting universal manhood suffrage, which increased the number of voters from three to fourteen million. In 1918, with the general acceptance of the practice of ministerial responsibility, for the first time a commoner, Takashi Hara, became prime minister of the empire. In 1926 another statesman of plebeian birth, Reejiro Wakatsuki, was appointed to the premiership. The rise of organized political parties like the liberal Kenseikai and the conservative Seiyukai gave promise of a parliamentary development following the pattern of the West. The growth of trade-unions and labor disputes, moreover, was interpreted by foreign observers to mean that the problems created by industrialism in Yokohama or Nagasaki were essentially not different from those in Pittsburgh or Düsseldorf.

Then came a rude awakening. The liberal policies pursued by Tokyo after the Treaty of Versailles proved to be only a passing phase. Not only did feudal traditions militate against the establishment of a democratic form of government, but economic and demographic developments played into the hands of the reaction as well. During the First World War an industrial boom arising out of military needs gave Japan a favorable trade balance of more than two billion dollars. Even after hostilities were over the prosperity of the early post-war years maintained its sales on the world market at a high level. But with the coming of the world depression the Nipponese economy suffered a disastrous decline. By 1930 the value of the exports of raw silk had fallen to little more than half of what it had been the year before, while the number of unemployed had risen to a million workers, and the size of the national debt had grown to three billion dollars. Population, on the other hand, was increasing at the rate of about a million a year. For a country with sixty-five million inhabitants in the home islands, squeezed together into an area only about half as large as Texas, the decline of international trade was a catastrophe. But the military leaders of the nation, allied with powerful agrarian and industrial interests, had a ready solution for hard times. For years they had been unhappy with the cautious policies adopted by the cabinets of the 1920's. Still, as long as financial prosperity and political reform maintained the faith of the lower classes in parliamentary government, there was little they could do except grumble. It was popular discontent aroused by the economic crisis which enabled the reactionaries to gain the upper hand.

After 1930 the jingoists began to exercise a growing influence. Sometimes they would achieve their purpose by abetting the assassination of political opponents, among them Prime Minister Ki Inukai and Finance Minister Korekiyo Takahashi. Sometimes they used threats of mass unrest or even armed insurrection. And sometimes they assumed ministerial office personally, as when Admiral Keisuke Okada became head of the government in 1934 or General Hideki Tojo in 1941. The result was an enfeeblement of representative institutions. While the form of parliamentary rule was retained, its spirit was crushed by the ruling clique of officers, bureaucrats, and industrialists. Moreover, the revival of authoritarianism in domestic affairs was the logical prelude to a return to imperialism in foreign affairs. For to the expansionists in Tokyo the establishment of a Japanese sphere of influence in eastern Asia was the answer to the problem of overpopulation and overproduction.

THE SINO-JAPANESE CONFLICT

In 1931 Japan launched an undeclared war against China, and after seizing Manchuria, transformed it into a satellite state named Manchukuo. As nominal ruler of the new country Tokyo chose the last Chinese emperor who had been deposed in 1912, Henry Pu Yi. The former boy monarch was now old enough to appreciate palaces and concubines, and wise enough to follow the suggestions of the mikado's generals. Chiang Kai-shek, unable to obtain any assistance from the League of Nations beyond moral support, was forced by the Tangku truce agreement of 1933 to acquiesce in the spoliation of his nation. But the sacrifice was in vain. Far from appeasing the militarists in Nippon, it merely strengthened them in the belief that nothing stood in their way. In 1935 they extended their political control over the provinces of Hopei and Chahar, and in 1937 they opened a new attack against China.

There followed a long period of warfare in the Far East which did not come to an end until the close of the Second World War. What the authorities in Tokyo had hoped would be a swift succession of victories turned out to be an exhausting struggle in which the flies gradually succeeded in conquering the flypaper. The Japanese armies had little trouble in occupying the great cities of the Chinese coastland like Peiping, Tientsin, Shanghai, Nanking, and Canton. Yet each triumph brought new complications. The invaders soon discovered that their jurisdiction reached no farther than the range of their artillery. The rural masses of the interior continued to defy the enemy despite air raids and punitive expeditions, and for the first time in his career Chiang found himself the head of a country united in purpose. Not only was the Kuomintang ready to support him in this hour of national danger, but most of the war lords like Chang Hsueh-liang and Yang Hu-cheng accepted his leadership as well. Even the communists agreed to join forces with him. At his headquarters in Chungking in the western province of Szechwan could also be found emissaries from both

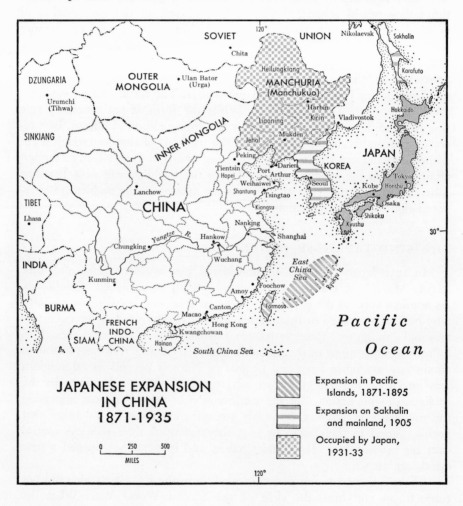

JAPANESE EXPANSION
IN CHINA
1871-1935

0   250   500
MILES

Expansion in Pacific
Islands, 1871-1895

Expansion on Sakhalin
and mainland, 1905

Occupied by Japan,
1931-33

The father of the Republic of China is shown at his headquarters in Canton in 1924. By both temperament and training he was eminently qualified to lead his country toward the goal of modernization. Chinese in culture and Christian in religion, at home in America as well as in Asia, he sought to synthesize Western and Eastern ideals in the program of the Kuomintang. More than any other man he was responsible for the liberation of his people from the decaying despotism of Manchu rule.

No one has commented on the political scene between the two world wars more incisively than the British artist David Low. In this cartoon which appeared during the 1930's he was suggesting that differences between London and Washington were in effect giving the Japanese a free hand in the Far East. The two buxom figures representing Great Britain and the United States occupy opposite ends of the seesaw, while a plump, pleased Nippon expresses the hope that "honourable foreign ladies continue to sit apart."

"The Great Soul" was more than the leader of a national awakening; he was the teacher of a universal ethic. Evolving his philosophy out of such diverse sources as the Indian Bhagavad-Gita *and the Christian* New Testament, *he spoke a language which transcends political boundaries and cultural differences. Fundamental to his thought was a profound belief in the sanctity of life: "Complete non-violence is complete absence of ill-will against all that lives. It therefore embraces even subhuman life, not excluding noxious insects or beasts. . . . Non-violence is therefore in its active form good-will toward all life. It is pure love. I read it in the Hindu scriptures, in the Bible, in the Koran." It was a tragic irony that he met his death at the hands of an assassin blinded by religious fanaticism.*

The tragedy of the black man's existence in the white man's scheme of things is portrayed in this photograph taken near the prosperous city of Johannesburg in the Transvaal. The primitive tribal society to which the ancestors of these natives belonged disintegrated under European influence. In its place came a Westernized social structure in which only the lowest positions were open to the Negro. The most urgent task which Africa faces is the improvement of the material welfare of the colored masses without the sacrifice of their dignity and freedom.

the United States and the Soviet Union, supplying him with loans and weapons.

The war in China was turning into a stalemate, when the outbreak of hostilities in Europe in 1939 provided the government in Tokyo with a new opportunity for territorial expansion. On September 22, 1940, it forced the demoralized French to admit Japanese troops to Indo-China. Five days later it entered into a military pact with Germany and Italy by which the signatory powers undertook "to assist one another with all political, economic, and military means when one of the three is attacked by a power at present not involved in the European war or in the Chinese-Japanese conflict." By allying itself with the Rome-Berlin Axis, however, Japan was running the risk of a conflict with the United States. Aware of the danger, it first sought to reach an understanding with Washington which would permit it to retain its conquests on the Asiatic mainland. But when this effort failed because of Roosevelt's insistence on the surrender of all Nipponese gains since 1931, the mikado's aircraft carriers began to sail eastward across the Pacific toward Pearl Harbor.

Within a few months early in 1942, Japanese arms won enough brilliant successes to satisfy the most ardent expansionist. But then came the counter-attack of the West. It began at Guadalcanal in August, 1942, continued on the Gilbert Islands in November, 1943, reached the Philippines in October, 1944, and conquered Okinawa in June, 1945. The last act was the atomic devastation of Hiroshima and the humiliating surrender in Tokyo Bay. The period in the development of the Far East which opened forty years before with the Russo-Japanese War had come to an end. It left behind it a political vacuum. As the tide of Japanese imperialism ebbed, the forces of liberalism and communism engaged in a conflict to decide what would take its place.

3 : India

NEVER DID the rule of Great Britain in India appear more secure than in the opening years of the twentieth century. The horror of the Sepoy Mutiny was only a memory, and the danger of a Russian attack vanished with the formation of the Triple Entente. Among the masses there was a mood of resignation to the rule of the foreigner, while the upper classes actively cultivated his customs. After the First World War broke out, more than a million Indians aided the military effort of the United Kingdom by serving abroad as soldiers and laborers. Their colonial government, moreover, presented a gift of five hundred million dollars to the exchequer in London. In recognition of this loyalty, Downing Street invited two Indians to participate in the imperial conference of 1917. Secretary of State for India Edwin S. Montagu also announced that the cabinet aimed at the "association of Indians in every branch of the administration and the gradual development of self-governing institutions with a view to the progressive realization of responsible government in India as an integral part of the British Empire." Two years later Lloyd George attempted to fulfill this promise with the Government of India Act. It provided for the establishment of provincial legislative councils invested with jurisdiction over such functions of government as public health and education. The members of these councils were to be chosen by a highly restricted suffrage system, which gave the franchise to fewer than six million persons out of a population of two hundred and thirty million in British India. As for the central authority, the viceroy and his executive council remained responsible to the English Parliament, although two advisory assemblies elected by barely a million voters were supposed to voice native opinion.

THE NATIONAL AWAKENING

If London thought that this half measure would satisfy Indian nationalism, it was sadly mistaken. The war years had greatly stimulated the growth of political consciousness on the subcontinent, leading to a close collaboration between the Hindu Indian National Congress and the All-India Moslem League. Civic discontent was aggravated by physical suffering, for soon after the hostilities a serious crop failure and a raging influenza epidemic took the lives of some five million persons. In the early 1920's a wave of agrarian uprisings directed against rapacious landlords and moneylenders swept over the nation. Before long proletarian unrest in the big cities became another powerful weapon in the hands of the opponents of foreign rule. In 1928 a series of strikes among textile workers and railroad employees made the task of governing the country still more difficult, while the rise of a radical movement in the northwest led by Abdul Ghafur Khan conjured up the specter of a communist revolution. Even the native bourgeoisie was ready to support a boycott campaign against goods imported from Great Britain.

Above this confusion of parties and slogans stood a universally respected symbol of the civic awakening. To most of his countrymen Mahatma Gandhi was a saint in politics who had made emancipation a secular religion. His hold on the masses derived not only from his indefatigable determination to achieve their liberation, but also from his skill as a compromiser of conflicting ideals. To fire-eating patriots he spoke of the need for national independence; to moderate reformers he preached peaceful non-cooperation. Before proletarian radicals he extolled social justice; before middle-class conservatives he advocated non-violent opposition. Moslems and pariahs heard him condemn the cruelty of caste exclusiveness; Brahmans approved his glorification of the ethical principles of Hinduism. The wizened little ascetic with the quaint crotchets about homespun clothes and frequent fasts also had a sharp eye for political advantage. His doctrine that the nation would have to achieve its freedom not by the use of force but by the refusal to co-operate with the foreign conqueror was more than idealistic; it was shrewd. An armed uprising against Great Britain invited the danger of military defeat. A militant non-violence, on the other hand, was bound to prevail in the long run. Gandhi therefore urged a strategy of passive resistance to English rule:

> What then is the meaning of Non-cooperation in terms of the Law of Suffering? We must voluntarily put up with the losses and inconveniences that arise from having to withdraw our support from a Government that is ruling against our will. Possession of power and riches is a crime under an unjust government, poverty in that case is a virtue, says Thoreau. It may be that, in the transition state, we may make mistakes: there may be avoidable suffering. These things are preferable to national emasculation. We must refuse to wait for the wrong to be righted till the wrong-doer has been roused to a sense of his iniquity. We must not, for fear of ourselves or others having to suffer, remain participators in it. But we must combat the wrong by ceasing to assist the wrong-doer directly or indirectly.[4]

The British authorities found themselves in the predicament of the lion thrown to the Christians. Their opponents actually invited martyrdom. It was hard to decide, moreover, whether a nationalist leader was more dangerous at large or behind bars. In prison he became an object of universal sympathy. But once he was released, he might organize a mass violation of some unpopular ordinance until the jails could no longer hold all the lawbreakers; or he would order thousands of his followers to lie down on railroad tracks thereby disrupting the movement of trains; or he surrounded government buildings with a sea of natives stretched out on the pavement, so that officials had to walk on human bodies in order to get to their place of work. No matter what the government did, it appeared either wicked or foolish. Sometimes the authorities opposed sedition with force, as when in 1919 General Reginald E. Dyer ordered his troops to open fire on a mass meeting in Amritsar. Almost four hundred persons died and three times as many were wounded. But the unfortunate "error of judgment," as a whitewashing army council characterized the affair, only stiffened resistance. Penal measures like the Rowlatt Acts of 1919 and the Public Safety Act of 1929 only proved that the nationalists could not be deterred by prison sentences any more than by bullets. Gandhi was arrested in 1922,

---

[4] M. Gandhi, *Young India* (New York: The Viking Press, 1923), p. 230.

in 1930, in 1932, and in 1933. Each time the subcontinent seethed with demonstrations and riots, while the distinguished prisoner terrified his jailers by embarking on well-publicized hunger strikes. The thought of what would happen if he died on their hands was so disturbing to the British that usually he was freed after only a brief period of confinement.

THE ROAD TO SELF-GOVERNMENT

By the early 1930's the cabinet in London was convinced that there was nothing to do but yield. At first it sought to limit itself to the administrative improvements recommended by an interparty parliamentary commission headed by Sir John Simon. The nationalists, however, refused to settle for a reform plan which avoided any reference to dominion status and which actually enlarged the authority of the viceroy. Prime Minister MacDonald then began to offer further concessions. But in a series of round-table conferences extending from November, 1930, to December, 1932, he discovered that it was impossible to reconcile the conflicting aspirations of Hindus and Moslems, of maharajas and radicals. Resolved at last to cut the Gordian knot, MacDonald issued in March, 1933, a white paper containing the proposal of a federal constitution. The plan was considered and revised by a legislative committee composed of members of both houses of Parliament, and on August 2, 1935, it became law with the passage of a new Government of India Act.

The measure provided for the establishment of eleven provincial administrations under the authority of elected assemblies and responsible ministers. They were to be overseen by appointed governors, who in times of emergency could issue ordinances with the force of law or even veto appropriation bills approved by the legislators. The central government was to consist of a parliament of two houses, chosen partly by election and partly by appointment. The viceroy, however, remained in charge of military defense and foreign affairs, and he continued to hold "reserved powers" in questions of religion, currency, and justice to foreigners. Because it extended the control of native voters over lawmaking and increased the size of the electorate to some thirty-five million persons, the act represented a significant improvement over the Government of India Act of 1919. But it disappointed the advocates of national self-determination by failing to bestow dominion status upon the country.

When the first elections to the provincial assemblies were held in 1937 the Indian National Congress won majorities or pluralities in nine of the eleven provinces. The victory led to a split in its ranks. The militants, under Jawaharlal Nehru and Subhas Chandra Bose, urged a program of noncollaboration with the imperial authorities which was calculated to paralyze the new constitution and force England to grant complete independence. The moderates, led by Rajendra Prasad and supported by Gandhi himself,

562

announced their readiness to form cabinets under the terms of the law, provided the governors agreed not to interfere with the details of daily administration. The British accepted this condition in substance, and for the time being the policy of the middle of the road prevailed.

But when the Second World War broke out the nationalists took advantage of Britain's involvement in hostilities to press anew their demands for self-government. They insisted in the fall of 1939 that the English recognize the right of the country to frame its own constitution. Since the viceroy refused to go beyond a promise that after the war London would consult with them regarding modifications of the Government of India Act of 1935, they adopted a policy of non-cooperation. Although in 1942 Sir Stafford Cripps, speaking for Prime Minister Churchill, gave them assurances of dominion status as soon as peace was restored, they continued to preach opposition to England and non-resistance to Japan. Their hope was that the crown would grant them immediate independence. Instead, Gandhi and Nehru found themselves under arrest, and for the next three years the British continued to rule by armed force over a sullen, restless people.

4 : Southeast Asia

BEYOND THE Brahmaputra River there was a similar national awakening. The lands of southeast Asia were politically less conscious and economically less advanced than their western neighbor, but in the interwar period they too became restive under foreign rule. From the time of its conquest in 1885 until the promulgation of the Government of India Act of 1935 Burma was administratively under the control of the viceroy in New Delhi. Yet even after their separation from India, the Burmese continued to feel the effects of the political storm on the other side of the frontier, and the movement for independence rapidly gained strength.

In French Indo-China the authorities attempted in 1922 to satisfy popular demands for a greater degree of self-determination by adding a number of elected members to the colonial council which assisted the governor-general. Five years later they went a step farther with the establishment of a government council to advise the official hierarchy. Yet the inadequacy of such temporizing measures was revealed in the serious riots which erupted in Tonkin in 1930–31. Although these were promptly suppressed by force, the colony continued to feel the effects of civic discontent among the native masses.

Siam pursued a policy of diplomatic self-assertion and political modernization. Through a series of treaties with the states of the West, the country succeeded in achieving complete tariff autonomy by 1926. A year later came the abolition of extraterritorial jurisdiction. Early in the thirties a group of liberal reformers who had formed the People's party seized control of the government and promulgated a constitution based on the principle of popular sovereignty. When King Rama VII showed himself unhappy with the new course they forced him into exile and replaced him with his ten-year-old nephew, who became Rama VIII. In 1939 they celebrated their accomplishments by renaming the nation Thailand, "the land of the free."

The islands off the coast of southeast Asia were also seized by the anti-imperialistic fever. The Dutch in the East Indies had tried to conciliate the indigenous population by exercising their rule largely through Indonesian princes and headmen. Furthermore, in 1916 they made an effort to adjust to changing political conditions with the establishment of a legislative council possessing advisory powers in military and financial affairs. Soon after the First World War this *Volksraad* was transformed into a representative parliament, receiving authority to pass on all official measures. Then came a thoroughgoing reform of the system of colonial administration, and in 1929 natives were assigned thirty of the sixty seats in the assembly. Still, the seventy million East Indians wanted more than parity with eight million Hollanders in the government of their country. The independence movement won a following among the poverty-stricken peasant masses; socialism and communism began to cast their spell over industrial labor; patriotic demonstrations and violent strikes became common occurrences; and in 1926–27 there were radical uprisings in Java. In the early thirties the authorities reacted to seditious agitation by imprisoning the leading advocates of self-government. Yet the mailed fist only made matters worse. In 1937 the *Volksraad* unanimously petitioned the crown for dominion status within ten years.

As for the Philippines, President McKinley had justified their acquisition by the United States in 1898 on the ground that "there was nothing left for us to do but to take them all, and to educate the Filipinos, and uplift and civilize and Christianize them." Actually, America could no longer Christianize the Filipinos, because the Spaniards had already done so three hundred years before. But it could and did engage in the work of educating and uplifting. The administrators sent out from Washington paved roads, built public schools, and established health clinics, although for a long time they remained silent about the right of self-determination. Finally, in 1916 Congress passed the Jones Act, which promised the colony its freedom "as soon as a stable government can be established therein." It was not until the Tydings-McDuffie Act of 1934, however, that a hard and fast commitment was made to bestow independence on the islands at the end of a decade.

While the Filipinos were awaiting the expiration of this transitional period the Second World War broke out. Its spread to the Far East in 1941 had a far-reaching effect on the growth of political awareness among colonial peoples. For reasons of their own, the armies of the mikado encouraged native patriotism in the regions which they occupied. At first the colored masses, seeing Europeans beaten and humiliated, greeted the Japanese as liberators. They soon discovered, to be sure, that they had merely changed masters. Yet they also remembered that it was possible for Orientals to defeat Occidentals. This realization worked a profound change in their attitude toward imperialistic rule. When Tokyo finally surrendered in 1945 the Westerners prepared to return to their plantations and clubs in the colonies as if nothing had happened. But the time for taking up the white man's burden was over. A new era had begun in southeast Asia.

5 : The Middle East

FOR ISLAM the most important effect of the First World War was the destruction of the symbol of religious unity represented by the institution of the caliphate. Its place was taken by new civic ideals based on geographic and cultural considerations. Since the fifteenth century the empire of the Ottoman Turks had provided Mohammedanism with a measure of political authority corresponding to its spiritual unity. Even after becoming the "sick man of Europe" the Sublime Porte continued to play an important role in international affairs. By 1914 it was the only Moslem government in the world still enjoying political independence. Its defeat on the field of battle marked the end of the theocracy of the dynasty of Osman, and prepared the way for a national reconstruction which completely altered the ideological foundations of the country.

THE NEW TURKEY

While the representatives of Sultan Mohammed VI in Constantinople were signing the humiliating Treaty of Sèvres in 1920, embittered patriots began to rally behind the war hero Mustapha Kemal who had formed a rival government in Angora. Provided with essential supplies by the Kremlin, which saw in him a useful ally against bourgeois imperialism, he reconquered the Armenian provinces of Ardahan and Kars, forced the Italians to evacuate Adalia, persuaded the French to withdraw from Cilicia, and finally inflicted a succession of serious defeats on the armies of Greece. The Entente Powers, in no mood for new military sacrifices in the Middle East, decided to accept the loss of the spheres of influence which had seemed to be in their grasp in 1918. By the Treaty of Lausanne of July 24, 1923, Turkey retained not only all of Asia Minor, but also the strategic straits between the Black Sea and the Aegean, and Eastern Thrace as far as the Maritsa River. Instead of the isolated vassal state which the peacemakers at Versailles had expected to establish in the interior of Anatolia, a mili-

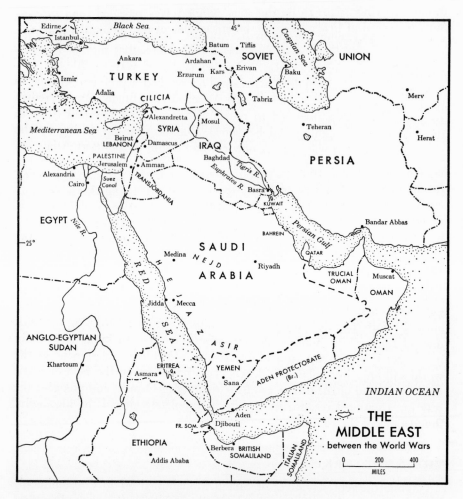

THE
MIDDLE EAST
between the World Wars

tant nation of thirteen million inhabitants emerged as a power to be reckoned with at the crossroads of Europe, Asia, and Africa.

To its victorious leader, however, the defeat of the foreign enemy was only the beginning of a process of civic revival. The old Turkey had been weak, he maintained, because it had made a fetish of tradition. The new must adopt a program of ruthless innovation in order to survive in a world of industrialism. Although in 1923 the nationalists proclaimed the establishment of a democratic republic, in fact Mustapha Kemal with the support of his People's party continued to exercise dictatorial power. Like Peter the Great in Russia two hundred years before, he used his authority to enforce the modernization of the country. First came the complete secularization of national life. In 1924 the caliphate was abolished; in 1925 polygamy was prohibited, religious orders were suppressed, and the fez was outlawed; in 1926 civil marriage was made compulsory; in 1928 the article of the constitution declaring Islam to be the state religion was repealed; and in 1935 Sunday instead of Friday became the official day of rest. Secondly, to hasten the course of Westernization new law codes were promulgated in 1926, based not on the teachings of the Koran but on the theories of European jurisprudence. The Latin alphabet was adopted in place of the Arabic in 1928; women were given the right to vote in 1934; and the use of family names was introduced in 1935. A concerted effort to extend elementary education reduced the rate of illiteracy from 85 per cent before the war to 42 per cent in 1932. Finally, to encourage the growth of manufacturing, the government in 1929 established a protective tariff; in 1934 it published a five-year plan of industrial expansion; in 1936 it enacted a law providing for the compulsory arbitration of labor disputes and regulating the hours and wages of factory employees; and by 1939 it succeeded in buying out the foreign railroad companies which formerly had played an important role in the national transportation system. Patriotic pride was stimulated by Turkifying geographic names—from Constantinople to Istanbul, from Angora to Ankara, from Smyrna to Izmir, from Adrianopole to Edirne. Furthermore, at the international conference in Montreux in 1936 Turkey won the right to fortify the Straits which had been denied by the Treaty of Lausanne, and through negotiation with France in 1939 it acquired Alexandretta in northern Syria. Mustapha Kemal died the year before the outbreak of the Second World War, but his friend and successor, Ismet Inönü, skillfully steered a neutral course in the conflict which raged around him, until in February, 1945, he decided that it was safe at last to declare war against Germany.

PERSIA

Persia, like Turkey, remained on the periphery of Islam. Yet it was separated from its co-religionists not by a new policy of secularization, but by the ancient linguistic barrier between its people and the Ottomans and Arabs. Even more important, its adherence to the Shi'ite form of Moslemism made it suspect in the eyes of its Sunnite neighbors. In 1907 Great Britain and Russia had divided the possessions of the shah into spheres of influence, and in 1915 his freedom of action was further curtailed by a new imperialistic agreement between London and St. Petersburg. With the overthrow of tsarism and the adoption of an anticolonial policy by the communists, the danger of aggression from the north came to an end for the time being. But in 1919 the English attempted to capitalize on the weakness of the Soviet Union by negotiating a treaty which gave them a dominant diplomatic influence in Teheran.

They failed, however, to take into account the force of native nationalism. The Majlis, the legislative assembly, refused to ratify the pact, and in the ambitious army officer Riza Khan the patriots found a leader of ability. Seizing control of the government in 1921, he became first minister of war, then head of the cabinet, and finally ruler as Riza Shah Pahlavi. The example of Mustapha Kemal inspired him to work for the modernization of his country by building railway lines, introducing financial reforms, and improving the system of education. In 1921 he concluded a convention with the Kremlin which freed the Caspian region from Russian domination, and twelve years later a new petroleum concession granted to the Anglo-Persian Oil Company provided his treasury with at least five million dollars annually in taxes and royalties. To signalize the opening of a new epoch for his kingdom he altered its name in 1935 to Iran.

Unfortunately, during the Second World War the shah overplayed his hand. When hostilities broke out he could not resist the temptation to play both ends against the middle. While flirting with the fascists, he also tried to ingratiate himself with the Allied camp. It was a dangerous game. In August, 1941, British and Russian troops crossed the frontier, forced the abdication of the shah, replaced him with his son Mohammed Riza Pahlavi, and remained in occupation until after the defeat of the Axis.

THE GROWTH OF ARAB NATIONALISM

The most significant development in the Middle East was taking place among the Arab countries. For more than five hundred years the people of this region had been politically subservient to the Ottomans, and before them to the Seljuks. But once the grip of the sultanate began to relax in the years after the Berlin Congress, new civic ideals arose on the sandy plains between Syria and Morocco. Sometimes their spokesmen were tribal chieftains, who saw in the slogans of freedom and unity a means of realizing personal ambitions. Sometimes they were Westernized intellectuals—lawyers, journalists, and teachers—familiar with the doctrines of nationalism and liberalism through study in European institutions of learning. Sometimes they were officers and bureaucrats in the service of the government in Constantinople, embittered by the inefficiency of Turkish rule. Whatever their motives, they shared a common belief that the liberation of their people from foreign domination would usher in a new era of national greatness for the Arabs.

When the First World War began the English proceeded to use this growing native patriotism for their own purposes by inciting the sheiks of the Arabian peninsula to an insurrection against the Turks. Thus, the British high commissioner in Egypt, Sir Henry McMahon, urged the sherif of Mecca, Hussein, to take up arms against the sultan in return for a promise of territorial independence: "I am convinced that this declaration will assure you beyond all possible doubt of the sympathy of Great Britain towards the aspirations of her friends the Arabs and will result in a firm and lasting alliance, the immediate results of which will be the expulsion of the Turks from the Arab countries and the freeing of the Arab peoples from the Turkish yoke."

The strategy followed by Downing Street proved effective. Its agents, among them the colorful Colonel Thomas E. Lawrence, succeeded in fomenting an uprising among the Arabs which contributed significantly to the successful outcome of the campaign waged by the Entente Powers in the Middle East. Once hostilities were over, however, the British discovered that in encouraging the rise of native nationalism they had helped create a political movement with a will of its own. The truth was that the victorious powers had not really wanted to establish self-governing countries on the ruins of the Ottoman Empire. What they hoped for was a complex of satellite states, nominally autonomous, actually dependent. Even while the war was still in progress and McMahon was painting pictures of liberation before Hussein, Sir Mark Sykes for England and Georges Picot for France concluded a secret agreement to divide the lands between the Mediterranean Sea and the Persian Gulf into spheres of influence. It was impossible to harmonize such completely contradictory commitments, although the peacemakers meeting at San Remo in the spring of 1920 bravely tried to square the circle. They recognized the independence of the Arabian peninsula. Egypt, under British occupation for more than thirty years, had officially become a protectorate of the crown a few months after the outbreak of the war. And the remaining Turkish possessions south of Anatolia were partitioned between the United Kingdom and France in the form of mandates, that is, territories to be trained for political independence at some unspecified time in the future. London received the lion's share with Iraq, Palestine, and Transjordania, but Syria and Lebanon, which went to Paris, were certainly no mean prize. As they contemplated their diplomatic handiwork, both Lloyd George and Clemenceau could take pride in the important gains which they had won in the Orient.

The Arabs were less pleased. Convinced that the statesmen of the West had cheated them, they decided to assert their rights by force. The English were compelled by demonstrations and riots to recognize the independence of Egypt in 1922; and they made the same concession to native nationalism in Iraq in 1927 and in Transjordania in 1928. Yet treaty provisions which gave Britain an important voice in the military and financial affairs of these countries left them subject to a high degree of foreign control. The French in Syria and Lebanon were even less conciliatory, and after failing to reach an agreement with the independence party they fell back in 1939 on the traditional methods of rule through the professional bureaucracy.

Nationalism, however, continued to make headway not only in the sovereign kingdoms and mandated territories, but also farther west in such older colonial possessions as Tripoli, Algeria, Tunisia, and especially Morocco, where for years Abd el-Krim stood off the armies of France and

Spain. In their personal ambitions and civic ideologies the native leaders were often bitterly divided. Some, like King Fuad of Egypt, accepted the principle of parliamentary government; others, like King Ibn Saud of Saudi Arabia, were benevolent despots pure and simple. There was Shukri el-Quwatli in Syria who talked of a Pan-Arab association of governments; and there was Emir Abdullah in Transjordania who seemed to be essentially a tribal particularist. A few, like the mufti of Jerusalem, Haj Amin el-Husseini, found something to admire in fascism; an even smaller group, which included the Iraqi reformer, Kamil Chadirchi, preached a vague socialism. What held them together despite this diversity of social philosophies was their opposition to alien domination.

THE ZIONIST MOVEMENT

The political situation in the Middle East was complicated by a fierce three-cornered conflict between Englishman, Arab, and Jew for the control of Palestine. Zionism, the movement seeking to re-create a Jewish state in the Holy Land, was a product of the nationalist doctrines current in Europe in the last years of the nineteenth century. Its leader, Theodor Herzl, argued that his people could escape persecution only by forming an independent community of their own in the country which they had left almost two thousand years before. Although invoking the traditional belief of Judaism in an eventual return of the children of Israel to their ancestral home, his ideology was actually modern and secular. At first it seemed to have but little chance of success. Not only was the Sublime Porte suspicious of any schemes for a large-scale immigration of foreigners, but European Jewry itself had serious misgivings about them. The pious were indeed convinced that some day they would be led back to Canaan, but this miracle would be the work of the Messiah, not of some worldly political organization. The liberals sought to end religious discrimination through parliamentary reform in their native countries. And the radicals hoped that a socialist revolution would emancipate all oppressed minorities.

THE STRUGGLE FOR PALESTINE

It was the First World War which transformed the Utopian vision of a handful of dreamers into an actuality. In order to enlist the support of Jewish opinion, British Secretary of State for Foreign Affairs Arthur J. Balfour announced on November 2, 1917: "His Majesty's Government view with favour the establishment in Palestine of a National Home for the Jewish people, and will use their best endeavours to facilitate the achievement of this object." While his assurances strengthened the position of England as long as hostilities were going on, they led to serious difficulties once peace returned. During the interwar period the Jews of central and eastern

Europe, victimized by the anti-Semitism of the authoritarian régimes, began to enter Palestine in growing numbers. In 1922 there were 83,790 of them in the Holy Land; in 1932, 180,793; in 1940, 463,535. The Moslem population in the same years numbered 589,177, 771,174, and 947,846. It still constituted a sizable majority of all inhabitants, but its lead was dwindling. The Arabs therefore insisted that Great Britain prohibit further immigration, and when the government hesitated to accede to their wishes, they proceeded to take the law into their own hands.

A confused political struggle ensued. When the authorities tried to restrict the admission of prospective settlers, the Zionists would organize violent demonstrations. When they consented to open the gates, the Mohammedans would riot. Both communities agreed that the English should withdraw from the mandate as soon as possible. In 1937 a royal commission headed by Lord Peel recommended that the country be partitioned among the two rival nationalities and the United Kingdom. But while the World Zionist Congress expressed cautious approval of the plan, the Pan-Arab Congress rejected it unconditionally, convinced that "the richest zone is to be given to the Jews, the holiest to the British, and the most barren to the Arabs." Two years later a new proposal provided for the creation of a united, independent state which was to safeguard the interests of each ethnic group, but which was also to limit the entry of immigrants. Parliament approved the scheme by a narrow margin, but this time neither the Jews nor the Arabs were willing to accept it. Palestine was approaching chaos, when war broke out in Europe. Zionism at once resolved to support Great Britain against fascist Germany, while Islam maintained an attitude of sullen neutrality. For six years the question of the Holy Land remained in abeyance, until the surrender of the Axis raised it again in an even more intense form.

6 : Africa

SINCE THE middle of the nineteenth century Africa had been the classic land of colonialism. In the Dark Continent tribal governments and armies were altogether primitive, while economic and social institutions were hopelessly backward. The great powers could therefore pose with some justification as the champions of a higher way of life which would bring lasting benefits to the Africans as well as the Europeans. At an international conference which met in Berlin in 1884–85 they solemnly agreed "to protect the natives in their moral and material well-being; to coöperate in the suppression of slavery and the slave trade; to further the education and civilization of the natives; to protect missionaries, scientists, and explorers."

Nevertheless, the pious declarations about uplifting the Negro were largely ignored during the scramble for overseas possessions which followed the meeting. The native masses soon discovered that while the conquerors spoke self-sacrificingly about the white man's burden, what they were really interested in was the black man's burden. But at least the ideal of an altruistic colonial administration survived. In Paris in 1919 the leading statesmen of the Entente Powers spoke of their imperialistic acquisitions as "a sacred trust of civilization," whose purpose was the education and development of peoples "not yet able to stand by themselves under the strenuous conditions of the modern world." Similarly, a parliamentary commission from the United Kingdom which visited East Africa in 1925 expressed the belief that "the status of trusteeship involves an ethical conception, that is to say, it imposes upon the trustee a moral duty and a moral attitude."

COLONIALISM IN THE DARK CONTINENT

In actual practice, colonialism meant first of all the development of natural resources and the improvement of shipping facilities. With a population of some one hundred and forty million people and with an area of eleven million square miles, almost equal to that of Europe and North America combined, Africa began to play a highly important role in the economy of the world. The palm oil and palm kernel of British West Africa, the cotton of the Sudan and Uganda, the cacao of Nigeria and the Gold Coast, the peanuts of Senegambia, the rubber of the Belgian Congo, and the gold of the Transvaal were exported in increasing volume from the Dark Continent to the four corners of the earth. The rise in the output of agriculture and mining made necessary an expansion of the transportation system. Even before the First World War ended it become possible to travel from Cape Town to Cairo by rail and water with only two short breaks. In 1931 came the completion of the first transcontinental railroad, running from Beira in Mozambique through Northern Rhodesia and Katanga Province of the Belgian Congo to Benguela in Angola. In 1920 Sir Helperus van Ryneveld and Sir Christopher Brand completed a flight from Egypt to the Union of South Africa, while at the same time Major Joseph Vuillemin of France was flying from Algiers to Gao on the Niger River and then to Dakar on the Atlantic Ocean. Later that year the Sahara was crossed by motor; the feat was repeated in 1923; and in 1929 a route from Algiers to Lake Chad was opened. The problem of sending goods through deserts and jungles continued to hamper the economic growth of the interior of Africa; but the locomotive, the automobile, and the airplane were providing a promising solution.

The material progress of the Dark Continent benefited the white man more than the black. For the most part, the Negro remained an exploited menial laborer living in a twilight zone between tribal barbarism and an alien civilization. Deprived of the sense of belonging which he had known as a savage, yet also barred from equal participation in the way of life of his conqueror, he became the spiritual victim of colonialism. The imperialistic states, however, were not entirely blind to his needs. Missionary organizations and philanthropic societies of which he had never heard were pleading his cause in high places. As early as the colonial conference of 1884–85 an effort was made to persuade the great powers to control the sale of liquor and firearms to Africans, although the only result was a vague statement about the desirability of regulating these traffics.

With the First World War came a new resolve to work for the welfare of the black man. The international agreement of 1919, which restricted the sale of weapons and the manufacture of intoxicants, could perhaps be considered a measure of self-defense on the part of the whites. But the antislavery convention of 1926, signed by twenty governments, was genuinely motivated by humanitarian considerations. And then there were the schools,

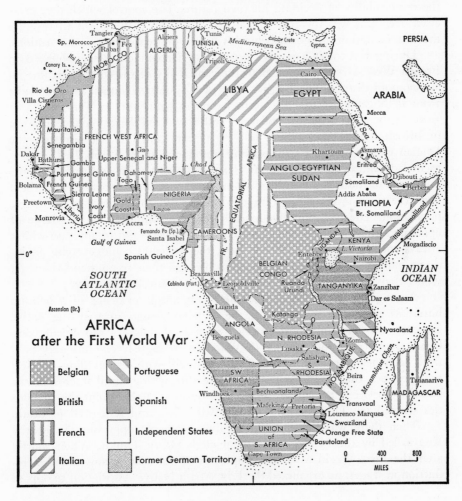

AFRICA after the First World War

Belgian | Portuguese
British | Spanish
French | Independent States
Italian | Former German Territory

libraries, hospitals, and orphanages, the suppression of tribal warfare, the improvement of agricultural techniques, and the reduction of the mortality rate. In the course of a single lifetime a tropical world was transplanted from the stone to the atomic age. Cities replaced kraals; factories rose where forests had grown. Never before had such a fundamental transformation of an entire continent been compressed into such a brief span of time.

IMPERIALISTIC RULE

The price of this swift advance was racial friction, because the relationship of the European to the African was that of master to servant. The colonial powers agreed that colored peoples should be governed in a spirit of benevolence, but not under conditions of political self-determination. The black man was too close to the jungle, they insisted, to be entrusted with the responsibility of deciding his own future. The control which they exercised over him was therefore dictatorial, although they sought to disguise the fact of authoritarianism behind a façade of representative institutions.

During the 1920's a partly-elective superior council was established in French West Africa, while Dakar, the capital city of the colony, became an autonomous district. The English formed a legislative council in Uganda in 1920; in Nigeria in 1921; in Sierra Leone in 1924; and in Tanganyika in 1926. At the same time they enlarged and liberalized the colonial legislature of British East Africa, which in 1920 was renamed Kenya. In 1922 the Belgian Congo received a measure of autonomy under a policy of governmental decentralization. Even the Portuguese in Angola and the Spaniards in Guinea introduced administrative improvements in the thirties. Still, there was little room in this benign imperialism for self-government by the native population. The representative assemblies were composed by and large of appointed members possessing only advisory powers, and in any case whites always constituted a majority. At best, the delegates could exercise an indirect influence over the administration through their recommendations. At worst, they degenerated into rubber stamps of the bureaucracy.

Among the masses of Africa there was ample evidence of a pent-up bitterness toward the whites. In the Belgian Congo in 1921 the native carpenter Simon Kimbangu founded a mystical religious movement combining exotic rites and apocalyptic visions with vaguely revolutionary political doctrines. At first he contented himself with expounding Biblical passages, but then his tone became more threatening, until it crossed the boundary between preaching and rabble-rousing. At that point the authorities stepped in. The prophet was arrested, tried, and sentenced to death.

Then there was the agitation against economic oppression in nearby Kenya, led by the Negro government clerk Harry Thuku. When shortly after the First World War the employers of the colony announced a reduction in wages, he organized the East Africa Native Association to oppose the exploitation of the black man. But the temptation to proceed from the criticism of labor conditions to an attack on imperialistic injustice was too much for him. In 1922 he, too, was placed under arrest on charges of sedition. The outcome was a wave of riots which did not end until some of the participants had been killed and their stormy leader deported.

Most important in the long run, however, was the growing conviction among educated natives that the position of colored peoples could be improved only through concerted civic action. In 1919 a Pan-African Congress called a conference in Paris to discuss ways and means of emancipating colonial lands. The charter of liberties which it drafted demanded from the great powers better educational opportunities, improved economic conditions, and greater political rights. It even urged the League of Nations to take the lead in the work of anti-imperialistic reform. Subsequent meetings continued to advance similar proposals throughout the interwar period.

RACIAL CONFLICTS

Yet the moment was not ripe for the emancipation of the Dark Continent. For one thing, the African who had only recently emerged from tribalism was in most cases unprepared to cope with the political complexities of national independence. For another, the great powers had no intention of surrendering their overseas possessions. As a matter of fact, they tried to encroach on those native states which had managed to retain their freedom. Liberia, for example, despite its participation in the First World War on the side of the victors and its membership in the League of Nations, was essentially little more than a dependency of the United States, or better still, of the Firestone Rubber Plantation Company. During the twenties the government in Monrovia had negotiated a loan of five million dollars from the company, which left it so completely at the mercy of its creditor that when the world depression came more than half of its annual revenue was absorbed by interest and amortization payments. The result was national bankruptcy. Although a more favorable financial agreement was worked out in 1935, the Negro republic remained in economic bondage to foreign rubber interests.

Ethiopia lost its independence altogether. In the early 1920's England and Italy had planned to partition the country into spheres of influence, but the support of France saved it for the time being. The accession of Emperor Haile Selassie in 1930 seemed to usher in a new era of enlightened reform. He promulgated a constitution, established a representative parliament, modernized the administration, improved education, suppressed slavery, and reorganized the army. But the very success of the program of Westernization hastened his downfall. Mussolini in Rome, who had long planned to round out his possessions in east Africa, did not propose to wait until his intended victim became strong enough to resist aggression. On Octo-

575

ber 3, 1935, Italian troops from Eritrea and Somaliland invaded the neighboring kingdom and remained as conquerors for six years. They were finally driven out during the Second World War by the armies of the United Kingdom, and in the spring of 1941 Addis Ababa welcomed back from exile its plucky little monarch.

The most violent conflict of interest between black and white developed in the Union of South Africa. There Europeans had settled in larger numbers than anywhere else in Africa, but their community was divided by the hostility between Englishman and Boer. Differing in speech, culture, outlook, and occupation, the two nationalities could not overcome the prejudices arising out of past struggles. And in the background were the Negro masses, outnumbering their masters four to one. Although dependent on the Occidentals for their livelihood, they little by little began to demand civic rights and economic improvements.

The British were by and large in favor of a conciliatory attitude toward the natives, while the Afrikaners insisted on an uncompromising policy of racial inequality. The two dominant minorities were at loggerheads, moreover, over such questions as the degree of governmental co-operation with the authorities in London, the use of Afrikaans as an official language on a par with English, and the replacement of the Union Jack with the old flag of the Transvaal, the *Vierkleur*. At first there were successful attempts to establish political collaboration between them. Such prominent public figures as Louis Botha and Jan Smuts, who had fought against Queen Victoria during the Boer War, formed the South African party advocating loyalty to her grandson, George V, in the First World War. But more and more of their compatriots were attracted to the Nationalist party, led by hard-bitten extremists like James Hertzog and Daniel Malan. In its ranks they talked loudly of secession from the British Empire, vowing to keep the Negroes in their place and flaunting the racialist slogan, "South Africa a white man's land!" It was an atmosphere ominously reminiscent of the American South before the Civil War.

When hostilities broke out in 1914 the Boers generally supported Great Britain, although a handful of irreconcilables under Christian de Wet and Christian Beyers did organize a rebellion, which was easily suppressed. After the war the moderates under Smuts continued to rule the country. But in 1924 the Nationalist party in alliance with the Labor party won a decisive victory at the polls. The white trade-unions, convinced that the government was in sympathy with the employers and fearful of the competition of cheap colored labor, gave their votes to Hertzog. They were rewarded two years later with the promulgation of the Color-Bar Bill excluding blacks from those skilled occupations which the Europeans considered their preserve.

Throughout the twenties Englishman and Afrikaner continued to argue about how closely the national flag should resemble that of the United Kingdom, and whether the national anthem should be "God Save the King" or "Die Stem van Suid-Afrika." But in 1933 hard times forced the major parties to form a coalition in order to combat the depression. The price which the racialists demanded for their co-operation was more discrimination against "God's stepchildren." In 1936 the Representation of Natives Act deprived the Negroes of the right to vote in the Cape Province. As a consolation prize they received the privilege of electing three whites to represent their interests in the federal legislature, and twelve out of twenty-two delegates to a council possessing advisory powers in native affairs. The collaboration between the moderates and the extremists continued until 1939, when the outbreak of war reawakened their latent political differences. After the legislative assembly voted eighty to sixty-seven to sever relations with Germany, a divided country took its stand beside the United Kingdom.

The Second World War quickened the forces of independence through-out the colonial world. The north coast of Africa was invaded by contending armies, but below the Sahara the struggle of the great powers produced an economic boom which stimulated self-confidence among the blacks. More important, the ideal of humanitarian fraternalism which the democracies preached and the defeat of the racialism advocated by the totalitarian states aroused new hopes in the slums of the native quarter. Finally, Asia's gains in the struggle against imperialism encouraged the colored races everywhere to resist foreign domination. The Dark Continent was still unable to defend its vital interests against the West. Yet it was slowly approaching the day of spiritual and material emancipation which William Pitt the Younger had prophesied in his speech of April 2, 1792, before the House of Commons:

> If we listen to the voice of reason and duty, some of us may live to see a reverse of that picture, from which we now turn our eyes with pain and regret. We may live to behold the natives of Africa en-gaged in the calm occupations of industry, in the pursuits of a just and legitimate commerce. We may behold the beams of science and philosophy breaking in upon their land. Then we may hope that even Africa shall enjoy at length those blessings which have descended so plentifully upon us in a much earlier period of the world.

Further Reading

The two most influential works on imperialism are John A. Hobson, *Imperialism: A Study* (New York: Macmillan, 1948), and V. I. Lenin, *Imperialism: The Highest Stage of Capitalism* (New York: International Publishers, 1939), both of them highly critical interpretations. For less rigid sociological analyses see R. Maunier, *The Sociology of Colonies*, 2 vols. (London: Routledge, 1949), and Joseph A. Schumpeter, *Imperialism and*

Social Classes (New York: Meridian M4, 1955). Kenneth S. Latourette, *A History of the Expansion of Christianity,* 7 vols. (New York: Harper, 1937–45), considers the connection between missionary activity and the colonial movement. E. M. Winslow, *The Pattern of Imperialism* (New York: Columbia Univ. Press, 1948), looks at the theoretical bases of overseas expansion, while E. Fisher, *The Passing of the European Age* (Cambridge, Mass.: Harvard Univ. Press, 1948), deals with the revival of the Orient. F. S. C. Northrop, *The Meeting of East and West* (New York: Macmillan, 1946), and Arnold J. Toynbee, *Civilization on Trial* (New York: Meridian M52, 1958), describe the cultural interaction of diverse peoples.

Good general accounts of the civic and economic problems of the Far East may be found in H. M. Vinacke, *A History of the Far East in Modern Times* (New York: Crofts, 1941); G. F. Hudson, *The Far East in World Politics* (New York: Oxford Univ. Press, 1937); Claude A. Buss, *War and Diplomacy in Eastern Asia* (New York: Macmillan, 1941); Bruno Lasker, *Asia on the Move* (New York: Holt, 1945); and Owen Lattimore, *The Situation in Asia* (Boston: Little, Brown, 1949). The following are sound histories of the republican régime in China: Owen and Eleanor Lattimore, *The Making of Modern China* (New York: Norton, 1944); N. Peffer, *China: The Collapse of a Civilization* (New York: Day, 1930); A. N. Holcombe, *The Spirit of the Chinese Revolution* (New York: Knopf, 1930); H. F. MacNair, *China in Revolution* (Chicago: Univ. of Chicago Press, 1931); and H. Gannes, *When China Unites* (London: Dent, 1938). H. A. Van Dorn, *Twenty Years of the Chinese Republic* (New York: Knopf, 1932), is valuable for non-political developments, and R. R. Pollard, *China's Foreign Relations, 1917–1931* (New York: Macmillan, 1933), deals with diplomatic affairs. L. Sharman, *Sun Yat-sen* (New York: Day 1934); E. T. Clark, *The Chiangs of China* (Nashville: Abingdon-Cokesbury, 1943); and Robert Payne, *Mao Tse-tung* (New York: Schuman, 1950), are solid biographical studies. E. O. Reischauer, *Japan: Past and Present* (New York: Knopf, 1946), and C. D. Carus and C. L. McNichols, *Japan: Its Resources and Industries* (New York: Harper, 1944), are excellent introductions to the modern development of Japan. H. E. Wildes, *Japan in Crisis* (New York: Macmillan, 1934), and A. M. Young, *Imperial Japan, 1926–1938* (New York: Morrow, 1938), describe the rise of militarism in Tokyo. For the growth of the Japanese economy see also K. L. Mitchell, *Japan's Industrial Strength* (New York: Knopf, 1942).

T. Walter Wallbank, *India* (New York: Holt, 1948), and *India in the New Era* (Chicago: Scott, Foresman, 1951), are useful surveys. A. Duncan, *India in Crisis* (London: Putnam, 1931); J. Coatman, *India: The Road to Self-Government, 1908–1940* (New York: Norton, 1942); and R. P. Dutt, *The Problem of India* (New York: International Publishers, 1943), portray the struggle for political independence. Louis Fischer, *Empire* (New York: Duell, 1943), attacks the British position in India, while F. Whyte, *India:*

A Bird's-Eye View (New York: Oxford Univ. Press, 1943), defends it. On economic affairs in the subcontinent there are V. Anstey, *The Economic Development of India* (New York: Longmans, 1932), and D. R. Gadgil, *The Industrial Evolution of India in Recent Times* (London: Oxford Univ. Press, 1942). Krishnalal J. Shridharani, *The Mahatma and the World* (New York: Duell, 1946), and Louis Fischer, *Life of Mahatma Gandhi* (New York: Harper, 1950), are admiring biographies of the saintly leader. He speaks for himself in Mohandas K. Gandhi, *Gandhi's Autobiography: The Story of My Experiments with Truth* (Boston: Beacon BP35, 1957). The following are important books about southeast Asia: Bruno Lasker, *Peoples of Southeast Asia* (New York: Knopf, 1944); Erich H. Jacoby, *Agrarian Unrest in Southeast Asia* (New York: Columbia Univ. Press, 1949); C. Du Bois, *Social Forces in Southeast Asia* (Minneapolis: Univ. of Minnesota Press, 1949); Robert I. Crane, *Aspects of Economic Development in South Asia* (New York: Institute of Pacific Relations, 1954); and B. Harrison, *South-East Asia* (New York: St. Martins, 1954).

H. A. R. Gibb, *Islamic Society and the West* (New York: Oxford Univ. Press, 1951); George Lenczowski, *The Middle East in World Affairs* (Ithaca: Cornell Univ. Press, 1952); and H. L. Hoskins, *The Middle East* (New York: Macmillan, 1954), are first-rate works. The modernization of Turkey is described in H. E. Allen, *The Turkish Transformation* (Chicago: Univ. of Chicago Press, 1935), and D. E. Webster, *The Turkey of Atatürk* (Philadelphia: American Academy, 1939). The best biography of the Westernizing Turkish dictator is D. von Mikusch, *Mustapha Kemal* (Garden City: Doubleday, 1931). On Iran see L. P. Elwell-Sutton, *Modern Iran* (London: Routledge, 1941), and R. N. Frye, *Iran* (New York: Holt, 1953). There are several good histories of the Arab world, among them B. Thomas, *The Arabs* (Garden City: Doubleday, 1937); Philip K. Hitti, *The Arabs* (Chicago: Regnery, Gateway 6033, 1956); and G. E. Kirk, *A Short History of the Middle East* (Washington: Public Affairs Press, 1949). For the growth of nationalism in the Middle East they should be supplemented with G. Antonius, *The Arab Awakening* (Philadelphia: Lippincott, 1939). A. Bonné, *The Economic Development of the Middle East* (New York: Oxford Univ. Press, 1945), and Doreen Warriner, *Land and Poverty in the Middle East* (London: Royal Institute of International Affairs, 1948), are significant studies of the economic problem. The rise of Zionism and the struggle for Palestine are examined in H. M. Kallen, *Zionism and World Politics* (Garden City: Doubleday, 1921); M. Samuel, *On the Rim of the Wilderness* (New York: Liveright, 1931); E. Sereni and R. E. Ashery, *Jews and Arabs in Palestine* (New York: Hechalutz Organization, 1936); and J. M. N. Jeffries, *Palestine* (New York: Longmans, 1939).

W. Fitzgerald, *Africa: A Social, Economic and Political Geography of Its Major Regions* (London: Methuen, 1945), is a handy guide to the Dark Continent. R. L. Buell, *The Native Problem in Africa,* 2 vols. (New York:

Macmillan, 1928); M. H. Hailey, *African Survey* (New York: Oxford Univ. Press, 1945); W. E. B. Du Bois, *The World and Africa* (New York: Viking, 1947); and A. Campbell, *The Heart of Africa* (New York: Knopf, 1954), deal with the conflict of black and white. For economic questions there are T. S. Githens and C. E. Wood, Jr., *The Food Resources of Africa* (Philadelphia: Univ. of Pennsylvania Press, 1943); A. W. Postel, *Mineral Resources of Africa* (Philadelphia: Univ. of Pennsylvania Press, 1943); and J. A. Noon, *Labor Problems of Africa* (Philadelphia: Univ. of Pennsylvania Press, 1944). S. H. Roberts, *History of French Colonial Policy, 1870–1925,* 2 vols. (London: King, 1929), and G. Padmore, *How Britain Rules Africa* (New York: Lothrop, 1936), are sound treatments of colonial administration. On the racial problem in South Africa see J. H. Hofmeyr and J. P. Cope, *South Africa* (London: Benn, 1952); L. Marquard, *The Peoples and Policies of South Africa* (New York: Oxford Univ. Press, 1952); and G. H. Calpin (ed.), *The South African Way of Life* (New York: Columbia Univ. Press, 1953).

Chapter 29

NEW PATTERNS OF CULTURE

THE GREAT political and economic transformation which followed the French Revolution brought with it important cultural innovations. Even amid the wars which overthrew benevolent despotism there were those who realized that the outlook of their society was undergoing a fundamental change. And only ten years after Waterloo the aging poet Johann Wolfgang von Goethe complained to the musician Karl Zelter of the restlessness of the new age:

> Wealth and speed are the things the world admires and for which all men strive. Railways, express mails, steamboats, and all possible means of communication are what the educated world seeks. . . . Actually this is the century of clever minds, of practical men who grasp things easily, who are endowed with a certain facility, and who feel their own superiority to the multitude, but who lack talent for the most exalted tasks. Let us as far as possible retain the ideals in which we were raised. We and perhaps a few others will be the last representatives of an era which will not soon return.[1]

With an old man's conviction that in his youth everything had been better, the great writer grumbled about the advent of industrialism which was changing the familiar landscape of Europe. For regardless of the material benefits which the progress of technology promised, it was destroying the placid world of enlightened princely absolutism in which he had grown up.

1 : The Scientific Image of Nature

THE CULTURE of the new century was bound to be affected by the common experiences of its society. The temper of ancient Hellas had been

---

[1] *Goethes Briefe* (50 vols.; Weimar: H. Böhlaus, 1887–1912), XXXIX, 216. Trans. by Theodore S. Hamerow.

shaped by the tradition of the Greek city-state with its fierce municipal loyalty. In the Middle Ages the constant preoccupation with the problem of salvation, the constant admonition *memento mori* ("remember that you must die") reflected the harshness of life on this earth. The confidence in the perfectibility of man and society characteristic of the Age of Enlightenment arose out of the stable political conditions introduced by the benevolent despots. As for the intellectual climate of opinion which prevailed after 1815, it was influenced by two major historic experiences, the progress of science and the growth of industrialism. One provided a new interpretation of nature and of man; the other created new cultural problems and demands. Formerly the arts and letters developed in an atmosphere of religious certainty and aristocratic patronage. Now they had to adjust to a world in which the scientist rather than the theologian answered questions about the cosmos, and in which the masses rather than the patriciate determined the canons of taste. The accompaniment of revolutionary changes in the production and distribution of material goods was thus a revolutionary change in the form of culture.

THE PROGRESS OF SCIENCE

The scientific image of the universe was completed in the nineteenth and twentieth century. To the astronomical discoveries of the age of Copernicus and the physical discoveries of the age of Newton was added a new understanding of force and matter. Hermann von Helmholtz and James Joule analyzed the relationship between heat and energy. Michael Faraday demonstrated that the rotation of a metal core within a magnetic field produced a flow of electricity. James Maxwell and Heinrich Hertz advanced the view that a fundamental unity existed between the waves of light and electricity. The examination of the chemical composition of matter by scientists like Jöns Berzelius and Dmitri Mendeleev showed that there is a fixed number of elements out of which all substance is created, and that the atom is the smallest unit of each element possessing its basic characteristics. Toward the end of the nineteenth century a new field of research was opened when Wilhelm Röntgen, Henri Becquerel, and Pierre and Marie Curie initiated the study of radiation, the emission of rays by such rare substances as radium and actinium. Finally, in the years preceding the First World War physicists like J. J. Thomson, Ernest Rutherford, and Niels Bohr provided evidence that the atom itself is composed of electrical particles, some with positive, others with negative charges, all revolving about each other at enormous speed and with vast force.

While chemistry and physics were discovering the cosmic forces underlying the behavior of matter, geology was advancing new theories about the origin of the world. When in the seventeenth century Archbishop James Ussher concluded that the earth had been created in the year 4004 B.C., his system of chronology was accepted and reprinted in the margins of the Authorized Version of the English Bible. Although even in his own day there were skeptics who scoffed at his views, it was not until two hundred years later that a systematic study of the evolution of the world was undertaken. To be sure, as early as 1785 James Hutton in his *Theory of the Earth* emphasized the importance of observation in geological research, and insisted that in the investigation of such phenomena as plant fossils and rock strata "no powers are to be employed that are not natural to the globe, no action to be admitted except those of which we know the principle." Yet geology achieved recognition as a science only after the appearance in 1830–33 of the *Principles of Geology* by Sir Charles Lyell. A work of popularization designed for the general public as well as the savant, it presented a naturalistic account of the formation of the earth. Contemporaneously, scholars like Alexander von Humboldt and Karl Ritter were laying the foundation of physical geography. By the time Henry M. Stanley wrote his famous account of how in 1871 he found David Livingstone in darkest Africa, the prevalent view of the geological and geographical environment of man had become completely transformed. After 1900 even the frozen wastes of the Arctic and the Antarctic were explored and charted.

The study of the nature of life aroused even greater popular interest. Perhaps the most important advance in the field of biology was the demonstration of the cellular structure of organic existence by Theodor Schwann and Matthias Schleiden. Out of it developed modern medical science, which in the course of a century almost doubled life expectancy in the West. The germ theory of disease owed its acceptance to the work of two brilliant pathologists, one a Frenchman, the other a German, united in a common dedication to the progress of knowledge. Louis Pasteur contributed to the growth of preventive medicine by analyzing the nature of microscopic organisms and demonstrating their relationship to human illness. Robert Koch proved that the same kind of microbe invariably caused the same sickness, and devised a technique for preparing pure cultures of bacteria which could be used for experimental study. The first effective use of an anesthetic was made in 1846 by the Boston dentist William T. G. Morton, and about twenty years later Joseph Lister introduced the practice of antiseptic surgery. Meanwhile, the studious monk Gregor Mendel was discovering the basic laws of heredity and publishing his findings in an obscure scientific journal in Brünn in Moravia. The embryologist Johann F. Meckel propounded the challenging hypothesis that the development of the organism during the period of gestation recapitulates the biological history of the species, a hypothesis which proved to be only partially true. And the outstanding botanist of the century, Wilhelm Hofmeister, conducted important investigations of the development of plant life and the process of its reproduction.

THE THEORY OF EVOLUTION

The scientific theory which made the deepest impression on the nineteenth century was the achievement of the retiring, hard-working naturalist Charles Darwin (1809–1882), who applied himself to the study of the evolutionary growth of living species. The notion that organic existence developed from the simple to the complex in the course of adaptation to a changing environment had long been familiar. Aristotle in the ancient world, Albertus Magnus in medieval times, and Francis Bacon and Gottfried von Leibnitz in the early modern period had suggested that the forms of life were not immutable. More recently the philosopher Immanuel Kant, the morphologist Georges de Buffon, and the zoologist Jean de Lamarck had advanced the doctrine of biological evolution. What Darwin therefore did was not to propound a new theory, but to present a new explanation of the way in which that theory operated.

From the demographic teachings of Thomas Malthus, Darwin concluded that in the animal kingdom as in human society the expansion of population invariably tended to exceed the increase in food supply, and that there was consequently a constant struggle for existence in nature by which the fit triumphed and the unfit perished. The gradual accumulation of those characteristics which enable the survivors to adjust to changing conditions produced in time new species. In what was to become perhaps the most influential book of the nineteenth century, *On the Origin of Species by Means of Natural Selection,* Darwin expressed his views in a language which must have sounded formidable even to dedicated scholars:

> If under changing conditions of life organic beings present individual differences in almost every part of their structure, and this cannot be disputed; if there be, owing to their geometrical rate of increase, a severe struggle for life at some age, season, or year, and this certainly cannot be disputed; then, considering the infinite complexity of the relations of all organic beings to each other and to their conditions of life, causing an infinite diversity in structure, constitution, and habits, to be advantageous to them, it would be a most extraordinary fact if no variations had ever occurred useful to each being's own welfare, in the same manner as so many variations have occurred useful to man. But if variations useful to any organic being ever do occur, assuredly individuals thus characterised will have the best chance of being preserved in the struggle for life; and from the strong principle of inheritance, these will tend to produce offspring similarly characterised.

Darwin himself was forced to admit that "my volume cannot be mere light reading, and some part must be dry and even rather abstruse"; while his publisher stated in confidence that he found the theory of evolution "as absurd as contemplating the fruitful union of a poker and a rabbit." Yet the work turned out to be a huge success not only among biologists, but also with the general educated public. What accounted for this popularity more than its scientific validity was its implication for economic and political life. To a generation of rugged individualists it offered a justification of the ethic of competition which supposedly insured the survival of the fittest. Indeed, in the hands of an astute systematizer like Herbert Spencer the doctrine of the struggle for existence became part of a civic faith. Industrialists could invoke it to oppose governmental regulation. Chauvinists found in it a divine endorsement of aggressive diplomacy. Imperialists and racialists were delighted with what they interpreted to be a vindication of the inherent superiority of the white man over the yellow and the black. And militarists were now more convinced than ever that only through war would the manly virtues triumph over sloth and decrepitude.

For the traditional theological outlook of the Occident, however, the theory of evolution was a serious challenge. By maintaining that in the course of countless millennia man had evolved from lower forms of life, Darwin contradicted the orthodox view that he had been created in the image of God at some fixed point in time. The struggle between science and religion, or rather between Darwinians and anti-Darwinians, raged furiously for about fifty years. Proselytizing naturalists, notably Ernst Haeckel and Thomas H. Huxley, preached the evolutionary gospel with an apostolic zeal. Opposed to it were eminent clergymen, among them Bishop Samuel Wilberforce of the Church of England, who once in the course of a public debate with Huxley coolly asked his learned opponent whether he was descended from an ape on his grandmother's or his grandfather's side. Their strictures, moreover, were endorsed by devout laymen like the American statesman William Jennings Bryan, widely known for his espousal of such lost causes as free silver, anti-imperialism, and fire-and-brimstone theology. Still, the weight of biological evidence was on the other side, and little by little the churches began to accept new interpretations of the origin of humanity. Catholicism allowed its communicants to construe the Book of Genesis figuratively, provided that they accepted the doctrine that at a specific moment in the process of gradual creation man was endowed with an immortal soul. Protestantism divided into a modernist and a fundamentalist wing, the former ready to make peace with science by an allegorical exegesis of the Bible, the latter insisting on the literal truth of every word of the Good Book.

THE NEW VIEW OF THE UNIVERSE

Even among the theological bitter-enders opposition to the theory of evolution became less rigid after the opening of the twentieth century. For scientific teachings were now increasingly regarded with an unquestioning respect which had formerly been reserved for religious doctrines. As a matter of fact, the laboratory probably inspired an even greater faith than the church, since its miracles were occurring in the present and its promises were being fulfilled in this world. Not only was it producing in ever greater abundance such necessities of life as food, clothing, and shelter, but through devices like the radio, the automobile, the motion picture, and the television set it was revolutionizing the way of life of human society. There seemed to be no end to the wonders emerging out of the test tube. The enlistment of the techniques of science in the service of economic progress was making possible a swiftly-rising level of material welfare. And the scientist himself was no longer a lonely genius experimenting in the attic of his home with primitive apparatus which he had bought at his own expense. In most cases he had become a highly trained, well-paid technician, hired by some great corporation to produce a tonic for the removal of dandruff or a fuel for guided missiles. The disciplined application of talent in physics, chemistry, and biology had in effect created an assembly-line method of experimentation by which invention could be made to order.

There was a growing gap in science between practical invention and theoretical investigation. The former continued to turn out new products and new models, until the appetite of the consumer had to be stimulated by the mumbo jumbo of the advertising profession. The latter, however, presented a picture of a cold, frightening universe in whose enormous vastness the individual dwindled into nothingness. The earth on which he lived became a mere speck floating through space around a star called the sun, which was only one of billions of stars constituting a galaxy named the Milky Way, which was only one of perhaps a million or more galaxies whose distances from each other were too great to envision. The matter with which he came in contact every moment of his life was not really the familiar solid substance it appeared to be, but rather an agglomeration of countless tiny particles known as electrons, protons, and neutrons. These in turn were nothing more than blobs of congealed energy which under certain conditions could assume a completely incorporeal form. Even the laws of atomic physics proved to be only statements of statistical probability. Finally, Albert Einstein advanced the bewildering theory that such fundamental categories as time, space, and mass were merely relative, so that a voyager in a rocket moving away from the solar system at a very high velocity would never grow old, while the weight of an athlete running at a sufficiently great speed would reach a ton.

The man in the street was clearly incapable of understanding the evidence supporting this image of the cosmos. For that matter, the average scientist in industry looking for some new detergent in which the housewife could wash dishes without roughening her hands was not always familiar with the findings of theoretical investigation. Indirectly, however, the world became conscious of the wild forces ruling its destiny and sensed their implication for human existence. Medieval man, sunk in poverty and ignorance, could find a source of strength in the knowledge that he was the greatest achievement of creation. God and Satan were locked in eternal combat for the possession of his soul. He mattered. But there was no such comforting certainty for man in the twentieth century. He had to contemplate a universe which was neither friendly nor hostile but simply indifferent, a universe in which his own position had become insignificant. He had to wrestle with the doubts aroused by science, which the empiricist thinker Bertrand Russell described:

> That man is the product of causes which had no prevision of the end they were achieving; that his origin, his growth, his hopes and fears, his loves and his beliefs, are but the outcome of accidental collations of atoms; that no fire, no heroism, no intensity of thought and feeling can preserve an individual life beyond the grave; that all the labours of all the ages, all the devotion, all the inspiration, all the noonday brightness of human genius are destined to extinction in the vast death of the solar system, and that the whole temple of man's achievement must inevitably be buried beneath the debris of a universe in ruins—all these things, if not quite beyond dispute, are yet so nearly certain that no philosophy which rejects them can hope to stand.[2]

2 : The Scientific Image of Society

THE EFFECTIVE application of the scientific method to natural phenomena suggested its value for a study of social institutions. Why could not the accumulation and classification of data lead to as precise an understanding of the community as of the universe? The achievements of the laboratory technique in the manipulation of inanimate matter seemed to promise equally impressive results in the reorganization of human society. Before long there arose a widespread demand for the creation of a science of man. Its most influential spokesman was the philosopher Auguste Comte (1798–1857), who had received his education in a polytechnical institute in Paris and had then become a teacher of mathematics. Yet the task which was closest to his heart was the improvement of humanity. A true son of the

---

[2] Bertrand Russell, "A Free Man's Worship," *Mysticism and Logic* (London: George Allen & Unwin Ltd., 1936), p. 44.

nineteenth century, he shared its passion for philanthropic reform and its respect for scientific investigation. Out of the basic cultural impulses of his age he formed a new philosophy of civilization known as positivism.

POSITIVISM

Essentially, Comte believed that in the course of its development every science, including that of man, had to pass through three distinct cultural levels. In the first, which he described as theological, natural events were explained in terms of the unpredictable actions of mythical gods and spirits. Then came the metaphysical state, when the questions posed by human experience were analyzed in abstract theories divorced from constructive action. Finally, thought entered the scientific or positivistic phase, in which observation and experimentation led to the discovery of fundamental laws. The world now stood on the threshold of the third stage. But while physicists, chemists, and biologists were solving the riddles of nature, the systematic study of civic problems was lagging behind. It was this deficiency which the founder of positivism proposed to make good:

> Though involved with the physiological, Social phenomena demand a distinct classification, both on account of their importance and of their difficulty. They are the most individual, the most complicated, the most dependent on all others; and therefore they must be the latest,—even if they had no special obstacle to encounter. This branch of science has not hitherto entered into the domain of Positive philosophy. Theological and metaphysical methods, exploded in other departments, are as yet exclusively applied, both in the way of inquiry and discussion, in all treatment of Social subjects, though the best minds are heartily weary of eternal disputes about divine right and the sovereignty of the people. This is the great, while it is evidently the only gap which has to be filled, to constitute, solid and entire, the Positive Philosophy. Now that the human mind has grasped celestial and terrestrial physics,—mechanical and chemical; organic physics, both vegetable and animal,—there remains one science, to fill up the series of sciences of observation,—Social physics.[3]

For Comte himself, positivism offered a blueprint of the good society. Temporal power would be concentrated in the hands of industrialists, bankers, and landlords, while a priesthood composed of social scientists rather than orthodox clergymen was to minister to the spiritual needs of mankind. He even worked out in detail a new religious cult complete with

---

[3] *The Positive Philosophy of Auguste Comte,* trans. by Harriet Martineau (2 vols.; London: Kegan Paul, Trench, Trübner & Co., 1893), I, 6.

theologians, saints, sacraments, and sacred writings, a kind of "Catholicism without Christianity." While few were ready to embrace this manufactured faith, the summons to study society with the same dispassionate precision as nature found a sympathetic hearing in scholarly circles.

THE SOCIAL SCIENCES

Positivism contributed directly to the development of the social sciences. These represented an attempt to examine the structure of society by means of statistical and comparative techniques. For more than two thousand years efforts to analyze civic institutions had been made in such works as Plato's *Republic*, Aristotle's *Politics*, Machiavelli's *Prince*, Jean Bodin's *Commonwealth*, and Hugo Grotius' *Law of War and Peace*. What distinguished the new school was its methodology borrowed almost bodily from the natural sciences. Behind it stood the assumption that the universe of matter and the community of man were essentially similar, so that the means employed to achieve an understanding of one could be applied with minor modifications to the other in order to discover constant laws of development.

Out of positivistic doctrines arose the discipline known as sociology, concerned with an analysis of the forces governing human society through the examination of social data. Frédéric Le Play was the author of more than thirty monographs dealing with the way of life of the working class of Europe; Charles Booth undertook a voluminous study of the *Life and Labour of the People in London;* and Herbert Spencer in England, Paul von Lilienfeld in Russia, Albert Schäffle in Germany, and Ludwig Gumplowicz in Poland applied biology and especially the theory of evolution to the process of civilization. At the same time anthropology was initiating the comparative study of culture designed to define the influence of heredity and environment on community institutions. In 1871 Edward Tylor, the first professor to teach the new subject at Oxford University, published his *Primitive Culture: Researches into the Development of Mythology, Philosophy, Language, Art, and Custom,* which for more than a generation remained the standard textbook in the field. Scholars like Jacques Boucher de Perthes, Sir John Lubbock, Lewis H. Morgan, and William Graham Sumner were gathering and classifying primitive artifacts or conducting investigations of the development of human beliefs. In economics the champions of laissez faire had for a century been preaching the primacy of natural law. But now their theories, which were basically a compound of logic and metaphysics, began to retreat before the empirical method of Alfred Marshall, the evolutionary approach of Gustav von Schmoller, and the statistical technique of William Stanley Jevons, who went so far as to maintain that a mathematical connection could be demonstrated between sunspots and business depressions. As for the traditional study of political philosophy, it came to be replaced by the new political science, whose students produced analytical accounts of national life like James Bryce's *American Common-wealth* or systematic examinations of corporate associations like Otto von Gierke's *Natural Law and the Theory of Society.*

Under the influence of positivism the traditional ties between the study of history on the one hand and literature, philosophy, and theology on the other began to weaken. As early as 1824 Leopold von Ranke, perhaps the greatest of modern historians, expressed the credo of a new historiography in the preface to his *Histories of the Romance and Teutonic Peoples:* "History has had assigned to it the task of judging the past, of instructing the present for the benefit of the ages to come. To such lofty functions this work does not aspire. Its aim is merely to show what actually occurred." Ranke himself was too discriminating a scholar not to perceive the fundamental difference between the historical and the natural disciplines. But after the middle of the nineteenth century historians began to create a science of history. They examined source materials, studied archaeological remains, gathered statistical data, weighed conflicting evidence, and published their findings in detailed monographic works buttressed by voluminous footnotes and vast bibliographies which only the specialist could appreciate. The result, they believed, was pure truth free from the personal prejudices and social predispositions which had marred scholarship in the past. Their attitude was that of the eminent medievalist, N. D. Fustel de Coulanges, who told an enthusiastic audience during one of his lectures: "Do not applaud me. It is not I that speak to you but history that speaks by my mouth." The employment of rigorous standards of judgment did, as a matter of fact, destroy many of the superstitions which earlier ages had accepted without question. Yet it also helped create a myth of its own, the myth that history can be apprehended directly by dispassionate study rather than indirectly through the mind of the historian. The will-o'-the-wisp of total objectivity could not transform the analysis of the past into an exact science, but it was to a large degree responsible for the growing gulf between the intelligent reading public and professional learning.

Even deeper was the effect of scientific progress on theology. Not only did scholarly hypotheses like the theory of evolution challenge ecclesiastical doctrines, but the technique of empirical investigation could be turned against religion itself by means of the so-called higher criticism. The comparative study of supernatural beliefs tended to encourage a theological relativism. James Frazer in his study of primitive superstitions and ceremonies entitled *The Golden Bough* (1890) shocked the devout by boldly asserting: "It is now easy to understand why a savage should desire to partake of the flesh of an animal or man whom he regards as divine. By eating the body of the god he shares in the god's attributes and powers. And when the god is a corn-god, the corn is his proper body; when he is a wine-god, the juice of the grape is his blood; and so, by eating the bread and drinking the wine, the worshipper partakes of the real body and blood of his god."

EUROPEAN CIVILIZATION
In the 19th Century (To 1913)

MILES 0   50   100   200   300

Number of volumes in public or institutional libraries
of cities about 1880

Over 2,000,000 volumes
500,000 to 2,000,000
200,000 to 500,000

Important scientific centers about 1900, as shown by
award of Nobel prizes in science 1901-1913

⊙ Two or more   ⊡ One

Odessa   Location of university founded during
1865   19th Century, with date of founding

•   Birthplace outside city

——   Boundaries in 1871

ROMANTICISM
To about 1850

REALISM AND POSITIVISM
After 1850
Advance of science and
vogue of science
Evolutionary ideas

**MODERNIZATION OF UNIVERSITIES
AND FOUNDATION OF NEW ONES**
Professionalization of research

IMPRESSIONISM IN THE ARTS
After about 1860
Primarily in France

**POST-IMPRESSIONISM,
EXPERIMENTATION, FUNCTIONALISM,
MODERN DESIGN**
After 1900

NOR
Bergen
1825

Ibser
1828

SCOTLAND

Glasgow   Edinburgh
Scott, 1771
Carlyle,
1795
Wordsworth,
1770

North

Sea

Belfast
Kelvin, 1824   ENGLAND

IRELAND

Dublin   Manchester   Leeds
G. B. Shaw,   1851   1887   Tennyson,
1856   1809
Yeats, 1865   Liverpool
Joyce, 1882   Darwin,   Spencer,
1809   1820
Aberystwith   Macaulay,
1872   R. Owen,   1800
1771

Cambridge
Oxford   Lister,
Bristol   1827
1876   Malthus,   London
1766   1828
Coleridge,   Turner, 1775
1772   Hardy,   Dickens,   Byron, 1788
1840   1812   Shelley, 1792
Keats, 1795
Newman, 1801
J. S. Mill, 1806
Browning, 1812

HOLLAND   G
Amsterdam
The Hague   Leiden   Hand

Maeterlinck,   Van Gogh,   Heine,   Götti
1862   1853   1797
Ghent
1817   Louvain   Marburg
Brussels
1834   Bonn
BELGIUM   1818   Wü

LUX.   Darmstadt,
Matisse,   Marx,   Heidelberg
1869   1818
Flaubert,   Verlaine,   Heg   Stu
1821   Nancy   1844   Strassburg   Ein
Tocqueville,   Poincaré,
1805   1854   Tübingen
Renan,   Chateaubriand,   Seine   Debussy,   Paris   Fourier, 1772   Freib
1823   1768   1862   St. Simon, 1760   Hugo, 1802
Corot, 1796   Proudhon, 1809
Michelet, 1798   Besançon   Cuvier,   Burckhard
Gobineau, 1816   1769   Zü
Baudelaire, 1821   Pasteur,   Bern
Loire   Manet, 1832   1822   SWITZERLA
Degas, 1834
Balzac,   Monet, 1840   Lamartine,
1799   Rodin, 1840   1792   A L
Zola, 1840   Lyon   Milau
Gauguin, 1848   1808   Manzoni
Renoir,   P. Curie, 1859   1785
1841   Bergson, 1859   Berlioz   Turin   Po
Gide, 1869   1803   Stendhal,
Proust, 1871   1783
FRANCE   Genoa
Ingres,   Mazzini
1780   1805
Bay of   Toulouse   Comte,   Guizot,
1798   1787   Cezanne,
Biscay   Toulouse-   1839
Lautrec,   Marseille
Unamuno,   1864   1854
Altamira   1864   Daumier,
Discovery of Old   1808
Stone Age cave   PYRENEES   CORSICA
paintings, 1879

SPAIN   SARDINIA

PORTUGAL
Duero

Madrid
Santayana,
Tagus   1863

Lisbon   BALEARIC ISLANDS

Guadiana

Mediter

Guadalquivir

Malaga
Picasso,
1881

From R. R. Palmer, *Atlas of World History* (Chicago, 1957), pp. 106-07.

• Bjornson,
1832
ristiania

SWEDEN

Sibelius,
1865

Helsinki
1828

St. Petersburg

Stravinsky,
1882

Rimsky Korsakov,
1844

Upsala

Stockholm
1878
Strindberg,
1849

Dorpat
1802

Mussorgsky,
1835

Bakunin,
1814

Gorki
1868

Moscow 1799
Pushkin, 1799
Dostoievsky, 1821
Kropotkin, 1842

RK

Copenhagen
Kierkegaard,
1813

Baltic

Danzig
Schopenhauer,
1788

Niemen

Mickiewicz,
1798

RUSSIA

Tolstoy,
1828

Lenin,
1870
(200 miles
east)

Düina

Turgeniev,
1818

Tchaikovsky,
1840
(In the Urals)

M A N Y

Berlin
1809
Tieck,
1773

Oder

Halle

Leipzig
Wagner,
1813

Dresden

Fichte,
1762

Breslau

Freytag,
1816

Hauptmann,
1862

Warsaw
Chopin, 1810
Mme. Curie,
1867

CARPATHIANS

Kharkov
1804

Gogol,
1809

Dnieper

Vistula

Cracow

Freud,
1856

Dniester

Prague

AUSTRIA

Dvorak,
1841

Jassy
1860

Odessa
1865

Danube

Vienna
Schubert, 1797
J. Strauss, 1825

Budapest

Cluj
1872

HUNGARY

RUMANIA

Black

enice

Bologna

Rossini,
1792

Leopardi,
1798

d'Annunzio,
1863

Croce,
1866

Rome

ITALY

Adriatic Sea

Belgrade
1863

SERBIA

Danube

Sea

Sofia
1888

OTTOMAN

Constantinople
Robert College
(American)
1863

EMPIRE

40°

Naples

Excavations at
Troy 1871 ff.

yrrhenian

Sea

Ionian

Sea

GREECE

Athens
1837
Schools of Classical
Archeology:
French, 1846
German, 1874
American, 1881
British, 1886
Italian, 1910

Palermo

SICILY

an

Sea

CRETE

David Friedrich Strauss subjected the Bible to a critical analysis, concluding that "an account is self-contradictory when one relation of events says what the other denies, as when one account makes Jesus appear definitely only, after the arrest of the Baptist in Galilee, but the other after he had already worked for some time in Galilee as well as in Judea." Ernest Renan who had at one time studied for the priesthood lost his professorship at the Collège de France because his *Life of Jesus* portrayed the founder of Christianity as a saintly but human figure. Such attacks were bound to weaken the fabric of theology. A sensitive poet like Matthew Arnold, lonely in a world suddenly deprived of religious certitude, could only mourn the loss of his belief:

> *The sea of faith*
> *Was once, too, at the full, and round earth's shore*
> *Lay like the folds of a bright girdle furl'd;*
> *But now I only hear*
> *Its melancholy, long, withdrawing roar,*
> *Retreating to the breath*
> *Of the night-wind down the vast edges drear*
> *And naked shingles of the world.*[4]

PSYCHOLOGY AND PSYCHOANALYSIS

The methodology of science was applied to man himself. Within twenty years after the enunciation of the evolutionary hypothesis Wilhelm Wundt was initiating the experimental study of the mind in a laboratory in Leipzig and publishing his pioneer work, *The Principles of Physiological Psychology*. Not long thereafter Ivan Pavlov began the observations of the behavior of dogs which enabled him to stimulate in his subjects conditioned reflexes, that is, forms of physical reaction independent of the reflective will. The investigation of such automatic physiological activities contributed to the rise of the school of behaviorism led by John B. Watson, who argued that mental processes can be understood solely in terms of the structure and activity of the body. On the other hand, members of the Gestalt school like Wolfgang Köhler and Kurt Koffka maintained that living organisms respond primarily not to simple physical stimuli but to total patterns of experience.

The most important advance toward an understanding of the mind, however, was made by the Viennese physician Sigmund Freud (1856–1939). In the last years of the nineteenth century he developed a technique known as psychoanalysis for dealing with emotional disturbances. From his clinical

---

[4] "Dover Beach," *The Poetical Works of Matthew Arnold* (New York: Thomas Crowell, 1897), p. 214.

experience he gradually arrived at a radically novel explanation of the mechanism of human behavior. At the heart of his theory was the view that the conduct of the individual is vitally affected by irrational impulses of which he is unaware because they are to a large extent subconscious. The repression of these instinctive drives, if severe enough, could lead to a psychological breakdown. More commonly it resulted in such maladjustments as phobias, compulsions, and complexes. In any case, the basic problem of the morbid personality was the conflict between conscience and desire which the trained diagnostician could help resolve:

> We come to the conclusion, from working with hysterical patients and other neurotics, that they have not fully succeeded in repressing the idea to which the incompatible wish is attached. They have, indeed, driven it out of consciousness and out of memory, and apparently saved themselves a great amount of psychic pain, *but in the unconscious the suppressed wish still exists,* only waiting for its chance to become active, and finally succeeds in sending into consciousness, instead of the repressed idea, a disguised and unrecognizable surrogate-creation ... to which the same painful sensations associate themselves that the patient thought he was rid of through his repression. This surrogate of the suppressed idea—the symptom—is secure against further attacks from the defenses of the ego, and instead of a short conflict there originates now a permanent suffering. We can observe in the symptom, besides the tokens of its disguise, a remnant of traceable similarity with the originally repressed idea; the way in which the surrogate is built up can be discovered during the psychoanalytic treatment of the patient, and for his cure the symptom must be traced back over the same route to the repressed idea. If this repressed material is once more made part of the conscious mental functions—a process which supposes the overcoming of considerable resistance—the psychic conflict which then arises, the same which the patient wished to avoid, is made capable of a happier termination, under the guidance of the physician, than is offered by repression.[5]

The image of man presented by psychoanalysis was essentially a secularized version of the view of orthodox Christianity. Both saw in the human spirit dark passions threatening to drown out the voice of reason. Both saw in intelligence only a thin veneer disguising "the submarine jungle of the half-conscious" with its wild, mysterious yearnings. For Freud as for Calvin, the curse of original sin and the total depravity of the soul were terrible realities. The sense of guilt found by scientific study to be at

---

[5] Sigmund Freud, "The Origin and Development of Psychoanalysis," *American Journal of Psychology,* XXI (1910), 195–96.

the root of so many mental disorders had been familiar to religion for two thousand years. The medical description of amoral drives at grips with the sense of propriety suggested the theological account of the struggle between will and intellect, instinct and morality. And was there really a great deal of difference between the psychoanalyst's couch and the priest's confessional?

As a therapeutic technique in the treatment of emotional illness psychoanalysis proved extremely valuable. Although many of the theories advanced by its founder were eventually rejected even by his own disciples, in particular Carl G. Jung and Alfred Adler, it remained fundamental for an understanding of the disordered personality. Yet by a curious irony the rational investigation of the mind proved only its irrationality. Gone was the hope that the progress of knowledge would subdue passion and create a brave new world of universal understanding. For two hundred years it had inspired great achievements in science, until science revealed that the road to truth eventually led back to the starting point. With Freud the circle was completed. In the spiritual universe of phobias and neuroses which the earnest young doctor discovered St. Augustine and Martin Luther would have felt perfectly at home.

CULTURAL PESSIMISM

Similarly, the psychological effect of the scientific study of society was not certainty but doubt. The questioning of accepted beliefs weakened the moral axioms which had provided the community with its scale of values. The sexual taboos recognized in Europe as universally valid were found to be ignored with impunity in Samoa. The competitive drive which the rugged individualism of America had assumed to be inherent in mankind could not be discovered among the Pueblo Indians. Standards of conduct thus lost their traditional meaning, and the result of an examination of established social norms without reference to a subjective system of truth was the rise of emotional insecurity.

Perhaps that was why so many of the attempts to synthesize the mass of information which scholarship had adduced concerning culture were conceived in a spirit of pessimism. During the French Revolution the philosopher Condorcet, outlawed and in hiding, could rise above his personal misfortune to announce in *The Progress of the Human Mind* that "nature has placed no bounds on the perfecting of the human faculties." For the twentieth century such a faith in the capacity of man for self-improvement became impossible. In Italy Vilfredo Pareto was emphasizing the irrational sources of political conduct in his *The Mind and Society* (1916). In Germany Oswald Spengler's *Decline of the West* (1918–22) was one long jeremiad about the imminent disintegration of the civilization of the Occident. In England Arnold Toynbee thought he saw a chance of salvation for modern society in a new dedication to religious truth, although his monumental *Study of History* (1934–54) did not sound very hopeful about the likelihood of such a conversion. Even in America, the most prosperous of nations, the sociologist David Riesman was warning his countrymen that their hunger for social approbation had largely displaced the inner strength which their ancestors had possessed. And the world in the meantime anxiously continued to search for some new statement of values which could give an ethical meaning to the social truths discovered by the scientific method.

3 : Philosophic Thought

FOR ABOUT fifty years after his death in 1804 Immanuel Kant dominated philosophic thought in the West. The bookish little professor from provincial Königsberg led a successful revolution against the empiricism which had ruled metaphysics for more than a century. To the argument that only physical experience could provide the raw material of thought he replied by drawing a sharp distinction between two categories of knowledge. He was prepared to render to Caesar the things that are Caesar's by conceding that scientific investigation was an effective instrument for the establishment of truth in the realm of natural phenomena. But he also insisted on the existence of another realm, the realm of feelings, judgments, and values, in which an instinctive understanding or "practical reason" supported the validity of religious and ethical principles.

IDEALISM

Essentially, idealism, as Kant called his system of philosophy, sought to create a universe of spiritual meaning lying beyond the reach of the critical weapons which the empiricists had used with devastating effect against traditional moral and theological assumptions. It translated into a cardinal doctrine the charming sentiment expressed by Blaise Pascal over a hundred years before: "The heart has its reasons, which reason knows nothing of." Thereby it helped release a torrent of intuitive, even mystical speculation in all branches of thought. And hence to his admirers the author of the *Critique of Pure Reason* (1781) remained "the presiding genius of the spiritual life," while his critics went on arguing that "he was a mere misfortune."

There could be no gainsaying, however, that in the early years of the nineteenth century his authority was enormous. All the powers of faith and imagination which had been held in check by the rigidity of empiricism were suddenly liberated in a great outpouring of idealistic thought. Johann

Gottlieb Fichte depicted life as an endless struggle for perfection in which the individual rose to new heights of moral strength by overcoming the forces of evil. F. W. J. von Schelling saw man and nature united in a common process of growth from lower to higher forms, from the unconscious to the conscious, from the amoral to the moral. Friedrich von Schlegel maintained that the ultimate aim of philosophy must be to perfect the inward life of the individual by the development within his mind of a sense of the divine. Nor were the Germans the only ones to rebel against the mechanical formulas of the Age of Enlightenment, although central Europe did gain a deserved reputation as the classic land of metaphysical speculation. In England such eminent writers as Samuel Taylor Coleridge and Thomas Carlyle fell under the spell of the new idealism. In France political writers like Louis de Bonald and Benjamin Constant questioned the doctrines of rationalism. Even on the other side of the Atlantic in far-off New England the transcendentalists—among them Ralph Waldo Emerson and Henry David Thoreau—preached that "within man is the soul of the whole; the wise silence; the universal beauty, to which every part and particle is equally related; the eternal one."

Idealism achieved its most lasting influence through the work of G. W. F. Hegel (1770–1831). Before the crowds of students who flocked to his lectures at the University of Berlin the brilliant philosopher expounded his analysis of political and social development in the light of an intuitive metaphysic. History to him was not a sum of discrete chance events but the concrete expression of a logical process originating in the divine will. It could be comprehended in terms of opposing spiritual principles which as thesis and antithesis were constantly in conflict until united in a higher synthesis, which in turn became a new thesis evoking a new antithesis and then merging in a new synthesis. This dialectical progression would continue until the end of time, but meanwhile it was evolving the ideals of justice, freedom, and virtue. As for the state, it was the institution which made possible and gave form to the forces of morality. Indeed, it was itself the embodiment of ethical values through which the individual could achieve union with the realm of eternal truth: "The State is the Divine Idea as it exists on earth. . . . It is the Idea of Spirit in the external manifestation of human will and its Freedom."

The bureaucracy of Prussia, delighted to learn that it was only one step removed from the angels, bestowed honors on the eminent scholar who defended its authority with such fervor. Yet it would be a mistake to consider Hegel simply a defender of the status quo. His emphasis on the rational foundation of existing political institutions was pleasing to a conservative ruler like Frederick William III. But his view that the essential characteristic of the historical process was change had progressive connotations. In the hands of Karl Marx it was even turned into a philosophic defense of revolutionary violence. In the final analysis, his thought was neither reactionary nor radical but authoritarian. The young men who hung on every word which the master uttered in the classroom did not understand the full meaning of what they were hearing. Only a hundred years later did the fascists and the communists reveal the implications of his doctrine that the heroic leader must bend the masses to his will:

> World-historical men—the heroes of an epoch—must, therefore, be recognised as its clear-sighted ones; their deeds, their words are the best of that time. Great men have formed purposes to satisfy themselves, not others. Whatever prudent designs and counsels they might have learned from others, would be the more limited and inconsistent features in their career; for it was they who best understood affairs; from whom others learned, and approved, or at least acquiesced in—their policy. For that Spirit which had taken this fresh step in history is the inmost soul of all individuals; but in a state of unconsciousness which the great men in question aroused. Their fellows, therefore, follow these soul-leaders; for they feel the irresistible power of their own inner spirit thus embodied.[6]

THE CRISIS IN PHILOSOPHY

Hegel was the last of the philosophic giants like Plato or St. Thomas Aquinas or Descartes who attempted to create a vast, all-embracing system of thought. Those who came after him were less daring because they were less confident. Bewildered by the complexity of the image of the universe which science was forming, they tended more and more to exalt emotion over reason, instinct over intellect. Since in the realm of nature they encountered only a cold immensity, their interest turned inward to the contemplation of their own consciousness. While idealism still reigned supreme in the universities, Arthur Schopenhauer was propounding the gloomy doctrine that man was the victim of an irrational will which drove him to incur suffering in a vain search for happiness. In his delusion he could not perceive that his lot on earth was simply "a striving without rest and without respite, a willing and a striving that may well be compared to an unquenchable thirst."

Before the century was over, Friedrich Nietzsche had launched his attack on conventional ethics in such works as *Beyond Good and Evil* and *Thus Spoke Zarathustra*, strange mélanges of mystical vision and poetic insight with a pinch or two of philosophy. The sickly erudite who spent the last years of his life in a state of complete mental collapse prophesied the

---

[6] G. W. F. Hegel, *Lectures on the Philosophy of History*, trans. by J. Sibree (London: George Bell, 1890), p. 32.

destruction of the accepted standard of values which protects the weak against the strong, and anticipated the reorganization of society by a new race of ruthless supermen free from the shackles of a slave morality: "What is good?—Whatever augments the feeling of power, the will to power, power itself, in man. What is evil?—Whatever springs from weakness. What is happiness?—The feeling that power increases—that resistance is overcome. Not contentment, but more power; not peace at any price, but war; not virtue, but efficiency. . . . The weak and the botched shall perish: first principle of our charity. And one should help them to it. What is more harmful than any vice?—Practical sympathy for the botched and the weak —Christianity."[7]

That the retreat from rationalism in philosophy did not neccessarily lead to a pessimistic outlook was demonstrated by Henri Bergson, whose lectures at the Collège de France cast a spell over an entire generation of French students. His view that the *élan vital,* the instinctive life urge implanted in the human subconscious, dominated the activity of man was not far removed from Schopenhauer's assertion of the primacy of will over reason. He was even ready to subordinate scientific knowledge to intuitive truth, because "we cannot sacrifice experience to the requirements of any system." Yet he found hope in his belief in "creative evolution," a mysterious elemental force carrying mankind onward to more perfect forms of existence. It was a poetic rather than a philosophic concept, and the language in which he described it had an appropriately lyrical quality: "The animal takes its stand on the plant, man bestrides animality and the whole of humanity, in space and in time, is one immense army galloping beside and before and behind each of us in an overwhelming charge able to beat down every resistance, and clear the most formidable obstacles, perhaps even death."

At the same time a group of American thinkers, among them Charles S. Peirce, William James, and John Dewey, were elaborating in a more prosaic mood the main tenets of pragmatism or instrumentalism. Making a virtue of necessity, they rejected as impracticable the search for absolute value. For them the true was not some eternal, immutable essence enthroned in the empyrean. It was variable; it was temporary; it was relevant to a practical human situation. Hence, the test of an idea or an institution was the effect which it produced in actual experience, in other words, whether it worked. The mind had to create and shape its own truth, because "to bid the man's subjective interests be passive till truth express itself from out the environment, is to bid the sculptor's chisel be passive till the statue express itself from out the stone."

---

[7] F. W. Nietzsche, *The Antichrist,* trans. by H. L. Mencken (New York: Alfred A. Knopf, 1927), pp. 42–43.

Still, pragmatism was a faith for the bold. What most men wanted from philosophy was what philosophy had traditionally given them, a sense of certainty. In the world of the twentieth century, however, it could no longer satisfy their need. The fault was not entirely the philosophers', who were as active and contentious as ever, perhaps more so. Among them were Neo-Aristotelians and Neo-Kantians, Platonists and Thomists, Phenomenologists and Fictionists, mystical idealists and logical positivists. But the clearest symptom of the philosophic distemper was the vogue of existentialism, a doctrine of despair which began to flourish after the Second World War. Assuming that the primary experience of life was frustration in an alien environment, it preached a standard of conduct in accordance with an inner sense of right. Through it man could at least face the hostile universe proudly, although in the struggle against destiny he was doomed to defeat. There was a good deal of pretentiousness about the youths who gathered in the arty Parisian cafés on the left bank of the Seine, drank cognac, grew beards, and played at being existentialists. Yet even their attitudinizing was a manifestation of the crisis of conscience through which their age was passing.

4 : Religion

THE DILEMMA of philosophy was bound to have a direct effect on theology. The great religions of the East—Hinduism, Mohammedanism, and Buddhism—had always exalted faith over reason. For them, therefore, the problem of understanding a changing universe in terms of a traditional belief was not critical. Besides, the masses of their followers continued to live in a social environment which was relatively stable, so that they did not have to grapple constantly with the moral uncertainty arising out of sudden political and economic innovation. But since the West had committed itself to a new way of life built on technological progress, Christianity was forced to adapt its ancient doctrines to a fundamentally altered order of society. The task was not unfamiliar to a theological system which had matured in the world of antiquity, which had learned to exercise a strong influence over medieval institutions, which had even succeeded in reaching an accommodation with the absolute monarchy. In the age of science and industry, however, it had to face a greater challenge than any of the past. Now its opponents were not barbaric chieftains like Attila the Hun or ambitious emperors like Henry IV, but secular ideologies like nationalism, socialism, fascism, and materialism. What made them so formidable was their reliance on spiritual rather than physical force, on those same techniques of moral suasion and logical demonstration which the church had previously employed with such success. In other words, they were basically new religions with a morality and salvation of their own, competing with older creeds for men's souls.

THE REVIVAL OF FAITH

In 1815, when peace finally returned to a Europe exhausted by twenty years of war and revolution, the climate of opinion was distinctly favorable to a religious revival. A generation of thinkers brought up in the theological indifferentism of the Age of Enlightenment had gone through a terrible experience which had shaken its confidence in human reason. In a chastened mood it began under the Restoration to preach a return to ancient beliefs. Philosophic idealism provided a theoretical foundation for this renaissance of faith, while political conservatism encouraged a spirit of piety which made the task of reactionary government easier.

True, there were some liberal theologians like Friedrich Schleiermacher who criticized accepted formulas, maintaining that "the usual conception of God as a single being outside of the world and behind the world, is not the beginning and end of religion, but only a way of expressing it that is seldom entirely pure and never adequate." But far more typical were the traditionalists seeking to recapture a departed medieval spirituality. They included Friedrich von Hardenberg, better known by his pen name as Novalis, Joseph de Maistre, Louis de Bonald, William Wordsworth, and, a little later, Friedrich Julius Stahl and John Henry Newman. In Catholicism many of them became ultramontanes, champions of papal influence over secular as well as spiritual affairs. In Protestantism their emphasis was usually on the political and ecclesiastical status quo, on altar, throne, and caste. For all of them religion was intimately associated with a sense of wonder before the mysteries of nature. "God of Christians!" exclaimed François René de Chateaubriand in the midst of a description of a sea voyage. "It is on the waters of the abyss, and on the expanded sky, that thou hast particularly engraven the characters of thy omnipotence! Millions of stars sparkling in the azure of the celestial dome; the moon in the midst of the firmament; a sea unbounded by any shore; infinitude in the skies and on the waves! ... Never did thy greatness strike me with profounder awe than in those nights when, suspended between the stars and the ocean, I had immensity over my head, and immensity beneath my feet!"[8]

Among the masses, however, religious feeling was different. The man in the street did not rhapsodize about nature, because his efforts were devoted almost entirely to the task of physical survival in a world of factories and banks. Most churchmen were too busy heaping ridicule on the theory of evolution, like Bishop Samuel Wilberforce, or defending the dogma that

---

[8] Viscount de Chateaubriand, *The Genius of Christianity*, trans. by Charles I. White (Baltimore and New York: John Murphy Co., 1856), pp. 171–72.

the sovereign pontiff was infallible in questions of faith and morals, like Pope Pius IX, to concern themselves with conditions in city slums. Radicalism, therefore, increasingly became the religion of the urban proletariat of Europe, while Christianity was left to the well-to-do, to peasants, and to women and children.

Here and there, to be sure, isolated efforts were made to divert missionary zeal from the conversion of the heathen to the improvement of the believer. Robert de Lamennais sought to equate Catholicism with political democracy and economic reform, yet his views led only to a condemnation by the Holy See. Charles Kingsley incurred the resentment of the respectable by his advocacy of labor associations within the framework of what was designated as Christian Socialism. The usual attitude was that of the popular American clergyman Henry Ward Beecher, who in 1877 assured fashionable churchgoers: "God has intended the great to be great and the little to be little. . . . I do not say that a dollar a day is enough to support a workingman. But it is enough to support a man! Not enough to support a man and five children if a man insists on smoking and drinking beer. . . . But the man who cannot live on bread and water is not fit to live." Similarly, the *Syllabus of the Principal Errors of Our Time,* which the Papacy issued in 1864, had little to say about the social problems created by the advance of technology. It simply lumped together in a single category "Socialism, Communism, Secret Societies, Biblical Societies, Clerico-Liberal Societies," warning the faithful that "plagues of this variety are reprobated in the strongest terms in various Encyclicals."

CHRISTIANITY AND INDUSTRIALISM

It took Christianity about a hundred years to recognize the moral implications of industrial capitalism, but by the end of the nineteenth century the work of such pioneer reformers as Bishop Wilhelm Emmanuel von Ketteler and Franz Hitze in Germany, Antoine Frédéric Ozanam and Philippe Joseph Buchez in France, and Frederick D. Maurice and Thomas Hughes in England was finally acknowledged as a valid expression of the spirit of the Holy Scriptures. Pope Leo XIII stated in 1891 in his famous encyclical *Rerum novarum:* "Religion teaches the rich man and the employer that their working people are not their slaves; that they must respect in every man his dignity as a man and as a Christian; . . . and that it is shameful and inhuman to treat men like chattels to make money by, or to look upon them merely as so much muscle or physical power." The practical application of this pronouncement became the concern of civic organizations like the *Action Libérale,* of labor unions like the *Christliche Gewerkschaften,* and of prominent statesmen like Count A. A. M. de Mun and Monsignor Ignaz Seipel. Within Protestantism Friedrich Naumann, Bishop

Charles Gore, Josiah Strong, and Richard T. Ely were among the many who sought to alleviate economic strife through the ideals of the Sermon on the Mount. Their point of view was epitomized by George Bernard Shaw in the quip that "the only trouble with Christianity is that it has never yet been tried." The churches voiced their views regarding social problems with particular firmness during the great depression, when bourgeois society found itself in the midst of a crisis which threatened to result in class warfare. In 1931 Pope Pius XI affirmed in the encyclical *Quadragesimo anno:* "The immense number of propertyless wage-earners on the one hand, and the superabundant riches of the fortunate few on the other, is an unanswerable argument that the earthly goods so abundantly produced in this age of industrialism are far from rightly distributed and equitably shared among the various classes of men." Similarly, in 1937 a Protestant World Ecumenical Conference held at Oxford asserted: "The existing system of property rights and the existing distribution of property must be criticized in the light of the largely nonmoral processes by which they have been developed."

Closely related to theological criticism of economic injustice was the movement popularly known as the social gospel. Essentially, it was an attempt to translate the ethical teachings of Christianity into a program of civic reform. Distrustful of dogmatic formalism, it identified the essence of religion with the impulse to do good. It often found expression in philanthropic organizations like the Salvation Army, founded in 1878 by William Booth to combat alcoholism, immorality, and godlessness among the lower classes. In a more sophisticated form it left its impress on the so-called Advanced Modernism which retained only a shadowy belief in the supernatural, substituting service to humanity for faith in God. Even eminent European theologians like Albrecht Ritschl and Ernst Troeltsch endorsed its emphasis on the spirit rather than the letter of the New Testament. And in America Walter Rauschenbush preached: "The Kingdom of God is a collective conception, involving the whole social nature of man. It is not a matter of saving human atoms, but of saving the social organism. It is not a matter of getting individuals to heaven, but of transforming the life on earth into the harmony of heaven."

THE SPREAD OF SECULARISM

The effect of the social gospel was greatest in the Anglo-Saxon countries, where it did much to loosen the bonds of rigid orthodoxy. But it also tended to transform the church from an instrumentality of salvation into an agency for the performance of charitable works or sometimes into little more than the locale of neighborhood social functions. Indeed, that was the danger which theological conservatism saw in the deification of the human and the humanization of the divine. For would not the progressive abandonment of such traditional concepts of religion as sin, penitence, and redemption lead to a slow erosion of belief? The Vatican thought so, because it attempted to buttress ecclesiastical authority by encouraging the revival of scholastic philosophy and condemning the teachings of Modernism in the encyclical *Pascendi gregis*. Among Protestants the opposition to liberal doctrine assumed several forms. In the United States its stronghold was the fundamentalism of the South and the Middle West with its insistence on an uncompromising adherence to religious orthodoxy. In Great Britain it was the Anglican High Church which maintained that the historic doctrines of Christianity constituted a living body, no part of which could be destroyed without injuring the whole. On the Continent the Neo-orthodox movement under the leadership of Karl Barth preached a return to tradition in theology. Especially after the First World War had demonstrated how blind the confidence of the liberals in human reasonableness had been, Europe began to rediscover the God of Calvin, stern but just, sitting in judgment on man's depravity.

In the final analysis, the dilemma of modern faith was the dilemma of modern man. It involved the search for a spiritual meaning in a mechanized world. Modernism and fundamentalism, liberalism and orthodoxy, each attempted to adapt a traditional belief to a changing environment. The account of the struggle of the church against the forces of secularism which Professor John Herman Randall, Jr., presented was based on the experience of America, but indirectly it also described the problem facing every religious institution affected by the advance of industrialism:

> We are apt to overlook the real religious revolution. . . , the crowding of religion into a minor place by the host of secular faiths and interests. For every man alienated from the Church by scientific ideas, there are dozens dissatisfied with its social attitudes, and hundreds who, with no intellectual doubts, have found their lives fully occupied with the other interests and diversions of the machine age. What does it matter that earnest men have found a way to combine older beliefs with the spirit of science, if those beliefs have ceased to express anything vital in men's experience, if the older religious faith is irrelevant to all they really care for? . . . Even when the Church embraces the new interests, it seems to be playing a losing game. There is little of specifically religious significance in the manifold activities of the modern institutional church; a dance for the building fund is less of a religious experience than a festival in honor of the patron saint. And any minister knows that his "social activities" spring less from real need than from the fervent

desire to attract and hold members. The church itself has been secularized. Its very members continue a half-hearted support, from motives of traditional attachment, of personal loyalty to the minister, of social prestige, because they do not want to live in a church-less community.[9]

5 : The Arts and Letters

THE FRENCH REVOLUTION overthrew not only an outworn system of government, but also a traditional standard of value in aesthetics. Benevolent despotism had become so closely associated with rationalistic philosophy, deistic theology, and classical art that its fall had a far-reaching effect on accepted canons of thought and taste. As a matter of fact, even before the storm broke in 1789 there were signs of an impending cultural crisis. Immanuel Kant ushered in a new intellectual age with his *Critique of Pure Reason,* and John Wesley initiated a great religious revival built on faith rather than reason with the establishment of Methodism. In literature and art the reaction against the Age of Enlightenment was already in full swing. The reading public wept over the suicide of the hero of Goethe's *Sorrows of Young Werther* and thrilled to the synthetic medieval flavor of poems like *Bristowe Tragedie or the Dethe of Syr Charles Bawdin* by Thomas Chatterton. The composition of music was still governed by moderation and restraint, but in the work of a Joseph Haydn or a Wolfgang Amadeus Mozart could be heard an impatience with classicism. As for painting, William Blake and Francisco Goya represented a growing scorn for the artificiality of such subjects as well-fed little cupids shooting arrows at pretty ladies, or shepherds and shepherdesses who had never been near a real flock gamboling on meadows whose greenness had never been defiled by real livestock. In short, the revolution against formalism in culture began in the last years of enlightened absolutism, and the great political upheaval which soon followed merely hastened its victory.

ROMANTICISM

The name applied to this aesthetic revolution was romanticism. Rejecting the elegant lucidity of the classical tradition, it exalted sentiment and instinct. The protagonist of Goethe's *Faust* gave up a life of academic study for the sake of direct experience:

---

[9] John Herman Randall, Jr., "The Forces That Are Destroying Traditional Beliefs," *Current History* (June, 1929), pp. 361–62.

> *Gray and ashen, my friend, is every science,*
> *And only the golden tree of life is green.*

And in William Wordsworth the same preference appeared in different words:

> *One impulse from a vernal wood*
> *May teach you more of man,*
> *Of moral evil and of good,*
> *Than all the sages can.*
>
> *Sweet is the love which Nature brings;*
> *Our meddling intellect*
> *Mis-shapes the beauteous forms of things:*
> *—We murder to dissect.*

This emancipation of feeling led the writer to seek new literary themes. Sir Walter Scott and Joseph Görres found beauty in a medieval past which the Age of Enlightenment had condemned as barbaric. Samuel Taylor Coleridge and François René de Chateaubriand sought the exotic in distant lands, the former in the Xanadu of Kubla Khan, the latter among the noble savages of the New World. Giacomo Leopardi and Adam Mickiewicz were inspired by a faith in the mission of their people. Lord Byron's Childe Harold, like Alexander Pushkin's Eugene Onegin, was a turbulent hero driven by an inward restlessness from adventure to adventure, from unhappiness to unhappiness. What tied together this great variety of subjects and forms in literature was their common rejection of the well-bred conventionalism of the previous age.

The change taking place in the arts was equally profound. Théodore Géricault's "Raft of the Medusa," portraying the agonized survivors of a shipwreck, and Eugène Delacroix' "Liberty Leading the People," with its glorification of the spirit of popular insurrection, were worlds removed from the pictures of Socrates drinking the hemlock or Adonis embracing Venus which had been popular fifty years before. Even the landscapists like John Constable and J. M. W. Turner saw in nature more than an idealized background for frisking satyrs and nymphs. In music the invention of new instruments and the improvement of existing ones made possible radical innovations in the technique of composition. Ludwig van Beethoven was a lonely titan whose observance of traditional musical forms still reflected a conservative influence. But the next generation of musicians lacked his respectful attitude toward aesthetic authority. The works of Felix Mendelssohn-Bartholdy, Robert Schumann, Franz Schubert, Frédéric Chopin, and Hector Berlioz on the concert stage, and of Karl Maria von Weber, Gioacchino Rossini, and Gaetano Donizetti in the opera house finally put an end to the reign of classicism. To a perceptive observer like the statesman Wilhelm von Humboldt it seemed that "there never was an epoch in which everywhere and at all points the old and the new ages appeared in such sharp contrast."

Yet romanticism was too intense, too theatrical a movement to exercise a lasting influence in the culture of the West. It tended to magnify and distort human experience, to make it seem bigger than life. There was an element of truth in the popular carricature of the romanticists as pale, artistic young men, living in a feverish agony of creativity, given to fits of coughing and spitting blood, and finally succumbing in their early thirties to tuberculosis, the fashionable disease of the Restoration. The age did suffer from a penchant for the melodramatic, and sooner or later a reaction against it was sure to come. After all, people had to live in a world of cities and machines, not among picturesque castles and Gothic cathedrals.

REALISM

By the middle of the nineteenth century the public had grown tired of the cult of feeling. It was all very well to criticize the primness of classicism, but could not an aggressive emotionalism be just as artificial? Industrial society began to look for an art which could mirror its own experiences, and it found what it was looking for in realism. The American novelist William Dean Howells described this new theory of aesthetics in the injunction that "we must ask ourselves before we ask anything else, Is it true?—true to the motives, the impulses, the principles, that shape the life of actual men and women." Of course, to argue that the function of the artist is to portray the truth which determines "the life of actual men and women" is to beg the question, since the classicists as well as the romanticists had been convinced that they were dealing with precisely that kind of truth. But the realists met the difficulty by equating social reality with the average and the prosaic. For them a great talent was one "robust enough to front the everyday world and catch the charm of its work-worn, care-worn, brave, kindly face."

If romanticism found the supreme literary form in poetry, realism soberly turned to prose, especially to the novel. Its pioneers were Honoré de Balzac, whose *Human Comedy,* composed of more than a hundred novels, presented a monumental account of life during the reign of Louis Philippe, and Charles Dickens, who won an immense popularity in the Victorian Era with his books compounded of just the right proportions of social criticism and old-fashioned sentimentality. Gustave Flaubert's *Madame Bovary* shocked the Second Empire with its portrayal of the moral impoverishment of French provincial life, while Émile Zola and Guy de Maupassant were the outstanding representatives of the realistic school in the early years of the Third Republic. In the meantime William Makepeace Thackeray, Thomas Hardy, and George Gissing in England, Gustav Freytag, Theodor Storm, and Theodor Fontane in Germany, and Ivan Turgenev, Feodor Dostoevski, and Leo Tolstoy in Russia were depicting the brutalized existence of the lower classes, or extolling the virtues of the bourgeoisie, or pondering the problems of morality.

The drama was brought down to earth, and the mythological heroes and dashing outlaws who had populated the stage began to give way before more mundane protagonists. The younger Alexandre Dumas blazed a new trail with his *La dame aux camélias,* whose central character was a courtesan. But the greatest playwright of the century was Henrik Ibsen. Dealing with such themes as the subordination of women in *The Doll's House* and the weakness of democracy in *An Enemy of the People,* he transformed the theater into a platform for the discussion of social issues. Before long, writers like August Strindberg, George Bernard Shaw, Gerhart Hauptmann, and Anton Chekhov had firmly established the new realistic tradition in dramaturgy. The art of the essay also revived in an age which wanted to understand more than it wanted to believe. The writings of Thomas Carlyle, Thomas Babington Macaulay, Matthew Arnold, John Ruskin, C. A. Sainte-Beuve, Hippolyte A. Taine, Ernest Renan, and Georg Brandes displayed a belletristic skill of the highest order. Even the poets responded to the prevailing intellectual currents, Robert Browning in his sensitive psychological portraits executed in verse form, and Alfred Tennyson in his songs in praise of industry, peace, and patriotism.

The reaction against romanticism in art was foreshadowed in the social satire of Honoré Daumier and the reverence for lowly labor of Jean François Millet. Yet it did not become a full-fledged school of painting until the rise of impressionism. Arguing that the task of the artist was not to impose his own sense of symmetry upon nature, but simply to depict what the eye saw, the impressionists became intoxicated with the qualities of light and color. They were prepared to sacrifice form and design for the sake of what was sometimes called "pictorial stenography." At their first exhibition held in Paris in 1874 they shocked the orthodox by their indifference to the accepted rules of composition. Edouard Manet was the leader of this movement for a new aesthetic realism, although his own work was less revolutionary than that of many of his followers. Claude Monet with his strangely misty landscapes, Pierre Auguste Renoir and the radiant women and children whom he liked to portray, the ballet dancers of Edgar Degas, the street scenes of Camille Pissarro, the outdoor etchings of James McNeill Whistler, whose artistic reputation fell victim to an unfortunate portrait of his mother—these were the best representatives of the impressionistic movement. Still, the view that the painter must record optical effects without intruding anything of himself did not go unchallenged. Paul Cézanne helped found post-impressionism by his renewed emphasis on

This portrait of the great scientist captures the quality of selfless dedication which was an essential part of his character. In advancing his theory of evolution he wanted to do no more than suggest a description of the basic process by which biological change occurs. Instead he initiated an intellectual revolution. Philosophy, politics, economics, sociology, and history seized on his ideas, adapted them to their purposes, and transformed them into a universal explanation of all social development. Only Marx and Freud have exercised a comparable influence over the thought of the last hundred years.

The famous founder of psychoanalysis is shown in a photograph taken during the spring of 1938. Perhaps the knowledge that his country was being overwhelmed by the forces of totalitarianism intensified the weariness which can be read in his face. A few months later the old man of eighty-two was forced to seek refuge in England from the anti-Semitic bigotry of the National Socialists. He died soon after the outbreak of the Second World War, that terrible confirmation of the irrationality deep in the soul of man which he had spent a lifetime studying.

This piece of delicious satire pokes fun at both the precious affectations of British aesthetes and the efforts of Yankee rustics to master the latest fashions in culture. The corpulent, long-haired Wilde, dressed in knee breeches and displaying a white lily, is holding forth to an audience of puzzled provincials. Abraham Lincoln, looking strangely sour, gazes from the portrait on the wall upon the curious confrontation of snobbery and artlessness. The cartoon was drawn by Max Beerbohm.

After a half-century of non-representational art this picture no longer seems especially daring. Indeed, it can be recognized without too much difficulty as an experimental effort to portray the positions assumed by a figure walking down a staircase, a sort of kaleidoscopic view of the dynamics of movement. But when it was first exhibited in 1913 at the Armory Show in New York, it created a sensation. While one enraptured critic hailed "the light at the end of the tunnel," most viewers tended to side with the wit who dubbed it "an explosion in a shingle factory."

form and dimension in painting. The half-mad Vincent van Gogh filled canvas after canvas with brilliantly burning suns and fields of grain emanating an unearthly luminosity. Paul Gauguin during his stay in the South Seas developed a style which was deliberately primitive in the use of color and the approach to composition. And Henri de Toulouse-Lautrec pictured the night life of Montmartre, the singers, the dancers, the roués, the harlots.

Since music was by its nature unable to give literal expression to everyday experience, its break with romanticism had to be less abrupt. Johannes Brahms seemed to be merely resuming where Beethoven had left off. The piano pieces of Franz Liszt revealed the influence of Chopin. Giuseppe Verdi wrote in the melodic tradition of his great compatriots Rossini and Donizetti. The composer, however, could not remain completly immune to the social thought of his age. The sense of nationality which so powerfully affected political developments was stimulated by the work of Edvard Grieg in Norway and Anton Dvořák in Bohemia. The emphasis on the actual appeared in such examples of program music as Peter Ilich Tchaikovsky's overture *The Year 1812,* which commemorated the defeat of Napoleon in Russia, or Paul Dukas' orchestral rendering of one of Goethe's ballads in his *Sorcerer's Apprentice.* The passion and sorrow of lower-class life formed the theme of those inseparable operatic twins, Pietro Mascagni's *Cavalleria Rusticana* and Ruggiero Leoncavallo's *I Pagliacci.* Even Richard Wagner, who arranged the shotgun wedding of all the art forms in his grandiloquent *Gesamtkunstwerke,* was only voicing the self-satisfied mood of the bourgeois Philistine. Behind the synthetic medievalism of his musical dramas could be heard all the ostentation of a parvenu Germany. Leo Tolstoy saw through this sham and left a devastating description of a performance of *Siegfried:* "When I arrived, an actor in jersey and tights was seated in front of an object intended to represent an anvil; his hair and beard were false; his hands, white and manicured, had nothing of the workman's; the carefree air, the bulging stomach, and the absence of muscle betrayed the actor. With an incredible hammer he struck, as no one ever struck, a sword that was no less fanciful. It was easy to see he was a dwarf because he bent the knee as he walked. He shouted for a long time, his mouth strangely open."

THE RISE OF AESTHETIC SUBJECTIVISM

After the opening of the twentieth century two divergent tendencies developed in the arts and letters. One was an outgrowth of realism, continuing to define the function of the artist as the interpretation of a socially shared experience. Among those subscribing to it were writers like Thomas Mann, who in his *Buddenbrooks* described the decline and fall of a patrician merchant family in Germany; Jules Romains, who in the nearly thirty interrelated novels of *The Men of Good Will* presented a brilliant picture of the spiritual crisis of France; John Galsworthy, whose *Forsyte Saga* depicted the growing insecurity of the middle class in England; and Sinclair Lewis, whose *Babbitt* was a portrait of the desiccating shallowness of small-town life in America. Also within this tradition were painters like George Grosz and Diego Rivera, concerned with themes of social injustice, and even Henri Matisse and Georges Rouault, with their unconventional techniques in the use of form and color. As for music, the works of Jean Sibelius, Richard Strauss, and Sergei Prokofiev revealed an approach to the problems of composition not radically different from that which had been traditionally taught in the conservatories.

At the source of the aesthetic principle of such artists was the need to communicate. Still conscious of the society about them, still eager to express some objective truth, they sought to remain within the framework of the accepted canons of art. The difficulty facing them, therefore, lay in the attempt to articulate a new truth in an old language. In a sense, of course, that was the dilemma which every theory of aesthetics in the past had had to resolve. But the process of artistic readjustment had become particularly arduous in a period of rapidly changing cultural values.

There was, however, an alternative. Why not ignore the environment of the artist and stress his inner world of emotion? Such a procedure involved the substitution of a psychological state for social reality as the object of creative enterprise. It led to the erection of an insuperable barrier between the connoisseur's ideal and public taste. For once the communication of universal experience ceased to be the main concern of art, the way was clear for the aesthetic assertion of purely individual feelings which the rest of the world often found incomprehensible.

The roots of this radical subjectivism extended into the late years of the nineteenth century, when in the decadent atmosphere of the *fin de siècle* writers like Stéphane Mallarmé, Paul Verlaine, Algernon Swinburne, and Oscar Wilde shocked their contemporaries with unconventional literary themes and imageries. Their countless imitators, striking artistic poses and reverently carrying the lily as the symbol of aesthetic purity, spread the cult of introspection. Its influence was felt in stream-of-consciousness novels like Marcel Proust's *Remembrance of Things Past* or James Joyce's *Ulysses,* and in the poetic obscurities of Gertrude Stein or E. E. Cummings.

Among artists the rejection of anything resembling literal representation culminated in such extreme movements as cubism and surrealism. It led to the melting watches and weird, spindly crutches of Salvador Dali and to Marcel Duchamp's "Nude Descending a Staircase," in which there is neither a nude nor a staircase nor any other identifiable object. In music the revolution against melody and harmony began with the haunting, sensuous dissonances of Claude Debussy who opposed "the stifling of emotion under the heap of motives and superimposed designs." It progressed with the highly original orchestral devices, or perhaps merely "cacophonic outrages and deviltries and tomfooleries," of Igor Stravinsky. And it assumed its most uncompromising form in the twelve-tone compositions of Arnold Schönberg. As for the artistic merit of these musical innovations, a moderate critic like Howard Taubman cautiously concluded that "the best atonal composers do say something." But others agreed with the unequivocal condemnation by R. O. Morris: "This complete upsetting of all traditional values, this disdain of all previously accepted melodic and harmonic relationships, suggests to me, not so much courage and sincerity, as an inflated arrogance of mind that can only be described as megalomania— a dreary wilderness of cacophony that somehow contrives to be pedantic and hysterical at the same time."

Aside from the question whether aesthetic modernism was good or bad, the fact remained that it represented a prevalent attitude. If the arts refused to speak an intelligible language, that was because the artists felt themselves estranged from their social surroundings. It did no good to scold them for failing to interpret the universe about them. For some reason they were seeking artistic truth within themselves, within their own consciousness or subconsciousness. In all probability a feeling of insecurity lay at the root of their subjectivism. Shakespeare, Goethe, even Tolstoy could feel in essential harmony with society, because basically they subscribed to its standard of private and public virtue. That sense of belonging vanished, however, when the artist found himself unable to perform the traditional function of his calling, the description of a universally recognizable reality. Once he lost his footing amid the shifting values of the modern world, all that was left for him to do was voice the indefinable anxiety of his age. His rejection of the material environment was an expression of a general escapist impulse. Besides, even when he decided to look for ultimate truth, how could he be sure what it was? Perhaps it was the elemental scientific process which Edgar Varèse tried to describe in a conglomeration of strange sounds entitled *Ionisation*. Perhaps it was the horror of total war portrayed with painful vividness in Pablo Picasso's "Guernica." Or perhaps it was simply the deadly monotony of a dehumanized urban existence suggested by the *Preludes* of T. S. Eliot:

> *The morning comes to consciousness*
> *Of faint stale smells of beer*
> *From the sawdust-trampled street*
> *With all its muddy feet that press*
> *To early coffee-stands.*
> *With the other masquerades*
> *That time resumes,*

One thinks of all the hands
That are raising dingy shades
In a thousand furnished rooms.[10]

6 : Changing Ideals of Learning

THE CULTURAL crisis arising out of industrialism was aggravated by a basic change in the social function of learning. With the growth of material welfare which accompanied technological progress came new problems of education. Until the nineteenth century intellectual training had been by and large a monopoly of the well-to-do whose interests and attitudes shaped the form of instruction. The masses were too absorbed in the daily struggle to keep body and soul together to exert any influence over culture. Primitive sagas, folk tales, popular ballads, and village dances provided the artist with material, but his creative talents were exercised for the benefit of a public which was essentially aristocratic in character. The paintings of Velásquez glorified the court of Spain; the plays of Molière were staged before the nobility of France; Haydn wrote his music to entertain the guests of the powerful magnates of Hungary.

Similarly, the substance of education mirrored the stratified, hierarchical social order maintained by monarchic absolutism. There was no system of general elementary instruction, because the peasant did not need to read in order to plow the lord's land. As a matter of fact, too much knowledge could be a bad thing for the lower classes; it could spoil them and make them dissatisfied with their station in life. All they needed was piety, which taught them obedience and resignation. Did not even the great Voltaire announce despite his religious skepticism that "it is a very good thing to make men believe that they have an immortal soul and that there is an avenging God who will punish my peasants when they steal my wheat and my wine?"

Institutions of higher learning, on the other hand, received generous support from the *ancien régime,* because they performed a valuable service for the state. First of all, they trained lawyers and clergymen for the bureaucracy and the church, the bulwarks of established authority. Perhaps even more important, they provided young gentlemen with a body of knowledge which raised them above the common run of humanity. The man who had learned to read Greek and Latin wore an invisible mark of distinction

---

[10] From *Collected Poems 1909–1935* by T. S. Eliot, copyright 1936, by Harcourt, Brace and Company, Inc.

identifying him as a member of the leisured class. True, in many cases he forgot most of what he had studied soon after leaving the classroom, and sometimes he had been too busy drinking and wenching to have learned much in the first place. Yet usually he retained enough to cite from time to time some classical authority. And this accomplishment sufficed for that conspicuous consumption of learning which in many circles passed for culture.

The advent of industrialism forced a fundamental change in the basis of education. To begin with, for the first time in history the laboring populace was freed from unremitting drudgery and provided with enough leisure to make universal literacy an attainable goal. Secondly, the complication of the processes of production and distribution created a demand for trained workers and made a mastery of the three R's essential for even the menial occupations. Finally, the shift of the center of political power from the upper to the lower classes which resulted from the growth of democracy in government necessitated a new program of popular instruction. "We must educate our masters" became the slogan of every government farsighted enough to realize that the era of the masses had arrived.

THE MODERNIZATION OF INSTRUCTION

An educational revolution occurred in the West in the latter part of the nineteenth century, as one country after another hastened to prepare its citizenry for new civic responsibilities. England in 1870 promulgated a law establishing a system of primary schooling open to all children, and ten years later classroom attendance became a legal obligation. France made elementary school instruction free and compulsory in 1882. Prussia nationalized its primary schools in 1872 and ended the payment of tuition in 1888. Basic education became obligatory in Switzerland in 1874, in Italy in 1877, in Holland in 1878, and in Belgium in 1879. Although enrollment in an elementary school was generally not required beyond the pupil's tenth year, illiteracy in Europe and America began to decline with remarkable rapidity. Within the lifetime of a single generation the essential tools of learning became available to the countless millions who from time immemorial had been condemned to an existence of total ignorance.

The content of education also changed. The classical curriculum, which originally served a practical purpose, had become a venerated idol. Its study was supposed to sharpen the intellect, purify morals, ennoble the spirit, and strengthen judgment. Moreover, it offered the advantage of differentiating between the gentleman and the boor, for no man who had to earn a livelihood by labor could afford to devote himself to it. Yet learning was too vital an enterprise to be permanently reduced to a social ornament. Among those demanding a thoroughgoing reform of instruction was Thomas H. Huxley, who brilliantly satirized the typical attitude of the

Victorian English family toward the academic training which its sons received:

> At the cost of from one to two thousand pounds of our hard-earned money, we devote twelve of the most precious years of your lives to school. There you shall toil, or be supposed to toil; but there you shall not learn one single thing of all those you will most want to know directly you leave school and enter upon the practical business life. You will in all probability go into business, but you shall not know where, or how, any article of commerce is produced, or the difference between an export and an import, or the meaning of the word "capital." You will very likely settle in a colony, but you shall not know whether Tasmania is part of New South Wales, or *vice versa* . . . . Very probably you may become a manufacturer, but you shall not be provided with the means of understanding the working of one of your own steam engines, or the nature of the raw products you employ; and when you are asked to buy a patent, you shall not have the slightest means of judging whether the inventor is an impostor who is contravening the elementary principles of science or a man who will make you as rich as Croesus. You will very likely get into the House of Commons. You will have to take your share in making laws which may prove a blessing or a curse to millions of men. But you shall not hear one word respecting the political organization of your country; the meaning of the controversy between free traders and protectionists shall never have been mentioned to you; you shall not so much as know that there are such things as economical laws. The mental power which will be of most importance in your daily life will be the power of seeing things as they are without regard to authority; and of drawing accurate general conclusions from particular facts. But at school and at college you shall know of no source of truth but authority; nor exercise your reasoning faculty upon anything but deduction from that which is laid down by authority.[11]

Little by little academic practice adjusted to new economic and political conditions. The natural sciences, the social sciences, the arts and letters, and modern languages began to appear among the course offerings of the secondary schools and universities. In Europe the reform of higher education was a slow process, for there institutions of advanced learning continued to draw their student body largely from well-to-do circles, and hence they retained an intellectually and socially aristocratic character. In the United

---

[11] Thomas H. Huxley, *Science and Education* (New York: D. Appleton and Co., 1898), pp. 95–96.

States, however, the democratization of formal study led to radical pedagogic innovations. For one thing, the increasing specialization of knowledge produced a department-store organization of subjects which lumped together literature and pottery, philosophy and football coaching. Secondly, under the influence of the undergraduate activities which came to dominate campus life, the average college seemed to resign itself to the performance of purely social functions. It frequently became little more than an ivy-covered resort where young men and women could form friendships with others of their class, establish future professional contacts, find prospective wives and husbands, and take the courses in business administration and home economics which would qualify them to take over father's insurance business or play the part of the enlightened housewife.

TRADITION AND PROGRESS IN CULTURE

Such a change in the nature of the educational process inevitably aroused the opposition of those accustomed to older forms of knowledge. As early as 1914 Paul Elmer More in an article suggestively entitled "Natural Aristocracy" protested against what he considered the vulgarization of learning:

> Let us, in the name of a long-suffering God, put some bounds to the flood of talk about the wages of the bricklayer and the trainman, and talk a little more about the income of the artist and teacher and public censor who have to remain in opposition to the tide. Let us have less cant about the great educative value of the theatre for the people and less humbug about the virtues of the nauseous problem play, and more consideration of what is clean and nourishing food for the larger minds. Let us forget for a while our absorbing desire to fit the schools to train boys for the shop and the counting-room, and concern ourselves more effectively with the dwindling of those disciplinary studies which lift men out of the crowd. Let us, in fine, not number ourselves among the traitors to their class who *invidiae metu non audeant dicere* [do not dare to speak out for fear of ill will].[12]

But the knights in shining armor who rode forth with sharpened pencils to fight the good fight of culture against barbarism were Don Quixotes tilting at windmills. Whether they liked it or not, the genteel tradition of learning was declining with the patrician environment which it had reflected. Its place was being taken by new concepts of pedagogy appropriate

---

[12] Paul Elmer More, "Natural Aristocracy," *The Unpopular Review*, I, No. 2 (April–June, 1914), 292.

to a civic order committed to the goal of mass welfare. John Dewey, the champion of progressive education, spoke for those who refused to seek truth in authority:

> The foundation of democracy is faith in the capacities of human nature; faith in human intelligence and in the power of pooled and cooperative experience. It is not belief that these things are complete but that if given a show they will grow and be able to generate progressively the knowledge and wisdom needed to guide collective action. Every autocratic and authoritarian scheme of social action rests on a belief that the needed intelligence is confined to a superior few, who because of inherent natural gifts are endowed with the ability and the right to control the conduct of others; laying down principles and rules and directing the ways in which they are carried out. It would be foolish to deny that much can be said for this point of view. It is that which controlled human relations in social groups for much the greater part of human history. The democratic faith has emerged very, very recently in the history of mankind. Even where democracies now exist, men's minds and feelings are still permeated with ideals about leadership imposed from above, ideas that develop in the long early history of mankind. After democratic political institutions were nominally established, beliefs and ways of looking at life and of acting that originated when men and women were externally controlled and subjected to arbitrary power persisted in the family, the church, business and the school, and experience shows that as long as they persist there, political democracy is not secure.[13]

The crisis in education created by the changing function of knowledge was only one aspect of a vast process of social reorganization arising out of industrialism. There was no doubt a good deal of cant in the professional pedagogical pontification about adjustment to life and training for citizenship in the classroom. Yet the alternative had to be more than a return to the good old days when the little red schoolhouse dispensed learning and discipline without fads or frills. Even in the halcyon days before the First World War a worried editor of the *Nation* was complaining about the declining level of intellectual achievement in the United States: "Boys come into college with no reading and with minds unused to the very practice of study; and they leave college, too often, in the same state of nature. There are even those, inside and outside of academic halls, who protest that our higher institutions of learning simply fail to educate at all. That is slander; but in sober earnest, you will find few experienced college professors, apart from those engaged in teaching purely utilitarian or practical subjects, who

---

[13] John Dewey, "Democracy and Educational Administration," *School and Society* (Chicago: University of Chicago Press, 1899), p. 67.

are not convinced that the general relaxation is greater now than it was twenty years ago." That must surely have been the lament of the good city fathers of Athens who put Socrates to death for corrupting the minds of the young; it must have been the view of the schoolmen of the medieval universities who solemnly proclaimed that the reading of those vulgarians Petrarch and Chaucer would distract students from the classics and prove the ruination of academic standards. In each age in which the form of learning changed under the influence of a new way of life there were those who made dire predictions about the decay of morality and the stultifying of intelligence. As far as they were concerned, every dawn looked red.

The point is that much of the criticism directed against mass culture ignored the essential character of modern society. Not that the strictures about popular taste were without foundation. The yellow press, the dime novel, the horror film, the "soap opera," the "juke box," the calendar illustration, each in its own way purveyed sensationalism or sentimentality. But were such forms of entertainment any more vulgar than the bearbaiting and cockfighting which used to amuse the aristocracy? Was the violence portrayed in thousands of neighborhood motion-picture theaters any more barbaric than the morbid curiosity which once attracted fashionable ladies and gentlemen to the public execution of criminals? It took centuries to transform a boorish, illiterate feudal chieftain into a connoisseur of art and a patron of literature. There was no reason to expect that the improvement of plebeian sensibilities would take less time.

The Greeks had once looked down on the Romans as intellectual parvenus; the Romans had considered the Germans country bumpkins; the nobleman had made fun of the bourgeois for being a *nouveau riche;* the bourgeois had derided the workingman trying to master good grammar and good breeding; and so it went. In the light of historical experience, however, no people and no class could claim a monopoly of culture. Every social order of the past had created its unique intellectual synthesis out of common scientific, aesthetic, philosophic, and educational experiences. The modern world was still engaged in the search for some new, all-embracing system of thought which could express its fundamental convictions in universal terms. It was only to be expected that in such a moment of moral crisis cries would be raised against the abandonment of the familiar old deities. But the twentieth century could not escape its own time. The civic faith which it was seeking to create had to express a basic belief in scientific progress, material welfare, social justice, and political democracy.

Further Reading

William C. Dampier, *A History of Science and Its Relations with Philosophy and Religion* (London: Cambridge Univ. Press, 1946), and F. Sherwood Taylor, *A Short History of Science and Scientific Thought* (New York: Norton, 1949), are standard works, although for a succinct, straightforward account nothing excels Humphrey T. Pledge, *Science since 1500* (New York: Philosophical Library, 1947). On physics see Carl T. Chase, *The Evolution of Modern Physics* (New York: Van Nostrand, 1947), and James Jeans, *The Growth of Physical Science* (New York: Fawcett, Premier D70, 1958); on chemistry, J. M. Stillman, *The Story of Early Chemistry* (New York: Appleton, 1924), and T. M. Lowry, *Historical Introduction to Chemistry* (London: Macmillan, 1936); and on geology, K. von Zittel, *A History of Geology and Palaeontology* (New York: Scribner, 1901), and H. B. Woodward, *History of Geology* (New York: Putnam, 1911). Charles Singer, *A History of Biology* (New York: Schuman, 1950), and R. H. Shryock, *The Development of Modern Medicine* (New York: Knopf, 1947), are solid but less readable than such works of popularization as Paul H. De Kruif, *Microbe Hunters* (New York: Pocket Book 49, 1958), and Hans Zinsser, *Rats, Lice, and History* (Boston: Little, Brown, 1935). The theory of evolution is described by Paul B. Sears, *Charles Darwin* (New York: Scribner, 1950); W. Irvine, *Apes, Angels, and Victorians* (New York: McGraw-Hill, 1955); and Jacques Barzun, *Darwin, Marx, Wagner* (Garden City: Doubleday, Anchor A127, 1958). Alfred N. Whitehead, *Science and the Modern World* (New York: Macmillan, 1925); Bertrand Russell, *The A.B.C. of Relativity* (New York: Harper, 1925); and Lincoln Barnett, *The Universe and Dr. Einstein* (New York: Sloane, 1952), consider the scientific image of nature.

J. T. Merz, *A History of European Thought in the Nineteenth Century,* 4 vols. (New York: Scribner, 1896–1914), has become almost a classic. There are also two briefer and livelier histories of ideas: John H. Randall, Jr., *The Making of the Modern Mind* (New York: Houghton, 1940), and Crane Brinton, *Ideas and Men* (Englewood Cliffs, N.J.: Prentice-Hall, 1950). The development of the social sciences is depicted in Harry E. Barnes, *The New History and the Social Studies* (New York: Century, 1925). P. A. Sorokin, *Contemporary Sociological Theories* (New York: Harper, 1928), is a sound guide to sociology; A. C. Haddon and A. H. Quiggin, *History of Anthropology* (New York: Putnam, 1910), to anthropology; C. Gide and C. Rist, *History of Economic Doctrines from the Physiocrats to the Present Day* (Boston: Heath, 1948), to economic theory; G. H. Sabine, *A History of Political Theory* (New York: Holt, 1950), to political science; G. P. Gooch, *History and Historians in the Nineteenth Century* (Gloucester, Mass.: P. Smith, 1949), to modern historiography; and E. R. Trattner, *Unraveling the Book of Books* (New York: Scribner, 1929), to Biblical criticism. G. Murphy, *Historical Introduction to Modern Psychology* (New York: Harcourt, 1929), is a good survey, but for psychoanalysis see in addition Sigmund Freud, *An Outline of Psychoanalysis* (New York: Norton, 1949); Fritz Wittels, *Freud and His Time* (New York:

Grosset, Universal Library 34, 1958); and E. Jones, *The Life and Work of Sigmund Freud,* 3 vols. (New York: Basic Books, 1953–57). H. S. Hughes, *Oswald Spengler* (New York: Scribner, 1952); Pieter Geyl, *From Ranke to Toynbee* (Northampton, Mass.: Smith College, 1952); and David Riesman, *The Lonely Crowd* (Garden City: Doubleday, Anchor A16, 1953), are studies in cultural pessimism.

H. Hoffding, *A History of Modern Philosophy,* 2 vols. (New York: Macmillan, 1900), is a well-known, substantial book. A. L. Lindsay, *Kant* (Gloucester, Mass.: P. Smith, 1934), presents an appraisal of the founder of philosophic idealism, while Herbert Marcuse, *Reason and Revolution: Hegel and the Rise of Social Theory* (New York: Oxford Univ. Press, 1941), deals with its most controversial exponent. Crane Brinton, *Nietzsche* (Cambridge, Mass.: Harvard Univ. Press, 1941), is an urbane biography of the prophet of the superman. E. Friedell, *A Cultural History of the Modern Age,* 3 vols. (New York: Knopf, 1930–32), and F. A. Lange, *The History of Materialism,* 3 vols. in 1 (New York: Harcourt, 1925), describe important modern intellectual movements. H. S. Leiper (ed.), *Christianity Today* (New York: Morehouse, 1947), advances a Protestant interpretation, while Philip Hughes, *A Popular History of the Catholic Church* (New York: Doubleday, Image D4, 1954), defends the Catholic position. A. C. McGiffert, *The Rise of Modern Religious Ideas* (New York: Macmillan, 1915), is a thoughtful and balanced exposition. E. A. Burtt, *Religion in an Age of Science* (New York: Stokes, 1929); Christopher Dawson, *Religion and Culture* (New York: Meridian M53, 1958); and W. Cunningham, *Christianity and Social Questions* (New York: Scribner, 1910), analyze the role of religion in an industrial society.

G. Brandes, *Main Currents in Nineteenth Century Literature,* 6 vols. (New York: Boni & Liveright, 1923), is a comprehensive work by an eminent literary critic. An adroit defense of the romanticists against the charge of irrationalism may be found in Jacques Barzun, *Romanticism and the Modern Ego* (Boston: Little, Brown, 1945). On realism and subjectivism in literature there is a perceptive book by Edmund Wilson, *Axel's Castle* (New York: Scribner, 1958). E. Faure, *History of Art,* 5 vols. (New York: Harper, 1921–30), and J. Pijoan, *History of Art* (New York: Harper, 1927–28), are established histories with an international reputation. For first-rate studies on a more modest scale see T. Craven, *Modern Art* (New York: Simon & Schuster, 1934), and M. Raynal, *The Nineteenth Century: Goya to Gauguin* (New York: Skira, 1951). P. H. Lang, *Music in Western Civilization* (New York: Norton, 1941), and C. Gray, *History of Music* (New York: Oxford Univ. Press, 1947), are two excellent accounts, the former more inclusive, and latter more discriminating. S. Giedion, *Mechanization Takes Command* (New York: Oxford Univ. Press, 1948), examines the effect of a mechanized economy on aesthetic judgment.

There are several works dealing with the relationship between the content of learning and the structure of society, among them J. H. Robinson, *The Humanizing of Knowledge* (Garden City: Doran, 1926); F. S. Chapin, *Cultural Change* (New York: Century, 1928); J. K. Folsom, *Culture and Social Progress* (New York: Longmans, 1928); and R. B. Fosdick, *The Old Savage in the New Civilization* (Garden City: Doubleday, 1928). The following are especially concerned with the problem of intellectual training in a democracy: W. H. Kilpatrick, *Education for a Changing Civilization* (New York: Macmillan, 1927); Bertrand Russell, *Education and the Modern World* (New York: Norton, 1932); C. H. Judd, *Education and Social Progress* (New York: Harcourt, 1934); and George S. Counts, *The Social Foundations of Education* (New York: Scribner, 1934). A description of changing pedagogic patterns in the Old World and the New appears in F. W. Roman, *The New Education in Europe* (New York: Dutton, 1930); E. P. Cubberley, *Public Education in the United States* (Cambridge, Mass.: Riverside, 1934); and R. G. Tugwell and L. H. Keyserling (eds.), *Redirecting Education,* 2 vols. (New York: Columbia Univ. Press, 1934–35). Critical reviews of recent trends in education are presented by Thorstein Veblen, *The Higher Learning in America* (New York: Sagamore S–7, 1957), and A. E. Bestor, *Educational Wastelands* (Urbana: Univ. of Illinois Press, 1953).

Chapter 30

THE POST-WAR SCENE

THE SECOND World War had the effect of destroying a system of international relations which had prevailed in the West for five hundred years. Ever since the fifteenth century, when the national monarchy became the dominant form of political organization, a balance of power among the major countries had been maintained by the art of diplomacy or by recourse to war. Whenever any state threatened to become strong enough to dominate the others, a coalition would be formed to restore the equilibrium. Charles V of the Holy Roman Empire, Louis XIV and Napoleon I of France, William II of Germany, each discovered that too much power could be as dangerous as too little. In a world in which diplomatic affairs were conducted in the spirit of Machiavelli's *Prince,* no ruler could allow his neighbor to acquire a preponderant influence. The weaker concerted to oppose the stronger, and in combination they succeeded in re-establishing the international equipoise. Sometimes the mere threat of force was enough to redress the balance; more commonly a war was required. In any case, the techniques of statesmanship reflected a diplomatic situation in which no one of the leading governments could achieve a position of hegemony.

1 : The New International Order

THE RESULT of the Second World War was to weaken the major states of Europe to the point where, with one exception, they could no longer be properly described as great powers. Not only were Germany and Italy forced to agree to unconditional surrender, but even such victorious countries as England and France were winners in name only. Enfeebled financially as well as ideologically, they ceased to play a leading role on the diplomatic stage. The traditional balance of power began to disintegrate because there were no longer several strong governments on the Continent. In its place there developed a dualism of power which reflected the fact that after 1945 there were only two great states, the Soviet Union and the United States. Having emerged from the Second World War in a stronger political and economic position than before, they were able to dominate international relations. Not since the days of the Roman Empire had there been such a high concentration of power. But whereas Rome had been able to provide its citizens with the *Pax Romana,* a period of tranquillity extending for almost three hundred years, the post-war world of the twentieth century was less fortunate. For the statesmen in Moscow and Washington were divided by fundamental differences in their philosophies of government.

THE COLLAPSE OF THE BALANCE OF POWER

As far as the Soviet Union was concerned, the defeat of the Axis meant that it could emerge from the isolation in which it had been kept by the capitalistic states during the first twenty years of its existence. It ceased to be a pariah among nations, and even began to exert a strong influence on countries beyond its borders. First of all, there were the secondary states of eastern Europe which during the interwar period had maintained a diplomatic barrier against the Soviet Union. In the final stages of the Second World War they had been overrun by the Red Army, so that Stalin could impose his will on their governments by the threat of armed force. Secondly, the defeat of the Wehrmacht by the Russian forces endowed the Kremlin with new prestige and strengthened the communist parties in western Europe. Finally, the economic decline resulting from the war won new converts for radical doctrines which promised the masses of the world financial security in the classless society of the future. Not since the chaotic days after the First World War had the chances of a Marxist victory been more favorable.

It was America which was primarily responsible for checking the expansionist designs of the Kremlin, because it alone possessed the necessary physical resources. In 1945, as in 1918, there was a strong desire among the people of the United States to demobilize their armies and regain that sense of cozy security which they had known through most of their history. Yet almost against their will they found themselves drawn into international complications which threatened to lead to a new war. Just as the Romans after the Carthaginian wars discovered that great political power brought with it heavy political responsibility, so the Americans after the Second World War found themselves compelled to assume duties for which they did not ask and to which they were not accustomed.

Since the domination of Europe by the Soviet Union would have left the Western Hemisphere isolated in a communist sea, self-interest demanded that Washington become the leader of the forces aligned against Russia.

It was too late to save the eastern borderlands of the Continent from the control of Moscow, but farther west economic and military assistance from the New World strengthened the opposition to Stalin. The result was the formation of two great alliances, one commanded by the Kremlin, the other directed from the White House.

THE REORGANIZATION OF THE CONTINENT

After hostilities came to an end in 1945, the reorganization of the Continent was carried out partly by an authoritarian communism, partly by a democratic capitalism. In the east Russia had a free hand. To begin with, she annexed several strategically located territories extending along her pre-war frontiers. Finland was forced to cede Petsamo and the western shore of Lake Ladoga; Estonia, Latvia, Lithuania, and part of East Prussia were incorporated into the Soviet Union; Poland gave up her eastern provinces; Romania lost Bessarabia and northern Bucovina; and Czechoslovakia surrendered Carpathian Ruthenia.

Moreover, in the years following the collapse of the Axis Moscow succeeded in gaining political control over its weak neighbors. The technique employed to achieve this end involved first the formation of a coalition government representing the Center and the Left. Then would come a gradual suppression of the bourgeois parties which left the radicals firmly in the saddle. Ultimately the state was reduced to a satellite fawning on the Kremlin. One after another the countries of eastern Europe underwent the transformation from "popular front" to "people's democracy." By the beginning of 1948 Mátyás Rákosi in Hungary, Marshal Tito in Yugoslavia, Ana Pauker in Romania, Joseph Cyrankiewicz in Poland, Georgi Dimitrov in Bulgaria, Klement Gottwald in Czechoslovakia, and Enver Hoxha in Albania were re-creating their states in the image of the Soviet Union. As for their foreign policies, a conference held in Warsaw in September, 1947, established the Communist Information Bureau (Cominform) to co-ordinate the diplomatic activities of all communist governments under the ultimate direction of Stalin.

In the meantime the United States was encouraging the revival of democratic governments and capitalistic economies in western Europe. Unlike the Kremlin, Washington did not use the weapon of the coup d'état, relying rather on the effects of civic and financial rehabilitation. Convinced that under normal social conditions the peoples of the Continent would continue to accept differences in class and property which were traditional in their culture, it made a determined effort to alleviate mass suffering in the Old World. The United Nations Relief and Rehabilitation Administration spent almost four billion dollars immediately after the war to provide the necessities of life to lands freed from the Axis. And its relief program was supplemented with direct loans advanced by the United

States to needy governments throughout the world. The results were grati-
fying from the American point of view. While the industrial proletariat of
Europe generally continued to accept Marxism, the middle class in alliance
with the peasantry, the bureaucracy, and the church succeeded in maintaining political control in the western states. France, Belgium, Holland, Norway, and Denmark all returned to the parliamentary form of government
under which they had lived before the war. Even Italy, after more than
twenty years of fascist dictatorship, decided, not without some prodding by
the occupying forces of the United States and Great Britain, to establish a
representative democracy.

The opposing camps met head on in central Europe. At the end of the
war their armies were in complete possession of enemy territory, and therefore their first serious disputes arose with regard to its administration. On
the punitive measures to be taken against Germany there was general
agreement. A policy of denazification was initiated throughout the country,
culminating in the trial and execution of ten of Hitler's close associates.
Demilitarization was also carried out with such thoroughness that not a
trace was left of the powerful war machine which had almost conquered the
Continent. Even on the question of reparations which Stalin demanded
there was little difference of opinion. As a result, a defeated nation, exhausted physically after six years of warfare, was crippled economically by
the confiscation of much of its remaining industrial equipment.

Yet while the victorious allies acted in harmony to effect the destruction
of fascism, they could not reconcile their views concerning a political system

to take its place. The Americans, the British, and the French, whose zones of occupation comprised more than two-thirds of the total area under military government, favored the creation of representative institutions similar to those of the Weimar Republic. The Russians, on the other hand, had no intention of allowing the establishment in the heart of Europe of a parliamentary, capitalistic state opposed to the Soviet Union. The outcome was the gradual formation of two Germanys, one a middle-of-the-road democracy with close ties to the United States, the other a communist dictatorship dependent on the support of Moscow.

THE UNITED NATIONS

Winston Churchill was one of the first democratic statesmen to realize that the great wartime alliance could not overcome the differences among its members regarding the organization of the peace. Even before the surrender of the Axis he had begun to distrust the intentions of the Kremlin. One year later, on March 5, 1946, he delivered a speech at Westminster College in Fulton, Missouri, bluntly describing the problem facing the parliamentary governments of the West: "From Stettin in the Baltic to Trieste in the Adriatic, an iron curtain has descended across the Continent. Behind that line lie all the capitals of the ancient states of central and eastern Europe . . . all these famous cities and the populations around them lie in what I might call the Soviet sphere." To oppose Russian aggression he urged close collaboration between America and the United Kingdom: "If the population of the English-speaking Commonwealth be added to that of the United States, with all that such co-operation implies in the air, on the sea, and in science and industry, there will be no quivering, precarious balance of power to offer its temptation to ambition or adventure. On the contrary there would be an overwhelming assurance of security."

To many of his listeners, however, talk of power politics and military alliances was a will-o'-the-wisp. The game of armed diplomacy had been played throughout history without preventing conflict among the great powers. Was there any reason why it should prove more effective in the post-war world? Surely it would be better to rely instead on some new form of international organization for the maintenance of world security. True, the League of Nations had failed to avert a ruinous war. But a careful study of its mistakes might make possible the formation of a more perfect association of peace-loving peoples.

So great was the longing of the masses of the West for political stability that while the Second World War was still in progress the grand coalition against fascism announced on October 30, 1943: "The Governments of the United States of America, the United Kingdom, the Soviet Union and China . . . recognize the necessity of establishing at the earliest practicable date a general international organization, based on the principle of the sovereign equality of all peace-loving states, and open to membership by all such states, large and small, for the maintenance of international peace and security." To implement this declaration exploratory conversations were held at Dumbarton Oaks in Washington, D.C., from August to October, 1944. Then early in February, 1945, Roosevelt, Stalin, and Churchill met at Yalta in the Crimea to concert plans for the military defeat of the Axis, the re-establishment of international stability, and the guarantee of the peace by a new league of nations. About two months later delegates from fifty countries gathered in San Francisco to draft the constitutional charter of the proposed association of states. Finally, on October 24, 1945, the United Nations came officially into existence.

The charter of the United Nations provided for the establishment of two major deliberative bodies, the General Assembly and the Security Council. The former, in which each state was to have one vote, possessed advisory rather than mandatory power. The latter, on the other hand, was endowed with considerable authority to deal with international conflicts. Composed of five permanent members, the United States, the Soviet Union, Great Britain, France, and China, and of six other nations elected by the General Assembly for terms of two years, it had the right to "take such action by air, sea, or land forces as may be necessary to maintain or restore international peace and security." The great powers were thus in effect entrusted with the primary responsibility for enforcing law and order among the lesser governments. Furthermore, the Economic and Social Council was formed to encourage co-operation among countries "with respect to international economic, social, cultural, educational, health, and related matters." The Trusteeship Council was designed to supervise the administration of those colonies taken away from the defeated nations in the two world wars which were not yet ready for self-government. Finally, the International Court of Justice was founded to help settle diplomatic disputes referred to it by sovereign states. The fundamental purpose of all these organizations was stated in the first article of the charter of the United Nations: "To maintain international peace and security, and to that end: to take effective collective measures for the prevention and removal of threats to the peace, and for the suppression of acts of aggression or other breaches of the peace, and to bring about by peaceful means, and in conformity with the principles of justice and international law, adjustment or settlement of international disputes or situations which might lead to a breach of the peace."

Yet the realization of this purpose was possible only as long as the leading states of the world, especially the United States and Russia, were able to continue the policy of collaboration which they had adopted during the struggle against the Axis. In other words, the success of the United Nations after the Second World War, like that of the League of Nations after the First World War or of the Quadruple Alliance after the Napoleonic era, depended on the maintenance of the diplomatic harmony among

THE UNITED NATIONS AND RELATED AGENCIES

(as of January 1959)

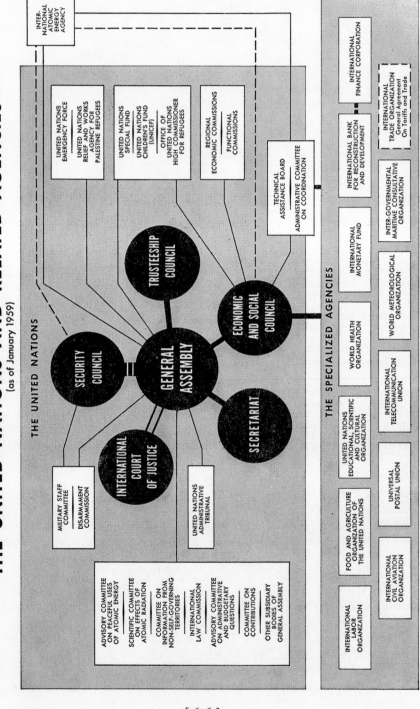

THE UNITED NATIONS

THE SPECIALIZED AGENCIES

INTER-NATIONAL ATOMIC ENERGY AGENCY

UNITED NATIONS EMERGENCY FORCE

UNITED NATIONS RELIEF AND WORKS AGENCY FOR PALESTINE REFUGEES

UNITED NATIONS SPECIAL FUND

UNITED NATIONS CHILDREN'S FUND (UNICEF)

OFFICE OF UNITED NATIONS HIGH COMMISSIONER FOR REFUGEES

REGIONAL ECONOMIC COMMISSIONS

FUNCTIONAL COMMISSIONS

TECHNICAL ASSISTANCE BOARD

ADMINISTRATIVE COMMITTEE ON COORDINATION

TRUSTEESHIP COUNCIL

SECURITY COUNCIL

GENERAL ASSEMBLY

ECONOMIC AND SOCIAL COUNCIL

SECRETARIAT

INTERNATIONAL COURT OF JUSTICE

MILITARY STAFF COMMITTEE

DISARMAMENT COMMISSION

UNITED NATIONS ADMINISTRATIVE TRIBUNAL

ADVISORY COMMITTEE ON PEACEFUL USES OF ATOMIC ENERGY

SCIENTIFIC COMMITTEE ON EFFECTS OF ATOMIC RADIATION

COMMITTEE ON INFORMATION FROM NON-SELF-GOVERNING TERRITORIES

INTERNATIONAL LAW COMMISSION

ADVISORY COMMITTEE ON ADMINISTRATIVE AND BUDGETARY QUESTIONS

COMMITTEE ON CONTRIBUTIONS

OTHER SUBSIDIARY BODIES OF GENERAL ASSEMBLY

INTERNATIONAL FINANCE CORPORATION

INTERNATIONAL BANK FOR RECONSTRUCTION AND DEVELOPMENT

INTERNATIONAL TRADE ORGANIZATION General Agreement On Tariffs and Trade

INTER-GOVERNMENTAL MARITIME CONSULTATIVE ORGANIZATION

INTERNATIONAL MONETARY FUND

WORLD METEOROLOGICAL ORGANIZATION

WORLD HEALTH ORGANIZATION

INTERNATIONAL TELECOMMUNICATION UNION

UNITED NATIONS EDUCATIONAL, SCIENTIFIC AND CULTURAL ORGANIZATION

UNIVERSAL POSTAL UNION

FOOD AND AGRICULTURE ORGANIZATION OF THE UNITED NATIONS

INTERNATIONAL CIVIL AVIATION ORGANIZATION

INTERNATIONAL LABOR ORGANIZATION

the victors which had been originally established under wartime conditions. Together the great powers could impose their will on the weaker countries and thus prevent an international dispute from developing into an armed conflict. But once they themselves became divided, the United Nations lost its effectiveness as an instrument for the enforcement of peace. Any consistent plan of action then became impossible, because Article 27 of the charter provided that each of the permanent members of the Security Council had the right to veto any important decision which it considered incompatible with its interests.

This provision came to be bitterly criticized in the democratic countries for enabling the Soviet Union to obstruct the efficient operation of the United Nations. But as a matter of fact at both the Yalta Conference and the San Francisco Conference American statesmen were as ready as the Russians to accept the veto. Remembering what had happened twenty-five years before when the Treaty of Versailles was submitted to a suspicious Senate, they decided to appease isolationist sentiment in the New World by an ironclad guarantee of the sovereignty of the United States. As it turned out, their precautions were unnecessary. In almost all significant questions Washington could count on the support of the great majority of the other governments, while Moscow was forced to oppose hostile votes with vetoes. Yet there could be little doubt that if the situation had been reversed, if America had found itself consistently outvoted in the United Nations, it, too, would have made use of the special right conferred upon it by the charter.

The disintegration of the wartime coalition meant that popular hopes for peace could not be realized. Instead, a diplomatic struggle between the communist and the capitalist states retarded the recovery of the world. Some observers of the international scene were reminded of the atmosphere of crisis which preceded the outbreak of the Second World War. There were even those who openly prophesied for the United Nations the same fate which had befallen the League of Nations. Yet much of their criticism was ill-founded. To be sure, the danger of a new armed conflict was real enough. But despite the fact that the United Nations failed to live up to the expectations of many of its supporters, the achievements to its credit were sufficiently impressive to justify its existence.

For millions of hungry people throughout the world the United Nations Relief and Rehabilitation Administration meant the difference between health and sickness. The International Bank facilitated economic progress in devastated or backward countries. The International Labor Organization urged improvements in the standard of living of the working class. The United Nations Educational, Scientific, and Cultural Organization sought to overcome national exclusiveness by encouraging intercultural understanding. Most important of all, the Security Council and the General Assembly constituted a stock exchange of diplomatic policies where opposing governments could discuss the political problems facing them. True, the debates between Russia and America sometimes reached the heights of futility. But as long as their delegates continued to argue around the conference table, they were not likely to start dropping bombs. Suggestions that the Soviet Union be expelled from the United Nations were therefore rejected by the democratic leaders, because to accept them would transform an international organization designed to maintain peace into an out-and-out military alliance directed against the communist states. It was better to let the long argument on the shores of the East River in New York go on, while the West recovered from the effects of a ruinous military conflict. Besides, there was always the hope that some day an agreement could finally be reached.

2 : The Recovery of the West

THE RIVALRY between the parliamentary and the communist states had an important effect on their internal development. In the case of the former, it meant an even greater political and economic dependence on the United States than would have been the case under conditions of diplomatic stability. For it was obvious that Europe could not resist the Soviet Union with its own resources. Only the strength of the New World made possible the survival of democratic capitalism in the face of Russian hostility.

THE UNITED STATES

By 1945 America had become a colossus among nations. While achieving a steadily rising standard of living for its own population, it was at the same time feeding and defending half of the world from Berlin to Tokyo. Despite the gloomy predictions of economists who could still remember the great depression, the end of the war failed to halt the growth of its productive capacity. Military expenditures to meet the threat of Russian aggression, the demand from abroad for foodstuffs and manufactured goods, and finally the appetite of the consumer at home for houses, automobiles, and television sets, all in combination generated the greatest wave of prosperity since the formation of the republic. At first the Democrats under President Harry S. Truman claimed credit for this material well-being. But good times proved to be non-partisan, and when the Republicans under President Dwight D. Eisenhower took over the administration in 1953 industry and agriculture went on producing as abundantly as before. Both parties, moreover, recognized the continuing need for welfare legislation by increasing public housing, raising the minimum-wage scale, subsidizing the farm population, financing flood control and soil conservation, and improving the social status of the Negro. And both pursued a diplomatic policy of opposition to Moscow by providing financial and military assistance to all governments ready to combat communism.

WESTERN EUROPE

The United Kingdom was the chief beneficiary of the generosity of the New World. Britain had undergone a serious relative economic decline since the nineteenth century, when its factories dominated the markets of the world. The movement for independence among colonial peoples, the competition of other great industrial states, and two world conflicts had left it in a condition of national exhaustion. The extent of popular dissatisfaction was clearly revealed in the election of 1945, when the indomitable prime minister of the war years, Winston Churchill, was soundly defeated, and the Labor party under Clement R. Attlee came to power.

In keeping with its campaign promises, the new government extended the social-insurance system and introduced a plan for free medical care. In 1946 it put the overseas cable and wire services and the coal mines under public ownership, and in 1947 it nationalized the railroads, canals, and docks. But social reform alone was not the answer to financial insecurity. Loans of some five billion dollars from the United States and Canada alleviated the economic problem without solving it, so that rationing of food had to be retained without substantial relaxation until 1948. Restrictions on the purchase of clothing remained in force even longer. Finally, in 1949 the pound sterling was devalued from $4.03 to $2.80 in order to stimulate the languishing export trade. Such Spartan measures succeeded little by little in restoring fiscal stability, but they did nothing to enhance the popularity of the socialist government. In the election of 1951 the Conservative party won a majority, just as the program of national austerity was beginning to show results. Two years later the coronation of the youthful Elizabeth II was greeted by millions of her jubilant subjects as inaugurating a reign like that of her illustrious sixteenth-century namesake. Yet it was clear that the country remained exposed to serious financial and political dangers.

While the difficulties which the English had to face were primarily economic, the French were afflicted by a crisis of national spirit. Their country had escaped severe physical damage during the war by a prompt capitulation to the enemy, and its population, which had hardly increased in more than seventy years, could still live in abundance on the most fertile lands of western Europe. But military defeat, colonial unrest, and the intensification of class resentment inflicted wounds which material well-being alone could not heal. In the post-war years the proletariat of France became more radical and the bourgeoisie less compromising than before. And there was still the conservative argument that ever since the French Revolution republicanism had divided and weakened the nation, so that only a return to some form of rule by the strong man could revive its sense of purpose.

Immediately after the liberation of Paris it looked as if a new spirit of civic unity had developed in France. On September 9, 1944, General Charles de Gaulle formed the Provisional Government of the French Republic, which initiated the work of economic reconstruction and political reorganization. By 1946 coal, gas, electricity, aviation, and banking had been nationalized, the armed forces had been modernized and enlarged, and an ambitious foreign policy befitting a major power had been initiated. But most Frenchmen were unwilling to sacrifice individualism for order. In the National Constituent Assembly elected on October 21, 1945, could be found the usual Gallic multiplicity of parties, and the new constitution adopted a year later was indistinguishable in most important respects from the old.

The Fourth Republic like the Third was plagued with ministerial instability and parliamentary confusion. In ten years some twenty cabinets came and went, each eventually overthrown because of its inability to reconcile the opposing forces on the political scene. On the Left, the Communist party was planning for a dictatorship of the proletariat. On the Right, the Reunion of the French People was preaching the need for a concentration of government authority. In the middle, moderate statesmen, among them Antoine Pinay, Joseph Laniel, Robert Schuman, Georges Bidault, Pierre Mendès-France, and Edgar Faure, continued to fight against revolutions in southeast Asia and North Africa and to struggle with inflated prices and labor strikes at home. Always in the midst of one crisis or another, the state went on muddling through in the familiar fashion of French republicanism, divided and confused. Finally, in June, 1958, a hopeless impasse in parliament and the threat of a mutiny in the army led to de Gaulle's return to power. Some three months later a new constitution won overwhelming popular approval, and the Fourth Republic was officially replaced by the Fifth.

In Italy there was a peaceful transition from authoritarianism to democracy. Yet at first the outlook was bleak, for a lost war had aggravated all the chronic economic ills of the country. It went without saying that fascism was discredited, but what would replace it? After the fall of Mussolini communism emerged as a powerful political movement supported by exploited factory workers and even by some landless peasants. Resisting it were the middle-of-the-road parliamentary parties expressing the views of the bourgeois businessman, the white-collar professional, and the church-going farmer. Their triumph in the struggle with radicalism was partly at least a result of the policy pursued by the democratic victor states.

To alleviate privation, the United Nations Relief and Rehabilitation Administration in 1946 alone shipped $450,000,000 worth of essential supplies to Italy. National pride, moreover, was flattered by the prompt return of political control over virtually the entire country to the government in

Rome. Under the terms of the peace treaty of February 10, 1947, the Italians suffered only minor losses of territory in Europe. The surrender of their costly overseas possessions and the reduction of their army to 300,000 men were actually blessings in disguise. And the presence of American and British troops provided security against a radical coup. On June 2, 1946, elections to the Constituent Assembly gave 207 seats to the moderate Christian Democratic party and 41 seats to the Liberal party, while the Socialist party received 115 and the Communist party 104. At the same time a national referendum decided in favor of the establishment of a republic by a vote of 12,717,923 to 10,719,284. After the adoption of a democratic constitution on December 22, 1947, Italy was ruled by the statesmen of the Center, of whom Alcide de Gasperi was the ablest. Poverty among the lower classes remained a serious problem. The Left continued to receive the endorsement of about a third of all voters. Even fascist and monarchist organizations revived. Yet the new régime displayed greater determination in dealing with economic and social questions than any which had been in power since the achievement of national unification almost a hundred years before.

Germany in the meantime provided proof that under conditions of modern warfare the distinction between winner and loser was often artificial. In 1945 a land of ruined cities and hungry people lay prostrate before the victorious powers. In the wake of defeat came despair, while the occupying forces demilitarized and denazified. To make matters still worse, the country was forced to receive almost ten million refugees and expellees from the east; its industrial output was reduced to half the volume of 1938; and it was deprived of territories normally providing about 25 per cent of its food supply by the assignment to Polish administration of the region beyond the Oder and the Neisse rivers. Never before had a leading state of the West suffered such a catastrophic collapse.

Yet before long the democratic powers decided that they could not go on indefinitely maintaining a slum in the heart of Europe. First of all, they would be endangering their own economic position. And secondly, in the developing struggle between capitalism and communism German factories and even German arms could play an important role. The introduction in 1948 of currency reform in the western zones of occupation was therefore designed to stimulate traditional Teutonic industriousness. One year later the territories under the control of America, England, and France formed the Federal Republic of Germany in accordance with a new democratic constitution. The first chancellor of the republic was Konrad Adenauer of the Christian Democratic party, a septuagenarian politician who governed his country like some stern but patient father controlling a houseful of unruly children.

The result of financial and civic reform was a surprisingly swift recovery. Ten years after unconditional surrender the industrial output of the western region of Germany far exceeded its level before the war. Moreover, the prerogatives of sovereignty, including even the right to maintain an army, had been restored. It was one of the ironies of the post-war scene that in 1950, while victorious England was still forced to retain a system of rationing, defeated Germany ended all restrictions on the purchase of goods. But prosperity had been bought with the low wages and long hours of the working class, and the undiminished strength of the Social Democratic party indicated that the urban proletariat remained loyal to the doctrines of Marxism.

The United States did not forget the small democracies. Belgium, Holland, Norway, Denmark, Greece, and Austria received funds to help revive their industry and agriculture which had been impaired by years of alien occupation. For that matter, the fascist countries were also enlisted in the struggle against radicalism. In 1953 the United States and Spain concluded an agreement by which the former obtained bases in the Iberian peninsula, while the latter received economic aid which strengthened the régime of General Franco. Similarly, the authoritarian government of Premier Salazar in Portugal succeeded in maintaining cordial relations with the democratic powers by allowing them to use airfields in the Azores during the war and by co-operating with them against Russia afterwards.

RUSSIA

The role which the Kremlin played on the other side of the iron curtain was similar to the one which the White House performed on this side. Russia, like America, had come out of the war in a stronger diplomatic and military position than when it went in. In foreign affairs its main concern became the consolidation and expansion of the important political gains which it had made during the hostilities. And at home it had to deal above all with the problem of repairing the vast damage caused by the invasion of the Axis. Both tasks were begun under the direction of Stalin, who was now at the pinnacle of his power. His domestic opponents had been purged; his enemies abroad had been defeated. The Red dictator could exercise greater authority than the tsars had ever possessed. In the army his word was law. Even the removal of the savior of Moscow and captor of Berlin, Marshal Georgi K. Zhukov, from the command of the armed forces evoked not a word of protest. Among biologists, he was accepted as the arbiter of scientific theories, championing Trofim D. Lysenko's teachings against those of Gregor Mendel, which the rest of the world accepted. He even assumed the role of music critic supreme, condemning the works of such eminent composers as Dmitri Shostakovich and Sergei Prokofiev for bourgeois tendencies. Like Ozymandias in Shelley's poem, he could boast: "Look on my works, ye Mighty, and despair!"

The legacy of his limitless power, however, was fear and hatred. After the death of the autocrat on March 5, 1953, the most damaging attack on his lifework came not from some conservative monarchist or middle-class liberal, but from one of his own protégés, Nikita S. Khrushchev:

> Stalin acted not through persuasion, explanation, and patient co-operation with people, but by imposing his concepts and demanding absolute submission to his opinions. Whoever opposed this concept or tried to prove his viewpoint and the correctness of his position was doomed to removal from the leading collective and to subsequent moral and physical annihilation.... Stalin originated the concept "enemy of the people." This term automatically rendered it unnecessary that the ideological errors of a man or men engaged in a controversy be proven; this term made possible the usage of the most cruel repression, violating all norms of revolutionary legality, against anyone who in any way disagreed with Stalin, against those who were only suspected of hostile intent, against those who had bad reputations.... In the main, and in actuality, the only proof of guilt used, against all norms of current legal science, was the "confession" of the accused himself; and as subsequent probing proved, "confessions" were acquired through physical pressures against the accused.[1]

But despite their criticisms, the successors of Stalin differed from him in temperament rather than objective. The apparatus of oppression was slightly relaxed, yet the dictatorship of the party remained. The government maintained its control over the economy, and the secret police continued to function. Moreover, while the cult of one man was replaced by an experiment in collective leadership, within the walls of the Kremlin a struggle for political mastery went on. In 1953 Lavrenti P. Beria appeared to be the power behind the scenes; in 1954 it was Georgi M. Malenkov; in 1955 Nikita S. Khrushchev. Although factions within the communist hierarchy vied for power, there was no evidence of popular opposition to the doctrines of Marxism. The man in the street probably remained convinced that the established order was in essence just. His faith was reinforced, moreover, by the economic and technological progress of his country, which in 1957 startled the capitalistic world by becoming the first to launch an artificial satellite revolving in an orbit around the earth. To a people which had never known political freedom or material well-being the promise of the future seemed to justify past sacrifices.

THE COMMUNIST SATELLITES

The vassal states of the Soviet Union meekly conformed to the wishes of the Kremlin. Soon after the war Poland, Romania, Hungary, Bulgaria,

---

[1] *New York Times,* June 5, 1956.

Yugoslavia, Albania, Czechoslovakia, and the German Democratic Republic, formed in the Russian zone of occupation, began to establish the dictatorship of the Communist party, to collectivize agriculture, to nationalize factories and banks, and to engage in a test of strength with the church. They organized security police systems and built corrective labor camps, launching periodic campaigns against ideological dissenters. Even dedicated left-wingers, among them Traicho Kostov in Bulgaria, Laszlo Rajk in Hungary, and Rudolf Slansky in Czechoslovakia, suffered imprisonment or death because of suspicions in Moscow that they were secretly planning to pursue an independent policy. Only Marshal Tito of Yugoslavia succeeded in defying Russia, and he was punished with expulsion from the communist camp in 1948.

With the death of Stalin the grip of the Kremlin began to loosen. There was much talk about following several paths to the classless society in accordance with special national conditions. In 1955 Khrushchev and Tito compromised the differences between their governments on terms which represented a moral victory for the latter. One year later the communist leader of Poland, Wladyslaw Gomulka, succeeded in winning a measure of autonomy for his country. Yet although the Soviet Union was prepared to tolerate some differences within the Marxist system, it remained opposed to any attack on the system itself. Thus, when in the fall of 1956 a popular uprising in Hungary sought to overthrow the radical government, the Red Army marched against the Magyars and suppressed the rebellion by force of arms. Disregarding all the pronouncements about "national sovereignty, mutual advantage, and equality," Moscow made it clear that it had no intention of permitting the re-establishment of the barrier of hostile states which had stood in its way in the interwar period.

After 1953 the Communist parties of the satellite nations, while still opposed to parliamentary democracy, relaxed some of their most oppressive economic and political restrictions. In the face of strongly antiradical popular sentiments, moreover, they advanced a program of reform which was not without beneficent results. They ended the dominant position of the conservative landed aristocracy; they increased the output of factories and mines; they improved the quality of popular instruction; they curbed the rampant chauvinism of the educated classes. Their rule was dictatorial and brutal, but they succeeded in destroying the historic social system of the eastern borderlands of the Continent. The lasting result of their activities was that even in the event of their fall from power, the task of restoring the old order would be like attempting to unscramble an omelet.

THE CONTINENT IN DECLINE

While the outcome of the struggle between democratic capitalism and authoritarian communism remained in doubt, there was no question that

Europe had suffered a political collapse. It could still manufacture goods and grow crops; it could still produce works of art and achieve advances in science. Indeed, the progress of technology assured for its masses a higher standard of living than they had ever known before. But it could no longer command obedience in a world which was increasingly adopting the way of life of the Occident. The ordeal of total war and the strain of colonial conflict had exhausted the Continent. Like Hellas after the death of Alexander the Great, it might continue to enlighten the barbarian. Its capacity for the subjugation of alien peoples, however, was dwindling. Not only was the colored man rebelling against the rule of the European with increasing success, but the European himself was no longer master in his own house. Whether he liked it or not, he had to choose between two alternatives neither of which would have been conceivable before the First World War. Either he allied himself with the United States, which lay beyond the frontiers of the Old World, or he was forced to become a satellite of Russia, a land only partly Occidental. The existence of this dilemma was a measure of his decline. Economic recovery remained an attainable goal, but political hegemony was a thing of the past. The heroic age of Europe had come to an end.

3 : The Orient in Revolt

The East was in the meantime experiencing the exhilaration of a great awakening. Its political revival, which had begun early in the twentieth century, was stimulated by military conflicts and social upheavals in Europe. Most of the Orient had escaped the devastation of war, and even in those regions which became battlefields economic backwardness actually facilitated recovery. It was easier to rebuild a Burmese village or a Bedouin encampment than Berlin, London, or Warsaw. Besides, from the point of view of native nationalism, physical suffering was a fair price for the relaxation of alien rule. After 1918 the English, the French, and the Dutch had been forced to make important political concessions to the colonial masses; after 1945 their resistance to anti-imperialistic demands began to collapse completely. For the Orient, therefore, the major developments of the post-war years were a logical extension of the administrative improvements and constitutional reforms initiated during the interwar period.

Some of the colonial powers, such as Great Britain and the United States, accepting gracefully what could not be changed, succeeded in maintaining cordial relations with their former possessions. Others, particularly France and Holland, attempted to hold their dependencies by force of arms, only to discover that they no longer had the military resources to suppress nationalism in the East. They were defeated, and what is more, the struggle cost them whatever good will they had retained among their emancipated subjects. For whether under the leadership of liberals, communists, or party bosses, the dark-skinned races were resolved to win the right of self-determination.

THE FAR EAST

In the Far East the most important political effect of the Second World War was the defeat of the country which for forty years had been paramount along the western shore of the Pacific. Japan, like Germany, paid the penalty of defeat by the loss of its position as a great nation. But, unlike Germany, it did not suffer the disaster of territorial partition. By surrendering under circumstances which in effect made the United States the major occupying power, it insured a uniform reorganization of its civic and economic institutions. The man entrusted with the task of governing the defeated enemy was General Douglas MacArthur, who played the role of Yankee proconsul with an enthusiasm inspiring the observation: "The Japanese emperor has renounced his divinity. It has been taken up by General MacArthur." Under his direction Japan adopted a program of far-reaching reform. A new constitution promulgated on November 3, 1946, declared the people to be the source of sovereignty; it introduced government by a cabinet responsible to parliament; it defined the freedom of the citizen in a bill of rights; it conferred on women a status of legal equality with men; and it proclaimed that war was "forever renounced as a means of settling disputes with other nations." At the same time the leading exponents of the pre-war policy of aggression were executed or imprisoned, and thousands of their followers were excluded from participation in politics. The armed forces were dissolved; the secret police was abolished; the system of popular education was liberalized; and the formation of labor unions was encouraged. Finally, measures were initiated to transform landless peasants into independent farmers and to break the power of the great industrial and financial combines known as the *zaibatsu*. The effect was a revolution from above democratizing the social structure of a country still dominated by an aristocracy of birth and wealth.

To demonstrate its faith in the new parliamentary régime as well as to win an important ally against communism, the United States on September 8, 1951, signed a peace treaty with Japan, by which the latter regained its national sovereignty. Yet the loss of all of its possessions outside the home islands meant that a population of some eighty-five million had to find subsistence in an area no larger than that on which twenty-eight million had lived a century before when Commodore Matthew C. Perry first sailed into Edo Bay. A security pact concluded with Washington, moreover, permitted American troops to remain in its territories. To be sure, they were no longer to act as an army of occupation, but rather "to deter armed attack." Yet expressions of mutual regard could not disguise the fact that the Land of the Rising Sun was still within the American sphere of influence.

The collapse of Japan enabled China to claim at last the position of the leading power in the Far East. Yet its triumph also exposed it once again to domestic strife. As long as they faced the Nipponese armies, the Kuomintang under Chiang Kai-shek and the Communist party under Mao Tse-tung were forced to collaborate against their common enemy. But once Tokyo had surrendered, old animosities began to rise to the surface.

From 1945 to 1950 the nation went through a civil war in which the leftists gradually won the upper hand. First of all, they received substantial support from the Soviet Union. Secondly, their armed forces proved superior in leadership and discipline to their opponents. And finally, their program of radical economic reform made a strong appeal to millions of poverty-stricken workers and peasants. The government of the republic, on the other hand, frittered away whatever political and military advantages it had possessed when the struggle began. As for the United States, immediately after the surrender of the Japanese it attempted to mediate between the two opposing camps. Even after the efforts of General George C. Marshall to arrange a truce had failed because of intransigency on both sides, Washington went on giving the Nationalists financial assistance, which by 1948 amounted to more than two billion dollars. But money alone could not buy honesty and efficiency in Nanking. As the Red armies continued to make headway against the anticommunists, the White House decided to cut its losses. Convinced that nothing less than the intervention of American troops could save the Kuomintang, it finally assumed a hands-off attitude.

The American policy of neutrality toward the struggle in China hastened the defeat of the Nationalists. By 1950 Chiang Kai-shek had been driven to the island of Formosa (Taiwan), leaving the mainland completely in the hands of the leftists. The latter proceeded to introduce an ambitious program of socialization and industrialization under the dictatorial leadership of the Communist party. Furthermore, a pact of friendship with the Soviet Union established a formal alliance between the two Marxist states.

Meanwhile the Nationalists on Formosa, now that the horse had been stolen, were rushing to lock the stable. The troops they managed to save from the debacle were reorganized and retrained; bureaucratic corruption was suppressed; the economy of the island was strengthened; and the system of administration was democratized. There was even bold talk about the reconquest of the mainland from communism. Yet the fact was that an insular province with a population of some eight million people and an army of perhaps six hundred thousand aging soldiers could hardly expect to undertake a military campaign against an enemy whose armed forces were among the largest in the world. Only in the event of a war between China and America, or of a successful revolution against the communist government in Peking, could the Kuomintang hope to regain political power.

INDIA

In India the victory of nationalism was easier. For one thing, there was a world of difference between the parliamentarians in London and the militarists in Tokyo. And secondly, the religious hostility of Hindu and Moslem was not as uncompromising as the ideological opposition of communist and conservative. As soon as the war was over, Prime Minister Attlee entered into negotiations with the political leaders of the subcontinent

INDIA AND
PAKISTAN
1950

Soon after the end of the Second World War the victorious governments established an International Military Tribunal at Nürnberg to sit in judgment on the chief civilian and military officials of Germany for crimes against peace and humanity. On October 1, 1946, twelve of the defendants were sentenced to death, seven were given prison terms of from ten years to life, and three were freed. Of those condemned to execution, Hermann Göring cheated the hangman by committing suicide, while Martin Bormann, who was tried in absentia, has never been found.

Here is that curious mixture of the ancient and the modern out of which was formed the state of Israel. The Star of David on the wall and the bearded elders wearing skullcaps in the foreground symbolize the age-old traditions of Judaism. The microphones broadcasting the ceremony and the uniformed figures standing in the background belong unmistakably to the twentieth century. The same contrast is personified in the president himself, an eminent scientist with an international reputation in chemistry, and a political dreamer seeking to re-create a nation which lost its independence long before the birth of Christ.

By the time of this historic meeting in the Crimea it was becoming increasingly difficult to reconcile the conflicts of interest among the leaders of the grand coalition. But victory over the Axis was now certain, and there was still great hope that the post-war world would be free from political insecurity. The British prime minister summoned a smile for the photographer, while even the dour Russian dictator seemed more or less relaxed. Only the American president looked haggard, a picture of total exhaustion. Two months later he was dead.

*Gathered around a conference table in Washington during the spring of
1949 are the representatives of eight governments opposed to the expansion
of the Soviet Union. From left to right they are LeGallais of Luxemburg,
Van Kleffens of the Netherlands, Silvercruys of Belgium, Morgenstierne of
Norway, Acheson of the United States, Bonnet of France, Wrong of Canada,
and Franks of Great Britain. Their deliberations led to the formation of
a vast military alliance covering an area of nearly 8,000,000 square miles,
with a population of more than 300,000,000 people.*

to determine the conditions under which the liberation of their country should take place. But no agreement was reached. The Indian National Congress, still loyal to the teachings of Gandhi, advocated the establishment of a united democratic state in which the various cultural communities could live peacefully side by side. This plan appealed particularly to the adherents of Hinduism, who constituted a majority of the nation. The All-India Moslem League under Mohammed Ali Jinnah, however, insisted on nothing less than the creation of a separate state for the followers of Islam, to be known as Pakistan. Otherwise, it maintained, there could be no effective protection of the Mohammedan minority against the bigotry of the Hindus. On August 15, 1947, after all efforts to find a mutually acceptable compromise had failed, two new countries were formed in India.

The Union of India, with a population of close to 400,000,000 people and an area of some 1,300,000 square miles, was politically the more important. Governed by Prime Minister Jawaharlal Nehru in the spirit of moderate socialism, it followed a policy of agricultural and industrial reform at home and of neutrality between Russia and America in foreign affairs. The essential objectives of its diplomacy were defined in 1954 in the five principles or Panch Shila: respect for other countries' territorial integrity and sovereignty; non-aggression; non-interference in other nations' internal affairs; equality and mutual benefit; and peaceful coexistence. But the Republic of Pakistan, with 76,000,000 inhabitants in two widely separated regions totaling 365,000 square miles, took its stand on the side of the capitalistic democracies. Influenced in its philosophy of state by the teachings of the Koran, it was naturally opposed to the antireligious doctrines of Marxism. Both nations suffered from overpopulation and underproduction, aggravated by the economic dislocation which political separation created. And yet despite their common history, despite their common needs and purposes, they remained divided by religious hostilities and territorial disputes. From the point of view of civic and material progress, the partition of the subcontinent was a surrender of national welfare to fear and prejudice.

SOUTHEAST ASIA

The neighboring states of southeast Asia also won their political independence. The British, once they recognized the inevitability of the decline of imperialism, adapted their colonial policies to changing conditions. Since they could not suppress native nationalism, they attempted to influence it by a program of conciliation. In 1946 Ceylon received the right of self-government in domestic affairs; in 1948 Burma was recognized as a free republic; and in 1957 Malaya won the status of a sovereign power. Similarly, the United States in 1946 redeemed the promise of the Tydings-McDuffie Act of 1934 with the establishment of the Republic of the Philippines, an act of generous statesmanship which was rewarded by a close political and economic collaboration between Manila and Washington.

The Dutch, however, were not disposed to part with their overseas possessions so easily. Immediately after the surrender of Japan they returned to the Netherlands East Indies, only to find that the nationalists under Achmed Soekarno and Mohammed Hatta had already proclaimed the independence of the islands. There followed four years of intermittent warfare, until on December 27, 1949, the government of Queen Juliana was forced to agree to the independence of the United States of Indonesia.

The French in Indo-China opposed demands for the end of imperialistic rule with even greater determination. Yet the result was the same. After fighting against their colonial subjects for nine frustrating years they were finally forced by the defeat at Dien Bien Phu in 1954 to admit the futility of further hostilities. The northern half of the country was surrendered to the communists led by Ho Chi Minh, while the southern part went to the moderates under Ngo Dinh Diem.

THE MIDDLE EAST

The conflicting objectives of European imperialism, Arab patriotism, and Jewish nationalism had created a diplomatic powder keg in the Middle East. Among Zionists the effect of the Second World War was to strengthen their determination to establish an independent nation in Palestine. The extermination by National Socialism of millions of their defenseless co-religionists served to emphasize the need for a sovereign authority capable of opposing anti-Semitism, while the plight of the hundreds of thousands of survivors of the holocaust who were in search of a place of refuge provided an additional argument for proclaiming a Jewish state in the Holy Land. The position of the Arabs was that the criminal atrocities of the Axis in eastern Europe were no justification for any change in the ethnic composition of western Asia. And the British had only one desire, to withdraw as soon as possible from a country in which both sides looked upon them as intruders.

After a proposal of the United Nations to partition Palestine had been rejected by the Arabs, the United Kingdom surrendered its mandate on May 14, 1948. That same day a Zionist provisional government under David Ben Gurion announced the formation of the state of Israel. The result was a war which continued for about a year between the new republic and its Arab enemies. The Jews held their own, and an uneasy armistice was finally concluded which left them in control of about half of the Holy Land. They adopted a system of government based on the principles of parliamentary democracy, and in the diplomatic struggle between the United States and the Soviet Union their sympathies were on the side of Washing-

ton. But serious dangers still threatened them. Economically, they managed to make ends meet only through the contributions of their co-religionists in the New World, since the arid soil of Palestine could not support a swiftly growing population of close to two million inhabitants. Militarily, moreover, they had to face hostile neighbors who had lost one campaign, but who were determined to avenge their defeat the moment an opportunity arose.

For the Arabs the conflict with Israel was only one aspect of a greater struggle against the political influence of the West. In 1945 there had been formed the League of Arab States, an association of countries which included Egypt, Syria, Lebanon, Iraq, Transjordania, Saudi Arabia, and Yemen, with a combined population of approximately forty-five million people and an area extending from the Persian Gulf to the Libyan Desert. Under its direction the lands of the Middle East proceeded to free themselves from the remnants of colonial rule. Foreign troops were withdrawn from Syria and Lebanon in 1946; national independence was achieved in Libya in 1951; and Morocco and Tunisia became sovereign states in 1956.

The most colorful of the leaders in the struggle against imperialism was Gamal Abdel Nasser, an officer in the Egyptian army, who became the dominant figure in the government in Cairo after the deposition of King Farouk in 1952. The impoverished masses of his countrymen idolized him as their deliverer from foreign oppression, while jealous politicians regarded him as only an ambitious climber exploiting the force of nationalism to further his own career. All agreed, however, that no other figure on the political scene in the Middle East possessed his flair for the dramatic. The supreme test of his skill as a statesman came in 1956, when as a result of the withdrawal of a promise of financial support by the democratic states he seized the Suez Canal Company. The reply to this move was a lightning military campaign by Israeli, British, and French troops against the Egyptian armed forces, which were easily defeated. The Nile lay defenseless before the invaders. And yet the dashing dictator actually managed to transform a military disaster into a diplomatic victory. Since neither the United States nor the Soviet Union wanted to antagonize patriotic sentiment within Islam, Nasser was saved from a total debacle by the intervention of the United Nations. The world organization deprived the victors of their conquests and left the vanquished to enjoy a major political triumph.

In the course of the hostilities the Kremlin had offered to help the Egyptians oppose the designs of "bourgeois imperialism." Thereafter the prestige of Russia rose throughout the Middle East. There were even important Arab leaders ready to enter into an alliance with Moscow, not because of any sympathy with Marxism, but in order to play off communism against capitalism. Such a course was tempting, although it was not without its dangers. In the diplomatic agreements which the Soviet Union had concluded with the countries of eastern Europe after the Second World War the Russians had consistently gotten the best of the bargain. Furthermore, leftist expansionism had proved as oppressive as rightist imperialism. Lastly, in the event of an armed conflict for control of the Mediterranean, the first victims of war would be the masses of Islam.

AFRICA

The influence of native nationalism was felt as far as the Dark Continent. In the interwar period there had already been evidence of the discontent of the black man with white rule, and after 1945 the demand for self-determination for Africa became more insistent. Sometimes it found expression in barbaric secret societies like the Mau Mau in Kenya, which launched a campaign of terror against colonial domination under the slogan: "Take back the land which the white man has stolen from us!" Sometimes it took the form of open demonstrations of political disaffection, as when some fifty thousand persons in the Gold Coast participated in a nationalist riot in 1948. And sometimes it was used by colored leftists like Jomo Kenyatta to advance radical doctrines in the guise of protests against imperialism.

The response of the whites to the growing civic consciousness of the Negro varied. In the Union of South Africa it was an even stricter program of racial segregation introduced in 1948 by the Boers of the Nationalist party under Prime Minister Daniel Malan. The Belgians and the Portuguese farther north attempted to oppose native nationalism with a policy of ethnic toleration and economic progress. For the French in West Africa and in Equatorial Africa, the ideal remained assimilation, that is, the acceptance by the educated and propertied blacks of the culture of the mother country in return for their admission to the rights of citizenship.

As for the possessions of Great Britain, they were governed on the assumption that the process of political development in colored colonies would not be essentially different from what it had been in white colonies. The authorities in London accordingly sought to prepare the way for a system of self-rule in which the Europeans would at least in the beginning be predominant, but in which the interests of the indigenous population would also be represented. In 1950, for example, new constitutions were promulgated for Nigeria and Sierra Leone which envisaged a considerable measure of participation in civic affairs by Negroes. In 1953 came the establishment of the Central African Federation, composed of Northern Rhodesia, Southern Rhodesia, and Nyasaland, and governed by a parliament of thirty-five members among whom were six natives. And in 1957 the Gold Coast became the free and sovereign state of Ghana, the first land in black Africa to complete the transition to national independence.

LIBERATION FROM IMPERIALISM

It was clear that the relationship between Occident and Orient was changing. The former was still preponderant in economic and military resources, but these were no longer sufficient to support its political domination. Occasionally through the use of persuasion, more commonly by the application of force, the dark-skinned races were freeing themselves from alien rule. The end of the era of imperialism, to be sure, was not always an unmixed blessing. In comparison with European standards, native methods of government were often less efficient and sometimes less honest. Moreover, in many cases colored politicans regarded the civic rights of their countrymen even more cavalierly than the foreign bureaucrats had done. Perhaps worst of all, economic ties which had been fostered under the auspices of the West were frequently severed by newly emancipated countries eager to assert their right of self-determination. Yet even after the first outburst of enthusiasm inspired by the proclamation of independence subsided, there was little nostalgia among the native masses for colonialism. In London, Paris, and The Hague disgruntled soldiers and administrators who had lost their jobs overseas went on predicting a dire future for their former colonies. The endless refrain was: "They'll be sorry." Yet for better or worse colored peoples preferred freedom to security or efficiency or even honesty. They were determined to make their own way in the world at all costs. And foreign criticism of their policy, no matter how justified, only intensified their determination. The truth was that imperialism was succumbing to the political resurgence of the Orient.

4 : The Cold War

THE MOST pressing problem confronting the post-war world was the danger of another great war. Modern military science had made any future armed conflict among the major states seem so devastating and comprehensive that a diplomacy of neutrality was becoming impossible. There could no longer be a distinction between combatants and non-combatants, only between winners and losers. For that matter, the unlimited capacity for destruction of new offensive weapons suggested that the difference between victory and defeat might prove meaningless, for each side was in a position to inflict enormous damage upon the other.

Never before the twentieth century had wars been waged for such objectives as "peace and justice in the life of the world" or "world order under law." Yet never before the twentieth century had peace treaties provided so little security for the world. The statecraft of reactionary aristocrats like Metternich and Castlereagh or of clever opportunists like Bismarck and Cavour had given the West a century of relative tranquillity. The idealism of democratic leaders like Woodrow Wilson and Franklin D. Roosevelt, on the other hand, produced only a brief truce after 1918 and an even briefer one after 1945. In his address of April 18, 1955, President Achmed Soekarno of Indonesia expressed the prevailing mood of a generation disillusioned by the constant frustration of its hopes: "Yes, we are living in a world of fear. The life of man today is corroded and made bitter by fear. Fear of the future, fear of the hydrogen bomb, fear of ideologies. Perhaps this fear is a greater danger than the danger itself, because it is fear which drives men to act foolishly, to act thoughtlessly, to act dangerously."

WARTIME DIPLOMACY

The origins of the diplomatic crisis which the post-war world faced lay in the war itself. The outbreak of hostilities in 1939 signified that the political structure of the West, weakened by the shock of the First World War, was in danger of total collapse. The question was what would replace it. Yet the victorious powers failed to deal with the organization of the peace until military operations were almost over. The democracies contented themselves with pious declarations like the Atlantic Charter of August 14, 1941, by which the United States and Great Britain promised to work together for a never-never land of brotherly love among nations. At the same time the Soviet Union was delivering vague pronouncements about the destruction of fascism and the friendship of peace-loving states. As Stalin put it: "It is not so difficult to keep unity in time of war since there is a joint aim to defeat the common enemy, which is clear to everyone. The difficult task will come after the war when diverse interests tend to divide the Allies."

From the point of view of military efficiency it was probably best to avoid discussion of controversial political issues until the Axis had been defeated. But at the same time the task of diplomatic negotiation became more difficult as the day of victory approached. The processes of war and peace could not be logically separated, since the outcome of one was bound to determine the conditions of the other. The decision to postpone serious consideration of the post-war settlement until the enemy was on the verge of surrender meant that by the time the statesmen finally met around the conference table there was little they could do except recognize an international situation which the generals had created by force of arms.

Early in February, 1945, Roosevelt, Stalin, and Churchill met at Yalta in order to reach an agreement concerning the organization of the peace. In an atmosphere of cordiality, heightened by the good news from the front, they succeeded in reaching a friendly understanding on most of the questions with which they had to deal. It was not difficult to make preparations for the establishment of the United Nations and for the occupation of the Third Reich. The fate of eastern Europe was a more delicate problem, but there the Soviet Union held all the trump cards. In its retreat westward the Wehrmacht had abandoned this region to the Red Army, which made sure that ministries friendly toward communism were formed in the countries which it "liberated." The democracies therefore decided to accept a state of affairs which they were powerless to alter in return for a promise by Moscow of "the earliest possible establishment through free elections of governments responsive to the will of the people." Finally, Russia agreed to enter the war against Japan on the condition that the territories and rights in the Far East which it had lost by the Treaty of Portsmouth of 1905 would be restored.

Since many of his military experts were warning him that it might take eighteen months or more to defeat the Japanese armies, Roosevelt consented to pay Stalin's price. As it turned out, his acquiescence was unnecessary, for Tokyo decided to sue for peace long before the Kremlin entered the conflict in Asia on August 8, 1945. Yet the criticism that the ailing president unleashed the demon of communism by making too many unnecessary concessions was by and large unjustified. Granted that he underestimated the political ambitions of the Kremlin and overestimated his own ability to charm Stalin into co-operation, even a statesman made of sterner stuff could not have halted the expansion of the Soviet Union.

The fact was that the total collapse of Germany and Japan created a power vacuum from which Moscow was bound to profit. Its neighbors in Europe were in effect occupied by the Red Army. Whether the democratic powers recognized the preponderance of Russia in the eastern borderlands or not, nothing short of a new major war could put an end to it. As for Asia, while it is true that Roosevelt invited the intervention of the Kremlin, Stalin would in any case hardly have consented to an extension of the influence of a capitalistic state over the entire western shore of the Pacific. With or without the approval of the United States he was sure to take advantage of the debacle of the Japanese by launching an invasion of China from bases in Siberia. Far from creating the problems which beset the post-war world, the Yalta Conference merely confirmed their existence. As James F. Byrnes, who had gone to the Crimea with the American delegation, pointed out: "It was not a question of what we would let the Russians do, but what we could get the Russians to do."

THE POST-WAR ALLIANCE SYSTEMS

Although the end of hostilities had been greeted in the victorious countries as the beginning of an era of international security, not many months passed before disillusionment set in. For there was obviously a vast difference of opinion among the wartime allies regarding the execution of the settlements reached at the Yalta Conference. To the democratic states they implied a guarantee of parliamentary capitalism in Europe. To the Kremlin, on the other hand, they meant an extension of the power of the Soviet Union commensurate with the magnitude of its victory over the Axis. No sooner had the enemy been defeated, therefore, than the grand coalition against fascism began to disintegrate.

First there was a dispute about the attempt of Moscow to maintain a foothold in Iran, which its troops had entered in the course of the war. Then appeared the new party line of the communist movement which once again became hostile toward bourgeois governments. Before long the régimes formed in eastern Europe under Russian auspices threw aside the mask of moderate reformism and revealed themselves as out-and-out satellites of Stalin. Finally, the impressive victories of the armies of Mao Tse-tung in China increased the prestige of the Kremlin among the nations of Asia. By 1947 there could no longer be any doubt about the political intentions of Moscow. As one Russian diplomatic success followed another, the statesmen of the democracies turned to the United States as the only power still capable of opposing the expansion of the Soviet Union.

When he first became chief executive on April 12, 1945, President Harry S. Truman was one of the millions of Americans who hoped for continuing collaboration among the victorious countries. The aggressive foreign policy pursued by Stalin, however, soon convinced him that only a strong stand by the parliamentary states could contain the radical dictator. When Russia began to menace Greece and Turkey, he decided that the moment had come to proclaim a new departure in the diplomacy of the United States. In a speech delivered on March 12, 1947, he made clear the readiness of his administration to accept the responsibility which communist expansion had thrust upon it. Urging Congress to extend financial aid to the two threatened nations, he told America that "the free peoples of the world look to us for support in maintaining their freedom."

Four months later the principles of the Truman Doctrine were applied in the Marshall Plan, a project advanced by General George C. Marshall who had recently been appointed Secretary of State. It provided long-term financial assistance by the United States to those countries of Europe which were ready to uphold representative institutions, but which were hampered in their efforts by material hardship. By 1952 the authorities in Washington had approved the expenditure of some thirteen billion dollars for the economic recovery of the Old World. The results were by and large satisfactory. While the Soviet Union still constituted a threat to the security of the democracies, the advance of the Kremlin on the Continent came to a halt, and the danger of revolution in western and southern Europe receded.

The employment of economic weapons to combat Moscow was followed logically by the mobilization of military resources. On April 4, 1949, the foreign ministers of the United States, Great Britain, France, Belgium, the Netherlands, Luxemburg, Italy, Portugal, Norway, Denmark, Iceland, and Canada signed the North Atlantic Treaty, which provided that an armed attack on any one of the parties was to be considered as an attack against all. The American Secretary of State Dean Acheson described the strategy dictating the formation of this alliance: "We have also learned that if the free nations do not stand together, they will fall one by one. The stratagem of the aggressor is to keep his intended victims divided, or, better still, set them to quarreling among themselves. Then they can be picked off one by one without arousing unified resistance. We and the free nations of Europe are determined that history shall not repeat itself in that melancholy particular." In the Far East a similar diplomatic alignment directed against communism came into existence in 1954 with the conclusion of the Southeast Asia Treaty by the United States, Great Britain, France, Australia, New Zealand, the Philippines, and Thailand. Its effectiveness, however, was limited by the absence of such important Asian states as India, Indonesia, and Burma.

At the same time the leaders of the Soviet Union were busy marshaling their forces. In 1950 a pact of mutual assistance negotiated by Moscow and Peking strengthened the influence of the Kremlin in Asia. And in 1955 the Warsaw Treaty authorized the Kremlin to station its troops in the satellite countries of eastern Europe and placed their armies under the command of Marshal Ivan Konev of Russia. Thus, ten years after the defeat of fascism, two armed camps divided by fundamental political and economic differences again confronted each other.

NEW INTERNATIONAL CONFLICTS

Even more ominous than the military alliances were the new international conflicts which followed the return of peace. In June, 1948, a diplomatic crisis arose when the Kremlin decided to score an inexpensive political success by forcing the democratic powers to evacuate their forces from Berlin. The former capital of the Third Reich, although deep within the region of Germany assigned to the Soviet Union, had been placed under the administration of all four occupying powers. By halting rail and road traffic between the city and the western zones, Moscow hoped to force the American, British, and French troops into a withdrawal from a starving metropolis. Only the transportation of essential supplies by air enabled the isolated western garrisons to hold out, until in May, 1949, the Russians admitted defeat by lifting the blockade.

One year later hostilities broke out in Korea. After its surrender by the Japanese at the end of the Second World War the country had been partitioned by Russia and the United States along the thirty-eighth parallel for the purpose of temporary administration. As in the case of Germany, the division proved to be lasting. Even when foreign troops were finally withdrawn after an occupation of almost four years, they left behind them two rival governments. The radicals led by Kim Il Sung controlled the north; the conservatives under Syngman Rhee were established in the south. On June 25, 1950, the armies of North Korea opened an invasion designed to unite the nation under a leftist régime. The result was a full-scale armed conflict which lasted three years. The Republic of Korea was supported by the troops of the United States and its allies, while the forces of the communist Korean People's Democratic Republic were reinforced by hundreds of thousands of "volunteers" from China. When a truce was finally concluded on July 27, 1953, total casualties were in the neighborhood of three million men, while the military expenditures of America alone were twenty-two billion dollars. As for the boundary between the two sides, it was just about where it had been before the shooting started, along the thirty-eighth parallel.

No sooner had the fighting in Korea come to an end, than developments in Indo-China threatened to lead to a major war. The struggle between the leftist nationalists under Ho Chi Minh and the colonial authorities reached a climax in 1954. The insurrectionists were clearly gaining the upper hand despite American dollars and French casualties. Their capture of the stronghold of Dien Bien Phu proved that they could not be defeated by the forces which the Fourth Republic had at its disposal. Only the armed intervention of the United States might crush the danger of Marxism in

Indo-China as it had almost done in Korea. President Eisenhower had to make a crucial decision. Having only recently brought to a conclusion one frustrating struggle in the Far East which had almost turned into a world war, he was in no mood to embark upon another. Besides, the involvement of American troops in the jungles of southeast Asia could tempt the Kremlin to seek gains in central Europe or along the Mediterranean. Washington therefore consented to an agreement which left the northern half of Indo-China to the radicals, while the south was placed under the control of a moderate native régime. Once again a conflict between communism and democracy had ended in a stalemate.

Most statesmen on both sides of the iron curtain wanted peace. Although they differed regarding the legitimate objectives of government, they also recognized that another world war would bring destruction to conqueror and conquered alike. Not only did the major countries therefore announce repeatedly that what they sought above all was international stability, but they conferred again and again concerning the best means to achieve it. The foreign ministers of the United States, the Soviet Union, the United Kingdom, and the French Republic met in London in 1945 to attempt to reach a friendly settlement. They met once more in Paris in 1946; then in Moscow in 1947. An even more important gathering took place in Geneva in 1955, when President Eisenhower, Russian Premier Nikolai A. Bulganin, British Prime Minister Anthony Eden, and French Premier Edgar Faure discussed the diplomatic situation. All in all, the declarations of pacific intentions issued by each of the powers would have filled volumes.

Yet the world knew no peace, because the two great alliance systems regarded each other with fear and hostility. They were almost convinced that "a house divided against itself cannot stand," that mankind could not remain indefinitely half authoritarian, half democratic. At times the United States insisted that its diplomacy aimed at nothing more than "containment," that is, a limitation of the gains of Marxism to the boundaries it had achieved by 1949. At other times, however, it spoke of "liberation," the suppression of communism in those regions in which it had become dominant after 1939. The Soviet Union was equally inconsistent in its statements of political objectives. There were occasions when it maintained that its purpose was "peaceful coexistence" with the capitalistic states in which the relative merits of the two rival economic systems could be tested by friendly competition. But then there were occasions when it returned to the more familiar theme that the proletarian fatherland must oppose by force the plutocratic democracies.

The most significant element of hope in this situation was the reluctance on both sides to precipitate open hostilities. New military weapons like atomic bombs, jet airplanes, rocket projectiles, and intercontinental missiles threatened to inflict such enormous damage on the combatants of the future that neither communism nor democracy could feel sure of its ability to survive the ordeal of war. Therefore, despite belligerent notes and pronouncements, despite even acts of direct provocation, neither the White House nor the Kremlin was ready to start shooting. Indeed, when it actually came to an armed conflict, as in Korea in 1950 or in Egypt in 1956, they used their influence to prevent it from developing into a major struggle. Yet in 1914 the great powers had also sought to avoid a major struggle, only to discover that they were no longer in a position to control the crisis which was driving them all to self-destruction. Was there any assurance that they would be more successful now in preventing a world war? There were still so many frustrated little countries ready to satisfy their national ambitions at all costs; there were still so many superpatriotic demagogues and chauvinistic dictators. Frightened and tired, the post-war world groped for a way out of an armed truce which was neither war nor peace.

5 : The Meaning of the Twentieth Century

THE EXPERIENCES of war, revolution, and depression have cast a pall of anxiety over the twentieth century. Ours is an age in which familiar institutions and attitudes are exposed to unfamiliar situations and demands. Such periods are not uncommon in the history of man, but they invariably produce a sense of bewilderment among those whom they force to abandon an accustomed way of life. Shortly after the First World War the British poet A. E. Housman expressed the anguish of a society shaken by a terrible physical ordeal:

> *And how am I to face the odds*
> *Of man's bedevilment and God's?*
> *I, a stranger and afraid*
> *In a world I never made.*[2]

He was echoing the sentiments of those who liked to think of themselves as the "lost generation." Yet only a hundred years earlier another British poet, William Wordsworth, was bewailing the England of his day:

> *She is a fen*
> *Of stagnant waters: altar, sword, and pen,*
> *Fireside, the heroic wealth of hall and bower,*
> *Have forfeited their ancient English dower*
> *Of inward happiness.*

Three hundred years before that a great political thinker, Niccolò Machiavelli, looked at his native country and lamented that "Italy should be

---

[2] A. E. Housman, *Last Poems* (New York: Henry Holt and Company, 1922), p. 28.

reduced to her present condition, and that she should be more enslaved than the Hebrews, more oppressed than the Persians, and more scattered than the Athenians; without a head, without order, beaten, despoiled, lacerated, and overrun, and that she should have suffered ruin of every kind." And some two thousand years before that the world-weary preacher of the Old Testament was warning mankind: "I have seen all the works that are done under the sun; and behold, all is vanity and vexation of spirit."

The point is that the very nature of social change imposes upon every age new tasks and responsibilities which at times seem insupportable to those who must struggle with them. Only long afterwards does the scholar look into the past and tell us that the despairing Wordsworth lived in the midst of that great outburst of creative energy known as romanticism; that Machiavelli bemoaned the fate of his nation in the shadow of the magnificent artistic achievements of the Renaissance; that the unknown disillusioned author of Ecclesiastes was the heir of a rich cultural tradition which gave mankind the ideal of universal monotheism. Similarly, it is safe to assume that what history will see in the twentieth century is not what the twentieth century sees in itself. For the price which today's existence demands in physical toil and mental strain is forgotten tomorrow, and only the vital accomplishment bequeathed by the present to the future remains. The problem is to recognize this accomplishment taking shape amid the hurly-burly of the market place where men labor for their daily bread. In order to solve it we must become detached observers of a world in which we are also active participants; we must rise above our own interests and commitments in the life which goes on around us. Clearly, a task of such complexity is to be approached with a sense of intellectual humility.

In the light of historical experience, the twentieth century appears to be concerned with social justice as intensely as the nineteenth century was concerned with political freedom. In other words, our age is one in which men are determined to free themselves from the economic inequities and insecurities which in the past were accepted as the inevitable accompaniment of life in the community. Parliamentarianism, socialism, fascism, each in turn has had to take into account this vast popular yearning for security and has had to make an accommodation to it. Seen from this point of view, the cold war becomes a struggle to determine whether a higher degree of mass welfare will be achieved under democratic capitalism or authoritarian communism.

This struggle may end in the ultimate victory of one side or the other; or it may result in a stalemate gradually leading to a mutual adjustment, such as that which followed the religious conflicts of four hundred years ago. In any case, unless a new world war accompanied by enormous physical destruction should suddenly depress the level of material civilization, the demand for a stable and paternalistic social order is bound to grow. The ideal of civic freedom and the institution of private property may solve the problems of the future as they overcame the dangers of the past, but only by recognizing the need to adapt themselves to the changing conditions of human progress. The strength of democracy lies not in a rigid adherence to outworn formulas, but in its ability to meet a new challenge in the spirit of liberty and honesty.

Perhaps even more important than the quest for social justice is the longing for national justice. The current reaction of the Oriental peoples against colonialism is nothing more than what the Occidental states experienced in the past. It is motivated by the same principle of nationalism; it aims at the same goal of self-determination. It is often guilty, moreover, of the same arbitrariness and jingoism. Yet successful resistance to its demands is in the long run impossible. For among colored as among white men the desire for political freedom cannot be suppressed. A recognition of the decline of imperialism need not imply an uncritical acceptance of all the extravagant claims of native patriotism. Asia and Africa have their demagogues no less than Europe and America. All can meet, however, in the common determination to work for a better world order. What the East wants from the West, even more than Goa or Aden or Dutch New Guinea, is understanding and respect. If the Occident can learn to satisfy this thirst for a status of dignity on the part of the Orient, it will succeed in coming to terms with those whom it formerly ruled. The two need each other more than they are prepared to admit, because the interdependence of the world which industrial progress has created makes their co-operation essential for the welfare of mankind. In view of the imminent end of the era of colonial domination, the twentieth century faces the task of forging new ties of friendship among the races of the earth.

Finally, we are in the midst of a technological revolution which in its far-reaching social effects can be compared only to that great communal revolution of six thousand years ago when men first began to live in cities. The advance of science harnessed to the demand for material welfare is creating a new civilization fundamentally different from any which the world has seen in the past. For the first time mankind looks forward to the day when the bugaboos which have haunted its history will disappear. Famines, epidemics, natural disasters, economic shortages, all the frustrations which have afflicted human society in the past are diminishing. With them will perhaps diminish the resentments and dissatisfactions which have traditionally driven nations to war. Moreover, the increase in the output of goods is still running ahead of the increase in the size of population, so that the time is in sight when the energies of the masses of humanity will no longer be completely absorbed by the process of mere physical survival. Leisure and the cultivation of the mind, which depends on leisure, will cease to be a monopoly of well-to-do classes deriving their power from political influence or economic advantage. Instead, the rationalization of production may make possible the emergence of a popular culture accessible to all strata of society.

For the twentieth century, as for every century before it, there is a promise of progress capable of inspiring men to action and sacrifice. Its realization is no easy task, and it must not give rise to that shallow optimism which marred the thought of so many well-intentioned intellectuals in the Age of Enlightenment. Yet neither is there need to despair of the fate of man who has historically displayed a remarkable talent for meeting the problems with which life confronts him. Before humanity lies the prospect of an exciting future. Its outline cannot be seen clearly, but it is surely suggested by the vision of one of the great thinkers of our age, the philosopher George Santayana:

> A man's feet must be planted in his country, but his eyes should survey the world. What a statesman might well aim at would be to give the special sentiments and gifts of his countrymen such a turn that, while continuing all vital traditions, they might find less and less of what is human alien to their genius. Differences in nationality, founded on race and habitat, must always subsist; but what has been superadded artificially by ignorance and bigotry may be gradually abolished in view of universal relations better understood. There is a certain plane on which all races, if they reach it at all, must live in common, the plane of morals and science.[3]

Further Reading

Good accounts of political developments since the end of the Second World War may be found in J. B. Harrison, *This Age of Global Strife* (Philadelphia: Lippincott, 1952); J. H. Jackson, *The World in the Postwar Decade, 1945–1955* (Boston: Houghton, 1956); and Hans W. Gatzke, *The Present in Perspective* (Chicago: Rand McNally, 1957). The collapse of the balance of power is described by F. W. Pick, *Peacemaking in Perspective* (Oxford: Pen-in-Hand, 1950); G. L. Arnold, *The Pattern of World Conflict* (New York: Dial, 1955); and Arnold and V. M. Toynbee, *The Realignment of Europe* (New York: Oxford Univ. Press, 1955). For the formation and organization of the United Nations there are the following works: S. Arne, *United Nations Primer* (New York: Rinehart, 1945); L. Dolivet, *The United Nations* (New York: Farrar, Straus, 1946); Vera M. Dean, *The Four Cornerstones of Peace* (New York: McGraw-Hill, Whittlesey

---

[3] George Santayana, *Reason in Society* (New York: Charles Scribner's Sons, 1905), p. 175.

House Publication, 1946); H. V. Evatt, *The United Nations* (Cambridge, Mass.: Harvard Univ. Press, 1948); and L. M. Goodrich and E. Hambro, *Charter of the United Nations* (Boston: World Peace, 1949). Julian Huxley, *UNESCO: Its Purpose and Philosophy* (Washington: Public Affairs Press, 1947); T. Besterman, *UNESCO: Peace in the Minds of Men* (New York: Praeger, 1951); H. D. Hall, *Mandates, Dependencies and Trusteeship* (New York: Carnegie Endowment, 1948); and W. N. Hogan, *The United Nations: Background, Organization, Functions, Activities* (New York: McGraw-Hill, 1952), deal with various agencies of the United Nations.

On the recovery of the West see Barbara Ward, *The West at Bay* (New York: Norton, 1948); Vera M. Dean, *Europe and the United States* (New York: Knopf, 1950); Crane Brinton, *The Temper of Western Europe* (Cambridge, Mass.: Harvard Univ. Press, 1953); and T. H. White, *Fire in the Ashes: Europe in Mid-Century* (New York: Sloane, 1953). Important studies of individual countries include, for the United States, Eric F. Goldman, *The Crucial Decade: America, 1945–1955* (New York: Knopf, 1956), and W. G. Carleton, *The Revolution in American Foreign Policy, 1945–1954* (New York: Random, 1954); for England, L. D. Epstein, *Britain: Uneasy Ally* (Chicago: Univ. of Chicago Press, 1954), and D. G. Somervell and H. Harvey, *The British Empire and Commonwealth* (London: Christophers, 1954); for France, G. Wright, *The Reshaping of French Democracy* (New York: Reynal, 1948), and A. Werth, *France, 1940–1955* (New York: Holt, 1956); for Italy, H. S. Hughes, *The United States and Italy* (Cambridge, Mass.: Harvard Univ. Press, 1953), and Muriel Grindrod, *The Rebuilding of Italy* (New York: Oxford Univ. Press, 1955); and for Germany, N. Muhlen, *The Return of Germany* (Chicago: Regnery, 1953), and H. C. Wallich, *Mainsprings of the German Revival* (New Haven: Yale Univ. Press, 1955). Hugh Seton-Watson, *From Lenin to Malenkov* (New York: Praeger, 1954), is useful for the last years of the Stalin régime. Events since then are examined by Edward Crankshaw, *Russia without Stalin* (New York: Viking, 1956), and David J. Dallin, *The Changing World of Soviet Russia* (New Haven: Yale Univ. Press, 1956). A sound analysis of the industrial expansion of Russia is to be found in Harry Schwartz, *Russia's Soviet Economy* (Englewood Cliffs, N.J.: Prentice-Hall, 1954). Doreen Warriner, *Revolution in Eastern Europe* (London: Turnstile, 1950), and Hugh Seton-Watson, *The East European Revolution* (London: Methuen, 1956), consider the communist satellites.

H. V. Hodson, *Twentieth-Century Empire* (London: Faber, 1948), and E. Staley, *The Future of Underdeveloped Countries* (London: Harper, 1954), look at the changing relationship of East and West. H. S. Quigley and J. E. Turner, *The New Japan* (Minneapolis: Univ. of Minnesota Press, 1956), describe the problems facing Nipponese democracy, while H. Feis, *The China Tangle* (Princeton: Princeton Univ. Press, 1953), and R. L. Walker, *China under Communism* (New Haven: Yale Univ. Press, 1955), survey the post-war development of China. T. G. P. Spear, *India, Pakistan, and the West* (New York: Oxford Univ. Press, 1952); A. Mellor, *India since Partition* (New York: Praeger, 1951); and R. Symonds, *The Making of Pakistan* (Hollywood-by-the-Sea, Fla.: Transatlantic, 1950), deal with the achievement of independence in the Indian subcontinent. For southeast Asia see T. Mende, *South-East Asia between Two Worlds* (London: Turnstile, 1955), and J. K. King, *Southeast Asia in Perspective* (New York: Macmillan, 1956). Nehla Izzeddin, *The Arab World* (Chicago: Regnery, 1953), and S. N. Fisher (ed.), *Social Forces in the Middle East* (Ithaca: Cornell Univ. Press, 1955), depict the civic aspirations of Islam, and J. C. Hurewitz, *The Struggle for Palestine* (New York: Norton, 1950), and G. de Gaury, *The New State of Israel* (New York: Praeger, 1952), treat the conflict in the Holy Land. C. W. Stillman (ed.), *Africa in the Modern World* (Chicago: Univ. of Chicago Press, 1955), is a thoughtful introductory work, while Chester Bowles, *Africa's Challenge to America* (Berkeley: Univ. of California Press, 1956), urges respect and sympathy for the Dark Continent.

B. G. Ivanyi and A. Bell, *Route to Potsdam* (London: Wingate, 1945), and W. L. Neumann, *Making the Peace, 1941–45* (Washington: Foundation for Foreign Affairs, 1949), describe the war aims of the victorious powers. J. L. Snell (ed.), *The Meaning of Yalta* (Baton Rouge: Louisiana State Univ. Press, 1956), is the best account of the crucial international conference. Walter Lippmann, *The Cold War* (New York: Harper, 1947), and K. Ingram, *History of the Cold War* (London: Darwen Finlayson, 1955), seek to analyze the struggle between democratic capitalism and authoritarian communism. The attempt of the United States to halt the advance of Russia through economic rehabilitation is examined by Seymour E. Harris, *The European Recovery Program* (Cambridge, Mass.: Harvard Univ. Press, 1948); George F. Kennan, *Realities of American Foreign Policy* (Princeton: Princeton Univ. Press, 1954); and H. B. Price, *The Marshall Plan and Its Meaning* (Ithaca: Cornell Univ. Press, 1955). H. Hoskins, *The Atlantic Pact* (Washington: Public Affairs Press, 1949), and D. Middleton, *The Defense of Western Europe* (New York: Appleton, 1952), explain the function of the North Atlantic Treaty. C. G. Haines (ed.), *The Threat of Soviet Imperialism* (Baltimore: Johns Hopkins Univ. Press, 1954), warns against the expansionist ambitions of the Kremlin. On the cold war there are such works as N. A. Graebner, *The New Isolationism* (Cardiff, Wales: Ronald, 1956); W. W. Kaufmann (ed.), *Military Policy and National Security* (Princeton: Princeton Univ. Press, 1956); and Henry L. Roberts, *Russia and America* (New York: Meridian MD182, 1956).

H. S. Hughes, *An Essay for Our Times* (New York: Knopf, 1950), and Raymond Aron, *The Century of Total War* (Boston: Beacon BP3, 1955), consider the contemporary world from a historical perspective. Roderick Seidenberg, *Posthistoric Man* (Boston: Beacon BP47, 1957), and

C. G. Darwin, *The Next Million Years* (New York: Doubleday, 1952), look into the distant future. Clyde Kluckhohn, *Mirror for Man* (New York: McGraw-Hill, 1949), applies the teachings of anthropology to social problems, while Reinhold Niebuhr, *The Children of Light and the Children of Darkness* (New York: Scribner, 1944), attempts to define the significance of theology for a democratic community. F. S. C. Northrop, *The Taming of the Nations* (New York: Macmillan, 1952), and A. H. Richmond, *The Colour Problem* (New York: Grove, 1955), plead for greater understanding among peoples and races. The effect of population growth on the standard of living is discussed by W. S. and E. S. Woytinsky, *World Population and Production* (New York: Twentieth Century Fund, 1953), and K. Sax, *Standing Room Only: The Challenge of Overpopulation* (Boston: Beacon, 1955). Julian Huxley, *Science and Social Needs* (New York: Harper, 1935); J. D. Bernal, *The Social Function of Science* (New York: Macmillan, 1940); C. H. Waddington, *The Scientific Attitude* (Baltimore: Penguin A84, 1941); and W. Esslinger, *Politics and Science* (New York: Philosophical Library, 1955), assess the influence of scientific progress on civic development. Barbara Ward, *Faith and Freedom* (New York: Doubleday, Image D73, 1958), is an eloquent plea for courage in a time of trouble.

LIST OF PHOTOGRAPHS
AND INDEX

List of Photographs

	following page
"Painel do Infante." Museu Nacional de Arte Antiga, Lisbon	30
Tikal, Temple I, Guatemala. The University Museum, Philadelphia	30
Temple of the Warriors, Chichén Itzá. Instituto Nacional de Antropologia e Historia, Mexico	30
The "Victoria." Brown Brothers	30
Wycliffe Bible. Courtesy of the Pierpont Morgan Library	62
Luther's Bible. Courtesy of the Pierpont Morgan Library	62
Gutenberg Bible. Courtesy of the Library of Congress	62
Erasmus' New Testament. Courtesy of the Pierpont Morgan Library	62
Martin Luther. Bildarchiv Foto Marburg	62
Ulrich von Hutten. The Bettman Archive	62
John Calvin. Courtesy of the New York Public Library	62
Philip Melanchthon. The Bettman Archive	62
Cardinal Wolsey. The Bettman Archive	62
Archbishop Cranmer. Courtesy of the National Portrait Gallery	62
Edward VI. Courtesy of the National Portrait Gallery	62
Illustration from Foxe's "Book of Martyrs." Courtesy of the New York Public Library	62
Council of Trent. The Bettman Archive	62
Pope Paul III. Anderson	62
St. Pius V (Pope). Brown Brothers	62
St. Ignatius Loyola. Courtesy of the New York Public Library	62
Isabella of Castile and Ferdinand of Aragon. Brown Brothers	126
Maximilian I. Courtesy of the Metropolitan Museum of Art, gift of Mortimer L. Schiff, 1919	126
Charles V. Anderson	126
Philip II. Alinari	126
Francis I. Archives Photographiques, Paris	126

CHÂTEAU OF BLOIS. Brown Brothers — 126

HENRY VII. The Bettman Archive — 126

HENRY VIII. Anderson — 126

MARY I. Courtesy of the National Portrait Gallery — 126

ELIZABETH I. Courtesy of the National Portrait Gallery — 126

THE ESCORIAL. Anderson — 126

HAMPTON COURT. British Information Services — 126

"ST. JEROME IN HIS STUDY." Courtesy of the Fogg Art Museum — 126

FONTAINEBLEAU. French National Tourist Office — 126

IVAN III. Sovfoto — 158

IVAN IV. Sovfoto — 158

MICHAEL ROMANOV. Brown Brothers — 158

PETER THE GREAT. Sovfoto — 158

THE GRABEN, VIENNA. Courtesy of the New York Public Library — 158

FREDERICK WILLIAM OF HOHENZOLLERN. The Bettman Archive — 158

LEOPOLD I OF HABSBURG. The Bettman Archive — 158

THE PALACE OF VERSAILLES. Courtesy of the New York Public Library — 158

LOUIS XIV. Archives Photographiques, Paris — 158

CHARLES I. Giraudon — 158

CHARLES II. Courtesy of the National Portrait Gallery — 158

WILLIAM III. The Bettman Archive — 158

OLIVER CROMWELL. Courtesy of Charles C. Abbott — 158

GALILEO GALILEI. Brown Brothers — 222

SIR FRANCIS BACON. The Bettman Archive — 222

RENÉ DESCARTES. Archives Photographiques, Paris — 222

SIR ISAAC NEWTON. Copyright reserved. Science Museum, London — 222

OTTO VON GUERICKE'S EXPERIMENT. The Bettman Archive — 222

HUYGENS' PENDULUM CLOCK. Photo Science Museum — 222

HOOKE'S COMPOUND MICROSCOPE. Crown copyright. Science Museum, London — 222

HUYGENS' AERIAL TELESCOPE. Crown copyright. Science Museum, London — 222

JOHN LOCKE. The Bettman Archive — 222

VOLTAIRE. Giraudon — 222

CHARLES DE MONTESQUIEU. Photo Marco Pillot, Studio Léoed — 222

JEAN JACQUES ROUSSEAU. Courtesy of the Board of Trustees of the National Galleries of Scotland — 222

DENIS DIDEROT. Giraudon — 222

"THE UPHOLSTERER." Courtesy of the New York Public Library — 222

"THE ROSARY MAKER." Courtesy of the New York Public Library   222

"THE PASTRY COOK." Courtesy of the New York Public Library   222

GEORGE WASHINGTON. Brown Brothers   254

THOMAS JEFFERSON. Courtesy of the New-York Historical Society   254

JOHN ADAMS. Brown Brothers   254

JAMES MADISON. Courtesy of the New-York Historical Society   254

"NÉ POUR LA PEINE." Photo Bibliothèque Nationale   254

"SANS-CULOTTE." Photo Bibliothèque Nationale   254

"CETTE FOIS CI . . . ." Photo Bibliothèque Nationale   254

THE TWO-FACED PRIESTLY ARISTOCRACY. Photo Bibliothèque Nationale   254

LOUIS XVI. Brown Brothers   254

MAXIMILIEN ROBESPIERRE. The Bettman Archive   254

CHARLES MAURICE DE TALLEYRAND-PÉRIGORD. The Bettman Archive   254

NAPOLEON I. Photo Bibliothèque Nationale   254

SIMÓN BOLÍVAR. Courtesy of the New York Public Library   254

JOSÉ DE SAN MARTÍN. Brown Brothers   254

AUGUSTÍN DE ITURBIDE. Brown Brothers   254

PEDRO I OF BRAZIL. Culver Service   254

AKBAR AT HOME. Victoria and Albert Museum, Crown copyright   318

K'ANG HSI IN OLD AGE. Courtesy of the Trustees of the British Museum   318

CHINESE PORCELAIN. Courtesy of the Trustees of the British Museum   318

THE SULTAN SCATTERING ALMS. Courtesy of the Topkapi Palace Library   318

JETHRO TULL. Courtesy of the Royal Agricultural Society of England   350

"TURNIP" TOWNSHEND. Courtesy of the National Portrait Gallery   350

ROBERT BAKEWELL. Courtesy of the National Portrait Gallery   350

ARTHUR YOUNG. Courtesy of the National Portrait Gallery   350

KAY'S FLYING SHUTTLE. Courtesy of the New York Public Library   350

HARGREAVE'S SPINNING JENNY. Crown copyright. Science Museum, London   350

CROMPTON'S MULE. Crown copyright. Science Museum, London   350

WHITNEY'S COTTON GIN. Courtesy of the New York Public Library   350

CUGNOT'S "AUTOMOBILE." Crown copyright. Science Museum, London   350

STOCKTON AND DARLINGTON RAILROAD. Photo Science Museum, London   350

TREVITHICK'S LOCOMOTIVE. Crown copyright. Science Museum, London   350

FITCH'S PADDLE BOAT. Courtesy of the New York Public Library   350

THE THIRD DUKE OF BRIDGEWATER. Courtesy of the National Portrait Gallery   350

JAMES WATT. Photo Science Museum, London   350

LIST OF PHOTOGRAPHS

RICHARD ARKWRIGHT. Photo Science Museum, London 350

MATTHEW BOULTON. Crown copyright. Science Museum, London 350

KARL MARX. The Bettman Archive 382

NAPOLEON III. Brown Brothers 382

ALEXANDER I. Copyright reserved 382

ANDREW JACKSON. The Bettman Archive 382

INAUGURATION OF THE SUEZ CANAL. Photo Bibliothèque Nationale 430

CECIL RHODES. Brown Brothers 430

YÜAN SHIH KAI. Underwood & Underwood 430

BURIAL OF A RUSSIAN OFFICER. From *The Tragedy of Russia in Pacific Asia,* by Frederick McCormick. By permission of the Macmillan Company 430

"THE LEGISLATIVE BELLY" 462

"MOSÉ IN EGITTO ! ! ! " Courtesy of *Punch* 462

OTTO VON BISMARCK. The Bettman Archive 462

WILLIAM II. Wide World Photo 462

THE BIG FOUR. United Press International Photo 526

LEON TROTSKY. United Press International Photo 526

THE SIGNATORIES OF THE MUNICH AGREEMENT. United Press International Photo 526

THE SURRENDER OF JAPAN. United Press International Photo 526

SUN YAT-SEN. Eastfoto 558

"RULE JAPANNIA." Reprinted by permission of David Low. Copyright © Low all countries 558

MAHATMA GANDHI. INFORMATION SERVICE OF INDIA 558

NEGRO SLUMS IN SOUTH AFRICA. United Press International Photo 558

CHARLES DARWIN. Courtesy of the National Portrait Gallery 606

SIGMUND FREUD. Wide World Photo 606

OSCAR WILDE LECTURING TO AMERICAN FARMERS ON AESTHETICISM. From *Rossetti and His Circle,* by Max Beerbohm, published by William Heinemann Ltd. and Doubleday & Co., Inc. Courtesy of the publishers and the Trustees of the Tate Gallery 606

"NUDE DESCENDING A STAIRCASE." Courtesy of the Philadelphia Museum of Art, Louise and Walter Arensburg Collection 606

THE LEADERS OF THE THIRD REICH ON TRIAL. Ewing Galloway 638

THE INAUGURATION OF CHAIM WEIZMANN AS FIRST PRESIDENT OF ISRAEL. Wide World Photo 638

CHURCHILL, ROOSEVELT, AND STALIN AT YALTA. Ewing Galloway 638

DRAFTING THE NORTH ATLANTIC TREATY. Wide World Photo 638

Index

Abd el-Krim, 569
Abdul Aziz, sultan of Turkey, 406
Abdul Hamid II, sultan of Ottoman Empire, 484
Abdullah, king of Jordan, 570
Absolute monarchy: rise of, 93
Abul Fazl, 303
Acheson, Dean, 647
Acre: fall of, 13
Adenauer, Konrad, 631
Adler, Alfred, 593
Aesthetic subjectivism, 607–10
Africa: early explorations, 439; European imperialism, 440–44; results of partition, 443–44; colonialism, 572–75; racial conflicts, 575–77
Agricultural Adjustment Act, 530
Agricultural Revolution: enclosure movement, 346–47; agricultural reformers, 347–48; improved animal husbandry, 348–49; farm tenancy, 349–50
Aix-la-Chapelle, Congress of, 280
Aix-la-Chapelle, Treaty of, 225, 227
Akbar, emperor of India, 293–96
Alaska: purchase by United States, 438
Albania: creation of, 495; communization under Enver Hoxha, 621, 634
Albert, archbishop of Mainz, 57–58
Albert I, king of Belgium, 471
Albert, Prince Consort of England, 388
Albert of Hohenzollern, 159
Albertus Magnus, 584
Albuquerque, Afonso de, 21
Alexander I, emperor of Russia, 274, 276, 278, 279, 403
Alexander II, emperor of Russia, 404–5, 406, 438, 478–80, 483, 493
Alexander III, emperor of Russia, 480, 493
Alexander I, king of Yugoslavia, 524
Alexander VI, Pope, 18, 53, 320
Alexis, tsar of Muscovy, 154–55
Alfonso XII, king of Spain, 399
Alfonso XIII, king of Spain, 523–24
All-India Moslem League, 560, 639
Alva, Fernando Alvarez de Toledo, duke of, 120–21
Amati, Nicolò, 234
American Academy of Science, 198

American Philosophical Society, 198
American Revolution: English colonial administration, 239–41; Navigation Acts, 240; colonial policies of George III, 241–44; Proclamation of 1763, 242; Revenue Act of 1764, 242; Stamp Act, 242–43; Townshend Acts, 243–44; Boston Massacre, 244; Boston Tea Party, 244; First Continental Congress, 245; Second Continental Congress, 245–46, 247; Declaration of Independence, 245–46; founding of the republic, 246–47; Saratoga, 247; French alliance, 247–48; Yorktown, 248; Treaty of Paris, 248–49
Ames, Oakes, 486
Amiens, Treaty of, 273
Amherst, Lord. See Pitt, William
Amundsen, Roald, 458
Amursana, ruler of West Mongols, 312–13
Anabaptists, 84–87, 88, 128
Anarchism, 464–65
Anarchosyndicalism, 465
Angostura, Congress of, 284
Anne, duchess of Brittany, 112
Anne, empress of Russia, 230
Anne, queen of England, 175, 176, 189
Anne of Cleves, 75
Anti-Comintern Pact, 534
Antipodes, 6
Apostolic Succession, doctrine of, 51, 79
Apprentices, Statute of, 374
Arab nationalism, 568–70
Arab States, League of, 641
Aragon: under Ferdinand and Isabella, 118
Ardennes offensive, 542
Argentina: revolt against Spain, 285–86; political progress after fall of Rosas, 415
Arkwright, Richard, 357, 358
Armed Neutrality, League of, 248
Armour, Philip D., 485
Arnold, Benedict, 248
Arnold, Matthew, 591, 606
Arthur, Chester A., 486
Arthur, prince of Wales, 107
Articles of Confederation, 247, 249
Artigas, José, 285
Asquith, Herbert, 509
Atahualpa, 39

Atlantic Charter, 644–45
"Atlantic Civilization," 407
Atlantic exploration, 13–34
Attlee, Clement R., 629, 638–39
Auerstädt, Battle of, 274
Augsburg, League of, 189
Augsburg, Peace of, 66, 117, 124, 125
Aulic Council, 113
Aurungzeb, emperor of India, 297–300, 304, 305
Ausgleich, 402, 477
Austerlitz, Battle of, 273
Australia: settlement of, 429–30; formation of Commonwealth, 469; acquisition of German Pacific colonies, 528
Austria: defeat of Napoleon, 267, 268, 273; gains from Congress of Vienna, 279; Seven Weeks' War, 395–96; movements for self-determination, 400–401; revolutions of 1848, 401; the March laws, 401, 402; reaction and the Bach system, 401–2; division of Austria and Hungary, 401–2; nationalism and constitutionalism, 477–478; disintegration of empire, 513; fascism under Dollfuss, 524; Nazi occupation of, 534; United States aid to, 632
Avilés, Pedrarias de, 36, 38
Axis. *See* Rome-Berlin Axis
Azores: discovery of, 13, 15
Aztec civilization, 25–26
Aztecs: earliest history, 25–26; conquest by Cortés, 36–38

Baber, emperor of India, 294, 303
Babeuf, "Gracchus," 382
Babylonian Captivity, 52, 54
Bach, Alexander, 401
Bach, Johann Sebastian, 234
Bach System, 401
Bacon, Francis, 131, 196, 345, 584
Bacon, Roger, 194
Baffin, William, 45
Baffin Island: discovery by Frobisher, 45
Bahamas: discovery by Columbus, 30–31
Bajazet II, sultan of Ottoman Empire, 319–20
Baker, Ray Stannard, 487
Baker, Samuel, 439
Bakewell, Robert, 348
Bakunin, Michael, 404, 465
Balance of power: principle of, 134; collapse after World War II, 620–21
Balboa, Vasco Núñez de, 35–36, 38
Baldwin, Stanley, 527
Balfour, Arthur, 468, 570–71
Balzac, Honoré de, 605
Baptists, 86. *See also* Anabaptists
Barbarossa, Khayr-ad-Din, 321, 324
Barents, Willem, 45
Barth, Heinrich, 439
Barth, Karl, 602
Baruch, Bernard, 509
Batavian Republic, 267, 268
"Battle of the Books," 207–8
"Battle of the Nations," 277
Bayle, Pierre, 170, 214

Beauharnais, Eugène de, 274
Beauharnais, Josephine de, empress of the French, 267, 275
Beaumarchais, Pierre Augustin de, 235
Bebel, August, 464
Beccaria, Cesare Bonesana, marchese di, 218, 229, 231
Bechuanaland, 441, 444
Becquerel, Henri, 582
Beecher, Henry Ward, 600
Beethoven, Ludwig van, 604, 607
Belgian Congo, 440, 441
Belgium: annexation to France, 274; under Leopold I, 392; establishment of Congo Free State, 441; labor unrest and socialism, 471; German invasion of, 495–96; return to parliamentary government, 623; United States aid to, 632
Belgrano, Manuel, 285
Belknap, William W., 486
Bell, Thomas, 358
Bellay, Joachim du, 465–66
Benavides, Óscar, 531
Ben Gurion, David, 640
Bennett, James Gordon, 440
Bentham, Jeremy, 381, 422–23
Berchtold, Leopold von, 478
Bergson, Henri, 597
Beria, Lavrenti B., 633
Bering Straits, 437
Berlin, Academy of, 198
Berlin blockade, 648
Berlin Congress (1878), 423, 483, 493, 494
Berlin Congress (1884–85): settlement of African boundary claims, 442
Berlioz, Hector, 604
Bernadotte, General. *See* Charles XIV, king of Sweden
Bernhardi, General Friedrich von, 467
Bernstein, Eduard, 464
Berzelius, Jöns, 582
Bethmann-Hollweg, Theobald von, 496
Beveridge, Albert J., 486
Beyers, Christian, 576
Bidault, Georges, 630
Bill of Rights (American), 250
Bill of Rights (English), 189, 218, 250
Bismarck, Otto von, 395–96, 423, 441–42, 472–73, 644
Black, Dr. Joseph, 359
Black Hole of Calcutta, 302
Blaine, James G., 486
Blake, William, 603
Blenheim, Battle of, 175
Blith, Walter, 347
Blum, Léon, 526
Bodin, Jean, 133, 589
Boer War, 432, 444–45, 489
Bohemia: growth of Protestantism, 115–16; Protestant revolt, 125
Bohr, Niels, 582
Boisdeffre, General Le Mouton de, 471
Boleyn, Anne, queen of England, 73–75, 109
Bolingbroke, Viscount (Henry St. John), 216
Bolívar, Simón, 284, 286, 412

Bolivia: liberation of, 286
Bologna, Concordat of, 88, 99
Bonald, Louis de, 385, 595, 599
Bonaparte, Jerome, 274
Bonaparte, Joseph, 274, 282, 286
Bonaparte, Louis, 274
Bonaparte, Lucien, 269
Bonaparte, Napoleon. *See* Napoleon I
Boniface VIII, Pope, 52
Bonomi, Ivanoe, 520
Book of Common Prayer, 74
Boorhaave, Herman, 179
Booth, Charles, 589
Booth, William, 601
Bora, Catherine von, 66
Borgia, Cesare, 132
Borodin, Michael, 555
Bose, Subhas Chandra, 562
Bossuet, Bishop Jacques Bénique, 171
Boston Massacre, 244
Boston Tea Party, 244
Boswell, James, 210
Botha, Louis, 445, 576
Boulanger, General Georges, 470
Boulton, Matthew, 359
Bourbon, Henry of, king of Navarre.
    See Henry IV, king of France (Henry
    of Navarre)
Bourbon, Louis de, prince of Condé, 100
Bourbon Dynasty: rise of, 100–102
Bourgeoisie: as factor in rise of early
    modern science, 194–95; rise to power,
    370–71
Bourgeois reformism, 462–63
Boxer Rebellion, 451–52, 551
Boyle, Robert, 195
Braddock, General William, 227
Braganza Dynasty, 414–15, 477
Brahms, Johannes, 607
Brand, Sir Christopher, 572
Brandenburg-Prussia. *See* Prussia
Brandes, Georg, 606
Brazil: discovery by Cabral, 21; early
    Portuguese settlements, 41; revolt against
    Portugal, 288–289; under the Braganzas,
    414–15; establishment of federal republic,
    489–90
Brazza, Savorgnan de, 440, 443
Brest-Litovsk, Treaty of, 508
Breughel, Pieter, the Elder, 130
Briand, Aristide, 533
Bright, John, 468
Brindley, James, 361–62, 363
Brissot, Jacques Pierre, 260
British East India Company, 110, 301–3,
    316, 423–26, 446
British North America Act, 411–12, 489
Brothers of the Common Life, 52–53
Browning, Robert, 606
Bruce, James, 438
Bruck, Artur Moeller van den, 520
Brüning, Heinrich, 522
Bryan, William Jennings, 585
Bryce, James, 590
Bucer, Martin, 64, 65, 71, 74, 76
Buchez, Philippe Joseph, 600
Buddhism: in Japan, 449

Buffon, Georges de, 584
Bukharin, Nikolai, 517
Bulganin, Nikolai A., 650
Bulgaria: autonomy established, 483; Treaty
    of Neuilly, 512; joins Axis, 539; com-
    munization under Georgi Dimitrov, 621,
    633–34
Bulnes, Manuel, 415
Bunyan, John, 190
Buonarotti, Filippo, 382
Burgoyne, General John, 247
Burke, Edmund, 258–59, 385, 386
Burma: annexation by British East India
    Company, 424; Japanese seizure of, 541;
    movement for independence, 563; foun-
    dation of republic, 639
Burton, Richard, 439
Byrd, William, 190
Byrnes, James F., 646
Byron, George Gordon, Lord, 604

Cabet, Étienne, 382
Cabinet government: invention in Great
    Britain, 386
Cabot, John, 32, 44, 108
Cabot, Sebastian, 32, 44
Cabral, Pedro Álvares, 19, 21
Cabrillo, Juan Rodríguez, 38
Caillaux, Joseph, 509
Cajetan, Cardinal, 59
Calonne, Charles Alexandre de, 254
Calvin, John, 72, 76, 89, 211, 592
Calvinism: teachings of, 68–70; spread of,
    83; legal recognition of, 128
Cambrai, Treaty of, 64, 115
Camões, 7
Campbell-Bannerman, Sir Henry, 468
Campo Formio, Treaty of, 268, 273
Canada: settlement of boundary question
    with United States, 408–9; peaceful es-
    tablishment of self-government, 411; Brit-
    ish North America Act, 411–12; develop-
    ment of, 432–33; achievement of do-
    minion status, 468–69, 489
Canary Islands: rediscovery of, 13; with-
    drawal of Portuguese claims, 15
Canning, Stratford, 406
Cánovas del Castillo, Antonio, 475
Cape Colony, 431–32, 444–45, 469
Cape Horn: discovery of, 45–46
Capelo, Hermenegildo, 440
Cape of Good Hope: discovery of, 17–18
Cape Verde Island, 16
Capitalism: basic institutions of, 340; inten-
    sification by Industrial Revolution, 369–70
Carlos I, king of Portugal, 477
Carlstadt, Andrew, 59, 62
Carlyle, Thomas, 595, 606
Carnegie, Andrew, 485
Carnot, Lazare Nicolas, 264
Carol II, king of Romania, 524
Carrera, Rafael, 414
Carranza, Venustiano, 490
Cartier, Jacques, 43, 99, 103
Cartwright, Edward, 357
Castellio, Sebastian, 88

Castile: under Ferdinand and Isabella, 117–18

Castlereagh, Viscount (Robert Stewart, Marquess of Londonderry), 278, 644

Cateau-Cambrésis, Treaty of, 99, 116, 123

Catherine I, empress of Russia, 230

Catherine II (the Great), empress of Russia, 224, 230–33, 235, 248, 330

Catherine of Aragon, queen of England, 73, 107, 109

Catholic League, 102, 123, 124

Catholic Reformation, 77–81, 123

Cavaignac, Godefroy, 381

Cavour, Count Camillo di, 398, 474, 644

Cawley, John, 358–59

Central African Federation, 643

Central America, United Provinces of, 288

Central Powers, 506–9

Cervantes Saavedra, Miguel de, 130

Cetshwayo, 432, 551

Ceuta: capture of, 14

Ceylon: achievement of self-government, 639

Cézanne, Paul, 606

Chadirchi, Kamil, 569

Chamberlain, Joseph, 468

Chamberlain, Neville, 527, 534–35

Champagne, Battle of, 506

Champlain, Samuel de, 43

Chancellor, Richard, 44

Chang Hsueh-liang, 558

Charles, archduke of Austria, 276

Charles, emperor of Austria, 510

Charles V, emperor of Holy Roman Empire, 33, 59, 61, 65, 66, 94, 114–17, 118

Charles VI, emperor of Holy Roman Empire, 176, 224

Charles I, king of England, 181–87, 190, 199

Charles II, king of England, 187–88, 198, 301

Charles VIII, king of France, 112

Charles IX, king of France, 100–102

Charles X, king of France, 389, 434

Charles I, king of Romania, 406

Charles II, king of Spain, 174, 175

Charles III, king of Spain, 282

Charles IX, king of Sweden, 147

Charles XII, king of Sweden, 156

Charles XIV, king of Sweden, 392

Charles, cardinal of Lorraine, 100

Charles Albert, king of Sardinia, 396–98

Charles Louis, elector of Palatinate, 127

Charles Louis, elector of Lower Palatinate, 127

Charles the Bold, duke of Burgundy, 94

Charter Act, 426

Chartered Company, 442

Chateaubriand, François René de, 599, 604

Chatterton, Thomas, 603

Chaumont, Treaty of, 277, 280

Chekhov, Anton, 606

Chia Ch'ing, emperor of China, 315–17, 446

Chiang Kai-shek, 555–58, 637

Chibcha civilization, 26–28

Chibchas: Spanish conquest of, 40

Ch'ien Lung, emperor of China, 312–15, 317, 446

Chile: conquest by Valdivia, 39; expansion during nineteenth century, 415

China: disappearance of European influence, 10; consolidation of Manchu power, 306–7; Kang Hsi, 307–8; internal administration by the Manchus, 308–10; Europeans in China, 310–12; Ch'ien Lung, 312–15; decadence of Manchu rule, 315–18; Opium War, 429, 446; Manchu Dynasty to end of Tai Ping Rebellion, 445–47; Tai Ping Rebellion, 447–48; European imperialism in, 450–52; Boxer Rebellion, 451–52; fall of Manchu Dynasty, 453–54; proclamation of republic, 454, 553; Sino-Japanese War, 448–50; abolition of extraterritoriality, 554–55; between the wars, 554–56; the Kuomintang, 554–56; rise of communism, 555; civil war, 637; defeat of Kuomintang, 637

Chinese Republic, 553

Chinese Revolution, 454

Ch'ing (Pure) Dynasty, 306–18, 454

Chopin, Frédéric, 604, 607

Chou En-lai, 555

Christian IV, king of Denmark, 125

Christian of Anhalt, 123

Christianity: revival of faith, 599–600; and industrialism, 600–601; spread of secularism, 601–3

Churchill, Sir Winston, 539, 555, 624, 629, 645

Cibola, Seven Cities of, 38

Cipriano de Mosquera, Tomás, 414

Cisalpine Republic, 268

Civil Constitution of the Clergy, 257, 258, 271

Civil War (United States), 410–11, 427

Clapp, Moses, 487

Clarendon Code, 188

Clark, George Rogers, 248

Clemenceau, Georges, 471, 509, 511, 569

Clement VII, Pope, 115

Cleveland, Grover, 455

Clive, Lord Robert, 227, 268, 302–3

Cobbett, William, 381

Cocceji, Baron Samuel, 228

Code, Napoleonic, 217, 271, 389

Coercive Acts, 244

Coke, Thomas William, 348

Colbert, Jean Baptiste, 171–73, 177, 198, 346, 355

Cold War, 651

Coleridge, Samuel Taylor, 595, 604

Coligny, Gaspard, Admiral de, 100

Cologne, Diet of, 113

Colombia: Chibcha culture, 26–28

Colonialism: Waning of, 548–77

Color-Bar Bill, 576

Columbus, Bartholomew, 35

Columbus, Christopher, 18, 30–31

Cominform (Communist Information Bureau), 621

Commerce: growth between East and West, 12–13

Commons, House of, 105

Communism: rise of, 513–19; Third Inter-

national, 519, 520; organization of party in Italy, 520; rise in China, 555
Company of the East Indies, 173
Company of the West Indies, 173
Compromise of 1850, 409
Comte, Auguste, 587–89
Conciliar Movement, 52
Condorcet, Marie Jean, marquis de, 593
Confederate States of America, 411
Congo: discovery of, 17
Congo Free State, 440, 441
Conkling, Roscoe, 486
Conservatism: restoration of, 383–85
Constable, John, 234, 604
Constance, Council of, 52
Constant, Benjamin, 595
Constitutional Charter of 1814, 279, 389
Constitution of Radom, 144
Constitution of 1791 (French), 257–58, 272
Constitution of 1795 (French), 266
Constitution of the Year VIII (1799) (French), 269
Constitution (United States), 249–50, 283
Consubstantiation, 64
Continental System, 275, 276
Cook, James, 430, 455–56
Coolidge, Calvin, 529
Copernicus, Nicolas, 6, 193–94
Coral Sea, Battle of, 541
Corneille, Pierre, 170
Corn laws, 341, 387
Cornwallis, Lord Charles, 248
Coronado, Francisco Vázquez, 38
Cortes, 118
Cortés, Hernán, 36–38
Coulanges, N. D. Fustel de, 590
Council of Five Hundred, 269
Council of the Indies, 41, 118
Council of Troubles, 121
Covenant (Scottish), 184
Covilhã, Pedro de, 17
Cranach, Lucas, the Elder, 130
Cranmer, Thomas, archbishop of Canterbury: the marriage question, 74, 109; growth of Church of England, 74–75; death of, 76
Crimean War, 391, 404, 406, 425, 438
Cripps, Sir Stafford, 563
Crispi, Francesco, 441, 475
Crompton, Samuel, 357
Cromwell, Oliver, 186–87
Cromwell, Thomas, 74
Crusades, 4, 8, 13
Cuba, 30–31, 475
Cugnot, Nicolas, 363
Cuius regio eius religio, 63–64, 66, 88, 117, 127
Cultural pessimism, 593–94
Culture System, 437
Cummings, E. E., 608
Cummins, Albert B., 487
Cunard, Samuel, 366
Curie, Marie, 582
Curie, Pierre, 582
Curzon, Viceroy George, 426
Cuza, Alexander, 406
Cyprus: British occupation of, 483
Czechoslovakia: vulnerability to attack, 531;

Nazi conquest of, 535; loss of Ruthenia to Soviet Union, 621; communization under Klement Gottwald, 621, 634
Czernin, Count Ottokar, 510

Daladier, Edouard, 526
Dali, Salvador, 608
Damascus, 12
Darby, Abraham, 360
Darnley, Lord (Henry Stuart), 180
Darwin, Charles, 549, 584–85
Das, Chitta Ranjan, 552
Daumier, Honoré, 606
Davis, John, 45
d'Azeglio, Marquis Massimo, 396
Debussy, Claude, 608–9
Decembrist Revolt, 403
Declaration of Independence, 241, 245–46, 379
Declaration of Indulgence, 188
Declaratory Act, 242–43
Degas, Edgar, 606
Deism, 213–14
Delacroix, Eugène, 604
Demarcation Treaty (Treaty of Tordesillas), 18–19. See also Tordesillas, Treaty of
Democracy: rise of 381–82
Denikin, General Anton, 514
Denmark: adopts Lutheranism, 67; Thirty Years' War, 125; adoption of constitution, 392; loss of Schleswig and Holstein, 395; democratic reform, 471–72; German seizure, 537; return to parliamentary government, 623; United States aid to, 632
Depretis, Agostino, 475
Derby, Lord, 467
Descartes, René, 196–97, 205
Despréaux, Nicolas-Boileau, 169
Dewey, John, 597, 614
d'Holbach, Baron, 214
Dias, Bartholomeu: discovery of Cape of Good Hope, 17
Díaz, Porfirio, 490
Dickens, Charles, 605
Diderot, Denis, 209, 214
Dimitrov, Georgi, 621
Diplomacy: beginning of, 133–34
Diplomatic Revolution of 1756, 225
Discovery, Age of, 5–26
Disraeli, Benjamin, 426, 432, 435, 467–68, 549
Divine right of kings, 132, 180–87, 203
Dole, Sanford B., 455
Dollfuss, Engelbert, 524
Dominicans, 80
Donizetti, Gaetano, 604, 607
Don John of Austria, 123, 328
Donne, John, 190
Dostoevski, Feodor, 606
Doumergue, Gaston, 526
Dover, Treaty of, 188
Drake, Sir Francis, 44, 110, 111, 122
Drayton, Michael, 131
Dreyfus case, 470–71
Dryden, John, 190–91, 298
Dubois, Pierre, 52

Duchamp, Marcel, 608
Dudley, Edmund, 107
Dukas, Paul, 607
Dumas, Alexandre, 606
Dumbarton Oaks Conference, 625
Dupleix, Joseph François, 302
Dürer, Albrecht, 130
Durham, Lord John, 411
Dutch East India Company: formation of, 45, 178
Dutch Republic, 177–80
Dutch War, 174
Dutch West India Company, 178
Dvořák, Anton, 607
Dyer, General Reginald, 561
Dynastic states: rise of, 93–97
Dzerzhinsky, Felix, 516

East Africa Native Association, 574
East Indies: Dutch imperialism, 435–37
Eck, Dr. John, 59, 60
Eden, Anthony, 649
Edward VI, king of England, 75, 109
Edward VII, king of England, 468
Egerton, Francis, duke of Bridgewater, 361–62
Egypt: under Mameluke rule, 320–21; British occupation of, 442–43; construction of Suez Canal, 435; independence granted, 569; deposition of King Farouk, 641; Nasser's rise to power, 641–42; seizure of Suez Canal, 642
Einstein, Albert, 586
Eisenhower, Dwight D., 542, 628, 649
Elcano, Sebastian de, 34–35
El Dorado, legend of, 27
Elgin, Lord James, 411
El-Husseini, Haj Amin, mufti of Jerusalem, 570
Eliot, T. S., 609
Elizabeth, empress of Austria, 465, 477
Elizabeth, empress of Russia, 225, 230
Elizabeth I, queen of England: growth of England as sea power, 44–45; birth of, 74; church settlement, 76–77; aid to Huguenots, 101, 102; reign of, 110–11; support of Dutch revolt, 122; and Philip II of Spain, 122; the Armada, 122
Elizabeth II, queen of England, 629
Elizabeth of York, 106
Ellenborough, Governor-General Lord, 424
El-Quwatli, Shukri, 570
Ely, Richard T., 601
Emerson, Ralph Waldo, 595
Empson, Richard, 107
Enclosure movement, 346–48
Encomienda system, 41–42
Engels, Friedrich, 383
England: early explorations, 44–45; Protestant Reformation, 72–77; rise of Parliament, 104–5, 183–89; Tudor Dynasty, 104–11; Henry VII, 105–8; Henry VIII, 108–9; Edward VI, 109; Mary I, 109; Elizabeth I, 110–11; gains from Treaty of Utrecht, 176; Thirty Years' War, 182; the Protectorate, 187; revolution in seventeenth cen-tury, 180–87; Stuart Dynasty, 180–91; reign of James I, 180–83; reign of Charles I, 181–87; the Civil War, 185–87; the Interregnum, 187; the Restoration, 187–88; succession of William and Mary, 189; the Glorious Revolution, 189; art and litera-ture during seventeenth century, 190–91; the Enlightenment, 210; Seven Years' War, 225–28; French and Indian War, 227–28; American colonial policy, 239–44; the American Revolution, 239–49; British East India Company activities in India, 301–3; reasons for permitting Industrial Revolution, 342–43; factors conducive to Industrial Revolution, 342–46; enclosure movement, 346–47; Agricultural Revolu-tion, 346–50; factory system, 350–55; In-dustrial Revolution, 355–75; growth of inventions, 356–57; changes in textile in-dustry, 356–58; the steam engine, 358–59; iron and steel, 359–60; revolution in transportation, 360–66; effects of Indus-trial Revolution, 366–75; Victorian Era, 386–88. See also Great Britain
England, Bank of, 345
England, Church of: Wolsey and the mar-riage question, 72–74; Act of Supremacy, 74, 76; Six Articles, 74, 76; Cranmer's role in founding of, 74–75; restoration of Catholic faith under Mary, 75–76; Acts of Repeal, 76; Marian persecutions, 76; Elizabethan settlement, 76–77; second Act of Supremacy, 77; Act of Uniformity, 77; spread of, 83–84; and Methodism, 212
Enlightened despotism: Prussia, 228; Habs-burg Empire, 229–30; Russia, 230–33
Enlightenment, Age of, 193–236
Entente Cordiale, 494
Entente Powers, 572
Enver Pasha, sultan of Ottoman Empire, 484
Erasmus, Desiderius, 54, 62, 129, 130
Ericson, Leif, 7
Esterhazy, M. C., 470–71
Estates-General: composition of, 105; royal triumph over, 97; under Henry IV, 103; position under Francis I, 100; called by Louis XVI, 254–55
Ethiopia: Italian conquest of, 575–76
Eugene, prince of Savoy, 175
Europe: world-wide expansion of influence in nineteenth century, 219–59; collapse of balance of power after World War II, 620–21
Evolution, theory of, 584–85

Facta, Luigi, 520
Factory system: household system, 351; handicraft system, 351–52; putting out system, 352–54; definition of, 354–55; social consequences, 372–75
Faraday, Michael, 582
Farel, William, 70
Farouk, king of Egypt, 641
Fascism: rise of, 519–25
Faure, Edgar, 630, 649

February Patent of 1861, 401
Federal Republic of Germany, 631
Fehrbellin, Battle of, 160
Fénelon, François de, 170
Ferdinand I, emperor of Holy Roman Empire, 114, 115–17
Ferdinand II, emperor of Holy Roman Empire, 125–26
Ferdinand III, emperor of Holy Roman Empire, 126
Ferdinand V, king of Aragon, 18, 96, 107, 108
Ferdinand I, king of Naples, 280
Ferdinand VII, king of Spain, 280, 281, 282–83, 284, 285, 286, 399
Feudalism: end of, 128
Feuillants, 260
Fichte, Johann, 276, 594–95
Fielding, Henry, 235
Fiji Islands: discovery of, 46
Filmer, Sir Robert, 203
First Coalition, 267
First Continental Congress, 245
First French Republic, 261–66
First International Workingmen's Association, 463
First Northern War, 147, 160
First World War: political background, 490–94; outbreak of hostilities, 495–96; stalemate on western front, 505–8; withdrawal of Russia, 508; entry of United States, 508–9; changes in modern total war, 509–10; Fourteen Points, 510–11; Treaty of Versailles, 510–13
Fitch, John, 365
Flaubert, Gustave, 605
Flodden Field, Battle of, 108
Florence, Council of, 151
Fontane, Theodor, 606
Formosa: conquest by Manchus, 307; stronghold of Kuomintang, 637–38
Forty-Two Articles of Religion, 74, 75
Fourier, Charles, 382–83
Fourteen Points, 510–11
Fox, Charles James, 386
Foxe, John, 76
Fragonard, Jean, 234
France: early explorations of America, 43–44; struggle of Valois with Habsburgs, 97–98; growth of royal absolutism under Francis I, 99–100; wars of religion, 100–102; founding of House of Bourbon, 102–4; peace under Henry IV, 102–4; Thirty Years' War, 126; Peace of Westphalia, 127; colonizing efforts under Richelieu and Colbert, 172–73; under Louis XIV, 166–77; ministry of Richelieu, 166–67; ministry of Mazarin, 167–68; the *Fronde,* 167–68; court and culture under Louis XIV, 171; Colbert and mercantilism, 171–73; War of Devolution, 174; the Dutch War, 174; War of the League of Augsburg, 174; War of Spanish Succession, 174–76; Treaty of Utrecht, 176; the Enlightenment, 207–10; under the *ancien régime,* 220–22, 251–53; alliance with United States, 247–48; the French Revolution, 250–66; Louis XV, 253; Louis XVI, 253–54, 263; Marie Antoinette, 253, 263; the constitutional monarchy, 254–57; Constitution of 1791, 257–58; war with Austria and Prussia, 258–61, 265; rise of the Jacobins, 260–61; the First Republic, 261–66; the Reign of Terror, 264–65; Constitution of 1795, 265–66; rise of Napoleon, 267; Treaty of Campo Formio, 268; defeat in Egypt, 268; Napoleon crowned emperor, 270; Napoleonic reforms, 270–72; the Coalitions, 273–74; Napoleonic Wars, 272–77; downfall of Napoleon, 275–77; Congress of Vienna, 277–81, 434; the Hundred Days, 278–79; activities in India, 300–301; restoration of the Bourbons, 388–90; Napoleon III, 390–91, 434; Franco-Prussian War, 391, 435, 469; Third Republic, 435, 469–71; construction of Suez Canal, 435; expansion in Africa, 441; annexation of Pacific islands, 456; Dreyfus case, 470–71; between the wars, 525–26; occupation of the Ruhr, 525; the Popular Front, 525; fall of, 537; return to parliamentary government, 623; post-war instability, 629–30; reconstruction under de Gaulle, 630; the Fourth Republic, 630; de Gaulle's return to power, 630; the Fifth Republic, 630; war in Indo-China, 649–50
Francia, José, 285
Francis I, emperor of Holy Roman Empire, 225, 259
Francis II, emperor of Holy Roman Empire, 274
Francis I, king of France: attitude toward Protestantism, 68, 100; exploration in New World, 98–99; supremacy in church affairs, 99; growth of bureaucracy and taxation, 99; struggle with Habsburgs, 115; and the royal court, 128; builds Fontainebleau, 130
Francis II, king of France, 100, 110
Francis, duke of Lorraine, 100
Franciscans, 80
Francis Ferdinand, archduke of Austria, 478, 495
Francis Joseph, emperor of Austria, 401, 402, 477, 495, 496
Francke, August Herman, 211–12
Franco, General Francisco, 524, 632
Franco, João, 477
Franco, Rafael, 531
Franco-Prussian War, 391, 396, 406, 491
Frankhausen, Battle of, 63
Franklin, Benjamin, 214, 235
Frazer, James, 590
Frederick III, emperor of Holy Roman Empire (Frederick I of Prussia), 161
Frederick I, king in Prussia, 160–61
Frederick II (the Great), king of Prussia, 223, 224, 225, 227, 228–29, 235
Frederick, elector of the Palatinate, 125, 182
Frederick III (the Wise), elector of Saxony, 58, 59, 61, 64
Frederick of Hohenzollern, elector and margrave of Brandenburg, 158

Frederick William I, king of Prussia, 160–62, 224

Frederick William III, king of Prussia, 274, 278, 595

Frederick William IV, king of Prussia, 393–95

Frederick William, elector of Brandenburg (the Great Elector), 159–60

Free will, 87–88

French Academy of Science, 198, 200, 210

French and Indian War, 225, 227

French Congo: conquest of, 441

French East India Company, 300–301

French Revolution: the *ancien régime,* 251–53; Louis XV, 253; Louis XVI, 253–54; the constitutional monarchy, 254; Constitution of 1791, 257–58; war with Austria and Prussia, 258–61, 265; rise of the Jacobins, 260–61; the First Republic, 261–66; death of Louis XVI and Marie Antoinette, 263; Committee of Public Safety, 264; the Reign of Terror, 264–65; Constitution of 1795, 265–66

Friedland, Battle of, 274

Freud, Sigmund, 591–93

Freytag, Gustav, 606

Frick, H. C., 485

Frobisher, Martin, 45

Fronde, 168

Fuad, king of Egypt, 570

Fulton, Robert, 365

Gage, General Thomas, 247

Gainsborough, Thomas, 234

Galilei, Galileo, 6, 195, 200, 201

Galsworthy, John, 608

Gama, Vasco da: expedition to India, 19

Gandhi, Mahatma, 560–63

Garfield, James A., 486

Garibaldi, Giuseppe, 398

Garrick, David, 210

Gaskell, P., 372

Gasperi, Alcide de, 631

Gauguin, Paul, 607

Gaulle, General Charles de, 630

General Assembly, 625, 627

General Trades' Union, 409

Geneva: Calvin's work in, 70–72

Gentz, Friedrich, 385

George I, king of England, 176, 189, 241

George II, king of England, 241

George III, king of England, 241, 242, 246, 314, 316, 422

George V, king of England, 496, 576

George, David Lloyd, 468, 511, 560, 569

George, Henry, 485

Géricault, Théodore, 604

Germanic Confederation, 279

Germany: Jesuit activities in, 81; Peasants' Rebellion, 86; under Maximilian I, 113; under Charles V, 115; Thirty Years' War, 127; revolution of 1848, 393–95; rise of Bismarck, 395–96; Seven Weeks' War, 395–96; Franco-Prussian War, 396; imperialistic expansion in Africa, 441–42;

supremacy under Bismarck, 472–73, 492–93; imperialism under William II, 473–74, 493–94; interest in Near East, 483; position after Franco-Prussian War, 491–92; Triple Alliance, 493–94; World War I, 506–9; Weimar Republic, 521–22; Versailles Treaty, 522; Hitler's rise to power, 522–23; the Third Reich, 523; Locarno Pact, 533; remilitarization of the Rhine, 533; Rome-Berlin Axis, 534, 559; conquest of Austria, 534; Munich, 534; Czechoslovakia, 534–35; invasion of Poland, 535; nonaggression pact with Russia, 535; World War II, 535–43; seizure of Denmark and Norway, 537; fall of France, 537; Battle of Britain, 539; subjugation of the Balkans, 539; invasion of Russia, 539; declaration of war on America, 541; Stalingrad, 541; Ardennes offensive, 542; collapse of the Third Reich, 542; currency reform in western zones, 631; formation of Federal Republic, 631; recovery, 631–32; denazification and demilitarization policy, 623; partition of, 622–24; Berlin blockade, 648

Ghana: founding of republic, 643

Gierke, Otto von, 590

Gilbert, Sir Humphrey, 110

Gioberti, Vincenzo, 396

Giolitti, Giovanni, 520

Girondins, 260, 264, 265

Gissing, George, 606

Gladstone, William Ewart, 423, 432, 444, 467

Glorious Revolution, 189

Godunov, Boris, 152–53

Goethe, Johann Wolfgang von, 581, 603, 607, 609

Gogh, Vincent van, 607

Golden Quivira, 38

Goldsmith, Oliver, 210

Gomulka, Wladyslaw, 634

Good Neighbor policy, 531

Gordon, Charles ("Chinese"), 447–48

Gore, Bishop Charles, 601

Görres, Joseph, 604

Goschen, Sir Edward, 496

Government of India Act (1919), 560

Government of India Act (1935), 562–63

Goya, Francisco, 234, 603

Grand Alliance, 175–76

Grand Remonstrance, 184–85

Grant, Ulysses S., 486

Great Britain: development of democracy during Victorian Era, 386; Crimean War, 406; subjugation of India by British East India Company, 423–26; Sepoy Mutiny, 425–26; development of India under the crown, 426–29; acquisition of Burma, Singapore, and Hong Kong, 426, 429; settlement of Australia and New Zealand, 429–31; occupation of South Africa, 431–32; Zulu War, 432; Boer War, 432, 444–45; development of Canada, 432–33; acquisition of control of Suez Canal, 435; imperialistic expansion in Africa, 441; occupation of Egypt, 442–43; Opium War,

446; annexation of Pacific islands, 456–57; political and social reform, 467–69; end of Victorian Era, 467–69; Gladstone and the Liberals, 467–68; Disraeli and the Conservatives, 467–68; Labor party, 468; Lloyd George, 468; problem of Ireland, 469, 528; occupation of Cyprus, 483; World War I, 506–9; post-war economic reverses, 526–27; general strike, 527; end of free trade, 527; decline in authority of government, 527–28; Statute of Westminster, 528; Munich, 534–35; Dunkirk, 539; attempted German invasion, 539; rise of Labor party, 629; return of Conservatives to power, 629; accession of Elizabeth II, 629; liberation and conciliation of colonies, 638–39, 643. *See also* England

Great Colombia, republic of, 284, 413
Great Northern War, 147, 156
Great Schism, 52
Greco, El (Domenico Theotocopuli), 130
Greece: revolts against Turks, 405; United States aid to, 632
Greenland: discovery of, 7
Gregory XIII, Pope, 78
Grenville Act, 242
Grévy, Jules, 470
Grey, Lady Jane, 75
Grey, Sir Edward, 496
Grieg, Edvard, 607
Groote, Gerard, 52
Grosz, George, 608
Grotius, Hugo, 134–35, 222, 589
Guadalcanal, Battle of, 541, 559
Guadalupe Hidalgo, Treaty of, 407
Guatemala: Mayan civilization, 24–25; Spanish conquest of, 38
Guericke, Otto von, 195
Guerrero, Vicente, 287
Guesde, Jules, 464
Guises: struggle for power in France, 100–102
Guizot, François, 379, 389
Gumplowicz, Ludwig, 589
Gustavus I, king of Sweden, 146
Gustavus Adolphus, king of Sweden, 125–26, 147
Guzmán Blanco, Antonio, 490

Haakon VII, king of Norway, 472
Habsburg Dynasty: dynastic marriages of, 94–95; struggle with Valois, 98–99; rule of Maximilian I over Holy Roman Empire, 112–14; reign and abdication of Charles V, 114–17; founding of Spanish line, 117; founding of Austrian line, 117; revival of Austrian house, 162–63; consolidation of power after Treaty of Karlowitz, 164–66; revolutions of 1848, 401; reaction under Francis Joseph, 401–2; separation of Austria and Hungary, 402
Habsburg Pragmatic Sanction Treaties, 225
Hackworth, Timothy, 364
Haeckel, Ernst, 585

Haile Selassie, emperor of Ethiopia, 533, 575–76
Hakluyt, Richard, 110
Halifax, Lord, 241
Haller, Karl Ludwig von, 385
Halley, Edmond, 200
Hals, Franz, 179
Hamilton, Alexander, 249
Hampton Court Conference, 183
Handicraft system, 351–52
Hanover Dynasty, 241
Hanseatic League, 143, 144, 146
Hardie, James Keir, 464
Hardy, Thomas, 606
Hargraves, Edward Hammond, 430
Hargreaves, James, 356
Harriman, E. H., 485
Harrison, Benjamin, 486
Harvey, John, 199
Hatta, Mohammed, 640
Hauptmann, Gerhart, 606
Hawaii: republic, 455; annexation of, 455
Hawkins, Sir John, 110, 111, 122
Hawkins, William, 301
Hay, John, 452
Haydn, Joseph, 234, 603, 610
Hayes, Rutherford B., 486
Heber, Bishop Reginald, 420–21
Hecker, Friedrich, 381
Hegel, G. W. F., 595, 596
Helfferich, Karl, 509
Helmholtz, Hermann von, 582
Helvetian Republic, 268
Henrietta Maria, queen of England, 182, 183
Henriquez, Friar Camilo, 283
Henry VII, king of England, 44, 105–8
Henry VIII, king of England, 72–75, 108–9
Henry II, king of France, 100
Henry III, king of France, 102
Henry IV, king of France (Henry of Navarre), 100, 101–4, 346
Henry, duke of Guise, 102
Henry, prince of Portugal (the Navigator), 14–16, 195
Henry of Valois: elected king of Poland, 144–45
Henry Pu Yi, 557
Herbert of Cherbury, Lord, 213, 214
Herder, Johann Gottfried, 466, 552
Hertz, Heinrich, 582
Hertzog, James, 576
Herzen, Alexander, 404
Herzl, Theodor, 570
Hidalgo, Miguel, 287
Hindenberg, Paul von, 508, 510, 522
Hinduism: rebirth among Marathas, 305–6
Hispaniola: discovery by Columbus, 30–31
Hitler, Adolf, 522–23, 541, 542
Hitze, Franz, 600
Hobbes, Thomas, 203–4, 205, 222
Hobson, Captain William, 431
Ho Chi Minh, 640
Hofmeister, Wilhelm, 583
Hogarth, William, 234
Hohenzollern Dynasty, 158–62, 396
Holbein, Hans, the Elder, 130
Holbein, Hans, the Younger, 130, 131

Holland: return to parliamentary government, 623; United States aid to, 632. *See also* Netherlands

Holy Alliance, 279–80

Holy League, 164, 328

Holy Roman Empire: under Maximilian I, 112–14; under Charles V, 114–17; Protestant Revolt, 116; Peace of Westphalia, 127–28; end of, 268, 274

Honduras: Mayan civilization, 24

Hong Kong: annexation by British, 429; Japanese seizure of, 541

Hoover, Herbert, 529

Horthy, Admiral Nicholas, 524

Hötzendorff, Conrad von, 478

Household system, 351

Housman, A. E., 650

Howard, Catherine, queen of England, 75

Howe, Admiral Richard, 247

Howe, Sir William, 247

Hoxha, Enver, 621

Howells, William Dean, 605

Huayna Capac, 30, 39

Hubertusburg, Treaty of, 227

Hudson, Henry, 45

Hudson's Bay Company, 433

Huerta, Victoriano, 490

Hughes, Thomas, 600

Huguenots, 100–104, 166

Humayun, emperor of India, 294

Humbert I, king of Italy, 464, 475

Humboldt, Alexander von, 583, 605

Hume, David, 216

Hundred Days, 278–79

Hungary: Jesuit activities in, 81; growth of Protestantism, 115–16; conquest by Austrians, 164–65; forceful conversion to Catholicism, 165; conquest by Ottomans, 324; Magyar movement for autonomy, 400; the March Laws, 401, 402; separation from Austria, 402, 477, 512; joins Axis, 559; communization under Rákosi, 621, 633–34; revolution of 1956, 634

Huntsman, Benjamin, 360

Huss, John, 52, 60, 72

Hussein, sherif of Mecca, 568

Hutten, Ulrich von, 62

Hutton, James, 583

Huxley, Thomas H., 585, 611

Huygens, Christian, 179, 195, 205

Ibn Saud, king of Saudi Arabia, 570

Ibsen, Henrik, 606

Idealism, 594–95

Iguala, Plan of, 287

Imperialism: background of Industrial Revolution, 370–71; Great Britain in nineteenth century, 423–24; reaction against, 548–49, 551–53; resurgence of, 549–51; in Africa, 574–75; liberation from, 643–44

Inca civilization, 28–30, 38–39

Index, Congregation of the, 80

India: growth of trade with Portugal, 19; Battle of Plassey, 227, 303; reign of Akbar, 293, 295–96; reign of the Moguls, 294–300; rise of European power, 300–

302; British domination, 302–3; religion and culture under the Moguls, 303–6; under the British East India Company, 423–25; Sepoy Mutiny, 425–26; development under the crown, 426–29; Indian National Congresses, 427–29; Government of India Act (1919), 560, 562; Gandhi, 560–63; passive resistance, 561–62; Government of India Act (1935), 562; road to self-government, 562–63; independence, 638–39; partition, 639

India, Union of, 639

Indian Congress party, 427–29, 560, 639

Indo-China, 563, 640, 648–49

Indonesia: independence of, 640

Indulgences, sale of, 79

Industrial Revolution: growth of inventions, 355–56; changes in textile industry, 356–58; the steam engine, 358–59; iron and steel, 359–60; road construction, 360–61; canal building, 361–63; steam transport, 363–66; effects of, 366–75; population growth and urbanization, 366–68; increased wealth, 368–69; intensified capitalism, 369–70; economic imperialism, 370–71; social consequences, 371–75

Innocent IV, Pope, 9

Inquisition, Court of the: revival of, 78; used by Ferdinand and Isabella, 96; in Spain, 118; in Low Countries, 121; in colonies, 282

Instrumentalism, 597–98

Intercursus Magnus, 108

Interim, 117

International Bank, 627

International Court of Justice, 625

International Labor Organization, 627

Intolerable Acts, 244

Iran: occupation during World War II, 568; Russian attempt to penetrate, 646

Ireland: under Henry VII, 107; rebellions, 111, 184, 187, 469

Irish Free State, 528

Isabella, queen of Castile, 18, 95, 96, 107, 118, 399

Ismail Pasha, viceroy of Egypt, 435

Israel: founding of, 640

Italy: under Napoleon, 268; expulsion of Austria, 396–98; Garibaldi, 398; imperialistic expansion in Africa, 441; establishment of kingdom, 474–75; colonial aspirations, 475; rise of socialism and anarchism, 475; rise of fascism, 520–21; Benito Mussolini, 520–21; Lateran Treaties, 521; declares war on America, 541; resignation of Mussolini, 541; conquest of Ethiopia, 576; transition to democracy, 630–31

Ito Hirobumi, prince, 449

Iturbide, Augustín de, 287–88

Iturrigaray, José de, 286

Ivan III (the Great), tsar of Muscovy, 149–51

Ivan IV (the Terrible), tsar of Muscovy, 109, 151–52

Ivan VI, emperor of Russia, 230

Ivens, Roberto, 440

Izvolski, Alexander, 467

Jackson, Andrew, 409
Jacobins, 260
Jainism, 304
James I, king of England, 112, 125, 180–83
James II, king of England, 188
James, duke of York, 188
James, William, 597
Jameson, Dr. Leander Starr, 444
Janissaries, 326, 330, 331
Jansen, Cornelius, 211
Jansenism, 211
Japan: opening of, 448–50; Meiji restoration, 448–49; Sino-Japanese War, 449–50; Russo-Japanese War, 452–53, 480–81; annexation of Pacific islands, 456; invasion of Manchuria, 533, 554, 557–59; withdrawal from League of Nations, 533; Anti-Comintern Pact, 534; bombing of Pearl Harbor, 539; war in the Pacific, 541–42, 559; the atomic bomb, 542, 559; defeat of, 636; reform under MacArthur, 636–37
Jaurès, Jean, 471
Jay, John, 249
Jefferson, Thomas, 244
Jehangir, emperor of India, 296–97
Jena, Battle of, 274
Jesuits: founding of order, 80–81; dissolution of, 211, 311–12, 315, 470
Jesus, Society of. See Jesuits
Jevons, William Stanley, 589
Jiménez, Cardinal Francisco, 77
Jinnah, Mohammed Ali, 639
Joanna, queen of Castile (the Mad), 94, 114
Jodl, General Alfred, 542
John I, emperor of Brazil, 285, 288
John I, king of Portugal, 14
John II, king of Portugal, 16–18, 31
John II, king of Sweden, 147
John of Leyden, 87
John of Pian del Carpine, 9
John Sigismund, elector of Brandenburg, 159
Johnson, Andrew, 434
Johnson, Hiram S., 487
Johnson, Dr. Samuel, 210
Johnson, Tom, 487
Joliet, Louis, 173
Jones, "Golden Rule," 487
Jones, Inigo, 130
Jones Act, 564
Jonson, Ben, 110, 131
Joseph I, emperor of Holy Roman Empire, 176, 225
Joseph II, emperor of Holy Roman Empire, 229–30
Josephine, empress of the French, 267, 275
Joule, James, 582
Joyce, James, 608
Juárez, Benito, 415
Juliana, queen of the Netherlands, 640
July Monarchy, 434
Jung, Carl G., 593
Jutland, Battle of, 506

Kalmar, Union of, 146
Kamehameha I, king of Hawaii, 455

Kamehameha II, king of Hawaii, 455
Kamenev, Leo, 517
Kang Hsi, emperor of China, 307–8, 309, 310, 311, 315
Kansas-Nebraska Act 409
Kant, Immanuel, 584, 594–95, 603
Karlowitz, Treaty of, 164–66, 329
Kautsky, Karl, 464
Kay, John, 356
Kay, Robert, 356
Keisuke Okada, Admiral, 557
Kellogg-Briand Pact, 533
Kemal, Mustapha, 565–67, 568
Kempis, Thomas à (von Kempen), 52–53
Kenya: British acquisition of, 441
Kenyatta, Jomo, 642
Kepler, Johannes, 200, 201
Kerensky, Alexander, 514
Ketteler, Bishop Wilhelm Emmanuel von, 600
Keynes, John Maynard, 511
Khan, Abdul Ghafur, 560
Khan, Genghis, 9, 12
Khan, Kublai, 9
Khrushchev, Nikita S., 633, 634
Ki Inukai, 557
Kijuro Shidehara, Baron, 556
Kimbangu, Simon, 574
King George's War, 227
Kingsley, Charles, 600
King William's War, 174, 227
Kipling, Rudyard, 421
Kitchener, Sir Herbert, 442–43
Knights of Labor, 485
Knights of St. John, 319, 324, 328
Knox, John, 111
Koch, Robert, 583
Koffka, Kurt, 591
Köhler, Wolfgang, 591
Kolchak, Admiral Alexander, 514
Konev, Marshal Ivan, 647
Korea: annexation by Japan, 453; republic of, 648
Korean People's Democratic Republic, 648
Korean War, 648
Korekiyo Takahashi, 557
Kossuth, Louis, 401
Kostov, Traicho, 634
Kropotkin, Prince Peter, 465
Kruger, Paul, 444
Kuang-hsü, emperor of China, 451
Kuomintang, 553, 554–57, 558, 637–38
Kwaresmian Empire: Mongol invasion, 9

Lafayette, Marie Joseph, marquis, de, 248, 260
La Follette, Robert M., 487
La Fontaine, Jean, 170
Laissez faire, 340–42, 380, 461
Lamarck, Jean de, 584
Lamennais, Robert de, 600
Lamoral, count of Egmont, 121
Lander, Richard, 439
Laniel, Joseph, 630
La Salle, Robert Sieur de, 173
Las Casas, Bartolomé de, 42

Lateran Treaties, 521
Latin America: revolts against Spain and Portugal, 281–89
Laud, William, archbishop of Canterbury, 184
Laurier, Sir Wilfrid, 489
Lausanne, Treaty of, 565, 567
Lavigerie, Cardinal, 443
Lawrence, Sir John, 427
Lawrence, Colonel Thomas E., 569
League of Nations, 532–33, 557, 575, 624, 625, 627
Lebrun, Charles, 169
Ledru-Rollin, A. A., 381
Leeuwenhoek, Anton van, 199
Leibnitz, Baron Gottfried Wilhelm von, 161, 196, 584
Leipzig, Battle of, 126
Lenin, V. I., 480, 514–17, 553
Le Nôtre, André, 169
Leo X, Pope, 57
Leo XIII, Pope, 600
Leoncavallo, Ruggiero, 607
Leopardi, Giacomo, 604
Leopold I, emperor of Holy Roman Empire, 163–66, 174, 224–25
Leopold II, emperor of Holy Roman Empire, 230, 259
Leopold I, king of the Belgians, 392
Leopold II, king of the Belgians, 440, 441, 443, 471
Lepanto, Battle of, 123, 327–28
Le Play, Frédéric, 589
Leroy-Beaulieu, Paul, 549
Lesseps, Ferdinand de, 406, 435
Levellers, 186, 203
Lewis, Sinclair, 608
Liberalism, 378–80
Liberation, Union of, 480
Liberia, 575
Libya: independence of, 641
Lichnowsky, Prince Karl Max, 496
Ligurian Republic, 268
Li Hung-chang, 448, 450
Lilburne, John, 186
Lilienfeld, Paul von, 589
Liliuokalani, Queen Lydia, 455
Linacre, Thomas, 131
Lincoln, Abraham, 410
Lin Tse-hsü, 446
Lister, Joseph, 583
Liszt, Franz, 607
Lithuania: German occupation of, 508
Livingston, Robert R., 365
Livingstone, David, 439–40, 583
Lloyd, Henry Demarest, 485
Lloyd George, David, 468, 511, 560, 569
Locarno Pact, 533
Locke, John, 202–6, 207, 209, 218, 345, 379
Lollard movement, 52, 72
London, Treaty of, 182
London Conference: limitation of naval armaments, 533
Long Parliament, 184, 187
Lords, House of, 105
Lorenzo the Magnificent, 100
Loris-Melikov, Michael, 478

Lorrain, Claude, 169
Louis XI, king of France, 94, 97, 133
Louis XIII, king of France, 103, 126, 166
Louis XIV, king of France: rivalry with Habsburgs, 163; War of the League of Augsburg, 164; reign of, 166–77; marriage to Maria Theresa of Spain, 168; building of Versailles, 168–69; art and literature, 169–71; absolutism, 171; Colbert and mercantilism, 171–73; wars of, 173–76; Treaty of Utrecht, 176; Treaty of Dover, 188; French Academy of Science, 198; and Jansenists, 211; deterioration of government after death of, 253
Louis XV, king of France, 253
Louis XVI, king of France, 253–54, 256, 257–59, 263
Louis XVII, king of France, 265
Louis XVIII, king of France, 277, 278, 279, 388–89
Louis Philippe I, king of the French, 389–90, 401, 434
Louis of Bourbon, prince of Condé, 100, 101
Louisiana Purchase, 407
Louvois, François Michel Le Tellier, 173
Loyola, Ignatius de, 80–81
Lubbock, Sir John, 589
Lübeck, Peace of, 125, 126
Ludendorff, General Erich von, 508–9
Ludwig, elector of the Palatinate, 61
Luiz I, king of Portugal, 399, 477
Lully, Jean Baptiste, 169
Lunéville, Treaty of, 273
Luther, Martin: protest against sale of indulgences, 49; youth and education, 56; doctrine of justification by faith, 57; the ninety-five theses, 57–59; debate with Eck and Carlstadt, 59–60; primary works, 60–61; Edict of Worms, 61; return to Wittenberg, 62; and Erasmus, 62; and the radicals, 62–65; and consubstantiation, 64; opinion of rulers, 89; and Diet of Worms, 116
Lutheranism: growth of, 65–67, 83, 146; and Pietism, 211–12
Lützen, Battle of, 126
Lyly, John, 131, 466
Lysenko, Trofim D., 632

MacArthur, General Douglas, 542, 636–37
Macarthur, John, 429
Macartney, Lord George, 314
Macaulay, Thomas Babington, 606
MacDonald, Sir John, 433
MacDonald, J. Ramsay, 527, 562
Machiavelli, Niccolò, 131–32, 589, 650–51
Machine Age, 357
MacMahon, M. E. P. M. de, 470
Madagascar: French conquest of, 441
Madeira Islands, 13, 15
Madero, Francisco, 490
Madison, James, 249
Magdeburg, sack of, 126
Magellan, Ferdinand, 32–35
Magna Carta, 183–84
Mahan, Alfred T., 549

Mahmud II, sultan of Ottoman Empire, 331
Maistre, Joseph de, 599
Malan, Daniel, 576, 643
Malaya: Japanese seizure of, 541; independence, 639
Malenkov, Georgi M., 633
Mallarmé, Stéphane, 608
Malplaquet, Battle of, 175
Malthus, Thomas, 380, 584
Malvy, Louis, 509
Mamelukes, 320–21, 330
Manchu Dynasty: consolidation of power in China, 306–7; reign of Kang Hsi, 307–8; internal administration, 308–10; Europeans in China, 310–12; Ch'ien Lung, 312–15; decline of Christianity, 315; decadence of rule, 315–17; society in Manchu China, 317–18; to end of Tai Ping Rebellion, 445–47; fall of, 453–54
Manco Capac, 28
Manet, Edouard, 606
Mann, Thomas, 607
Mansart, Nicolas François, 169
Manuel I, king of Portugal, 19, 21
Manuel II, king of Portugal, 477
Mao Tse-tung, 555, 637, 646
Marburg, Colloquy of, 64
Marchand, Major Jean-Baptiste, 443
March Laws, 401, 402
Margaret, duchess of Parma, 120
Margaret of Valois, 103
Margaret Tudor, 110
Maria I, queen of Portugal, 288
Maria II, queen of Portugal, 399
"Marian Exiles," 76
Mariana, Juan de, 133
Maria Theresa, empress of Austria, 224, 225, 229
Marie Antoinette, queen of France, 253–54, 256, 259, 263
Marie Louise, empress of the French, 275
Marlborough, John Churchill, duke of, 175
Marlowe, Christopher, 131
Marne, Battle of the, 506
Marquette, Father Jacques, 173
Marroquín, José, 490
Marshall, Alfred, 589
Marshall, General George C., 637, 647
Marshall Plan, 647
Martov, Julius, 480
Marx, Karl, 382–83, 463, 595
Mary I, queen of England, 44, 73, 75–76, 109, 122
Mary II, queen of England, 189
Mary, queen of Scots, 100, 110, 111–12, 180
Mary of Burgundy, 112
Masaryk, Thomas G., 531
Mascagni, Pietro, 607
Mason, George, 244
Masurian Lakes, Battle of the, 508
Mateo Sagasta, Práxedes, 475
Matisse, Henri, 608
Matteotti, Giacomo, 520
Matthias, emperor of Holy Roman Empire, 125
Maupassant, Guy de, 605

Maurice, Frederick D., 600
Maximilian, duke of Bavaria, 123, 126, 127
Maximilian I, emperor of Holy Roman Empire, 59, 94, 112–14
Maximilian, emperor of Mexico, 391, 415, 434, 477
Maxwell, James, 582
Mayan civilization, 24–25
Mazarin, Cardinal Jules, 126, 167–68
Mazzini, Giuseppe, 381, 396–98, 466
McAdam, John Loudon, 361
McKinley, William, 465, 486, 564
McMahon, Sir Henry, 568–69
Meckel, Johann F., 583
Medici, Catherine de', 100–102, 128, 169
Medici, Marie de', 103, 166
Mehemet Ali, pasha of Egypt, 330, 331
Meiji restoration, 448–49
Melanchthon, Philip, 62, 64, 65, 74
Melbourne, Lord William, 467
Mendel, Gregor, 583, 632
Mendeleev, Dmitri, 582
Mendelssohn-Bartholdy, Felix, 604
Mendès-France, Pierre, 630
Menelik, 441
Mensdorff, Albert von, 496
Mercantilism, 103, 171–73, 216–17
Merchant Adventurers, Company of the, 109
Mestizos, 42
Metcalf, John, 361
Methodism, 211–12, 374, 603
Metternich, Clemens, Prince, 278, 280, 393, 396, 401, 644
Mexican War, 407
Mexico: Mayan civilization, 24–25; Aztec civilization, 25–26; conquest by Cortés, 36–38; revolt against Spain, 286–87; Plan of Iguala, 287; Iturbide crowned emperor, 287–88; expulsion of the French, 391; Mexican War, 407; Benito Juárez, 415; downfall of Maximilian, 415, 434; the revolution, 490
Mexico City: founding of, 25–26
Mickiewicz, Adam, 604
Middle Ages: geography and travel, 6–11
Middle class: influential in rise of early modern science, 194–95; rise to power, 371–72
Midway, Battle of, 541
Miliukov, Paul, 514
Mill, John Stuart, 462, 466–67
Millerand, Alexandre, 464
Millet, François, 606
Milton, John, 190
Ming Dynasty, 306
Miranda, Francisco, 283–84
Missouri Compromise, 409
Mitchel, John Purroy, 487
Mitre, Bartolomé, 415
Moctezuma II, 36, 37
Mogul Empire: reign of Baber, 294; reign of Akbar, 295–96; Jehangir, 296–97; Shah Jehan, 297–98; Aurungzeb, 298–300; rise of European power, 300–302; British domination, 302–3; culture of the Mogul period, 303–4; religion, 304–6
Mohammed II, sultan of Ottoman Empire, 318

Mohammed V, sultan of Ottoman Empire, 484

Mohammed VI, sultan of Ottoman Empire, 565

Mohammed Kiuprili, 164

Mohammed Riza Pahlavi, 568

Molière (Jean Baptiste Poquelin), 170, 610

Moltke, Field Marshal Helmuth von, 395, 496, 506

Monagas, José Gregorio, 414

Monck, General George, 187

Monet, Claude, 606

Monroe, James, 281

Monroe Doctrine, 281, 407

Montagu, Edwin S., 560

Montaigne, Michel de, 130

Montcalm, Louis-Joseph, marquis de, 227

Monteagudo, Bernardo, 283

Montecuccoli, Raimondo, count of, 164

Montesinos, Antonio de, 42

Montesquieu, Charles Louis, baron de, 214, 218–19, 231, 235, 379

Monteverde, General, 284

Montmorency, Anne de, 100, 101

Montt, Manuel, 415

Morazán, Francisco, 414

More, Paul Elmer, 613

More, Sir Thomas, 129, 130

Morelos, José, 287

Moreno, Mariano, 285

Morgan, J. P., 485

Morgan, Lewis H., 589

Morocco: independence of, 641

Morton, John, archbishop of Canterbury, 107

Morton, William T. G., 583

Morris, R. O., 609

Moslem League, 560, 639

Mozart, Wolfgang Amadeus, 234, 603

Mühlberg, Battle of, 66, 117

Müller, Adam, 385

Mumtaz Mahall, 297

Mun, Count A. A. M. de, 600

Munich Agreement, 534–35

Müntzer, Thomas, 63

Murat, Joachim, 274

Muraviev, Nikolai, 438

Murray, "Alfalfa Bill," 287

Mussolini, Benito, 441, 520–21, 533–34, 537, 575, 630

Mutsuhito (Meiji), emperor of Japan, 448–449

Nachtigal, Gustav, 439

Nahuas, 25

Nanking, Treaty of, 446–47

Nantes, Edict of, 103, 166, 171

Napier, General Sir Charles, 424

Napier, John, 196

Naples, kingdom of, 274

Napoleon I, emperor of the French: recovery of Toulon, 265; youth and background, 267; early military career, 267; campaigns in Austria and Italy, 267–68; Battle of the Nile, 268–69; First Consul, 269; crowned emperor, 270; administrative reforms, 270;

fiscal reforms, 270–71; legal reforms, 271; reconciliation with the church, 271–72; educational reforms, 272; Second Coalition, 273; Third Coalition, 273; sale of Louisiana, 273; Trafalgar, 273; Austerlitz, 273; Jena and Auerstädt, 274; Friedland, 274; Tilsit, 274; failure of the Continental System, 275; Peninsular War, 276; Russian campaign, 276–77; exile to Elba, 277; Hundred Days, 279; exile to St. Helena, 279; attempt to gain control of Spanish colonies, 282–83; invasion of Egypt, 330; and proposed submarine, 365

Napoleon II, king of Rome, 275

Napoleon III, emperor of the French, 390–91, 398, 404, 434

Nasser, Gamal Abdel, 641–42

Nationalism: and the Protestant Reformation, 87–88; growth among non-Europeans, 421–22; rise of, 465–67, 552–53; Japan, 557–59; India, 559–63; Siam, 563–64; Netherlands East Indies, 564; Turkey, 565–67; Persia, 567–68; the Arabs, 568–70; Zionism, 570

National Industrial Recovery Act, 530

National Labor Relations Act, 530

Natural religion: during Enlightenment, 212–13

Naumann, Friedrich, 600

Navigation Acts, 240

Nehru, Jawaharlal, 562–63, 639

Nelson, Lord Horatio, 268, 273

Neoguelph movement, 396

Nerchinsk, Treaty of, 310–11, 438

Netherlands: early Arctic exploration, 45; expedition to Indies, 45; formation of Dutch East India Company, 45; discovery of Cape Horn, 45; circumnavigation of Australia, 45; revolt against Spain, 120; gains under Treaty of Utrecht 176; rise and decline of Dutch republic, 177–80; Dutch colonial expansion, 178–79; annexation of Holland to France, 274; independence of Holland, 277; growth of constitutionalism, 391–92; imperialism in Indies, 435–37

Netherlands East Indies: Japanese seizure of, 541; independence movement, 564

Neuilly, Treaty of, 512

New Amsterdam, 240

Newcomen, Thomas, 358–59

New Deal, 529–30

New Granada: formation of, 41; revolt against Spain, 283–84

Newman, John Henry, 599

New Model Army, 186–87

New Spain: formation of, 41; vice-royalty of, 119–20. See also Mexico

Newspapers: growth of, 235

Newton, Isaac, 195, 196, 200–202, 205, 206; 207, 209, 215

New World: earliest civilizations, 22, 30; earliest migrations to, 22, 24

New York harbor: discovery of, 43

New Zealand: discovery by Tasman, 46; achievement of dominion status, 469

Ngo Dinh Diem, 640

Nicholas I, emperor of Russia, 403–4, 406, 438
Nicholas II, emperor of Russia, 450, 480–81, 495, 514
Nietzsche, Friedrich, 596–97
Nitti, Francesco, 520
Nigeria: British acquisition of, 441
Nikolaievich, Grand Duke Nicholas, 508
Nikon, Patriarch, 154
Nile, Battle of the, 268
Norfolk System, 348
Norris, George W., 487
North, Lord Frederick, 241, 244, 248
North America: Mayan civilization, 24–25; Nahua civilization, 25–26
North Atlantic Treaty Organization (NATO), 647
North German Confederation, 396
Norway: representative government in, 392; dissolution of union with Sweden, 472; German seizure of, 537; return to parliamentary government, 623; United States aid to, 632
Noske, Gustav, 464
Novalis (Friedrich von Hardenberg), 599
Novara, Battle of, 398
Nurmahal, 297
Nystadt, Treaty of, 161

Oceania: European partition of, 454–57
Ockham, William of, 194
October Diploma of 1860, 401
October Manifesto, 481
O'Higgins, Bernardo, 285–86
Oliva, Treaty of, 147
"Open Door" policy, 452
Opium trade, 424
Opium War, 429, 446
Orange Dynasty, 178, 391
Orange Free State, 431–32, 444–45
Orellana, Francisco de, 39–40
Orlando, Vittorio, 511, 520
Oscar I, king of Sweden, 392
Otis, James, 242
Ottawa Imperial Economic Conference, 527
Ottoman Empire: Battle of Lepanto, 123, 327–28; conquests of Mohammed II, 318–19; acquisition of caliphate, 319–21; Suleiman the Magnificent, 321–27; decline of the empire, 328–31; Selim III, 330; struggle between Russia and England for influence, 405–6; Crimean War, 406; birth of Romania, 406; the Suez Canal, 406–7; Westernization under Abdul Aziz, 406; democracy and nationalism, 481–84; foreign interests, 481–84; revival of absolutism, 484. See also Turkey
Oudenarde, Battle of, 175
Owen, Robert, 382
Oyama, Field Marshal, 453
Ozanam, Antoine Frédéric, 600

Pacific, War of the, 490

Pacific islands: partition of, 454–57
Padua Circular, 259
Páez, Federico, 531
Páez, José, 414
Paine, Thomas, 245
Pakistan: founding of republic, 639
Palacky, Francis, 400
Palestine: Balfour White Paper, 570–71; suggestion for partition, 571, 640; World War II, 571; founding of Israel, 640–41
Palmerston, Lord Henry John, 387, 435, 467
Pan-African Congress, 575
Panama: founding of, 36
Panama, Isthmus of: discovery of, 31
Pan-American conference of 1938, 531
Papacy: beginnings of national opposition to, 54–55; weakened position of, 52; Lateran Treaties, 521
Paraguay: revolt against Spain, 285
Pareto, Vilfredo, 593
Paris, Treaty of (1763), 227, 241
Paris, Treaty of (1783), 248–49
Paris, Treaty of (1814), 277
Paris, Second Treaty of (1815), 279, 280
Paris, Treaty of (1856), 406
Park, Mungo, 438, 439
Parliament: rise of in England, 104–5, 183–89
Parliament Bill, 468
Parr, Catherine, queen of England, 75
Pascal, Blaise, 594
Passive resistance, 561–62
Pasteur, Louis, 583
Patrons of Husbandry, 485
Pauker, Ana, 621
Paul III, Pope, 78
Paul, Lewis, 357
Pavia, Battle of, 115
Pavlov, Ivan, 591
Pearson, Karl, 549–50
Peary, Robert, 458
Peasants' Revolt, 63, 86, 87
Pedro I, emperor of Brazil, 286, 288–89, 414
Pedro II, emperor of Brazil, 414–15, 489
Pedro V, king of Portugal, 399
Pedro, prince of Portugal, 14–15
Peel, Sir Robert, 467
Peel, Lord William, 571
Peirce, Charles S., 597
Peninsular War, 276
People's Charter, 397
Pérez, José Joaquín, 415
Permanent Court of International Justice, 533
Perrault, Claude, 207–8
Perry, Commodore Matthew C., 448, 636
Pershing, General John J., 490
Persia: rise of nationalism, 567–68; modernization under Riza Shah Pahlavi, 568; change in name to Iran, 568; occupation during World War II, 568. See also Iran
Perthes, Jacques Boucher de, 589
Peru: Inca civilization, 28–30; conquest by Pizarro, 38–39; the vice-royalty, 41, 119; revolt against Spain, 286
Peruvian-Bolivian Confederation: struggle with Chile, 413

Pétain, Marshal Henri-Philippe, 537
Peter I (the Great), emperor of Russia, 155–58, 177, 329
Peter II, emperor of Russia, 230
Peter III, emperor of Russia, 225, 230–31
Petition of Right, 183
Philip, Captain Arthur, 429
Philip II, king of Spain: the Armada, 44; marriage to Mary Tudor, 76, 109; role in French wars of religion, 101, 102; character and aims, 118; succession to throne of Portugal, 119; overseas expansion, 119–20; revolt of the Netherlands, 120–22; and Elizabeth of England, 122–23; builds Escorial, 130; closing of Lisbon to Dutch trade, 178
Philip V, king of Spain (Philip of Anjou), 175
Philip, duke of Burgundy, 94, 112, 114
Philip of Flanders, 108
Philip of Hesse, 64
Philippine Islands: Spanish colonization of, 119–20; expulsion of Spaniards, 456, 475; Japanese seizure of, 541; American reoccupation, 542; American control, 564–65; World War II, 564–65; establishment of republic, 639–40
Philosophes, 207, 215–20, 222–23, 282, 284, 403
Picasso, Pablo, 609
Picot, Georges, 569
Picquart, Colonel Georges, 471
Pietism, 211–12
Pillnitz, Declaration of, 259
Pilsudski, Marshal Joseph, 524
Pinay, Antoine, 630
Pissarro, Camille, 606
Pitt, William, 316, 386, **577**
Pius V, Pope, 78, 80
Pius VI, Pope, 268
Pius VII, Pope, 271
Pius IX, Pope, 396, 600
Pius XI, Pope, 601
Pizarro, Francisco, 38–39
Plassey, Battle of, 227, 303
Plekhanov, George, 480
Pobiedonostsev, Constantine, 480
Poincaré, Raymond, 526
Poland: Jesuit activities in, 81; gains under Treaty of Karlowitz, 164; partition by Russia and Prussia, 232; partition by Congress of Vienna, 279; German invasion of, 508, 535; under Marshal Pilsudski, 524; loss of territory to Soviet Union, 621; communization under Joseph Cyrankiewicz, 621, 633–34; partial autonomy under Gomulka, 634
"Poland, Republic of," 144–46
Political science: development of, 589–90
Politiques, 102, 133
Polo, Marco, 5, 10
Polo brothers: trip to China, 9
Poltava, Battle of, 156
Ponce de León, Juan, 38
Poniatowski, Stanislaus, 232
Pontiac's Rebellion, 241–42
Poor Law of 1601, 374

Pope, Alexander, 206, 234–35
Population growth, 342–44, 366–67
Portsmouth, Treaty of, 480, 645
Portugal: explorations under Pedro and Henry, 14–16; explorations under John II, 16–19; exploration under Manuel I, 19, 21; da Gama's expedition to India, 19; discovery of Brazil, 19, 21; empire in the East, 19–22; growth of trade with India, 19, 21; under Habsburg rule, 119; attacked by Napoleon, 275; revolt of Brazil, 288–289; missionaries in India, 297; trading efforts in China, 311; during nineteenth century, 399–400; expansion in Africa, 442; proclamation of the republic, 477; Salazar dictatorship, 524, 632; United States aid to, 632
Positivism, 588–90
Poussin, Nicolas, 169
Pourtalès, Friedrich von, 496
Poyarkov, Vasili, 310
Poyning's Law, 107
Pragmatic Sanction of Bourges, 55, 88, 99
Pragmatism, 597–98
"Prague, Defenestration of," 125
Prague, Treaty of, 126
Predestination, 69, 87
Presbyterianism, 83, 111
Pressburg, Treaty of, 273
Prester John, legend of, 8–9, 14, 16, 17
Primo de Rivera, General Miguel, 524
Princip, Gavrilo, 495
Proclamation of 1763, 242
Prokofiev, Sergei, 608, 632
Proletarian radicalism, 463–65
Protectionism: growth of, 549
Protestantism: extirpation in Bohemia, 125; extirpation in Hungary and Transylvania, 165
Protestant Reformation: in Germany, 56–67; in Sweden, 67; in Denmark, 67; in Slovenia, 67; in Geneva, 67–72; in England, 72–77; Catholic and Protestant views of, 81–83; growth of sects and sectarianism, 83–87; growth of nationalism, 87–88; and democracy, 89; and rise of capitalism, 89–90. *See also* Protestant Revolt
Protestant Revolt: effect on Holy Roman Empire, 116; in Low Countries, 121
Protestant Union, 124, 125
Proust, Marcel, 608
Prussia: rise of, 158–62; under the Great Elector, 159–60; First Northern War, 160; growth as military power under Frederick William, 161–62; gains under Treaty of Utrecht, 176; under Frederick the Great, 228–29; Treaty of Tilsit, 274; defeat by Napoleon, 274; gains from Congress of Vienna, 279; revolution of 1848, 393–95; rise of Bismarck, 395–96; Seven Weeks' War, 395–96; Franco-Prussian War, 396
Psychology and psychoanalysis: development of, 591–93
Public Safety Act, 561
Public Works Administration, 530
Pufendorf, Baron Samuel von, 222
Pugachev, Emelian, 232

Puritans: and the early Stuarts, 183–85; the Civil War, 185–87; the Restoration, 187–88; literature, 190
Pushkin, Alexander, 604
Putting out system, 352–54
Pyrenees, Treaty of the, 174

Quadruple Alliance, 280, 281, 625
Quebec Act, 244
Queen Anne's War, 174, 227
Quesnay, François, 217
Quinault, Philippe, 169
Quintuple Alliance, 280, 387

Rabelais, François, 130
Racine, Jean, 170
Radek, Karl, 517
Radetzky, Field Marshal Joseph, 401
Rajk, Laszlo, 634
Rákosi, Mátyas, 621
Raleigh, Sir Walter, 110, 131
Rama VII, king of Siam, 564
Rama VIII, king of Siam, 564
Ramillies, Battle of, 175
Ranke, Leopold von, 590
Rauschenbush, Walter, 601
Realism, 605–7
Realpolitik, 133–34, 395, 467, 511
Reconstruction Finance Corporation, 529
Reejiro Wakatsuki, 556
Reformation. See Catholic Reformation; Protestant Reformation
Reign of Terror, 264–65
Reinsurance Treaty of 1887, 493
Reinsurance Treaty of 1890, 493
Rembrandt, 179
Renan, Ernest, 591, 606
Renoir, Pierre Auguste, 606
Representation of Natives Act, 577
Restitution, Edict of, 125
Restrepo, Carlos, 490
Revenue Act of 1764, 242
Reyes, Rafael, 490
Reynolds, Sir Joshua, 234
Rhee, Syngman, 648
Rhine, Confederation of the, 273–74
Rhodes, Cecil, 441, 442, 444
Rhodesia, 441, 444, 445
Ricardo, David, 380
Ricci, Matteo, 311
Richardson, Samuel, 235
Richardson, William A., 486
Richelieu, Armand Jean du Plessis, cardinal-duke of, 126, 166–67, 182
Riesman, David, 594
Rigaud, Antoine, 169
Rights of Man, Declaration of, 256, 271, 283
Riksdag: composition of, 105
Risorgimento, 396, 474
Ritschl, Albrecht, 601
Ritter, Karl, 583
Rivera, Diego, 608
Riza Shah Pahlavi (Riza Khan), 568
Robespierre, Maximilien, 260, 264, 265, 381
Rocco, Alfredo, 524

Rochambeau, Jean Baptiste, comte de, 248
Rochefoucauld, François de la, 170
Rockefeller, John D., 485
Rocroi, Battle of, 126
Roe, Sir Thomas, 301–2
Roger-Ducos, 269
Romains, Jules, 607–8
Roman Catholic church: role on eve of Protestant Reformation, 50; early dissenters, 51–53; criticisms of, 53–56; sale of church offices, 53; sale of dispensations, 53–54; sale of indulgences, 54; traffic in sacred relics, 54; church levies, 55; excommunication of Henry VIII, 74; dissolution of monasteries in England, 74; restoration under Mary, 75–76; passages of Six Articles in England, 74; efforts at reform, 77–78; papal reforms, 78; revival of Inquisition, 78; Council of Trent, 78–80; creation of Congregation of the Index, 80; founding of Society of Jesus, 80–81; regains Poland, Bohemia, Hungary, 84; and Jansenism, 211; dissolution of Jesuit order, 211; confiscation of church lands in France, 256–57; Concordat with Napoleon, 271–72; missionary activity in China, 311–12; decline in China, 315; missionary activities in Africa, 443
Romania: birth of, 406; independence, 483; under Carol II, 524; joins Axis, 539; loss of territory to Soviet Union, 621; communization under Ana Pauker, 621, 633–34
Roman law: Grotius' study of, 135
Romanov, Michael, tsar of Muscovy, 154
Romanov Dynasty, 152–58
Roman Republic, 268
Romanticism, 603–5, 651
Rome: sack of, 115
Rome-Berlin Axis, 534, 559
Rommel, General Erwin, 541
Röntgen, Wilhelm, 582
Roosevelt, Franklin D., 529–30, 531, 541, 559, 644, 645–46
Roosevelt, Theodore, 453, 486
Rosas, Juan Manuel de, 415
Rossini, Gioacchino, 604, 607
Rouault, Georges, 608
Rousseau, Jean Jacques, 219–20, 381
Rowlatt Acts, 561
Rubens, Peter Paul, 130
Rudolf, crown prince of Austria, 478
Rump Parliament, 186–87
Rurik Dynasty, 150–52
Ruskin, John, 606
Russell, Bertrand, 587
Russell, Lord John, 467, 468
Russia: under the Tartars, 147–49; emergence in fifteenth century, 149; rise to power under Ivan III (the Great), 149–51; Rurik Dynasty, 150–52; subjugation of nobility by the Rurik tsars, 151–52; growth of serfdom, 151–52; colonizing efforts of Cossacks, 152; Ivan IV (the Terrible), 152; Romanov Dynasty, 152–58; Time of Troubles, 153–54; First Northern War, 154; wars with Poland, 154; Don Cos-

sack revolt, 154; church reforms, 154; reign of Alexis, 154–55; Peter the Great, 155–58; Great Northern War, 156; under Catherine the Great, 230–33; Treaty of Tilsit, 274; defeat by Napoleon, 274; Napoleonic campaign in, 276–77; gains from Congress of Vienna, 279; penetration into China, 310–11; struggles with Turks, 329–30; Alexander I, 403; absolutism under Nicholas I, 404–5; Crimean War, 404, 438; Alexander II and the beginning of reform, 404–5; imperial expansion, 437–38; Russo-Japanese War, 452–53; closing years of Romanov Dynasty, 478–81; beginning of revolution, 481, 508, 514–16; World War I, 506–9; Treaty of Brest-Litovsk, 508; economic recovery, 516–17; Five-Year Plans, 516–17; Stalin dictatorship, 517–19; Moscow purges, 517; diplomacy of, 518–19; entrance into League of Nations, 518; Third International, 519; non-aggression pact with Germany, 535; German attack, 539; Battle of Stalingrad, 541; entry into war with Japan, 542. See also Soviet Union
Russo-Japanese War, 452–53, 480–81
Rutherford, Ernest, 582
Royal Society of London, 198, 210, 345, 347
Ryneveld, Sir Helperus van, 572

Sadi-Carnot, Marie François, 465
Sahara Desert: French absorption of, 441
Saïd Pasha, viceroy of Egypt, 435
St. Bartholomew's Day, Massacre of, 101–2
Sainte-Beuve, C. A., 606
St.-Germain, Treaty of, 512
St. Gotthard, Battle of, 164
St. Petersburg Academy, 198
Saint-Simon, Count Henri de, 382, 383
St.-Simon, Louis, duc de, 170
Salazar, Antonio de Oliveira, 524, 632
Salisbury, Lord Robert, 468
Salvation Army, 601
Samoa, 455–56, 528
San Francisco Conference, 625, 627
San Martín, José de, 285–86, 412
San Stefano, Treaty of, 483
Santa Anna, Antonio López de, 414, 415
Santa María, Domingo, 415
Saratoga, Battle of, 247
Sarmiento, Domingo, 415
Savery, Thomas, 358
Sazonov, Sergei, 496
Schäffle, Albert, 589
Scharnhorst, Gerhard von, 276
Schelling, F. W. J. von, 595
Schenck, Robert, 486
Schlegel, Friedrich von, 595
Schleiden, Matthias, 583
Schleiermacher, Friedrich, 599
Schlieffen, General Alfred von, 495
Schmalkaldic League, 65, 66, 117
Schmalkaldic War, 117
Schmoller, Gustav von, 589
Schön, Wilhelm von, 496

Schönberg, Arnold, 609
Schopenhauer, Arthur, 596–97
Schouten, Willem, 46
Schubert, Franz, 604
Schuman, Robert, 630
Schumann, Robert, 604
Schwann, Theodor, 583
Schwarzenberg, Felix zu, 401
Science: rise of, 193–96; philosophy and organization of, 196–99; achievements of, 199–200; Newton and the Newtonian synthesis, 200–202
Scotland: growth of Presbyterianism, 111; formation of the Covenant, 184
Scott, Sir Walter, 604
Second Coalition, 268
Second Continental Congress, 245–46, 247
Second International, 463–64
Second World War: immediate background, 535–37; Axis successes, 537–39; Battle of Britain, 539; Pearl Harbor, 541; Allied victories, 541–42; end of hostilities, 542; costs of the war, 542–43
Secularism: spread of, 601–3
Security Council, 625, 627
Sedan, Battle of, 391, 435
Seipel, Monsignor Ignaz, 600
Selim I, sultan of Ottoman Empire, 320–21
Selim II, sultan of Ottoman Empire, 325, 327–28
Selim III, sultan of Ottoman Empire, 328, 330
Sepoy Mutiny, 425–26, 447, 551
Serbia: revolts against Turks, 405; independence of, 483
Serpa Pinto, Alexandre, 440
Settlement, Act of, 189
Seven Weeks' War, 395–96, 398, 402
Seven Years' War, 225–27, 241, 302
Sévigné, Madame de, 170
Sèvres, Treaty of, 512, 565
Seymour, Edward, duke of Somerset, 75
Seymour, Lady Jane, 75
Sforza, Francesco, duke of Milan, 115
Shakespeare, William, 110, 131, 609
Shaw, George Bernard, 601
Sheridan, Thomas, 210
Shimonoseki, Treaty of, 450
Shinto: growth in Japan, 449
Short Parliament, 184
Shostakovich, Dmitri, 632
Siam: modernization, 563–64; change in name to Thailand, 564
Sibelius, Jean, 608
Sickingen, Franz von, 62
Sidney, Sir Philip, 131
Sieyes, Emmanuel-Joseph, 269
Sigismund II, king of Poland, 144
Sigismund III, king of Poland and Sweden, 147
Sikhism, 304
Silk trade: growth of, 11–12
Simon, Sir John, 562
Sinclair, Upton, 487
Singapore: acquisition by British, 429
Sino-Japanese War, 449–50
Sivaji, 305–6

Six Articles, 74, 75
Sixtus V, Pope, 78
Slansky, Rudolf, 634
Slavery question, 409–10
Smeaton, John, 359
Smetona, Antonas, 524
Smith, Adam, 217, 340, 380
Smith, Sir Thomas, 181
Smollett, Tobias, 235
Smoot-Hawley Tariff, 529
Smuts, Jan, 445, 576
Sobieski, John, king of Poland, 164, 329
Social gospel, 601
Socialism, 381–83, 463–65
Social sciences: development of, 589–90
Social Security Act, 530
Sociology: development of, 589
Soekarno, Achmed, 640, 644
Soil Conservation Act, 530
Solano López, Francisco, 413
Somme, Battle of the, 506
Sophia, electress of Hanover, 189
Sophia Augusta Fredericka, princess of An-
    halt-Zerbst. See Catherine II (the Great),
    empress of Russia
Sophia Charlotte of Hanover, 161
Sorel, Georges, 465
Soto, Hernando de, 38
South Africa: British occupation of, 431–32;
    Boer War, 432, 444–45, 489; formation
    of union, 445, 469; expansion of, 528;
    English-Boer differences, 576–77; Jan
    Smuts, 576; discriminatory policies of
    Boers, 576–77, 642–43
South America: Chibcha civilization, 26–28;
    Inca civilization, 28–30
Southeast Asia Treaty Organization
    (SEATO), 647
Soviet Union: emergence as great world
    power after World War II, 620; annexa-
    tion of strategic lands after World War
    II, 621; creation of the satellite states,
    621, 633–34; the Iron Curtain, 624; Yalta,
    625; position in the United Nations, 625–
    28; the veto, 627; death of Stalin, 632–33;
    power struggle, 633; Hungarian revolu-
    tion, 634; rising prestige in Middle East,
    642; agreement to enter war against
    Japan, 645–46. See also Russia
Spain: exploration by Columbus, 30–31; ex-
    ploration by Vespucci, 31–32; Magellan's
    circumnavigation of globe, 32–35; colon-
    ization of Panama, 35–36; conquest of
    Mexico, 36–38; conquest of Peru, 38–39;
    conquest of the Chibchas, 40; formation of
    vice-royalties, 41; unification under Ferdi-
    nand and Isabella, 118; under Philip II,
    117–23; under Bonaparte rule, 274; the
    Peninsular War, 275–76; colonial policies,
    281–82; revolt in New Granada, 283–85;
    revolt in the South, 285–86; revolt in
    Mexico and Guatemala, 286–88; during
    the nineteenth century, 399; activities in
    Africa, 442; political unrest under parlia-
    mentarians, 475–77; Spanish-American
    War, 475; proclamation of the republic,
    524; civil war, 524, 534

Spanish-American War, 456, 475, 486
Spanish Armada, 110, 111
Spanish Concordat, 88
Speke, John Hanning, 439
Spencer, Herbert, 589
Spener, Philipp Jacob, 211–12
Spengler, Oswald, 216, 593
Spenser, Edmund, 110, 131
Speyer, Second Diet of, 64
Spice trade, 12, 21
Stahl, Friedrich Julius, 599
Stalin, Joseph, 517–18, 555, 620–21, 623,
    632–33, 634, 645–46
Stalingrad, Battle of, 541
Stamp Act, 242
Stanley, Henry Morton, 440, 583
Star Chamber, 107, 184
State sovereignty: fascist principle of, 524–25
Staupitz, John von, 56
Stavisky, Sergei, 526
Steam engine, 358–59
Steen, Jan, 179
Steffens, Lincoln, 487
Stein, Gertrude, 608
Stein, Heinrich, baron vom, 276
Stephenson, George, 364–65
Sterne, Laurence, 235
Steuben, Frederick, baron von, 248
Stevin, Simon, 195
Stolypin, Peter, 481
Storm, Theodor, 606
Stradivari, Antonio, 234
Strauss, David Friedrich, 591
Strauss, Richard, 608
Stravinsky, Igor, 609
Stresemann, Gustav, 533
Strindberg, August, 606
Strong, Josiah, 601
Struve, Gustav von, 381
Suárez, Francisco, 132
Sublime Porte, 481–84, 565, 570
Sucre, General Antonio José de, 284, 286
Suez Canal: completion of, 406–7; French
    construction, 435; British acquisition of
    voting control, 435, 468; seizure by Nas-
    ser, 642
Sugar Act, 242
Sukhomlinov, General Vladimir, 496
Suleiman I (the Magnificent), 116, 123,
    321–27
Sumner, William Graham, 589
Sung, Kim Il, 648
Sun Yat-sen, 454, 553, 554–55
Supremacy, Act of, 74, 109
Sweden: adopts Lutheranism, 67; Thirty
    Years' War, 126; Peace of Westphalia,
    127; revolt against Denmark, 146; growth
    of Protestantism, 146; territorial expan-
    sion under Gustavus I, 146; First North-
    ern War, 147; gains under Treaty of
    Westphalia, 147; Great Northern War,
    147; industrialization, 472; dissolution of
    union with Norway, 472
Swift, Jonathan, 208
Swinburne, Algernon, 608
Sykes, Sir Mark, 569
Symington, William, 365

Tadeo, José, 414
Taine, Hippolyte A., 606
Tai Ping Rebellion, 447–48
Takashi Hara, 556
Talleyrand, Charles de, 278, 422
Tamerlane, 12
Tannenberg, Battle of, 508
Tao Kuang, emperor of China, 446
Tasman, Abel Janszoon, 46, 178, 430
Tasmania: discovery of, 46
Tata, Jamshedi, 427
Tawney, R. H., 89, 90
Tchaikovsky, Peter Ilich, 607
Telford, Thomas, 361, 363
Temple, Sir William, 208
Tennyson, Alfred, 606
Tenochcas. See Aztecs
Tenochtitlán, 25–26, 37–38
Tetzel, John, 58
Teutonic Knights, 143–44, 158–59
Texas, Republic of, 407
Textile industry: and the Industrial Revolution, 356–58
Thackeray, William Makepeace, 606
Thailand: modernization of, 563–64; change in name from Siam, 564
Theodore III, emperor of Russia, 155
Thiers, Adolphe, 469
Third Republic, 435
Thirty-Nine Articles of Faith, 77
Thirty Years' War, 125–26
Thomson, J. J., 582
Thoreau, Henry David, 595
Thorhall the Hunter, 7
Three Emperors' League, 493–94
Thuku, Harry, 574
Tibet, 308, 313–14, 426
Tilly, Johann, count of, 125–26
Tilsit, Treaty of, 274
Tirpitz, Admiral Alfred von, 473, 494, 496
Tito, Marshal, 621
Togo, Admiral Heihachiro, 453
Tojo, General Hideki, 557
Tolstoy, Leo, 606, 607, 609
Toltecs, 25
Tordesillas, Treaty of, 18–19, 22, 31, 32, 34
Torgau, League of, 64, 117
Torricelli, Evangelista, 195
Toulouse-Lautrec, Henri de, 607
Townshend, Charles, viscount, 348
Townshend Acts, 243–44
Toynbee, Arnold, 216, 339, 593–94
Trade, House of (Casa de Contratación), 118
Trade and Plantations, Board of, 239, 241
Transubstantiation, 64, 74
Transvaal Republic, 431–32, 444–45, 469
Treitschke, Heinrich von, 421
Trent, Council of, 78–80
Tresaguet, Pierre, 361
Trevithick, Richard, 363–64
Trianon, Treaty of, 512
Triple Alliance, 493–94
Triple Entente, 494, 506–9, 559, 565
Troeltsch, Ernst, 601
Troppau, Congress of, 403
Trotsky, Leon, 514–17, 555

Truman, Harry S., 628, 646–47
Truman Doctrine, 647
Trusteeship Council, 625
Tsushima Strait, Battle of, 453
Tudor Dynasty, 104–11, 130–31
Tukaram, 305
Tull, Jethro, 348
Tunisia: independence of, 641
Turenne, Marshal, 126
Turgenev, Ivan, 606
Turgot, Anne Robert, Baron de Laune, 254, 423
Turkey: threats to Holy Roman Empire, 116; decline of power, 124; threats to Europe in seventeenth century, 164; the Ottoman Empire, 318–31; victories under Mustapha Kemal, 565–66; modernization under Mustapha Kemal, 566–67; abolition of the caliphate, 566; neutrality in World War II, 567; Ismet Inönü, 567. See also Ottoman Empire
Turner, J. M. W., 604
Tydings-McDuffie Act, 564, 639–40
Tylor, Edward, 589

Uganda: British acquisition of, 441
Uniformity, Acts of, 75, 77
United Kingdom. See England; Great Britain
United Nations: formation of, 624–28; Dumbarton Oaks, 625; Yalta, 625; San Francisco, 625; structure of, 625–27; the veto, 627; achievements of, 627–28; intervention in Suez Canal dispute, 642
United Nations Economic and Social Council, 625
United Nations Educational, Scientific, and Cultural Organization, 627
United Nations Relief and Rehabilitation Organization, 621–23, 627, 630
United Provinces of Central America, 413–14
United States of America: English colonial background, 239–46; emergence of, 246–49; American Revolution, 246–48; Treaty of Paris, 248–49; the Constitution, 249–50; Louisiana Purchase, 273, 407; War of 1812, 407; Monroe Doctrine, 407; Mexican War of 1846–48, 407; the slavery question, 409; Civil War, 410–11; purchase of Alaska, 438; "Open Door" policy in China, 452; annexation of Hawaii, 455; Spanish-American War, 455, 456; Reconstruction, 485; the robber barons, 485–86; political corruption, 486; imperialism, 486; growth of reform, 486–89; intervention in Central America, 486; entry into World War I, 508–9; post-war prosperity, 528–29; stock market crash, 529; New Deal, 529–30; Pearl Harbor, 539; World War II, 541–42; control of the Philippines, 564–65, 639–40; emergence as great world power after World War II, 620; post-war relief program in Europe, 621–23; post-war boom, 628–29; Korean War, 648. See also American Revolution
Unkiar Skelessi, Treaty of, 406

Urbanization, 342–44, 366–68
Uruguay: wins independence from Brazil, 413
Ussher, Archbishop James, 582
Utrecht, Treaty of, 176, 227, 345
Utrecht, Union of, 122

Valdivia, Pedro de: conquest of Chile, 39
Valera, Eamon de, 528
Valéry, Paul, 458
Valois Dynasty, 98–99, 130
Van Diemen, Anton, 178
Van Rijn, Rembrandt, 179
Varèse, Edgar, 609
Vargas, Getulio, 531
Vasa Dynasty, 146–47
Vau, Louis le, 169
Velásquez, 610
Velázquez, Diego, governor of Cuba, 36
Venetian Republic, 268
Venezuela, 40, 283–84
Venice: gains under Treaty of Karlowitz, 164
Verdi, Giuseppe, 607
Verdun, Battle of, 506
Vereeniging, Treaty of, 445
Vergil, Polydore, 131
Verlaine, Paul, 608
Verona, Congress of, 280, 281
Verrazano, Giovanni da, 43
Versailles, palace of, 168–69
Versailles, Treaty of, 510–13, 529, 534, 627, 656–66
Vesalius, Andreas, 193–94
Vespucci, Amerigo, 31–32
Veto power, 627
Vico, Giambattista, 216
Victor Emmanuel II, king of Italy, 398
Victor Emmanuel III, king of Italy, 520
Victoria, queen of England, 388, 426, 468
Victorian Era, 386–88, 467–69
Vienna, Congress of, 278–79, 434
Villa, Francisco, 490
Vinland: Norse discovery of, 7, 8
Virginia Resolves, 244
Vivaldi, Ugolino, 13
Vivaldi, Vadino, 13
Voltaire (François Marie Arouet), 208–9, 214, 215–16, 217, 235–36, 257, 379, 610
Vuillemin, Major Joseph, 572

Wages and Hours Law, 530
Wagner, Richard, 607
Waitangi, Treaty of, 431
Waldseemüller, Martin, 31–32
Wallenstein, Albrecht von, duke of Friedland and Mecklenburg, 125–26
"War between Ancients and Moderns," 207–8
War of Austrian Succession, 224–27
War of Devolution, 174
War of Jenkins' Ear, 224

War of Spanish Succession, 174–77, 227
War of the League of Augsburg, 174, 227
"War of the Three Henrys," 102
War of 1812, 407
Wars of the Roses, 104, 105
Warsaw, grand duchy of, 274
Warsaw Treaty, 647–48
Washington, George, 227, 244, 245, 247, 249
Washington Conference, 533, 556
Waterloo, Battle of, 279
Watson, John B., 591
Watt, James, 359
Watteau, Antoine, 169, 234
Weber, Karl Maria von, 604
Weber, Max, 89, 90
Weimar Republic, 522–23, 526
Wellington, duke of (Sir Arthur Wellesley), 276, 281, 532
Wells, H. G., 510
Welsers of Augsburg, 40
Wesley, Charles, 212
Wesley, John, 212, 603
Westernization: material benefits and political subjugation, 551
Westminster, Statute of, 528
Weston, Sir Richard, 347
Westphalia, kingdom of, 274, 279
Westphalia, Peace of, 127–28
Wet, Christian de, 576
Whistler, James McNeill, 606
White Lotus Rebellion, 314, 316
White Mountain, Battle of, 125
Whitney, Eli, 357
Wilberforce, Bishop Samuel, 585, 599–600
Wilberforce, William, 386
Wilde, Oscar, 608
Wilhelmina, queen of Holland, 471
Wilkinson, John, 359, 360
William II, emperor of Germany, 451, 473–74, 493, 494, 496, 509
William III, king of England, 174, 175, 178, 188–89
William I, king of Holland, 392, 437
William II, king of Holland, 437
William III, king of Holland, 471
William V, king of Holland, 267
William I, king of Prussia, 395, 396
William of Orange (the Silent), 121, 122
Willoughby, Hugh, 44
Wilson, Woodrow, 487, 510–11, 644
Windischgrätz, Prince Alfred zu, 401
Witte, Sergei, 480
Wittenberg Concord, 64
Wolfe, General James, 227
Wolsey, Cardinal Thomas, 72–73, 108–9, 130
Wordsworth, William, 599, 604, 650–51
Workingmen's party, 409
Works Progress Administration, 530
World War I. See First World War
World War II. See Second World War
Worms, Edict of, 61, 63–64
Wren, Sir Christopher, 190
Wundt, Wilhelm, 591
Wyatt, John, 357
Wycliffe, John, 52, 60, 72

Yalta Conference, 625, 627, 645–46
Yang Hu-cheng, 558
Yehonala, dowager empress of China, 451–52
Yorktown, Battle of, 248
Young, Arthur, 349, 373
Young Turks, 484
Ypres, Battle of, 506
Yüan Dynasty, 308
Yüan Shih-Kai, General, 454, 554
Yudenitch, General Nikolai, 514
Yugoslavia: communization under Marshal Tito, 621, 633

Zanzibar: British acquisition of, 441
Zápolya, John, 115
Zenta, Battle of, 164
Zhukov, Marshal Georgi K., 632
Zimmermann, Arthur, 494
Zinoviev, Gregory, 517
Zionism: struggle for Palestine, 570–71; Balfour White Paper, 570–71
Zola, Émile, 471
Zollverein, 393
Zulu War, 432, 551
Zwickau "saints," 63
Zwingli, Ulrich, 64, 65

PRINTED IN U.S.A.